# TAX
# HANDBOOK
## 2000–01

A. Foreman

PEARSON EDUCATION LIMITED

Head Office:
Edinburgh Gate
Harlow CM20 2JE
Tel: +44 (0)1279 623623
Fax: +44 (0)1279 431059

London Office:
128 Long Acre, London WC2E 9AN
Tel: +44 (0)20 7447 2000
Fax: +44 (0)20 7240 5771
Websites: www.business-minds.com
www.pearsoned-ema.com

This edition first published in Great Britain in 2000

ISBN 0 273 650 43 2

*British Library Cataloguing in Publication Data*
A CIP catalogue record for this book can be obtained
from the British Library

Typeset by M Rules
Printed and bound in Great Britain by
Biddles Ltd, Guildford and King's Lynn

*The Publishers' policy is to use paper manufactured
from sustainable forests.*

# CONTENTS

# ABBREVIATIONS

| | |
|---|---|
| ACT | Advance Corporation Tax |
| ADR | American depositary receipt |
| AIM | Alternative Investment Market |
| APPP | appropriate personal pension plan |
| AVC | additional voluntary contribution |
| BES | Business Expansion Scheme |
| CAA | Capital Allowances Act 1990 |
| CGT | capital gains tax |
| COMPS | contracted-out money purchase scheme |
| COP | Code of Practice |
| CPO | compulsory purchase order |
| CTO | Capital Taxes Office |
| CY | current year |
| DSS | Department of Social Security |
| EIS | Enterprise Investment Scheme |
| ESC | extra-statutory concession |
| EU | European Union |
| FA | Finance Act |
| F(No 2)A | Finance (No 2) Act |
| FPCS | fixed profit car scheme |
| FRS | Financial Reporting Standard |
| FSAVC | free-standing additional voluntary contribution |
| FURBS | funded unapproved retirement benefit scheme |
| GCD | General Claims District |
| GMP | guaranteed minimum pension |
| HP | hire-purchase |
| IHT | inheritance tax |
| IHTA | Inheritance Tax Act 1984 |
| IRC | Inland Revenue Commissioners |
| ISA | Individual savings account |
| LAPR | life assurance premium relief |
| LIBOR | London inter-bank offer rate |

| | |
|---|---|
| LIFO | last in, first out |
| MIRAS | mortgage interest relief at source |
| NIC | national insurance contribution |
| NRE | net relevant earnings |
| NSB | National Savings Bank |
| pa | per annum |
| para | paragraph |
| PAYE | pay as you earn |
| PEP | personal equity plan |
| PHI | permanent health insurance |
| PILON | payment in lieu of notice |
| PPP | personal pension plan |
| PRAS | pension relief at source |
| PRP | profit-related pay |
| PSO | Pension Schemes Office |
| PY | preceding year |
| reg | regulation |
| RPI | retail prices index |
| s (ss) | section (sections) of an Act |
| SAYE | save as you earn |
| Sched | Schedule of an Act |
| SDRT | stamp duty reserve tax |
| SERPS | State earnings-related pension scheme |
| SI | Statutory Instrument |
| SP | Inland Revenue Statement of Practice |
| SSAP | statement of standard accounting practice |
| SSAS | small self-administered scheme |
| STC | Simon's Tax Cases |
| TA | Income and Corporation Taxes Act |
| TC | Tax Cases |
| TCGA | Taxation of Chargeable Gains Act 1992 |
| TESSA | tax-exempt special savings account |
| TMA | Taxes Management Act 1970 |
| USM | Unlisted Securities Market |
| VAT | value added tax |
| VATA | Value Added Tax Act 1983 |
| VCT | venture capital trust |
| WFTC | working family tax credit |

# GLOSSARY

**Actual basis of assessment**   This describes the situation where a person carrying on a trade or profession is assessed according to the profits which he has actually earned during the tax year concerned. See 2.3.

**Accounting reference date**   The date to which accounts are made up for a company. In practice, when a company is formed, the accounting reference date will normally be the last day of the month in which the anniversary of its incorporation falls.

**Additional voluntary contribution (AVC)**   A contribution by an employee to secure additional benefits under his employer's approved pension scheme. See 12.11.

**Ad valorem duties**   Duties which are charged as a percentage of the value of the asset concerned, particularly stamp duty. See Chapter 26.

**Advance Corporation Tax**   Tax payable by companies on dividend payments, etc up to 5 April 1999 which would be offset against the company's mainstream corporation tax liability. See Chapter 24.

**Agricultural buildings allowances**   A form of **capital allowance** given in respect of expenditure on buildings used for agricultural purposes. See 2.5.

**Agricultural property relief**   This is a relief given for **inheritance tax** purposes. The relief is either 50% or 100% of the value of agricultural land. In order to qualify, the land must be situated in the UK, Channel Islands or Isle of Man. See 17.9.

**All-employee share scheme**   A new approved scheme for employees to receive shares tax free. See 3.15.

**Alternative Investment Market**   The Stock Exchange launched the AIM in June 1995 to enable investors to deal in shares in unquoted companies. AIM has replaced the Unlisted Securities Market, an earlier market for unquoted companies.

**Annual exemption**   An individual is entitled to an annual exemption for CGT purposes of £7,200 for 2000–01. See 13.1. There are two types of annual exemption for **inheritance tax**. An individual may give away up to £250 to any number of people in a tax year; this is generally called the 'small gifts exemption'. Separately from this, an individual is allowed to make chargeable transfers of up to £3,000 pa which are treated as exempt. See 17.5.

**Approved profit sharing schemes**   These are schemes under which employees of companies may be given shares without an income tax charge provided the shares are retained for a minimum period of three years. See 3.12.

**Approved share option schemes**   There are two types of approved share option scheme: SAYE linked schemes, which are democratic in nature and must be made available to all employees, and executive share option schemes, which can be restricted to directors and senior executives. See 3.15.2–3.15.4. See also **Enterprise Management Incentives**.

**Associated companies**   Companies controlled by the same person or groups of people.

**Basis period**   The period on which your (usually Schedule D) profits for the tax year are based.

**Bed and breakfasting**   A widely used way of establishing CGT losses by selling shares and repurchasing the next day. Anti-avoidance rules took effect from 17 March 1998 to prevent this. See 20.7.

**Benefits in kind**   Perks received by a director or employee which are taxed as employment income and which are generally subject to NICs from 6 April 2000. See 3.4.

**Beneficial loans**   Loans to an employee at less than a commercial rate of interest (see official rate). See 3.7.

**Business property relief**   This is a deduction of either 50% or 100% which is made from the value of business property when it is assessed for **inheritance tax** purposes. See 17.8.

**Capital allowances**   These are allowances given in respect of plant and machinery, industrial buildings and commercial property in **enterprise zones**. In general terms, capital allowances represent a form of relief which corresponds to depreciation. See 2.5.

**Capital expenditure**   Capital expenditure is expenditure of a once and for all nature to achieve an enduring benefit for a trade. It is not a cost which may be deducted in arriving at profits for tax purposes, although **capital allowances** may be available. See 2.4.5.

**Cash accounting**   A method of accounting to Customs & Excise for VAT as and when payment is received rather than according to when VAT invoices are issued. See 25.6.3.

**Chargeable transfer**   A gift or other transfer of value made by an individual which is not covered by any of the various exemptions and which is therefore a transfer for **inheritance tax** purposes. See 17.2–17.5.

**Charitable trust**   A trust where all income must be used for charitable purposes. In England and Wales, most charities have to be registered with the Charity Commissioners.

**Class 1A NICs**   These are special national insurance contributions charged on an employer in respect of cars made available to employees for private use. The contributions are levied on the 'scale' benefits which are used to arrive at the employees' taxable benefit. See Chapter 23.

**Class 1B NICs**   It is proposed to introduce Class 1B contributions with effect from 6 April 1998 where an employer settles tax in respect of employees' benefits under a **PSA**. See Chapter 23.

**Close company**   A company where the directors control more than half of the voting shares or where such control may be exercised by five or fewer people and their associates.

**Corporate venturing**   A new relief for companies which invest in small trading companies by subscribing for ordinary shares on or after 1 April 2000. See 24.13.

**Corporation tax**   This is a tax levied on companies' profits. The full rate is 30% but many companies will qualify for the **small companies rate**.

**Covenant**   A payment under a deed of covenant in favour of a charity will normally transfer income to the charity. The person making the payment under the deed of covenant must deduct tax at basic rate but the charity can reclaim this. See 10.5.

**Current year basis**   This is the Schedule D basis of assessment, whereby an individual will be assessed on his profits for the firm's year which ends in the tax year. It came into effect from 1997–98 onwards. See 2.3.1.

**CY basis**   Current year basis.

**Deeds of variation**   This is a special term for **inheritance tax** purposes. Where the provisions of a person's Will are varied by mutual consent of the beneficiaries, and the necessary deed of variation is executed within two years of the relevant death, inheritance tax may be computed as if the deceased's Will had contained the revised provisions from the outset. A similar treatment may apply where a person has died without making a valid Will, and the individuals who would benefit under the intestacy rules mutually agree to vary the position. See 17.4.6.

**Deregistration**   Deregistration occurs when a trader who has been registered for VAT purposes is permitted to deregister. Once the trader has deregistered, he must not charge VAT on any supplies subsequently made by him in the course of his business. See Chapter 22.

**Discretionary trust**   This is a type of trust where the trustees can vary the way that they use the trust monies and can choose how they pay out (or 'distribute') income to members of a class of potential beneficiaries. This is different to other types of trust where the trustees are bound to pay the income over to a particular beneficiary.

**Dispensations**   An employer is required to make annual returns of payments and benefits provided to employees (form P11D). A dispensation may be negotiated with the Revenue whereby certain expenses and other payments need not be reported on form P11D.

**Distribution**   A distribution of a company's assets to its members (ie shareholders), for example a payment of a dividend. Distributions may also be made by a liquidator. Where assets are distributed to members of the company during the course of a liquidation, there is said to be a distribution *in specie*.

**Dividends**   A dividend is a cash amount paid to a member of a company according to the number of shares held by him. Dividends may only be declared out of distributable profits.

**Domicile**   This is a legal concept which can be very important where a person transfers property situated outside the UK. A person generally has a foreign domicile if he does not regard the UK as his real home and he retains strong links with another country.

   The concept of domicile is not exactly the same as that of nationality although if you are a foreign national, this will be very helpful in establishing that you are not domiciled in the UK. Your domicile of origin will normally be that of your father when you reached age 16 (or that of your mother if she was unmarried or your father died while you were still a minor). The relevant age is 14 for individuals who are domiciled in Scotland.

Your domicile of origin continues to remain in force until such time as you acquire a new domicile of choice by making a permanent home elsewhere. See 22.1.

**Earnings basis** Accounts should be prepared so as to reflect a trader's earnings for a year rather than just cash received. Thus, accounts should include debtors, ie bills which have been issued but which have not been paid by the year end. See 2.4.

**Earnings cap** An employee's earnings in excess of the cap are generally disregarded for the purpose of arriving at his benefits under an approved pension scheme. A similar rule applies for determining maximum contributions under a **personal pension scheme**. See 12.8.

**Election to waive exemption** A VAT term used in commercial land and property transactions. Otherwise known as the option to tax. A landowner has the option to make what would otherwise be an **exempt supply** into a taxable supply. Formal notification to Customs is required. See 25.3.

**Enhancement expenditure** This is a term used in the context of CGT. In computing a person's capital gain, it is possible to deduct the costs incurred in acquiring the asset and any enhancement expenditure on improvements etc which is reflected in the state of the asset at the date of disposal. See 14.2.4.

**Emoluments** Normal remuneration, bonuses and other employment income received by a director or employee. See 3.2.1 and 19.1.2.

**Enterprise Investment Scheme** This is a scheme under which individuals may receive income tax and CGT relief when investing in qualifying unquoted trading companies. See 11.6.

**Enterprise Management Incentives** A new **approved share option scheme** which allows up to 15 key employees to receive options over shares worth up to £100,000 in a small trading company. See 3.13.

**Enterprise zones** The Government has designated certain areas as enterprise zones. Designation normally lasts for a period of ten years. During that period, a person carrying on a business within the enterprise zone is exempt from business rates. There is also considerable freedom from planning controls.

Expenditure on commercial buildings situated in an enterprise zone qualifies for **capital allowances**. The acquisition of an unused commercial building, or a building which has been let only during the preceding two years, attracts a 100% allowance. See 2.5.13.

**Equity partner** A term used to distinguish between a salaried partner taxed under Schedule E and proprietors of the business or 'full partners' taxed under Schedule D.

**ESOP** Employee Share Ownership Plan.

**ESOT** Employee Share Ownership Trust.

**EU** The European Union comprises Austria, Belgium, Denmark, Finland, France, Germany, Greece, Ireland, Italy, Luxembourg, the Netherlands, Portugal, Spain, Sweden and the UK.

**Exempt supplies**   Supplies which are not liable to VAT. A person who makes only exempt supplies will not be able to recover **input VAT** suffered by him.

**Exempt transfers**   The following transfers are exempt from **inheritance tax**: gifts to spouse; normal expenditure out of income; £250 small gifts exemption; annual £3,000 exemption; exemption for marriage gifts; gifts to charities; gifts for national purposes; gifts for public benefit; gifts to political parties; certain transfers to employee trusts. See 17.5.

*Ex-gratia*   A person makes an *ex-gratia* payment when he does so without admitting liability, eg a payment by an employer on terminating an employment.

**Existing obligation**   Liability to make court order or other maintenance payments to a former spouse and/or children, where the obligation pre-dated 15 March 1988. See 8.2.

**Filing date**   An individual or trustee must file his **self-assessment** return on or before 31 January following the end of the tax year concerned. See pages 1–5.

**Financial Reporting Standards**   Issued by the Accounting Standards Board which are mandatory for companies.

**Form CT61**   A quarterly return required for a company in respect of dividends and annual payments made under deduction of tax. See Chapter 24. Dividends paid after 5 April 1999 no longer need to be reported in this way.

**Form P11D**   An annual return made by employers of expenses payments and **benefits in kind** provided for an employee.

**Full-time working directors and managers**   This is a concept which applies for the purposes of CGT **retirement relief**. A person selling shares in a company qualifies for retirement relief only if he is a officer or manager, ie someone who is required to spend the greater part of his time working for the company in a managerial capacity. See 15.11.

**FURBS**   Funded Unapproved Retirement Benefit Scheme. See 12.12.

**Gross income**   This is income from which no tax has been deducted. It may still be taxable income.

**Groups of companies**   There are various different rules under which companies may be regarded as part of a group. A parent company may have subsidiaries, ie other companies in which the parent company has a majority shareholding. The companies constitute a group for company law purposes.

   The conditions which need to be satisfied for companies to form a group for tax purposes vary but in general, the parent company needs to have a 75% interest in its subsidiaries (see 24.9).

**Group registration for VAT purposes**   Companies which are under common control may register for VAT purposes as a single unit or VAT group. Where this happens, all supplies between the companies concerned are disregarded for VAT purposes. VAT is charged only on supplies outside the group. See 25.4.1.

**Hold-over relief**   This is the relief given to a donor or other transferor of business assets. Where an individual etc is entitled to hold-over relief, his gain is not charged but is deducted from the asset's market value in determining the transferee's acquisition value for CGT purposes. See 15.6.

**Income from savings**   This is income which is taxed at only 20% unless you are a higher rate taxpayer. Income from savings includes interest, dividends and purchased life annuities.

**Income received gross**   See **Gross income** above.

**Indexation**   This is an adjustment made for CGT purposes to allow for inflation up to April 1998. The adjustment is computed by reference to the increase in the retail price index between the month of acquisition (or March 1982 if later) and the month of disposal (or April 1998 if earlier). Replaced by taper relief for individuals and trustees in relation to periods after April 1998. See 14.5.

**Individual savings account**   A new savings scheme which came into operation on 6 April 1999. All income and capital gains are free of tax. See 11.1.

**Industrial buildings**   Buildings which are occupied for the purposes of a qualifying trade may qualify as industrial buildings. The significance of this is that a person who incurs expenditure on an industrial building may claim industrial buildings allowances. Normally, allowances are given at the rate of 4% pa over a two-year period. See 2.5.15.

**Inheritance tax**   Inheritance tax is a combination of a gift tax and death duties. Tax is payable on chargeable transfers made by an individual during his lifetime and on his estate at the time of his death. See Chapter 17.

**Input VAT**   The VAT paid to suppliers of goods and services. Where a person has paid for such goods and services and he is himself VAT registered, he may recover input VAT by offsetting the tax paid by him against tax charged on his own supplies. See 25.4.3.

**Interest in possession trust**   An interest in possession exists where the beneficiary is entitled to income arising from the trust capital and is legally entitled to demand that the trustees pay that income to him or her. An interest in possession can also exist where the trust owns a property and the beneficiary is entitled to live there rent free.

**Investment companies**   An investment company is a company which exists wholly or mainly for the purpose of carrying on a business of managing investments.

**Know-how**   Certain expenditure by a person carrying on a trade to acquire information required to carry out certain industrial or manufacturing processes may qualify for a form of **capital allowances**.

**Mainstream corporation tax**   Corporation tax payable on a company's profits. See Chapter 24.

**Market value rule**   Where an asset is transferred to a person by way of a gift or some other disposal which is not an arm's length transaction, CGT may be charged as if the person making the disposal had in fact received market value.

**MIRAS**   Mortgage interest relief at source. See 9.1. It was abolished from 6 April 2000.

**National insurance contributions**   These are Social Security Contributions. **Class 1 NICs** are payable by an employer and employees. Class 2 and Class 4 NICs are payable by self-employed individuals. The national insurance system is administered by the Department of Social Security.

**Official rate**   A rate of interest set by Parliament which is supposed to be a commercial rate. Loans from an employer are generally treated as a benefit in kind if interest is paid at less than the official rate. See 3.7.

**Opening years' rules**   There are special rules for the opening years under the Schedule D **CY basis**. See 2.3.1.

**Options**   An option is a legally binding contract under which one party to the contract is bound to buy or sell an asset to the other party. A call option is an option under which the person granting the option agrees to sell an asset to the other party if he exercises his option. A put option is where a person has the right to require the other party to buy an asset from him.

**Output tax**   VAT chargeable on goods or services supplied in the UK. The trader must account for VAT charged on such supplies by completing a VAT return, normally on a quarterly basis. See 25.4.2.

**Outworkers**   Some industries have outworkers who work on their own premises. However, depending upon the circumstances, outworkers may be regarded as employees and not as self-employed individuals. This means that payments made by the person using the services of outworkers may be subject to **PAYE** and employers **national insurance contributions**. See 2.2.

**Overlap relief**   Under the Schedule D **CY basis** of assessment, there are special provisions to cover the way in which profits are assessed during the opening years. The general principle is that total amount of profits which are assessed over the life of the business should precisely equal the actual profits earned by the business. Overlap relief covers situations where a particular year's profits are assessed more than once (usually under the **opening years' rules**) and is effectively an adjustment to ensure that this does not result in excessive amounts being assessed overall.

   Overlap relief is given by way of a deduction from an individual's profits when he ceases to carry on his business or profession, or when the accounting date of the firm is changed to a date which falls later in the tax year. See 2.3.

**Partially exempt traders**   This is a VAT concept. A partially exempt trader is a person who makes a mixture of standard rated or zero rated supplies and supplies which are exempt for VAT purposes. A partially exempt trader may not be able to claim full credit for his input tax. See 25.4.5.

**Pay As You Earn (PAYE)**   This is a compulsory system for deduction of tax at source from cash payments to employees. There are different rules for PAYE and **national insurance contributions** and an individual's earnings may be different for the purposes of these two systems.

**Payment in lieu of notice (PILON)**   The Revenue may argue that payments to an employee are taxable where the employment contract refers to the possibility of the employer making a PILON. See 3.22.8.

**Personal equity plan**   A Government approved way of investing in stocks and shares. Replaced by ISAs from 6 April 1999.

**Personal trading company**   Term used in the context of CGT **retirement relief**. A company is an individual's personal trading company only if he can exercise at least 5% of the voting rights. See 15.11.

**Personal pension scheme**   These are approved pension schemes run by insurance companies, banks, building societies or unit trust groups. An individual who is self-employed or who is in non-pensionable employment may make contributions to a personal pension scheme. See 12.8.

**Plant and machinery**   Plant and machinery attracts **capital allowances** if used by a person in the course of a business carried on by him. There is no statutory definition of plant and machinery although certain rules have evolved through decided cases. See 2.5.

**Potentially exempt transfers**   An outright gift made by an individual to another individual or to an interest in possession or accumulation and maintenance trust is a potentially exempt transfer (PET). This means that the gift will be exempt from **inheritance tax** provided the donor survives seven years. If the donor does survive for that period the potentially exempt transfer becomes an actually exempt transfer. If he dies during the period the transfer will prove not to have been exempt. See 17.6.

**Preceding year basis**   The old Schedule D system, which applied for an individual who commenced business prior to 6 April 1994. The normal basis of assessment for a tax year was the preceding year basis, ie the assessment for the tax year 1994–95 was based on the firm's, accounts for a period which ended during the tax year 1993–94. This came to an end in 1995–96.

**Prescribed accounting periods**   VAT term for periods covered by VAT returns. Normally periods are of three-month duration ending on the dates notified in the certificate of VAT registration.

**Pre-trading expenditure**   Certain expenditure incurred in connection with a trade which is about to be carried on may qualify for tax relief once the trade is commenced. See 2.6.

**Premium**   A lump sum payment to a landlord in order to obtain a lease is regarded as a premium for tax purposes. Where the lease is for a period of less than 50 years, part of the premium will normally be treated as income for the landlord. See 4.3.

**PAYE Settlement Agreements (PSAs)**   Formerly known as Annual Voluntary Settlements (AVSs), these provide employers with the mechanism to meet tax liabilities arising on a wide range of staff costs which would otherwise be assessed to tax on the employees concerned as **benefits in kind**.

**Purchase of own shares**   A company may purchase its own shares. A public company is normally permitted to do so only in so far as it has distributable profits or the purchase of own shares is being funded by the proceeds from an issue of new shares. A private company may purchase its own shares out of capital. In all situations, there is a set procedure which must be followed in order for the purchase to be in accordance with company law.

A special tax treatment may apply where a private trading company purchases its own shares. See 5.9.7–5.9.8.

**PY basis**   Another name for preceding year basis.

**Qualifying corporate bonds**   A loan stock issued by a company may be an exempt asset for CGT purposes (ie it qualifies for exemption). On the other hand, any loss realised on a disposal of a QCB is not normally allowable for CGT purposes. See 13.3.2.

**Qualifying loans**   An individual who is a partner is entitled to relief for interest paid on qualifying loans, ie loans used to acquire an interest in the firm or loans which have been taken to enable the individual to make a loan to his firm for use in the ordinary course of the firm's business. See 9.3.

Shareholders in a close company may also be able to raise qualifying loans to acquire shares or make loan capital available to the company. See 9.4–9.5.

**Readily convertible assets**   This is a term used for PAYE and NICs purposes and replaced the former term 'tradeable assets' from 17 March 1998. PAYE and NICs have to be paid if an employee receives readily convertible assets as part of his remuneration. See 3.2.1 and 19.1.2.

**Rebasing**   This is a technical term for CGT purposes whereby an individual who held an asset at 31 March 1982 may have his capital gain computed as if his cost were the market value of the asset at that date. See 14.3.

**Relevant earnings**   Schedule D profits and earnings from a non-pensionable employment. An individual may make contributions into a **personal pension scheme** based on a percentage of his relevant earnings for a tax year. See 12.8.

**Relief for reinvestment in unquoted shares**   CGT relief was available up to 5 April 1998 where an individual or trust invested in a qualifying unquoted trading company within three years of the date of a disposal which gave rise to a capital gain. See 15.5.

**Rent-a-room relief**   A special relief for individuals who let rooms in their home. See 4.4.

**Relevant discounted security**   A loan stock which is issued at a discount of more than ½% for each year of its life (or more than 15% if the stock has a life of more than 30 years). A gain on the sale of a relevant discounted security is taxed as income. See 5.7.

**Reservation of benefit**   This is an **inheritance tax** term. Where a person makes a gift but reserves a benefit, the transaction is not regarded as a **potentially exempt transfer**. The asset remains part of the individual's estate for as long as he continues to reserve a benefit. If he has not relinquished his reserved benefit by the time of his death, the market value of the asset will be brought into account for inheritance tax purposes just as if he still owned the asset. See 17.7.

**Restrictive covenant**   An undertaking not to do something in the future. Where an employee receives a cash sum in return for entering into such a covenant, the cash is taxed as employment income. See 3.20.

**Retirement annuity**   These are similar to **personal pension schemes**. In effect, they are approved contracts under which a person who was self-employed or in non-pensionable employment could provide for their retirement prior to the introduction of personal pension schemes in July 1988. Many retirement annuity policies make provision for premiums to be paid in subsequent years and, whilst no new retirement annuity policies are now issued, contributions under existing policies will thus continue to attract relief for some years to come. See 12.9.

**Retirement benefits scheme**   Technical term for a pension scheme. See Chapter 12.

**Retirement relief** This is a special relief for CGT purposes which applies where an individual aged 55 or over disposes of his business or an interest in a business (eg an interest in a firm). See 15.9.

**Revenue expenditure** Expenditure which is deductible in arriving at a company's profits. Contrast **capital expenditure**.

**Reverse charge** VAT charging mechanism which obliges the customer to account to Customs for VAT on the price charged for goods or services. The VAT charged is recoverable as input VAT, subject to the normal rules. See 25.5.3.

**Roll-over relief** This is a CGT relief which applies where an individual disposes of a business or an asset used in a business and spends the proceeds on acquiring replacement assets during a qualifying period (normally up to one year before and up to three years after the date of disposal of the original asset). See 15.5.

**Roll-up fund** A colloquial term for an offshore collective fund where the managers do not pay out income but accumulate it within the fund. See 6.2.

**Salaried partner** A salaried partner is an individual who is subject to the supervision and direction of equity partners and who is therefore no more than a very senior employee. Salaried partners are assessable under Schedule E rather than under Schedule D.

**Schedule D** A self-employed person's profits are assessed under Schedule D. See Chapter 2.

**Schedule E** Directors and employees are assessed under Schedule E. The normal basis of assessment for Schedule E income is the receipts basis, ie an individual is assessed according to remuneration received by him during the year. See Chapter 3.

**Scientific research allowances** Certain expenditure incurred by traders on scientific research may attract allowances. **Revenue expenditure** is allowed in full. **Capital expenditure** may attract 100% **capital allowances**. See 2.5.18.

**Self-administered pension scheme** A pension scheme with no more than 12 members where one or more of the members is a trustee or the company which established the scheme is a trustee. See 12.10.

**Self-assessment** New system for assessing tax and payment of tax liabilities which came into force in 1996–97 for individuals and trustees. See pages 16–19. Companies moved onto a self-assessment system for accounting periods ending on or after 1 July 1999.

**Shares Valuation Division** A specialist section of the Capital Taxes Office which negotiates valuations of unquoted shares where such a valuation is required for tax purposes.

**Small companies rate** Corporation tax is charged only at 20% unless the company concerned has profits in excess of the lower limit. The lower limit is at present £300,000 provided that there are no **associated companies**. If there are associated companies, the lower limit is divided by the number of associated companies. See 24.3.

**Sole traders** An individual is a sole trader if he carries on business on his own account rather than in partnership or through a company. Similarly an individual carrying on a profession on his own account is termed a 'sole practitioner'.

**Stakeholder pensions**   These are a new type of personal pension schemes which will become available from 6 April 2001. See 12.8.9.

**Stamp duty**   Duty payable at ½% on transfers of shares and at 1–4% on transfers of property. See Chapter 26.

**Surcharge**   A penalty based on the amount of tax payable which will be imposed automatically if an individual has not paid the tax due on his self-assessment return by one month after the filing date. A further surcharge will normally be imposed if tax remains unpaid after a further six months have elapsed.

**Taper relief**   Capital gains may be reduced by taper relief, depending on the number of complete years of ownership after 5 April 1998, and depending on whether the asset disposed of is a business asset. See 14.6.

There is also a taper relief for **inheritance tax** where an individual dies within seven years of making a **potentially exempt transfer**. See 17.6.

**Tax invoice**   An invoice issued by a supplier which must show specific information. It is the document on which VAT accounting and control procedures are based. See Chapter 25.

**Tax point**   The time at which a transaction is regarded as taking place for VAT purposes, and when VAT becomes payable or recoverable. See **Cash accounting** above.

**TESSA**   Tax Exempt Special Saving Account – available for new investors up to 5 April 1999. The interest is tax free if it is not drawn for a period of five years. See 11.4.

**Time apportionment basis**   Where an asset was owned at 6 April 1965, and no universal **rebasing** election has been made, it is sometimes possible for a capital gain to be computed on the apportionment basis. This means that only a proportion of the gain achieved over the total period of ownership is brought into charge. See 14.3.

**Transitional relief**   Where a firm has been assessed on the **PY basis** for 1995–96, the firm will normally be assessed under the transitional basis for 1996–97. In practice, this normally means that the assessment for 1996–97 will be based on 12 months' share of the profits for a period commencing immediately after the end of the basis period for 1995–96 and ending on the date to which accounts are drawn up during the tax year 1996–97. See 2.3.6.

**Trust**   Property is held in trust where trustees hold it for the benefit of clearly identified beneficiaries. The trustees must use the capital and income as directed by the trust deed and in accordance with trust law. See Chapter 18.

**Unincorporated businesses**   A company is an incorporated business. Businesses carried on by a **sole trader** or by a partnership are unincorporated businesses.

**Universal rebasing election**   An irrevocable election which may be made under which the 31 March 1982 value of assets held by that person is treated as if it were the original cost. See 14.3.

**Venture Capital Loss Relief**   Where an individual has subscribed for shares in an unquoted trading company, any losses may be set against the individual's income for the year in which the loss is realised. This is known as Venture Capital Loss Relief. See 15.2.

**Venture Capital Trust**  A type of investment trust established under the provisions of the Finance Act 1995. VCTs must invest in unquoted trading companies with net assets of no more than £15m. See 11.7.

**Wasting assets**  A wasting asset is an asset with an expected useful life of less than 50 years. See 14.10.2.

**Zero-rating**  A VAT term for a sale on which no VAT is charged. A person making zero-rated supplies may nevertheless still be able to recover input VAT. See 25.3.2.

# KEY CHANGES BROUGHT ABOUT BY THE FINANCE ACT 2000 AND RECENT COURT DECISIONS ETC

## Coping with self-assessment

- Inland Revenue takes a tougher line on returns which include provisional figures (pages 19–20)

## Chapter 2: Self-employment income

- IR35 rules come into operation for companies and partnerships providing personal services (2.2.1 and 19.3)
- Revenue concedes defeat on tax relief for provisions (2.4.9)
- First year allowances for SMEs put on a permanent basis (2.5.5)
- 100% first year allowances for IT expenditure by small businesses (2.5.6)

## Chapter 3: Taxation of employment income

- Changes in the taxation of company cars from 6 April 2002 (3.5.1)
- New all-employee share scheme (3.13)
- Enterprise Management Incentive scheme (3.17)

## Chapter 5: Income from savings

- Exemption for bank compensation payments to holocaust victims and their descendants (5.1.7)

## Chapter 7: Personal allowances

- Many allowances phased-out from 6 April 2000 (7.5–7.8)
- Introduction of Working Family Tax Credits (7.11)

## Chapter 8: The taxation of maintenance

- Extra relief for 'existing obligations' abolished from 6 April 2000 (8.2)

## Chapter 9: Interest on qualifying loans

- MIRAS finally phased-out from 6 April 2000 (9.1)

## Chapter 10: Annual payments which attract tax relief

- Radical changes extending the Gift Aid scheme (10.2)
- New relief for gifts of AIM or quoted shares to charities (10.4)

## Chapter 11: Tax efficient investment

- Higher limit for ISA investments made in 1999-2000 extended one further year (11.11.1)
- Five-year retention period for EIS and VCT investors reduced to three years (11.6.14, 11.7.2)
- Various anomalies and pitfalls for EIS and VCT companies removed

## Chapter 12: Life assurance and pensions

- Pensions earnings cap increased to £91,800 for 2000–01 (12.10.4, 12.10.5)
- Stakeholder pensions to replace personal pensions from 6 April 2001 (12.8.9)

## Chapters 13–16: Capital gains tax

- Annual exemption increased to £7,200 (13.1.1)
- Major improvements to rate of taper relief on business assets (14.6)
- Substantial widening of the definition of business assets (15.3)
- Hold-over relief no longer available for gifts to companies (15.6.2)

## Chapter 19: Deducting tax at source – and paying it over to the Inland Revenue

- Major changes to the Construction Industry Tax Deduction scheme (19.2)
- IR35 changes came into effect from 6 April 2000 (19.3)

## Chapter 20: Anti-avoidance legislation

- Interest-free loans from overseas trusts may constitute a benefit (20.4.7)

## Chapter 23: National insurance contributions

- Class 1 NICs apply to most benefits in kind from 6 April 2000 (23.1.4)
- Employee can agree to pay his employer's NICs on exercising share options granted after 5 April 1999 (23.1.7)

## Chapter 24: Tax and companies

- Corportion tax self-assessment now fully operative (24.8)
- Corporate venturing (24.13)
- R&D tax credits for SMEs (24.14)

## Chapter 26: Stamp Duty

- Another increase in the rates (26.1.2)
- Exemption for transfers of intellectual property rights after 27 March 2000 (26.1.3)

## Chapter 28: Charities and not-for-profit organisations

- Major reforms to the tax treatment of charities (28.1)

# PREFACE

This book covers a wide field and is aimed at both the professional and non-professional reader. It deals with income tax, capital gains tax, inheritance tax, corporation tax and VAT. It also covers (in rather less detail) stamp duty and that other levy on our income, a tax in all but name, national insurance contributions.

Our aim is to make this Handbook 'user friendly', and at the same time provide a comprehensive analysis of the relevant legislation. The overall style of the book should help people from all walks of life who have to grapple with unfamiliar areas of taxation and the new demands imposed by the self-assessment regime. We reproduce the relevant pages of the Revenue forms, cross-referenced to this book. We have tried to go into sufficient detail for professionals whose daily work brings them face to face with our complex tax system – Accountants, Solicitors, and Company Secretaries, and draw attention to areas of uncertainty, potential pitfalls and tax planning points. However, it really goes without saying that this Handbook deals only with general principles and is no substitute for expert advice which takes full account of the specific facts and circumstances of your case. Readers should normally seek professional advice where substantial amounts are involved.

This book is a team effort. My PKF colleagues – Roger Bleasby, Louise Delamere, Sharna Edwards, Richard Heap, Mark Francis, Sudeep Ganguli, Peter Harrup, Peter Jun Tai, Sheena Sullivan, Colin Walker, Colin Williams and Mike Wilkes have all updated chapters and provided a considerable amount of new material. Sue Parr has compiled the tables. Vince Jerrard and Stuart Reynolds of Allied Dunbar have once again provided a chapter on the taxation of life assurance and pensions. Amelia Lakin and the editorial staff at Pearson Education have gone over the entire text with a fine-tooth comb and managed to see us through extremely tight deadlines.

Finally, Gerald Mowles has once again acted as deputy editor and has been of enormous help in trying to make the material more accessible to the non-specialist.

Tony Foreman

# Other titles in the Allied Dunbar Handbook series

### EXPATRIATE TAX & INVESTMENT (7th edition)
'Expat's bible' – *What Investment*

Written by experts, the *Allied Dunbar Expatriate Tax & Investment Handbook* gives you comprehensive coverage of every aspect of expatriate tax and investment from the effect of the single currency to advice on working abroad. It is the essential guide for expatriates wishing to manage their financial affairs to their greatest possible advantage.

### PENSIONS (7th edition)

This is the complete guide for business owners, company directors, the self employed and professional pension planners. It gives you a detailed investigation of all the choices available for successful pension planning.

### RETIREMENT PLANNING (7th edition)

The *Allied Dunbar Retirement Planning Handbook* is an essential addition to your book-shelf. It ensures that you are fully aware of long and short term investment opportunities and examines the options available for improving retirement prospects.

─── AVAILABLE SOON ───

### INVESTMENT & SAVINGS 2000/2001

The *Allied Dunbar Investment & Savings Handbook* guides you through the complexities surrounding the abundance of financial products available, so that you can make informed choices for your investment strategy. Completely up-to-date with the latest legislation (it features changes resulting from the Spring 2000 budget and the Finance Act 2000), it highlights the significant changes in the law and how they will impact on your investments and savings.

### ESTATE PLANNING & TAXATION OF CAPITAL (7th edition)

The *Allied Dunbar Estate Planning & Taxation of Capital Handbook* provides an easy and straightforward way of understanding the principles of capital taxation on personal business and family wealth and how, by careful planning, its impact can be, legally, mitigated.

### BUSINESS TAX & LAW (3rd edition)

With detailed information and astute advice, the *Allied Dunbar Business Tax & Law Handbook* makes business planning easier. It details the important taxation and legal considerations that affect a business; and considers both the legal environment in which businesses operate and the taxation obligations which must be met.

**For further information contact your local bookseller,
telephone Pearson Education Ltd on 01704 50 80 80
or e-mail at customer.orders@pearsoned-ema.com**

# COPING WITH SELF-ASSESSMENT
## (AND OTHER ASPECTS OF OUR TAX SYSTEM)

In this chapter, we look at the following:

(1) Some basic principles of UK taxation.
(2) The Inland Revenue.
(3) Understanding your responsibilities and rights.
(4) Complaints and compensation.
(5) Self-assessment.
(6) Revenue enquiries into tax returns.
(7) Internet filing of self assessment tax returns.
(8) Finding your way around the self-assessment form.
(9) Ten golden rules for dealing with your 2000 tax return.

## SOME BASIC PRINCIPLES OF UK TAXATION

Despite the introduction of self-assessment, many of the basic principles of the UK tax system still go back to the 19th century.

### Income charged under different schedules

When Lord Addington reintroduced income tax in 1801, it was not thought to be proper or appropriate for a civil servant to be supplied with full details of an individual's total income. Consequently, income tax was made payable under several schedules, each with its own system of assessment. This made it possible for a taxpayer to report the income taxable under each schedule to a separate Inspector and so avoid the full extent of his income being known ✳ by any one official. This legacy remains with us today. Over the past two centuries, a great number of different rules have grown up so that the way in which income is assessed under each different schedule varies.

Income tax is now charged under four schedules, as follows.

### Schedule A

Schedule A applies to income from property (ie land and buildings) and includes rent and certain lease premiums. Since 1995–96, income from furnished lettings has also been taxed under Schedule A.

## Schedule B

This schedule applied to the taxation of woodlands managed on a commercial basis with a view to making a profit. It was abolished with effect from 6 April 1988.

## Schedule C

This used to cover paying agents (eg bankers) who have the responsibility for handling the income from UK gilt-edged securities and any public revenue organisations based overseas. Schedule C was abolished in the Finance Act 1996 but this was no more than a change in name as the requirements for paying agents to withhold tax was simply transferred to Schedule D.

## Schedule D

This schedule is itself sub-divided into six cases as follows:

- Cases I and II cover the profits or gains arising from trades (Case I) or professions or vocations (Case II), ie income from self-employment.
- Case III is primarily concerned with the taxation of interest and annual payments, but a whole range of related items has been included over the years.
- Cases IV and V cover the overseas income of UK-resident individuals. Case IV is concerned with interest on overseas securities (unless already covered by Schedule C); Case V covers income from overseas possessions.
- Case VI covers miscellaneous profits which do not fall into other cases of Schedule D and are not taxed through any of the other schedules.

## Schedule E

Schedule E covers the taxation of all wages, salaries, benefits etc resulting from employments (including directorships). It is divided into three cases as follows:

- Case I applies to earnings received by UK-resident and ordinarily resident individuals.
- Case II applies to earnings received by individuals who are resident but not ordinarily resident in the UK.
- Case III applies to work carried out abroad.

## Schedule F

This schedule covers dividends and other distributions by companies.

## Income tax – an annual tax

Income tax is an annual tax in that it arises on an individual's income for a tax year which ends on 5 April. Capital gains tax (CGT) is also an annual tax in this sense. In contrast, inheritance tax (IHT) may be levied by reference to a person's chargeable transfers during a seven-year period.

There is one other way in which income tax is an annual tax. It is an obligation imposed by each year's Finance Act (unlike CGT, which is imposed by the Taxation of Chargeable Gains Act 1992). This can have some surprising consequences. For example, where an individual is made bankrupt after the Finance Act for the current year has received royal assent, his liability for that year comes to an end and is recoverable only out of the assets held by the individual's trustee in bankruptcy. At the end of the tax year concerned, the individual loses this exemption from income tax since a fresh liability for the following year is imposed by that year's Finance Act.

## The Budget and Finance Bill

Each year, the Chancellor of the Exchequer introduces his Budget. Shortly after the Budget (usually during the same week) the Chancellor introduces the Finance Bill and it is said to have a 'first reading'. However, this is somewhat misleading since the Bill is not actually printed for a further three weeks.

It is then read in Committee, at which time points of detail are considered and amendments are made.

It is then brought back for a 'third reading' – in this case a formal vote of approval by the House of Commons. It is then approved by the House of Lords (actually their Lordships cannot amend it because it is a 'Money Bill' and since 1911 the House of Lords has been debarred from making changes to such Bills). It then receives the Royal Assent and becomes an Act. This last stage must happen by 5 August as otherwise the Provisional Collection of Income Tax Act would cease to apply and there would no longer be a legal requirement to deduct tax at source (eg under PAYE).

The whole period during which the Chancellor's proposals move from being a Finance Bill to becoming an Act is less than 100 working days for Parliament. The draft legislation is often complex (several recent Finance Acts have been so long that they have had to be printed in two volumes) and it is not surprising when it subsequently emerges that the legislation is ambiguous or uncertain – hence the need for statements of practice and extra-statutory concessions (see page 13).

## THE INLAND REVENUE

No book on UK taxation would be complete without an overview of the Inland Revenue and how it operates. The following is therefore an overview of the Revenue and how it deals with its 'clients', the taxpayers.

## Inland Revenue organisation and structure

The Inland Revenue is the government department that has responsibility for assessing and collecting direct taxes (income tax, corporation tax, CGT, petroleum revenue tax, IHT and stamp duty) and national insurance contributions (NICs). It also has responsibility for enforcing the national minimum wage, payment of the Working Families and Disabled Persons Tax Credits and the collection of student loans. In dealing with Revenue officials, taxpayers should bear in mind that there are three main divisions of responsibilities:

(1) Inspectors of taxes.
(2) Certain specialist offices such as:
    (a) the Capital Taxes Office (CTO) – responsible for collecting IHT and valuing shares in unquoted companies;
    (b) the Valuation Office Agency – responsible for providing valuations for land and business;
    (c) the Financial Intermediaries and Claims Office (FICO) – four offices providing specialist services on a range of subjects such as UK charities and residence/domicile issues;
    (d) the National Insurance Contributions Office (NICO) – responsible for collecting and recording NICs; and
    (e) the Stamp Duty Office – responsible for assessing and collecting stamp duty
(3) Collectors of taxes – responsible for collecting tax and NICs. There are various collection offices around the country. Staff at the Collector's office do not get involved at all in assessing the tax payable; this is the job of the Inspector of Taxes.

Each individual taxpayer dealt with by the Revenue has a single tax district or tax office, which deals with all aspects of his income tax and CGT liabilities. A director or employee's tax district is determined by his employer's address. Where a taxpayer is self-employed, the main tax district will be decided by the address from which the business is carried on. Individuals who have only investment income are normally dealt with by the tax district which deals with the area in which they live.

The Revenue has three main types of tax office (Taxpayer Service Office, Tax District Office and Integrated Office) which are supported by the Tax Enquiry Centres and various specialist offices.

### Taxpayer Service Office (TSO)

TSOs combine assessment with preliminary collection work to improve customer service. They deal specifically with personal tax matters, such as:

- PAYE coding
- Assessments and personal reliefs

- Employer-based (including PAYE-related) compliance work
- Checks and telephone calls to taxpayers on certain local collection action cases (although in London, this involves all local collection action, including enforcement)
- Income tax accounts processing.

### Tax District Office (TDO)

TDOs are locally based to handle investigation and compliance work, including the following:

- All corporation tax
- In-depth accounts examination and income tax compliance, including Schedule D
- Local recovery action, including enforcement.

### Integrated Office (IO)

These are single offices set up in some areas to cover all TSO and TDO functions.

### Tax Enquiry Centre

Tax Enquiry Centres perform the following services:

- Answering enquiries and providing assistance by telephone or in person
- Providing leaflets and forms
- Arranging for staff from the three main offices (above) to provide specialist help
- Accepting payments where a taxpayer wishes or needs to pay tax locally.

## The Revenue's Code

The Revenue publishes codes of practice, some of which are examined in this chapter, explaining their approach and procedures in certain areas of work, which set out the legal rights of taxpayers (and the Revenue) and explain what the taxpayer can expect to happen. The codes of practice (which can be found at the Inland Revenue's website (www.inlandrevenue.gov.uk/leaflets/) include the following:

| | |
|---|---|
| COP1 | Mistakes by the Inland Revenue |
| COP2 | Investigations |
| COP3 | Review of employers' and contractors' records |
| COP4 | Inspection of schemes offered by financial intermediaries |
| COP5 | Inspection of charities records |

| COP6 | Collection of tax |
|---|---|
| COP7 | Collection of tax due from employers and contractors in the construction industry |
| COP8 | Special Compliance Office investigations. Cases of other than suspected serious fraud |
| COP9 | Special Compliance Office investigations. Cases of suspected serious fraud |
| COP10 | Information and advice |
| COP11 | Enquiries into tax returns by local offices |
| COP14 | Enquiries into Company Tax Returns |
| COP17 | Enquiries into applications for Working Families' Tax Credit or Disabled Person's Tax Credit |
| Consultation | Code of Practice on Consultation |

## The Revenue's open government policy

In April 1994, the Government introduced the *Code of Practice on Access to Government Information* and in May 1995, the Revenue published leaflet IR141, *Inland Revenue: Open Government*. This leaflet explains how the Revenue is complying with the promise of increased openness and accountability so as to improve the democratic process and public's understanding of the way the Government works. The Revenue is committed to make information about policies and decisions more extensively available.

The Revenue makes certain information generally available through press releases, leaflets, booklets and other publications including their internal guidance manuals, which were published at the end of 1995. This information covers:

(1) details of major policy proposals and decisions which the Government considers to be relevant and important;
(2) explanatory material on the Revenue's dealings with the public; and
(3) information about standards of service, complaints procedures and other aspects of the way the Revenue runs its services.

Except where there is an established convention or legal authority not to do so, the Revenue will provide reasons for administrative decisions affecting individual taxpayers. It will also respond to questions about the general working of the tax system where taxpayers need the information, say to complete their tax returns, or to understand how their tax is worked out, or to appeal.

In addition, the Revenue will generally meet requests for information about Government policy on taxes, their actions and decisions, and interpretation of legislation where it has a settled view. Information will not be given if it is in the public interest for it to remain confidential. Such examples are where it would prejudice the assessment or collection of tax, or assist tax avoidance or evasion.

The Revenue will charge for providing some information. The charge is based upon the nature of the request and the time needed to deal with it, and calculated at a rate of £15–20 per hour, unless it is of a specialist nature. A flat-rate charge of £15 applies for dealing with straightforward requests where the estimated cost is less than £50. There is no charge for Revenue leaflets, which explain different aspects of the tax system, copies of the Taxpayer's Charter, codes of practice or other similar types information which sets out the services provided by the Revenue and the standards it aims to achieve. Explanations of the reasons for decisions, answers to questions about the general working of the tax system and information about the right of appeal or how to complain are also free.

The Revenue's code of practice on open government sets a response date target of 20 working days from receipt of a straightforward request and outlines the complaints procedure

## Revenue information and advice

COP10 outlines Revenue practice in giving post-transactional rulings, statutory clearances and approvals, together with interpretations of tax law (in certain circumstances) and provides details of the other information published. Post-transaction rulings are rulings given by the Revenue on the application of tax law to a specific transaction after it has taken place. Such rulings will bind the Revenue unless material information was withheld. The scheme requires the following information to be submitted before a ruling can be obtained:

- The taxpayer's name and tax reference
- Full particulars of the transaction or event
- A statement of the issue(s) to be considered
- Copies of all relevant documents, with the relevant passages identified
- A statement that to the best of the taxpayer's knowledge and belief, the facts as stated are correct and all relevant facts have been disclosed
- A statement of the specific point(s) of difficulty giving rise to the ruling request
- A statement of the ruling requested or suggested as appropriate by the applicant
- Particulars of sections of the Taxes Acts considered to be relevant
- Particulars of any case law, statements of practice, extra-statutory concessions etc considered to be relevant
- Particulars of any previous discussions or correspondence about the tax treatment of the transaction, or of any similar transaction between the taxpayer and any Revenue office; also when the taxpayer or his advisers are aware of correspondence on the transaction between any other person and any Revenue office, particulars of that correspondence
- A statement of the applicant's opinion of the tax consequence of the transaction, along with reasons to the extent that they are capable of being supplied.

The following information is available from the Revenue:

- Explanatory leaflets, booklets and helpsheets, designed to explain different aspects of the tax system and provide assistance with tax return completion
- Statements of practice (SP) explain the Revenue's interpretation of legislation and the application of the law in practice
- Extra-statutory concessions (ESC), which are relaxations providing a reduction in tax liability that would not be available under the strict letter of the law
- Press Releases announce a proposed change in the law, in Revenue practice or other change
- The *Tax Bulletin* provides insight into the thinking of technical Revenue specialists on technical issues and interpretation of tax law. It is published every two months
- Internal Guidance Manuals cover the Revenue's interpretation of tax law and the operation of the tax system.

With the exception of the last item, most of the above information is available on the Revenue's Internet website (www.inlandrevenue.gov.uk). Any Revenue Enquiry Centre, Tax Office or the Revenue Information Centre should be able to provide leaflets, booklets, statements of practice and ESCs and certain items can be obtained through the Self Assessment Orderline.

The above website is a significant and valuable source of information, not only in the large amount of information it makes available, but also in the speed in which it is updated. As well as providing the aforementioned information, return forms (eg self-assessment and employers forms) can be downloaded and there are a number of specialist featured areas such as:

- Construction Industry Scheme
- e-business and e-commerce
- IR35 Proposals
- Employee Share Schemes
- Working Families Tax Credit.

Over the last few years, access to the Revenue's Internal Manuals has increased and at present over 50 different manuals are in the public domain, covering a wide range of subjects. The manuals are available for reference in Inland Revenue Enquiry Centres or can be purchased from independent publishers. It is hoped that they will shortly be made available on the Revenue's website.

It must not be forgotten that the Revenue's information sources do not have the force of law, but are merely interpretations of the legally binding statute and case law. Therefore, potentially they could be open to challenge through the courts.

# UNDERSTANDING YOUR RESPONSIBILITIES AND RIGHTS

The Inland Revenue is now increasingly run more like a business. At the same time, the Government requires it to operate quality management and to assess its efficiency in terms of 'satisfied customers'.

It is the Revenue's policy to help taxpayers understand their rights and obligations, to get their tax affairs right and pay their tax on time. Their standards in dealing with the public are explained in *Our Service Commitment to You*. The work must be done thoroughly, timely, cost-efficiently and its staff must get it right first time. Targets are set each year and regularly measured to see if they are being achieved. The Revenue has also issued a joint charter with Customs & Excise (see below), a Charter for Inland Revenue taxpayers (IR167) and a charter for national insurance contributors (CA4):

---

**Our overall approach to customer service**

This Charter covers the service provided to customers with regard to income tax, corporation tax and capital gains tax, by a network of local tax offices within the ten Regional Executive Offices, together with the two Accounts Offices, and Enforcement Office.

For each tax, our aim is to provide an efficient, effective and fair service. This Charter has been developed after consultation with our customers and staff, and sets out:

- how we will provide you with help and assistance
- the standards of service you can expect
- how you can help us deliver an effective service and make suggestions for further improvement
- where you can obtain information about your legal rights and other entitlements, and
- how to complain, if you are unhappy with the service we provide.

**Providing help and assistance to you**

We provide help:

- through a wide range of clearly written leaflets and booklets. Each explains a particular aspect of tax, or what to do in specific circumstances (for example, setting up a business). These are summarised in our IR list 'Catalogue of leaflets and booklets' and most are available from Inland Revenue offices. Information is also available on the Internet at **www.inlandrevenue.gov.uk**
- over the telephone, in writing or, at Inland Revenue Enquiry Centres, in person. Inland Revenue leaflet 'How to contact the Inland Revenue', available from all Inland Revenue offices, sets out the main sources of help and information available to you.

---

## Contacting us

*Opening hours*
Inland Revenue Enquiry Centres are open for at least 40 hours a week. Most are open from 8.30am to 4.30pm, Monday to Friday. And some are also open outside these hours.

*Telephone service*
Switchboards in tax offices are open at least 40 hours a week including the period 9.00am to 4.30pm, Monday to Friday. Again, many offices provide a telephone service outside these hours.

*Addresses*
The address and telephone number of your own tax office will be at the top of any correspondence they have sent you. Alternatively, details of tax offices in your area can be found in your phone book under 'Inland Revenue'.

## Our standards of service

If you **telephone us**, we aim to:

- answer within 30 seconds (ten rings) at the switchboard
- connect you to the right extension first time (unless your call has gone direct).

If you **visit** our Inland Revenue Enquiry Centres, we aim to see you within 15 minutes of arrival if you have not previously made an appointment.

If you **write** to our tax offices, we aim to respond to every question or issue you have raised within 28 calendar days. Where this is not possible, we will tell you why and when you can expect a full reply.

However you contact us, we will:

- provide a clear, accurate and helpful response
- make clear what action you need to take next, and by what date
- give our names, and
- be courteous and professional.

In addition, we aim to:

- get every aspect of your affairs right first time by making full and correct use of the information available to us
- deal with your repayment claims sent to our specialist repayment offices, within 28 calendar days.

## Specific targets and previous year's results

We deliver a national service on income tax, corporation tax and capital gains tax through ten Regional Executive Offices, supported by two Accounts Offices and Enforcement Office.

The Regional Executive Offices annually produce customer service leaflets showing:

- performance against the previous year's customer service targets
- targets for the current year.

Inland Revenue Enquiry Centres can supply a copy of their Region's leaflet.

Leaflets showing similar information for the Accounts Offices and Enforcement Office are available from those Offices.

Information on customer service standards and achievements, together with the service standards operated by the Inland Revenue's specialist tax offices, is also found in the Department's annual report, available from The Stationery Office and on the Internet.

**Privacy and confidentiality**

In handling your affairs, we will:

- deal with them on a strictly confidential basis, within the law
- respect your privacy
- find a private room or space for you if you visit us to discuss your affairs, should you prefer it.

**Any special needs**

If you have any special needs (for example, related to a disability), we will provide whatever help we reasonably can. Most Inland Revenue Enquiry Centres have already been equipped with ramps, hearing loops and other aids, and we are installing Minicom systems (for people with hearing difficulties). Some of our leaflets are being converted, on a rolling programme, to Braille, audio and large print. Details of specific services can be found in the Regional Executive Office Customer Service leaflets (available from Inland Revenue Enquiry Centres).

If you need to see us, but you have a disability which prevents you from coming to our office, please phone or write explaining the problem and what you need from us. We will make the necessary arrangements to visit you.

Please discuss any other requirements with the Customer Service Manager of the office with which you are dealing (you can get their name from any member of staff in the office). They will explain what they can offer to help you.

**Your legal rights and our Codes of Practice**

The Inland Revenue produces Codes of Practice explaining our approach and procedures in certain areas of work (especially tax investigations). The Codes set out, as appropriate, your legal rights and the rights of the Inland Revenue, and explain what you can expect to happen. Copies of the Codes are available from Inland Revenue Enquiry Centres and tax offices.

**How you can help us**

To help us deal with your tax affairs accurately and quickly, we sometimes need help from you. For example, we may ask you for more information. If we make such a request, please respond as quickly as you can, checking you have provided everything asked for.

If you contact us, please have ready your tax reference number (shown on your tax return, provided in our correspondence with you and given on your pay slips).

It is also useful if you can tell your tax office when your circumstances change – for example, when you get married or change your address.

You are required by law:

- to keep proper records of your income and expenses
- to complete any return we send to you accurately and on time
- if you do not receive a tax return to complete, to let us know about any income or gains which have not been fully taxed.

It saves everyone trouble if you pay your tax on time. If you experience difficulty, please advise your tax office immediately.

### If you disagree with us

You may disagree with our interpretation of the law or the way we have applied it to your particular circumstances. If so, you should tell us why you disagree. Alternatively, if we have already made a formal decision in respect of your tax liability, you are entitled to appeal against what we have done. We will explain how you can appeal when we give you our decision. If we can not resolve your appeal, you can refer it to the General or Special Commissioners – independent appeals tribunals whose decision is binding on both parties. Appeals on the Commissioners' interpretation of the law can be made through the civil courts.

### If you wish to complain

If you are unhappy about the way we have dealt with your affairs (because, for example, of delays, mistakes or a failure to act on information you have given us), you should complain first of all to the Officer in Charge of the office or unit you are dealing with. Their name is displayed at the head of all correspondence.

If you are still not satisfied, you can refer the complaint to the Director with overall responsibility for that office or unit. (The name and address of the Director is shown in leaflet IR120 'You and the Inland Revenue' and can also be obtained from any Inland Revenue office).

If you are dissatisfied with the Director's response, you can ask the Adjudicator to look into your complaint. Finally, you can ask your MP to refer your case to the independent Parliamentary Commissioner for Administration (the Ombudsman). The Ombudsman will accept referral from any MP, but you should approach your own MP first. IR leaflet IR120 explains these options.

The Adjudicator's Office also produces a leaflet (AO1) explaining its role and procedures. Copies of the Adjudicator's leaflet are available from The Adjudicator's Office (Haymarket House, 28 Haymarket, London SW1Y 4SP) or any Inland Revenue office.

### Listening to your suggestions

We welcome your suggestions and use them to improve our service and supporting processes. We supplement these with:

- an annual national postal survey covering all major customer groups
- local and Regional office surveys, as appropriate
- feedback from complaints.

Please make any suggestions for improvement (including this Charter) direct to your Customer Service Manager at your tax office or Inland Revenue Enquiry Centre.

**Revision date**

This Charter came into force at 1 April 1999; it will be reviewed annually and (if not amended before then) will be reissued at 1 April 2002.

## What this means in practice

In practice, this means that a taxpayer should attend promptly to correspondence from the Inland Revenue and complete tax returns within a reasonable period. If you find that there are some aspects of your tax return which are complex and which prevent you from completing the entire form, you should contact the Inspector and explain the reason for the difficulty.

## Statements of practice and extra-statutory concessions

It is extremely important that the Inland Revenue operates a uniform interpretation of the tax legislation. This is all part of the Taxpayer's Charter which requires the Revenue to deal with two taxpayers in the same way if their circumstances are identical.

In cases where the legislation is obscure, or its precise implication is uncertain, the Revenue publishes statements of practice (SPs). These operate as a shield for the taxpayer rather than a sword for the Revenue. You can rely upon the Revenue applying these SPs but they do not affect your statutory rights and, if you believe that the Revenue interpretation is wrong, it is still open to you to appeal to the Commissioners.

The Revenue also publishes extra-statutory concessions (ESCs). These apply in cases where the legislation is quite clear, but the letter of the law produces an unreasonable result. In effect, the Revenue recognises that Parliament could never have intended to impose certain tax liabilities, and ESCs are commonsense rules which the Revenue applies so as to avoid an unreasonable result. Once again, the Revenue publishes these ESCs because it recognises the need to treat all taxpayers alike. In general, and unless your circumstances are special, or you are seeking to apply an extra-statutory concession so as to avoid tax, you can rely on the Inspector of Taxes applying a published extra-statutory concession if it covers your particular circumstances.

## If you and the Revenue cannot reach agreement

There will be cases from time to time where an Inspector and a taxpayer (or his professional adviser) form different conclusions as to whether, or how, tax should apply to a particular transaction. In such cases where there is an honest difference of opinion, or even in cases where there is an argument as to the actual facts, the Revenue does not have the last word. The procedure for resolving such disputes is to require an appeal to be heard by the Commissioners.

There are two types of Commissioners, General Commissioners and Special Commissioners, but the difference lies mainly in the type of disputes that each type of Commissioner is best equipped to deal with. Questions of fact, requiring local knowledge, are best heard by General Commissioners. Special Commissioners are generally lawyers and are normally regarded as more competent to deal with technical issues arising from the interpretation of the legislation.

The Commissioners are an independent body and are not connected with the Inspector of Taxes or the Inland Revenue. Their findings on matters of fact are normally final, but if a taxpayer (or the Revenue) is dissatisfied with his (or its) decision on a point of law, an appeal may be made to the courts. Normally, the appeal is heard by the High Court (or the Court of Session in Scotland). It is even possible to appeal against decisions by the courts and ultimately the matter may go right up to the House of Lords for a decision.

## COMPLAINTS AND COMPENSATION

If a taxpayer is not happy with the way he has been treated by the Revenue he is entitled to complain. In this first instance, it is recommended that the complaint be raised with the Officer in Charge of the local district before approaching the Director or Controller with overall responsibility for that office. Further details are provided in leaflet IR20. If this still proves unsatisfactory, the complaint should be raised with the Adjudicator (see leaflet AO1) and failing that, the case could be referred through the taxpayer's local MP to the independent Parliamentary Commissioner for Administration (the Ombudsman).

If the Revenue makes a mistake or causes unreasonable delay, the taxpayer is entitled to an apology, an explanation of what went wrong and, if appropriate, details of the steps taken to ensure the mistake does not reoccur. If reasonable and possible, the Revenue will also have the mistake corrected.

The Revenue has a 28-day target for replying to all letters and enquiries and if there is a delay in excess of six months, without good reason, it will give up interest on unpaid tax and pay repayment interest on overpaid tax arising because of the delay. Furthermore, any reasonable costs incurred as a direct result of the delay will also be paid. The Revenue's policy on remitting tax where there has been a delay in using information provided to it is explained at page 29.

If the mistake or delay is serious, it may be possible to claim additional costs arising from the mistake. According to the Revenue's internal Redress Manual, a serious error is something which no responsible person, acting in good faith and with proper care, could reasonably have done; this would indicate that a non-serious error was a pardonable error, or even an innocent misunderstanding. Although the interpretation of 'serious' is dependent upon the facts of each situation, the Revenue considers the following to fall within the definition:

(1) taking a wholly unreasonable view of, as opposed to having a genuine difference of opinion about, the law;

(2) starting or pursuing enquiries into matters which were obviously trivial on the basis of the facts available at the time;

(3) making what would normally be a simple or trivial mistake, but the particular circumstances required more care because the Revenue should have known that such a mistake could have serious consequences.

Even if the mistakes are not serious, reasonable costs may be paid for persistent errors (eg where the Revenue makes the same type of mistake or continues in the mistake even after it has been revealed, unless there is a genuine difference of opinion). If a number of unconnected mistakes were made in any 12-month period, for the same tax year or for the same period of assessment, this may also be regarded as persistent (eg if an assessment keeps being amended because of new facts, but each time the Revenue gets the amendment wrong).

The reasonable costs that may be paid extend to professional fees, incidental personal expenses, or wages or fees which would have been earned but were lost through having to sort things out. They could also include such items as postage and telephone charges.

In exceptional cases, where a serious error has resulted directly in a significant and unwarranted intrusion into the taxpayer's personal life, the Revenue will consider making a payment as consolation for any worry and distress suffered as a direct result of that error. Significant and unwarranted intrusions may comprise confidentiality breaches, inappropriate use of information, poorly handled investigations, and misleading advice or mistakes affecting vulnerable taxpayers (such as those suffering medical or physical illness, emotional trauma (eg bereavement) or the elderly). If the unreasonable delay exceeds more than two years, a consolatory payment may also be made. In handling the complaint itself, if there has been significant delay for no good reason or where it has been seriously mishandled, consolatory payments may be made. Unsurprisingly each case will be considered on its own merits and payments are likely to be in the region of £50–250, although could be higher in more extreme cases, but unlikely to ever exceed £2,000.

## Revenue Adjudicator

If you find that you are dissatisfied with the treatment you receive from the Revenue (or Customs and Excise) you can ask an independent body to investigate your complaint. The matter should be referred to

Revenue Adjudicator's Office
3rd Floor
Haymarket House
28 Haymarket
London SW1Y 4SP
Tel: 020 7930 2292

The Revenue Adjudicator has issued a leaflet, *How to Complain about the Inland Revenue*.

## SELF-ASSESSMENT

The chances are that if you are going to receive a 2000 self-assessment (SA) tax return, you will have received it just after the start of the new tax year in April. If you do not receive a form and you had a new source of income or capital gains in the year just ended, you should report this to the Inland Revenue by 5 October 2000. If you have received the form then this must be filed no later than 31 January 2001; if you want the Revenue to work out your tax for you, you need to file your return by 30 September 2000.

### An overview of the self-assessment system

Do not be put off by the fact that the form seems complicated. The Revenue has produced a number of helpsheets and your tax office will be only too pleased to clarify anything which is not covered by the notes. There are still teething problems, but the system is proving to be a great improvement on what went before: a system designed afresh rather than a set of procedures which evolved gradually in a piecemeal fashion over the previous 200 years. For example, you only need to deal with one tax office. Also, you or the Revenue work out the tax that you owe (or are owed) as a global figure, whereas in the past many taxpayers have had to contend with several different tax districts making assessments on particular types of income, sometimes from opposite ends of the country.

The Revenue form contains a 'core' section which applies to all taxpayers. Beyond that, there are a number of special schedules which you need to complete only if you have a specific type of income, etc.

The basic principle is that by completing the form you should work out your own tax liability and you should settle what you owe by 31 January. However, provided an SA return is delivered to the Revenue not later than 30 September following the end of the tax year, the Revenue will calculate the amount of tax payable for you. Where a person does not submit the forms by 30 September he has until the following 31 January to complete the form (ie the SA return for 1999–2000 will need to be filed by 31 January 2001).

The legislation contains a number of 'incentives' to ensure that people comply with their obligations. If a person does not send back his SA return by the 31 January deadline, he will become liable for a fixed penalty of £100. If the return has still not been sent in by six months later, there will be a further £100 fixed penalty. If taxpayers continue to be dilatory, the Revenue may apply to the Commissioners for further penalties to be imposed of up to £60 per day that the SA returns are still outstanding.

The penalties for late submission of the return forms are in addition to surcharges which may be imposed on outstanding tax (see below).

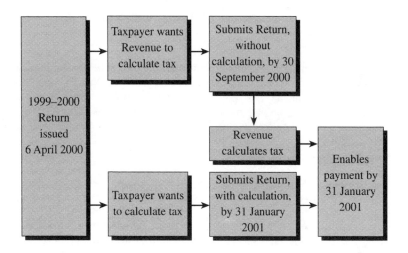

## Payment of tax

Where a person submits an SA return form, he will need to settle his tax liability for the year concerned. Of course, some income will have borne tax during the course of the year, either under PAYE or because a self-employed person has made payments on account of his tax liability. If tax is still outstanding after the 31 January payment date, interest is charged and the following surcharges are imposed:

(1) a 5% surcharge on any tax which is unpaid by 28 February after the end of the tax year (a month after the tax fell due);

(2) a further 5% surcharge on any tax still outstanding by 31 July (ie six months after the date that the tax fell due for payment on 31 January).

A taxpayer will also need to make payments on account of the current year.

## Payments on account

When a person files an SA return, he may also be required to make payments on account of his tax liability for the current year. Basically, the person should take his total tax liability for the previous year (ie the year covered by the SA return) and deduct CGT and tax withheld at source. If the balance is £500 or more, the taxpayer must make equal payments on account on 31 January and 31 July, which add up to this amount.

## Example

A files an SA return for 1999–2000 in January 2001. There is tax to pay of £10,000, but £4,500 of this is CGT. A must pay £2,750 on 31 January 2001 as a payment on account for 2000–01 and he must make a similar payment on account on 31 July 2001.

There is also no need to make payments on account if 80% of your liability (ignoring any CGT) is covered by tax deducted at source. You can apply for a reduction in your 2000–01 payments on account if you have reason to believe that your tax liability will be lower than that for 1999–2000, but if you turn out to be mistaken you will be charged interest.

## Process now, check later

The Revenue has designed the SA return with its own data processing in mind. The returns are normally read by an OCR (optical character recognition) machine or some returns may be submitted electronically – the Revenue would much prefer that their 'customers' use the ELS method of filing. Past experience has shown that many returns need correcting because of arithmetical errors, figures being transposed, amounts being entered in the wrong column etc. When the Revenue officer identifies such mistakes he will issue a notice to the taxpayer advising him of the correction (or 'repair') needed. The taxpayer can object, but if the Revenue does not hear further within three months, the correction is deemed to form part of the return.

Routine checking and making corrections must not be confused with Revenue officers carrying out an enquiry. The Revenue will need to issue a formal notice within a period of 12 months of the filing date (31 January) unless the return is submitted after that date. The Revenue need not give any reason for wanting to check a return and, indeed, between 5,000 and 10,000 taxpayers will be selected each year on a totally random basis. The Revenue has said that it expects to carry out around 40,000 enquiries each year.

## Protection against unnecessary enquiries

The Revenue has issued a number of codes of practice and has stressed to its staff that enquiries should be brought to an end as soon as possible. Furthermore, the Revenue cannot open fresh enquiries into a return once the original enquiry has been brought to a conclusion.

## Keeping proper records

Because the Revenue operates on a 'process now, check later' basis, you need to keep records in order to be able to back up your entries on your SA return. The length of time that you need to retain your records depends upon whether you have a business or are letting property. If you do, the required period is five years and ten months after the end of the tax year. If you do not have either of these sources of income, the minimum period for retaining your records is normally one year and ten months after the end of the tax year concerned. You may find it helpful to read Revenue leaflet SA/BK4, *Self Assessment: a general guide to keeping records*.

## REVENUE ENQUIRIES INTO TAX RETURNS

Self-assessment has been with us since 6 April 1996, so we now have a fairly good understanding of how the regime works in practice. Fundamentally, the Revenue has a period of 12 months from the 31 January filing date to issue a notice that it is carrying out an enquiry into a tax return. Once that enquiry is completed, the position becomes final and the Revenue cannot reopen enquiries into that year unless it can show 'discovery', that is that the taxpayer acted negligently or fraudulently so that key information was withheld from the Revenue. Enquiries can be made into partnership returns under the same rules as apply to individual returns, but any amendments to partnership profits then need to be taken through to the individual partners' tax returns.

## Inclusion of provisional figures, estimates and valuations

The maximum time permitted for completion and submission of a return is ten months (ie for 2000–01, 6 April 2001 to 31 January 2002). Inevitably, final figures may not always be available by the submission deadline and therefore it will be necessary to estimate these amounts. The Revenue recognises this and has said that this is acceptable in certain circumstances. Initially, the Revenue's attitude to provisional figures was somewhat relaxed and it did not normally regard a return containing provisional figures as incomplete, provided the taxpayer took all reasonable steps to obtain the final figures and that the estimate was corrected as soon as the figures are available.

However, in *Tax Bulletin* September 1998, the Revenue announced that it would regard provisional returns as incomplete in circumstances where the taxpayer had made little or no effort to obtain the final figures. It stated that general pressure of work or complexities of tax affairs did not validate provisional figures and in the case of accounts information it must be genuinely impossible for final figures to be submitted. A single figure of estimated business profit would only likely to be acceptable for a newly commenced business, where the first accounting period does not end until close to or after the submission date. A change of accounting date may also give rise to provisional standard accounts information, and this should fulfil the requirements as being a complete return. Despite all this, the Revenue confirmed that it would not reject such returns, but would process them as received and flag them for enquiry review if the ultimate figures were not supplied by the expected date. However, the Revenue's leniency narrowed further in December 1999, when it stated returns would be rejected if an 'acceptable explanation for the delay' were not included in the return along with a date by which final figures were expected.

There will be situations where an estimated figure is submitted, which will not be amended in the future (eg where there is inadequate information to reach a precise figure). If the estimate is considered to be sufficiently reliable to make a complete return (eg where it is based upon detailed records for a sample representative period, in the case of private proportion expenses (eg motoring expenses)), it is not necessary to specifically refer to the estimate. However, if the figure is not so reliable (eg because the records may have been lost or destroyed), the Revenue requires identification of the amounts and an explanation of its calculation.

The Revenue also draws a distinction between estimates and judgmental figures. A valuation at 31 March 1982 for CGT is a good example of a judgmental figure. That is, there is no right or wrong answer, and the figure to be included is basically the taxpayer's best judgement as to the figures, which could be agreed with the Revenue. Again, the Revenue requires identification of, and details about, the valuation. The Revenue has agreed that where no enquiry is made into a valuation within the 12-month enquiry period, and the valuation falls within the range of bona fide valuations which could arise in negotiations between valuers who were fully instructed on the facts, it will not try to reopen the position.

## Return amendments by the taxpayer and the Revenue

The taxpayer may give a notice to the Revenue amending his SA return. This notice may be given within 12 months of the filing date (in most cases, 31 January).

The Revenue may amend an SA return within nine months of receiving it to correct obvious errors of principle, transpositions of figures and arithmetical errors. Such amendments are called 'repairs'. The Revenue is required to issue a notice in this connection and the taxpayer can then accept the repair or file an objection.

## Selection of returns for Revenue enquiries

The Revenue has a statutory power to enquire into any tax return without giving a reason. However, because of its limited resources, the Revenue has

## Diary under self-assessment

| Date | Who is affected | What happens |
|------|-----------------|--------------|
| 6 April 2000 | Everybody who gets a tax return | Self-assessment tax return for 1999–2000 sent out |
| 31 May 2000 | Employees | Employer should have given employee P60 for 1999–2000 by this date |
| 6 July 2000 | Employees who receive expenses and benefits in kind (not covered by a dispensation) | Employer should have given employee details of expenses and benefits for 1999–2000 by this date |
| 31 July 2000 | Some people: the Revenue will notify in advance where it applies | Second interim payment on account of 1999–2000 tax |
| 30 September 2000 | People who want the Revenue to calculate their 1999–2000 tax | Send in tax return by now |
| 30 September 2000 | People who pay tax under PAYE and want the Revenue to collect any tax due (up to £1,000) through their PAYE code during 2000–01 | Send in tax return by now |
| 5 October 2000 | People with new sources of income or capital gains arising in 1999–2000, who have not received a return | Report to Revenue by now or risk penalty |
| 31 January 2001 | Everybody who receives a return | This is the deadline for sending in the return and paying the tax due (£100 penalty for those failing to comply) |
| 31 January 2001 | Everybody who had an income tax liability for 1999–2000 of more than £500 and less than 80% of liability not accounted for by tax deducted at source | First interim payment on account in respect of 2000–01 tax |
| 28 February 2001 | Everybody who has not paid tax due on 31 January 2001 | Automatic surcharge will arise |
| 6 April 2001 | Everybody who gets a tax return | Tax return for 2000–01 will be sent out |

to be selective. It is more likely to target cases where it is perceived that there is a larger amount of tax at risk and enquiries are also likely to arise in cases where the Revenue's internal procedures require a mandatory review. However, a number of returns not suspected of being incorrect will also be selected at random each year.

An examination of the Revenue's Internal Enquiry Handbook indicates that Revenue staff are required to review certain returns such as:

- Returns filed late
- Returns which include provisional figures
- Cases which involve large capital gains
- Situations where there has been a change in accounting year, and
- Returns for Lloyd's Names.

## Revenue procedure for enquiries

The Revenue must give written notice that an enquiry is going to be made into an SA return. This notice must be served within a strict time limit:

(1) 12 months after the date that the SA return was delivered; or
(2) where the SA return is delivered after the normal 31 January filing date, the quarter date following 12 months after delivery.

For these purposes, the quarter dates are 31 January, 30 April, 31 July and 31 October. Thus, if an SA return is not in fact delivered until 31 March, the Revenue can give notice that it is starting an enquiry up to 30 April of the following year.

The Revenue will not give any reason for having opened an enquiry. However, it should soon become apparent whether the enquiry is initially an 'aspect enquiry' into one particular aspect of the return or a 'full enquiry' under which the Revenue requires access to all the taxpayer's records. An aspect enquiry can extend into a full enquiry as the Revenue receives information, so the distinction is not completely clear cut.

The opening of an enquiry is not meant to imply that the Revenue believes that anything is untoward, merely that it is carrying out checks to test the accuracy and reliability of the return.

The Enquiry Handbook repeatedly states that Revenue officers should adopt a non-confrontational approach and keep an open mind. The Revenue intends that the opening of enquiries should be less contentious, and that their aim is to develop a more neutral and less confrontational approach in this area. It is acknowledged that the information initially available in the return and elsewhere is unlikely to be sufficient to establish whether the return is incorrect, and even where it appears incorrect it could be that the information is incomplete, misleading or capable of explanation. The Handbook advises officers that unless they are reasonably certain that there have been omissions, and often it will not be possible for them to be certain, they should ask the taxpayer in a neutral way whether there is anything further that he has to say, taking account of what has already been said. They should make it clear that they are not making any allegations at this point. When the Revenue opens an enquiry, it will issue details of its code of practice, which will be either the full code or a short version in straightforward cases.

## Information required

The Revenue is instructed to informally request any information needed, rather than using its formal powers to require the production of the information. A formal notice would, however, be issued for documents in the taxpayer's power or possession, if he had refused to co-operate with the informal request or had failed to comply within the specified timescale. Such a notice must allow the taxpayer at least 30 days to comply. Moreover, the taxpayer may appeal to the Commissioners if he thinks that the notice is invalid. If the Commissioners decide that the notice is valid, the documents must then be produced within 30 days of their decision.

The Revenue can only request information and documents which are relevant and reasonably required to determine whether the self-assessment is correct. Its approach varies according to whether the taxpayer is a business taxpayer (ie a taxpayer whose is self-employment or in receipt of income from property). In the case of a full enquiry into the business taxpayer's affairs, the Revenue considers that the following items can be reasonably requested without providing an explanation:

- Business records generally
- Cash book, petty cash book, sales and purchase invoices and bank account statements
- Details of how any adjustments by the accountant had been calculated
- An analysis of drawings, and
- Details of any balancing figures or estimates used in the accounts.

Private bank statements are not normally required at the initial stage of an enquiry.

Where there is a full enquiry into a non-business taxpayer, which is a complex case, officers should seek to verify in the first place the income and gains declared by reference to any third party information held (eg a form P11D). The information requested directly might then comprise:

- Dividend vouchers
- Certificates of loan interest paid
- Form PPCC (ie a certificate confirming payment under a personal pension scheme)
- A detailed CGT computation
- A copy of a property valuation
- An account of the precise use made of a company asset such as a private plane.

As for business taxpayers, the advice to officers is that they should not ask to see private bank statements at this early stage unless it can be demonstrated that the statements are relevant to the return and can be reasonably required for checking the return's accuracy.

In aspect cases, the information requested should, unsurprisingly, concentrate upon information relevant to the particular point under review.

## Meetings with the Revenue

The Enquiry Code of Practice states that taxpayers are not obliged to attend any meeting requested by the Revenue, but taxpayers are expected to provide promptly any information considered essential to the enquiry. The Revenue believes meetings allow taxpayers to clarify and explain any points that may have been misunderstood, and to ask questions of the Revenue. The taxpayer will be told if the Revenue considers correspondence is an inadequate substitute for a meeting. However, it is not possible for an officer to insist that a taxpayer attends any meeting, and his only alternative in terms of asking questions of the taxpayer face-to-face is to take an appeal to a personal hearing before the Commissioners and put his question to the taxpayer during cross-examination (assuming that the taxpayer is put forward as a witness).

There is no reason in principle why enquiries should not be conducted entirely through correspondence. Code of Practice 11 commits the Inspector to being mindful of the taxpayer's compliance costs and it may be possible to agree with the officer that matters should proceed by way of correspondence without this being viewed as lack of co-operation on the taxpayer's part. However, it should be borne in mind that a refusal to attend a meeting may in certain circumstances be seen as a lack of co-operation when it comes to assessing penalties in the event that the enquiry reveals an under-declaration of tax.

Generally, a request for a meeting should be taken as an indication that the officer, having considered the information initially supplied, has concluded that there are grounds for doubting the return's accuracy or that there are matters that require further detailed enquiry. Officers are instructed that where irregularities are suspected they would need to consider how to give the taxpayer the opportunity to disclose them and to co-operate actively in quantifying them. Whether the taxpayer does take this opportunity could have a bearing on the level of penalty that could be levied on him. Officers are instructed to seek early meetings.

## Closure of the enquiry

The legislation does not specify any time limit in which the Revenue must complete its enquiries. However, if the taxpayer feels that the Revenue has had sufficient information, he may appeal to the Commissioners for them to direct the Revenue to bring the enquiry to an end.

When the Revenue officer who has conducted the enquiry has completed his investigation, he must issue a notice stating this and setting out his conclusions of the correct amount of tax which should be payable for the year in question. Once such a notice has been issued, the Revenue is debarred from starting new enquiries in relation to that return.

## Faster Working enquiries

The Revenue is keen to reduce the time taken to deal with enquiries into business returns and therefore introduced 'Faster Working'. Since April 1998, business taxpayers whose returns are selected for enquiry have had the opportunity to elect for Faster Working. Faster Working is voluntary for taxpayers, and either side can pull out of the agreement if, for instance, the enquiry proves to be unexpectedly complex. It involves setting an agreed but flexible timetable for the enquiry and the total time will vary according to circumstances. The Revenue's aim is for enquiries under Faster Working to be completed within about six months. Leaflet IR162, *A better approach to local office enquiry work under self-assessment*, and *Tax Bulletin Supplement to Special Edition 2* provide more information. Despite the Revenue's intentions, there is little evidence that Faster Working has been embraced by local districts, which are rumoured to be reluctant to agree to it, even if it is specifically requested.

## Future changes

The Revenue in December 1999 announced the commencement of a review of its procedures for self-assessment enquiries. Revenue officials will look at the impact of the current procedures on taxpayers and tax advisers and consider possible improvements, both administrative and legislative, with a view to introducing any changes in the 2001 Finance Bill. They state that their review will include the following:

- Codes of practice
- Faster Working
- Letters opening enquiries
- Use of the correction power and its link with enquiries
- Enquiries limited to particular entries on a return, including CGT enquiries
- Enquiries into partnerships
- Use of formal self-assessment information powers
- Contract settlements and penalty determinations
- Litigating points in dispute.

# Protection from discovery assessments

Even though an assessment has been accepted, the time limit for starting an enquiry has expired and all enquiries have been completed, the Revenue may still revisit the past if fresh information comes to light or if it turns out that the taxpayer had negligently or fraudulently withheld that information. An assessment to collect underpaid tax in these circumstances is called a 'discovery assessment'.

No discovery assessment may be made where the Revenue could reasonably have been expected to identify the point at issue from information provided in an SA return. Moreover, information provided in SA returns for the two previous years is also to be taken into account in this connection. It follows that taxpayers should provide the Revenue with too much information rather than too little to avoid discovery assessments. The provision of business accounts is particularly useful in this context, although the Revenue guidance notes for taxpayers state that it is not necessary to send them.

An additional form of protection may be secured by obtaining post-transaction rulings (see pages 7 and 8 above).

## What happens if the SA return is found to be incorrect?

If the Revenue's enquiry shows that the taxpayer has self-assessed and paid too much tax, he will be refunded the difference, together with interest (normally from the date of payment). However, if the enquiry reveals material errors in the taxpayer's favour he is likely to be charged interest from the 31 January filing date plus a surcharge for the tax unpaid at 28 February and 31 July following that filing date. If the errors revealed in the enquiry were duplicated in previous tax years, the Revenue is likely to raise discovery assessments for those years and to seek interest and surcharges. Penalties may also be imposed where the enquiry reveals under-declarations, which amount to negligence or fraud.

## What penalties can the Revenue impose?

### Deliberate deception

Anyone who has deliberately understated his taxable income or chargeable gains may be prosecuted for fraud, false accounting, theft or the beautifully old-fashioned, but still rather serious, offence of 'cheating our Sovereign Lady the Queen'. If business profits have been understated, there has been failure to declare all investments or the taxpayer has claimed allowances to which he is not entitled, he is in serious trouble and at risk of imprisonment. A taxpayer in this position should seek the advice of a solicitor or accountant experienced in settling 'back duty' cases immediately, even if the Revenue has not yet shown signs of suspecting the deception. Although, it is very difficult for the Revenue to amass enough evidence to mount a successful criminal prosecution, an unrepresented taxpayer may find himself out of his depth at a Revenue enquiry.

## Failure to submit a return

If a taxpayer fails to submit his SA return by the required filing date, usually 31 January following the end of the tax year, there is an automatic flat-rate penalty of £100. For continuing failure, the Commissioners may impose an additional penalty of up to £60 per day. If there has been no application for an additional daily penalty and the return has not been submitted within six months of the filing date a further automatic £100 penalty arises. If the return is still outstanding within 12 months of the filing date a penalty not exceeding the tax that would have been payable under the return will be charged – in other words, there can be a double assessment. However, according to the Revenue's SA/BK6 these late return fixed penalties cannot exceed the tax liability for the year payable at the filing date, which is after taking into account payments made on account or otherwise. For example:

|  |  | £ | £ |
|---|---|---|---|
| 1999–2000 SA shows total liability |  |  | 50,000 |
| *Less*: payments on account | 31/1/2000 | 23,000 |  |
|  | 31/7/2000 | 23,000 |  |
| Additional payment on account | 20/1/2001 | 2,000 |  |
| Tax deduction under PAYE for (1999–2000) |  | 1,925 | 49,925 |
| Balance payable at filing date | 31/1/2001 |  | 75 |

Any penalties for late submission in respect of 1999–2000 would be reduced to £75. If, however, the additional payment of £2,000 had been made after the filing date (say 20 February 2000 rather than 20 January 1999), the automatic penalties would not be reduced. It is possible to appeal against the penalties if the taxpayer can satisfy the Commissioners as to having had a reasonable excuse throughout the period of default.

The same fixed penalties apply for failures to submit partnership returns, although there is no tax-geared penalty or provision for reducing the penalties as for individuals. Each partner will be liable to a £100 penalty if the partnership return is submitted late.

## Failure to notify Revenue of taxable income or gains

A taxpayer who has not received a return form is still obliged to inform the Inspector of any taxable income or gains (other than income taxed under the PAYE scheme, income taxed by deduction at source and income and gains already assessed) within six months of the end of the year of assessment. If he fails to do so, he becomes liable to a penalty equal to the tax unpaid at the filing date.

## Submission of an incorrect return

If a taxpayer submits an incorrect return, he is liable to a penalty equal to the difference between the tax charged on the income or gain returned and the true income or gain. Strictly, such a penalty is only chargeable if the taxpayer has been fraudulent or negligent, but the Revenue's approach has always been that the mere fact that the return is wrong proves that the taxpayer must have been guilty at least of negligence. Moreover, the taxpayer is not allowed to blame a third party (eg his accountant) for the error, although he may be able to insist that the accountant reimburses any penalty suffered.

Similar provisions apply for partnership returns; penalties for incorrect partnership returns may be levied on each partner.

## Mitigation of penalties for incorrect return

The penalty for an error in a return (including, of course, a set of business accounts submitted with a return) is, therefore, a potential doubling of the tax chargeable on the income or gains under-declared. This could be levied in addition to any interest charge. However, the Revenue's practice is to reduce or mitigate the potential penalty by reference to three factors. Taking the maximum penalty as a surcharge of 100%, the possible reductions are as follows:

(1) For disclosure, a maximum of 30% if the taxpayer goes to the Inspector admitting that a mistake has been made and a maximum of 20% if the taxpayer makes a complete disclosure as soon as he is challenged by the Inspector.

(2) For co-operation, a maximum of 40%. 'Co-operation' means, for example, answering the Inspector's questions and providing any back-up documentation within a reasonable timespan.

(3) For reduced culpability, a maximum of 40%. For example, nothing will be allowed under this head if it is clear, even though the Inspector cannot prove it, that the taxpayer set out deliberately to cheat the Revenue. A reduction of perhaps 15–25% will be allowed if the taxpayer has been guilty of gross carelessness and between 30% and 40% where he has simply misunderstood information supplied by a third party (eg where he has entered the net instead of the gross interest received on a building society account).

The usual procedure is for the Inspector to suggest an overall settlement figure to include underpaid tax, interest and any penalty. However, he will also provide a computation showing how the overall figure was calculated and it is open to the taxpayer to argue for a bigger reduction of the penalty element. If the Inspector does not agree, he must submit the case to his Head Office, which is sometimes willing to accept a lower settlement than originally proposed by the Inspector.

Payment by instalments is possible where the taxpayer does not have readily realisable capital, but this will of course increase the interest (though not the penalty) payable.

## Certificates of tax deposit

A taxpayer can make deposits with Collectors of Taxes to cover tax liabilities. A certificate is issued and the deposit held for the general benefit of the individual until such time as he surrenders all or part of the certificate to cover tax liabilities.

Where a deposit is used to cover a tax liability, interest on overdue tax cannot run from the date that the deposit was made. They are therefore commonly used to cover a tax liability which cannot easily be quantified, eg a capital gain on a sale of unquoted shares where a value at 31 March 1982 needs to be negotiated with the Shares Valuation Division.

Interest is credited from the date the deposit is made to the date it is used (or cashed) for a maximum of six years. The rate of interest is fixed by reference to money market rates and is taxable. Interest is paid at a lower rate where deposits are encashed rather than used to settle tax liabilities.

Deposits are not transferable except to personal representatives of a deceased person. They cannot even be transferred to a spouse, although the Collector of Taxes will accept a certificate on the basis that it is treated as encashed with the resultant proceeds being applied to cover a spouse's tax liability. The problem with this procedure is that it does not protect the spouse from a liability to interest on underpaid tax. The Revenue has confirmed that a certificate of tax deposit held in the name of a partnership may be used to discharge personal tax liabilities of any of the partners.

## Remission of tax by the Revenue

The Revenue's policy, detailed in ESC A19, is to give up arrears of tax which have arisen because of failure by the Revenue to make proper and timely use of information supplied. Remission of tax in this way is normally available where the taxpayer could have reasonably believed that his tax affairs were in order and was notified of the arrears more than 12 months after the end of the tax year in which the Revenue was informed. Alternatively, in the case of an over-repayment, it is available if the taxpayer was notified after the end of the tax year following the year in which the repayment was made.

## Error or mistake relief

Sometimes errors are made against the taxpayer and relief can be claimed against any over-assessment to income tax or CGT due to an error or mistake in a return. However, relief does not extend to an error or mistake in a claim included in the return. Relief will not be available on the ground of an alleged error in the basis of computation of liability if the return was made on the basis of or in accordance with the practice generally prevailing at the time when the return was made. According to the Revenue's internal manuals at IM3751A the term 'error or mistake' includes errors of omission such as the non-deduction of an admissible expense, errors of commission (eg computational or arithmetical errors), errors arising from a misunderstanding of the law and erroneous statements of fact.

The relief is also available for an error or mistake in a partnership statement by reason of which the partners claim that their self-assessments were excessive. If the claim results in an amendment to the partnership statement, any necessary amendments to the partners' individual self-assessments will be made by notice by the Board of the Revenue.

Relief may be claimed within five years of 31 January following the tax year to which the return relates. For years prior to self-assessment, a six-year time limit applied.

## Tax underpaid or overpaid for pre-self assessment years

### Interest on underpaid tax
(TMA 1970, s 86)

Despite the Revenue's endeavours, there are still assessments for pre-self assessment years (1995/96 and earlier) which are under appeal. If it transpires that too much tax was postponed, and the final liability exceeds the amounts paid on account, interest may be charged under s 86 where an estimated assessment was inadequate but the taxpayer has made an appeal and the tax paid on account is less than that ultimately found to be payable. The rules for determining the date from which s 86 interest runs are complex.

#### Assessments made before 6 April 1998
Interest on a Schedule A, Schedule D or CGT assessment usually ran from the date shown in the table below or 30 days after the date the assessment was made (if later). Interest on a Schedule E assessment made before 6 April 1998 ran from 14 days after the Collector first applied for payment of the relevant tax, although a payment application could not be made until the Inspector had issued the assessment notice.

*Interest calculation dates ('reckonable date') following appeal and postponement of tax*

| Type of income or gain | Interest runs from |
|---|---|
| Higher rate (for individuals) and additional rate (for trustees) on income received net of basic rate tax | 1 June 14 months following the end of the year of assessment |
| All other income charged under Schedule A or Schedule D | 1 July following the year of assessment |
| Capital gains | 1 June 14 months following the end of the year of assessment |

### Assessments issued after 5 April 1998

In this case, interest is charged by reference to the date that the tax was technically due and payable, which is 31 January following the tax year to which the assessment relates. This is, of course, six months before the dates in the table above. Interest is charged from this date even if the tax is paid within 30 days of the assessment being issued.

### Tax outstanding at a person's death

ESC A17 applies where a person dies after receiving an assessment, but before paying the tax. Section 86 interest ceases to run until probate or letters of administration are obtained.

### Rate of interest charged

The rate of interest charged varies according to the general level of interest rates. The rates for the last six years are given in Table 29.9. A ready reckoner, entitled *Interest Factor Tables*, is available, free of charge, from:

> Inland Revenue Public Enquiry Room
> Somerset House
> Strand
> London WC2R 1LB

## Default interest
(TMA 1970, s 88)

Where the Revenue has been unable to issue an assessment at the proper time, because the taxpayer either failed to submit his return or submitted an incorrect or incomplete return, interest may be charged under s 88 rather than s 86 from the date the tax should have been paid to the date of payment.

Interest under s 88 is not normally charged for 1995–96 and earlier years where a taxpayer did not submit his full return on time provided the Revenue had been given sufficient information to raise an estimated assessment by 31 October following the tax year. For example, if a large capital gain was made in 1995–96, it should have been possible to at least advise the gross proceeds by 31 October 1996, even if the exact taxable gain could not be calculated, perhaps because 31 March 1982 valuations were required.

## Repayment supplement on tax overpayments
(ICTA 1988, s 824)

The Revenue is required to pay interest or 'repayment supplement' on overpayments of tax for 1995–96 or previous years. However, the Revenue is required to give repayment supplement only from 12 months after the end of the year of assessment concerned. Furthermore, where an assessment is issued more than 12 months after a year of assessment, repayment supplement runs only from the end of the year of assessment in which the tax was paid.

The period during which interest on underpaid tax may accrue and the period in which entitlement to repayment supplement may arise do not match up. There may be a period of nine months during which an overpayment does not qualify for repayment supplement even though interest may be accruing under s 86 on an assessment for the same tax year raised under a different schedule.

Special rules apply where tax has been overpaid under Schedule E. Where Schedule E assessments for different years are raised at the same time, the net tax overpaid at the end of a year is normally carried forward to the next year's assessment. For the purposes of attributing a repayment, the Revenue's practice is to treat an overpayment as arising in the earliest year possible. Difficulties may arise where there are overpayments for earlier years, which are extinguished by an underpayment for a subsequent year.

# INTERNET AND E-COMMERCE

## Overview – sitemap

The computer is now a well-established part of most people's everyday life and the Government is keen to ensure that the UK workforce is up to coping with the new technology. There exist within the tax legislation incentives designed to aid individuals and companies come to terms with new technology or increase their know how on IT.

## Tax incentives: vocational training

Individuals used to be able to obtain tax relief on certain courses, including those designed to enhance their knowledge of computing. The relief was restricted to basic rate in the 1999–2000 tax year and was phased out after 5 April 2000 because of the introduction of Individual Learning Accounts (see below *re* the latter and 10.6 for further details on vocational training).

## Individual Learning Accounts

The Government is introducing new legislation to encourage the UK's adult population to acquire new skills and qualifications. The first accounts will be available in the current tax year and extended to all by 2000–01. The legislation will specifically target certain courses, including computer literacy, by offering greater discounts on those courses.

## Personal use of computers by employees

Legislation introduced by FA 1999 enables employers to lend their staff computers of a value up to £2,000 for home and private use. The legislation only applies provided the loans are not limited solely to senior staff and directors (see 3.4.8).

## Capital allowances – computer software

If the software has a short life usage (ie less than two years), this may be treated as a revenue expense. Where a company incurs capital expenditure on computer software outright, this is treated in the same way as plant and machinery for capital allowances (see 2.5). Similar rules apply to software acquired under a licence after 10 March 1992.

## INTERNET FILING OF SELF-ASSESSMENT TAX RETURNS

The Revenue is now allowing individuals with simple tax affairs to file their tax returns over the Internet. As an incentive there is a £10 one-off payment to anyone who boldly goes. To file your return over the Internet you first visit the Revenue website (www.inlandrevenue.gov.uk/), or alternatively you can go straight to the registration form (ir-efile.gov.uk/register.htm). To register you will need the following three pieces of information:

● Your ten-digit tax reference
● Your postcode
● Your national insurance number.

Additionally you are given the opportunity to give your e-mail address. This is to be recommended, as once you have successfully registered you will receive an e-mail which will explain how to register.

Once you have successfully registered you will then need to download the Revenue's software, which was available at the end of May 2000.

## Discounts for Internet filing

Legislation in FA 1999 enabled Customs and the Revenue to develop new electronic services as an alternative to traditional paper-based communication.

Small VAT-registered businesses (with a turnover of below £600,000) are now able to submit their VAT returns via the Internet. From April 2001 a discount of £50 is available if they file via the Internet and pay the tax due electronically. This scheme is being introduced by Customs for one year only. This discount will only be available if the VAT returns are filed and the payments made at the appropriate times.

There will be similar £50 discounts for electronic filing of PAYE returns, with an additional £50 discount available for small employers who pay tax credits to their employees under the Working Families' Tax Credit or Disabled Person's Tax Credit systems.

Individual taxpayers who file their SA returns via the Internet and pay their tax electronically will also qualify for a one-off discount of £10.

While the discounts offered are modest in amount, they do reflect the Government's commitment to embrace new technology and to encourage others to do likewise.

## Purchasing tax software

It is beyond the scope of this book to review and recommend software that can be used to assist with tax and business affairs. Though it is to a large extent a question of 'you pays your money and you takes your choice', price is by no means a guarantee that the software you purchase will be the right one. Indeed software downloaded free from the Internet may prove to be perfectly adequate for your requirements.

Consider the following when deciding which software is appropriate for you:

(1) If this is the first time you have used a personal finance package, seek out a product with good interactive tutorials, as this will help you get over the initial hurdles.

(2) Try to buy a package that dovetails with your own knowledge or degree of expertise or knowledge.

(3) You must have a computer with a CD-ROM drive, since most software is usually supplied on CD.

(4) Check that any accounting package produced by a non-UK software company has been properly anglicised.

(5) If you deal with any overseas matters, the chances are that you will need to handle foreign currencies. Also check the ability to handle the euro correctly.

(6) All accounting and personal finance software should be fully Millennium-compliant, but check this out if you are concerned. Make sure dates beyond 31 December 1999 are handled properly (see above).

(7) Not all accounting software is multi-user. If you want to use a package on a particular network operating system, make sure it is compatible. Make sure that your computer hardware and software are compatible with your operating system.

(8) If you expect your business to expand significantly, make sure that any package is scaleable to meet increased demands. Alternatively, choose a product from a compatible range of products.

(9) The Internet is being used increasingly for commerce. Check what Internet features a particular package has and look for possible future enhancements.

## Surfing the web – useful websites

Surfing or browsing the web can be as rewarding as it is frustrating. To get the most out of the web you do need a fast processor (say, a Pentium II 266Mhz), a great deal of memory (32Mb+) and hard disk space (64Mb), a

56k modem + and a fast graphics card with at least 16Mb of memory on board. A tip – if your machine struggles with fancy graphics, try disabling them.

A good website, almost like a person, can be judged by the company it keeps. For a website this means the interactive links with other useful related websites. The following sites offer a snapshot of the Internet and should be used as a gateway to a more productive use of the Internet.

## Government

| | |
|---|---|
| Inland Revenue | www.inlandrevenue.gov.uk/ |
| Treasury | www.hm-treasury.gov.uk/ |
| NICs – Contributions Agency | www.inlandrevenue.gov.uk/ |
| Customs & Excise | www.hmce.gov.uk/ |
| House of Commons | www.parliament.uk/ |
| The Stationery Office | www.tsonline.co.uk/ |

## Professional bodies

| | |
|---|---|
| Chartered Institute of Taxation | www.tax.org.uk/ |
| Institute of Chartered Accountants of England and Wales | www.icaew.co.uk/ |
| The Institute of Chartered Accountants of Scotland | www.icas.org.uk/ |
| The Institute of Chartered Accountants of Ireland | www.icai.ie/ |
| The Law Society | www.lawsoc.org.uk/ |
| Gray's Inn Tax Barristers | taxbar.com |

## Media

| | |
|---|---|
| *The Guardian* | www.guardian.co.uk/ |
| *Financial Times* | www.ft.com/ |
| *The Times* (money page) | www.times-money.co.uk/ |
| BBC | www.bbc.co.uk/ |

## Computing

| | |
|---|---|
| *PC Magazine* | www.pcmag.co.uk/ |
| LYCOS | www.lycos.com |
| Yahoo! | www.yahoo.com/ |
| Hotbot | www.hotbot.com/ |
| Hotmail | www.hotmail.com/ |

### General

| | |
|---|---|
| The publishers | www.pearsoned-ema.com/ |
| Pannell Kerr Forster | www.pkf.co.uk/ |
| Allied Dunbar | www.allieddunbar.co.uk/ |

## You've got mail – useful e-mail addresses

Electronic mail (e-mail) is becoming the fastest, easiest and most reliable way to keep in contact with clients. When using e-mail keep in mind the Inland Revenue rules under self-assessment concerning documentation and also the rules relating to point of business. The following can be contacted via e-mail:

| | |
|---|---|
| The author | tony.foreman@uk.pkf.com |
| The deputy editor | gerald.mowles@soctax.com |

## FINDING YOUR WAY AROUND THE SELF-ASSESSMENT FORM

When you examine page 2 of your return, you will see the following questions which we have cross-referred to this book (see opposite).

The part of the return reproduced on page 38, as cross-referenced, shows question 10 of the return. Boxes 10.1–10.14 require figures to be inserted in respect of each specific type of income. Boxes 10.15–10.32 require amounts for different types of dividend income.

## TEN GOLDEN RULES FOR DEALING WITH YOUR 2000 TAX RETURN

The self-assessment system requires that you carry out certain tasks by fixed deadlines. If you fail to deal with your tax affairs in a business-like way, you will be charged interest and surcharges (and possibly worse).

The SA tax return may still be unfamiliar but is not as difficult as it seems at first glance. A review carried out by the Revenue showed that 30% of returns contained clerical errors which needed correction (such as arithmetical mistakes, figures entered in the wrong columns etc), but 90% of the mistakes could be readily identified to enable the return to be 'processed' and the taxpayer's details entered on the Revenue computer. The standard eight-page return may need to be supplemented by additional schedules so this is probably your first task: to see if you have been sent all the extra schedules that you will need. The tax legislation can be very complicated but the Revenue has gone to considerable expense to provide detailed notes and 'helpsheets' which accompany the extra schedules and should enable you to cope with most straightforward situations.

**Inland Revenue**

## INCOME AND CAPITAL GAINS *for the year ended 5 April 2000*

**Step 1**

Answer Questions 1 to 9 below to find out if you have the right supplementary Pages. Please read pages 6 and 7 of your Tax Return Guide if you need help. The Questions are colour coded to help you identify the supplementary Pages and their guidance notes. If you answer 'No', go to the next question. If you answer 'Yes', you must complete the relevant supplementary Pages. Turn to the back of your Tax Return to see if you have the right ones and look at the back of the Tax Return Guide to see if you have guidance notes to go with them. **Ring the Orderline on 0845 9000 404, or fax on 0845 9000 604 for any you need** (open 7 days a week between 8am and 10pm). If I have sent you any Pages you do not need, ignore them.

*Check to make sure you have the right supplementary Pages and then tick the box below.*

**Q1** Were you an employee, or office holder, or director, or agency worker or did you receive payments or benefits from a former employer (excluding a pension) in the year ended 5 April 2000?  NO  YES

EMPLOYMENT YES  — See Chap. 3

**Q2** Did you have any taxable income from share options, shares (but this does not include dividends - they go in Question 10) or share related benefits in the year?  NO  YES

SHARE SCHEMES YES — See 3.11–3.16

**Q3** Were you self-employed (but not in partnership)? (Tick 'Yes' if you were a Name at Lloyd's.)  NO  YES

SELF-EMPLOYMENT YES — See Chap. 2

**Q4** Were you in partnership?  NO  YES

PARTNERSHIP YES — See 2.10

**Q5** Did you receive any rent or other income from land and property in the UK?  NO  YES

LAND & PROPERTY YES — See Chap. 4

**Q6** Did you have any taxable income from overseas pensions or benefits, or from foreign companies or savings institutions, offshore funds or trusts abroad, or from land and property abroad or gains on foreign insurance policies?  NO  YES

See 6.4, 20.4 and 12.4

Have you or could you have received, or enjoyed directly or indirectly, or benefited in any way from, income of a foreign entity as a result of a transfer of assets made in this or earlier years?  NO  YES

Do you want to claim tax credit relief for foreign tax paid on foreign income or gains?  NO  YES

FOREIGN YES

See 6.11 and Chap. 17

**Q7** Did you receive, or are you deemed to have, income from a trust, settlement or deceased person's estate?  NO  YES

TRUSTS ETC YES

**Q8** Capital gains
- Have you disposed of your only or main residence? If 'Yes', read page 7 of your Tax Return Guide to see if you need the Capital Gains Pages.  NO  YES
- Did you dispose of other chargeable assets worth more than £14,200 in total?  NO  YES
- Were your total chargeable gains more than £7,100?  NO  YES

Please see page 7 of the Tax Return Guide if you wish to claim a capital loss.

CAPITAL GAINS YES — See Chaps 13–15

**Q9** Are you claiming that you were not resident, or not ordinarily resident, or not domiciled, in the UK, or dual resident in the UK and another country, for all or part of the year?  NO  YES

NON-RESIDENCE ETC YES

See Chaps 21 and 22

**Step 2** Please use blue or black ink to fill in your Tax Return and please do not include pence. Round down, to the nearest pound, your income and capital gains and round up your tax credits and tax deductions. **Now fill in any supplementary Pages BEFORE going to Step 3.**

Tick this box when you have filled in your supplementary Pages.  

**Step 3** Now fill in Questions 10 to 23. If you answer 'No' to a question, go to the next one. If you answer 'Yes', fill in the relevant boxes.

**Remember**
- You do not have to calculate your tax - I will do it for you if you send your Tax Return to me by 30 September. This will save you time and effort.
- The Tax Calculation Guide I have sent you will help if you decide to calculate the tax yourself.
- You do not have to wait until 30 September 2000, or 31 January 2001, to send me your Tax Return.

BMSD 12/99     TAX RETURN: PAGE 2

## INCOME *for the year ended 5 April 2000*

**Q10** Did you receive any income from UK savings and investments?  NO  YES   *If yes, fill in boxes 10.1 to 10.26 as appropriate. Include only your share from any joint savings and investments.*

■ *Interest*

● Interest from UK banks, building societies and deposit takers

|  | | Taxable amount | |
|---|---|---|---|
| - where **no tax** has been deducted | | **10.1** £ | See 5.1 |

| | Amount after tax deducted | Tax deducted | Gross amount before tax | |
|---|---|---|---|---|
| - where **tax has** been deducted | **10.2** £ | **10.3** £ | **10.4** £ | See 5.2 |

● Interest distributions from UK authorised unit trusts and open-ended investment companies (dividend distributions go below)

| Amount after tax deducted | Tax deducted | Gross amount before tax | |
|---|---|---|---|
| **10.5** £ | **10.6** £ | **10.7** £ | See 5.8 |

● National Savings (other than FIRST Option Bonds and the first £70 of interest from a National Savings Ordinary Account)

| | Taxable amount | |
|---|---|---|
| **10.8** £ | | See 11.2 |

● National Savings FIRST Option Bonds

| Amount after tax deducted | Tax deducted | Gross amount before tax | |
|---|---|---|---|
| **10.9** £ | **10.10** £ | **10.11** £ | |

● Other income from UK savings and investments (except dividends)

| Amount after tax deducted | Tax deducted | Gross amount before tax | |
|---|---|---|---|
| **10.12** £ | **10.13** £ | **10.14** £ | See Chaps 5 and 6 |

■ *Dividends*

● Dividends and other qualifying distributions from UK companies

| Dividend/distribution | Tax credit | Dividend/distribution plus credit | |
|---|---|---|---|
| **10.15** £ | **10.16** £ | **10.17** £ | See 5.8 |

● Dividend distributions from UK authorised unit trusts and open-ended investment companies

| Dividend/distribution | Tax credit | Dividend/distribution plus credit | |
|---|---|---|---|
| **10.18** £ | **10.19** £ | **10.20** £ | See 5.8 |

● Scrip dividends from UK companies

| Dividend | Notional tax | Dividend plus notional tax | |
|---|---|---|---|
| **10.21** £ | **10.22** £ | **10.23** £ | See 5.8.5 |

● Non-qualifying distributions and loans written off

| | Notional tax | Taxable amount | |
|---|---|---|---|
| | **10.25** £ | **10.26** £ | See 5.9 |
| **10.24** £ | | | |

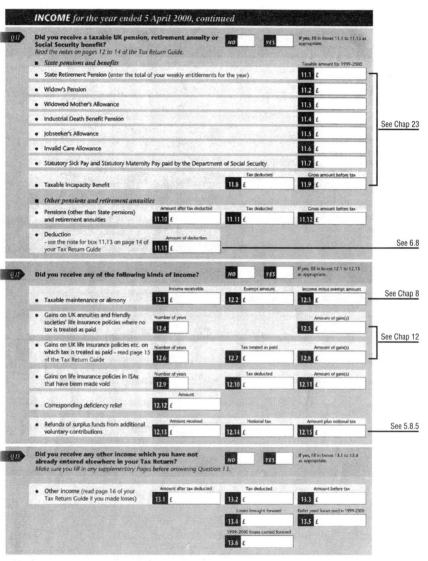

**INCOME** *for the year ended 5 April 2000, continued*

**Q11** Did you receive a taxable UK pension, retirement annuity or Social Security benefit? NO YES
If yes, fill in boxes 11.1 to 11.13 as appropriate.
*Read the notes on pages 12 to 14 of the Tax Return Guide.*

■ *State pensions and benefits*
Taxable amount for 1999-2000

● State Retirement Pension (enter the total of your weekly entitlements for the year) 11.1 £

● Widow's Pension 11.2 £

● Widowed Mother's Allowance 11.3 £

● Industrial Death Benefit Pension 11.4 £

● Jobseeker's Allowance 11.5 £

● Invalid Care Allowance 11.6 £

● Statutory Sick Pay and Statutory Maternity Pay paid by the Department of Social Security 11.7 £

See Chap 23

Tax deducted / Gross amount before tax
● Taxable Incapacity Benefit 11.8 £ 11.9 £

■ *Other pensions and retirement annuities*

● Pensions (other than State pensions) and retirement annuities
Amount after tax deducted 11.10 £ | Tax deducted 11.11 £ | Gross amount before tax 11.12 £

● Deduction
- see the note for box 11.13 on page 14 of your Tax Return Guide
Amount of deduction 11.13 £
See 6.8

**Q12** Did you receive any of the following kinds of income? NO YES
If yes, fill in boxes 12.1 to 12.15 as appropriate.

Income receivable / Exempt amount / Income minus exempt amount
● Taxable maintenance or alimony 12.1 £ | 12.2 £ | 12.3 £
See Chap 8

● Gains on UK annuities and friendly societies' life insurance policies where no tax is treated as paid
Number of years 12.4 | Amount of gain(s) 12.5 £

See Chap 12

● Gains on UK life insurance policies etc. on which tax is treated as paid - read page 15 of the Tax Return Guide
Number of years 12.6 | Tax treated as paid 12.7 £ | Amount of gain(s) 12.8 £

● Gains on life insurance policies in ISAs that have been made void
Number of years 12.9 | Tax deducted 12.10 £ | Amount of gain(s) 12.11 £

● Corresponding deficiency relief
Amount 12.12 £

● Refunds of surplus funds from additional voluntary contributions
Amount received 12.13 £ | Notional tax 12.14 £ | Amount plus notional tax 12.15 £
See 5.8.5

**Q13** Did you receive any other income which you have not already entered elsewhere in your Tax Return? NO YES
If yes, fill in boxes 13.1 to 13.6 as appropriate.
*Make sure you fill in any supplementary Pages before answering Question 13.*

● Other income (read page 16 of your Tax Return Guide if you made losses)
Amount after tax deducted 13.1 £ | Tax deducted 13.2 £ | Amount before tax 13.3 £

Losses brought forward 13.4 £ | Earlier years' losses used in 1999-2000 13.5 £

1999-2000 losses carried forward 13.6 £

BMSD 12/99          TAX RETURN: PAGE 4

## RELIEFS for the year ended 5 April 2000

**Q14** **Do you want to claim relief for pension contributions?** NO ☐ YES ☐    If yes, fill in boxes 14.1 to 14.17 as appropriate.

*Do not include contributions deducted from your pay by your employer to their pension scheme, because tax relief is given automatically. But do include your contributions to personal pension schemes and free-standing AVC schemes.*

■ *Retirement annuity contracts*

| | | Relief claimed | |
|---|---|---|---|
| Qualifying payments made in 1999-2000 **14.1** £ | 1999-2000 payments used in an earlier year **14.2** £ | | See 12.9 |
| 1999-2000 payments now to be carried back **14.3** £ | Payments brought back from 2000-2001 **14.4** £ | box 14.1 *minus* (boxes 14.2 and 14.3, but not 14.4) **14.5** £ | |

■ *Self-employed contributions to personal pension plans*

| | | Relief claimed | |
|---|---|---|---|
| Qualifying payments made in 1999-2000 **14.6** £ | 1999-2000 payments used in an earlier year **14.7** £ | | See 12.8 |
| 1999-2000 payments now to be carried back **14.8** £ | Payments brought back from 2000-2001 **14.9** £ | box 14.6 *minus* (boxes 14.7 and 14.8, but not 14.9) **14.10** £ | |

■ *Employee contributions to personal pension plans (include your gross contribution – see the note on box 14.11 in your Tax Return Guide)*

| | | Relief claimed | |
|---|---|---|---|
| Qualifying payments made in 1999-2000 **14.11** £ | 1999-2000 payments used in an earlier year **14.12** £ | | See 12.8 |
| 1999-2000 payments now to be carried back **14.13** £ | Payments brought back from 2000-2001 **14.14** £ | box 14.11 *minus* (boxes 14.12 and 14.13, but not 14.14) **14.15** £ | |

■ *Contributions to other pension schemes and free-standing AVC schemes*

• Amount of contributions to employer's schemes **not deducted** at source from pay    **14.16** £

• Gross amount of free-standing additional voluntary contributions paid in 1999-2000    **14.17** £    See 12.11

**Q15** **Do you want to claim any of the following reliefs?** NO ☐ YES ☐    If yes, fill in boxes 15.1 to 15.12, as appropriate.

• Payments you made for vocational training (read the box 15.1 note on page 20 of your Tax Return Guide)    Amount of payment **15.1** £

• Interest eligible for relief on loans to buy your main home (other than MIRAS)    Amount of payment **15.2** £    See 9.1

• Interest eligible for relief on other qualifying loans    Amount of payment **15.3** £    See 9.3–9.5

• Maintenance or alimony payments you have made under a court order, Child Support Agency assessment or legally binding order or agreement

   Amount claimed under 'new' rules **15.4** £

| Amount claimed under 'old' rules up to £1,970 | Amount claimed under 'old' rules over £1,970 | |
|---|---|---|
| **15.5** £ | **15.6** £ | See Chap 8 |

• Subscriptions for Venture Capital Trust shares (up to £100,000)    Amount on which relief claimed **15.7** £    See 11.7

• Subscriptions under the Enterprise Investment Scheme (up to £150,000)    Amount on which relief claimed **15.8** £    See 11.6

• Charitable covenants or annuities    Amount of payment **15.9** £    See 10.1

• Gift Aid and Millennium Gift Aid    Amount of qualifying payments **15.10** £    See 10.2

• Post-cessation expenses, pre-incorporation losses brought forward and losses on relevant discounted securities, etc.    Amount of payment **15.11** £    See 2.8, 2.99 and 5.7

• Payments to a trade union or friendly society for death benefits    Half amount of payment **15.12** £    See 10.8

## ALLOWANCES for the year ended 5 April 2000

16 You get your personal allowance of £4,335 automatically. **If you were born before 6 April 1935, enter your date of birth in box 21.4** - you may get higher age-related allowances.

**Do you want to claim any of the following allowances?** NO [ ] YES [ ]

If yes, please read pages 23 to 26 of your Tax Return Guide and then fill in boxes 16.1 to 16.28 as appropriate.

Date of registration (if first year of claim)     Local authority (or other register)

- **Blind person's allowance** 16.1 / / 16.2

See 7.10

- **Transitional allowance** (for some wives with husbands on low income if received in earlier years).

- Tick to claim and give details in the 'Additional information' box on page 8 (please see page 23 of your Tax Return Guide for what is needed) 16.3

- If you want to calculate your tax, enter the amount of transitional allowance you can have in box 16.4  16.4 £

- **Married couple's allowance for a married man** - see page 24 of your Tax Return Guide.

- Wife's full name 16.5
  - Date of marriage (if after 5 April 1999) 16.6 / /
- Wife's date of birth (if before 6 April 1935) 16.7 / /
  - Tick box 16.8 if you or your wife have allocated half the allowance to her 16.8

box number 16.9 is not used
  - Tick box 16.10 if you and your wife have allocated all the allowance to her 16.10

See 7.5

· · · · · · · · · · · · · · · · · · · · · · · · · · · · · · · · · · · · · · · · · · · ·
- **Married couple's allowance for a married woman** - see page 24 of your Tax Return Guide.

  - Date of marriage (if after 5 April 1999) 16.11 / /
- Husband's full name 16.12
  - Tick box 16.13 if you or your husband have allocated half the allowance to you 16.13
box number 16.14 is not used
  - Tick box 16.15 if you and your husband have allocated all the allowance to you 16.15

- **Additional personal allowance** (available in some circumstances if you have a child living with you - see page 25 of your Tax Return Guide).

  - Tick box 16.16A if you are claiming the married couple's allowance **and** additional personal allowance because your spouse was unable to look after themselves because of illness or disablement, throughout the year ended 5 April 2000 16.16A

See 7.8

- Name of the child claimed for 16.16
  - Child's date of birth 16.17 / /
  - Tick if child lived with you for at least part of the year ended 5 April 2000 16.18

- Name of university etc/type of training if the child is 16 or over on 6 April 1999 and in full time education or training 16.19

**Sharing a claim**

Name and address of other person claiming
16.20
  - Enter your share as a percentage 16.21 %
  - If share not agreed, enter the number of days in the year ended 5 April 2000 that the child lived with
Postcode
    - you 16.22 days
    - other person 16.23 days

- **Widow's bereavement allowance**
  - Date of your husband's death 16.24 / /

- **Transfer of surplus allowances** - see page 26 of your Tax Return Guide before you fill in boxes 16.25 to 16.28.

- Tick if you want your spouse to have your unused allowances 16.25
- Tick if you want to have your spouse's unused allowances 16.26

**Please give details in the 'Additional information' box on page 8** - see page 26 of your Tax Return Guide for what is needed.
If you want to calculate your tax, enter the amount of the surplus allowance you can have.

- Blind person's surplus allowance 16.27 £
- Married couple's surplus allowance 16.28 £

The next thing to take on board is that the Revenue has powers enabling it to check up on taxpayers. Tax officials will be using these powers and will not find it amusing if you are audited and found wanting, even where the shortcomings amount only to carelessness. The Inland Revenue Enquiry Manual makes it quite plain that self-assessment will not be allowed to degenerate into 'pay what you like'. Furthermore, even though there is a set time limit for the Revenue to announce that a return will be audited ('selected for enquiry'), the Revenue will be able to reopen back years if the taxpayer has omitted key information (this is called 'discovery').

Therefore, you are advised to do the following:

(1) Get organised. Start to collect together the information that you will need (see summary).

(2) Do not throw anything away for the time being. In fact, you should keep your 1999–2000 records until 31 January 2002 (2006 if you run a business or receive rental income). Remember that the Revenue policy is 'process now, check later'. The Revenue will be able to open an enquiry into your 1999–2000 return by serving a notice before 1 February 2002 – and it will not have to give any justification for doing so.

(3) Do not leave everything until the last minute. There will be an automatic £100 penalty if you are late in filing your return and, while 31 January 2001 is a long way off, it will be easier to tackle the return while things are still fresh in your mind. If there are any gaps in your records (you have been under a legal obligation to keep adequate records since 6 April 1996) you may be able to reconstruct them by getting down to the task before the trail goes completely cold.

(4) Do not try sending in an incomplete return, as it will be rejected. If you had benefits in kind such as a company car or a mobile telephone, you will need to put down a figure for your taxable benefit: just reporting 'per form P11D' or 'as PAYE' is not acceptable.

(5) Start to put cash aside now so that you can settle your 1999–2000 tax and make a payment on account for 2000–01 next 31 January. If you are short of funds after Christmas you may find yourself exposed to interest (APR currently 8.5%). Worse still, if you are unable to clear your 1999–2000 tax by 28 February, you will be liable for an automatic 5% surcharge (equal to an APR of over 60%).

(6) Consider filing by 30 September. Somerset House has given repeated assurances that filing early will not increase the likelihood of your return being selected for enquiry. On a positive note, the Revenue will collect underpayments of up to £1,000 via the PAYE system if you submit your return by end September. This may be much more convenient than having to make a lump sum payment.

(7) Work on the basis that your return will be selected for enquiry. The Revenue will be selecting around 10,000 returns each year on a random basis; this means there is less than a 1% chance of being selected, but that you are considerably more likely to be selected for random

enquiry than to win the National Lottery. Tax offices are also expected to check another 30,000 returns with the selection being made on a more scientific assessment of risk of undeclared tax.

(8)  Remember to tick the box if your return contains any estimated or provisional figures. It will probably be in your own best interests to give an explanation of how you have arrived at the figures concerned as this may pre-empt queries from the Revenue. It may also afford a degree of protection against the Revenue coming back after 31 January 2002 and reopening 1999–2000 by making a 'discovery assessment'.

(9)  Think twice about not drawing attention to any assumptions that you have made in completing your return which could be challenged by the Revenue. You do not have to follow the Revenue's line on everything, especially if you receive advice that the Revenue's interpretation of the legislation is open to doubt, but you should not be coy about this. From time to time the Revenue is shown to be wrong (a recent instance is the treatment of Cheltenham & Gloucester investors), but the Revenue wins more often than it loses and you could be liable for penalties if the courts uphold the Revenue interpretation and it emerges that you had not put all your cards face up on the table.

(10)  Finally, get professional advice if your affairs are complicated. Do-it-yourself tax returns may be a false economy if your situation is non-standard, however hard the Revenue has tried to explain the rules in its helpsheets.

## Information you will need

| If you are employed: | |
|---|---|
| Form P60, ie the annual certificate of pay and tax deducted at source.<br>Taxable figures for any benefits in kind (company car, mobile 'phone, cheap loans in excess of £5,000) from your employer.<br>Details of amounts paid to you under the Fixed Profit Car Scheme for using your own car for company business. | Your employer should have provided this automatically by 5 July 2000. |
| If you changed jobs during the year ended 5 April 2000, details of benefits provided by your previous employer. | You may have to ask for this. |
| Advice from your employer as to what to report if you received free shares or exercised (or were given) a share option in 1999–2000 | Speak to your Personnel Department. |

| | |
|---|---|
| *If you were self-employed:* | |
| You will need to prepare accounts or have an accountant do this for you. The Revenue requires your details in a set format so that it can use its computer to assist it in identifying cases which should be taken up for enquiry. | See 2.4.1 and 2.4–2.5. |
| *If you have rental income:* | |
| You should keep an analysis of rents receivable for 1999–2000 and a note of any bad debts, details of expenditure such as fees paid to managing agents, repair bills and redecoration, replacement of electrical goods and furniture. If you have borrowed to fund your property 'business', the interest should be an allowable expense. | Rent charged for 1999–2000 will normally be taxable even if you did not receive it until after the end of the year. |
| *If you have income from savings:* | |
| Keep a copy of your bank deposit account statements, your building society passbook and dividend vouchers. | |
| *If you had trust income:* | |
| You need form R185 which sets out the amount of income paid to you and the tax deducted at source. | |
| *If you have made capital gains:* | |
| You will need the stockbroker's contract notes for sales of shares and copies of the sale contract and completion statement if you made real estate sales. If you gave assets to your children you may be liable for CGT as if you had sold at market value so seek advice in such situations. | The gains are exempt if they totalled less than £7,100. |

![1]

# MANAGING YOUR TAX AFFAIRS – AND SAVING TAX

Managing your tax affairs and planning ahead are really inextricably connected with one another: you cannot really plan in an effective way unless you are on top of your responsibility to file returns and you are aware of key deadlines.

In this chapter we cover:

### General strategy

(1) Key points to bear in mind.

### Some specific situations where you need to plan ahead

(2) If you are thinking of becoming self-employed.
(3) If you are already in business.
(4) If you are employed.
(5) Managing your investments.
(6) Tax deductible investments.
(7) Your family affairs and personal financial planning.

### Managing your tax affairs

(8) Ensure that all important deadlines are kept.

## 1.1 KEY POINTS TO BEAR IN MIND

There is no simple solution to the question of how to pay less tax – if only there were! And there are plenty of ways of going wrong and increasing your tax problems. However, you will almost certainly do well to adopt the following basic principles of effective tax management and planning:

### Carry out some background research

Your tax affairs need to be taken seriously. It is important to fill out your tax return in a meticulous way. You should carefully read the notes issued with

ALLIED DUNBAR TAX HANDBOOK

the tax return and, if there are areas on which you are not quite sure, you should seek advice, either from the Inland Revenue itself or from a practising accountant.

## Deal with your self-assessment return issued in April 2000

Under self-assessment you need to submit your tax return, together with a cheque covering your outstanding tax, by 31 January following the tax year. If you fail to do this, you will automatically become liable for interest and penalties.

## Do not get involved in evasion

Before you take any action, ask yourself whether you would be happy for all the documentation to be put before the Inspector of Taxes. If in fact a scheme relies upon non-disclosure, you may be getting involved in evasion. If you are found out you will become liable for interest and penalties and you might be subject to prosecution.

The Government seems increasingly to put tax avoidance in the same category as tax as evasion. However taxpayers are under no obligation to arrange their tax affairs in such a way that they maximise their tax liability and in fact the "avoidance of tax" has been described as the only worthwhile pursuit left.

## Plan ahead

Part of practical tax planning is to anticipate what could change in the future. For example, it may be that you are likely to sell your present home in two or three years' time when you reach retirement. If you have let a property in the past, you need to look into the position now to see whether there could be a CGT charge when you sell the property and, if there is a potential problem, what steps you might take to avoid the problem. If you are going to sell your business when you retire in a few years' time, you need to find out what tax may be payable and what you can do to reduce this.

## Do take all taxes into account

It is important to be aware that steps you might take to avoid income tax may have CGT consequences, or vice versa. For example, you may be able to get a tax deduction if you set aside part of your home for work. However, if a couple of rooms are set aside exclusively for business purposes, this may affect your main residence exemption and could result in a CGT charge when you sell the property. There may well be ways in which you could both have your cake and eat it, but you need to look into the fine detail of the rules concerning the main residence exemption.

## Be flexible

It makes no sense to invest in a savings plan because the return is free of tax if the plan is not suited to your personal requirements and the capital is tied up for (say) ten years. You should bear in mind that circumstances may change and it may therefore be unwise to put all your spare investments into a trust for the benefit of your children if your own situation might change. In recent years, many individuals have suffered unexpected demands on their capital (spare a thought for members of Lloyd's) and some people are now regretting that they gave away capital which is no longer surplus to their requirements.

## Do not forget the law may change

Tax legislation is subject to a review at least once a year in the Chancellor's Budget. Moreover, decisions by the courts are constantly resulting in changed interpretations. This is another area where you need to be flexible rather than lean too heavily upon a favourable tax situation afforded by the present rules.

At one time, it was possible to obtain income tax relief for all interest payments. When the law was changed, individuals were given relief for a transitional period on existing borrowings. Nevertheless, the withdrawal of interest relief came as a serious blow to those who had come to depend upon it. So before you carry out any tax planning which will affect your situation in future years, ask yourself how much various tax reliefs are worth to you and how you could rearrange your affairs if the law were changed and the reliefs curtailed or abolished.

## Do not be fooled by G&T tax advice

One of the things that all professional advisers complain of is that clients invariably know someone who assures them that, quite legitimately, he is paying virtually no tax at all. Be wary of advice given over a Gin and Tonic: very often, the individual himself does not understand all the ramifications of his own affairs. Worse still, some of the schemes put forward often turn out to involve evasion (which is illegal) rather than avoidance. Even where there is some substance to what is being said, your friend's or colleague's situation may be quite different from yours. For example, someone who advises you that he pays no tax on his earnings from work carried out outside this country may have a foreign domicile (see Chapter 22) and so be entitled to reliefs which are not available to you as a UK domiciliary.

## Don't wag the dog

Investment first, tax second – tax breaks may be a consideration when considering an investment but normal investment criteria should be the deciding factor. For example, you may be able to defer gains by investing in EIS companies but what is the benefit if the EIS company's business plan is poorly thought out?

## Take professional advice

Unless your affairs are extremely straightforward, you could probably do with a financial 'health check' from time to time, ie a discussion with an accountant or tax adviser to go over your affairs and look for ways in which you might improve your situation and pay less tax. A good accountant should be able to more than cover the fees that he charges by pointing out ways in which you can reduce personal taxes or avoid penalties.

If your affairs are more complex, you probably need to take professional advice on a regular basis. It will also make sense for a tax accountant or adviser to take over the detailed work of preparing your tax return, agreeing payments and making sure that deadlines are not missed.

## Bear in mind the anti-avoidance provisions

The tax legislation contains extensive anti-avoidance provisions intended to make sure that you cannot save tax by carrying out transactions in a round-about way. In particular, much legislation is aimed at preventing a person from converting interest income into capital gain. There are also provisions aimed against the use (or, to be more specific, the abuse) of settlements. In the main, you will be assessed on income arising to trustees of a settlement if you created that settlement and there is any way in which you, or your spouse, may benefit under the settlement.

If you are considering taking steps for tax planning which you hope will help you to escape tax, but which are contrary to the spirit of the legislation, you will need to take a particularly close look at the anti-avoidance provisions. This is a situation where it is normally necessary to take professional advice. Remember that tax evasion is illegal, but tax avoidance, maybe to the annoyance of the Treasury, is not. Arrange your tax affairs in a way that reduces your exposure to taxation. Tax avoidance, some say, is the only profitable past-time left.

## Check on back years

You may well still be receiving communications from several branches of the Inland Revenue and the Department of Social Security. Do not take it as read that all the Civil Servants concerned liaise among themselves. While the position has dramatically improved with the introduction of self-assessment, it is quite possible that at the very time that you are receiving demands for payment of tax for other income or capital gains for years before 1996–97 you may be owed tax on other back years.

Mistakes do happen, and in the past you may have failed to claim all the allowances to which you were entitled. You should therefore carry out a periodic check or 'audit' to ensure that you (and members of your family such as your minor children or your elderly dependent relatives) have claimed all the tax allowances and reliefs to which you are entitled. If you find that mistakes have occurred, you need to file a repayment claim within the six-year time limit or five years and ten months for tax years commencing 6 April 1997 under the self-assessment regime. If not, the overpaid tax will be lost to you forever.

## 1.2 IF YOU ARE THINKING OF BECOMING SELF-EMPLOYED

### 1.2.1 Will the Revenue accept that you are self-employed?

The first question to address is whether the Revenue is likely to accept that you are self-employed. If the main thing that you have to sell is your time, and you are subject to supervision in the way in which you carry out your work, the Revenue may well regard you as an employee. It cuts no ice that your contract may state that you are self-employed.

One reason why the Revenue will look into this so closely is that, if you are self-employed, you will be able to claim certain expenses which are not allowable deductions for employees. So you should take all possible steps to ensure that your claim for self-employed status can stand up to scrutiny by the Revenue (see 2.2).

In theory, the risk of the Revenue's reclassifying a self-employed person as an employee lies with the employer. If the Revenue's view is eventually upheld, the employer will be liable to pay Class I national insurance contributions (NICs) and the Revenue may well require him to pay over the tax that he ought to have withheld under PAYE. Where this happens, the consequences can be disastrous. In law, an employer is precluded from collecting arrears of Class I NICs by deducting them from subsequent payments to the individual concerned. In other words, if the employer does not get it right first time round, he cannot correct his mistake later on. Similarly, the primary responsibility for deducting tax under PAYE and paying it over to the Revenue lies with the employer. The Collector of Taxes is normally reluctant to get into time consuming disputes with the employee and will simply demand the tax from the employer, leaving him to make any adjustment by agreement with the employee. Nevertheless, most self-employed individuals also have a vested interest in the Revenue's accepting that they are genuinely self-employed. If a dispute arises with someone to whom you provide services, he is unlikely to want to deal with you again in the future, certainly not on a self-employed basis.

## 1.2.2 Keep the Revenue informed

Once you start to be self-employed, your best interests are safeguarded by keeping the Revenue advised as to what you are doing. Make your existence known to your local tax district by completing form CWF3 and advise them as to when they may expect to receive accounts. An Inspector of Taxes is like anyone else, he is likely to be more reasonable if he is handled properly rather than irritated by the fact that he constantly has to chase you for information.

There are various other practical matters. You should make enquiries of your local VAT Office to see if you will need to be registered for VAT (see 25.4.1). You should also advise the Department of Social Security that you are self-employed and start to pay Class 2 NICs as a self-employed person.

The Revenue issues a starter pack for new businesses which can be obtained by either visiting www.inlandrevenue.gov.uk/employers/new-bus.htm or calling 08457 646 646.

## 1.2.3 Should you employ your spouse?

Depending upon the type of business you carry on, it may be appropriate for you to employ your spouse, or even to have your spouse as a partner (see 1.3.4 below). This may be a particularly good idea if your spouse would otherwise have little or no taxable income. However, if you employ your spouse, do not pay an unrealistic salary. The Revenue is almost bound to challenge a situation where the salary is disproportionate. The Revenue's argument is that you will be due a deduction only for a reasonable rate of remuneration paid to your spouse in return for services and expertise provided.

Do be careful on this; in principle you could suffer double taxation if you get it wrong since your spouse will still be taxed on his or her full salary even if only part of that salary is allowed as a deduction in arriving at your business profits for tax purposes. Problems could also arise if you are deemed to pay your spouse too little; you should obtain advice on the implications of the minimum wage legislation (see 1.3.4).

## 1.2.4 Provide for tax

Finally, when you commence self-employment, do think ahead and make provision for the tax payments that you will need to make over the next 18 months to two years. Get into the habit of setting aside part of your earnings each month so that you will have something in hand to pay the Revenue when the assessments are eventually issued. Under self-assessment the first tax payment can often be crippling as it represents a payment of tax for your first year plus a 50% payment on account.

**Example**

> A becomes self-employed during the tax year to 5 April 2001 and draws up his
> accounts on a fiscal year basis. He was formerly an employee who paid all his tax
> under PAYE. On 31 January 2003 A will have to pay all of the tax due for the
> year to 5 April 2002 plus a payment on account in respect of the year to 5 April
> 2003 equal to 50% of the 2001–02 tax.

## 1.2.5 Take advice on IR35

If you are setting up a limited company to supply your services, bear in
mind that new provisions in the Finance Act could mean that the company
must pay over PAYE tax on 19 April 2001 on notional salary which you
have not actually taken out. The legislation is aimed at individuals who provide their services via intermediary companies (or partnerships) and who
would otherwise be regarded as employees of the end customer. The effect
of the new rules is that your company is required to account for tax on its
income from 'relevant engagements' as if that income was your Schedule E
earnings subject to PAYE.

# 1.3 IF YOU ARE ALREADY IN BUSINESS

## 1.3.1 Keep good records

Much of what has already been said applies to the same extent if you have
been in business for a number of years already. In many businesses, some
figures have to be estimated (for example, the extent to which a trader's
telephone bill relates to business calls as opposed to private calls). There is
nothing wrong with estimates, but do try to keep some sort of record so that
the estimate can be supported if the Revenue challenges it.

Your self-assessment return will have to indicate where any entries are
estimates. The Revenue may enquire into this and the Inspector may well
want to go back to previous years if he looks into the position later on and
decides that an estimate is unreasonable. The main defence against this
would be where the Inspector was already on notice as to the way in which
the estimates were arrived at.

Keep your records: the Revenue may call for them up to five years and
ten months after the end of the tax year. Remember that this applies to all
your tax affairs, not just the records relating to your business.

If you are a partner, keep tabs on the partnership's tax affairs. One of the
partners (the 'representative partner') will be responsible for filing a partnership return and you will not be able to complete your personal return
without reference to this.

## 1.3.2 Do not cut corners on PAYE

Beware of situations where you should withhold tax, especially where you are paying casual or freelance workers whom the Revenue may regard as employees. The Revenue has teams of investigators who carry out regular reviews of PAYE compliance.

## 1.3.3 Take VAT seriously

VAT is a constant source of problems. Whenever you carry out a major transaction you should ask a VAT specialist for advice. Also, bear in mind that Customs and Excise make regular control visits to examine accounting records. Penalties can be levied if mistakes are uncovered during visits so it is well worth having a review carried out in good time for errors to be corrected prior to a visit.

## 1.3.4 Remunerating your spouse

Think carefully about the salary that you pay your spouse. If the salary is less than you have to pay to an ordinary employee, increase the amount (if only to the £3.70 per hour required under the minimum wage legislation). Perhaps you should set up a pension scheme for your spouse as your contributions will be tax deductible.

Think also about bringing your spouse into partnership. However, this is a complex matter on which it is probably best to seek professional advice which will take account of the nature of your business, and the time, expertise or capital brought to the business by your spouse.

## 1.3.5 Financing a partnership

There are some interesting possibilities for accelerating tax relief by you and your partners raising personal loans to put money into the firm to enable it to clear borrowings. Suppose your firm makes up accounts to 30 April 2001: interest on the firm's borrowings will be an expense in arriving at 2001–02 taxable profits, whereas interest paid in 2000–01 by the partners on personal loans will be a deduction from their taxable income for 2000–01 – so you get your tax relief one year earlier.

## 1.3.6 Relief for losses

If your business has not been going so well, and you have been suffering losses, look into the best way in which you can get relief. In some cases, you may be able to carry the losses back and set them against your other income (see 2.9). In other situations, the choice that is open to you will be to set your losses against your income for the year of the loss, or against your income of the following or preceding year, or carry the losses forward to be set against trading income received in later years. Obviously, it is going to make a great deal of difference if you take relief in a year in which you are otherwise going to be subject to 40% tax rather than in a year in which your other income is relatively low and tax relief will be obtained at only 20% or 23%.

### 1.3.7 Personal pension schemes (see 12.8)

It is particularly important for self-employed individuals to provide for their retirement since they qualify only for the basic State pension and not for SERPS. The Government has played its part in recent years in improving matters and the maximum contributions which may be paid to a personal pension scheme are now much greater than in earlier years – unless you are caught because your profits exceed the 'earnings cap' (£91,800 for 2000–01).

Contributions to a personal pension scheme are tax deductible. Furthermore, the pension scheme is not subject to tax of any kind and so the fund is likely to grow at a far faster rate than personal investments which are subject to tax.

It is possible to take the benefits from a personal pension scheme at any time after you reach age 50. Up to 25% of the fund may be taken as a tax-free lump sum. The balance must eventually be used to purchase an annuity, although this can be postponed until age 75 if you opt for income withdrawals (see 12.8.6).

You should also take advice on the replacement of personal pension schemes by the new stakeholder pensions. There may well be scope for using up your unused relief for previous years before the rules change on 6 April 2001.

### 1.3.8 Should you transfer your business to a company?

If your business is going really well, you should consider whether to incorporate your business, ie transfer your business to a company. There are some general principles set out in 24.16 but once again this is a matter where you would probably be best advised to consult an accountant or tax adviser. You will also have to consider the new rules in respect of service companies, discussed at 19.2.

### 1.3.9 Plan for retirement and handing the business on to the next generation

Finally, do plan ahead, both for retirement and for passing on your business in due course to your family. There are key questions to be addressed in relation to CGT planning (make sure that any gains that you realise on disposing of your business are going to be covered by retirement relief or that you maximise the advantages of taper relief available on business assets – see 15.9). Will IHT be payable on your death or can matters be arranged so that 100% business property relief will be due? See 17.8 on this.

## 1.4 IF YOU ARE EMPLOYED

Whether you are a company director, a senior executive, a manager or an ordinary employee, there are all manner of ways you may be able to reduce your tax liabilities.

### 1.4.1 Claim expenses

It is important to claim all allowable expenses (see 3.3). If you have to belong to a professional institute, the subscription is normally an allowable expense. There are fixed deductions for workers in certain industries. If you are required to provide certain equipment yourself (for example, a fax machine at home) make sure that you put in a claim for the expenses associated with it, and claim capital allowances.

### 1.4.2 Keep records

If you are required to travel extensively, especially overseas, keep a note of your itinerary and the main types of expense that you incur. By doing this, you will be well placed to answer any queries from the Inspector and you should be able to demonstrate that there is no benefit in kind if all the expenses were business related.

Keep a note of your business mileage if you have a company car, especially if you are around the 2,500 and 18,000 margins (see 1.4.3). If you need to use your own car in the course of your employment, find out whether the Fixed Profit Car Scheme applies (see 3.4.9). If it does not, or the mileage payments exceed the FPCS rates, you need to keep a detailed note of your business and private mileage so that any benefit in kind can be calculated. Even if the mileage paid to you by your employer is within the FPCS scale, do let the Revenue know if you have taken a bank or HP loan to buy your car, as part of the interest that you pay should be allowable.

Under self-assessment the keeping of good records is no longer simply a matter of 'good housekeeping' but a necessity (see page 19).

### 1.4.3 Reduce car scale benefits

If you made a capital contribution towards the cost of your company car, this should be deducted in arriving at your benefit in kind. The scale benefit is normally 35% of the list price of your company car as reduced by any capital contribution made by you up to a limit of £5,000.

Also bear in mind that the scale benefit is reduced if your business mileage is 2,500 miles or more pa and the scale benefit is further reduced if you have business mileage of 18,000 miles or more pa (see 3.5). If you are close to either of these margins, it may be worthwhile bringing forward some business trips to make sure that you qualify.

The rules on company cars are changing from 6 April 2002 so look into how this will affect you when your existing car is replaced.

### 1.4.4 Go for benefits which do not attract NICs

The cost of traditional benefits packages are becoming more onerous for employers due to the imposition of the Class 1A NICs charge at 12.2% (see 23.1.8). Why not suggest a package of benefits which are not subject to Class 1A, such as computers for home use, mobile phones and approved share schemes?

### 1.4.5 Other tax efficient benefits

If you have any influence over the way in which your remuneration package is made up, take account of the fact that some benefits are more tax efficient than others. For example, it is well worth having an interest free loan of £5,000 since no benefit in kind is assessed whatsoever. The benefit of having the right to occupy a company flat is often taxed on a favourable basis, especially where it originally cost your company £75,000 or less (see 3.8 on this).

### 1.4.6 Pension schemes (see 12.10)

Pension benefits are particularly attractive as they are not normally taxable. If you do not need all your salary to cover your living costs, it may well be attractive if you can reach a 'deal' with your employer so that he makes contributions towards your pension instead of giving you a larger annual pay rise.

Quite separately from this, do carefully consider the merits of making additional voluntary contributions. If you are not in a company pension scheme, you are most strongly advised to start a personal pension scheme.

### 1.4.7 Share incentives

Company directors and senior executives are often offered an opportunity to acquire shares in their company. However, there are various pitfalls which can apply if you acquire shares through an unapproved scheme (see 3.14) and this is an area where you need professional advice. Also plan ahead. If you have been given approved share options in the past (see 3.15), give some thought as to how you will reap the benefit. Do not forget that CGT may be payable when you exercise your share options if you go on to sell the shares that you have acquired.

The two new approved schemes offer significant advantages (see 3.13 and 3.17).

# 1.5 MANAGING YOUR INVESTMENTS

It is important to keep tax planning in perspective. In general, investment considerations should dictate your investment policy. These will naturally vary according to an individual's perspective, ie his age, need for short and medium-term liquidity, income requirements, the degree of risk that is acceptable, expectations as to future levels of inflation and perception of the economic climate etc. Tax planning has to be fitted in around these investment considerations. Having said all that, there are some quite simple steps which should be considered and which may help you to reduce the tax payable on your investment income and gains.

## 1.5.1 Use all your family's allowances

A married couple both have their own personal allowances and their income is taxed completely separately. If your spouse has little or no income, or is liable only at 20 or 22% whereas you have to pay 40% tax, there may be advantages in transferring income to him or her. There is a fairly straightforward way of doing this, ie hold bank deposit accounts and other investments in your joint names. The basic rule is that where investments are held in this way, half of the resulting income is taxed on each spouse.

If you open an account in your child's name, the interest will only be treated as your income for tax purposes if the total income arising from such potential gifts exceeds £100 pa (see 20.5.3), so there may be some limited opportunity for achieving tax-free savings, especially if you have several children (the £100 limit is per child).

Your spouse will have his or her own £7,200 CGT annual exemption and you should look for ways of using this each year, possibly by transferring investments (transfers between spouses are deemed to take place on a no gain/no loss basis) in order to put your spouse in a position to realise a gain on a sale to a third party. This is often appropriate where a gain has built up on quoted securities. A judicious transfer to your spouse of stocks and shares which show a paper gain can save significant amounts of tax even if the transfer takes place shortly before the securities are sold. But take care: the Revenue will often look very closely at the paperwork on such interspouse transfers and you will need to show that beneficial ownership of the securities actually passed to your spouse before a firm of stockbrokers was instructed to sell the shares. All other things being equal (which they seldom are) it is generally best to allow a few days to elapse between the transfer of the shares to your spouse and the sale by him or her.

Sometimes there may be scope for using your children's annual CGT exemption as the £100 limit for income tax purposes does not apply for capital gains. Bear in mind that this is more difficult since a gift of shares etc to anyone other than your spouse is normally treated as a disposal which is deemed to take place for CGT purposes at market value. However, if you hold shares in unquoted trading companies, and you can see an opportunity coming up whereby you will be able to realise those shares at a large gain, it may be worth transferring part of your shareholding to your children. Because the shares are in unquoted trading companies, it may be possible to 'hold over' any capital gain so that your child (or other relation or friend) takes over the shares at your original acquisition value (see 16.5). This means that you will have no capital gain. The recipient of the gift will have a gain on disposal of the difference between your acquisition value (as adjusted for inflation) and the sale proceeds. However, if you plan carefully you can probably ensure that the child etc realises a gain which is just within his or her £7,200 annual exemption – so no one pays tax on the capital gains. When there is a new share listing, consideration should also be given to subscribing in your child's name as well as your own.

For CGT planning generally, see Chapter 16.

### 1.5.2 Take full advantage of tax efficient investments

Investments in an Individual Savings Account are totally free from tax (see 11.1), so if possible you should open ISAs for yourself and your partner. National Savings Certificates also offer a safe and tax-free return, albeit at a relatively low rate of interest.

For longer term investments, qualifying life insurance policies are often attractive. Once a policy has been in force for ten years, there is normally no tax charge whatsoever on the policy being cashed in.

### 1.5.3 Planning for some special situations

If you have suffered losses in the past on 'one off' transactions which are dealt with under Schedule D Case VI (see 5.17) look out for ways of realising Case VI gains. The point is that Case VI profits may generally be set against Case VI losses brought forward from previous years, and the profits do not have to arise from the same source.

It might be, for example, that you suffered losses on a property which you let out as furnished accommodation before 1994–95. Perhaps you have sold the property or ceased to let it and you assumed that your losses would go to waste. However you may be able to 'access' these Case VI losses by selling gilts shortly before they go ex-div. The point is that the sale of gilts cum-interest will normally give rise to a Case VI charge on notional income by virtue of the 'Accrued Income Scheme' (see 5.6). Another alternative way of generating Case VI profits is to invest in offshore roll-up funds. In many cases, such investments are very similar to having money on a bank deposit overseas. The point is that no income is deemed to arise until the investor realises the investment. When this happens, the profit is charged under Schedule D Case VI.

Your circumstances may be special in another way. It may be that you plan to work overseas for a few years and will therefore cease to be resident in the United Kingdom. In such a case, it will obviously make sense to defer taxable income until after you have ceased to be resident as this will mean that no tax will arise. Once again, a possible way of doing this is to invest in offshore roll-up funds, rather than bank deposit accounts, with a view to cashing in the offshore roll-up investments after you have ceased to be a resident.

### 1.5.4 Property investments

Investments in real estate tend to be longer term investments. For that reason, the tax planning considerations also tend to be long term in nature.

One planning point is relevant at the time that you acquire an investment property. As explained at 9.2, interest on a qualifying loan may be set against any rental income which is taxable under Schedule A, ie any income from properties in the United Kingdom which are let out for rent. However, it is not normally possible for a person who already owns a property to take a qualifying loan later on. The planning point is therefore very simple; you should normally borrow at the outset unless you are quite sure that you will not need to borrow money to finance your property investments later on. Even if you do have sufficient capital, it may be best to borrow to make property investments and use your spare capital for other purposes. For example, it would not be good tax planning to use your capital to purchase an investment property and at the same time take a long-term non-qualifying loan to finance (for example) school fees.

Do not plan for one tax in isolation. If you let part of your home, or if you let your home for a period while you are living elsewhere, check on the CGT implications (see 14.13). There are a number of reliefs and extra statutory concessions, but you need to be very careful not to put your extremely valuable main residence exemption into jeopardy.

If you do let part of your home, bear in mind the special rent-a-room relief (see 4.4) which may mean that rental income of up to £4,250 is totally exempt from tax.

### 1.5.5 Qualifying loans for company directors

If you work full time for a close company (see 9.4) or hold more than 5% of the shares, and you wish to purchase further shares, you may be able to raise a qualifying loan. The interest will attract tax relief at your top rate and there is no £30,000 limit as formerly applied under MIRAS.

### 1.5.6 Plan ahead when buying a private company

If you purchase the whole of the share capital of a private trading company, and things do not go to plan, you will not normally be due income tax relief for any loss. Of course, you may be able to get a loss allowed for CGT purposes, but capital losses may be set only against capital gains, not against income, and therefore it may be some years before you get effective relief.

There may be a way around this if you follow certain steps when you acquire the company. You should speak with your accountant, but basically what will be involved is for you to form a new company, subscribe cash for new shares in that company and have the company acquire the shares in the private trading company. At the end of the day, your position will be almost exactly the same, except that you will hold shares in a company with a wholly-owned subsidiary rather than hold shares in the subsidiary itself. What is important is that by dealing with matters in this way, you will be entitled to s 574 relief on any capital loss (see 15.2), ie you will be able to set the loss against your income for the year of loss or the preceding tax year.

If you need to raise equity from outside investors, see if you can structure your company in a way which qualifies under the Enterprise Investment Scheme (see 11.4). Also consider Venture Capital Trusts as a potential source of equity investment (see 11.7).

## 1.6  TAX DEDUCTIBLE INVESTMENTS

There are basically four types of investment which attract income tax relief when you make the investment:

- Pension contributions
- Investment in enterprise zone properties
- Investments under the Enterprise Investment Scheme (EIS)
- Investments in Venture Capital Trusts (VCTs).

### 1.6.1  Pension contributions

We keep coming back to pension contributions because the tax situation is so attractive. There is no other type of investment where you can get tax relief when you pay money in, enjoy the benefits of a fund which pays no tax on its income and gains, and take part of the fund as a lump sum which is not taxable. The last aspect is one of the most important; contributions to pension schemes allow a person to effectively convert taxable income into a tax-free capital sum.

It is precisely because the tax treatment is so beneficial that restrictions have been introduced in recent years. For example, there is the 'cap' on pensionable earnings (presently £91,800) which means that you cannot make personal pension contributions based on your actual earnings if they exceed this amount. On the other hand, the percentage limits which vary according to your age have been improved, so it is now possible to make larger contributions on the first £91,800 of your annual earnings. Further- more, if you have not made the maximum contributions in earlier years, you can pick up the relief now by paying a one-off contribution which covers all or part of the unused relief for the last six years.

It is worth noting that if you make payments into a retirement annuity policy, ie a policy similar to a personal pension plan which was taken out before 1 July 1988, the earnings cap does not apply. This means that if your earnings for 2000–01 are £200,000, you can get income tax relief for retirement annuity premiums based on £200,000 and not on £91,800. However, be careful: the tax situation is quite complicated where an individual pays a mixture of retirement annuity and personal pension plan contributions and this is an area where you need advice from a specialist.

FA 2000 contains legislation on stakeholder pensions. Basically from April 2001 an individual will be able to make a payment of up to £3,600 regardless of net relevant earnings. The pension payments will be made net of basic rate tax even if he has no taxable income. On the other hand, the introduction of the new scheme will stop the carry forward of unused relief under the personal pension scheme legislation which remains in force for the current tax year. You may be well-advised to mop up all unused relief from earlier tax years in the year to 5 April 2001.

## 1.6.2 Investment in enterprise zone properties

A 100% allowance is available where a person invests in a commercial building located in an enterprise zone. Basically, the building must be unused or you must make your investment within two years of it having first been let.

The enterprise zones were designated for a period of ten years and this period has now run out for many of the zones. Nevertheless, there are still a number of enterprise zone property investments available.

Many people prefer to invest via a syndicate or fund. These funds are often called enterprise zone property trusts. Basically, a person who invests in such a trust is entitled to relief for the corresponding proportion of the trust's investments in enterprise zone properties.

## 1.6.3 Investments under the Enterprise Investment Scheme

Wealthy individuals should consider making selective investments under the EIS. It is now possible to invest up to £150,000 pa under the EIS. Investors are entitled to 20% income tax relief and may also be able to claim CGT deferral relief (see 11.6). The income and CGT reliefs may add up to 60% of your investment. Any capital gain on a disposal of the EIS shares after three years is totally tax free.

The Government has also made the EIS more attractive in other ways. Many of the restrictions and anti-avoidance rules have been abolished. It is now possible for an investor to become a paid director and take a full part in the management of the company. If you have gains in excess of

£150,000, or you have made gains in the last few years which you would like to 'roll over', you may be able to obtain CGT deferral relief by investing further amounts under the EIS. Also, one of the requirements for EIS investors to qualify for the 20% income tax relief is that they must not have more than 30% of the equity. This rule does not apply if you are investing in an EIS company only in order to secure CGT deferral relief (see 11.6).

### 1.6.4 Venture Capital Trusts

An individual is allowed to invest up to £100,000 pa in VCTs. Be careful, because these may be relatively high risk investments. However, there are significant tax advantages in that if you subscribe for new VCT shares you will be entitled to 20% income tax relief and CGT deferral relief. In addition, the dividends that you receive from your investment and any capital gain when you eventually dispose of it can be tax free (see 11.7).

## 1.7 YOUR FAMILY AFFAIRS AND PERSONAL FINANCIAL PLANNING

There are important personal financial planning issues to be addressed (eg making sure you claim all that is due to you under the Working Family Tax Credits (see 23.6.2 and Table 23.2), mortgages, tax implications of marriage (and separation and divorce), life assurance, funding school fees, providing help to elderly dependent relatives, assisting your children in buying their first home etc). Looking further ahead, there are longer term matters which need to be kept in mind, such as the way in which your Will, and possibly the way in which your spouse's Will, should be drawn up. IHT planning also needs to be considered.

### 1.7.1 House purchase

When you purchase your home, there are several different types of mortgage available. You should take advice as to whether an ordinary repayment, endowment, or pension mortgage is the most appropriate for you.

If you took out a PEP mortgage in the past, you need to reconsider your options now that PEPs have been abolished. One alternative is to open ISAs and use this type of tax privileged savings to build up capital to enable you to clear the mortgage in due course.

### 1.7.2 Life assurance

Income tax relief is not given for life assurance premiums on policies taken out after 13 March 1984.

If you are self-employed, it is possible to obtain income tax relief at your top rate for life assurance premiums paid under a personal pension plan. You should consult your adviser about the possibility of taking out a 'section 621' policy. However, bear in mind that if you use up part of your relief for personal pension contributions in this way, it may limit the amount which you can pay into a personal pension plan in order to secure pension benefits.

## 1.7.3 Marriage

Many of the tax planning issues which arise in connection with marriage concern CGT or IHT.

### Capital gains tax

Bear in mind that if you transfer shares or other chargeable assets to your intended spouse before your marriage, you will be deemed to have made a disposal at market value and a capital gain may therefore arise. From this point of view, it may be better to delay matters until after you are married as no capital gain arises on transfers between spouses who are living together.

Of course, if you are thinking of transferring an asset on which a capital loss would arise, it may be best to crystallise this loss by making the transfer before you get married.

Something else to bear in mind is the position if both of you already own your own home. Basically, you will have three years grace to resolve the position, but at the end of that time only one property can qualify as your main residence (see 14.14.5). The property concerned may be a new home or one of you may move into the other's existing home.

### Inheritance tax

No IHT arises on transfers of assets by one spouse to another unless the transferor is domiciled in the UK and the transferee is not (see 17.5.1).

## 1.7.4 If you and your partner are not married

In the main, the tax legislation does not recognise common law marriages or same sex relationships. CGT and IHT are likely to be much more of an issue here and you need advice if significant capital assets are involved.

## 1.7.5 Separation and divorce

Relief for maintenance payments under pre-14 March 1988 court orders was abolished with effect from 6 April 2000. Furthermore, now that the married man's allowance has been phased out there is no relief for maintenance payments whatsoever.

So far as CGT is concerned, you could find yourself in a Catch 22 situation. The legislation provides that a man and his wife are connected persons for CGT purposes until the marriage comes to an end. The marriage comes to an end when there is a decree absolute, not a decree nisi. However, the exemption for transfers between spouses applies only if you are living together. You may therefore find yourself in a situation where a CGT charge may arise because you are required to transfer assets to your spouse as part of your divorce settlement.

As so often, it is possible to get round this problem if you plan ahead. The basic rule that transfers between spouses are not subject to CGT applies to transfers made during a tax year in which you have been living together at some time. Thus, if you and your wife separate on (say) 10 April 2000, a transfer of assets between you will not give rise to a CGT charge provided the transfer is made before 6 April 2001.

### 1.7.6 Funding school fees

If grandparents or other relatives are able to help, advantage could be taken of your children's tax allowances. One way of doing this is for your relatives to set up trusts and for the trustees to distribute income to your children. This money could then be used to pay school fees.

Bear in mind that this will not work if you make a trust for your own children as any income which is paid out before they attain age 18 will be treated as if it were your income.

Where grandparents etc cannot assist, things are more difficult but not necessarily impossible. You should start saving as early as possible and take full advantage of privileged investments such as ISAs and qualifying insurance policies. Take advice from a specialist.

### 1.7.7 Providing for elderly dependants

Many readers will be making a contribution towards the support of elderly parents or other relatives. Unfortunately, recent Chancellors of the Exchequer have significantly reduced the scope for obtaining assistance towards these costs through tax relief. In particular, it is no longer possible to transfer income by means of a deed of covenant and the income tax allowance for dependent relatives has been abolished altogether.

One area where it may be possible to secure tax relief is where it is necessary to purchase a property which is used by the relative as his or her home. There is no tax relief for a mortgage taken out for this purpose, but it may be possible to secure CGT exemption in due course if you follow a fairly involved route.

The CGT exemption is not available if you own the property yourself (unless you owned the property prior to 5 April 1988). However, if you form a trust and put money into it to enable the trustees to buy the dependant's home, the trustees may be entitled to an exemption as and when they eventually sell the property. Furthermore, this exemption is not affected by your being a beneficiary under the trust yourself. So the answer may be to set up a trust under which your elderly father or mother is entitled to occupy the property during their lifetime, with the trust coming to an end on their death and the property passing to you as a beneficiary of your own trust.

There are other aspects to be considered, not least the IHT position if the property has a value in excess of £234,000. You therefore need to talk this through with a specialist tax adviser to see whether this solution would work in your particular circumstances.

### 1.7.8 Assisting your children in making tax privileged investments

If you can afford it, it may make sense for you to lend your adult children the money so that they can use their quota of tax exempt and tax privileged investments such as ISAs.

### 1.7.9 Inheritance tax

This is a highly specialised area (see further Chapter 17), but in general a person should:

(1) Make use of the annual exemptions.
(2) Preserve (and maximise) business property and agricultural reliefs.
(3) Make a valid will
(4) Consider making exempt transfers by a deed of variation.
(5) Make potentially exempt transfers which escape IHT after the donor has survived seven years.
(6) Fund insurance policies so as to provide cash to meet IHT payable on death.

## 1.8 ENSURE THAT ALL IMPORTANT DEADLINES ARE KEPT

It is pointless trying to arrange your affairs tax efficiently unless you get the basics right and keep your affairs tidy. This means watching deadlines for action (eg paying tax) and making elections.

The most important tax planning deadlines are listed below. This section should, however, be read subject to three cautions:

(1) Most of the deadlines are dates by which a return, claim or election must be received by the Inspector of Taxes, or a payment received by the Collector. Obviously, a document or payment must be posted at least one working day before the deadline and, because of the danger of postal delays, ideally at least a week.

(2) To keep this checklist to a manageable size, only those deadlines likely to apply to the majority of people have been included. The checklist is not, therefore, fully comprehensive.
(3) Many deadlines cannot be included because they are fixed by reference to the facts of the individual case. For example, if a Will has been varied by a deed of variation, you must submit the deed to the Revenue within six months. Similarly, most corporation tax deadlines are fixed by reference to the end of the company's accounting period.

## 1.8.1 **2000 deadlines**

**April 19**  PAYE/NICs payments due at the Accounts Office by today. Interest chargeable after this date.
**May 19**  Employers who do not file end-of-year returns (on Forms P14, P35 and P38/P38A) by today may be fined.
**May 31**  Last date for giving a 1999–2000 form P60 to each relevant employee.
**July 6**  Substantial fines may be imposed on employer who does not submit Form P11D (Returns of benefits, etc provided for employees) by today (see 3.4.1). In addition details of benefits shown on P9D or P11D forms must also be supplied to each employee.
**July 19**  Due date for payment for 1999–2000 Class 1A NICs (company cars and fuel) (see 23.1.7).
PAYE quarterly payment date for small employers.
**July 31**  Second interim tax payment for 1999–2000 due.
**October 5**  To avoid the danger of incurring penalties, individuals with new sources of income in 1999–2000 should have notified the Revenue by 4 pm today if no tax return has been received.
**October 19**  PAYE quarterly payment date for small employers.
**December 31**  Closing date for claiming, on grounds of low income, repayment of Class 2 NICs paid in 1999–2000 (see 23.2.3).

## 1.8.2 **31 January 2001 deadlines**

A large number of claims and elections must be made within 22 months of the end of the tax year in question.

### Deadlines in relation to the tax year 1998–99

#### *Personal tax*

(1) Claiming a set-off for industrial buildings allowances on enterprise zone investments made in 1998–99 (see 11.8 and 4.6.3–4.6.4).
(2) Electing to split rents received from a furnished letting in 1998–99 between Schedule A and Case VI assessments.

(3) Claiming relief against income tax for 1998–99 for a loss on the disposal (in 1997–98 or 1998–99) of shares in a qualifying trading company (see 15.2).

### Capital gains tax

(1) Electing to compute all gains and losses on assets acquired before 31 March 1982 by reference to values on that day (possible only where the first relevant disposal took place after 5 April 1998) (see 14.3.2).
(2) Claiming that an asset became of negligible value during 1998–99 (see 13.4.9).
(3) Claiming relief in respect of a rolled-over or held-over gain which crystallised in 1998–99 (see 14.3.5).
(4) Claiming a set-off against capital gains assessed for 1998–99 in respect of a loss incurred on a qualifying loan to a trader (see 15.1).

### Business tax

(1) Claiming that a trading loss incurred in 1998–99 should be set against other income of 1998–99 (see 2.9.2).
(2) Claiming that a trading loss incurred in 1998–99 should be set against a capital gain realised in 1998–99 (see 2.9.6).
(3) Claiming that a trading loss incurred in 1998–99 be carried back, where this is permitted under the 'new business' rules (see 2.9.5).
(4) Claiming CGT retirement relief in respect of a disposal made in 1998–99, where that claim is based on ill health (see 15.9.3).
(5) Electing to treat plant or machinery purchased in 1998–99 as a short-life asset for capital allowance purposes (see 2.5.9).
(6) Electing for post-cessation receipts received in 1998–99 to be taxed for the year the trade was discontinued (see 2.7).

## 1.8.3 5 April 2001 deadlines

Most claims to personal allowances and reliefs for pre-self assessment years have to be made within six years, so that claims for 1994–95 must be made by 5 April 2000.

The list below shows, for each year of assessment, the claims or elections which must be made by 5 April 2001. It must be emphasised that, owing to the complexity of the legislation, this table is not comprehensive.

### Deadlines in relation to the tax year 1994–95

#### Personal tax

(1) Claiming personal allowances for 1994–95 (see 7.2.1).
(2) Claiming relief for interest paid in 1994–95.
(3) Claiming relief for pension contributions paid in 1994–95.
(4) Claiming 'top-slicing' relief in respect of life assurance policy gains arising in 1994–95 (see 12.3.4).

(5) Claiming relief to correct an error or mistake made by the taxpayer which resulted in an excessive assessment being made in the year to 1994–95.
(6) Electing to have a Case III source of income assessed on the current year basis rather than the preceding year basis, where 1994–95 was the third year.
(7) Claiming to exclude from assessment rent due in 1994–95 which was never in fact received.

### Capital gains tax

Claiming roll-over and hold-over relief in respect of disposals which took place in 1994–95 (see 15.4 and 15.6).

### Deadline in relation to the tax year 1995–96

### Personal tax

Requesting the Inspector formally to assess 1995–96 Schedule E liabilities.

## 1.8.4 Other 2001 deadlines

**April 19**  PAYE/NICs payments due at the Accounts Office by today. Interest chargeable after this date.
**May 19**  Employers who do not file end-of-year returns (on Forms P14, P35 and P38/P38A) by today may be fined.
**May 31**  Last date for giving a 2000–01 form P60 to each relevant employee.
**July 6**  Substantial fines may be imposed on employer who does not submit Form P11D (Returns of benefits, etc provided for employees) by today (see 3.4.1). In addition details of benefits shown on P9D or P11D forms must also be supplied to each employee.
**July 19**  Due date for payment for 2000–01 Class 1A NICs (company cars and fuel) (see 23.1.7).
PAYE quarterly payment date for small employers.
**July 31**  Second interim tax payment for 2000–01 due.
**October 5**  To avoid the danger of incurring penalties, individuals with new sources of income in 2000–01 should have notified the Revenue by 4 pm today if no tax return has been received.
**October 19**  PAYE quarterly payment date for small employers.
**December 31**  Closing date for claiming, on grounds of low income, repayment of Class 2 NICs paid in 2000–01 (see 23.2.3).

# 2

# TAX AND SELF-EMPLOYMENT

SHEENA SULLIVAN

If you are self-employed, either in business on your own or in a partnership, you will be taxed under Schedule D Case I (if you carry on a trade) or Case II (if your business is regarded as a profession). In practice, the rules for determining taxable profits are virtually the same and therefore all references in this chapter to a person carrying on a trade apply equally to a person who is engaged in a profession.

The following key aspects of taxation of the self-employed are covered in this chapter:

(1) How self-employed individuals pay tax.
(2) Are you really self-employed?
(3) Basis of assessment.
(4) How taxable profits are computed.
(5) Capital allowances.
(6) Pre-trading expenditure.
(7) Post-cessation receipts.
(8) Post-cessation expenses.
(9) Relief for trading losses.
(10) Partnerships

## 2.1 HOW SELF-EMPLOYED INDIVIDUALS PAY TAX

### 2.1.1 Payment of tax

Unlike employees who suffer deduction of tax from their earnings under PAYE, self-employed individuals pay tax directly to the Revenue. Taxation payable by self-employed individuals for 2000–01 needs to be paid in two instalments: on 31 January 2001 and 31 July 2001. The amount payable for each instalment is normally half the liability for 1999–2000. If you started self-employment fairly recently, and previously almost all your tax was collected under PAYE, you may find that you do not have to make instalment payments for 2000–01. However, the system will catch up with you on 31 January 2002 as you will then have to settle the whole of your 2000–01 tax and make the first payment on account for 2001–02.

## 2.1.2 Completing your tax return

You will need to complete a special schedule as part of your self-assessment tax return; this asks for details of the type of business that you are carrying on. It also asks whether your sales exceed £15,000 pa.

### Very small businesses

If your sales are less than £15,000 pa you can simply file your tax return on the basis of three entries: sales, expenses and profit. There is no obligation to prepare accounts, although it may be advisable to do so for other reasons.

## 2.1.3 Ascertaining taxable profits based on accounts

If your sales (or 'turnover') exceeds £14,999 you will need to complete further forms and, in order to do this, you will need accounts for your business. We would normally advise that accounts are sent in with the self-assessment return, whether or not the Revenue wants them, as this limits the scope for the Revenue to reopen back years by making 'discovery assessments'.

Very often, accounts are drawn up for other reasons as well (eg for production to banks and other lenders) and it is important to bear in mind that there may need to be some specific adjustments for tax purposes. There are also specific rules which govern the amount of 'capital allowances' that a trader may claim – in broad terms, capital allowances are an adjustment for depreciation or wear and tear on equipment etc used in the business. This is dealt with in greater detail at 2.4.

## 2.2 ARE YOU REALLY SELF-EMPLOYED?

## 2.2.1 Introduction

It is not possible to elect to be self-employed; whether you are self-employed is a matter of fact. However, since the Taxes Acts do not define self-employment the rules have evolved through decisions handed down by the courts.

The real distinction between being self-employed and an employee is that there is no 'master-servant' relationship. However, in practice it is often difficult to discern the dividing line and the Revenue may take a different view from the parties concerned. For example, freelance workers may not necessarily be recognised as being self-employed and salaried partners may be classified as employees. Before 6 April 1999, the position could be further complicated in that the Contributions Agency were responsible for assessing liability for national insurance contributions and occasionally reached a different conclusion from the Revenue.

These grey areas can sometimes result in companies treating freelance workers as if they were employees and deducting tax and NICs under PAYE accordingly. This reflects the Revenue's practice of seeking unpaid tax from employers in cases where a company has not operated PAYE. As a result, it is very difficult, for example, for workers in the computer field to secure payment on a self-employed basis. Similar problems are often experienced by workers in the TV industry, journalists, actors and artistes and many other industries where freelance workers are required to work 'on-site'.

The Revenue has addressed this issue by the introduction of new legislation with effect from 6 April 2000, known colloquially as IR35. These rules are covered in more detail at 19.3 as they deal primarily with individuals who offer their services through a service company. However, during the consultation period leading up to the introduction of the new legislation the Revenue consolidated its statements on the dividing line between being employed and self-employed. These can be found in *Tax Bulletin* 45 available at www.inlandrevenue.gov.uk/bulletins/tb45.htm. See also leaflet IR175, *Supplying Services*.

## 2.2.2 The Inland Revenue's criteria

Guidelines issued by the Revenue in conjunction with the DSS to clarify employment status (leaflet IR56, *Employed or self-employed?*) included the following points:

(1) An employee generally does the work in person (and does not hire someone else to do it) working at times and places and in the way specified by the firm for whom the work is done and normally paid at hourly, weekly or monthly rates, possibly including overtime.

(2) A self-employed person may hire and pay others to do the work, or do it personally, in either case specifying the time and the way it is done, providing major items of equipment, being responsible for losses as well as profits and correcting unsatisfactory work in his own time and at his own expense.

These criteria, however, are only for guidance and in some cases the Commissioners and the courts have held that a person who did not fulfil the requirements in (2) above was nevertheless self-employed. Thus, a journalist who worked as a freelance sub-editor at various national newspapers was held by the Commissioners to be self-employed even though she carried out all the work at the newspapers' offices. Similarly, a test case sponsored by Equity resulted in the Special Commissioners finding that actors engaged in London West End theatre work are not employees.

Commissioners' decisions, unlike court decisions, do not set binding legal precedents. It was therefore even more important that the Court of Appeal held in *Hall v Lorimer* [1994] STC 23 that a TV vision mixer was self-employed even though he failed to satisfy virtually all of the above tests or, as the courts put it, 'indicators'. In this case the taxpayer used extremely expensive equipment which was provided by the TV companies concerned and his work was rigorously controlled.

The moral is to take professional advice if you are a borderline case rather than simply accept a 'ruling' from the Revenue. The borders are constantly shifting; for example, FA 2000 contains provisions which can treat certain partnership income as if it were employment income subject to PAYE.

## 2.3 BASIS OF ASSESSMENT

The same rules apply for both Schedule D Cases I and II. A self-employed person may draw up accounts to any date that he chooses; there is no requirement that accounts be made up to 5 April in order to fit in with the fiscal year, although the Revenue will encourage him to adopt a fiscal year basis. All self-employed individuals are now taxed on the 'current year' basis.

### 2.3.1 Current year basis

The assessable profits of a business are dealt with on the current year basis. This means that the assessment will be determined by the profits for the accounting year which ends in the year of assessment. Thus a business with a 31 May year end will be assessed for 2000–01 on its profits for the year ended 31 May 2000. Taxable profits for these purposes are after deducting capital allowances (see 2.5).

Special rules govern the first tax year since there will normally be no accounts which end in that tax year (see below).

#### Opening years

Special rules apply for the first two tax years;

(1) The first tax year's assessment is made by reference to profits actually earned during that year.
(2) The second tax year's assessment is normally determined by the profits of the first 12 months.
(3) The third tax year's assessment will be on the current year basis.

## Example of opening years rules under the current year basis

*A* starts in business on 6 October 1999. His accounts for the year to 5 October 2000 show profits of £48,000. Profits for the year ending 5 October 2001 are £72,000. *A* will be assessed as follows:

|   | £ |
|---|---|
| 1999–00 'actual' basis ($\frac{6}{12} \times$ £48,000) | 24,000 |
| 2000–01 first 12 months' profits | 48,000 |
| 2001–02 current year basis | 72,000 |

## Example of position where first accounts are not drawn up for a 12-month period

The precise way in which the opening year rules work is slightly more complicated where there are no accounts for a period of 12 months ending in the second tax year. This is covered by the following examples:

(1) *B* starts in business on 1 January 1999. The first set of accounts are made up to 30 April 1999, then to 30 April 2000. *B* will be assessed on profits computed as follows:

| *1998–99* | $\frac{3}{4} \times$ profits of period 1 January–30 April 1999. |
| *1999–00* | profits of first 12 months, ie |
| | $\frac{4}{4} \times$ profits of period 1 January–30 April 1999 |
| *Plus* | $\frac{8}{12} \times$ profits for year ended 30 April 2000. |

(2) *C* starts up on 1 March 1998 and the first set of accounts are made up to 30 April 1999 ie there are no accounts ending in the second year. *C*'s assessable profits are:

| *1997–98* | $\frac{1}{14} \times$ profits for 14 months ended 30 April 1999. |
| *1998–99* | profits of first 12 months, ie |
| | $\frac{12}{14} \times$ profits for 14 months ended 30 April 1999. |
| *1999–00* | $\frac{12}{14} \times$ profits for 14 months ended 30 April 1999. |

## 2.3.2 Final year of trading

Where an individual ceases to carry on a business, he is taxed under the current year basis on his profits for a notional period which starts immediately after the basis period for the previous tax year and ends on the date that he ceases. This can be illustrated by a case where a person makes up accounts to 30 April. Assume her profits for the year ended 30 April 2000 are £80,000. She ceases business on 30 November 2000 and her profits for the final six months amount to £50,000. The assessable income for 2000–01 is her share of profits for the period 1 May 1999–30 November 2000, ie

£80,000 plus £50,000 (but subject to either overlap or transitional relief – see below).

## 2.3.3 Overlap relief

Because of the way that a new business is assessed under the current year basis for the first two tax years, some profits may be taxed more than once. To compensate for this, and to ensure that over the life of the business tax is paid only on the actual amount of profits, overlap relief is given when the business is discontinued or, in the case of partners, when they leave the firm.

If the overlap relief exceeds the taxable profits for the final year, the balance may be treated as an allowable loss and either set against the individual's other income for that year or the preceding year, or carried back against Schedule D Case I profits of the last three years as terminal loss relief (see 2.9.9).

### Example of overlap relief

In the first example at 2.3.1, in which $A$'s first accounts end on 5 October 2000, $\frac{6}{12}$ of the first 12 months' profits are assessed twice. Accordingly, a figure of £24,000 is carried forward and is deducted from $A$'s profits for the final year of trading. Thus, if $A$ retires on 5 October 2001, and his final year's profits are £60,000, the assessment for 2002–03 will be as follows:

|  | £ |
|---|---|
| Current year basis | 60,000 |
| *Less*: overlap relief | 24,000 |
| Taxable profits | 36,000 |

### Change of accounting dates

Unless a business from the date of commencement draws up annual accounts ending in the period 31 March–5 April there will be overlap relief.

### Example – change of accounting dates

$A$ starts trading on 1 October 2001. The profit for the first year of trading is £45,000. The basis of assessment for the opening years would be:

| 2001–02 | 1/10/2001 to 5/4/2002 |
| 2002–03 | 12 months to 30/9/2002 |
| 2003–04 | 12 months to 30/9/2003 |

The overlap period is the 187 days to 5 April 2002 which will be assessed both in 2001–02 and 2002–03. The overlap profit is £23,055.

If during the lifetime of the business the accounting date is extended to bring it nearer to 5 April the overlap relief is utilised. The intention of the legislation is to give relief in full when accounts are drawn up on a fiscal year basis ie for the year to 5 April.

If the accounting period is shortened then additional overlap relief is created.

### Example – change of accounting dates

> *A* changes his accounting date to 30 April 2006. The profit in the year to 30 September 2005 was £90,000.
>
> | 2005–06 | 12 months to 30/9/2005 |
> | 2006–07 | 12 months to 30/4/2006 |
>
> The period of overlap is 1 May 2005–30 September 2005. The overlap profit is therefore £37,726 over 153 days which is combined with the earlier overlap profit to give an overlap profit of £60,781 over 340 days.
>
> If *A* extends his basis period towards the 5 April then the overlap relief is used and logically if *A* were to extend the accounting date to 5 April then all of the relief would be utilised.

## 2.3.4 Preceding year basis
(TA 1988, s 60)

In the past, the profits on which an individual was taxed were normally determined on the 'preceding year' basis so that a self-employed person's assessment on profits for 1995–96 was determined by his profits for an accounting year which ended some time between 6 April 1994 and 5 April 1995. For further details on the preceding year basis in 1995–96 and earlier years, see *Allied Dunbar Tax Handbook 1997–98* at 2.3.12–2.3.17.

## 2.3.5 1996–97 – the transitional year

The preceding year basis was abolished altogether from 5 April 1996. The 1995–96 assessment on a trader who was in business before 6 April 1994 will normally have been made on the preceding year basis. The 1996–97 assessment was generally based on the average profits for the two years' accounts which ended in the tax year 1996–97.

For further details on the way in which businesses were assessed for 1996–97, see *Allied Dunbar Tax Handbook 1998–99* at 2.3.5–2.3.6.

## 2.3.6 Transitional relief

As explained above, a pre-6 April 1994 business has been assessed on the current year basis for 1997–98 onwards (see 2.3.1). Thus, a businessman with a year end of 5 May was assessed for 1997–98 on the whole of the business's profits for the year ended 5 May 1997 even though he was assessed for 1996–97 on a full year's profits. It was argued that this amounted to double taxation, and the legislation therefore allows 'transitional relief' which works like overlap relief (see 2.3.3 above). The relief represents the amount which will be assessed under the current year basis for 1997–98 but which was earned before 6 April 1997. Thus, if a business made up accounts to 5 May, the 1997–98 assessment was based on profits for the year ended 5 May 1997 and the transitional relief will be $\frac{1}{12}$ of those profits. Incidentally, the Revenue is content to split years in these situations by either months or days providing there is consistency.

Transitional relief will be enjoyed when the accounting date is moved to be a point which is later in the tax year, or the individual ceases to carry on business.

### Example

> A makes up his accounts to 5 June and has been in business for many years prior to 1994. His 1995–96 assessment was made on the preceding year basis. His 1996–97 assessment was made on 50% of the profits for the two years ended 5 June 1996. Assume that this computation produced an assessment for 1996–97 of £100,000.
>
> For 1997–98, A was assessed on the current year basis, ie his assessment was made on the profits for the year ending in 1997–98. Thus, if A's profits for the year ended 5 June 1997 amounted to £180,000, that was his assessable income for 1997–98.
>
> If A ceases to carry on the business in 2000–01, he will be entitled to transitional relief equal to $\frac{10}{12}$ of £180,000, ie £150,000. This amount will be allowed as a deduction in arriving at his assessable profits for 2000–01.

## 2.4 HOW TAXABLE PROFITS ARE COMPUTED

### 2.4.1 Self-assessment tax return

At the centre of self-assessment for the self-employed is the schedule which contains a series of boxes designed to adjust account figures for tax purposes (see page 77).

## Example

Z's profit and loss account for the year ended 31 December 1999 show the following:

|  | £ | £ |
|---|---|---|
| Income |  | £97,500 |
| Expenses |  |  |
| Wages | 27,500 |  |
| Rent | 6,000 |  |
| Insurance | 1,650 |  |
| Utilities | 1,060 |  |
| Repairs | 2,100 |  |
| Telephone | 980 |  |
| Accountancy | 500 |  |
| VAT surcharge | 400 |  |
| Depreciation | 1,400 |  |
| Entertaining | 1,200 |  |
| Miscellaneous | 250 |  |
|  |  | 43,040 |
| Net profit |  | £54,460 |

*Notes*
(1) Goods taken out for personal use and not reimbursed at full cost £600.
(2) Telephone costs not relating to business £200.
(3) Non-staff entertaining £565.

## 2.4.2 What type of accounts are required?

The nature and complexity of accounts should be governed by the business. An individual in business as a window-cleaner can keep his accounts as simple as possible. Moreover, the Revenue allows certain 'short-cuts'; for example, if you use your car for business you generally can use the FPCS rates designed for employees (see 3.4.9) and merely claim (say) 4,000 miles at the appropriate rate rather than keep all your motoring bills and claim capital allowances.

Larger businesses require more complex accounting. The following covers the rules which govern the tax treatment of income and expenses and deals with adjustments to accounts which are required for tax purposes. For example, a set of accounts prepared for commercial reasons may include a provision for wear and tear to a building. Such a provision needs to be 'added back' (as no relief is available for depreciation as such, relief is due only via the capital allowances system).

## 2.4.3 Accounts should be on the 'earnings basis'

The Revenue's view is that accounts should normally be prepared to reflect a trader's earnings for a year rather than just the cash received. For example,

## Income and expenses - annual turnover £15,000 or more

You must fill in this Page if your annual turnover is £15,000 or more - read the Notes, page SEN2

If you were registered for VAT, do the figures in boxes 3.16 to 3.51, include VAT? **3.14** ☐ or exclude VAT? **3.15** ✓

Sales/business income (turnover) **3.16** £ 97,500

| | Disallowable expenses included in boxes 3.33 to 3.50 | Total expenses |
|---|---|---|
| Cost of sales | 3.17 £ | 3.33 £ |
| Construction industry subcontractor costs | 3.18 £ | 3.34 £ |
| Other direct costs | 3.19 £ | 3.35 £ |

box 3.16 minus (box 3.33 + box 3.34 + box 3.35)

Gross profit/(loss) **3.36** £ 97,500

Other income/profits **3.37** £

| | Disallowable | Total expenses |
|---|---|---|
| Employee costs | 3.20 £ | 3.38 £ 27,500 |
| Premises costs | 3.21 £ | 3.39 £ 7,650 |
| Repairs | 3.22 £ | 3.40 £ 2,100 |
| General administrative expenses | 3.23 £ 200 | 3.41 £ 2,040 |
| Motor expenses | 3.24 £ | 3.42 £ |
| Travel and subsistence | 3.25 £ | 3.43 £ |
| Advertising, promotion and entertainment | 3.26 £ 565 | 3.44 £ 1,200 |
| Legal and professional costs | 3.27 £ | 3.45 £ 500 |
| Bad debts | 3.28 £ | 3.46 £ |
| Interest | 3.29 £ | 3.47 £ |
| Other finance charges | 3.30 £ | 3.48 £ |
| Depreciation and loss/(profit) on sale | 3.31 £ 1400 | 3.49 £ 1,400 |
| Other expenses | 3.32 £ | 3.50 £ 650 |

Put the total of boxes 3.37 to 3.32 in box 3.53 below

total of boxes 3.38 to 3.50

Total expenses **3.51** £ 43,040

boxes 3.36 + 3.37 minus box 3.51

Net profit/(loss) **3.52** £ 54,460

## Tax adjustments to net profit or loss

total of boxes 3.17 to 3.32

| | | |
|---|---|---|
| Disallowable expenses | 3.53 £ 2,165 | |
| Goods etc. taken for personal use and other adjustments (apart from disallowable expenses) that increase profits | 3.54 £ 600 | |
| Balancing charges | 3.55 £ | |

boxes 3.53 + 3.54 + 3.55

Total additions to net profit (deduct from net loss) **3.56** £ 2,765

| Capital allowances | 3.57 £ |
|---|---|
| Deductions from net profit (add to net loss) | 3.58 £ |

boxes 3.57 + 3.58

**3.59** £

boxes 3.52 + 3.56 minus box 3.59

Net business profit for tax purposes (put figure in brackets if a loss) **3.60** £ 57,225 the accounts should include debtors, ie bills which have been issued but which have not been paid by the year end. Similarly, the accounts should include work in progress.

### 2.4.4 Sound commercial accountancy principles

The Master of Rolls stated in *Gallagher v Jones* [1993] STC 537, CA that:

> Subject to any express or implied statutory rule . . . the ordinary way to ascertain the profits or losses of a business is to apply accepted principles of commercial accountancy. That is the very purpose for which such principles are formulated. As has often been pointed out, such principles are not static: they may be modified, refined and elaborated over time as circumstances change and accounting insights sharpen. But so long as such principles remain current and generally accepted they provide the surest answer . . .

In practice, there are two fundamental concepts which underlie accounts drawn up on normal commercial accountancy principles:

(1) The accruals concept where income and costs are accrued, in other words recognised as they are earned or incurred rather than according to when money is received or paid. In general, income (or 'revenue') and costs should be 'matched' so that revenues are set against associated costs and expenses. However, it may sometimes be necessary to depart from this rule because of the 'prudence' concept.

(2) The prudence concept requires that revenue and profits should not be anticipated but rather should be recognised only when realised. Moreover, provision should be made for costs or expenses for which liability has arisen, with the provision being made on an estimated basis in the light of the information available.

Certain types of expenditure are disallowed for tax purposes even though it may be sound accounting practice to deduct such costs in a trader's accounts, for example entertaining customers. There are also issues concerning the point in time when it is appropriate to recognise income or expenditure. While this remains a grey area, increasingly the trend is for the courts to endorse accounts which are drawn up in accordance with recognised accountancy principles unless the tax legislation specifically overrides these principles. See *Johnston v Brittannia Airways* which is discussed in 2.4.9.

### 2.4.5 Expenditure which is specifically disallowed
(TA 1988, ss 74 and 577)

As mentioned above, certain types of expenditure are disallowed, although it may be sound accounting practice to deduct such costs in a trader's accounts. See Table 2.1 for a summary contained in the Revenue guide. The rest of this section looks more closely at specific types of business expenses.

## Capital expenditure
(TA 1988, s 74)

The acquisition of a capital asset is not a cost which may be deducted in arriving at profits for tax purposes. This may seem obvious where an asset such as a building is acquired, but the definition of capital expenditure goes a long way beyond the acquisition of tangible assets. The generally accepted definition was given by Lord Cave in *British Insulated and Helsby Cables Ltd v Atherton* (1925) 10 TC 155; he stated:

> when an expenditure is made . . . with a view to bringing into existence an asset or an advantage for the enduring benefit of a trade . . . there is very good reason (in the absence of special circumstances leading to the opposite conclusion) for treating such expenditure as properly attributable not to revenue but to capital.

The acquisition of goodwill, for example, would be capital expenditure. Less obviously, a lump sum payment to secure release from an onerous liability such as a lease at a high rent or a fixed rate loan would also be regarded as capital expenditure.

## Entertaining
(TA 1988, s 577)

Any expenses relating to entertaining customers or suppliers which are included in a set of accounts normally need to be added back. There is a modest exemption which may apply where the entertaining is provided by a hotelier, restaurateur or by someone else who provides entertainment in the ordinary course of his trade. Staff entertainment is also an allowable expense but the individual employee may be assessed on a benefit in kind.

## Gifts to customers etc
(TA 1988, s 577)

The cost of gifts to customers and to potential customers and introducers is also disallowed by s 577 unless the gift carries a conspicuous advertisement and is neither food, drink, tobacco or a voucher exchangeable for such goods, nor an item which costs more than £10 per recipient per year.

## Illegal payments

A specific provision disallowing illegal payments such as bribes came into force on 11 June 1993 (the date that the relevant clause was introduced in the committee stage of the Finance Bill 1993). Prior to 11 June 1993, it was open to a business to claim a deduction for such payments where they were incurred wholly and exclusively for the purposes of the trade – although this will often have been difficult to prove in practice.

The disallowance was extended by FA 1994 to cover payments made on

## Table 2.1 – Inland Revenue summary of allowable and non-allowable business expenses

|  | *Allowable* | *Not allowable* |
|---|---|---|
| **Basic costs** | Light, heat and power; telephone; insurance; stationery and postage; business rates and rent; advertising; protective clothing; repairs; replacement loose tools (unless capital allowances claimed instead); transport of goods to customers or materials from suppliers; subcontractors (see Leaflet IR14/15) | Private and personal expenses; non-business part of running costs of premises used only partly for business; own insurance; ordinary, everyday clothing even if bought specially for business use; parking and other fines; buying, altering or improving fixed assets; depreciation or losses on sale of fixed assets |
| **Employee costs** | Employees' wages and salaries; employers' National Insurance; redundancy payments; pension contributions on employees' behalf; employees' expenses and benefits | Own wages or salary and drawings from the business; own pension payments and other benefits; own National Insurance contributions |
| **Finance costs** | Interest on loans and overdrafts used solely for business purposes; costs of arranging such finance | Repayment of loan or overdraft (as opposed to the interest) |
| **Professional** | Accountancy fees; preparation of ordinary business costs agreement; debt recovery (if debt is for a taxable receipt); renewing leases of less than 50 years (where no premium is paid); defending business rights; appeals against business rates. | Costs of settling tax disputes; legal costs of buying fixed assets (treated as part of the cost of fixed asset); costs and fines or penalties for breaking the law |
| **Travel** | Travel on business to meet customers, suppliers, etc; travel between business premises; accommodation and reasonable cost of meals on overnight business trips; vehicle running expenses (less proportion of private use) | Travel between home and place of business (unless agreed with the Tax Office that your home is your base); costs of buying vehicles (but capital allowances can be claimed); meals (except on overnight business trips) |
| **Bad debts** | Irrecoverable debts written off, if taxed when they arose; recovery costs; provisions against specific doubtful debts; debts recovered later should be shown in box 3.16 or 3.37 of the self-assessment return | General bad debts reserve; debts not taxed when they arose, eg because they relate to sale of a fixed asset |
| **Subscriptions** | Payments to certain professional bodies (Tax Office can tell you which) | Payments to political parties; most payments to clubs, charities or churches |
| **Entertaining** | Costs of entertaining staff; gifts (not food or drink) up to £10 per person per year which advertise your business | All other entertaining and hospitality |
| **VAT** | Any VAT which is not recoverable is an allowable expense. This does not include any input VAT paid on capital items. However, this can be included in their cost if a claim can be made to capital allowances for them.<br><br>Where allowable expenses net of recoverable input VAT are shown then the turnover should be shown on the same basis, that is net of output VAT charged. Alternatively, you may prefer to show receipts and allowable expenses gross of VAT and the net payment to Customs and Excise as an expense or the net repayment as a taxable receipt. | |

or after 30 November 1993 in response to threats, menaces, blackmail and other forms of extortion.

### Lease rentals on expensive cars
(CAA 1990, s 35)

Where a trader uses a leased car or provides a motor car to an employee and the original cost was £12,000 or more (£8,000 prior to 10 March 1992), part of the lease rentals must be added back as a disallowable expense. The amount disallowed is the following proportion of the lease rental:

$$\tfrac{1}{2} \times \frac{(\text{Cost of car} - £12,000)}{\text{Cost of car}}$$

Thus, if a car which cost £16,000 is leased for a rental of £2,400 pa, the amount disallowed is:

$$\tfrac{1}{2} \times \frac{(£16,000 - £12,000)}{£16,000} \times £2,400, \text{ ie } £300$$

This treatment does not apply to maintenance costs included in the lease rentals provided they are identified separately under the terms of the leasing agreement. Amounts paid under an HP agreement are dealt with differently (see 2.4.6).

### Provisions for bad debts
(TA 1988, s 74(j))

A general provision against bad debts is not allowable, but provisions against specific debts are a proper deduction for tax purposes provided that it can be shown that the amount is a reasonable provision. (This is discussed further in 2.4.8.)

### Remuneration not paid within nine months of the year end
(FA 1989, s 43)

Bonus payments to employees may be made after the end of a year. If they clearly relate to a period of account, it would be normal for the trader's accounts to include a provision. However, this provision is allowable only if the remuneration is paid within nine months of the year end.

### Pension contributions for employees
(FA 1993, s 112)

A deduction is due only if the contribution is paid during the course of the trader's year. This applies whether the contribution is paid to an approved or unapproved scheme.

Pension contributions for the trader himself are not an allowable deduction in computing profits although relief is available as a deduction from taxable profits (see 12.8–12.9 for details of the method of dealing with personal pension contributions).

## Expenditure not wholly for the purposes of the trade
(TA 1988, s 74(a))

The legislation requires the expenditure to be incurred 'wholly and exclusively' for the purposes of the trade. Consequently, expenses which are incurred partly for trade purposes and partly for personal reasons are not allowable.

The Revenue has invoked s 74(a) to disallow the cost of black dresses worn in court by a female barrister on the grounds that the expenditure had a dual purpose (warmth and decency as well as the need to dress in a particular way when appearing in court). The Revenue has also relied upon s 74(a) to disallow the cost of meals incurred by a self-employed carpenter when he was working away from home.

Where an expense is incurred for mixed purposes the whole amount is disallowed; this rules out relief where an individual travels abroad mainly to have a holiday but carries out some work while abroad. However, where it can be shown that an additional cost was incurred wholly for business reasons, a deduction may be due for this. Consequently, if a person uses part of his home for business, the extra heat and light bills are an allowable expense for tax purposes. In practice quite a number of expenses are apportioned between private use (not allowable) and business use (an allowable expense). Telephone bills and car expenses are two particular examples which arise often.

In *McKnight v Sheppard* legal expenses were incurred by a stockbroker in defending charges brought by the Stock Exchange. He was found guilty of gross misconduct and suspended from trading. However, because a suspension would have resulted in the destruction of his business, he appealed and his suspension was reduced to a fine. He was allowed tax relief for his legal expenses because these had been incurred wholly and exclusively for the purposes of the trade. The fines imposed were disallowed.

## Payments of reverse premiums

FA 1999 provides that no relief shall be due to a trader who pays a reverse premium to induce a tenant to take a lease.

## Sums recoverable from an insurance policy etc
(TA 1988, s 74(c))

Where a trader can get back from an insurance company the money that he has paid out, there is no deduction due for the expenditure. The same treatment applies where a trader has been indemnified against a particular cost.

### Annual payments
(TA 1988, s 74(p) and (q))

Certain annual payments (eg patent royalties) generally need to be paid net of tax at the basic rate. The payments are not deductible in arriving at profits which are assessable under Schedule D Case I or Case II, although they are allowed as a deduction for higher rate purposes.

## 2.4.6 Other expenditure where adjustments may be required

### Interest

Interest payments on loans taken by partners are allowable (if at all) against the partner's general income (see 9.3). Interest paid by a sole trader or by a partnership may be deducted in arriving at the taxable profits of the business provided it passes the 'wholly and exclusively' test (see above).

Problems may arise where overdraft interest is charged in a set of accounts and the proprietor's capital account is overdrawn. The Revenue is likely to argue that the interest (or, at any rate, part of the interest) was incurred not for the purposes of the business but to finance drawings. If you find yourself in this situation you should take advice from an accountant.

### Cost of raising business finance
(TA 1988, s 77)

There are often certain costs in raising long-term finance and for many years these were regarded as capital expenditure by the Revenue. A statutory deduction is now available provided certain conditions are satisfied:

(1) The costs must be wholly and exclusively incurred for the purposes of obtaining loan finance, providing security or repaying a loan.
(2) The costs must represent expenditure on professional fees, commissions, advertising, printing or other incidental expenses in relation to raising finance.

In some cases a deduction will be available even though the expenditure failed and the loan finance was not in fact obtained.

### Lease rentals

The way in which lease rentals are treated depends upon the type of the lease. If the lease is an 'operating lease', ie a lease for a period which is less than the asset's anticipated useful life, it is normal for rentals to be deducted in arriving at the profits for the period to which the rentals refer. In practice, most leasing agreements provide for rentals to be payable in advance. For example, if a trader pays lease rentals of £12,000 on 1 December which cover a period of six months, and he makes up accounts to the following 31 March, the amount deducted in arriving at the profits for the year ended 31 March would be:

$$\frac{4 \text{ months}}{6 \text{ months}} \times £12,000 = £8,000$$

A different treatment is required where a trader pays rentals under a 'finance lease', ie a lease agreement under which the trader acquires almost all the benefits of outright ownership. There is a special accounting standard which governs the accounting treatment of such leases, and the Revenue's view is that the amount which should be deducted is that charged in the trader's accounts in accordance with SSAP 21 (ie the relevant Statement of Standard Accounting Practice issued by the Institute of Chartered Accountants).

### Hire purchase

Where equipment is acquired under an HP contract, the cost of the equipment counts as capital expenditure (in most cases capital allowances will be available). The 'interest' element is apportioned over the term of the contract and relief is given for the amount of interest which relates to the accounting period concerned.

### Example – Adjustments for HP contracts

A trader acquires a computer under a three-year HP agreement. The cost of the computer was £12,000, but the trader pays 36 monthly HP payments of £420.

The interest payable over the three years totals £3,120. This would normally be allocated roughly as follows:

| | | |
|---|---|---|
| Year one | – | £1,715 |
| Year two | – | £1,040 |
| Year three | – | £365 |

This type of allocation reflects the amount of the HP 'loan' which is outstanding during each year.

### Legal and professional expenses

Where an Inspector of Taxes examines a trader's business accounts, he normally asks for an analysis of any substantial amounts relating to legal and professional expenses. Legal costs in connection with the acquisition of capital assets are disallowable as capital expenditure as are legal costs in connection with renewing a lease of more than 50 years. In contrast, legal costs which are incurred to protect a capital asset are generally allowable as a revenue expense.

Professional costs incurred in connection with tax appeals are not allowable on the grounds that such costs relate to tax on profits rather than an expense incurred in earning profits. However, in practice the costs of preparing and agreeing tax computations are usually allowed.

### 2.4.7 Relief for premiums
(TA 1988, s 87)

A trader may be required to make a lump sum payment to a landlord to obtain a lease. In cases where the lease is for a period of less than 50 years, part of the lump sum may be treated as income in the landlord's hands (see 4.3) and the trader may claim a deduction for this amount as if it were rent payable over the period of his lease. The part which is taxed in the landlord's hands is 100% of the premium less 2% for each complete year of the lease other than the first year.

There is no relief if the lease is for more than 50 years or if the premium is paid to someone other than the landlord since such a third party (for example, an outgoing tenant) is not subject to income tax under Schedule A.

Sometimes the lease will require a tenant to have certain building work carried out which will increase the value of the landlord's interest in the property. The landlord may be assessed under Schedule A on a notional premium (see 4.3.3). Where this applies, the trader is able to claim a deduction just as if he had been required to pay a premium in cash. However, the notional premium will generally be far less than the actual cost of carrying out the work concerned.

#### Example – Treatment of premiums

B pays a premium for a lease of ten years of which £40,000 is treated as income of the landlord for Schedule A purposes. Of this sum, 82% (ie, £32,800) is taxed in the landlord's hands as income for the year in which the premium is payable.

B can claim a deduction in his accounts for the ten years as if he had paid rent of £3,280 pa. If it were not for s 87, the expenditure would be treated as capital expenditure and would attract no relief.

### 2.4.8 Provision for bad or doubtful debts

The Revenue has explained its approach with regard to provisions for bad or doubtful debts. Its interpretation is that a trader may be entitled to a deduction provided the following circumstances are satisfied:

(1) the debt existed at the balance sheet date; and
(2) before the accounts were finalised, the company's trader/directors

discovered that the debtor's financial position at the balance sheet date was such that the debt was unlikely to be paid.

The Revenue stated that a common example of this is where a debtor at the balance sheet date goes into administration or liquidation shortly after the balance sheet date and before the date on which the financial statements are approved by the trader. Where the administration or liquidation commences after the balance sheet date, its occurrence before the accounts were finalised normally sheds light on the debtor's financial position at the balance sheet date. If the period between the balance sheet date and approval of the accounts is short, it is unlikely that a debtor would have gone from financial good health to insolvency in that period. In these circumstances it would normally be reasonable for the trader to regard the debt as doubtful. The acceptable amount of provision would depend upon the information available.

The Revenue contrasts this with a situation where a debtor is an habitually slow payer and there are no grounds to believe his financial position has changed. In such a case, the Revenue argues that the length of time that a debt has been outstanding is not in itself a sufficient reason to regard the debt as doubtful.

### 2.4.9 Provisions against liability to pay sums after the year end

This is an aspect of a trader's accounts to which Inspectors of Taxes pay particular attention. The Revenue needs to be satisfied that relief is not sought for expenditure which will be incurred only in the future. Consequently, an Inspector will almost certainly withhold relief unless he is satisfied that a trader became liable to make the payment concerned before the year end. For example, in the past it was not generally possible to secure a deduction for redundancy costs unless the necessary redundancy notices were served by the end of the trader's accounting period. Similarly, the Revenue will argue that a provision for an amount which may be due to a client for professional negligence is not allowable unless the client's claim has been admitted by the year end.

This interpretation is not free from doubt, but the difficulty of persuading an Inspector of Taxes to adopt a more favourable interpretation should not be underestimated. Again this is a situation where professional advice is required if sizeable amounts of tax are at issue.

The Revenue's rather restrictive approach was successfully challenged in *Johnston v Britannia Airways Ltd* [1994] STC 763. This case concerned a company which operated as an airline. Civil Aviation Authority rules required each aeroplane to have a certificate of airworthiness. This would not be issued unless each engine was overhauled every 17,000 flying hours which, in Britannia's case, meant every three to five years. Accordingly, a provision for the overhaul costs was made in each year's accounts based on the average cost of the overhaul per hour flown and the number of hours flown in the period.

The Inspector took the view that the correct treatment was to make no provision before the cost of the major overhaul was incurred, to capitalise the overhaul cost when incurred, and then to write it off gradually over the period up to the next overhaul.

The Special Commissioners found that the accruals method used by Britannia gave the most accurate picture of the airline's profits and was more effective in matching costs with revenue than the capitalise and amortise method favoured by the Revenue. Furthermore the company's method was in accordance with ordinary principles of commercial accountancy. Accordingly, since there was nothing in statute or case law to contradict it, the company's appeal succeeded. This decision was then upheld by the High Court.

Bear in mind that accountancy principles are constantly being refined and updated and FRS12 now sets out 'best practice' on provisions for sums payable after the year end. The Revenue will resist an accounting treatment which does not comply with FRS12. The decision in *Britannia Airways* has since been overtaken by changes in generally accepted accountancy principles.

There are sometimes circumstances where a payment will almost certainly be required in the future, although the precise amount has yet to be ascertained. An example contained in a Revenue publication concerns an insurance broker who may be required to refund commission to an insurance company if clients allow policies to lapse. The Revenue has accepted that a provision may be allowable in these circumstances provided it is arrived at scientifically by reference to past experience. A 'rough and ready' general provision is not allowable.

During 1999 the Revenue decided not to appeal against a High Court decision on provisions for sums that would be payable only in the future. The case concerned a firm of solicitors who had taken long leases over office premises which turned out to be surplus to their requirements. The offices could only be sub-let at a much lower rent and the solicitors' accounts made a provision for the loss which would accrue in later years. The Revenue's decision not to appeal followed from its acceptance that the accounting treatment was in accordance with generally accepted accountancy principles. See *Herbert Smith v Honour* [1999] STC 173.

Another case involving these issues was the so-called *Jenners* case where the Commissioners held that a company operating a department store was able to make provisions for repairs which would have to be carried out in later years. Once again, the Revenue decided not to appeal and accepted that provisions made in accordance with generally accepted accountancy principles were allowable for tax purposes.

## 2.4.10 Valuation of stock and work in progress

A trader's accounts should include his stock in hand at his year end. Individual items of stock should be valued at the lower of cost or realisable value. Cost should normally include a proportion of overheads.

Similarly, work in progress should be valued at the year end on the same basis. Where the accounts relate to a profession, it is not necessary to include in cost the time value of work put in by the sole proprietor or partner since this represents the proprietor's profit rather than a cost incurred in carrying on the profession.

The treatment of long-term work in progress can involve complex issues and should be discussed with the firm's accountant.

## 2.4.11 Withdrawal of 'cash basis' practice for professions

Relatively large businesses have been able to prepare accounts purely on a cash receipts basis without taking into account income from unpaid invoices nor the value of work in progress. The cash basis was widely used by barristers, solicitors, surveyors, actuaries, doctors and accountants, supported by a Revenue Statement of Practice which allowed such businesses to use this basis subject to conditions – that profits were computed on the earnings basis for the first three fiscal years and thereafter could be accounted on a purely cash basis. The cash basis also applied to expenses.

This has now been abolished. Businesses must use the earnings basis for accounting periods starting on or after 6 April 1999. Furthermore, there is a one-off catching-up charge based on the value of work in progress and debtors, net of creditors, at the start of the first accounting period affected.

The catching-up charge will be payable over ten years of assessment starting with the 2000–01 year of account. The amount chargeable in each year except the last will be restricted to the smaller of:

(1) one-tenth of the total charge; and
(2) 10% of the 'normal' profit.

In the tenth year, the balance of the catching-up charge will be taxed.

### Example of catching-up charge

*B* has prepared his accounts on a cash basis for many years using a 31 October year end. He will have a catching-up charge based on the value of his work in progress and debtors less creditors as at 1 November 1999. The first of his ten instalments will be taxable for the year 2000–01 and the tax will be due on 31 January 2001.

## 2.4.12 Other consequences of the catching-up charge

Although the charge itself is not welcome, there are some measures of relief:

(1) as the catching-up charge will be taxed under Schedule D Case VI, it will not be liable to Class 4 NICs.

(2) There will be no charge in a loss-making year, unless this is the final year of the business.

(3) Existing losses arising from the same business can be set against the charge.

(4) Relief will be given for any initial double charge.

### Example of initial double charge

C began to practise on 1 May 1990, preparing his accounts to 30 April each year. For the first three years, he used the earnings basis to compute his profits. With effect from 1 May 1991, he used a purely cash basis. Closing debtors on 30 April 1991 were £40,000. He was taxed on profits as follows:

| Year of assessment | Basis period | |
|---|---|---|
| 1990–91 | 1 May 1990–5 April 1991 | Earnings basis |
| 1991–92 | 1 May 1990–30 April 1991 | Earnings basis |
| 1992–93 | Year ended 30 April 1991 | Earnings basis |
| 1993–94 | Year ended 30 April 1992 | Cash basis |

In addition to the normal overlapping of early profits, he will have been taxed yet again when he received payment for the £40,000 unpaid invoices, following adoption of the cash basis in 1992. (This could also work the other way around, resulting in a net saving from changing the way that the accounts were prepared.)

## 2.4.13 Cessation of trade

Where a business ceases, the ten-year spread of the charge will continue. However, there will be no 10% profits cap because there are no longer any profits.

## 2.4.14 Barristers and advocates

Barristers (in Scotland, advocates) have always been regarded as a 'special case': few other professions experience such delay between completing an assignment and being paid. In recognition of the particular difficulties facing new barristers especially, they will be allowed to remain on the cash basis until the seventh anniversary of the start of their practice. They will then have to change to the earnings basis and meet the catching-up charge at that time.

It is possible for a barrister to change to preparing accounts within the seven-year period, but this decision will depend on a number of factors, including his marginal rate of income tax and the reliability of future profit projections (see 27.2 re barristers generally).

## 2.4.15 Use of 'true and fair view' approach

The 'true and fair view' approach to computing taxable profits and losses is intended merely to ensure that profits are calculated in accordance with appropriate accounting standards and that time is not wasted on immaterial amounts. The Revenue has confirmed that sole traders and partnerships do not need to have an audit even though their taxable profits must now be based on accounts which would comply with the true and fair view recognised for audited accounts.

Guidance on the application of accounting principles for traders who were formerly on the cash basis is contained in *Tax Bulletin* December 1998. See also the ICAEW technical release Tax 30/98.

## 2.4.16 Miscellaneous matters

### Enterprise allowance should not be included
(TA 1988, s 127)

Where a trader has received an enterprise allowance, this should not be included in the computation of profits assessable for Schedule D Case I purposes. The allowance is taxable, but is charged to tax under Schedule D Case VI rather than Case I.

### Class 4 NICs

A deduction was available for half of the trader's liability for Class 4 NICs (see 23.4) in arriving at the trader's income tax liability. This relief was withdrawn from 1996–97 onwards.

### Gifts in kind to charities

FA 1999 gives relief for traders who donate computers or other equipment to charities. Relief is also due for the employer costs of staff seconded to educational establishments.

## 2.5 CAPITAL ALLOWANCES

### 2.5.1 Introduction

A trader is entitled to capital allowances on plant and machinery which is used in the trade. Capital allowances are also available on commercial buildings located in an enterprise zone, agricultural buildings, industrial buildings and hotels. Allowances may also be claimed for expenditure on know-how and scientific research expenditure. All these are dealt with differently, and various rates of initial and annual allowances are given.

Capital allowances are treated like any other business expense. The allowances are computed on the current year basis, but once again with special rules for the first tax year.

## 2.5.2 What is plant and machinery?

Until recently there was no definition of 'plant and machinery' within the Taxes Acts. Even after the introduction of specific legislation, in FA 1994, the position remains unclear. The statutory definition focuses mainly on what is not plant as it forms part of a building and the Revenue's practice and interpretation are still largely based on decisions handed down by the courts.

The earliest judicial definition was provided in *Yarmouth v France* (1887) 19 QBD 647, in which Lindley LJ stated:

> in its ordinary sense, it includes whatever apparatus is used by a businessman for carrying on his business – not his stock-in-trade, which he buys or makes for sale, but all goods or chattels, fixed or movable, live or dead, which he keeps for permanent employment in his business . . .

Some items are clearly within this definition, for example, typewriters, dictating machines, telephone equipment, computers, manufacturing equipment, vans and other motor vehicles. What is less obvious is that a building may contain items which are plant and machinery. In some cases the plant will have become part of the building, for example a lift. Also, there may be structures which are items of plant, for example a dry dock or a grain silo, or a mezzanine floor put into a factory to create storage space. Capital allowances are also due on building work which is needed to enable plant and machinery to be installed – this would apply if a floor had to be strengthened to install a computer.

You should take professional advice if you acquire a building or adapt premises to meet the requirements of your trade in order to ensure that you obtain the Inspector of Taxes' agreement on the full amount which is eligible for capital allowances.

## 2.5.3 Allowances for plant and machinery
(CAA 1990, s 24; FA 1993, s 115)

Plant and machinery qualifies for a 25% writing-down allowance. Writing-down allowances are computed on the balance of the 'pool' at the year-end. The opening balance of the pool represents the cost of plant and machinery brought forward from previous years, less the capital allowances already received. A trader receives writing-down allowances based on the opening balance plus the cost of additional plant and machinery acquired during the year, less any disposal proceeds.

### Example – Writing-down allowances

A and B are in partnership. In their year to 31 March 1999 they had acquired plant and machinery at a cost of £30,000 and received capital allowances of £7,500. During their year ended 31 March 2000, they sell some of this plant for £2,000 and buy new plant for £20,000. Their pool would be as follows:

|  | £ |
|---|---|
| Written-down value brought forward at 1 April 1999 | 22,500 |
| Additions during year ended 31 March 2000 | 20,000 |
|  | 42,500 |
| Less: disposal proceeds | 2,000 |
|  | 40,500 |
| Writing-down allowances (25%) | 10,125 |
| Written-down value carried forward | 30,375 |

## 2.5.4 Expenditure treated as incurred in a period

Expenditure is deemed to be incurred in a period if a trader enters into an unconditional contract; it is not necessary that the trader should actually have paid for it or have brought it into use by his year end. There is an exception for plant and machinery acquired under an HP contract where entitlement to allowances arises only when the plant and machinery is actually brought into use.

## 2.5.5 First year allowances for small and medium-sized businesses

The first Labour budget in July 1997 introduced a first year capital allowance of 50% for a 12-month period for investment in plant and machinery. The allowance was available to unincorporated businesses and to companies provided that they qualified as SMEs (small or medium-sized businesses). The 25% writing-down allowance applies for the second and subsequent years.

Expenditure on plant or machinery incurred during the 12 months from 2 July 1997 to 1 July 1998 qualified for a first year allowance of 50%. The rate of first year allowance was then reduced to 40%. At first, the first year allowance was renewed on a year-by-year basis but FA 2000 has now put the relief on a permanent basis. In order to establish whether a business is regarded as 'small' or 'medium-sized' the tax legislation relies on the Companies Act definitions. Three conditions arise from the legislation:

(1) turnover of not more than £11.2m;
(2) assets of not more than £5.6m; and
(3) there are no more than 250 employees.

Provided two of the above three conditions are satisfied for the current or the previous year, the business is regarded as 'small' or 'medium-sized'.

Specifically in the case of companies, the company must be small or medium-sized for the year in which the expenditure is incurred. If the company is a member of a group, the group as a whole must satisfy two of the three conditions.

The first year allowances apply to businesses carried on by individuals and partnerships made up of individuals, provided the business would qualify if it were carried on by a company. There are two specific exclusions:

(1) expenditure on plant and machinery for leasing, cars, sea-going ships and railways assets;
(2) expenditure on LLAs (long life assets – plant and machinery which has an expected useful life of at least 25 years) bought on or after 26 November 1996 under a contract entered into before that date (such assets were outside the rules on LLAs under transitional provisions).

There are special rules which still apply to LLAs, but the £100,000 pa limit (see 2.5.10) should exclude the majority of small and medium-sized businesses. Where such special rules do still apply, the first year allowance under the new proposals will be 12% in the year ending 1 July 1998 followed by 6% pa on the reducing balance (although it is perhaps unlikely that a small or medium-sized business will spend over £100,000 on LLAs).

### Northern Ireland

A provision was introduced into the 1998 Finance Bill when it was halfway through the process of becoming an Act. Expenditure incurred by small and medium-sized businesses on plant and machinery for use in Northern Ireland during the period 12 May 1998–11 May 2002 may qualify for 100% first year allowances. Such allowances are not available for expenditure on plant used for leasing or for cars, long-life assets, sea-going ships, aircraft and railway assets.

## 2.5.6 100% allowances for IT equipment

Small businesses which invest in information and communications equipment (ie computers, software and Internet-enabled mobile telephones) over the period 1 April 2000–31 March 2003 are entitled to 100% allowances. The definition of a small business for this purpose is that the business must satisfy two of the following requirements:

(1) turnover of not more than £2.8m;
(2) a balance sheet total of not more than £1.4m; and
(3) not more than 50 employees.

## 2.5.7 Assets kept separate from the pool
(CAA 1990, ss 34 and 79)

Motor cars which cost more than £12,000 (£8,000 prior to 10 March 1992) need to be kept separate. The maximum writing-down allowance for such a car is £3,000, but a balancing allowance (or charge) arises on disposal.

### Example – Writing-down allowances for motor cars

*A* operates an advertising business. He makes up his accounts to 30 April. On 1 May 1997 he acquired a car which costs £30,000 and this was used by an employee. After two years, the car is sold for £10,000.

The car is deemed to be in a separate pool and the position is as follows:

|  |  | £ |
|---|---|---:|
| Year one – | cost | 30,000 |
|  | writing-down allowances |  |
|  | for 1997–98 | 3,000 |
|  |  | 27,000 |
| Year two – | writing-down allowances |  |
|  | for 1998–99 | 3,000 |
|  |  | 24,000 |
| Year three – disposal proceeds |  | 10,000 |
| Balancing allowance for 2000–01 |  | 14,000 |

Motor cars which cost less than £12,000 were kept in a separate pool until the start of the accounting period which includes 6 April 2000.

### Other assets kept separate
(CAA 1990, s 79)

Certain other assets are kept separate from the pool. One particular category is assets which are used partly for the purposes of the trade and partly for other purposes. For example, a van used by a sole trader as to 40% for business and 60% for private motoring would be deemed to form a separate pool. The trader would be entitled to 'scaled down' allowances, ie he would receive 40% of the full writing-down allowance and 40% of any balancing allowance.

'Short life' assets are also kept separate (see 2.5.9).

## 2.5.8 Assets brought into use part way through year
(CAA 1990, ss 24(2) and 60)

An asset which is acquired towards the end of a trader's accounting period still attracts the full 25% allowance unless the trade has not been going for 12 months. In such a case, the 25% allowance may be scaled down.

### Example – Assets bought in year in which trade is commenced

> B commenced trading on 5 October 1999. On 5 April 2000 he acquired plant and machinery for £60,000. The capital allowances due to him for 1999–2000 are:
>
> $$\tfrac{6}{12} \times 25\% \times £60,000, \text{ ie } \underline{\underline{£7,500}}$$
>
> Allowances are normally due where a trader incurred qualifying expenditure by his year end by entering into an unconditional contract to purchase the plant and machinery. He does not need actually to have brought it into use by his year end.

## 2.5.9 'Short life' assets

(CAA 1990, ss 37–38)

Where expenditure is added to the pool, the trader receives writing-down allowances which are likely to get smaller and smaller. For example, a trader invests expenditure of £100,000 on plant in year one. He does not acquire any other plant and machinery for five years. His writing-down allowance in year one will be £25,000 (ie 25% of £100,000), £18,750 in year two (ie 25% of the residual £75,000) and so on. By the end of year five, the written-down value will be just under £24,000 but the equipment itself may be worn out and have a scrap value of only, say, £2,000.

To cover this type of situation, the legislation allows for a trader to designate certain assets as short life assets. The cost of these assets is kept in a separate pool and a balancing allowance (or charge) arises on a sale within five years, or on the assets being scrapped by then. If an asset is not sold within that period, the written-down value of the asset is transferred to the pool.

(1) In the above example, if the plant and machinery were actually scrapped at the start of year five and the trader received no scrap value at all, he would receive a balancing allowance of £31,640.

(2) Again using the same basic facts, if the plant and machinery were still in use at the end of year five, the written down value of £23,730 would be transferred to the trader's pool of other plant and machinery.

The following cannot be short life assets:

(1) Motor cars.
(2) Assets used partly for non-trade purposes.
(3) Assets originally acquired for non-trade purposes (eg assets acquired prior to the trade being commenced).
(4) Ships.
(5) Certain assets leased out in the course of a trade.

An election needs to be made for an asset to be treated as a short life asset. This needs to be submitted to the Inspector of Taxes within two years of the accounting period in which the short life asset is acquired. The Inspector will require sufficient information to be able to identify the assets at a later stage (see SP1/86).

## 2.5.10 Long life assets
(CAA 1990, ss 38A–38H)

FA 1997 added to the already complex rules on capital allowances by introducing the concept of long life assets (LLAs). An LLA is one with an expected working life of 25 years or more. Where a trader incurs expenditure of more than £100,000 on an LLA, capital allowances are restricted to 6%.

This rule affects assets purchased on or after 26 November 1996, but not those purchased before 31 December 2000 where the contract was entered into prior to 26 November 1996. A number of categories of expenditure are specifically excluded from the general definition. Thus LLAs do not include any machinery or plant which is a fixture in, or is used in, a dwelling house, retail shop, showroom, hotel or office or for ancillary purposes. Also there are specific exclusions for motor or hire cars, sea-going ships and railway assets (the last two until 2011). There is a transitional exception for expenditure contracted for before 2 November 1996 and incurred by 31 December 2000 and to which the long life rules do not apply. Expenditure on LLAs is segregated into a separate pool which qualifies for writing-down allowances at 6% instead of 25%. This categorisation of an asset as long life is irrevocable and it cannot later be reclassified as non-long life.

The LLA rules do not apply where second-hand plant is purchased from a person who qualified for 25% writing-down allowances.

## 2.5.11 Expenditure on landlord's fixtures
(CAA 1990, s 52)

The decision in *Stokes v Costain Property Investments Ltd* [1984] STC 204 established that capital allowances were not due on expenditure on plant by a tenant where the plant became part of a building and therefore became a landlord's fixture. The reason for this was that the items of plant did not 'belong' to the tenant. This was clearly unsatisfactory as tenants are often required to install plant within a building such as lifts, air conditioning and so on. Accordingly, the legislation was amended and now specifically provides that a tenant who incurs expenditure in these circumstances can receive allowances but a balancing charge may be made on the expiry or surrender of the lease, according to the market value of the plant at that time. There are complex provisions dealing with situations where more than one person incurs expenditure on the same fixture or where expenditure is incurred by an equipment lessor.

## 2.5.12 Acquisition of second-hand buildings

FA 1997 contained anti-avoidance provisions which:

(1) prevent allowances being given on fixtures as machinery and plant and under some other category (eg enterprise zones or scientific research);
(2) limit allowances given on fixtures as machinery and plant in total to the original cost of the fixtures (or where capital allowances were claimed on the fixtures for periods before 24 July 1996, the cost price to the most recent claimant). This applies only where the disposal by the previous claimant took place on or after 24 July 1996;
(3) treat a fixture as sold at its tax written-down value if it is sold for less than that value to accelerate allowances (other than where the disposal is for good commercial reasons and is not part of a tax avoidance scheme).

## 2.5.13 Buildings located in an enterprise zone
(CAA 1990, s 1)

Qualifying expenditure on a commercial building which is located in an enterprise zone can qualify for a 100% initial allowance. A commercial building is defined as a building or structure, other than an industrial building or hotel, which is used for the purposes of a trade, profession or vocation or is used as an office. The definition specifically excludes a building which is wholly or partly used as a dwelling house. Certain conditions must be fulfilled:

(1) The building must have been constructed under an unconditional contract entered into before the enterprise zone came to the end of its designated life.
(2) The building must be acquired unused or within two years of its having been let for the first time.

The part of the purchase price which relates to the cost of the land does not qualify for capital allowances.

Plant and machinery contained in the building which have become an integral part of the building may also qualify for the 100% allowance.

The initial allowance can be disclaimed, in whole or in part, and the remaining amount of qualifying expenditure is then available as 25%. The 25% writing-down allowances are given on a straight line basis over four years rather than on the reducing basis which applies for plant and machinery.

### Example – Capital allowances on buildings in an enterprise zone

An enterprise zone building is acquired for £200,000. The land cost is £20,000, so £180,000 qualifies for capital allowances. The purchaser disclaims the whole of the initial allowance. He will then receive annual allowances as follows:

|  | £ |
|---|---|
| Year of expenditure | 45,000 |
| Year two | 45,000 |
| Year three | 45,000 |
| Year four | 45,000 |

If the purchaser had disclaimed only £80,000, the position would have been:

|  | £ |
|---|---|
| Year of expenditure | |
|    Initial allowance | 100,000 |
|    Annual allowance | 45,000 |
| | 145,000 |
| Year two annual allowance | 35,000 |
| Year three annual allowance | nil |
| Year four annual allowance | nil |

The point to note is that the annual allowances are based on the total qualifying costs, not on the balance left over after deducting the initial allowance.

### Example – Disposal of a building in an enterprise zone

A disposal of an enterprise zone building within 25 years of acquisition gives rise to a balancing charge.

A acquires an enterprise zone building in year one and takes the full 100% initial allowance on the qualifying expenditure of £95,000. In year four he disposes of the building. If he receives disposal proceeds of £75,000, there will be a balancing charge of £75,000. If he receives £120,000 (ie more than the trader's qualifying expenditure) the balancing charge is limited to £95,000.

## 2.5.14 Agricultural buildings allowances
(CAA 1990, s 123)

Expenditure on agricultural buildings qualifies for a 4% annual allowance given on a straight line basis. A balancing allowance or charge may arise on a disposal which takes place within a period of 25 years.

The term 'agricultural buildings allowances' is slightly misleading in that the expenditure does not need to be on a building. The allowances are given in respect of expenditure on farmhouses, farm or forestry buildings, cottages, fences, ditches, drainage and sewerage works. The land must, of course, be used for agricultural purposes.

Expenditure incurred during the year ended 31 October 1993 qualified for an initial allowance of 20%. If the buildings etc were brought into use during the trader's accounting period, he also qualified for the 4% annual allowance for that year.

## 2.5.15 Industrial buildings
(CAA 1990, ss 3 and 18)

Expenditure on an industrial building which is brought into use for a trade by the year end qualifies for a 4% annual allowance, again given on the straight line basis. An 'industrial building' is a building or structure which is used for the purpose of a trade consisting of:

(1) the manufacture or processing of goods or materials; or
(2) the maintaining or repairing of goods or materials for customers; or
(3) the maintaining or repairing of goods or materials owned by the trader himself provided that the relevant trade consists of the manufacture or processing of goods or materials; or
(4) the storage of:
  (a) raw materials for manufacture;
  (b) goods to be processed;
  (c) goods manufactured or processed, but not yet delivered to any purchaser;
  (d) goods on arrival by sea or air into the UK; or
(5) the working of mines, oil wells etc or foreign plantations.

In addition, a sports pavilion provided for the welfare of workers employed in any trade qualifies for industrial buildings allowances. Qualifying expenditure once again excludes the land element in the purchase price.

Expenditure on an unused industrial building which was incurred during the year ended 31 October 1993 qualified for an initial allowance of 20%. If the building was brought into use during that year, a 4% annual allowance was also due.

A balancing charge or allowance may arise on a disposal within 25 years.

### Example – Disposal of industrial buildings

An industrial building was acquired in August 1993 for a cost of £250,000. The land element was £20,000. If the purchaser brought the building into use immediately, allowances would be due as follows:

|  |  | £ |
|---|---|---:|
|  | Qualifying cost | 230,000 |
| Year one – | initial allowance | 46,000 |
|  |  | 184,000 |
| Year one – | annual allowance | 9,200 |
|  | Residue | 174,800 |
| Year two – | annual allowance | 9,200 |
|  | Residue | 165,600 |

If the building is sold in year three, a balancing allowance or charge will arise according to whether the proceeds exceed £165,600. If the proceeds were £175,000 there would be a balancing charge of £9,400. If the proceeds were £150,000 there would be a balancing allowance of £15,600. The maximum balancing charge would be £64,400, ie the allowance received in year one and year two.

## 2.5.16 Hotels
(CAA 1990, ss 7 and 19)

A qualifying hotel attracts industrial buildings allowances (see 2.5.15). A qualifying hotel must fulfil the following conditions:

(1)  Accommodation must be provided in a building of a permanent nature.
(2)  The hotel must be open for at least four months during April–October.
(3)  There must be at least ten bedrooms available for letting to the public in general which must not normally be in the same occupation for more than a month.
(4)  The services provided must normally include the provision of breakfast and evening meals, making beds and cleaning rooms.

## 2.5.17 Expenditure on 'know-how'
(TA 1988, s 530)

Expenditure on acquiring know-how for use in a trade attracts capital allowances.

'Know-how' means any industrial information and techniques of assistance in manufacturing or processing goods or materials, or working or searching for mineral deposits, or which may be relevant to agricultural, forestry or fishing operations. Allowances are given on 'qualifying expenditure' which is the aggregate of any capital expenditure on know-how during the basis period, together with any unused balance of expenditure brought forward from the previous basis period and less any disposal value for know-how which has been sold.

Writing-down allowances are given at the rate of 25%.

## 2.5.18 Expenditure on scientific research
(TA 1988, s 530)

Any capital expenditure incurred by a trader on scientific research related to a trade attracts a 100% allowance. 'Scientific research' has traditionally been defined as activities in the fields of natural or applied science for the extension of knowledge. It has been redefined in FA 2000 to make it clear that it includes scientific research:

(1)  which may lead to or facilitate an extension of trade; or
(2)  of a medical nature which has a special relation to the welfare of workers employed in particular industries.

### 2.5.19 Capital allowance basis periods
(CAA 1990, s 160)

The basis period for a business is usually the same as the period which is taken in arriving at the profit. However, where basis periods overlap, expenditure in the common period is normally treated as incurred only in the earlier period. Expenditure incurred in a gap between two periods is treated as incurred in the later period.

## 2.6 PRE-TRADING EXPENDITURE
(TA 1988, s 401, as amended by FA 1989, s 114 and
FA 1993, s 109; CAA 1990, s 83(2))

A person may incur expenditure before he starts to trade such as:

(1) Rent for business premises
(2) Rates, insurance, heating and lighting
(3) Advertising wages or other payments to employees
(4) Bank charges and interest
(5) Lease rentals on plant and machinery and office equipment
(6) Accountancy fees.

Expenditure qualifies for relief only if it is incurred within seven years of the date that the trade is commenced. In the past pre-trading expenditure has not been deducted in arriving at the profits of the trade but can be allowed as if it were a loss incurred at the date that the trade actually commences (see 2.9 on relief for trading losses). A different rule applies where the trade is commenced after 5 April 1995; the expense is now treated as an ordinary trading expense incurred on the day that the trader starts business.

Pre-trading capital expenditure which qualifies for capital allowances is always treated as having been incurred at the date the trade is commenced.

## 2.7 POST-CESSATION RECEIPTS
(TA 1988, ss 103–104)

Where a person has been assessed on the cash basis (see 2.4.3) special rules apply if the trade or profession is discontinued. Subsequent receipts are normally taxed under Schedule D Case VI as income for the year in which they come in, although an election may be made for the post-cessation receipts to be treated as arising in the year of discontinuance.

Expenses may be deducted in so far as they were incurred wholly and exclusively for business and are not otherwise allowable. For example, a solicitor who had post-cessation receipts would be able to deduct premiums paid on a professional indemnity policy where the cover related to the period after the solicitor had ceased to carry on his profession.

A similar charge may arise where a change occurs in the treatment of a trader's profits so that the cash basis ceases to apply and his profits are assessed on the earnings basis. Amounts received from customers after the change which relate to invoices issued when the business was dealt with on the cash basis are treated as post-cessation receipts.

## 2.8 POST-CESSATION EXPENSES
(FA 1995, s 82)

Until FA 1995 was enacted, no tax relief was available for expenditure incurred after a trade or profession had ceased (except to the extent to which the expense could be set against post-cessation receipts). This gave rise to serious problems for professional people such as architects who need to retain professional indemnity insurance after they have retired, in case a defect should subsequently come to light. The Revenue proved most intractable on this and stated that even if an insurance premium was paid prior to cessation, the part of the premium relating to the post-cessation period was not considered to be an allowable expense.

FA 1995 corrected this anomaly and expenditure may now be allowable if it is incurred within seven years of a business ceasing. The following types of expenditure may qualify for this relief:

(1) the costs of remedying defective work done, goods supplied, or services rendered while the trade or profession was continuing and damages paid by the taxpayer in respect of such defective work, goods or services whether awarded by a court or agreed during negotiations on a claim;

(2) insurance premiums paid to insure against the above costs;

(3) legal and other professional expenses incurred in connection with the above costs;

(4) debts owed to the business which have been taken into account in computing the profits or gains of the trade or profession before discontinuance but which have subsequently become bad;

(5) the costs of collecting debts which have been taken into account in computing the profits of the trade before discontinuance.

The amount of the relief will be reduced by any expense allowed as a deduction in the final accounting period which remains unpaid at the end of the year of assessment in which the new relief is given.

Expenditure which qualifies for the relief will be set against income and capital gains of the year of assessment in which the expense is paid. Where there is insufficient income or capital gains to cover the expenditure, the unrelieved expenditure of that year cannot be carried forward under the relief arrangements against future income or capital gains. However, the unrelieved expenditure will still be available to be carried forward under the existing rules and set against subsequent post-cessation receipts from the trade or profession.

The legislation requires a formal claim to be made within 22 months of the end of the year of assessment in which the expense is paid.

## 2.9 RELIEF FOR TRADING LOSSES

Relief may be available for a loss incurred by an individual in a trade or profession. Relief may also be due for pre-trading expenditure which is treated as a loss incurred when the trade was commenced (see 2.6). The provisions which govern the relief for trading losses are complex and there are several ways in which you may claim that losses be utilised.

### Table 2.2 – Losses under self-assessment for 1998–99

| Reference | Description | Deadline |
|---|---|---|
| TA 1988, s 380 FA 1991, s 52 | Deduction from income or gains for 1998–99 | 31 Jan 2001 |
| TA 1988, s 380 | Deduction from income or gains for earlier years | 31 Jan 2001 |
| TA 1988, s 381 | Loss in first four years of trade carried back | 31 Jan 2001 |
| TA 1988, s 385 | Carry forward against future profits | 31 Jan 2005 |
| TA 1988, s 388 | Terminal loss relief | 31 Jan 2005 |

### 2.9.1 Carry forward relief against subsequent assessments
(TA 1988, s 385)

A loss incurred by a sole trader or a partner's share of his firm's trading loss may be carried forward and deducted in assessments for later years in respect of the same trade or profession. With the introduction of the current year basis of assessment (see 2.3.1), capital allowances are treated as trading expenses and can therefore increase or create a loss. Where losses are carried forward in this way, they must be used against the assessable profits for the first subsequent year in which profits arise. The loss which is carried forward in this way may also be relieved against certain income which is connected with the trade even though it is assessed under a different schedule (eg interest earned on temporary investment of trade receipts and dividends from trade investments). There is no limit on the number of years for which a loss may be carried forward provided that the same trade is carried on.

Prior to self-assessment a claim was required within six years of the end of the year of assessment in which the loss arose (ie a loss arising within the year ended 6 April 1996 to be carried forward must be claimed by 5 April 2002). For 1996–97 onwards the loss must be claimed within five years of the filing date (ie for a loss arising in 1998–99 by 31 January 2005).

## 2.9.2 Relief against general income
(TA 1988, s 380)

Where a sole trader or partner incurs a loss and the trade was carried on with a view to profit, the loss may be relieved against his general income for the year of assessment in which it was incurred (ie his total income for the year). Relief may also be claimed against the individual's general income for the preceding tax year. This type of relief was introduced for 1996–97 and future years. For years up to 1995–96 it was instead possible to set the loss against the individual's income for the following tax year. This relief was available only if the relevant trade, profession or vocation was carried on by the individual at some time during that year.

The claim for a loss to be set against an individual's general income for the preceding tax year is an alternative to the claim for the loss to be relieved against income of the year of loss. In other words, either the loss may be set against income of the current year (with any balance being set against income of the following year) or the individual may forgo the chance to set the loss against his income for the current year and set the full amount against income of the preceding year.

Where an individual takes relief for trading losses against his general income, he must use up the losses to the extent to which he has taxable income. It is not possible for a claim to be made to restrict the amount of losses so as to enable sufficient income to be left to make use of the individual's personal allowances. On the other hand, the legislation permits the individual to deduct certain items before arriving at his general income against which trading losses can be offset. These items include relief for allowable expenses for Schedule E purposes, retirement annuity and personal pension contributions, interest relief and relief for donations to charities by deed of covenant or gift aid.

Relief for losses of 1996–97 and subsequent years must be claimed within 22 months of the end of the tax year in which the loss arises (ie one year after the filing date for the return relating to that year of assessment) so that a 1998–99 loss must be claimed by 31 January 2001.

## 2.9.3 Relief by aggregation

Where the profits of different accounting periods are time apportioned (eg on commencement of a business) a loss may be relieved by aggregation with a profit. This situation could arise if a first period of trading were less than 12 months.

## Example – Loss relief by aggregation

*A* started business on 1 January 1998. He made a loss of £6,000 for the period ended 30 September 1998 and a profit of £24,000 for the year ended 30 September 1999. Relief by aggregation would produce the following result:

| | |
|---|---|
| Profits assessable 1997–98 | Nil |
| Profits assessable 1998–99 | Nil |
| Profits assessable 1999–00 | £24,000 |

The reason for this is that the first 12 months' trading would be deemed to produce a net loss computed as follows:

| | £ |
|---|---|
| Loss for period 1 Jan–30 Sept 1998 | (6,000) |
| $\frac{3}{12}$ of profit for year ended 30 Sept 1999 | 6,000 |
| | Nil |

If a loss is set against other income, it cannot also be relieved by aggregation. Thus, if *A* had claimed relief for the £3,000 loss that he had incurred in 1997–98, only the balance of the loss for the period ended 30 September 1999 which relates to the period 6 April–30 September 1999 could be taken into account in arriving at the profits of the first 12 months' trading. The 1998–99 assessment would then be £3,000.

## Example – Loss set against other income

*B* commenced trading on 1 August 1998. He has a loss during the nine months ended 30 April 1995 of £36,000. He has profits for the year ended 30 April 2000 of £60,000.

If the 1998–99 and 1999–2000 losses are used by being set against *B*'s other income, the Schedule D assessments will be as follows:

| | | £ |
|---|---|---|
| *1998–99* | | Nil |
| *1999–00* | Profits of first 12 months: | |
| | nine months ended 30 April 1999 | Nil |
| | $\frac{3}{12}$ × profits for year ended 30 April 2000 | 15,000 |
| | | 15,000 |
| | Current year basis profits for | |
| | year ended 30 April 2000 | 60,000 |

Contrast this with the situation where relief for the loss is obtained by aggregation.

| 1998–99 | | Nil |
|---|---|---|
| 1999–00 | Loss for 9 months to 30 April 1999 | (36,000) |
| | ³⁄₁₂ × profits for year ended 30 April 2000 | 15,000 |
| | Loss carried forward | (21,000) |
| 2000–01 | Profits assessed on current year basis | 60,000 |
| | less loss brought forward | (21,000) |
| | | 39,000 |

## 2.9.4 Losses arising from a business taxed under current year basis

Under the current year basis (see 2.3.1), losses are attributed to a tax year in the same way as profits are assessed. This means that once the business has got past the opening years, a loss will be treated as arising in the tax year in which the trader's accounting period ends. Losses for the opening years are computed on exactly the same basis as profits.

## 2.9.5 Losses in early years of a trade
(TA 1988, s 381)

In certain circumstances, relief may be claimed against an individual's general income for the three years of assessment preceding the year in which the loss is incurred. Relief is given against income for the earliest year first.

There are certain preconditions for a loss to be claimed in this way.

(1) The loss must arise during the first four tax years in which the business is carried on.
(2) Where a trade is acquired from a spouse, the four years run from the date that the spouse first commenced trading (unless the trade is taken over on the death of the spouse).
(3) The trade must be carried on a commercial basis and with a reasonable expectation of profits.

A claim for a 1998–99 loss to be relieved in this way must be made by 31 January 2001.

## 2.9.6 Relief for trading losses against capital gains
(FA 1991, s 72)

An individual who has incurred a trading loss may have the loss set against any capital gains which arise in the same year or the preceding year.

It is not possible to claim relief for trading losses in this way without first having made a claim for relief under s 380 for the loss to be set against the individual's general income for the year (see 2.9.2 for the time limit for making such a claim).

## 2.9.7 Terminal loss relief
(TA 1988, s 388)

Where a trade, profession or vocation is permanently discontinued, a loss incurred during the last 12 months can be deducted from the profits charged to tax in the three tax years before the final year. The relief can include a claim for the loss arising in the tax year in which the cessation takes place, and a proportion of the loss for the previous tax year.

Capital allowances for the final tax year may also be claimed, as can an appropriate proportion of the preceding year's capital allowances, representing the allowances due for the period beginning 12 months prior to the cessation.

The terminal loss may be carried back against profits from the same trade for the three tax years preceding the year of cessation. The relief is given against the latest year's profits first.

If interest and dividends would have been included as trading profits, (except that they were subject to deduction of tax at source), the terminal loss may be set against such income.

## 2.9.8 Anti-avoidance provisions

### Farming losses
(TA 1988, s 397)

Restrictions may apply to losses suffered by farmers. The legislation may prevent a farming loss being set against the individual's other income where he has suffered losses for each of the preceding five tax years. The only way of avoiding this restriction is for the individual to show that no reasonably competent farmer would have expected to have made a profit during the period in question.

### Losses from limited partnerships
(TA 1988, s 117)

Limited partnerships were widely used in tax avoidance arrangements. The House of Lords decided in *Reed v Young* [1986] STC 285 that a limited partner could be entitled to loss relief for an amount which exceeded his actual liability under the Limited Partnership Act. This led to specific legislation to limit the amount of loss relief to the capital which is 'at risk'. Any losses incurred beyond this amount have to be carried forward to be set against any future share of profits received by the limited partner from the firm.

The provisions of s 117 apply to individuals who are limited partners or members of a joint venture arrangement under which their liability is limited to a contract, agreement, guarantee etc.

## 2.9.9 Loss relief where a business has been transferred to a company
(TA 1988, s 386)

Where a business has been carried on by an individual (either as a sole trader or in partnership) and the business is transferred to a company, it is possible for any unused trading losses to be relieved against the individual's income from the company in subsequent years.

This relief is available only if the business is transferred to a company wholly or mainly in return for an allotment of shares and then only if the individual has retained ownership of those shares throughout the tax year concerned. In practice, the Revenue does not withhold relief provided the individual has retained at least 80% of the shares.

## 2.9.10 Schedule D Case V losses
(TA 1988, s 391)

Profits from a trade managed or controlled abroad are taxed under Schedule D Case V. Loss relief is calculated in the same way as for a loss incurred in a trade, profession or vocation taxed under Schedule D Case I or II.

Relief for such losses is given in the same way as relief is given for UK trading losses, except that where a loss is to be set against other income, a Case V loss can be deducted only from:

(1) profits from other foreign trades assessable under Schedule D Case V;
(2) foreign pensions and annuities where a 10% deduction is available;
(3) foreign emoluments assessable under Schedule E.

## 2.10 PARTNERSHIPS

A partnership's profits are computed in the same way as a sole trader's profits (see 2.4–2.5). However, there are a number of additional complications.

### 2.10.1 Salaried partners

A salaried partner is engaged under a contract of employment. He is normally taxed under Schedule E rather than under Schedule D. His remuneration is treated as a normal employee cost in arriving at the firm's profits. Sometimes partners have a fixed share of profits. It is not always easy to determine whether they are Schedule D or salaried partners. The key indicators that a partner is assessable under Schedule D are that the individual has capital at risk and that he is not subject to the control and direction of the Schedule D partners.

## 2.10.2 **How partnership profits are taxed**

There was a difference between firms which were carrying on business on or after 6 April 1994 and those carrying on business before that date. The difference in treatment disappeared in 1997–98 with the introduction of the current year basis for *all* unincorporated businesses.

Partners in a firm which started business on or after 6 April 1994, or who are deemed to have started a new business because the old firm had a cessation, have always been taxed separately. Assessments are raised on the individual partners rather than on the firm as a whole. There is no principle of partners being jointly and severally liable for the firm's tax. The cessation provisions do not apply and no election need be made when a partner retires or a new partner joins a firm.

Where a pre-1994–95 business was concerned, assessments were made on the firm rather than on individual partners. The partnership's assessable profits for a year were assessed in one amount payable by the firm as a whole with each partner jointly and severally liable. The assessment reflected the way in which income was divided among the partners, their allowances etc. This came to an end in 1996–97 and partners are now always assessed separately.

## 2.10.3 **Treatment of partners under the current year basis**

### Partners assessed individually

Assessments under the current year basis have always been made on individual partners rather than on the firm itself. Each partner is responsible for settling his own tax liabilities and is not jointly and severally liable for the total amount of tax payable by the partners. There may be a minor exception to this where there are non-resident partners in the firm.

### Application of the current year basis to partners

Basically, each partner is treated separately and the rules described at 2.3.1–2.3.3 are applied.

### Example of how partners' taxable income is computed

*A* and *B* start a new firm on 6 October 1997. They share profits equally. On 6 January 1999, *C* joins them and takes a one-third entitlement to profits. Accounts to 5 October 1998 show a profit of £132,000. The accounts for the years to 5 October 1999 and 5 October 2000 show a profit of £240,000 and £300,000 respectively. The position is as follows:

*1997–98* *A* and *B* are each assessed on the actual basis, ie the firm's profits of £66,000 for 1997–98 (%12 × £132,000 profits for the year ended 5 October 1998) are divided equally between them. *A* and *B* are therefore each assessed on £33,000.

*1998–99*   *A* and *B* are assessed on their share of the firm's profits for the first 12 months, ie profits of £132,000 are divided equally and each is assessed on £66,000. *C* is assessed on the actual basis, because 1998–99 is her first tax year as a partner in this firm, so she is assessed on £20,000 ($\frac{3}{12}$ × her one-third share of the profits for the year ended 5 October 1999).

*1999–00*   *A* and *B* are assessed on the CY basis on their share of the firm's profits for the year ended 5 October 1999, ie £80,000 each. *C* is assessed on the profits for her first 12 months, (ie $\frac{9}{12}$ × £80,000 plus $\frac{3}{12}$ × £100,000).

*2000–01*   All three partners are assessed on the CY basis, ie their $\frac{1}{3}$ share of the firm's profits for the year ended 5 October 2000 of £300,000.

Similarly, the provisions on overlap relief are applied separately in relation to each partner. Thus, in the above example, if *A* retired on 5 October 2000, he will be entitled to overlap relief in arriving at his taxable profits for 2000–01. The other ongoing partners would get their overlap relief only when they retire or the firm changes its accounting date – see below. Their overlap relief is as follows:

|   | £ |
|---|---|
| A | 33,000 |
| B | 33,000 |
| C | 25,000 ($\frac{3}{12}$ × £100,000). |

### 2.10.4 Treatment of partnership interest and other investment income

A partner may be entitled to a share of interest earned by the firm on surplus cash – or indeed any other investment income. Each partner is assessed on his share of such income, but it is assessed on the current year basis. Thus, if a firm makes up accounts to 31 May, the partners will be assessed for 2000–01 on their share of investment income in the firm's accounts for the year ended 31 May 1999. This is so even though the relevant income may actually have been received during the tax year 1998–99.

### 2.10.5 How catching up charge affects partnerships formerly on cash basis

The catching up charge for businesses which were taxed on the cash basis up to 1998–99 is described at 2.4.11. The total catching-up charge for partnerships will be based on the first accounting period starting on or after 6 April 1999 as for individuals. The part of the charge allocated to the first year will then be allocated to the persons who were members of the partnership:

(1) during the 12 months ending on the date that the catching-up charge is calculated;

(2) using the profit-sharing arrangements for that 12-month period.

The same method will be used for the parts of the charge being levied in future years, using the profit-sharing arrangements for the 12 months ending on the anniversary of the catching-up charge which falls into the tax year. This will apply irrespective of a future change in accounting date.

## 2.10.6 Limits and changes in partners

The one-tenth and 10% limits will operate at partnership level for the first nine years as they do for individuals. A partner will only remain liable for his share of the catching-up charge for the period up to the date that he leaves the partnership. Similarly anyone joining the partnership during the ten-year spreading period will become liable for his share of the charge in the future.

## 2.10.7 Partnership tax returns

As well as requiring returns from individual partners, the Revenue issues a partnership tax return to the 'nominated partner'. The return requires full details of the firm's profits and capital gains and the way in which profits (and losses) are divided between the partners. A partner needs to refer to the self-assessment reference under which the partnership return has been filed.

The legislation means that all business expenses must be claimed on the partnership return, even where the expenditure is borne by an individual partner (eg his car expenses or the purchase of a fax machine for business use at home). However, the Revenue states in Helpsheet IR231 that:

> the only legal basis for giving relief for expenditure that qualifies for capital allowances is as a deduction in the calculation of the profits of the partnership business (unless there is a formal leasing agreement between the partner and the partnership, when the allowances will be due against the leasing income).
>
> However, this does not mean that any legitimate expenditure incurred by a partner – *that is any expense that would be allowable if met from partnership funds* – can only be relieved if it is formally included in the partnership accounts. Nor does it mean that capital allowances can only be claimed on vehicles, or other assets, that feature in the partnership accounts.
>
> Providing that:
>
> ● any expenditure, or claim to capital allowances, is correctly calculated for tax purposes, and
> ● records relevant to those calculations are made and kept *as if* the expenditure, or assets, were part of the partnership accounts
>
> the Inland Revenue will accept entries in the relevant sections of the Partnership Tax Return which, though based on the partnership accounts, include adjustments for such expenditure, or allowances. But once the adjustments have been made the expenditure will be treated, for all practical purposes, as if it had been included in the partnership's accounts.

## 2.10.8 Interest paid by partners on personal loans

Where a partner has taken a personal loan to finance his buying into the firm or to provide part of its working capital, he can claim relief for the interest paid by him on such borrowings. However, this relief is given by way of a deduction from his total taxable income rather than as an expense in computing his Schedule D profits (see 9.3).

## 2.10.9 Partnerships controlled outside the UK
(TA 1988, s 112)

A UK-resident individual may be a partner in a partnership which is controlled outside the UK. His earnings from such a partnership are normally assessable under Schedule D Case V rather than under Schedule D Case I or II (however, profits which are earned by a UK branch are taxed under Schedule D Case I or II).

## 2.10.10 Current year basis

Where an individual became a partner in a foreign partnership on or after 6 April 1994, his income from the partnership is assessable on the current year basis (see 2.3.1).

Special rules applied up to 1996–97 to individuals who became partners before 1994–95, but from 1997–98 onwards they are assessable on the current year basis. See *Allied Dunbar Tax Handbook 1998–99* at 2.9.11.

# EMPLOYMENT INCOME

LOUISE DELAMERE

This chapter deals with the following matters:

(1)  Basis of assessment.
(2)  How tax is collected.
(3)  Allowable expenses.
(4)  Benefits in kind in general.
(5)  Company cars.
(6)  Free use of assets.
(7)  Beneficial loans.
(8)  Living accommodation.
(9)  Miscellaneous benefits.
(10)  Profit-related pay.
(11)  Gifts of shares.
(12)  Profit-sharing schemes.
(13)  New All-Employee Share Schemes.
(14)  Non-approved share options.
(15)  Approved share option schemes.
(16)  Restricted shares and shares in subsidiary companies.
(17)  Enterprise Management Incentives.
(18)  Options to acquire company assets.
(19)  Golden hallos.
(20)  Restrictive covenants.
(21)  Redundancy payments.
(22)  Golden handshakes and other termination payments.
(23)  Special rules for working outside the UK.
(24)  Designing a 'tax efficient' remuneration package.
(25)  Completing your self-assessment tax return.

## 3.1 BASIS OF ASSESSMENT

### 3.1.1 Introduction
(TA 1988, s 19)

An individual who holds an office or employment is taxed under Schedule
E. There are three different cases of Schedule E which depend upon the

residence, ordinary residence and domicile of the individual and where the duties of the employment are carried out:

### Table 3.1 – Schedule E

**Case I**    Individual resident and ordinarily resident in the UK. Tax due on total remuneration received.

**Case II**    Individual resident but not ordinarily resident in the UK. Tax due on total remuneration received (subject to special treatment of foreign emoluments (see 22.2), and remuneration taxed under Case III (see below)).

Individual not resident in the UK. Tax due on total remuneration received for duties performed in the UK.

**Case III**    Individual resident but not ordinarily resident in the UK where the duties are performed outside the UK. Case III may also apply to foreign domiciled individuals' earnings from duties performed outside the UK. Tax is due on earnings which are brought into the UK.

The remainder of this chapter concentrates on employees who are taxed under Schedule E Case I. See Chapter 22 for the taxation of foreign domiciled individuals under Schedule E Case III.

## 3.1.2 Receipts basis
(TA 1988, s 202A)

The amount which is assessable for a tax year is the amount of earnings received in that year.

## 3.1.3 Date remuneration is deemed to be received
(TA 1988, s 202B)

Special provisions define the date that an individual is deemed to receive remuneration as the earlier of:

(1) the date when payment is actually made; and
(2) the time when the employee becomes entitled to payment.

In the case of directors, the date can be earlier than above, in that payment is deemed to take place on the earliest of (1) and (2) and

(3) the date that income is credited to the director in the company's accounts or records;
(4) the date when the amount of income for a period is determined;
(5) the end of a period if the director's remuneration for a period is determined before the period has expired.

The employer is required to operate PAYE when payment is deemed to take place (see 19.1).

### 3.1.4 Amounts deducted in arriving at pay
(TA 1988, s 202)

Contributions made by an employee to an approved retirement benefit scheme and contributions to a payroll giving scheme ('give as you earn') are deducted from an individual's salary in arriving at taxable pay for the purposes of both PAYE and Schedule E. Profit-related pay must also be left out of account provided that it does not exceed the limits set out in 3.10. Note that NICs are based on pay before such amounts are deducted (see 23.1).

### 3.1.5 Amounts added in arriving at pay

With effect from 6 April 2000, an employer is required to pay working families' and disabled persons' tax credits (see 23.6).

## 3.2 HOW TAX IS COLLECTED

### 3.2.1 Tax deductions under PAYE

All payments of 'emoluments' by a UK-resident employer to directors and employees are subject to Pay as You Earn (PAYE). Emoluments are cash payments (salary, wages, bonus etc) other than expense payments.

#### PAYE code numbers

The Inland Revenue issues code numbers which determine the amount of PAYE deductions. Such code numbers are based on the latest information available to the Revenue and are intended to ensure that the amounts withheld under PAYE approximate closely to the individual's actual liability. Nevertheless, deduction of tax under PAYE is provisional in that if the actual liability exceeds the amount withheld under PAYE, the Revenue may collect the balance either by increased PAYE deductions in subsequent years or by raising an assessment.

Although the top rate of tax is 40%, the Revenue may issue 'K' codes under which increased deductions may be taken of up to 50% of an individual's pay. The principle behind K codes is that notional pay is added to an employee's actual pay, and PAYE is operated accordingly. This is intended to cover the situation where the benefits in kind which are taxable exceed a person's allowances.

### 3.2.2 Foreign employers who are unable to operate PAYE

Where a person is employed by a foreign employer which has no place of business in the UK, PAYE is not normally operated. Tax is payable by the employee as if he were self-employed, ie two payments on account based on the previous year's tax bill plus a balancing payment on 31 January following the end of the tax year.

### 3.2.3 Schedule E under self-assessment

An employee has until 31 January following the year of assessment to file a return and pay any additional tax due (ie for 1999–2000 by 31 January 2001).

If the employee wants the tax underpaid (of up to £1,000) to be collected by way of an adjustment in the code operated against his salary, he is requested to file the return by 30 September following the year of assessment (ie for 1999–2000 by 30 September 2000).

Where the taxpayer fails to notify the Revenue and pay any tax due by 31 January, interest penalties and surcharges may arise.

A practical point when completing the self-assessment form is to have copies of your PAYE Codings (P2) to hand. For 1999–2000, question 18.1 on the main form asks for 'unpaid tax included in your tax code for 1999–2000', and question 18.2 asks for 'tax due for 1999–2000 included in your tax code for a later year'. The former should be taken from the last P2 notice of coding received for 1999–2000 and the latter from your current 2000–01 form. If in doubt, contact your PAYE district office.

### 3.2.4 Schedule E assessments – old rules

In respect of years up to and including 1995–96, a Schedule E assessment could be made after the end of a tax year. Tax became payable as and when the actual liability was determined, either by the Inspector issuing an agreed assessment or by an appeal being determined under the Taxes Management Act (TMA) 1970, s 54 or by the appeal being determined by the Commissioners.

For further details see *Allied Dunbar Tax Handbook 1999–2000* at 3.24.

## 3.3 ALLOWABLE EXPENSES

### 3.3.1 Schedule E expenses
(TA 1988, s 198)

The rules governing the amounts which may be deducted for tax purposes from remuneration which is subject to Schedule E tax are extremely strict. The legislation provides for a deduction to be made only in respect of expenses which are wholly, exclusively and necessarily incurred in the performance of the duties of the employment or office.

#### Wholly, exclusively . . .

The courts have held that the following expenses are not deductible for Schedule E purposes because they were not deemed to have been incurred wholly and exclusively in the performance of the duties of the employment:

(1) Meal expenses paid out of meal allowances
(2) Rent of telephone installed for business reasons but not used wholly and exclusively in the performance of duties
(3) Cost of domestic assistance where the taxpayer's wife was employed
(4) Cost of looking after a widower's children
(5) Cost of ordinary clothing.

### . . . and necessarily . . .

The situation often arises that the employer has reimbursed the expense because it is regarded as essential. This is helpful, but not conclusive. The Revenue will assess the amount paid to a director or P11D employee (see 3.4.1) but may then seek to disallow the claim by the individual in respect of the expenditure on the grounds that it is not necessary. Two of the leading cases involved reimbursed expenditure by journalists on newspapers and other periodicals and the point at issue was whether reading such newspapers was part of, or inherent in the performance of, the journalists' duties. The key point here is that it is not the employer's decision which determines the case. The employer may be fully prepared to reimburse the expenditure but the Revenue may still argue that the expenditure fails to meet the very strict guidelines on what constitutes 'necessary'.

### . . . in the performance of the duties

Other expenses were rejected on the grounds that they were not incurred in the performance of the duties of the relevant employment:

(1) Employment agency fees (although entertainers are now specifically entitled to claim a deduction for such expenses up to 17½% of their earnings)
(2) Headmaster's course to improve background knowledge
(3) Articled clerk's examination fees
(4) Travelling costs from home to the place where the duties of the employment were performed
(5) Living expenses paid out of living allowances paid to an employee when working away from home.

### Cases where the taxpayer has succeeded

There have been cases where travelling expenses have been allowed because the courts were satisfied that a person's duties started as soon as he left home. For example, in *Gilbert v Hemsley* [1981] STC 703, the duties of a director of a plant-hire company involved his using his home as a base and travelling to various sites. The court therefore held that once he left home he was travelling in the course of his duties. Similarly, in *Pook v Owen* (1969) 45 TC 571, a doctor was 'on call' and his duties started once he was telephoned by the hospital to ask him to attend.

117

### 3.3.2 Expenses which are allowable
(TA 1988, s 201)

There are certain expenses which are specifically allowable, such as the cost of professional subscriptions to an approved body which is relevant to the individual's employment (eg the annual subscription to the Institute of Chartered Accountants or The Law Society). Also, flat rate expenses are given to employees in certain industries to cover expenditure on tools, overalls, special clothing etc.

Despite the very restrictive rules outlined in 3.3.1, you may be able to secure a deduction under s 198 if you pay interest on a loan used to purchase equipment used by you in the course of your employment (eg a car or a fax machine at your home which you use for business purposes).

In addition to claiming a deduction for loan interest, relief may be due for expenses such as running costs and (in the case of a fax machine) the line rental. Capital allowances may also be due, subject to a restriction if the equipment is used for private purposes as well as for your employment.

Until recently, directors or employees could not obtain tax relief for expenditure on items such as directors' and officers' liability insurance, or professional indemnity insurance. FA 1995 introduced relief for such premiums where they are paid by employees. Moreover, tax relief is also available where an employee has to meet his own uninsured liability.

The relief for insurance or payment of uninsured liabilities is also available to former employees who incur such expenses within a period of six years after the year in which the employment ceased.

## 3.4 BENEFITS IN KIND IN GENERAL

### 3.4.1 Directors and 'higher paid employees'
(TA 1988, ss 153–168)

The legislation distinguishes P11D employees (ie directors and employees earning at the rate of £8,500 or more pa) from other employees. An employer is required to submit form P11D in respect of each P11D employee who may then be assessed on the cost to the employer of benefits in kind received by them. Other employees are normally taxed on benefits only if they are convertible into cash.

An employee will fall within the P11D category where remuneration, together with benefits and reimbursed expenses, is £8,500 pa or more. Such employees were formerly called 'higher paid' employees. The threshold of £8,500 was set in 1979 and, in accordance with the Government's intentions that all employees should pay income tax on the whole of their earnings whether received in cash or in kind, this limit has not been increased. By 1989 the term 'higher paid' had become inappropriate and consequently, while there was no change made in the level of the threshold, references to higher paid employees were deleted from the legislation.

Employees are treated as earning £8,500 or more if they are remunerated at the rate of £8,500 pa or more. For example, a person whose employment began on 1 January 1999 and who had received a salary of £2,000 and reimbursed expenses of £200 by 5 April 1999 would be within the P11D category as the total amount of £2,200 would give an annual rate greater than £8,500.

All reimbursed expenses and other benefits have to be reported on form P11D and count towards the £8,500 limit, even though they may be justified as being for business purposes and no taxable benefit in kind ultimately arises, unless a dispensation has been agreed by the Inland Revenue (see below).

Directors are normally within the P11D regime, regardless of whether their remuneration reaches or exceeds the £8,500 limit (subject to one exception – see below). Furthermore, individuals who control a company's affairs and who take management decisions may be treated as directors even if they do not hold a formal position with the company and even though they may have another title or job description within the company.

A person remunerated at a rate below £8,500 by a particular company is still within the P11D category if a directorship is held with another company in the same group, or if the total remuneration from group companies amounts to £8,500 pa whether or not any directorships are held. Certain directors are exempt from the above rules by virtue of s 168 and are therefore excluded from the definition. To qualify for this favourable treatment, certain conditions need to be satisfied. The director:

(1)  must not hold more than 5% of the company's ordinary share capital (holdings by his 'associates' may need to be included as if he held the shares); and
(2)  must be employed on a full-time basis (or the company must be a non-profit making organisation); and
(3)  must be receiving remuneration and benefits which in aggregate are less than £8,500 pa.

An employer must provide employees with details of the taxable amounts for benefits shown on his form P11D. This must be done before 5 July following the tax year unless the employee had left the firm before the end of the tax year (in which case the employer must provide the information within 30 days of the former employee requesting him to do so). The P11D must include the cost of benefits provided by third parties where they were arranged by the employer.

### 3.4.2 Dispensations

The Revenue may grant a dispensation so that certain reimbursed expenses need not be reported on form P11D. This is clearly useful in reducing administration and accounting work and, wherever possible, employers should apply for a dispensation. The expenses covered by it will be set out by the Revenue and any expenses not covered must still be reported. Any changes in the method of reimbursing expenses or scales of allowances must be notified to the Revenue.

### 3.4.3 Benefits in kind provided by third parties
(Extra-statutory concession A70; TA 1988, s 155(7))

It is not uncommon for wholesalers and distributors to offer benefits in kind to the employees of retailers with whom they do business. Subject to certain *de minimis* rules, such benefits are taxable just as if they had been provided by the retailer himself. However, non-monetary gifts costing no more than £150 (£100 up to 1994–95) which an employee or his family receives from someone other than his employer, will generally be exempt from income tax. Likewise, no income tax liability will usually arise on entertainment which an employee receives from a third party. These concessions only apply, however, where the gift or entertainment is not provided directly or indirectly by the employer and, furthermore, it is not provided as a reward for, or in recognition of, specific services done or to be done by the employee.

Where the third party benefits have not been arranged by the employer, the provider must give the employee details of any taxable benefits by 5 July following the tax year.

### 3.4.4 Benefits for director's family
(TA 1988, s 154(1))

A fundamental point is that an assessment may arise even though the director or employee has not personally received a benefit in kind. A tax liability may arise if the benefit was made available to a member of the director's or employee's household by reason of his employment. The Revenue may argue that substantial benefits in kind enjoyed by a director's family are provided by reason of that person's employment even though the recipient may also be a company employee. The Revenue is especially likely to argue this where a director's spouse is employed by the company and receives abnormally large benefits in kind for employees of that category.

### 3.4.5 Scholarships
(TA 1988, ss 331 and 165(1))

There is a general exemption for scholarships but the provision of scholarships to children by reason of their parents' employment is normally treated as a benefit in kind of the parent concerned. The benefit is taxable unless it can be shown that the scholarship was not awarded by reason of the employment and 75% of the scholarships awarded by the fund are awarded to children whose parents are not employed by the company.

### 3.4.6 Benefits which may result in a tax charge for non-P11D employees

The general rule is that employees who are not within the P11D category are assessable only on benefits capable of being converted into cash or on any benefits provided through an employer meeting an employee's own personal liability. This principle has been modified to some extent so that, for instance, credit vouchers are an assessable benefit even if the employee is not within the P11D category. However, the principle continues to hold good with regard to benefits such as the provision of a company car, free use of assets, beneficial loans etc.

Table 3.2 below sets out the position.

### 3.4.7 Tax treatment of specific benefits where received by a non-P11D employee

#### Benefits capable of being converted into cash

Where the benefit is convertible into cash, the measure of assessable benefit is the amount of cash which could be realised. For example, an employee provided with a new suit by the employer would be taxable on its second-hand value.

#### Table 3.2 – Treatment of benefits received by non-P11D employees

|  | Taxable | Non-taxable |
|---|---|---|
| Benefits capable of being turned to pecuniary account ie convertible to cash | ✓ | |
| Luncheon vouchers in excess of 15p per working day | ✓ | |
| Credit tokens and vouchers | ✓ | |
| Transport vouchers (ie any ticket, pass or other document or token intended to enable a person to obtain passenger transport services) | ✓ | |
| Living accommodation | ✓ | |
| Payment of employees' personal liabilities | ✓ | |
| Company cars | | ✓ |
| Free use of assets | | ✓ |
| Beneficial loans | | ✓ |
| Medical insurance | | ✓ |

## Credit tokens and vouchers
(TA 1988, s 142)

The taxable amount in respect of credit tokens and vouchers is the cost to the employer of providing them. Vouchers other than cheque vouchers are deemed to be taxable emoluments as and when they are allocated to a particular employee, not when they are used by that employee.

## Transport vouchers
(TA 1988, s 141)

Specific legislation was introduced in 1976 to ensure that season tickets provided by employers should be taxable. Once again, the measure of the assessable benefit is the cost to the employer of providing the voucher.

## Living accommodation
(TA 1988, s 145)

The assessable amount is the greater of the gross rateable value of the property or the rent payable by the employer, less any amount made good by the employee. Following the abolition of domestic rates, estimated values are used for new or substantially altered properties. No assessable benefit arises where the employee occupies representative accommodation (see 3.4.8).

## Payment of employee's personal liabilities

A liability arises where the employer pays a personal liability of the employee. This would include such items as home heating and lighting bills and water rates, but special rules apply where the employee is in representative accommodation (see 3.4.8).

## 3.4.8 Benefits which are not taxable for any category of employees

There are certain benefits that are not usually taxable even when the employee is within the P11D category. The most widely used tax-free benefits are:

Retirement benefits
Luncheon vouchers
Staff canteen and dining facilities
Sports facilities
Workplace nurseries and crèches
'Green commuting' facilities
Changing facilities
Late travel

Rail strike costs
Relocation expenses
Long service awards
Awards under suggestion schemes
Use of company computers
Use of a pooled car
The provision of representative accommodation
Retraining
Certain gifts.

## Retirement benefits

Payments by an employer to an approved occupational pension scheme to secure retirement benefits for an employee do not give rise to an income tax liability for that employee. Payments into a non-approved scheme are taxable as additional remuneration for the year that the employer makes the relevant contribution. To secure approval, a pension scheme must be established for the sole purpose of providing 'relevant benefits' (ie pensions, death-in-service payments, and widow's and dependants' pensions). In addition, an employee's contributions must not exceed 15% of his remuneration. The pension benefits payable by an approved scheme must not exceed certain limits. Pension schemes are covered in more detail in Chapter 12.

## Luncheon vouchers

Non-transferable luncheon vouchers (ie vouchers which are not capable of being exchanged for cash) are exempt from income tax up to a limit of 15p per working day. Vouchers for larger amounts are partly exempt, with the excess over 15p being taxable in full, whether or not the employee is within the P11D category.

## Staff canteen and dining facilities

No taxable benefit in kind arises where the canteen etc is used by all staff. Furthermore, the use of a separate room by directors and more senior staff does not prejudice this exemption, unless the meals provided are superior. The Revenue also accepts that facilities provided by a hotel or restaurant for staff to 'eat in' may come within the definition of a 'canteen', provided that the meals are taken at a time or place when they are not being served to the public or where part of the restaurant or dining room is specifically designated as being for the use of staff only.

## Sports facilities
(FA 1993, s 75)

No taxable benefit arises in respect of the use or availability of sports facilities owned by the employer. In the past, no assessment was normally made where an employer took out corporate membership of an outside sports club so that all the employees were able to use the club's facilities. However, the Revenue's current literature states that the exemption is not available for sports facilities which are available to the general public.

## Workplace nurseries and crèches

Since 6 April 1990, employees have been exempt from income tax on the benefit derived from the use of a workplace nursery provided by the employer. The exemption applies only to nurseries run by employers alone or jointly with other employers or bodies, either at the workplace or elsewhere. The provision by an employer of cash allowances to employees for childcare, or the direct meeting of an employee's childcare bills by an employer, are taxable benefits.

## 'Green commuting' facilities

A number of measures have been introduced to encourage green commuting. With effect from 6 April 1999, there is no taxable benefit in respect of:

- works buses with a seating capacity of 12 or more;
- subsidies to public bus services, provided the employee pays the same fare as other members of the public;
- bicycles and cycle safety equipment made available for employees to get to and from work; and
- workplace parking for bicycles and motorcycles.

## Changing facilities

For employees who may need to change clothes and to shower after arriving at the office because, for example, they cycle or run to work, tax is not chargeable on the free use by employees of changing room and shower room facilities at an employer's premises, provided these facilities are generally available to all employees.

## Late travel

There is an exemption for the cost to an employer of providing transport to get an employee home (after 9 pm) where public transport is not available or it is not reasonable for the employer to expect the employee to use it. The exemption does not apply if the employee has to work late on a regular or frequent basis.

The exemption has been extended to cover extra travel costs where car sharing arrangements temporarily break down. This can include situations where the employee travels home at his normal time (eg where the employee whose car he shares is unexpectedly kept late).

## Employees' rail strike costs

Somerset House has confirmed that ESC A58 covers extra costs incurred by employees in getting to work because of a rail strike. The concession (which may also cover the cost of hotel accommodation near the place of work) means that no Schedule E tax is payable where the employer meets these expenses.

## Relocation expenses
(FA 1993, s 76)

There is an exemption from tax on certain removal expenses borne by an employer when an employee has had to change his residence to take up a new job within the same organisation, or to take up completely new employment. It is not necessary for the employee to sell his former home but the exemption is available only where it would be unreasonable to expect him to work at the new location without moving closer to it. Abortive costs where a particular purchase falls through can be covered by the exemption provided the employee does eventually move house. The exemption is subject to a ceiling of £8,000 in respect of any one move.

The Revenue changed its practice on compensation payments with effect from 6 April 1993, and payments made to compensate employees for losses on the sale of their old houses are now regarded as taxable.

The Revenue has published a guide for employees on relocation packages and their tax treatment (IR134 obtainable from tax offices and tax enquiry centres). Sometimes employers provide guaranteed selling prices for the employee's former home, either directly or through a relocation agency. The Revenue published its views on the tax consequences of such arrangements in *Tax Bulletin* May 1994, which may be obtained from Somerset House.

## Long service awards

Awards to directors and employees to mark long service are exempt provided the period of service is at least 20 years and no similar award has been given to the employee within the previous ten years. The gift must not consist of cash and the cost should not exceed £20 pa of service. An Inland Revenue concession has extended the exemption to gifts of shares in the company which employs the individual or in another group company.

## Awards under suggestion schemes
(Extra statutory concession A57)

Provided the employee concerned is not engaged in research work, he may receive a tax-free payment under a firm's suggestion scheme. The making of suggestions should not, however, be regarded as part of the employee's job. The size of the award should also be within certain limits, ie £25 or less where the suggestion, although not implemented, has intrinsic value. Where the suggestion is implemented, the amount should be related to the expected net financial benefit to the employer. In any event, any excess over £5,000 will be taxable.

## Use of company computers

Since 6 April 1999, employees have been able to take up the loan of a computer without being faced with a tax charge. This concession applies to computer equipment with a value of up to £2,000. The normal benefit in kind rules (20% × market value) will apply to any excess over £2,000. The exemption will not be given if the equipment is confined to directors and senior staff.

## Pool cars
(TA 1988, s 159)

No tax charge arises by reason of the use of a pooled car. A car qualifies as a pooled car only if all the following conditions are satisfied:

(1) It is available for, and used by, more than one employee and is not ordinarily used by any one of them to the exclusion of the others.
(2) Any private use of the car by an employee is merely incidental to its business use.
(3) It is not normally kept overnight at or near the residence of any of the employees unless it is kept on premises occupied by the employer.

The above requirements are strictly interpreted. Note that a car only qualifies as a pooled car for a tax year. There is a danger therefore in a car being taken out of pooled use and allotted to a specific employee towards the end of a tax year. As the car now no longer qualifies as a pooled car, any employee who has had the car available for private use during the same tax year may be assessed. Therefore, if the car is ordinarily parked overnight near the home of one of the users, it will not qualify as a pooled car and will create a tax problem for any other employees who use it.

## Disabled employees' travel costs

Assistance with costs of travelling between home and work is not taxable where it is given to disabled persons. This includes contributions towards the cost of travel by public transport. A car provided for home to work travel is not taxed where:

(1) the employee is severely and permanently disabled; and
(2) the car has been specially adapted; and
(3) no private use is made other than travel from home to work.

## Representative accommodation
(TA 1988, s 145(4))

Living accommodation qualifies as representative accommodation if any one of the following conditions is satisfied:

(1) It is necessary for the performance of the employee's duties that he should reside in the accommodation.
(2) The accommodation is provided for the better performance of the employee's duties and it is customary to provide accommodation for such employees.
(3) The employee has to live in the accommodation because of a special threat to his security.

The exemption under the first two conditions is usually only available to directors who (together with their associates) hold 5% or less of the company's ordinary share capital and are full-time working directors. Where the employer pays for heating, lighting, repairs, maintenance etc, the representative occupiers cannot be assessed in respect of such benefits on more than 10% of their emoluments of the employment.

The main occupations which satisfy the conditions for exemption are:

(1) agricultural workers living on farms or agricultural estates;
(2) lock-gate and level-crossing gatekeepers;
(3) caretakers who live on the premises for which they are responsible;
(4) stewards and greenkeepers who live on the premises they look after;
(5) managers of public houses who live on the premises;
(6) wardens of sheltered housing who live on the premises;
(7) police officers and Ministry of Defence police;
(8) prison governors, officers and chaplains;
(9) clergymen and ministers of religion, unless engaged on administrative duties only;
(10) members of the armed forces;
(11) members of the Diplomatic Service;
(12) managers of newspaper shops that have paper rounds;
(13) managers of traditional off-licences (ie those with opening hours which are the same as for public houses);
(14) head teachers and teachers at boarding schools who have pastoral responsibility, if the accommodation is at or near the school;
(15) veterinary surgeons who live near their practice so that they can respond regularly to emergency calls;
(16) managers of camping and caravan sites living on or near the premises.

## Retraining
(TA 1988, ss 588–589)

Where an employer pays the cost of a course undertaken by an employee (or former employee) for the purpose of providing him with skills for future employment elsewhere, the cost of the course can be a deductible expense of the employer, and may not be a taxable benefit of the employee. The employee must have been full time and have completed at least two years' service.

The exemption is normally dependent upon the employee leaving his job no later than two years after completing the course.

## Sandwich courses
(Statement of Practice SP4/86, reissued November 1992)

Where an employee is released by his employer to take a full-time educational course at a university, technical college or similar educational institution which is open to the public at large, payments for periods of attendance may be treated as exempt from income tax. There are various conditions which attach to this exemption, ie:

(1) The course must last for at least one academic year with an average of at least 20 weeks of full-time attendance.
(2) The rate of payment must not exceed the greater of £7,000 and the rate of payment that an individual would have received had he been granted a public grant.

Where the rate of payment exceeds the above limits, the full amount is taxable but where the amount of payment is increased during a course, only subsequent payments are taxable.

## Gifts

Certain gifts received by an employee are exempt if all the following conditions are satisfied:

(1) the gift consists of goods or a voucher or token only capable of being used to obtain goods;
(2) the person making the gift is not the employer or a person connected with the employer;
(3) the gift is not made either in recognition of the performance of particular services in the course of the employment or in anticipation of particular services which are to be performed;
(4) the gift has not been directly or indirectly procured by the employer or by a person connected with the employer;
(5) the gift cost the donor £150 or less; and
(6) the total cost of all gifts made by the same donor to an employee, or to

members of his family or household, during the income tax year is £150 or less.

## 3.4.9 Expenses relating to directors and P11D employees

This section deals with problem areas which regularly arise in practice where expenses are paid on behalf of directors or reimbursed to them.

### Travelling expenses
(TA 1988, s 153)

Travel between home and the ordinary place of work does not rank as business travel. Where an individual is 'on call' and assumes the responsibilities of the employment upon leaving home, it may be possible to argue that home to work travel is business and not private travel, but this usually applies only in exceptional cases. Other travelling expenses are not normally treated as a benefit in kind so long as the individual has a 'normal place of work' which he attends the majority of the time. Where an employee performs incidental duties of the employment at another location and travels there directly to or from his home, the allowable expense is the lesser of the travel and subsistence expenses actually incurred, and the expenses which would have been incurred if the journey had started and finished at the normal place of work.

In order to secure tax relief on reimbursed travelling expenses, the employee must keep adequate records so as to distinguish business from non-business travel. Ideally, expenses claims to the employer should show the actual cost of such travel and, if the employer is to obtain a dispensation, the Revenue will need to be satisfied that such internal controls exist.

Mileage allowances should not be so large as to create a 'profit' element which would of course be taxable. The Revenue has been especially concerned about high business mileage drivers who are paid the standard AA and RAC rates. Maximum rates have been agreed with the Revenue and are referred to as Fixed Profit Car Scheme (FPCS) rates. The rates for 1997–98 to 2000–01 are:

| | Amount per mile | |
| --- | --- | --- |
| Engine size | up to 4,000 miles | over 4,000 miles |
| up to 1000cc | 28p | 17p |
| 1001–1500cc | 35p | 20p |
| 1501–2000cc | 45p | 25p |
| Over 2000cc | 63p | 36p |

Where reimbursement is not linked to engine size, the rates are 40p up to 4,000 miles pa and 22.5p thereafter. Provided these rates are not exceeded and mileage is for business purposes, no benefit in kind will arise. Interest paid on a loan taken out for the purchase of a car used for business purposes may qualify for tax relief. Relief for interest is not included in FPCS rates and needs to be claimed separately.

Where an individual is required to use his own car for business, and he is reimbursed at less than the FPCS rates, he can claim a deduction equal to the shortfall. An employer must give employees a summary of FPCS payments made to them by 5 July following the tax year.

## Using your bicycle for business

Employees are now able to claim capital allowances on bicycles used for business travel on a proportion of cost. A tax-free cycling allowance of 12p per business mile has been introduced for employees using their own bicycles. Where the employer pays less than this rate, the employee can claim a tax deduction for the excess.

## Subsistence
(TA 1988, s 153)

The Revenue's view is that it is strictly only the extra costs of living away from home which are allowable. If there are continuing financial commitments at home, the whole cost of living away from home is normally allowed. This concession is not available if the employee has no permanent residence, for example an unmarried person who normally lives in a hotel or club and who gives up that accommodation when away on a business trip. There is a specific exemption where an employee performs his duties wholly overseas and needs board and lodging abroad to do so.

## Miscellaneous personal expenses

FA 1995 introduced a statutory exemption for employees' miscellaneous personal expenses when they are required to stay away from home overnight on business. This exemption took effect from 6 April 1995 and allows employers to meet expenses of up to £5 a night (£10 if overseas). Under the previous rules, incidental personal expenses such as newspapers, laundry and telephone calls home were often met by employers but, because relief is only available for expenses necessarily incurred in the performance of the duties, these were liable to tax. Under the new rules, payments up to the aforementioned *de minimis* limits will be exempt which should reduce employers' compliance costs and simplify their administrative procedures. But there is a sting in the tail. If the limits are exceeded the whole of the expense payment is taxable, not just the excess.

## Employees' travel and subsistence – rules for 1998–99 onwards

New rules in respect of travel and subsistence came into operation on 6 April 1998.

### Triangular travel

Triangular travel occurs where an employee with a normal place of work travels not between home and normal place of work, but between home and another place at which he is required to perform the duties of his employment.

## Example of triangular travel

An employee usually commutes by car from home in Oxford to a normal place of work in London. This is a daily round trip of 114 miles. On a particular day, the employee drives instead to a temporary place of work in Brighton, a round trip of 120 miles.

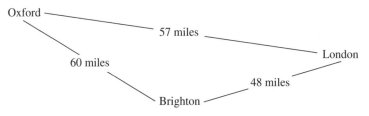

The new rules allow a claim for the full mileage cost of 120 miles. It is not necessary to restrict the claim for the normal commuting costs which would have been incurred if the employee had travelled to London.

Of course, nothing in tax is ever as straightforward as this; for example, the Revenue would not allow the cost of the employee travelling to Brighton if he worked there so regularly that it became a normal place of employment. The Revenue's criterion here is that a place of work becomes a normal place of employment if the employee spends 40% of his time there.

The Revenue has issued a comprehensive guide, *Tax relief for business travel*, to employers.

The new rules affect employees in employment which involves travel where tax relief is available for travel between home and various places visited. The Revenue will review whether the travelling is 'on the job', as opposed to 'to the job'. Such employees will be expected to visit a number of places each day and have no base to which they regularly report. Thus, the definition of 'permanent workplace' may create difficulties where an employee reports regularly to a head office or regional base, say, every Tuesday.

Employees who are based at home may also come under scrutiny. The issue will be whether the home base is an objective requirement of their duties rather than a personal choice.

Area-based employees whose duties are defined by reference to a specific area (ie a county) will have their tax relief restricted if they live outside of that area. Tax relief will only be due on necessary business journeys within the designated area or to a temporary workplace outside the area.

There are specific anti-avoidance measures (including a 'necessary attendance rule') which require attendance to be an objective requirement of the duties, and not from personal choice or to claim tax relief. It is also a requirement that any changes to a workplace must be significant in the effect on the journey. The Revenue has suggested adopting a ten-mile 'common sense' rule.

Employers should review their travel and subsistence expenses reimbursement policies in the light of the new legislation and determine if changes need to be made.

### Site-based employees

The new rules allow a deduction for the costs of travel to or from any place where attendance at that place is in the performance of the duties of a person's employment. The subsistence costs of site-based employees are also an allowable expense.

### Temporary absence from normal place of work

Where an employee is required to work temporarily at a place other than his normal workplace, the deductions for travel expenses described above are available.

### Temporary relocation to another office etc

The Revenue has recently clarified the circumstances in which employees who are temporarily absent from their normal place of work can claim a deduction for travelling and subsistence expenses. Normally an employee is regarded as temporarily absent from his normal place of work if:

(1) the absence is not for more than 24 months; and
(2) the employee returns to the normal place of work at the end of the period.

If these conditions are satisfied, the employer can pay a subsistence allowance free of tax.

The Revenue takes the view that an individual may also qualify if these conditions are expected to be satisfied at the outset but circumstances subsequently change. Relief is available for the period up to the time when it becomes clear that either condition will be breached.

## Overseas travelling expenses
(TA 1988, ss 193–194)

Where some or all of the duties of an employment are performed abroad, the expenses of travelling to and from the UK to carry out these duties are specifically regarded as having been necessarily incurred in the performance of the overseas employment. It follows, therefore, that if those expenses are reimbursed by the employer, no benefit in kind arises. Legislative changes have relaxed the rules further, so that, while the employee is serving abroad, the employer may pay for an unlimited number of journeys made by the employee to and from the UK without any tax charge arising. However, these journeys must be made wholly and exclusively for the purpose of performing the duties of the employment.

Moreover, where an employee travels between places where different jobs are performed, and one or more of these jobs is performed wholly or partly overseas, the expenses incurred in travelling overseas are also deemed to be necessarily incurred in performing the duties carried out overseas, so that once again no benefit in kind arises. In many cases, there is dual purpose in travelling and a taxable benefit in kind arises on the private element. Consequently, where travel expenses relate partly to a foreign holiday taken at the end of the business trip, there would be a taxable benefit in kind.

Similarly, a benefit in kind may be assessed on some or all of the expense where a spouse accompanies a director or employee and where this is not necessary for business purposes.

The maximum allowance to cover an employee's miscellaneous personal expenses is £10 per night when the employee is abroad.

A director or employee who travels overseas should be able to substantiate a claim that expenses were necessarily incurred for business purposes by producing details of the expenses and the time spent away from home. A brief itinerary should be available where travel is undertaken within the overseas country or countries. Inspectors of Taxes will normally expect that an employer will properly control expenditure but in certain cases they may wish to see receipted bills or other vouchers.

## Spouse's travelling and subsistence expenses

Where a spouse or other member of the family accompanies the director or employee abroad on a business trip, it will be helpful in satisfying the Revenue that no benefit in kind arises if the board of directors minutes its decision that the director should be so accompanied. However, this is not generally sufficient in itself and it must be shown that the spouse or other relative was able to perform certain tasks which could not be performed by the director.

It may be possible to show this if the spouse has some practical qualification, for example an ability to speak the foreign language concerned. A relative's expenses might also be allowable where the director or employee is in poor health and to travel alone would be impracticable or unreasonable. Where the individual's presence is for the purpose of accompanying his or her spouse at business entertainment functions, the expenses of the trip may be disallowed in calculating the employer's tax liability under the entertainment legislation, even though the expenses may be allowable in determining the employee's tax liability.

### Employees working overseas – family visits
(TA 1988, s 194)

Where an employee is abroad for a continuous period of 60 days or more, there is an exemption for amounts borne by the employer in respect of the travelling expenses for visits by the employee's spouse and minor children. The exemption is only available for two journeys by the same person in each direction in a tax year. There is no relief if the employee ultimately bears the expense personally.

### Entertaining expenses and round-sum allowances

It is not uncommon for directors or employees to have a round-sum allowance to cover such things as travelling, subsistence and entertaining. In the case of travelling and subsistence, the allowance counts as the taxable income of the director or employee, but a tax deduction may be claimed in respect of any part of the allowance which can be shown to have been spent for business purposes. It is very important to have a record-keeping system which enables such claims to be substantiated. In some situations, it may be better for the employer to dispense with round-sum allowances and reimburse the director or employee for properly substantiated expenditure since no benefit in kind should then arise.

In the case of entertaining expenditure, the situation is rather more complex. If an employer reimburses a director's or employee's entertaining expenditure or pays a round-sum allowance which is specifically intended for entertaining, the expense to the employer is disallowed for tax purposes. The reimbursement or allowance is entered on the director's or employee's P11D but a deduction may be claimed for all the expenditure which is for genuine business purposes. If, on the other hand, the director or employee is given a round-sum allowance not specifically designated as being for entertaining, there is no question of the allowance being disallowed in the employer's tax computation. However, the director or employee would only escape liability on any part of the allowance which could be shown to have been used for business expenditure other than entertainment.

## 3.5 COMPANY CARS
(TA 1988, s 157)

### 3.5.1 Car benefits for 1999–2000 onwards

The most widespread benefit is the company car made available for private use. The taxable benefit is currently based not on the cost, but on the car's list price at the time that it was first registered.

Where a company car is used for less than 2,500 miles in a tax year, the benefit is 35% of the list price. If business use is between 2,500 and 17,999 miles, the benefit is 25%. In cases where business use amounts to 18,000 miles or more, the benefit is 15%. Where, in exceptional circumstances, a second car is used for more than 18,000 business miles, the benefit is 25% of the list price.

Each of the above benefits is reduced by one-quarter if the car is at least four years old at the end of the tax year. However, where a car is more than 15 years old at the end of the tax year, has a market value of at least £15,000 and the market value exceeds the list price, the benefit in kind is calculated by reference to the market value rather than original list price (or £80,000 if less).

The list price includes delivery charges, standard accessories and optional accessories fitted when the car was first made available to the employee. A separate addition to the list price is also made where accessories are fitted after the car was made available, but accessories with a list price of less than £100 are left out of account. Costs of converting a company car for use by a disabled person are not included in the list price. The list price is 'capped' at £80,000.

The scale figures are reduced where an employee is provided with a company car part way through the tax year, or where he ceases to have a company car. However, there is no reduction where the car was not available for use because of repairs, unless it was incapable of being used for at least 30 consecutive days.

The Revenue will provide a Helpsheet, on request, to enable you to check the benefits reported by your employer on form P11D: ask for Helpsheet IR203.

### Reform of company car taxation – New measures from 6 April 2002

The Government has confirmed that it will introduce an environment-friendly tax charge on company cars from 6 April 2002. The new tax charge will be based on a percentage of the car's price graduated according to the level of its carbon dioxide ($CO_2$ emissions). The charge will start at 15% of the car's price for cars emitting 165 grammes per kilometre (g/km) $CO_2$, with 1% increments for additional g/km over/km. The maximum charge, as now, will be 35% of the car's price. Diesel cars will be subject to a 3% supplement, within the 35% maximum. The existing business mileage and age related discounts will be abolished.

The effect will be to increase the tax charge for high business mileage drivers who drive over 18,000 business miles from 15% (or less if the car is over four years old) to 35%. Many employers are already reconsidering their car policies and looking at cash alternatives

Further discounts for environmentally friendly cars and low emission diesel cars are being considered and are open for consultation – in the longer term the authorised mileage rate will also be reviewed for environmental reasons.

### 3.5.2 Car benefits from 1994–95 to 1998–99

The taxable benefit was normally 35% of the list price, but was reduced by one-third where use was at least 2,500 business miles in the tax year. There was a reduction of a further one-third where the business mileage was at least 18,000 miles pa. The taxable benefit is also reduced by one-third where the car was at least four years old at the end of the tax year.

### 3.5.3 Car benefits where car is changed during tax year

In *Henwood v Clarke*, the taxpayer changed company cars during the course of the tax year. The court held that the mileage test should be pro rated for each vehicle.

#### Example – Car changed during tax year

On 5 August, *X* changed his company car from a Renault to a Ford. He had travelled 1,600 business miles in the Renault and 1,000 business miles in the Ford by the end of the tax year. In the light of the case law, the rules must be applied to each car separately.

Although *X* has travelled more than 2,500 miles in total during the year, he has only exceeded the limit, reduced pro rata, in the Renault. The cash equivalent of the Ford will be uplifted by 50% because its business mileage was less than the relevant threshold of 1,664 miles.

### 3.5.4 Tax treatment of employee contributions

Contributions made by an employee towards the cost of the car can be deducted from the list price, subject to a maximum deduction of £5,000. Capital contributions made before 6 April 1994 may be deducted in this way, even though there was no deduction prior to 1994–95.

#### Example – Employee contributions to company cars

Two employees are entitled to company cars. One contributes £4,000 towards the car which has a list price of £18,000 while the other contributes £11,000 towards a car with a list price of £25,000. Their assessable benefits in kind for 1998–99 are:

|  | A | B |
|---|---|---|
|  | £ | £ |
| List price | 18,000 | 25,000 |
| *Less*: capital contribution income of: |  |  |
| (A) amount contributed | (4,000) |  |
| (B) deduction for capital contribution limited to |  | (5,000) |
|  | 14,000 | 20,000 |
| 35% thereof | 4,900 | 7,000 |
| Assessable benefits | 4,900 | 7,000 |

Annual payments made by employees in respect of private use of a car may still reduce the assessable benefit on a £1 for £1 basis. In the above example, *B* would be better off to reduce his initial capital contribution and make annual payments in return for being allowed to use the vehicle for private purposes.

### 3.5.5 Private petrol
(TA 1988, s 158)

An additional scale benefit applies where an employer provides private petrol for use in a car to which a scale benefit charge arises. The scale charge depends entirely on engine size (for cars with a recognised cylinder capacity) as follows:

|  | 1999–2000 | | 2000–2001 | |
| --- | --- | --- | --- | --- |
|  | *Petrol* | *Diesel* | *Petrol* | *Diesel* |
|  | £ | £ | £ | £ |
| Up to 1400cc | 1,210 | 1,540 | 1,700 | 2,170 |
| 1401 to 2000cc | 1,540 | 1,540 | 2,170 | 2,170 |
| More than 2000cc | 2,270 | 2,270 | 3,200 | 3,200 |

For cars without a cylinder capacity, the scale charge for 1999–2000 was £2,270 and has been increased to £3,200 for the current tax year 2000–01.

The scale figures apply regardless of the amount of private fuel provided. If any is provided, the fuel scale charge will always apply unless the employee reimburses his employer for the full cost. In some cases it may be cost effective for an employee to do this and the position should therefore be reviewed before the start of each new tax year.

This charge does not apply where an employer provides fuel for the private use of a van. If an employer provides fuel for the private use of the employee's own car, the amount paid is a benefit which has to be reported on form P11D.

### 3.5.6 Other related costs

The car benefit does not cover the salary of a chauffeur. If a director is allocated a chauffeur, the full cost to the employer of providing one should be included on the director's form P11D and therefore will be potentially assessable as a benefit in kind (subject to a claim for business usage).

At one time, the Revenue accepted that no private use arose where a driver chauffeur drove an employee to or from his home in order that he could work in the car on confidential papers. However the Revenue have treated this as private use since 1996–97.

### 3.5.7 **Car parking spaces**
(FA 1988, s 46)

The provision of a car parking space at or near the employee's place of work has not been treated as a taxable benefit since 1988–89. Where, however, an employee pays for car parking himself, he will not be able to claim a deduction for those charges.

### 3.5.8 **Private use of company vans**
(FA 1993, s 73)

FA 1993 introduced a scale charge for employees who have private use of company vans. An employee may be assessed on a standard amount of £500 pa in respect of private use of a van. The amount is reduced to £350 for vans which are four or more years old at the end of the tax year. Any vehicles in excess of 3.5 tons are exempt from tax altogether (unless the vehicle is used wholly or mainly for the employee's private purposes). Where an employee has two or more vans made available for private use at the same time, tax is charged on the scale figure for each van. The standard amount will be reduced pro rata where the van is only available part of the year. As for company cars a £1 for £1 reduction is made for any contributions made by the employee towards the private use. Where a van is shared among several employees the standard amount is apportioned among the employees.

It is possible for employees to elect to pay tax on a flat benefit of £5 for every day that the van was made available to them for private use.

## 3.6  FREE USE OF ASSETS
(TA 1988, s 156)

A taxable benefit arises where an asset is made available by an employer for use by a director or P11D employee. The annual amount is 20% of the asset's market value when it was first made available for use by the employee, unless the asset was made available before 6 April 1980, in which case the annual value is 10%. Assets which may be involved include yachts, furniture, television sets, stereo equipment, company vans etc, ie virtually any asset apart from living accommodation and company cars. If the employer rents or hires the item concerned for a sum in excess of 20% of the asset's original market value, the higher rental charge is substituted as the assessable benefit. A deduction is allowed for any contribution or rental payable by the employee.

A further charge may arise if the ownership of assets is eventually transferred to the employee. The amount may be determined either by the market value of the asset at the time of transfer of ownership, or, where a higher figure results, by the original cost of the asset at the time it was first made available as a benefit for any person, less any amounts already charged as benefits in connection with the availability of the asset.

The second alternative does not apply to cars.

## Example – Transfer of assets

A company provides an employee with the use of a yacht which costs £40,000 with the employee paying a rental of £2,000 pa. After two years the yacht is sold to the employee for its second-hand market value of £20,000. The assessable benefit would be:

|  |  | Benefit £ |
|---|---|---|
| Year one: | £40,000 x 20% | 8,000 |
|  | *Less*: rental paid | (2,000) |
|  |  | 6,000 |
| Year two: | £40,000 x 20% | 8,000 |
|  | *Less*: rental paid | (2,000) |
|  |  | 6,000 |
| Year three: | Cost of yacht | 40,000 |
|  | *Less*: benefits assessed in years one and two | (12,000) |
|  | Amounts paid by employee | (24,000) |
|  |  | 4,000 |

Where an asset which has previously been made available to an individual is transferred to him (or to another employee), at a time when its market value is still high, it is possible that the total amount charged as a benefit for tax purposes exceeds the original cost. In other cases, the rules may operate to impose a high benefit charge upon the transfer of an asset despite the value of the asset having rapidly depreciated during the period of use.

Such rules must therefore be carefully considered when planning the provision of an asset for use by an employee or arranging for its transfer to the employee. It may be that transfer of ownership should be avoided where assets have a relatively short useful life if a tax-efficient remuneration package is desired.

## Example – Ownership of assets

A company provides employees with the use of suits which remain the property of the company. The suits cost £200 and have a useful life of two years, after which they are scrapped. An employee could therefore have an effective benefit of £200 but would be charged tax on only £40 for each of the two tax years.

## 3.7 BENEFICIAL LOANS
(TA 1988, s 160)

### 3.7.1 Type of loans which are caught

A charge generally arises for directors and P11D employees on the annual value of beneficial loan arrangements. The annual value of a loan is taken as interest at the 'official rate' less the amount of interest (if any) paid by the employee. The official rate is now set annually in advance and is 6.25% for 2000–01. An additional taxable benefit arises if the loan is subsequently written off or forgiven. The beneficial loan provisions can also apply if a loan is made to a member of an employee's family.

Moreover, the Revenue is able to assess benefits even though there may be no formal loan, where credit has been involved. In particular, a director who overdraws his current account with the company will be regarded as having obtained a loan.

Almost all loans by employers (and persons connected with them) will be caught as the legislation deems such loans to have been given by reason of the employment. Originally there was only a single exception in that this rule did not apply where the employee was related to the employer and it could be shown that the loan was given for family reasons. Since 6 April 1994, loans made by an employer whose business includes the lending of money to the general public do not give rise to a charge on the employees provided the loans are made on similar terms to the public.

### 3.7.2 Beneficial loans used for qualifying purpose

No charge arises in respect of a cheap loan where the money which has been borrowed has been applied for a qualifying purpose, eg for the purchase of shares in a close company in which the individual has a material interest or where he is employed full time in the conduct and management of the company's business.

### 3.7.3 *De minimis* exemption

All cheap or interest free loans made to an individual employee which do not exceed £5,000 are exempt. This figure excludes loans which qualify for tax relief such as loans of up to £30,000 for house purchase.

### 3.7.4 Employee loans written off

If the loan is written off, the amount forgiven is treated as assessable income for that year even if the person concerned is no longer employed by that company. The only exception here is if the loan is forgiven on the death of the employee.

Some care needs to be taken if it is decided to clear a loan by making an *ex gratia* or compensation payment to an employee upon the termination of the employment. An income tax liability will arise if the loan is formally written off. On the other hand, no liability normally arises if the employee receives a cheque as an *ex gratia* or compensation payment and uses that sum to clear his outstanding loan. It is recommended that professional advice be taken in such circumstances.

### 3.7.5 Further information

The Revenue has issued a leaflet, IR145, which explains how loans provided by employers to employees are taxed.

## 3.8 LIVING ACCOMMODATION
(TA 1988, ss 145–146)

### 3.8.1 Introduction

The income tax charge which generally applies where an employee is provided with accommodation (unless it is representative accommodation – see 3.4.8), depends upon whether the property is owned or rented by the employer. In the past, where the employer owned the property, the assessable amount was usually the gross annual value for rating purposes. Despite the abolition of domestic rates, this treatment continued to apply for properties on existing rating lists (see 3.4.7). For new properties, and those where there have been major improvements, the Revenue makes an estimate of what the gross annual value would have been had rates continued.

Where the property is rented by the employer, the assessable amount is the greater of the rent paid and the annual value as above. In addition a charge may arise on the annual value of any furniture and fixtures, and on any occupier's expenses borne by the company such as water rates, decorations, gardener's wages etc.

An additional charge may arise where the employer paid more than £75,000 to acquire the property. The amount assessable is a percentage of the excess of the cost of the property over £75,000. The percentage to be applied is the official rate of interest used for beneficial loans (see 3.7) as at the beginning of the tax year.

### Example – Charge on living accommodation in excess of £75,000

A company director occupies a property owned by the company which has a gross annual value of £2,000. The cost of the property in 1994 was £95,000. The director will be assessed on the following amount for 1999–2000:

|  | £ | £ |
|---|---|---|
| Gross annual value |  | 2,000 |
| Additional charge: |  |  |
| Cost in 1994 | 95,000 |  |
| *Less*: | (75,000) |  |
| Total | 20,000 |  |
| Assessment on £20,000 at |  |  |
| the official rate of 6.25% | 1,250 |  |
| Total |  | 3,250 |

## 3.8.2 Properties owned for more than six years

Where the property is made available to an employee after 31 March 1983, and it has been owned by the company for at least six years, the figure taken into account in computing the additional charge is the market value at the time it was made available rather than the cost. The actual cost (including improvements) to the employer is still used to determine whether or not the provisions apply. Consequently, properties whose actual cost was less than £75,000 (including the cost of any improvements) are not within the scope of this additional charge even if their market value exceeds £75,000. Where the actual cost exceeded £75,000, the additional charge is based on the market value.

### Example – Charge on living accommodation purchased over six years ago

In the example in 3.8.1, assume that the company has owned the property for more than six years and that in May 1994, when the director first occupies it, the market value is £191,000. As the original cost of the property exceeded £75,000, the director will be assessed on the following amount for 1999–2000:

|  | £ | £ |
|---|---|---|
| Gross annual value | 2,000 |  |
| Additional charge: |  |  |
| Market value in 1994 | 191,000 |  |
| *Less*: | (75,000) |  |
| Total | 116,000 |  |
| Assessment on £116,000 at |  |  |
| the official rate of 6.25% |  | 7,250 |
| Total |  | 9,250 |

### 3.8.3 Possible reduction in taxable amount

It may be possible to reduce the taxable amount where the employee is required to occupy a property which is larger than would normally be needed for his or her own purposes. In *Westcott v Bryan* (1969) 45 TC 476 a director was required to live in a large house so that he could entertain customers. He was allowed a reduction in the taxable amount to cover the relevant proportion of the annual value and the running expenses.

Some care is needed if it is intended to claim relief in this way. This claim succeeded because the house was larger than needed for the director and his family. It would not have succeeded had the property merely been more expensive than he would have chosen. It was also helpful that the directors of the company had approved board minutes setting out their requirement and the business reason for it.

Where part of the property is exclusively used for work, the taxable amount may be reduced on a pro rata basis. Revenue Helpsheet IR202 contains working sheets which enable you to compute your taxable benefits in this situation.

### 3.8.4 Possible increase in taxable benefit

It will sometimes be the case that an employer offers a choice: salary of £x or salary of £y plus a house. In this situation, the difference between £x and £y may be taxed if this exceeds the normal benefit in kind calculated along the lines set out in 3.8.1–3.8.2 above.

### 3.8.5 Holiday accommodation and foreign properties

Some employers buy holiday flats or cottages etc for use by staff. In practice, the Revenue generally apportions the assessable amount for the year among those employees who have occupied the property. The assessment can be reduced by letting the accommodation to third parties when it is not required by directors and employees.

A practical problem arises with regard to overseas properties. Because there is no rateable value, the benefit is the annual rent which the property would normally command on the open market. However, where this applies, there is normally no additional charge based on the excess of the cost of the property over £75,000 (see 3.8.1). An extra-statutory concession avoiding such a double charge was published on 28 November 1995.

## 3.9 MISCELLANEOUS BENEFITS

### Council tax

Where an employer pays the council tax on behalf of an employee, this will normally be chargeable as part of the employee's remuneration package, resulting in a charge to both income tax and NICs. The one exception to this is where the employee is a representative occupier (see 3.4.8).

## Mobile telephones (charge abolished from 6 April 1999)
(FA 1991, s 30)

Tax was charged on a standard amount of £200 pa per telephone where it was used privately. Private use means making personal calls or accepting reverse charge calls; it does not include receiving normal personal calls.

The tax charge did not arise where the employee was required to make good the whole cost of any private use. The Revenue interprets these provisions so that the requirement to make good the full costs of private calls must have existed throughout the year.

The charge was made on a proportionate basis where the telephone was not available for part of the tax year. However, unless the phone was withdrawn for at least 30 consecutive days, short periods of non-availability were ignored.

## Telephone rental

The Revenue treats the full amount of the rental paid by the employer as a taxable benefit in kind even though the telephone may be partly (or mainly) used for business calls. The decision in *Lucas v Cattell* (1972) 48 TC 353 was that the expenditure on rental had a dual purpose (ie that a telephone is intended to be used for both business and personal use) and therefore no part of it was allowable.

## Liability insurance and payment of uninsured liabilities

FA 1995 provides that employees shall not be subject to tax on a benefit in kind where their employer pays premiums on items such as a directors' and officers' liability insurance or a professional indemnity insurance policy. Furthermore, the Act also provides that payment of an employee's uninsured liabilities will not give rise to a benefit in kind provided they arise from the employee's work. This is subject to the overriding requirement that the liabilities could have been insured against and this means that those arising from, for example, criminal convictions cannot attract relief.

## Medical insurance
(TA 1988, s 155(6))

The cost of medical insurance is normally assessable on P11D employees. Where the employer has a group scheme, a proportion of the total premiums is related to individual employees. There is an exception in that the premiums are exempt to the extent that they provide cover for an employee working outside the UK.

## Club subscriptions

A benefit in kind is deemed to arise where an employer pays or reimburses an employee's subscription to a club, even though the employee may only belong to the club in order to entertain the employer's customers.

## In-house tax and financial advice

This is a type of expenditure which the Revenue has ignored in the past, but certain Inspectors of Taxes are now treating this as a benefit in kind where the cost can clearly be allocated to particular employees. Similarly the Revenue will seek to assess directors on a benefit in kind where work on their personal taxation affairs has been carried out by the company's auditors, the cost being recovered in whole or in part from the company.

## Christmas parties and other functions

The Revenue does not assess a benefit in respect of 'modest' expenditure on a Christmas party for staff, provided the party is open to all staff. The limit for expenditure to be regarded as modest in this context is currently £75 per head (£50 up to 1994–95). If the cost (including VAT) amounts to £76 or more, the whole amount is taxable, not just the excess. Although this rule is generally attributed to Christmas parties, it may apply to a function at another time of year. Since 1995–96 the £75 annual 'allowance' can be used to cover the cost of more than one function.

## Legal fees

There may be expenditure which is incurred for the benefit of the company's business but nevertheless is deemed to give rise to a benefit in kind. A leading case in this connection concerned a director of a company who was accused of dangerous driving. It was necessary for the company's business that he should not be imprisoned and the company paid his legal expenses. Although the lawyers engaged by the company were more expensive than the director would have used himself, the expenditure by the company was treated as a benefit in kind.

## Outplacement counselling
(FA 1993, s 108)

The value of outplacement services provided to employees made redundant is exempt from income tax. Such services may include assistance with CVs, job searches, office equipment provisions and advice on interview skills.

## Goods and services provided at a discount to the normal price ('in-house benefits')

Where employees are allowed to purchase goods or services from their employer, no tax charge arises provided they pay an amount equal to the employer's cost. The House of Lords eventually decided that 'cost' meant marginal cost and not average cost (*Pepper v Hart* [1992] STC 898). This will normally produce a significantly lower benefit.

Following this case the Revenue published a statement of practice with regard to teachers, employees within the transport industry and other employees who receive goods or services from their employer. It stated that the decision in *Pepper v Hart* means that:

(1) rail or bus travel by employees on terms which do not displace fare-paying passengers involves no or negligible additional costs;
(2) goods sold at a discount which leave employees paying at least the wholesale price involve no or negligible net benefit;
(3) where teachers pay 15% or more of a school's normal fees, there is no taxable benefit;
(4) professional services which do not require additional employees or partners (eg legal and financial services) have no or negligible cost to the employer (provided the employee meets the cost of any disbursements).

### Funded Unapproved Retirement Benefit Schemes (FURBS)
(TA 1988, s 595)

Some employers make contributions to unapproved pension schemes, or FURBS. The creation of the scheme has to be reported to the company's Inspector of Taxes within three months. The employer's contributions also need to be reported on Form P11D and the employee is treated as if he had received a benefit the cost of which is equal to the amount paid into the FURBS. For further details on FURBS, see 12.12.

### Making good benefits in kind for previous years

The cash equivalent of any benefit chargeable to tax under TA 1988, s 156 is the cost of the benefit 'less so much (if any) of it as is made good by the employee to those providing the benefit'. The Revenue accepts that there is no time limit for making good and, provided the relevant year's assessment has not been determined, there could be some merit in the person concerned taking further remuneration now and using the net cash left to him after PAYE to make good benefits provided for earlier years. This could be a particularly good idea where a director of a family company is faced with a Schedule E assessment plus penalties and interest in respect of prior year incorrect returns because benefits have not been reported properly in the past.

146

Where beneficial loans are concerned, however, the Revenue's view is that the cash equivalent can only be reduced by a payment in a later year if the interest is paid under an obligation which existed at the time of the loan. Also, the scale benefit on a mobile phone can be reduced by a payment from the employee only if he was required to make the contribution and paid it during the tax year concerned.

## 3.10 PROFIT-RELATED PAY
(TA 1988, ss 169–171)

The rules on profit-related pay schemes are complex in so far as they concern the companies which set up a scheme. They are relatively straightforward from the point of view of the employee.

### 3.10.1 PRP exempt from income tax
Where an individual receives profit-related pay (PRP) under a registered scheme, all or part of the PRP is exempt from income tax. The exemption is available on the lowest of:

(1) 20% of total remuneration for the year;
(2) £4,000;
(3) the actual PRP received in the tax year.

Where an individual participates in more than one PRP scheme, the £4,000 exemption has to be divided between the amounts payable under each PRP scheme.

PRP forms part of a director or employee's earnings for NICs.

### 3.10.2 Conditions required for a PRP scheme to be registered
The following conditions need to be satisfied before the Revenue will register a PRP scheme:

(1) The scheme rules should provide for at least 80% of relevant employees to participate. Relevant employees are those who are in the pay unit concerned (these need not necessarily be the company as a whole but could, for example, be a division within the company).
(2) The PRP legislation requires that employees must participate 'on similar terms'. This does not necessarily mean that all employees should receive the same amount (although a scheme could be established on such a basis). Instead, the scheme rules may provide for payments to vary in order to reflect the following factors:
    (a) levels of remuneration;
    (b) length of service;
    (c) hours worked;
    (d) other similar objective factors.

(3) Individuals who have more than a 25% shareholding in a company (either alone or taken together with associates) cannot participate in a PRP scheme.

### 3.10.3 **PRP final year**

PRP became a victim of its own success and FA 1997 phased out the relief over a four-year period by reducing the ceiling on the relief (see 3.10.1 above). The maximum amount which may be exempt is as follows:

Phase 1 – profit periods commencing prior to 1 Jan 1998: £4,000;
Phase 2 – profit periods commencing between 1 Jan 1998 and 31 Dec 1998: £2,000;
Phase 3 – profit periods commencing between 1 Jan 1999 and 31 Dec 1999: £1,000;
Phase 4 – profit periods commencing on or after 1 Jan 2000: nil.

## 3.11  GIFTS OF SHARES

A gift of shares to an employee will normally be a taxable benefit, the charge being based on the market value of the shares. Much the same applies where an employee buys shares for less than their real market value. If the shares are given to the employee by a shareholder, he will normally be treated as if he had made a disposal of the shares at their market value, and may therefore be liable for CGT.

The tax position where an employee is allowed to subscribe for new shares at an undervalue is broadly the same. The employee will be taxed on the difference between the amount that he pays to subscribe for the shares and their market value. However, dealing with matters in this way will usually avoid any CGT problems for the shareholders (since there is no disposal by the existing shareholders or the company, merely an issue of new shares).

A company needs to report the acquisition of shares by an employee within 30 days of the end of the relevant tax year to:

Inland Revenue
Employee Share Schemes Unit
Savings and Investment Division
First Floor, South West Wing
Bush House, Strand
London WC2B 4RD

PAYE will need to be accounted for if the shares are marketable securities or trading arrangements are in place.

## 3.12 PROFIT-SHARING SCHEMES
(TA 1988, ss 186–187)

These operate by means of a trust, with the trustees receiving payments from the company's profits to enable them to buy shares on behalf of the employees. In computing its profits, the company should get a deduction for the sums paid so long as the trustees apply the money in accordance with the approved scheme rules. The amount which may be appropriated to an employee under the scheme cannot exceed £3,000 or, if greater, 10% of the employee's remuneration for PAYE purposes, with an overall limit of £8,000.

The employee will be entitled to dividends paid on the shares during the period of retention by the trustees. The trustees must retain the shares for a period of two years; if the shares are then retained by the trustees for a further year, there will be no income tax charge on him. If they are sold by the employee within three years of appropriation, an income tax charge will arise based on the 'locked-in value', ie the lower of the market value of the shares when they were appropriated by the trust fund or the sale proceeds. This charge is reduced by 50% where the individual is no longer an employee because of his leaving through injury, disability, redundancy or reaching pensionable age.

Provided that the shares are held in trust for three years, normally the only liability arising to the employee will be to CGT when he disposes of the shares appropriated to him. The capital gains liability will arise on the difference between the disposal proceeds of these shares less their open market value on the day on which they were appropriated to him. The growth in value from the date of acquisition by the trust to the date of appropriation is tax free.

For further details, see Revenue leaflet IR95.

### Anti-avoidance

FA 2000 contains special rules which were introduced in order to prevent approved profit-sharing schemes being used as a substitute for PRP. With effect from 21 March 2000, schemes may not be approved if they involve shares in service companies which provide services to a business whose proprietors control the service company. Similarly, a scheme may not involve shares which are subject to special restrictions which do not apply to all ordinary shares.

## 3.13 NEW ALL-EMPLOYEE SHARE SCHEMES

FA 2000 has established a new type of share scheme which enjoys a much more generous range of tax reliefs than any previous all-employee share scheme. The new scheme may involve one or more of the following elements:

- Free shares
- Partnership shares
- Matching shares.

The basic principle behind this scheme is that all employees should participate on similar terms. However, if an employer awards free shares the award may be partly or wholly by reference to performance targets. Under the scheme, shares in the employing company or the holding company of a group are acquired by trustees. No Schedule E tax or NICs are payable on the award of shares. All income and capital growth which arises while the shares are held by the trustees will normally be tax free. The shares must be fully paid-up ordinary shares in a company which is not controlled by another company or shares in a quoted subsidiary of a company which is not a close company (see 24.12).

## Free shares

An employee may be awarded free shares with a value of up to £3,000 pa. The shares may be awarded partly by reference to criteria based on salary, length of service etc. In such a case, other employees may be awarded shares by reference to performance provided the highest performance-linked award does not exceed four times the highest award by reference to non-performance linked criteria. In other cases (eg where all awards are by reference to performance), the employer must demonstrate to the Revenue's satisfaction that the performance targets are broadly comparable.

Wherever awards are to be made by reference to performance, the targets and other criteria must be communicated to employees in advance. Performance criteria may be linked to individual, team, divisional or corporate performance.

Free shares must be held by the trustees for a period of between three and five years. Shares can be awarded so that they will be forfeited if the employee leaves within three years, but this is not an essential feature of a scheme; it is up to the employer whether such a rule should apply.

## Partnership shares

Employees may relinquish up to £1,500 of their pay in return for 'partnership' shares being acquired by the trustees on their behalf. No Schedule E tax or NICs arise on salary foregone in this way but the employing company receives a deduction in arriving at its taxable profits equal to the amount which is relinquished. The partnership shares cannot be subject to forfeiture but the rules of a scheme can require the trustees to pay out on the employee leaving.

Where an employee withdraws from the scheme within three years, income tax and NICs are payable on the shares' market value at the date of withdrawal. Where he withdraws after three but before five years have elapsed, the employee is charged on the lower of the initial value of the shares or their market value at the time that he withdraws.

Where an employment comes to an end because of disability or redundancy, the shares may be withdrawn tax free even if this happens within the three-year period.

### Matching shares

If an employer so wishes, matching shares can be awarded to employees on a basis of up to 2:1 (ie shares worth £3,000 for an employee who relinquished salary of £1,500 in order to 'buy' partnership shares worth £1,500). An award of matching shares may be made on the basis that they are forfeited if the employee leaves within three years or withdraws his partnership shares during that period.

### Dividends

The legislation gives employers a choice as to whether to offer dividend reinvestment. If dividends are paid out they will be taxable income for the employees. On the other hand, dividends may be reinvested tax free up to £1,500 pa.

## 3.14 NON-APPROVED SHARE OPTIONS
(TA 1988, ss 135 and 162; FA 1988, ss 77–87)

### 3.14.1 Introduction

A Schedule E income tax charge may arise on the exercise of a share option which was granted by reason of the individual's office or employment. The legislation was introduced on a piecemeal basis and it is often difficult to discern any clear or logical structure or principles which underlie the legislation.

### 3.14.2 Non-approved share options
(TA 1988, s 135)

A tax charge may arise either on the grant or on the exercise of the option.

### Grant of the option

A charge may arise only if the option has a potential life of more than ten years (seven years for options granted before 17 March 1998). Even if the option is capable of being exercised more than ten years later, the Revenue is unlikely to assess a value greater than the difference between the value of the shares at the time the option is granted and the aggregate of the amount (if any) paid for the grant of option and the amount payable under the option.

## Exercise of the option

A person who is subject to tax under Schedule E Case I (see 3.1.1) may be subject to an income tax charge when he exercises a non-approved share option which has been granted to him by reason of his office or employment. The charge is not dependent upon his selling the shares but arises on any profit or gain that he is deemed to have made by exercising the option. Normally the profit will be simply the difference between the shares' market value at the time that he exercises his option and the price payable under the option.

## Example – Exercise of share options

*A* was granted an option to acquire 1,000 shares in XYZ Ltd at a price of £2 per share. After five years have elapsed, he exercises the option and pays £2,000 to acquire the 1,000 shares. By this time the shares have grown in value to £5 per share. *A* will be assessed for the year in which he exercises the option. His profit will be assessed as £3,000, ie:

|  | £ |
|---|---|
| Market value of 1,000 shares | 5,000 |
| *Less*: amount paid | (2,000) |
|  | 3,000 |

If the employee agrees to pay his employer's NICs on the profit from exercising the option, the NICs are deducted in arriving at the taxable amount.

## 3.14.3 Residence status of the employee

No charge arises under these provisions if the employee was not resident and ordinarily resident in the UK at the date that the option was granted. This is because the individual has to be UK-resident and ordinarily resident if he is to be chargeable to tax under of Schedule E Case I. The charge will, however, still arise where an individual who was resident and ordinarily resident when the option was granted ceases to be UK-resident before the option is exercised.

### 3.14.4 Other employee share options
(TA 1988, s 162)

Where an individual exercises an option which was granted to him as an employee, but at a time when he was not chargeable to tax under Schedule E Case I, and he retains the shares, an income tax charge may arise on the eventual disposal of the shares. The legislation on beneficial loans contains deeming provisions which treat the difference between the market value of the shares at the time that the option is exercised and the amount payable to exercise the option as if it were a loan. On a subsequent sale or disposal of the shares the loan is deemed to be written off and a Schedule E charge arises if the individual is resident in the UK at that time. If you think that you may be in this situation, you should seek professional advice.

### 3.14.5 Reporting requirements

Ask your accountant to obtain a copy of *Tax Bulletin* February 1994 for your reference. The grant or exercise of options will need to be notified by 6 May following the end of the tax year.

PAYE will need to be accounted for on profits from options which are both granted and exercised after 25 November 1996 and where the shares are marketable securities or trading arrangements are in place.

## 3.15 APPROVED SHARE OPTION SCHEMES
(TA 1988, s 185 and Sched 9)

### 3.15.1 Introduction

There are two main types of approved share option schemes for employees: save as you earn (SAYE) linked share option schemes and executive share option schemes.

Approved SAYE linked share option schemes were introduced in 1980. The main features of these schemes are that there is a limit on the value of the shares which may be allocated to an employee and that participation in the scheme must be open to all full-time employees who have completed five years' service.

In 1984 the Government introduced a further category of approved share options intended to cover special arrangements for senior executives. The maximum amounts involved are much more generous and there is no requirement that the option be granted to all employees.

It is possible for an employer to establish both types of scheme and, indeed, to grant non-approved share options as well.

## 3.15.2 Approved SAYE linked share option schemes

These schemes entail the grant of an option for employees to purchase company shares at a price which must not be 'manifestly less' than 80% of their market value at the time that the options are granted. The employee is required to take out an SAYE linked savings scheme (maximum £250 per month) and may use the proceeds to exercise the share option three, five or seven years later, depending upon the rules of the particular scheme. No income tax liability arises on the grant of the options or upon their exercise. CGT is charged on an eventual disposal of the shares.

For further details obtain a copy of the Revenue leaflet IR97.

## 3.15.3 Executive share option schemes

The general principle is that an income tax charge may arise on the exercise of a share option, but certain approved share option schemes may be established which avoid such an income tax liability. CGT may still apply but only on a subsequent disposal of the shares concerned.

## 3.15.4 Conditions for approval

In order to receive Revenue approval, the following conditions must be satisfied:

(1) Participation in the scheme must be open only to full-time directors or employees or to part-time employees working at least 20 hours a week. Part-time directors may not participate in this scheme. The Inland Revenue has indicated that it regards a director who works 25 hours per week as full-time. The employer may choose which of the employees are to be permitted to participate in the scheme.

(2) Where the employer is a close company, no participant must own (or be entitled to acquire as a result of the grant of the option) more than 10% of the company's shares. Furthermore no individual who has owned more than 10% of the company's shares within the previous 12 months is able to participate.

(3) The price at which the option is to be exercised must not be 'manifestly less' than the value of the shares at the time that the option is granted.

(4) There is a limit on the number of shares over which a particular employee may be granted options. The scheme must limit the employee's options to shares with a market value at the time that the options are granted which does not exceed £30,000.

(5) The shares issued under the scheme must be fully paid ordinary shares of the company or its parent company. They must either be shares quoted on a recognised stock exchange or shares in a non-close company which is controlled by a quoted company or shares in a company not under the control of another company.

(6) Options must not be transferable. The exemption from income tax applies only to options which are exercised between three and ten years after they are granted. Moreover, there is an income tax charge on individuals who exercise options under the scheme more than once every three years. This three-year time limit is waived if a director or employee dies, in which case the option must be exercised by the personal representatives within one year of death.

You may find it helpful to obtain a copy of Revenue leaflet IR101.

### 3.15.5 Options granted before 17 July 1995

Different rules applied up to 17 July 1995. Basically an executive could be granted approved options over shares with a market value of up to four times his remuneration. Furthermore, in certain circumstances, options could be granted at a discount of up to 15% on the market value.

Profits realised from the exercise of such options are still exempt from income tax (provided the other conditions in 3.15.4 are satisfied).

## 3.16 RESTRICTED SHARES AND SHARES IN SUBSIDIARY COMPANIES
(FA 1988, ss 77–87)

### 3.16.1 General

FA 1988 contains provisions which may apply to any shares acquired by reason of an individual's employment which is charged under Schedule E Case I (see 3.1.1). The legislation may apply to any shares acquired in this way whether by exercise of an option, subscription for new shares or purchase of existing shares. Liability to tax under Schedule E may arise:

(1) when any restrictions affecting the employee's shares are removed; or
(2) when the employee shareholder receives any special benefit by virtue of ownership; or
(3) where the shares are in a 'dependent subsidiary'.

Tax charged in this way can be especially serious as the individual may not have realised any cash.

### 3.16.2 Removal of restrictions

Tax may be charged on the increase in value which accrues from the removal of restrictions. There are, however, certain circumstances in which restrictions can be removed without a tax charge – see the flow chart overleaf.

## Does removal of restrictions mean there is an income tax charge under Schedule E?

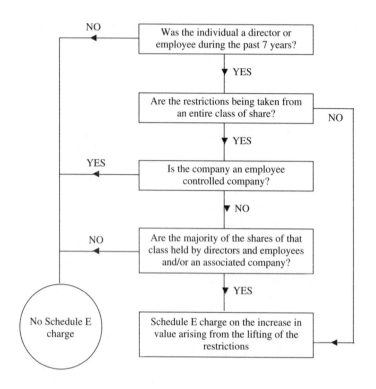

### Example of tax charge on removal of restrictions

X acquires 1,000 shares in the company for which he works. The shares do not have any rights to dividend. Two years later, the restrictions are removed so that the shares have normal dividend rights. Suppose the figures work out like this:

| | |
|---|---|
| Value of shares with full dividend rights | £3 per share |
| Value of shares with no dividend rights | £1 per share |
| Increase in value from removal of restrictions | £2 per share |

X will therefore be taxed on £2,000 (1,000 x £2 per share)

### 3.16.3 Shares in a dependent subsidiary

A company is regarded as a dependent subsidiary if there is any significant amount of trading with the parent company or another member of the group. A company which is a subsidiary is deemed to be a dependent subsidiary unless the directors certify each year that it is not and the auditors confirm their agreement to this. There is a two-year deadline for the directors to issue their certificate; if they fail to do so the subsidiary is automatically regarded as a dependent subsidiary. Attempts to persuade the Revenue to extend this period have been consistently rebuffed.

Where an employee holds shares in a dependent subsidiary, a tax charge may arise on the growth in the value which takes place at the earliest of the following times:

(1) the time when he actually disposes of the shares;
(2) the date that the company ceases to be a dependent subsidiary;
(3) the expiry of seven years from the date of acquisition.

A charge may arise even though the company was not a dependent subsidiary when the person acquired his shares if it subsequently becomes a dependent subsidiary.

The self-assessment return pack contains some very useful 'helpsheets' which should enable you to compute your taxable benefit.

### 3.16.4 Long-term incentive plans

FA 1998 introduced two new provisions.

#### Shares subject to forfeiture

An award of shares to employees can be subject to certain targets being met, or sometimes the shares are given at the outset on condition that they will be forfeited if a target is not met. The risk of forfeiture is lifted when a target is met and the employee then becomes the unconditional owner of the shares.

The tax position was clarified by FA 1998. There will be a charge to tax when shares are first awarded if there is a risk of forfeiture more than five years after they are first awarded. Otherwise there is no charge to income tax until the risk of forfeiture is lifted or, if sooner, when the shares are sold.

These provisions apply to shares awarded on or after 17 March 1998. Advice on the treatment of shares awarded prior to 17 March is contained in *Tax Bulletin* June 1998.

#### Convertible shares

An income tax charge will arise on the value of any new class of shares, less an allowance for any income tax already paid, when a share conversion takes place. This is designed to cover schemes where an employee receives shares with a low value which are later converted to shares with a much higher value.

These provisions apply to shares awarded on or after 17 March 1998 but will not normally apply if the majority of the shares of the class converting are held by people who are not employees or directors.

PAYE will also have to be operated where any shares or conversions are readily convertible assets.

## 3.17 ENTERPRISE MANAGEMENT INCENTIVES (EMI)

Key aspects of the new EMI option scheme are as follows:

(1) Share options can be issued to up to 15 key employees.
(2) The shares over which options are granted can have a value of up to £100,000 per employee. This refers to the value at the time the options are granted.
(3) The price at which options may be exercised may be more or less than market value at the time that the options are granted.
(4) The only income tax charge is on exercise of the options and is equal to the difference between the shares' market value at the time of grant less the exercise price. If the options are granted at the market value then no tax will be payable.
(5) If the shares are readily convertible assets at the time that the option is exercised, NICs will be charged at 12.2% on the same basis as the income tax charge described above. If the options were issued at market value then there will be no charge.
(6) There are also significant CGT benefits for the employees. The shares acquired by the employees will qualify for the business asset rate of taper relief. Taper relief provides relief for CGT for individuals based on the length of ownership. Under the EMI rules the period of ownership is deemed to start from when the share options are granted. The rules for other share option schemes are that the period of ownership starts when the shares are acquired. Overall this means that provided the shares are sold four years after the options are granted (calculated by income tax year), the CGT rate will be 10%.

Only certain companies will be able to operate the scheme, and certain employees may be ineligible. A summary of the rules is as follows:

(a) The company must be independent and not under the control of another company
(b) The company must be carrying on a qualifying trade defined as for EIS purposes (see 11.6.4). This trade must be carried on mainly in the UK.
(c) The company's gross assets cannot exceed £15m at the time the options are granted.
(d) The employee must be employed for at least 25 hours per week, or if less 75% of his working time.
(e) The employee must not own more than 30% of the shares in the company.

(f)  An employee can only participate in one Revenue-approved share option scheme.

## 3.18 OPTIONS TO ACQUIRE COMPANY ASSETS

The treatment of non-approved employee share options can be disadvantageous but this is due to specific legislation on share options; the rules governing options involving other assets are quite different. An income tax charge may arise at the time that an option is granted if the option has a market value. However, if the price at which the option may be exercised is higher than the asset's present market value, it is arguable that the option has little or no value at the time that it is granted.

No Schedule E income tax charge would normally arise upon the exercise of the option. Furthermore, on a subsequent disposal of the asset there would normally be liability only for CGT on the profit over the amount paid. Although special care needs to be taken where the director or employee is connected (perhaps as a shareholder) with the company which grants the option, this type of option can provide substantial benefits.

### Example – Option to acquire assets

A company director, who is not a shareholder, is granted the option to purchase surplus development land owned by the company for £150,000 at any time during a period of ten years. The land has a market value of only £125,000 at the time the option is granted and the option, therefore, has only a small value at that time. When the option is exercised the land has a market value of £250,000 and the director has in effect acquired a capital asset at a discount of £100,000 on its current market value. This discount would not normally be subject to income tax.

## 3.19 GOLDEN HALLOS

These are payments made to induce a prospective employee to take up employment with the company and are occasionally not taxable. A case involving a chartered accountant, *Pritchard v Arundale* (1971) 47 TC 680, concerned the senior partner in a firm of chartered accountants who was approached by a client to leave his practice and become a director of that client's company. In order to induce him to do this, he was given shares in the company which were held to be not a reward for services to be rendered in the future but an inducement to leave his practice and take up the employment. It was therefore not taxable.

Another case, *Vaughan-Neil v IRC* [1979] STC 644, concerned a barrister who received £40,000 to induce him to give up practising as a barrister and join a company as its 'in-house adviser'. Once again it was held that the payment was not taxable. By contrast, in *Glantre Engineering Ltd v Goodhand* [1983] STC 1, a payment by an engineering company to induce an employee of a firm of accountants to join them was held to be taxable.

The principles which emerge from these three cases are as follows:

(1) it must be clear from the facts that the payment is an inducement and not a reward for future services;
(2) the payment must not be returnable if the person does not take up the employment; and
(3) it is probably more likely that the payment will be accepted as non-taxable if the recipient has previously been in practice or self-employed rather than an employee of another company.

*Shilton v Wilmshurst* [1991] STC 88 extended these principles by deciding that a payment made by a football club to a footballer about to transfer as an inducement to him to join his new club was taxable. The House of Lords held that an emolument from an employment meant an emolument for being or becoming an employee and therefore would include a sum paid by a third party as an inducement to enter into a contract of employment to perform services in the future. It was not necessary for the payer to have any interest in the performance of those services.

## 3.20 RESTRICTIVE COVENANTS
(FA 1988, s 73)

Where the present, past or future holder of an office or employment gives an undertaking which restricts his conduct or activities, any sum paid in respect of that restrictive covenant is treated as remuneration from the office or employment for the year in which the payment is received. This rule applies even where the restrictive covenant is not legally valid. In some cases, valuable consideration other than money is given for the restrictive covenant and in such a situation a sum equal to the value of that consideration is treated as having been paid. The payment may not necessarily come from the employer and so a payment to an employee which was made by a major shareholder in a family company might well be caught under these provisions.

## 3.21 REDUNDANCY PAYMENTS
(TA 1988, s 579)

A statutory redundancy payment made under the Employment Protection (Consolidation) Act 1978 is exempt from tax although it may need to be taken into account in computing the tax payable on a termination payment (see 3.22). Payment to an employee under a non-statutory redundancy scheme is generally treated by the Revenue as exempt under SP1/94 where the following conditions are satisfied:

(1) payments are made only on accounts of redundancy as defined in Employment Protection (Consolidation) Act 1978, s 81;
(2) the individual has at least two years' continuous service;
(3) payments are made to all relevant employees and not merely to a selected group of employees;
(4) the payments are not excessively large in relation to earnings and length of service.

In *Mairs v Haughey* [1993] STC 569, the Revenue sought to tax a payment made to an employee for giving up contingent redundancy rights. The Revenue argued that the payment constituted an emolument of the employment, but it was held that a redundancy payment is not an emolument and a lump sum paid in lieu of a right to receive such a redundancy payment is equally not an emolument. This case has also cast doubt on the view generally held within the Revenue that a termination payment is always taxable where the employee is contractually entitled to it.

## 3.22 GOLDEN HANDSHAKES AND OTHER TERMINATION PAYMENTS
(TA 1988, s 148)

### 3.22.1 Introduction

Where a director's or employee's contract of service is terminated, it may be possible for a compensation payment or ex gratia payment to be made which is either wholly or partly tax free provided the employee is not entitled to the compensation under a contract of service and the payment is not deemed to be a benefit under a retirement benefit scheme. Where the individual receives compensation under a term of his contract of employment, the Revenue's view is that it is taxable under Schedule E in the usual way. A payment made to a director as compensation for accepting a reduced salary or any other variation of his service contract is not regarded as a termination payment, and the amount received is normally taxable in full.

### 3.22.2 Exemptions from the charge under s 148

There are various types of termination payment which are exempt:

(1) Payments made under TA 1988, s 188 because of termination of employment through death, injury or disability. Disability covers not only a condition arising from a sudden affliction but also covers a continuing incapacity to perform the duties of an office or employment

because of the culmination of a process of deterioration of physical or mental health caused by chronic illness (see SP10/81).

(2) Terminal grants and gratuities to members of HM forces.

(3) Lump sum payments from Commonwealth government superannuation schemes or compensation for loss of career due to constitutional changes in Commonwealth countries.

(4) A special contribution by an employer into an approved retirement benefit scheme.

(5) A lump sum payment under TA 1988, s 188(3) where the employment has constituted foreign service which exceeds the following limits:

  (a) three-quarters of the whole period of service;

  (b) the last ten years;

  (c) one-half of the period of service provided that this amounted to at least 20 years and subject to at least ten of the last 20 years of service being foreign service.

'Foreign' service is defined as meaning a period of service during which the earnings were not assessable under Schedule E Case I either because the individual was not resident in the UK or because the 100% deduction was available because the period spent working overseas exceeded 365 days (see 3.23).

### 3.22.3 Basic £30,000 exemption
(TA 1988, s 188(4))

Where a termination payment is not wholly exempt, the first £30,000 is normally free from tax and only the balance is chargeable. Where an individual receives both statutory redundancy payments and a termination payment, the amount of the statutory redundancy payments uses up part of the £30,000 exemption and only the balance is available to cover part of the termination payment.

### 3.22.4 Employment includes a period of foreign service

The £30,000 exemption may be increased where the employment has included 'foreign service'.

#### Example – Increased exemption due to foreign service

B was non-resident in the UK from 1980 to 1988. He then qualified for the 100% deduction from1988 to 1990, so that he was not subject to UK tax on his salary even though he was resident. He retired in December 2001 and received compensation of £80,000. The exemption is found by using the fraction:

$$\frac{\text{Foreign service}}{\text{Total period of employment}}, \text{ ie in this case } \frac{10 \text{ years}}{21 \text{ years}}$$

This fraction is applied to the amount of the golden handshake after deduction of the £30,000 exemption. The taxable amount would be arrived at as follows:

|  | £ |
|---|---|
| Compensation | 80,000 |
| *Less*: 'normal exemption' | (30,000) |
|  | 50,000 |
| ¹⁰⁄₂₁ thereof | (23,809) |
| Taxable amount | 26,191 |

## 3.22.5 Year for which a termination payment may be taxed

Until recently, the time when a termination payment is made has not affected the tax liability as it has always been treated as taxable income for the year in which the employment is terminated. However, from 1998–99 onwards, it is the year of receipt that counts and termination payments are taxed as income of the year in which they are received.

## 3.22.6 Taxation of continuing payments and benefits

Redundancy and other termination settlements often include provisions for payments to be made or benefits to continue after termination. The legislation which applied up to 5 April 1998 was regarded as unfair and to some extent unworkable, as what was taxed was the value of the promise to provide the ongoing benefits rather than the benefits themselves. Valuing the entitlement of a future benefit could be difficult and normally involved a significant up-front tax charge at a time when the former employee could least afford it. The assessment, once finalised, could not later be adjusted to reflect the level of benefit actually enjoyed or received.

Where cash was paid after termination of the employment, it was also assessed in the year of termination but in practice a charge could not arise before the payment was made. A former employee's tax liability for the year of termination might therefore have to be revised on several occasions if he continued to receive payments in later years. This caused problems under self-assessment which is designed to provide certainty for the taxpayer. It required the taxpayer to self-assess by estimating the value of the right to receive continuing benefits.

An optional alternative approach was applied for 1996–97 and 1997–98 allowing the ex-employee to elect for ongoing benefits to be taxed only to the extent that they are received. However, the tax charge still arose in respect of the year of termination, not the year of receipt.

The new rules should be fairer and simpler and involve less l administrative costs for employers. Benefits are taxable only as they arise: both benefits and payments will be taxable in the year when received or enjoyed (not in the year of termination).

### Example – Benefits in kind following redundancy

*M* is made redundant on 6 October 1999 and receives a lump sum of £20,000 plus a further £20,000 on 6 April 2000. She also continues in the company medical insurance scheme for 18 months at an ongoing cost to the employer of £350 in 1999–2000 and £650 in 2000–01.

In 1999–2000 *M* receives a combined redundancy package of £20,350 which is covered by the £30,000 exemption. The balance of £9,650 exemption is carried forward to the following year. In 2000–01 she receives the balance of the package of £20,650, of which £9,650 is exempt. The medical benefit of £650 is covered by the balance of the exemption as is £9,000 of the cash payment, leaving £11,000 to be taxed at the basic rate under PAYE.

## 3.22.7 *Ex gratia* payments

There has been concern that *ex gratia* payments may be subject to tax under Schedule E as unapproved retirement benefits taxable under TA 1988, s 596A. If this charge arises, the £30,000 exemption is not available. The Revenue issued SP13/91 in October 1991 and has subsequently clarified the position. An *ex gratia* payment is normally regarded as a retirement benefit taxable under s 596A only where it is paid in connection with an individual's retirement. The Revenue has also given the following guidelines on hypothetical situations:

(1) A person who has worked for a company for 20 years leaves at age 54 to take a senior executive position in another company – 'golden handshake'.

(2) A long-service employee leaves to take a senior executive position in another company at the age of 60 – borderline, probably retirement.

(3) A division of a company is sold and the 55-year-old manager responsible for running it leaves to take a job with the purchaser – 'golden handshake'.

(4) A person in his 50s has a heart attack and is advised by his doctor to leave and seek a less stressful position – 'golden handshake'.

(5) An employee aged 35 is involved in an accident and suffers disabilities that make him unable to continue with his job – 'golden handshake'.

(6) An employee aged 50 leaves to take a job nearer home to be able to nurse her aged parents – borderline, 'golden handshake'. If the employee did not take a new job, or was nearer normal retirement age, this situation would be treated as retirement.

## 3.22.8 Payments in lieu of notice (PILONs)

Payments in lieu of notice are often referred to as 'PILONs'. They have increasingly featured in employment contracts in recent years as employees have tried to formalise their rights and employers have wanted to be able to enforce restrictive covenants and prevent ex-employees using confidential information that they have acquired in the course of their employment. The Inland Revenue has set out its opinion in a lengthy article in *Tax Bulletin* August 1996. In large measure, the Revenue's interpretations have been upheld by the courts (see *EMI Electronics Group Ltd v Coldicott*).

The term 'PILON' is sometimes loosely used to include payments to employees on 'garden leave'. This is not correct as an employee who is on garden leave is still an employee. He cannot take another job until the end of the notice period. All that has changed is that he is not required to carry out any duties. Payments to such an employee are taxable in the normal way and the employer should deduct tax under PAYE.

There are also situations where the employee's service contract actually provides for a PILON, usually at the employer's option. The Revenue view is that where an employer decides to make a PILON, the payment is made under the contract rather than as compensation for the contract having been broken. As such, it remains taxable in full and PAYE deductions should be made.

Rather more controversially, the Revenue argues that there may be an implied term to an employment contract where an employer customarily makes PILONs. This is common in certain industries (IT, stockbroking and asset management) where the last thing that an employer wants is for an employee who is serving out a notice period to have continued access to confidential information (or clients). You should take professional advice if you are an employer who has a history of regularly making PILONs.

Virtually the only circumstances in which you can be completely confident that a PILON will be treated as a golden handshake (see 3.22.1) is where the payment is a 'one off' exception to your normal rule, and there is no reference to the possibility of such a payment in the service contract or related documents such as the staff handbook. In this situation, the first £30,000 will normally be exempt from tax.

## 3.23 SPECIAL RULES FOR WORKING OUTSIDE THE UK ABOLISHED ON 17 MARCH 1998
(TA 1988, s 193 and Sched 12)

### 3.23.1 Introduction

Where a person is resident and ordinarily resident in the UK but worked overseas for a continuous period of at least 365 qualifying days, a 100% deduction was available up to 17 March 1998. This meant that no UK tax was payable on the earnings concerned.

A qualifying day was a day when the individual is absent from the UK at midnight and the following conditions are fulfilled:

(1) the individual has spent that day working abroad under his contract of employment; or

(2) the individual has spent part of that day travelling overseas to perform duties under his contracts of employment; or

(3) the day is one of at least seven consecutive days which (taken as a whole) are substantially devoted to performing duties overseas.

There are specific rules on what counts as a qualifying day for people working on board ship or aircraft and travelling to a foreign destination.

It was possible to aggregate shorter periods so as to make up the 365-day period provided the periods were not separated by more than 62 consecutive days spent in the UK, or by a total period greater than one-sixth of the periods being aggregated.

### 3.23.2 Abolition of 100% deduction

With effect from 17 March 1998 the 100% deduction ceased to be available except to seafarers. The Revenue has confirmed that where a qualifying 365-day period straddled 17 March 1998, the relevant proportion of the individual's earnings for 1997–98 qualified for relief.

Because of the loose definition of seafarer, it was possible for employees who worked on particular types of oil rigs to be treated as such. The definition of 'seafarer' was therefore restricted in order to prevent abuse. The High Court has recently decided that a worker on a jack-up oil rig which could be moved but was normally fixed to the sea bed was not entitled to the deduction.

### 3.23.3 Double tax relief

Where a UK-resident individual works abroad, he may be liable for foreign tax. Now that the 100% deduction is not available, there will usually be a UK tax liability.

## 3.24 DESIGNING A 'TAX EFFICIENT' REMUNERATION PACKAGE

Where an individual has a real degree of influence over the way in which his total remuneration package of salary and benefits is made up, the following should be borne in mind.

(1) Pension schemes are very tax efficient.

(2) Approved share options are treated more favourably than non-approved options.

(3) The legislation on benefits in kind still leaves some scope for manoeuvre.

(4) Golden handshakes are not always taxable.

### 3.24.1 Advantages of pension funds in general

There can be no better medium to long-term investment than a pension scheme. The fact that pension schemes are not subject to tax internally because of the funds' exemption from UK income tax and CGT, combined with the facility to take a tax-free lump sum at retirement means that the overall return will almost certainly beat any comparable investment.

### 3.24.2 Pension schemes which are not subject to the earnings cap

Some individuals may be in a company pension scheme which they had joined prior to 17 March 1987. If there is any element of choice, and the individual can afford to do so, it may well be better to forgo salary in return for an increased level of funding for the company pension. The fact that there is no ceiling on the tax-free lump sum of one and a half times final remuneration is obviously extremely attractive.

In practice, even if the company operates a first class pension scheme, there is likely to be some scope for augmenting the individual's pension entitlement. For example, many company pension schemes do not define final remuneration so as to include the maximum amount which the Revenue would permit. In these cases, it may be possible for an individual to have his pension entitlement increased to take account of 'fluctuating emoluments' such as benefits in kind, etc.

### 3.24.3 Schemes where the individual is subject to the earnings cap

Where an individual is subject to the earnings cap (see 12.10.4) because he has taken up employment after 31 May 1989, or has become a member of a company pension scheme only after that date, there may still be considerable scope for increasing the level of benefits. If the individual can afford it, he should pay the maximum additional voluntary contributions and arrange matters so that his employer funds the scheme to the maximum extent permitted. In most cases, the individual will not receive the full pension if he accrues benefits at the standard rate of $\frac{1}{60}$ final remuneration for each year of service, whereas the Revenue will permit a scheme to be funded so that the full pension is due after 20 years' service (see 12.10.5).

In the case of a family company, where both spouses are active in the business, it may well be possible for each to have the maximum permitted pension benefits.

### 3.24.4 Approved share option schemes

The tax treatment of an individual who exercises an approved share option or who receives shares via an approved profit-sharing scheme is significantly better off than someone who benefits via an unapproved arrangement. Basically, no tax charge arises on the exercise of an approved share option provided that the necessary conditions have been observed (see 3.15).

The conclusion must be that wherever an individual has a choice, he should normally participate via an approved rather than a non-approved scheme.

The new approved schemes which have just been introduced in FA 2000 must also be borne in mind, especially the Enterprise Management Incentive scheme (see 3.17).

## 3.24.5 Tax efficient benefits in kind

Despite the Government's long-term intention to remove any discrimination between the tax treatment of benefits in kind and cash remuneration, there are still certain benefits in kind which are favourably treated for tax purposes. If a person is a company director, or someone else who has a degree of say in the way in which his remuneration package is made up, significant tax benefits can be secured by a judicious choice of benefits in kind.

### Company cars

Because of the high rate of depreciation in the first year, it may well be advantageous for a director to arrange for his company to purchase a car with a view to its being sold to him after it has been used for a period. Provided that he pays the full market value for the car in its second-hand condition, there will be no Schedule E charge on the difference between the cost of the car to the company and the amount at which the director purchases it. Admittedly, there is a scale benefit for the period the company owns the car, but this is often significantly less than the depreciation of the vehicle during the period concerned.

### Car fuel

It is clearly beneficial that an individual should have as much free petrol as possible as the scale benefit does not vary according to how much private petrol is provided to an employee.

### Interest-free loans

There is a *de minimis* limit so that, if an individual has a beneficial loan from his company, no Schedule E charge arises unless the loan exceeds £5,000.

### Company accommodation

It may be possible to secure a reduction in the taxable benefit which arises where a director or employee occupies a company property. This is a complex area where you should take professional advice.

## 3.24.6 Golden handshakes are not always taxable

Despite the rules being tightened up, a termination payment can still be favourably treated, either because of the £30,000 exemption or because it qualifies for total exemption (see 3.22).

# 3.25 COMPLETING YOUR SELF-ASSESSMENT TAX RETURN

If you were employed in 1999–2000, you will need to complete the additional schedule reproduced on pages 170–73. We have annotated and cross-referred these forms to this book. You will also need to tick the 'yes' box on question 2 of the main tax return if you exercised share options or were given shares (unless you received them under a Revenue-approved scheme).

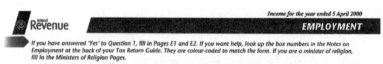

Income for the year ended 5 April 2000

**EMPLOYMENT**

*If you have answered 'Yes' to Question 1, fill in Pages E1 and E2. If you want help, look up the box numbers in the Notes on Employment at the back of your Tax Return Guide. They are colour-coded to match the form. If you are a minister of religion, fill in the Ministers of Religion Pages.*

**Fill in a separate copy of these Pages for each employment from which you received any income.**

### Details of employer

Employer's PAYE reference - may be shown under 'Tax Office number and reference' on your P60 or 'PAYE reference' on your P45

**1.1**

Employer's name

**1.2**

Date employment started
(only if between 6 April 1999 and 5 April 2000)

**1.3**    /    /

Employer's address

**1.5**

Date finished (only if between 6 April 1999 and 5 April 2000)

**1.4**    /    /

Postcode

Tick box 1.6 if you were a director of the company

**1.6**

and, if so, tick box 1.7 if it was a close company

**1.7**

### Income from employment

■ *Money - see Notes, page EN3*

● Payments from P60 (or P45 or payslips)    Before tax  **1.8** £

● Payments not on P60 etc.  - tips    **1.9** £

  - other payments (excluding expenses entered below and lump sums and compensation payments or benefits entered overleaf)    **1.10** £

● UK tax deducted from payments in boxes 1.8 to 1.10    Tax deducted  **1.11** £

*Your employer should give you your form P60 by 31 May*

■ *Benefits and expenses - see Notes, pages EN3 to EN6. If any benefits connected with termination of employment were received, or enjoyed, after that termination and were from a **former** employer you need to complete Help Sheet IR204, available from the Orderline. Do not enter such benefits here.*

● Assets transferred/ payments made for you    Amount  **1.12** £

● Vouchers/credit cards    Amount  **1.13** £

● Living accommodation    Amount  **1.14** £

● Mileage allowance    Amount  **1.15** £

● Company cars    Amount  **1.16** £

● Fuel for company cars    Amount  **1.17** £

● Vans    Amount  **1.18** £    See 3.5

  See 3.4

● Interest-free and low-interest loans    Amount  **1.19** £    See 3.7

  See 3.4

*box 1.20 is not used*    See 3.8

● Private medical or dental insurance    Amount  **1.21** £    See 3.9

  See 3.4.9

● Other benefits    Amount  **1.22** £    See 3.6, 3.9

● Expenses payments received and balancing charges    Amount  **1.23** £    See 3.5

  See 3.5

BMSD 12/99    TAX RETURN ■ EMPLOYMENT: PAGE E1    *Please turn over* ➤

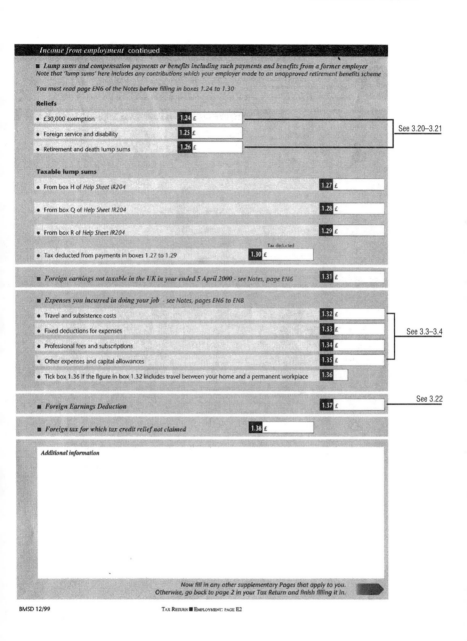

**Income from employment** continued

- **Lump sums and compensation payments or benefits including such payments and benefits from a former employer**
Note that 'lump sums' here includes any contributions which your employer made to an unapproved retirement benefits scheme

You must read page EN6 of the Notes before filling in boxes 1.24 to 1.30

**Reliefs**

- £30,000 exemption — 1.24 £

- Foreign service and disability — 1.25 £

- Retirement and death lump sums — 1.26 £

See 3.20–3.21

**Taxable lump sums**

- From box H of Help Sheet IR204 — 1.27 £

- From box Q of Help Sheet IR204 — 1.28 £

- From box R of Help Sheet IR204 — 1.29 £

- Tax deducted from payments in boxes 1.27 to 1.29 — 1.30 £    *Tax deducted*

- **Foreign earnings not taxable in the UK in year ended 5 April 2000** - see Notes, page EN6 — 1.31 £

- **Expenses you incurred in doing your job** - see Notes, pages EN6 to EN8

- Travel and subsistence costs — 1.32 £

- Fixed deductions for expenses — 1.33 £

- Professional fees and subscriptions — 1.34 £

- Other expenses and capital allowances — 1.35 £

- Tick box 1.36 if the figure in box 1.32 includes travel between your home and a permanent workplace — 1.36

See 3.3–3.4

- **Foreign Earnings Deduction** — 1.37 £

See 3.22

- **Foreign tax for which tax credit relief not claimed** — 1.38 £

**Additional information**

*Now fill in any other supplementary Pages that apply to you.
Otherwise, go back to page 2 in your Tax Return and finish filling it in.*

**Income for the year ended 5 April 2000**

**SHARE SCHEMES**

Inland Revenue

Fill in these boxes first

Name

Tax reference

If you want help, look up the box numbers in the Notes.

## Share options

Read the Notes, pages SN1 to SN5 before filling in the boxes

### ■ Approved savings-related share options

Name of company and share scheme

Tick if shares unlisted

Taxable amount

| | | | |
|---|---|---|---|
| ● Exercise | 2.1 | 2.2 | 2.3 £ |

See 3.15.2

| ● Cancellation or release | 2.4 | 2.5 | 2.6 £ |

### ■ Approved discretionary share options

Name of company and share scheme

| ● Exercise | 2.7 | 2.8 | 2.9 £ |

See 3.15.3

| ● Cancellation or release | 2.10 | 2.11 | 2.12 £ |

### ■ Unapproved share options

Name of company and share scheme

| ● Grant | 2.13 | 2.14 | 2.15 £ |

| ● Exercise | 2.16 | 2.17 | 2.18 £ |

See 3.14

| ● Cancellation or release | 2.19 | 2.20 | 2.21 £ |

## Shares acquired

Read the Notes, page SN6 before filling in the boxes

Name of company and share scheme

| ● Shares acquired from your employment | 2.22 | 2.23 | 2.24 £ |

See 3.11 and 19.1.4

| ● Shares as benefits | 2.25 | 2.26 | 2.27 £ |

| ● Post-acquisition charges or lifting of risk of forfeiture | 2.28 | 2.29 | 2.30 £ |

See 3.16.4

● Total of the taxable amounts boxes (boxes 2.3, 2.6, 2.9, 2.12, 2.15, 2.18, 2.21, 2.24, 2.27 and 2.30)

total column above

2.31A £

● Any taxable amounts included in boxes 2.6 to 2.30 which are included in the Pay figure on your P60 or P45(Part 1A)

2.31B £

**Total taxable amount**

box 2.31A minus box 2.31B

2.31 £

*Additional information*

SA102

BMSD 12/99

Tax Return ■ Share schemes: page S1

You must complete a separate copy of this Page for each taxable event in the year ended 5 April 2000 that relates to your share options or shares acquired. If you had more than one taxable event in the year, ask the Orderline for more copies, or photocopy this Page. (If you use a photocopy, please put your name and tax reference at the top.)

## Share options

Read the Notes, pages SN2 to SN5 before filling in the boxes

Name of company and share scheme | Class of share (for example, 10p Ordinary)

2.32 | 2.33

| | Grant | Exercise | Cancellation/Release |
|---|---|---|---|
| 2.34 Date option was granted | / / | / / | / / |
| 2.35 Date option was exercised | | / / | |
| 2.36 Number of shares | | | |
| 2.37 Exercise price/option price per share | £ . | £ . | |
| 2.38 Amount paid for option | £ . | £ . | £ . |
| 2.39 Market value per share at date the option was granted | £ . | | |
| 2.40 Market value per share at date the option was exercised | | £ . | |
| 2.41 Amount received in money or money's worth | | | £ . |

## Shares acquired

Read the Notes, page SN6 before filling in the boxes

Name of company and share scheme | Class of share (for example, 10p Ordinary)

2.42 | 2.43

| | Shares acquired | Post-acquisition charge |
|---|---|---|
| 2.44 Date shares acquired or forfeiture lifted | / / | / / |
| 2.45 Number of shares | | |
| 2.46 Amount paid per share | £ . | |
| 2.47 Market value per share at date of acquisition or forfeiture lifted | £ . | £ . |
| 2.48 Give details of the nature of the post-acquisition event | | |

BMSD 12/99      TAX RETURN ■ SHARE SCHEMES: PAGE S2

Printed in the U.K. by St Ives Direct, St Ives plc. R0H2111 12/99.

173

# 4

# INCOME FROM UK PROPERTY

This chapter deals with rental income from land or property in the UK. All such income is now taxed under Schedule A. Rents received from letting an overseas property are taxed under Schedule D Case V and the tax treatment of such income is covered in Chapter 5.

The following matters are covered in this chapter:

(1)  Basis of assessment and administration.
(2)  How to calculate your taxable profit.
(3)  Lump sums deemed to be rent (premiums).
(4)  'Rent-a-room' relief.
(5)  Furnished holiday accommodation.
(6)  Capital allowances on investment properties.
(7)  Mineral royalties.
(8)  Woodlands.
(9)  The old Schedule A rules.
(10)  Completing your self-assessment tax return.

Finally, do not overlook VAT. It is possible to register many rental businesses for VAT purposes and this can mean that you will recover input tax. On the other hand, you will have to charge VAT on the rent. For further details, see 25.3.6.

## 4.1 BASIS OF ASSESSMENT AND ADMINISTRATION

### 4.1.1 All rental activities treated as single business

All rental income received by an individual from UK properties is now assessed under Schedule A, whether the property is let unfurnished or furnished. All the income and expenses are brought together in a single business of letting UK property. The income is brought in on normal commercial accountancy principles. Expenses are allowed if they satisfy the test that the expense is incurred wholly and exclusively for business purposes and this rule applies to interest (including overdraft interest) just as for any other expense.

### 4.1.2 Exceptional types of rental income

Rental income for Schedule A purposes includes ground rents. It also includes 'other receipts from an estate' in land such as charges levied by a landlord in return for maintaining a block of flats and payments made to a landowner for sporting rights. However, Schedule A income does not include admission charges made by hotels, boarding houses, theatres etc since the profits of such businesses are chargeable to tax under Schedule D Case I.

The income from taking in lodgers is also generally treated as trading income rather than rental income assessable under Schedule A. However, see 4.4 on 'rent-a-room' relief.

### 4.1.3 Schedule A assessed on fiscal year basis

An individual must report his income on a tax year basis, ie he must draw up accounts to 5 April.

### 4.1.4 Partnership income dealt with separately

Rental income received by a partnership is treated as a separate source. If the partnership does not have any trading income, the rental income is assessed on a fiscal year basis, irrespective of the date to which the partnership draws up accounts. In contrast if the partnership also has some trading income taxed under Schedule D Case I or II, its Schedule A income is assessed on the same basis. Thus, if a trading partnership has a 30 April year end, the partners will be assessed for 1999–2000 on their share of the partnership's Schedule A income for the year ended 30 April 1999. For 1996–97 the transitional year rules apply so that the partners are assessed on 50% of the income for the two years ended 30 April 1996 unless the partnership commenced after 5 April 1994 (see 2.10.6).

### 4.1.5 Schedule A income is investment income

Although all rental income is treated as arising from a single business of letting property, the income is still treated as investment income. Any losses can only be carried forward for off-set against Schedule A income and cannot be set against the individual's other income for the year (there is an exception to this for deficits arising from letting agricultural properties where the deficit may be set against other income: see 4.1.6 below).

Schedule A income is not 'income from savings'.

### 4.1.6 Deficiency on an agricultural property
(TA 1988, s 33)

Where an estate consists of, or includes, agricultural land, a deficiency may be set against any Schedule A income. Any balance which cannot be relieved in this way may be set against the individual's other income for the year, or the following tax year.

Agricultural land is defined as land, houses or other buildings in the UK occupied wholly or mainly for the purposes of husbandry. An estate means any land and buildings managed as one estate. Where only part of the estate is used for husbandry, only a proportion of any deficiency can be relieved in this way.

## 4.2 HOW TO CALCULATE YOUR TAXABLE PROFIT

The legislation requires that landlords should calculate their income and expenses in accordance with normal accountancy principles but subject to the same specific rules which apply for Schedule D Case I purposes.

You may find it helpful to obtain a copy of Revenue booklet IR150, *Taxation of Rents*. You should also study the notes and help sheets issued by the Revenue to enable landlords to complete their self-assessment tax returns. The Revenue's guide to the self-assessment return sets out the normal treatment of certain common expenses.

### 4.2.1 Rent receivable

The Revenue confirms in its booklet that you do not bring rent into a year's tax computation merely because you receive it in the year or because it is due to be paid to you in the year. Equally, you do not exclude rent merely because you receive it outside the tax year or it is due outside the tax year. You bring in the proportion of the rent which is earned in the year from the tenants' use of the property in the year. You exclude the proportion which is earned from the tenant's right to use the property outside the year. You may therefore need to make an adjustment where rent is receivable on (say) a quarterly basis, either in advance or in arrears.

Incidentally, the Revenue's notes to the self-assessment return point out that rental income includes receipts in kind as well as in cash.

### 4.2.2 Bad debts

The landlord can claim a deduction for rent which is due to him but has not been paid where the debt is clearly irrecoverable. A deduction can also be claimed for doubtful debts. Such a deduction is available only where the landlord has taken all reasonable steps to recover the debt. Furthermore, if the outstanding rent is collected in a later tax year, the landlord should bring the recovery into his accounts as a receipt for his rental income for that year.

No deduction is available for a general bad debt reserve (ie a landlord cannot deduct 5% of the outstanding rents due to him at the year end just to be on the safe side). Tax relief is available for provisions for doubtful debts only if the provisions relate to specific debts and the facts relating to each debtor have been taken into account. Furthermore, as the Revenue literature makes clear, you cannot deduct a bad or doubtful debt merely because the tenant is always a slow payer. There has to be good reason for thinking the debt is likely to be bad.

### 4.2.3 Rent-free periods

The Revenue approach follows the accounting principles set out in SSAP No 21. If, for example, the landlord grants a lease for a five-year period with no rent being payable in the first year and rent of £10,000 being payable in years two to five, the landlord should spread the total amount of rent receivable over the five years (ie £40,000) and bring into his accounts one-fifth of that total income for each year of the lease. In other words, the treatment reflects the substance of the transaction; in essence there is not really a rent-free year at all since the £40,000 payable over the first five years is rent for the whole of that period.

### 4.2.4 Expenses

Expenses should also be brought into account on normal accountancy principles. This means that a landlord should deduct any allowable expenses which relate to work done, or goods or services supplied to him, for a particular year. There is no requirement that the supplier should have been paid during the tax year. Thus if you have raised a loan for the purchase or improvement of repairs of properties which are let out, you can claim relief for interest which has accrued up to 5 April even though the bank or building society may debit interest on a different basis (eg at 30 June and 31 December).

Expenses are deductible only if they meet the 'wholly and exclusively' rule (ie expenditure which is part business/part private is not allowable). For example the cost of travelling to Wales to supervise repairs to a holiday cottage is not an allowable deduction for tax purposes if the landlord also took a holiday while he was in Wales, and the visit had a dual purpose. On the other hand, where a definite part or proportion of an expense is wholly incurred for business purposes, that part may be deducted. This might well arise where a landlord lives in part of the property which is rented out and in such a case, a proportion of the insurance premium relating to the property as a whole may be deducted in the landlord's Schedule A computation. It should be remembered that where expenditure is partly for business and partly for personal use, you have to complete a specific box on the self-assessment return.

### 4.2.5 Repairs, maintenance and renewals

Examples of common repairs which are normally deductible in computing income for tax purposes are:

- exterior and interior painting and decorating
- stone cleaning
- damp and rot treatment
- mending broken windows, doors, furniture and machines such as cookers or lifts
- re-pointing
- replacing roof slates, flashing and gutters.

On the other hand, substantial repairs carried out shortly after a landlord has occupied a property to put the property into a fit state are generally disallowed as constituting capital expenditure.

The *Jenners* case (see 2.4.9) means that a specific and scientifically calculated provision for the cost of repair work to be carried out in the future might be allowable. However, you will need to take specialist advice on whether making such a provision accords with the generally accepted accountancy principles as set out in FRS12.

## 4.2.6 Renewals

The landlord can claim the cost of replacing furniture, furnishings and machinery. However, expenditure on renewals is not available where the landlord claims a standard 10% wear and tear allowance (see 4.2.9 below).

Where expenditure on renewals is claimed, the landlord should bring into account of his income any amounts that he receives for items which have been scrapped or sold. Also, expenditure on renewals should not normally include the cost of items which represent a significant improvement or addition to the furniture and furnishings, etc which were previously made available to the tenant.

## 4.2.7 Legal and professional costs

The Revenue view is as follows:

### Non-allowable expenses

(1) Expenses in connection with the first letting or sub-letting of a property for more than one year. These include, for example, legal expenses (such as the cost of drawing up a lease), agents' and surveyors' fees and commission.
(2) Any proportion of the legal, etc costs which relate to the payment of a premium on the renewal of a lease.
(3) Fees incurred in obtaining planning permission or on the registration of title when buying a property.

### Allowable expenses

(1) Expenses for granting a lease of a year or less.
(2) The normal legal and professional fees incurred on the renewal of a lease, provided the lease is for less than 50 years (the Revenue has confirmed in its *Tax Bulletin* that the costs of granting a lease to a new tenant will normally be allowable provided the replacement lease follows closely on the previous one and is broadly similar in terms).
(3) Professional fees incurred in evicting an unsatisfactory tenant, with a view to re-letting.

(4) Professional fees incurred on an appeal against a compulsory purchase order.

(5) Professional fees in drawing up accounts.

## 4.2.8 Costs of services provided, including wages

Where a landlord provides any service to a tenant (eg gardening, the provision of a porter, cleaning, etc) the landlord can claim the cost of these services (provided they are incurred wholly and exclusively for the purposes of the letting).

## 4.2.9 10% wear and tear allowance

Where a landlord lets a dwelling house as furnished accommodation, he can claim (as an alternative to claims on a renewals basis) an allowance amounting to 10% of the rent received after deducting charges or services which would normally be borne by the tenant but which are, in fact, borne by the landlord (eg council tax). This allowance, which is known as 'wear and tear allowance', is accepted by the Revenue as broadly covering the cost of normal renewals of furniture.

Where a landlord lets non-residential property such as offices, etc, he will normally be able to claim capital allowances for any items, such as furniture, which are provided.

### Table 4.1 – Computing your Schedule A income (straightforward situation)

For each property, bring in the rental income which relates to the tax year (ie if rent is receivable on 25 March 2000 for the quarter ending 24 June 2000, include a proportion – $^{11}\!/_{91}$ – for the period 25 March–5 April 2000).

**Deduct**

- Charges made by an agent for rent collection and management.
- Any rent you have to pay on the property such as ground rent.
- Any service charges that you have to pay (this is particularly likely to apply if you are letting out a flat).
- Insurance premiums paid for the period covered by the tax year – if you pay insurance for a calendar year, include $^3\!/_2$ of the premium for 1999 + $^9\!/_2$ of the premium for 2000.
- Repairs and similar expenses (eg gardening) incurred in the tax year. Note that the expense need not actually have been in the tax year so long as it is clear that it relates to the tax year.
- Interest on borrowings used to finance the original purchase of a property, improvements or repairs.

Aggregate all the income and expenses for your different properties except for properties which are not let on a commercial basis; any deficit on that property will almost certainly not be allowable. Also add in any lump sums taxable as premiums (see 4.3).

## 4.3 LUMP SUMS DEEMED TO BE RENT (PREMIUMS)
(TA 1988, ss 34–39)

### 4.3.1 Introduction

A landlord faced with the choice of letting a property for five years at £10,000 pa, or taking a lump sum in return for granting a lease for five years at an annual rent of £100, would regard the two transactions as very similar in their overall consequences. The purpose behind the tax legislation which deals with such lump sums (or 'premiums') is to ensure that the tax treatment of the two types of transaction is also similar in nature. The principle is that a proportion of a premium received by a landlord for granting a lease of less than 50 years should be taxed as if it were rent.

The following sections apply only where the person who receives the premium is the landlord, ie a person who continues to hold a superior interest in the property. An outgoing tenant who assigns the whole of his interest in the property is not regarded as receiving a premium for Schedule A purposes.

### 4.3.2 How premiums are apportioned between income and capital
(TA 1988, s 34)

The rule is that the full amount of the premium is treated as rent except for 2% for every complete year of the lease after the first year. For example, if a ten-year lease is granted for a premium of £25,000, the amount which is subject to tax under Schedule A is 82% of £25,000, ie £20,500. See Table 4.2 below.

#### Table 4.2 – Extract from Inland Revenue Helpsheet

| Working sheet for chargeable premiums – leases up to 50 years | | |
|---|---|---|
| Premium | **A** | £ |
| Number of **complete periods of 12 months** in lease *(ignore the first 12 months of the lease)* | **B** | £ |
| A multiplied by B | **C** | £ |
| C divided by 50 | **D** | £ |
| A less D | **E** | £ |
| Copy figure in box E to box 5.22. | | |

### 4.3.3 Payments in kind
(TA 1988, s 34(2))

It is provided that if a tenant is required to carry out work as a term of his lease, the whole of the benefit accruing to the landlord is deemed to be a premium receivable at the commencement of the lease.

### 4.3.4 Deemed premiums
(TA 1988, s 34(5))

Any lump sum paid by a tenant to vary the lease can be treated as a premium receivable at the time that the contract for the variation is entered into.

#### Example – Deemed premium

A is the landlord of a property used as offices and let on a 15-year lease. It is a term of the lease that the tenant should not use the premises for any other purpose.

The tenant secures planning consent to use the property for light industrial use. He makes a payment to A of £12,000 in year four to induce him to vary the lease so that the property can be used for industrial purposes. A is deemed to receive a premium in year four. The taxable amount is:

|                          | £       |
|--------------------------|---------|
|                          | 12,000  |
| *Less*: $(10 \times 2\%)$ | (2,400) |
|                          | 9,600   |

Similarly, if A had received a lump sum to induce him to waive the relevant term in the lease, the lump sum would be treated as a premium.

### 4.3.5 Sale with right to repurchase the property
(TA 1988, s 36)

Where the freehold or leasehold of a property is sold subject to a condition that at a future date the purchaser may be required to sell the property back to the vendor at a lower price, the vendor is liable to tax under Schedule D Case VI on the excess of the sale price over the repurchase price. The difference is treated as a premium so that the amount charged is reduced by 2% for each complete year between the date of sale and the date of resale less one year. A similar rule applies where a vendor sells a property, but retains an option to repurchase it.

### 4.3.6 Which year?

The self-assessment return pack and the Inland Revenue's internal guidance indicate that the taxable amount of any premiums should be taxed as income for the year in which the landlord becomes entitled to them. This could be challenged on the grounds that the income for granting (say) a five-year lease should be spread evenly over the period, with part of the premium being taxed for each of the years to which it relates. Seek professional advice if substantial amounts are involved.

## 4.4 'RENT-A-ROOM' RELIEF
(F(No 2)A 1992, s 59 and Sched 10)

There is a special relief which is available to an individual who receives payment for letting furnished accommodation in a qualifying residence. The relief provides total exemption from income of £4,250 unless sums accrue to another person in respect of lettings of furnished accommodation in the same property, in which case the exemption is reduced to £2,125.

A qualifying residence is a residence which is the individual's only or main residence at sometime in the basis period for the year of assessment in relation to the lettings. Residence means a building (or part of a building) occupied or intended to be occupied as a separate residence.

Rent-a-room relief is available automatically unless the taxpayer elects otherwise or the gross sums received exceed the £4,250 limit.

Where the gross sums received exceed the £4,250 limit for the year of assessment (or the £2,125 limit where some other person receives income from furnished lettings within the same property), the taxpayer may elect for his profits or gains for the basis period to be treated as equal to the excess. For example, if a taxpayer has gross rent of £5,000, he may compute his taxable income as £750 or he can compute it in the normal way by reference to the expenses that he actually incurred.

### Need for caution

The Revenue has commented upon the suggestion that rent-a-room relief might be available where part of an individual's residence is let to a company for use as an office (or for some other trade or business purpose). The Revenue view is that rent-a-room relief is available only where the person paying rent uses the premises for residential purposes.

### 4.4.1 Possible restriction on relief for interest

If you claim rent-a-room relief for a year of assessment, you will not be entitled to any relief for interest for that year on a loan used to buy that property apart from the relief under MIRAS (see 9.1). This could be a disadvantage if you carry on a trade or business from home as well as letting out rooms.

## 4.4.2 Inland Revenue leaflets

For further information on rent-a-room relief, obtain copies of leaflets IR87, *Rooms to let*, and IR223, *Rent-a-Room for Traders*.

# 4.5 FURNISHED HOLIDAY ACCOMMODATION
(TA 1988, ss 503–504)

## 4.5.1 Definition of furnished holiday accommodation

Where a person lets furnished holiday accommodation (this includes caravans), it may be treated as a trade provided the following conditions are satisfied:

(1) The property must be situated in the UK.
(2) It must be let on a commercial basis.
(3) It must be let as furnished accommodation.
(4) It must be available for commercial letting to the public as holiday accommodation for at least 140 days in a 12-month period.
(5) It must be let for at least 70 such days.
(6) It must not normally be occupied by the same person for more than 31 consecutive days at any time during a period of seven months within the 12-month period.

Where a person has more than one property let as furnished holiday accommodation, the 70 day test may be satisfied by averaging any or all of the accommodation let by that person. A claim for averaging must be made within 22 months of the end of the tax year (ie for 1999–2000 by 31 January 2002).

## 4.5.2 Consequences where lettings are classified as furnished holiday lettings

The following consequences will follow if a property is treated as being let as furnished holiday accommodation.

### Relief for interest

Interest on loans used to purchase the property, and to finance the lettings, should qualify as an expense incurred in the trade. In some cases, the inclusion of such interest will give rise to a loss for tax purposes.

### Capital allowances for plant and machinery

Equipment and furniture and furnishings may attract allowances for the capital allowances system.

### Relief for pre-trading expenditure

Expenditure incurred before the business of letting the properties as furnished holiday accommodation actually commences may be allowed as a loss incurred at the point in time when the lettings commence as pre-trading expenditure (see 2.6).

### Relief for losses

Because the activity of letting property as furnished holiday accommodation is regarded as a trade for the purposes of Schedule D, it will be possible to obtain relief for losses against the individual's other income (see 2.9). This will apply whether the loss arises from interest, capital allowances or pre-trading expenditure or for other reasons provided that it can be shown that the activity was carried on on a commercial basis.

### Profits classified as earned income

The legislation provides that profits arising from letting furnished holiday accommodation should be treated as earned income. This is not dependent on the owner taking any active involvement in the lettings: the whole activity can be dealt with by an agent where this is desired. Because the profits are regarded as earned income, they rank as 'relevant earnings' for the purposes of personal pension contributions and retirement annuity premiums (see 12.8 and 12.9).

### Capital gains tax

Roll-over and retirement reliefs may be available – see 15.4 and 15.9.

## 4.6 CAPITAL ALLOWANCES ON INVESTMENT PROPERTIES

### 4.6.1 Introduction

Capital allowances are usually given when the Revenue assesses the profits of a trade. However, it is possible to qualify for capital allowances in respect of expenditure on investment properties. The allowances must first be set against the income of a defined class (see below) but any surplus of allowances may be set against the individual's other income. The legislation states that such allowances may be given by way of 'discharge or repayment of tax'.

### 4.6.2 Agricultural buildings allowances
(CAA 1990, ss 132(3) and 141)

Agricultural buildings allowances (see 2.5.18) are available for relief by 'discharge or repayment of tax' if the landlord does not carry on a trade of farming. The allowances must first be set against agricultural or forestry rental income.

It is necessary to make a claim under CAA 1990, s 141 within two years of the end of the year of assessment in order that agricultural buildings allowances may be set against other income rather than carried forward. If the individual wishes, the surplus allowances may be set against income of the following tax year.

### 4.6.3 Industrial buildings allowances
(CAA 1990, ss 9 and 141)

An individual who owns the relevant interest in an industrial building may qualify for industrial buildings allowances (see 2.5.15) because the property is occupied and used for a qualifying trade. Similarly, an individual who owns a property in an enterprise zone will generally qualify for allowances where the building is occupied for commercial purposes.

The allowances on such buildings must first be set against rental income from the industrial buildings and then against any balancing charge which arises on the disposal of an interest in an industrial building. If there is a surplus of allowances, these allowances may then be set against the individual's income for the year, or the following tax year. Once again, a formal claim is required under CAA 1990, s 141.

### 4.6.4 Enterprise zone trust

It is possible to invest in properties in enterprise zones through a syndicate or 'enterprise zone property trust'. An individual who invests in the enterprise zone property trust is treated as if he had incurred a proportion of the trust's expenditure on enterprise zone properties and the allowances may be set against his other income in the same way as described at 4.6.3 above. In some cases, there may be a delay in that an individual invests in a trust at the end of one tax year and becomes entitled to allowances only for the following year (because that is the year in which the trust acquires the relevant properties).

## 4.7 MINERAL ROYALTIES
(TA 1988, s 122 and Sched 6)

Mineral royalties are normally received net of tax at the basic rate. However, only part of the royalties is taxable as income.

Where the recipient is resident or ordinarily resident in the UK, one half of the mineral royalties is treated as capital gains rather than income. Similarly, only 50% of any management expenses or other sums deductible for Schedule A purposes may be set against the part of the mineral royalties treated as income.

When the mineral lease comes to an end, the person may claim a capital loss as if he had disposed of the land at its market value at that time. The loss may be set against capital gains for the year in which the mineral lease expires or against capital gains taxed on mineral royalties during the preceding 15 years.

'Mineral royalties' are defined so as to include rents, tolls, royalties and other periodic payments which relate to the winning and working of minerals (other than water, peat and topsoil) under a lease, licence or other agreement.

## 4.8 WOODLANDS
(FA 1988, s 65 and Sched 6)

At one time, profits arising from the occupation of woodlands in the UK were taxed under Schedule B. This charge was abolished with effect from 6 April 1988. Profits or gains arising from the occupation of woodlands are now exempt and woodlands are not chargeable under Schedule A.

In some cases, woodlands were owned prior to 15 March 1988 and an election was made for profit or losses to be taxed under Schedule D. Such an election ceases to have effect at 6 April 1993 and profits which arise after that date are not taxed under Schedule D and are therefore exempt income.

## 4.9 OLD SCHEDULE A RULES

Different rules applied for individuals and trustees up to 1994–95 and for companies up to 31 March 1998. For details, see *Allied Dunbar Tax Handbook 1998–99* at 4.9.

## 4.10 COMPLETING YOUR SELF-ASSESSMENT TAX RETURN

The relevant schedule is reproduced opposite, with cross references to the previous paragraphs.

Income for the year ended 5 April 2000

**LAND AND PROPERTY**

Inland Revenue

Fill in these boxes first

**Name**

**Tax reference**

If you want help, look up the box numbers in the Notes

**Are you claiming Rent a Room relief for gross rents of £4,250 or less?**
(Or £2,125 if the claim is shared?)
Read the Notes on page LN2 to find out
- whether you can claim Rent a Room relief; and
- how to claim relief for gross rents over £4,250

No ☐  Yes ☐

If 'Yes', and this is your only income from UK property, you have finished these Pages

See 4.4

**Is your income from furnished holiday lettings?**
If 'No', turn over and fill in Page L2 to give details of your property income

No ☐  Yes ☐

If 'Yes', fill in boxes 5.1 to 5.18 before completing Page L2

See 4.5

### Furnished holiday lettings

- Income from furnished holiday lettings — **5.1** £

■ *Expenses* (furnished holiday lettings only)

- Rent, rates, insurance, ground rents etc. — **5.2** £
- Repairs, maintenance and renewals — **5.3** £
- Finance charges, including interest — **5.4** £
- Legal and professional costs — **5.5** £
- Costs of services provided, including wages — **5.6** £
- Other expenses — **5.7** £

total of boxes 5.2 to 5.7 **5.8** £

**Net profit** (put figures in brackets if a loss) — box 5.1 minus box 5.8 **5.9** £

■ *Tax adjustments*

- Private use — **5.10** £
- Balancing charges — **5.11** £

box 5.10 + box 5.11 **5.12** £

- Capital allowances — **5.13** £

**Profit for the year** (copy to box 5.19). If loss, enter '0' in box 5.14 and put the loss in box 5.15 — boxes 5.9 + 5.12 minus box 5.13 **5.14** £

**Loss for the year** (if you have entered '0' in box 5.14) — boxes 5.9 + 5.12 minus box 5.13 **5.15** £

■ *Losses*

- Loss offset against 1999-2000 total income — **5.16** £
- Loss carried back — see Notes, page LN4 **5.17** £
- Loss offset against other income from property (copy to box 5.38) — see Notes, page LN4 **5.18** £

SA105

BMSD 12/99 — TAX RETURN ■ LAND AND PROPERTY: PAGE L1 — *Please turn over* ➤

# ALLIED DUNBAR TAX HANDBOOK

## Other property income

### Income

| | | |
|---|---|---|
| | copy from box 5.14 | |
| Furnished holiday lettings profits | 5.19 £ | |
| Rents and other income from land and property | 5.20 £ | Tax deducted 5.21 £ — See 4.3 |
| Chargeable premiums | 5.22 £ | |
| Reverse premiums | 5.22A £ | boxes 5.19 + 5.20 + 5.22 + 5.22A 5.23 £ |

### Expenses (do not include figures you have already put in boxes 5.2 to 5.7 on Page L1)

| | | |
|---|---|---|
| Rent, rates, insurance, ground rents etc. | 5.24 £ | |
| Repairs, maintenance and renewals | 5.25 £ | |
| Finance charges, including interest | 5.26 £ | See 4.2 |
| Legal and professional costs | 5.27 £ | |
| Costs of services provided, including wages | 5.28 £ | |
| Other expenses | 5.29 £ | total of boxes 5.24 to 5.29 5.30 £ |

**Net profit** (put figures in brackets if a loss)   box 5.23 minus box 5.30  5.31 £

### Tax adjustments

| | | |
|---|---|---|
| Private use | 5.32 £ | |
| Balancing charges | 5.33 £ | box 5.32 + box 5.33 5.34 £ |
| Rent a Room exempt amount | 5.35 £ | |
| Capital allowances | 5.36 £ | See 4.6 |
| 10% wear and tear | 5.37 £ | See 4.2.9 |
| Furnished holiday lettings losses (from box 5.18) | 5.38 £ | total of boxes 5.35 to 5.38 5.39 £ |

Adjusted profit (if loss enter '0' in box 5.40 and put the loss in box 5.41)   boxes 5.31 + 5.34 minus box 5.39  5.40 £

Adjusted loss (if you have entered '0' in box 5.40)   boxes 5.31 + 5.34 minus box 5.39  5.41 £

Loss brought forward from previous year   5.42 £

**Profit for the year**   box 5.40 minus box 5.42  5.43 £

### Losses

Loss offset against total income (read the note on page LN8)   5.44 £

Loss to carry forward to following year   5.45 £

Pooled expenses from 'one-estate election' carried forward   5.46 £

Tick box 5.47 if these Pages include details of property let jointly   5.47

*Now fill in any other supplementary Pages that apply to you.
Otherwise, go back to page 2 of your Tax Return and finish filling it in.*

BMSD 12/99    Tax Return ■ Land and property: page L2

Printed in the U.K. by St Ives Direct, St Ives plc. R0H2116 12/99.

188

# 5

# INCOME FROM SAVINGS

This chapter deals with the types of income which need to be reported on page 3 of the self-assessment tax return (which is reproduced on page 38). Such income does not fit neatly into the traditional categories or 'Schedules'. The chapter encompasses:

## Income taxed under Schedule D Case III

(1) Bank and building society interest.
(2) Other interest income.
(3) Loans to individuals and other private loans.
(4) Gilts and loan stocks.

## Interest received net of tax

(5) Rate of tax deducted at source.

## Interest taxed under Schedule D Case VI

(6) Accrued income scheme.

## Other interest-type income

(7) Relevant discounted securities.

## Dividends from UK companies

(8) Dividends.
(9) Sundry receipts treated as for dividends.

Certain interest and dividends received from foreign companies are taxed as income from savings, but this is dealt with in Chapter 6 as they need to be reported on another part of the self-assessment tax return. Income from savings is always taxed at 20% unless the taxpayer is liable for higher rate tax.

# INCOME TAXED UNDER SCHEDULE D CASE III

## 5.1 BANK AND BUILDING SOCIETY INTEREST

### 5.1.1 Circumstances in which interest receivable without tax deduction source

The National Savings Bank (NSB) always pays interest without deduction of tax. The first £70 interest paid on an ordinary NSB account is exempt (see 11.2.2), but interest on an NSB investment account or from deposit bonds, income bonds or capital bonds is taxable in full.

Interest payments by UK banks or building societies on deposit accounts are normally subject to deduction of tax at source unless the depositor completes form R85. This form requires the depositor's full name, address, date of birth and national insurance number and contains a declaration that the depositor is unlikely to be liable for income tax.

Banks are permitted to pay interest without deduction on non-transferable fixed deposits for amounts of £50,000 or more and where the deposit is for a fixed period not exceeding five years.

Interest payments may be made without deduction of tax on certificates of deposit provided the deposit is for at least £50,000 and the bank or building society takes the deposit for a fixed period (the period must not exceed five years). Interest may also be paid without deduction of tax on deposits where no certificate of deposit has been issued, but the depositor would be entitled to a certificate if he called for one to be issued.

Interest may also be received without tax being deducted at source from loans to individuals, deposits held by a solicitor and on certificates of tax deposit (see 5.2).

### 5.1.2 How taxable amount is arrived at

The preceding year basis was replaced by the current year basis in 1997–98, ie the assessable income is now the actual income which arises during the tax year. This means that for 1999–2000 the assessable income is the income receivable for the year ended 5 April 2000.

### 5.1.3 Basis of assessment for 1996–97 and earlier years

See *Allied Dunbar Tax Handbook 1999–2000* at 5.1.3.

### 5.1.4 Date of receipt

Interest is regarded as received when it is credited to the account. From time to time, cases arise where an individual is required to make a deposit with a bank as a condition of the bank advancing money to a company. In some situations, the individual is precluded from making withdrawals from the deposit account as long as the company's borrowings are outstanding.

The courts have held that an individual who has a deposit account which is subject to such a block may nevertheless be taxed on interest credited to that account. Furthermore, there is no relief if the individual never receives the interest because the company goes into liquidation and the bank appropriates the money outstanding to his credit on the deposit account.

### 5.1.5 Minor children's accounts

An individual will generally be charged tax on interest credited to an unmarried minor child's account where he is a parent and the person who provided the capital, unless the total income from such parental gifts does not exceed £100 (see 20.5.3 on aggregation of minor children's income in general).

### 5.1.6 Rate of tax on income from savings

All interest income assessed under Schedule D Case III counts as income from savings. Tax is charged at only 20% unless the recipient is liable for the 40% higher rate.

**Example**

B receives untaxed interest in the year ended 5 April 2000 of £15,000. She is single and has other income of £12,000, so she is not subject to higher rate tax. She will pay tax on the interest as follows:

|  | £ |
|---|---|
| Non-savings | 12,000 |
| Savings | 15,000 |
|  | 27,000 |
| *Less* allowance | (4,335) |
|  | 22,665 |
| Non-savings income |  |
| Covered by personal allowance 4,335 | Nil |
| Starting rate £1500 @ 10% | 150.00 |
| Basic rate £6165 @ 23% | 1,417.95 |
| Savings income |  |
| Lower rate £15,000 @ 20% | 3,000.00 |
| Tax due | 4,567.95 |

Note that for 1999–2000, where an individual's income consists wholly of income from savings, it is taxed at 20% (ie the 10% rate on the first £1,500 taxable income does not apply).

### 5.1.7 Compensation paid on bank accounts owned by Holocaust victims

Compensation paid by banks on dormant accounts opened by Holocaust victims and frozen during World War II is exempt from tax. See the Inland Revenue Press Release dated 8 May 2000.

## 5.2 OTHER INTEREST INCOME

### 5.2.1 Interest payable by a solicitor

Interest may be received without deduction of tax from client's accounts held by a firm of solicitors or accountants. Such income is taxable under Schedule D Case III.

### 5.2.2 Interest receivable on compulsory purchase monies

Where a property is the subject of a compulsory purchase order which goes to appeal, and the amount payable is increased, interest will generally be payable on the increase. This is regarded as income for the year in which the entitlement arises, ie when the CPO appeal is settled by agreement or on appeal and the interest is received. This principle is not affected by the fact that the interest may have accrued over several years and may be calculated using six monthly rests.

### 5.2.3 Certificates of tax deposit

Interest is credited to an individual where he has invested in certificates of tax deposit which are either applied to cover tax payable by assessments or are encashed. The interest is taxable and is income for the year of receipt.

### 5.2.4 Exempt interest

Interest paid by the Inland Revenue or Customs & Excise on over-payments of tax is not itself subject to tax. This type of interest is called 'repayment supplement' (see 19.9). However, interest paid by Customs in respect of official error is taxable.

### 5.2.5 Interest awarded by the courts

This may be exempt. The treatment turns on whether the court order or arbitration award provides for payment of interest as such (taxable) or is merely an element which is taken into account in arriving at the amount to be awarded (in which case it is capital and not income taxable under Schedule D Case III).

## 5.3  LOANS TO INDIVIDUALS AND OTHER PRIVATE LOANS

Interest on a private loan to an individual or trust will generally be received without deduction of tax. Interest paid by cheque is received when the sum is credited to the recipient's account, not when the cheque is received.

Interest is not assessable where an individual waives the interest before it falls due for payment provided he receives no consideration for such a waiver.

## 5.4  GILTS AND LOAN STOCKS

Interest payments on British Government Securities ('gilts') can be received gross from 1998–99 onwards, although this must be requested where interest was previously received net. There are two exceptions:

(1)  Interest on 3½% War Loan is always paid without deduction.
(2)  Where interest is paid on gilts which are held on the National Savings Bank register, interest is also automatically paid without deduction.

Interest payments on loan stocks issued by companies are normally subject to deduction of tax at source.

Once again, interest from gilts and loan stocks is regarded as income from savings and so qualifies for the 20% rate from 1996–97 (see 5.1.6).

## INTEREST RECEIVED NET OF TAX

## 5.5  RATE OF TAX DEDUCTED AT SOURCE
(TA 1988, ss 480A–482)

Interest payments made by UK banks and building societies are normally subject to deduction of tax at source (for exceptions see 5.1.1).

Interest paid on gilts may also be paid net of tax except in the case of 3½% War Loan and stocks held on the NSB register. Interest paid on local authority loan stocks and company loan stocks and debentures is subject to deduction of tax, as indeed is all interest paid by UK companies to persons other than group companies.

Because such income is income from savings, tax is deducted at 20% and the 10% starting rate does not apply.

# INCOME TAXED UNDER SCHEDULE D CASE VI

## 5.6  ACCRUED INCOME SCHEME
(TA 1988, ss 710–728)

### 5.6.1 Introduction

An individual who sells a gilt or fixed interest loan stock may sell either cum-interest or ex-interest. In the former case, the buyer will receive the next interest payment; in the latter situation the seller receives the next interest payment even though it is paid after he has sold the gilt or loan stock. In practice, gilts etc are quoted on an ex-interest basis from six weeks or so before interest is due for payment.

The price at which a gilt or loan stock is sold generally reflects an adjustment for accrued interest. For example, if a gilt pays interest every six months, a person who sells at the end of month four will receive a price which reflects four months' accrued interest. Conversely, a person who sells at the end of month five would normally sell on an ex-interest basis and the purchaser would take a deduction for one month's interest (as the seller would receive this).

### 5.6.2 Accrued income taxable

The accrued income scheme may apply where the nominal value of gilts or loan stocks held at any point in the year exceeds £5,000. It brings into charge the interest credited to sellers of gilts and loan stocks. The interest which is deemed to accrue on a daily basis is treated for tax purposes as if it had been received by the vendor. The amount of any adjustments in the other direction (interest received but not earned over the period of ownership) is deducted and the net amount is charged to tax under Schedule D Case VI on the current year basis.

#### Example

$A$ subscribes £30,000 for a new Government Stock, 5% Treasury Stock 2050 issued on 1 August 1999. He holds the stock for 86 days and then sells it to $B$ who holds the stock at 1 February 2000 when the first six months' interest is payable. $A$ will be assessable for income tax purposes on £353, ie $^{86}/_{183} \times £750$ (the half-yearly interest payable on stock). $B$ will be entitled to a deduction of the same amount in computing his taxable income. His position will therefore be as follows:

|  | £ |
|---|---|
| $B$ receives six months interest of | 750 |
| He deducts 'rebate interest' | 353 |
| Taxable income | 397 |

### 5.6.3 Types of securities within accrued income scheme
(TA 1988, s 710)

The scheme applies to acquisitions and disposals of virtually all types of fixed interest securities by UK-resident individuals. The securities must be loan stock not shares, but the scheme may apply to foreign securities as well as to UK loan stocks.

Savings certificates, certificates of deposit and zero coupon bonds are excluded. Bills of exchange and Treasury bills are not regarded as securities for this purpose because certificates of deposit are excluded and they are within the definition of certificates of deposit for the purposes of the accrued income scheme.

### 5.6.4 Types of disposal which may be caught
(TA 1988, s 710)

The scheme applies to transfers. This term is widely defined in TA 1988 and includes:

(1) a sale (s 710(5));
(2) an exchange (s 710(5)) or a conversion of securities (s 710(13));
(3) a gift (s 710(5));
(4) any transfer otherwise (s 710(5));
(5) death (s 721(1));
(6) a change in the true ownership where a person entitled to securities becomes a trustee in relation to them (s 720(4)).

### 5.6.5 Year of assessment
(TA 1988, s 714)

The assessment is under Schedule D Case VI. It is made for the tax year in which the interest period ends, ie if a loan stock pays interest on 30 April, a disposal of the stock on a cum-interest basis on 5 April 1999 will produce taxable income for 1999–2000.

### 5.6.6 Income from savings

Amounts of accrued income taxed under Schedule D Case VI count as income from savings (see 5.1.6) for 1998–99 onwards.

### 5.6.7 Calculation of the accrued amount and the rebate amount
(TA 1988, ss 710, 713 and 714)

Where transactions go through the Stock Exchange, the accrued amount and the rebate amount are calculated by the broker and appear on the contract note. Where the transaction does not go through the market the calculation is made in the same way.

If there is more than one transaction in 'securities of the same kind', the accrued amounts and rebate amounts can be netted off. This term is interpreted strictly: £5,000 9% Treasury Stock 2020 is 'of the same kind' as £10,000 9% Treasury Stock 2020, but is not 'of the same kind' as some other issue of Treasury stock.

Separate calculation of all accrued amounts and rebate amounts is necessary. Relief is given for a rebate amount against the next interest received on that security or, if a transfer intervenes, against the accrued amount. Thus it is possible for a rebate amount in one tax year to be set against interest received in the next tax year.

# OTHER INTEREST-TYPE INCOME

## 5.7 RELEVANT DISCOUNTED SECURITIES
(FA 1996, Sched 13)

### 5.7.1 Introduction

Schedule D Case III may also bring sums into charge which are deemed to be interest income.

A loan stock may be issued at a discount, or be redeemable at a premium. In either case, the borrower undertakes that when the loan is repaid the borrower will receive more than the amount originally paid on the issue of the stock. A typical situation is where a loan stock is issued at £80 for every £100 nominal and when the loan stock is redeemed the investor is entitled to receive £100. There are no provisions for the payer to deduct tax from discount.

The discount or premium is charged to tax under Schedule D Case III where the loan stock is within the definition of a relevant discounted security and the company which issues the bond is a UK company. If the issuer is an overseas company, the discount is charged under Schedule D Case V.

### 5.7.2 Definition of relevant discounted security
(TA 1988, Sched 4, para 1)

A loan stock will not be a relevant discounted security just because it is issued at a discount; it must be issued at a deep discount. A discount is regarded as a deep discount only where it exceeds 0.5% for every year of the intended life of the loan stock, or where the discount exceeds 15% in total.

The following types of loan stock cannot be a relevant discounted security:

(1) indexed-linked gilts.

(2) gilts issued prior to 14 March 1989;

(3) a loan stock which is convertible into shares; and

(4) certain corporate loan stocks whose redemption price is linked to shares or other assets.

### Examples – Relevant discounted security

(1) A five-year loan stock is issued at £95 for every £100 nominal. This is a relevant discounted security because the discount exceeds 0.5% pa.

(2) A 35-year loan stock is issued at £80 for every £100 nominal. This is a relevant discounted security, even though the discount is less than 0.5% pa, because it exceeds 15% in total.

## 5.7.3 Events which give rise to a tax charge
(TA 1988, Sched 4, para 4)

A disposal of a relevant discounted security can give rise to a charge under Schedule D Case III. The whole of the profit is taxable as if it were interest.

### Example – Disposal of deep discount security

A bond is issued at £82, redeemable at £100 after two years. This reflects a compound interest rate of approximately 10% since $82 \times (^{110}\!/_{100})^2 = 100$. If the holder sells for £93 after 12 months, he will be assessed on the difference between £82 and £93, ie £11. If the purchaser holds the bond until it is redeemed in Year 2 he will be chargeable under Schedule D Case III on the redemption profit of £18 as income for that year.

## 5.7.4 Stripped gilts

There is one exception to the general rule that individuals and trustees are taxed on discounted securities only when a disposal takes place. Where a stripped gilt is held, it is necessary to re-value it at the end of each tax year and the owner must pay tax on any increase in value as if it were income.

## 5.7.5 Income from savings

Discounts which are taxed under Schedule D Case III count as income from savings (see 5.1.6).

## 5.7.6 Losses

An individual who realises a loss on the disposal of a relevant discounted security is allowed to deduct this from his taxable income for the year. However, the loss cannot be carried back or forward to a future year.

### 5.7.7 Pre-1996–97 legislation

Similar, but more complex, legislation applied before 6 April 1997 to 'deep discount bonds' and 'deep gain securities'. For further details, see the *Allied Dunbar Tax Handbook 1996–97* at 5.6–5.7.

## DIVIDENDS FROM UK COMPANIES

## 5.8 DIVIDENDS

### 5.8.1 Dividends are taxable for year in which they fall due for payment
(TA 1988, s 834(3))

The dividends which need to be reported on a tax return, and which are income for a tax year, are the dividends which were due for payment in the year. If you have shares in a company which declared a dividend which was payable on 5 April 2000, you will have to report the dividend as 1999–2000 income. This is not affected by the fact that you may not have received the dividend cheque until early in the next tax year.

The period for which the dividend is paid is not relevant. A final dividend for a company's year which ended on 31 December 1997 would be income for 1999–2000 if it was paid in (eg) June 1999.

A dividend from a UK company carries a tax credit (see 5.8.4).

### 5.8.2 Dividends paid by unit trusts

Dividends from unit trusts are treated in exactly the same way as dividends from companies except in regard to 'equalisation'. This is an amount paid to holders of units who have acquired them since the last dividend was paid. The equalisation payment is not taxable as income but is instead treated as a return of capital.

### 5.8.3 Treatment of dividends received in 1999–2000

The treatment of tax credits changed on 6 April 1999. The fundamental changes are:

(1) the rate of tax credit decreased from $^{20}\!/_{\!90}$ to $^{1}\!/_{\!9}$ of the dividend; and

(2) the tax credit became non-refundable.

As far as taxpaying individual shareholders are concerned, the lower and basic rates of income tax on dividends will become 10% so the tax exactly eliminates any tax liability. Higher rate taxpayers will pay 32.5% on the dividend income, which means that they will be in the same position as at present. This is demonstrated in the following example:

## Example

|  | 1998–99 | From 6 April 1999 |
|---|---|---|
|  | £ | £ |
| Cash dividend received | 80.00 | 80.00 |
| Tax credit (²⁰‰ and ¹‰) | 20.00 | 8.89 |
| Taxable income | 100.00 | 88.89 |
| Higher rate tax (40% and 32.5%) | (40.00) | (28.89) |
| After tax income | 60.00 | 60.00 |

Both before and after 6 April 1999, it can be seen that a cash dividend of £80 received by a higher rate taxpaying individual results in a tax liability of £20.

Trustees are now taxed at 25% to compensate for the reduction in the rate of tax credit to 10%. Prior to 6 April trustees were taxed at 34% on their dividend income.

## 5.8.4 Tax credits – Treatment prior to 6 April 1999
(TA 1988, 231; FA 1993, s 78)

When a UK company paid a dividend before 6 April 1999, it had to account for advance corporation tax (see 24.6.2). The corollary of this was that the recipient is entitled to a tax credit of 20%. A dividend of £75 was therefore treated as gross income of £93.75.

Where the individual is liable for tax at 40%, he has to pay additional tax at 20% on his dividend income (ie 40% less the 20% tax credit). However, where an individual is not subject to higher rate tax, the tax credit is deemed to satisfy any liability to the basic rate.

### Example – Tax treatment of a person who received dividend income in 1998–99

A receives dividend income of £80,000 in 1998–99. The tax credits total £20,000 and the 'gross income' is therefore £100,000. If A's other taxable income (after allowances and reliefs) is £20,000 he will be liable to tax:

- at 20% on the first £4,300
- at 23% on the next £15,700
- at 20% on £7,100 (ie the balance of the basic rate band)
- at 40% on £92,900.

He will therefore be liable for higher rate tax of £18,580 (ie 20% of £92,900).

## 5.8.5 Stock dividends
(TA 1988, s 249)

A company may make a 'scrip' or bonus issue so that shareholders receive new shares in proportion to their existing shareholdings. This is not taxable income since in reality all that has happened is that the company has subdivided its share capital by issuing new shares.

In contrast to this, a company may offer shareholders the choice between a cash dividend or additional shares to a similar value. This is called a 'stock dividend' and is taxable income. Sometimes, stock dividends are referred to as 'enhanced scrip dividends'. These are merely a special type of stock dividend where the company offers a premium to shareholders who take stock rather than cash and makes prior arrangements to enable the shareholders to dispose of the shares that they have acquired by taking the stock alternative.

## 5.8.6 How stock dividends are assessed
(Statement of Practice SP A8)

A shareholder who accepts extra shares in lieu of a cash dividend is normally treated as if he had received a dividend equal to the cash that he could have taken. Tax is deemed to have been paid at the lower rate.

A slightly different treatment applies where the value of the shares taken as the stock dividend differs from the cash dividend by 15% or more. In such a case, the shareholder is deemed to have received a dividend equal to the value of the shares at the date of issue. The shareholder may therefore be required to pay higher rate tax on the 'grossed up' value of the dividend or the shares.

### Example – Taxation of dividends

In 1999–2000, A was entitled to a dividend of £2,100 or extra shares in X plc. He took the shares. If the shares were worth £1,900, he will nevertheless be charged higher rate tax on £2,100 plus an amount equal to the tax credit; the amount charged to higher rate tax for 1999–2000 is £2,210 (£2,100 grossed up for the 10% tax credit).

If the shares were worth £2,600 when they were issued, he would be charged higher rate tax on £2,600 'grossed up', ie £2,860.

## 5.8.7 No basic rate repayment
(TA 1988, s 249(4))

Prior to 6 April 1999, although the stock dividends were treated as if they had borne 20% tax at source, no repayment can be made to the shareholder if he was not liable for tax.

### 5.8.8 Consequences for CGT of taking a stock dividend

In the example in 5.8.6, the shareholder's acquisition value for CGT purposes of the shares that he acquires through the stock dividend is the amount on which he is assessed for higher rate purposes less basic rate tax.

### 5.8.9 Trustees and enhanced scrip dividends

Where trustees hold shares in a company which offers an enhanced scrip dividend, the tax treatment of trustees and beneficiaries can involve complex issues. The Revenue issued a Statement of Practice in May 1994 and you should refer to this for guidance.

### 5.8.10 Dividends which form part of a demerger
(TA 1988, s 213)

A dividend may take the form of an issue of shares formerly held by the company in a subsidiary. Where the necessary Revenue clearances have been obtained, such a dividend is treated as capital and not as taxable income. The documentation issued by the company will normally state that clearance has been obtained from the Revenue and that the demerger is an exempt distribution.

### 5.8.11 Foreign income dividends

It was possible for a UK company paying a dividend between July 1994 and 5 April 1999 to elect for it to be treated as a foreign income dividend; this had tax advantages for the company. So far as the shareholder is concerned, he is treated in the same way as if he had received any other UK dividend unless he is entitled to reclaim tax. No tax can be recovered on foreign income dividends. On the other hand, a basic rate taxpayer has no tax liability on foreign income dividends and a 40% taxpayer is merely liable for the difference between 40% and a notional 20% tax credit.

### 5.8.12 Other dividend income

See 5.9 on sundry receipts from UK companies which are treated as distributions. See also 6.10.2 on dividends paid by foreign companies and which are treated as income from savings.

## 5.9 SUNDRY RECEIPTS TREATED AS FOR DIVIDENDS

### 5.9.1 Deemed dividends
(TA 1988, s 209)

There are various transactions which can count as a distribution, particularly where a person holds shares in a close company (see 24.12). From the point of view of the recipient, a distribution is for all practical purposes the same as a dividend.

## 5.9.2 Interest at more than a commercial rate
(TA 1988, s 209)

Interest which is paid to a shareholder may constitute a distribution in so far as it exceeds a normal commercial rate.

## 5.9.3 Issue of redeemable shares
(TA 1988, 209(2)(c))

An issue to shareholders of redeemable preference shares (or other redeemable shares) counts as a distribution. The value of the redeemable shares at the date that they are issued is treated as if it were a dividend paid in cash at that time. This rule does not apply where the redeemable shares are issued for new consideration.

## 5.9.4 Bonus issue following repayment of share capital
(TA 1988, s 210)

Where a company has repaid share capital in the past, a subsequent bonus issue is treated as a dividend paid to the shareholders who receive the bonus shares. The shareholders who receive the bonus shares may not be the same people whose shares were previously bought back by the company, but this does not make any difference to the way in which the current shareholders are taxed on receipt of a bonus issue of shares in these circumstances.

## 5.9.5 Benefits in kind provided to shareholders
(TA 1988, s 418)

Where shareholders in a close company (see 24.12) are provided with benefits in kind, they may be assessed under Schedule E. However, if they are not employed by the company, it will not be possible for the Revenue to assess benefits in kind under Schedule E. In these circumstances, the company may be deemed to have made a distribution equal to the value of the benefits in kind concerned.

## 5.9.6 Assets transferred by or to a close company
(TA 1988, s 209(4))

A deemed distribution may arise where assets are transferred from the members of a company to the company at a price which exceeds their market value, or company assets are transferred to shareholders at a price which is less than market value.

## 5.9.7 **Purchase by a company of its own shares**
(TA 1988, s 209)

The general rule is that where a company buys back its shares, the amount paid by the company is treated as a distribution in so far as it exceeds the original issue price of the shares.

The amount treated as a distribution is not affected by the value of the shares at the time when they were acquired by an individual. Consequently, where a person has acquired shares by inheritance, or bought them from an existing shareholder, his acquisition value may exceed the original issue price (ie the amount which was paid to the company in return for the shares being issued). In the event of a purchase of own shares by a company, it is the issue price which is important.

### Example – Purchase by company of own shares

> A acquires 1,000 shares in X Ltd for £10,000. The shares were originally issued at their par value of £1 per share. It subsequently transpires that A cannot get on with the directors of the company. If A's shares are bought back by the company at £9 per share A is deemed to have received a distribution of £8,000, even though he had actually made a capital loss.

## 5.9.8 **Relief under TA 1988, s 219**

In certain circumstances it may be possible for a company to purchase its own shares without the transaction being treated as giving rise to a distribution. Clearance needs to be obtained from the Revenue that the purchase of own shares is for the benefit of the company's trade. The conditions which must be satisfied are:

(1) the company must be unquoted;
(2) it must be a trading company or the holding company of a trading group;
(3) the vendor must be resident and ordinarily resident in the UK;
(4) the vendor must have owned the shares for at least five years;
(5) the vendor's interest in the company must be 'substantially reduced';
(6) the purchase must be undertaken to benefit the company's trade.

# 6

# OTHER INCOME

This chapter deals with both income received without deduction of tax and income received net of tax.

### Income from which no tax is deducted at source

*Investment income taxed under Schedule D Case VI*

(1)  Sale of certificates of deposit.
(2)  Gains from roll-up, and other offshore, funds.

*Schedule D Cases IV and V: untaxed income from abroad*

(3)  Foreign interest and dividends.
(4)  Foreign real estate income.
(5)  Alimony and maintenance payments.
(6)  Investment in overseas partnerships.
(7)  Double tax relief.
(8)  Pensions taxable under Schedule D Case V.

*Other income taxed under Schedule D Case VI*

(9)  Sundry income assessed under Case VI.

### Income received net of tax

(10)  Foreign interest and dividends received via UK paying agents.
(11)  Other income received net of tax.

## INCOME FROM WHICH NO TAX IS DEDUCTED AT SOURCE

## INVESTMENT INCOME TAXED UNDER SCHEDULE D CASE VI

### 6.1  SALE OF CERTIFICATES OF DEPOSIT
(TA 1988, s 56)

A certificate of deposit is a document which entitles the holder to receive the amount held on deposit. An owner of such a deposit can assign the deposit to someone else. Where this is done for valuable consideration the profit is taxable under Schedule D Case VI.

At one time it was possible to avoid having taxable income by assigning ownership of a deposit without there being a certificate of deposit. However, profits on such transactions are now also caught as income which is taxable under Schedule D Case VI. They are not treated as income from savings.

## 6.2 GAINS FROM ROLL-UP, AND OTHER OFFSHORE, FUNDS
(TA 1988, ss 757–763)

A Schedule D Case VI charge may arise on gains from disposals of certain offshore funds. The type of funds concerned are generally collective investment schemes similar to unit trusts. In many cases the fund earns bank interest which is accumulated within the fund rather than distributed as dividend. When the shareholder disposes of his investment he receives the benefit of this accumulated interest in the price that he obtains for his shares.

### 6.2.1 No charge on distributor funds
(TA 1988, s 760 and Sched 27)

Gains from distributor funds are generally exempt from the charge under s 757. Offshore funds qualify for distributor status where at least 85% of investment income received by the fund is distributed as dividend. In the case of commodity funds, the 85% distribution requirement is reduced to 42.5%.

Where a fund does not qualify as a distributor fund, a Case VI charge is charged on a disposal. This includes certain disposals which are not taken into account for CGT purposes such as a share exchange on a takeover of a fund. It also includes a deemed disposal on the death of the shareholder.

The charge arises on the gain as it would be computed for CGT purposes, but with no allowance for indexation.

#### Example – Tax on offshore funds

A has held shares in an offshore fund since June 1992. The shares cost £14,000 and are worth £17,000 when sold in August 1999. If the offshore fund does not have distributor status, the gain of £3,000 is Case VI income for 1999–2000.

If the offshore fund had distributor status the gain would have been charged to CGT rather than as income. The amount charged would have been less than £3,000 because of indexation allowance and the gain may have been covered by A's annual exemption for CGT purposes (see 13.1.1).

## 6.2.2 Equalisation arrangements
(TA 1988, s 758)

Where an overseas fund has distributor status, and there are equalisation arrangements, any sum paid to a shareholder on the sale of his shares or units and which is treated as equalisation is income for the purposes of Schedule D Case VI. There is no income tax charge on the balance of the disposal proceeds.

## 6.2.3 Gains realised by foreign domiciliaries
(TA 1988, s 762)

A gain from a disposal of an offshore fund by a person of foreign domicile is taxed under Schedule D Case V rather than under Case VI, and the remittance basis applies (see 22.9).

## 6.2.4 Gains not income from savings

Gains realised from the disposal of offshore funds are taxed under Schedule D Case VI, not Case III, and do not count as income from savings (see 5.1.6).

# SCHEDULE D CASES IV AND V: UNTAXED INCOME FROM ABROAD

If you have untaxed income from abroad, a special schedule of your self-assessment tax return must be completed (see opposite).

# 6.3 FOREIGN INTEREST AND DIVIDENDS

Debenture and Government bond interest and dividends paid by overseas companies are taxed under Case IV or Case V only if they fall outside the paying agent procedures described in 6.11. Interest on overseas bank deposits and private loans are always taxable under Case V. Such income is normally treated as income from savings.

## 6.3.1 How the taxable amount is computed

The current year basis has applied since 1997–98. Until 1995–96, the basis of assessment was the preceding year basis as for Schedule D Case III (see 5.1.3). A point to watch with all foreign investments is that income tax is charged on the interest credited or dividends received, without reference to any exchange gain or loss on the money deposited or invested.

*Income and gains and tax credit relief for the year ended 5 April 2000*

Inland Revenue **FOREIGN**

Fill in these boxes first

| Name | Tax reference |
|---|---|
| | |

*If you want help, look up the box numbers in the Notes*

## *Foreign savings*

**Fill in columns A to E, and tick the box in column E if you want to claim tax credit relief.**

| | Country A | tick box if income is unremittable ▼ | Amount before tax B | UK tax C | Foreign tax D | Amount chargeable E | tick box to claim tax credit relief ▼ |
|---|---|---|---|---|---|---|---|
| ■ ***Interest, and other income from overseas savings*** *- see Notes, page FN4* | | | £ | £ | £ | £ | |
| | | | £ | £ | £ | £ | |
| | | | £ | £ | £ | £ | |
| | | | £ | £ | £ | £ | |
| | | | £ | £ | £ | £ | |
| | | | £ | £ | £ | £ | |
| | | | £ | £ | £ | £ | |
| | | | £ | £ | £ | £ | |
| | | | £ | £ | £ | £ | |
| | | | £ | £ | £ | £ | |
| | | | £ | £ | £ | £ | |
| | | | | total of column above 6.1 £ | | total of column above 6.2 £ | |
| ■ ***Dividends*** *- see Notes, page FN4* | | | £ | £ | £ | £ | |
| | | | £ | £ | £ | £ | |
| | | | £ | £ | £ | £ | |
| | | | £ | £ | £ | £ | |
| | | | £ | £ | £ | £ | |
| | | | £ | £ | £ | £ | |
| | | | £ | £ | £ | £ | |
| | | | £ | £ | £ | £ | |
| | | | £ | £ | £ | £ | |
| | | | £ | £ | £ | £ | |
| | | | £ | £ | £ | £ | |
| | | | £ | £ | £ | £ | |
| | | | £ | £ | £ | £ | |
| | | | | total of column above 6.1A £ | | total of column above 6.2A £ | |

SA106

BMSD 12/99net

TAX RETURN ■ FOREIGN ETC: PAGE F1

*Please turn over*

### Example – Foreign currency deposit account

In June 1998, *F* deposited £10,000 with a foreign bank. At the then exchange rate of £1 = 20 units of foreign currency, that sum was credited as 200,000 units. In June 1999, when the exchange rate was £1 = 25 units, interest of 30,000 units was credited to the account. In June 2000, *F* closed the account, receiving back his original capital, the interest credited in June 1999 and a further 20,000 foreign currency units as interest to close. However, by then the exchange rate was £1 = 30 units, so the sterling equivalent of the 250,000 units was only £8,333.

In commercial terms, *F* has suffered a loss of £1,667, but for tax purposes he received interest of £1,200 in June 2000 (30,000 units at £1 = 25) and £667 in June 2000 (20,000 units at £1 = 30) and income tax must be paid on that interest. He has, however, also made a capital loss of £3,534, calculated as follows:

|  |  |  | £ | £ |
|---|---|---|---:|---:|
| Proceeds of | 250,000 | units |  | 8,333 |
|  | 200,000 | units cost (June 1998) | 10,000 |  |
|  | 30,000 | units cost (June 1999) | 1,200 |  |
|  | 20,000 | units cost (June 2000) | 667 |  |
|  |  |  |  | 11,867 |
| Capital loss |  |  |  | (3,534) |

Unfortunately, that capital loss may only be used by set-off against capital gains on the disposal of other assets. If *F* has no such gains, he cannot utilise the loss and so has paid tax on a profit of £1,867 when he has in fact made a loss of £1,667.

### 6.3.2 Income from savings

Foreign dividends and interest taxed under Schedule D Cases IV or V count as income from savings unless the income is taxed under the remittance basis (see 22.9).

## 6.4 FOREIGN REAL ESTATE INCOME

It is not unusual for a UK resident to have bought – or inherited – a villa or flat abroad. It is less usual to own commercial premises, but the tax rules are the same. And the same rules also apply to properties bought under 'time-share' arrangements.

### 6.4.1 Basis of assessment

The current year basis of assessment has applied since 1997–98. Rents from overseas properties were normally assessable for 1995–96 and earlier years under the usual Case V preceding year rules. For further details see *Allied Dunbar Tax Handbook 1999–2000* at 6.4.1.

## 6.4.2 How income is computed

In calculating the assessable rent, the landlord may deduct expenses paid, such as repairs, redecoration, insurance, maid service, gardening, management fees and advertising. If the landlord sometimes uses the property himself, then an apportionment of these expenses must be made, in the same way as for a UK property (see 4.2).

There are three important differences between the tax treatment of rent from real property in the UK and rent from property abroad:

(1) The 'rent-a-room' scheme (see 4.4) applies only to properties in the UK. Therefore this exemption cannot be claimed against rents from an overseas property.
(2) Similarly, the special rules allowing the provision of furnished holiday accommodation to be treated as a trade (see 4.5) apply only where the relevant property is situated in the UK.
(3) If the rental income statement for an overseas property shows a deficit for a year (that is to say, if expenses excluding interest paid exceed rent received), that deficit may be carried forward and deducted from the rent received in respect of the same property in the next year (and the deduction may be rolled forward indefinitely until there is rental income against which it can be set). However, no other form of loss relief is available. In particular, the deficit may not be set against rents received from other properties, whether in the UK or abroad.

Interest payments have been deductible since April 1995, whether the interest is paid in the UK or overseas. For the treatment of interest paid before 6 April 1995 on loans taken out to buy investment property, see *Allied Dunbar Tax Handbook 1997–98* at 5.10.2.

## 6.4.3 Accounts

In the past, rental income statements should have been drawn up to 5 April but in practice the Revenue often accepted statements drawn up to any convenient date. For example, the rental statement for the calendar year will often have been taken as the measure of the income for the tax year. This is no longer acceptable and it is necessary to report the income, which has actually arisen in the tax year.

One possible complication is that income may be received, and expenses may be incurred, in either UK or local currency. In practice, the Revenue will accept any reasonable basis of currency conversion. For example, if the rents are collected by a local agent, who disburses local expenses and remits a net sum to the landlord, that net amount may be converted at the spot rate for the day it was remitted. However, the Revenue will expect the same basis of conversion to be retained from one year to the next.

The form which you will have to complete as part of your self-assessment tax return is reproduced overleaf.

## Income from land and property abroad

*Fill in one Page F4 if:*
- *you have only one overseas let property, or*
- *you have more than one but all your overseas let properties are in the same country, or*
- *you have more than one and they are in different countries but there has been no foreign tax deducted from any of the income.*

*If your overseas let properties are in different countries and some foreign tax has been deducted you must fill in a copy of Page F4 for each property letting. (Take copies of Page F4 before you start or ask the Orderline for more copies of the Foreign Pages.) Please put your name and tax reference next to the address box on each copy.*

*If you are using Page F4 to return income from more than one property please use the address box below for the first property and the 'Additional information' box on Page F5 for the addresses of your other overseas let properties.*

Address of property

|  |
|--|
|  |
|  |
|  |
| Postcode |

- Income - total rents and other receipts (excluding chargeable premiums) — **6.11** £
- Tick box 6.11A if box 6.11 contains income from more than one property — **6.11A**

■ *Expenses - see Notes, page FN7*

- Rent, rates, insurance, etc — **6.12** £
- Repairs, maintenance and renewals — **6.13** £
- Finance charges, including interest — **6.14** £
- Legal and professional costs — **6.15** £
- Costs of services provided — **6.16** £
- Other expenses — **6.17** £ | **6.18** £

- show loss in brackets — **6.19** £

■ *Tax adjustments - see Notes, page FN8*

- Private use proportions — **6.20** £
- Balancing charges — **6.21** £ | **6.22** £

- Capital allowances — **6.23** £
- 10% wear and tear — **6.24** £ | **6.25** £

(if loss, enter '0' here, and enter loss in box 6.27) — **6.26** £

(if you have entered '0' in box 6.26) — **6.27** £

## 6.5 ALIMONY AND MAINTENANCE PAYMENTS
(TA 1988, s 347A(4))

A UK resident may receive maintenance or alimony payments from a spouse, former spouse or parent resident abroad. The tax treatment used to depend on whether that maintenance or alimony was paid under a UK or a foreign court order (or under a UK or foreign agreement). Payments under UK orders and agreements were taxed under Case III of Schedule D (as explained in 8.2.1) up to 5 April 2000. Payments under foreign orders and agreements were taxed under Case V of Schedule D. All of this was subject to the overriding rule that payments under both UK and foreign court orders and agreements were not taxable unless the relevant order or agreement counted as an 'existing obligation'. Broadly, an existing obligation was one that was created by an order or agreement made before 15 March 1988 either in the UK or abroad (for further detail see 8.2). Furthermore, even payments under existing obligations were taken out of charge from 6 April 2000.

## 6.6 INVESTMENT IN OVERSEAS PARTNERSHIPS
(TA 1988, s 391)

A UK resident may be a sleeping partner in a business carried on abroad. For example, a man might provide the finance for his son to set up in business abroad, in return for a share of the profits. He will then be a sleeping partner in the son's business. In some situations it may be difficult to tell whether the father has become a sleeping partner in the son's business or has made a loan at interest to the son. If the father is entitled to a stated proportion of profits (say one-quarter), then he will certainly be a sleeping partner. However, if he is entitled to a fixed annual sum, he may be a sleeping partner or may simply have made a loan. In practice this is not important, as both interest and a sleeping partner's profit share are taxed according to the usual Case IV/Case V rules.

The important question is whether the UK resident is a sleeping or an active partner. If he is an active partner the partnership business is likely to be carried on at least partly within the UK and complex questions arise, which are outside the scope of this book.

If the sleeping partner is entitled to a fixed sum, at annual or other intervals, and that sum is stated in a foreign currency, then each instalment must, for tax purposes, be converted into sterling at the spot rate for the date it falls due. If he is entitled to a stated proportion of profits, and the business accounts are prepared in a foreign currency, then the appropriate profit figure must be converted into sterling at the spot rate for the last day of the accounting period. If the sleeping partner is obliged to bear a share of a trading loss, that loss may be relieved against overseas trading and pension income, but not against overseas investment income or any UK income. In most cases therefore it will be relieved by deducting the amount of the loss from the partnership profit share assessable for a later year.

## 6.7 DOUBLE TAX RELIEF
(TA 1988, s 790)

Basically put, foreign tax paid can be deducted from the UK tax charged on the same income.

### Example – Double tax relief

D, a basic rate taxpayer, receives an interest payment of £1,000 from abroad, on which the foreign tax is £150. The UK tax position is:

|  | £ |
|---|---|
| Gross interest | 1,000 |
| Foreign tax deducted or paid | 150 |
| Net receipt | 850 |
| UK tax at 23% of £1,000 | 230 |
| *Less*: foreign tax paid | 150 |
| UK tax to be paid | 80 |
| After-tax income | 770 |

If D were liable for tax at only 10%, the foreign tax would bring his UK tax liability down to nil, but he would not be entitled to reclaim the difference of £50.

### 6.7.1 An important practical point

Relief for overseas tax will not be given unless the individual can prove that he has indeed paid the tax. It is not sufficient simply to demonstrate that tax is payable under foreign law: the claimant must be able to show that he has indeed paid that tax by producing an official receipt or tax deduction certificate.

### 6.7.2 Foreign tax adjustments

The Revenue must be notified if an amount of foreign tax paid is later adjusted and this means that too much credit has been allowed as double taxation relief. Failure to notify the Revenue within one year of an adjustment will result in a taxpayer becoming liable to a penalty (not exceeding the tax underpaid) because of the claim which has proved to be excessive.

If a foreign tax adjustment means that you have not claimed enough, you are under no statutory duty to report this but it is clearly in your own interests to do so.

# 6.8 PENSIONS TAXABLE UNDER SCHEDULE D CASE V
(TA 1988, s 58)

Certain pensions are taxable under Case V rather than Schedule E:

(1) Pensions paid by a person outside the UK.
(2) Pensions paid on behalf of a person outside the UK.
(3) Voluntary pensions paid by a person outside the UK.

Pensions which are charged to tax under Schedule D Case V are assessed on pensioners who are:

(1) resident, ordinarily resident and domiciled in the UK – 90% of the pension is charged to tax;
(2) resident but not ordinarily resident in the UK – the pension is assessed on the remittance basis by reference to sums brought into the UK;
(3) resident and ordinarily resident in the UK but not domiciled in the UK – the pension is assessed on the remittance basis.

Pensions assessed under Schedule D Case V are taxed on the current year basis for 1997–98 and subsequent years. They were taxed on the preceding year basis up to 1995–96. The 1996–97 assessment will normally be half of the income for the two years ended 5 April 1997.

### Nazi compensation pensions
(TA 1988, s 330)

Annuities and premiums paid under German or Austrian law to victims of Nazi persecution are exempt from income tax. These are pensions paid because of serious damage to the individual's health and are also exempt from tax in Germany and Austria.

# OTHER INCOME TAXED UNDER SCHEDULE D CASE VI

# 6.9 SUNDRY INCOME ASSESSED UNDER CASE VI
(TA 1988, s 15)

Tax may be charged under Schedule D Case VI in respect of any annual profits or gains which do not fall under any other case of Schedule D and which are not charged by virtue of any other schedule.

Post-cessation receipts (see 2.7) and enterprise allowances are charged under Case VI. In addition, Case VI applies to gains from roll-up funds, profits under the accrued income scheme and gains on foreign life policies. Furthermore, where tax is charged under various anti-avoidance provisions (see Chapter 20) the charge is normally made under Case VI.

In addition, profits from certain 'one off' or isolated business activities in the nature of a trade have been charged under Case VI. Thus, the following have been held by the courts to be Case VI income:

(1) commission for guaranteeing overdrafts;
(2) underwriting commission on share issues;
(3) insurance commission;
(4) receipts for the use of copyright material;
(5) payments made to the wife of a train robber for their life story;
(6) profits realised by an 'Angel', ie a person who sponsored a play and was entitled to a share of the profits.

Case VI income may be earned income or investment income.

### 6.9.1 Schedule D Case VI losses
(TA 1988, s 392)

Case VI losses may be set against any profits assessable under Case VI, whether or not the profits arise from the same activity. However, they may not be set against income which is taxed under any other schedule.

Where an individual has suffered losses from an isolated transaction in the past, it may be sensible to arrange matters so that income arises which is taxable under Case VI. For example an investment in an offshore roll-up fund (see 6.2) could be made with a view to producing a predictable level of Case VI profits which will be tax free because of the relief for Case VI losses.

## INCOME RECEIVED NET OF TAX

## 6.10 FOREIGN INTEREST AND DIVIDENDS RECEIVED VIA UK PAYING AGENTS
(TA 1988, ss 17, 44 and 123, and Sched 3; F(No 2)A 1992, Sched 11)

### 6.10.1 Foreign interest income

Interest on bonds issued by overseas Government or companies may be received via a 'paying agent'.

The paying or collecting agent receives, from the overseas Government or company, a remittance representing the interest due less the foreign tax payable on that interest. The rate at which foreign tax is deducted depends partly on the laws of the country concerned and partly on the terms of any double tax treaty between the UK and that country. At worst, tax will be deducted at the full rate payable by residents of the overseas country. At best, no foreign tax at all will be deducted. More usually, however, tax will be deducted at a 'treaty' or 'withholding' rate of, typically, 10% for interest and 15% for dividends.

Before paying the interest over to the individual bondholders, the paying agent must deduct UK tax so that the total tax paid (foreign and UK) equals tax at 20% (at basic rate for years up to 1995–96). The interest is treated as income from savings.

### Example – Tax deducted by paying agent

*A* has a holding of foreign Government bonds on which the interest, payable annually through a British bank, is 500 dinars, equivalent to £100 sterling. Foreign withholding tax is charged at 10%. The bank will send *A* a cheque for £80 (or will credit his account with that amount) and provide a voucher showing:

|                                   | £    |
| --------------------------------- | ---- |
| Gross income                      | 100  |
| *Less*: foreign withholding tax   | (10) |
|                                   | 90   |
| *Less*: UK income tax             | (10) |
| Net payment                       | 80   |

The bank will, of course, pay the £10 UK income tax over to the Revenue.

If *A* is a basic rate taxpayer, that is the end of the story: the deduction made by the paying agent clears his basic rate liability and gives him relief for overseas tax paid. If he is a higher rate taxpayer, he is in the same position as if he had received income on a British Government security: his total liability is £40 (40% of £100) of which he has paid £20 by deduction. He must therefore pay a further £20, probably on his annual tax assessment.

However, if *A* is not a taxpayer at all, the Revenue will repay only the £10 UK income tax deducted by the British bank – it will not repay the £10 foreign tax deducted by the foreign Government. In certain circumstances it may, theoretically, be possible to reclaim this money direct from the foreign authorities, but it is certain to be a difficult and time-consuming process, especially if correspondence in a foreign language is necessary. In almost all cases, it simply will not be worth the effort.

Care is needed with regard to foreign dividends as in some cases the tax shown as 'deducted' on the dividend certificate is really tax suffered by the foreign company on its profits rather than foreign tax withheld from the dividend, and such tax is not eligible for double tax relief. This is often the case where the company is based in Australia or the Channel Islands.

## 6.10.2 Foreign dividends

If the shareholder was liable to higher rate tax, the rate on foreign dividends for 1998–99 was 40%, but the top rate went down to 32.5% from 6 April 1999 in line with the rate of tax on UK dividends.

A UK paying agent deducts UK tax so as to bring the total of foreign tax and UK tax up to 20%. Foreign dividends are income from savings.

### 6.10.3 High overseas tax rate

In some instances, overseas tax may be deducted at a rate higher than the 20% UK rate on dividends. In such a case, the UK paying agent will simply pass on whatever net payment is received from overseas.

#### Example – High overseas tax rate

> B has a shareholding in a foreign company, on which a dividend equivalent to £100 is declared during 1999–2000. However, the foreign authorities withhold tax at 30%. The net remittance received by B will be £70.
>
> If he is a basic rate taxpayer, no UK tax will be payable on the foreign dividend, because the UK tax is reduced to nil by relief for the £30 foreign tax paid. However, the excess foreign tax paid cannot be set against B's UK tax liability on other sources of income – it is simply lost. If B is a higher rate taxpayer, his UK liability of £32.50 (32.5% of £100) will be reduced to £2.50 by deducting the £30 foreign tax paid.
>
> There are thus two basic rules. First, the Revenue will never refund tax paid to a foreign government, and secondly, foreign tax paid in respect of a particular source of income may only be set against UK tax charged on that same source.

### 6.10.4 Which year of assessment?
(TA 1988, s 835(6) and Sched 3, para 8; F(No 2)A 1992, Sched 11)

Interest and dividends within the 'paying or collecting agent' scheme count as income of the year in which they are paid to the investor by the UK paying or collecting agent. Accordingly, the operative date is the date the agent issues a cheque or authorises a credit transfer. This cannot be before, but may be a few days after, funds become available in the UK. Therefore it is still possible that a dividend or interest payment due, say, at the end of March 2000 will be assessable as income of the 2000–01 tax year. The payment date will of course be clearly shown on the paying or collecting agent's voucher, so no particular difficulty should arise.

### 6.10.5 Stock dividends and other peculiarities
(TA 1988, s 249)

As explained in 5.8, an investor who opts to take a stock dividend (that is to say, additional shares in lieu of a cash dividend) from a UK company is taxed as if he had received an equivalent amount in cash. This rule does not apply where a stock dividend is paid by a company not resident in the UK.

A higher rate taxpayer offered the choice between a stock and a cash dividend is therefore usually better off taking the stock dividend. However, this assumes that the additional shares offered are worth at least as much as the cash option and that they are readily saleable. As always, the 'tax-saving' tail must not be allowed to wag the 'sensible investment policy' dog. Moreover, in one court case it was suggested that, if stock dividends are taken year after year, and the shares so obtained are sold to provide the shareholder with an income, then income tax may be charged on that income. However, the Revenue is unlikely to take this point unless a substantial amount of money is at stake.

In a number of other cases also, payments by an overseas company may escape tax where an equivalent payment by a UK company would be taxable as a dividend. Most often this occurs where a payment which under UK law would count as a distribution of profits counts, under the relevant foreign law, as a partial return of the shareholders' original investment. The correct position is usually advised by the overseas company or the UK paying agent.

### 6.10.6 Reporting the income

Interest and dividends from foreign companies collected by paying agents should be included on the form reproduced on page 207.

## 6.11 OTHER INCOME RECEIVED NET OF TAX

### 6.11.1 Annuities
(TA 1988, ss 349 and 656–658)

Annuities which are paid by an insurance company are dealt with at 12.5. Where an annuity is payable by an individual or a private company, the payer must deduct tax at basic rate. Note that such income is not treated as savings income and therefore tax is still deducted at basic rate and not at 20% where payment is made.

#### Example – Annuity income received net of basic rate tax

A sells his business to B for a cash sum plus an annuity of £10,000 a year payable by B out of the profits of the business. In 1999–2000, B paid A only £7,700 (£10,000 less tax at 23%).

(1) A may set any available personal allowances against the annuity, so that if he is aged 67, is single, and has no other income, the position for 1999–2000 will be:

|  | £ |
|---|---|
| Annuity (gross amount) | 10,000.00 |
| Personal allowance (over-65 rate) | 5,720.00 |
| Tax payable on | 4,280.00 |
| £1,500 charged at 10% | 150.00 |
| £2,780 charged at 23% | 639.40 |
| Total tax due | 789.40 |
| *Less*: tax paid by deduction | 2,300.00 |
| Inland Revenue will repay | 1,510.60 |

(2)  If $A$'s other income is sufficient to utilise both his personal allowances and the lower rate band, there will of course be no repayment. If he is a higher rate taxpayer, he will have to pay additional tax on the annuity, as follows:

|  | £ |
|---|---|
| Higher rate tax on annuity (40% of £10,000) | 4,000 |
| *Less*: Already paid by deduction | (2,300) |
| Additional tax payable by assessment | 1,700 |

(3)  The buyer, $B$, can obtain relief for the annuity paid to $A$ not as a trading expense, but as a deduction in computing total taxable income.

(a) If he is only a basic rate taxpayer, he obtains the relief to which he is entitled by keeping for himself the £2,300 difference between the gross amount of the annuity and the £7,700 actually paid to $A$.

(b) If he is a higher rate taxpayer, additional relief is given by not charging higher rate tax on an amount equal to the gross annuity paid – a process usually referred to as 'extending the basic rate band'.

(4)  Suppose $B$'s profits are £50,000, he has no other income and is entitled only to the basic personal allowance of £4,335. If he did not have to pay the annuity, his tax position would be:

|  |  | £ |
|---|---|---|
| Income |  | 50,000 |
| Personal allowance |  | 4,335 |
| Tax payable on |  | 45,665 |
| £1,500 | charged at 10% | 150 |
| £26,500 | charged at 23% | 6,095 |
| £17,665 | charged at 40% | 7,066 |
| £45,665 |  | 13,311 |

(5)  As he does have to pay the annuity, the basic rate band is extended by the gross amount of that annuity (£10,000), so the position becomes:

|  |  | £ |
|---|---|---|
| £1,500 | charged at 10% | 150 |
| £36,500 | charged at 23% | 8,395 |
| £7,665 | charged at 40% | 3,066 |
| £45,665 |  | 11,611 |

This is a reduction of £1,700 and so overall the position is:

|  | £ |
|---|---|
| Gross annuity | 10,000 |
| Net payment to $A$ | 7,700 |
| Basic rate tax relief | 2,300 |
| Reduction in tax payable by assessment | 1,700 |
| Total tax relief (40% of £10,000) | 4,000 |

## 6.11.2 Income from trusts

Income paid to a beneficiary of a fixed interest trust will normally be taxed at source at 20%. However, tax will sometimes have been charged on the trustees at basic rate on income received by them which is not income from savings. For example, rental income falls into this category. In such a situation, the beneficiary will have a credit for basic rate tax on that element of his income from the trust which represents income which is not income from savings.

Income payments to discretionary beneficiaries carry a credit of 34% for 1996–97, 1997–98 and 1998–99 (35% for 1995–96 and previous years).

## 6.11.3 Estates of deceased persons
### (TA 1988, ss 695–702)

When someone dies, it takes time for his executors or personal representatives to identify all his assets, pay all his debts, settle any IHT liability and work out the best way of dividing the estate between those entitled (eg one beneficiary may want to take specific investments, another may prefer cash). During this time, known as 'the administration period', it is quite likely that income will be received by the executors or personal representatives, both on the deceased's existing investments and, for example, as interest on a bank account into which the executors have paid money collected on behalf of the estate.

The executors or personal representatives must pay tax on all income received. Items such as share dividends and bond interest will be received net of 20% tax in 1998–99 and this will cover the executors' liability. Other income will be subject to tax at the basic rate and, where no tax has been withheld at source (eg rental income) the executors will need to go through the self-assessment procedures.

The executors or personal representatives will therefore have a pool of income on which tax has been paid. That pool must be divided between the beneficiaries in accordance with the terms of the deceased's will, or of the laws of intestacy if he left no will.

### Example – Tax treatment of estate income

The gross income from an estate is £200, on which the executors have paid tax of £46. The deceased's son is, under the will, entitled to half that income. He will receive a cheque for £77 plus a certificate, signed by the executors, confirming that tax of £23 has been paid to the Revenue. The son's income for tax purposes is £100, but he is treated as having already paid basic rate tax on that £100. If he has personal allowances or other reliefs available, he can obtain (from the Revenue) a repayment of some or all of the £23 tax paid; if he is a higher rate taxpayer, he will have to pay over to the Revenue the difference between basic and higher rate tax.

In some cases, the executors will have suffered tax at only 20%, rather than at basic rate, and the certificate issued by them to the beneficiary must make this clear.

### 6.11.4 Allocation of estate income to particular tax years

The tax treatment of beneficiaries of deceased person's estates was simplified by FA 1995, with a view to facilitating the introduction of self-assessment. With effect from 6 April 1995, payments made to beneficiaries out of the income of the residue of an estate are taxable as income for the year of payment.

This treatment applies both to estates of individuals who die after 5 April 1995 and to existing estates still in the course of administration at 6 April 1995. In summary, a payment to a residuary beneficiary is deemed to be income to the extent that the estate has received income.

More complex rules applied in the past for ascertaining beneficiaries' income. These rules apply only if the estate was wound up before 6 April 1995 (see *Allied Dunbar Tax Handbook 1995–96* at 6.6.6–6.6.8).

# 7

# PERSONAL ALLOWANCES

This chapter looks in detail at the various personal allowances that may be claimed by individual taxpayers. The following topics are covered:

(1) What are personal allowances?
(2) Who may claim personal allowances?
(3) The basic personal allowance.
(4) Calculating 'total income'.
(5) Married couple's allowance.
(6) Pensioner couples.
(7) Widow's bereavement allowance.
(8) Additional personal allowance.
(9) Additional allowance for disabled spouse.
(10) Blind persons.
(11) Working Families' Tax Credits

## 7.1 WHAT ARE PERSONAL ALLOWANCES?
(TA 1988, ss 256–278)

Income tax is not charged on the whole of a person's income. In calculating the amount on which tax must be paid, an individual may deduct both relief for certain types of expenditure (eg subscriptions to work-related professional bodies – see 3.3.2) and one or more 'personal allowances'. Entitlement to personal allowances depends on individual circumstances, as explained later in this chapter, but the three examples below illustrate the principles involved.

Consequently, it is possible for three people to earn exactly the same salary but, because of differing personal circumstances, to pay differing amounts of income tax.

### Examples – Principles of personal allowances

(1)  *A*, a single man aged 35, earns an annual salary of £15,000, out of which he pays a qualifying professional subscription of £135. His tax bill for 1999–2000 will be £2,226.90, calculated as follows:

|  | £ |
|---|---|
| Gross salary | 15,000 |
| Professional subscription | 135 |
|  | 14,865 |
| Basic personal allowance | 4,335 |
| Tax payable on | 10,530 |

| | | |
|---|---|---|
| £1,500 | charged at 10% | 150.00 |
| £9,030 | charged at 23% | 2,076.90 |
| £10,530 | | 2,226.90 |

(2)   *B* is a single mother, also earning £15,000 and paying a qualifying professional subscription of £135. Her tax bill for 1999–2000 will be only £2,029.90, calculated as follows:

|  | £ |
|---|---|
| Lower and basic rate tax payable | |
| (calculated as for (1) above) | 2,226.90 |
| *Less*: additional personal allowance | |
| (£1,900 at 10%) | 197.00 |
|  | 2,029.90 |

(3)   *C*, a widower, is aged 67 but is still in full-time employment. He also earns £15,000 pa and pays a qualifying professional subscription of £135. He is entitled to the higher personal allowance for the over-65s (see 7.3.1) and so his tax bill will be £1,908.35, calculated as follows:

|  | £ |
|---|---|
| Gross salary | 15,000 |
| Professional subscription | 135 |
|  | 14,865 |
| Higher personal allowance | 5,720 |
| Tax payable on | 9,145 |

| | | |
|---|---|---|
| £1,500 | charged at 10% | 150.00 |
| £7,645 | charged at 23% | 1,758.35 |
| £9,145 | | 1,908.35 |

## 7.2  WHO MAY CLAIM PERSONAL ALLOWANCES?
(TA 1988, s 278; British Nationality Act 1981, s 37)

Personal allowances may be claimed by anyone resident in the UK. There is no minimum age requirement so that, for example, a new-born baby is entitled to a personal allowance. Sometimes it is possible, through the use of trusts or settlements, to redirect part of a family's income to a child, so that it may (being covered by the child's personal allowance) be enjoyed tax-free (although the scope for transferring taxable income in this way has been whittled down by a succession of complex anti-avoidance provisions – see 20.5.3).

Personal allowances may also be claimed by British subjects and certain other categories of people not resident in the UK.

### 7.2.1 Time limit for claims
(TMA 1970, s 43)

Under self-assessment a claim to any allowance (unless the legislation specifies to the contrary) must be made within five years of 31 January following the year of assessment to which the claim relates (ie for the year ended 5 April 2000 by 31 January 2006).

Exceptionally, if you failed to claim a relief because you were misled by the Revenue or any other Government Department, you may ask for the last 20 years to be reopened.

Late claims should be avoided if possible, because they may cause difficulties. Although the Revenue should in theory retain papers for at least the last six years, in practice the files for Schedule E taxpayers (those in employment, rather than in business on their own account) are often 'weeded out' after only two or three years. Therefore, unless you have yourself kept papers such as tax assessments and Form P60 (employer's annual statement of pay and tax deducted), it may be impossible to determine how much tax was paid and how much is now repayable.

A final point is that the Revenue usually refuses to grant any relief (other than the basic personal allowance) until the claimant has submitted his tax returns for all relevant years. The Revenue argues that, until it has the returns, it cannot be sure that any relief claimed would not be cancelled out by the tax due on sources of income of which it is unaware.

## 7.3 THE BASIC PERSONAL ALLOWANCE
(TA 1988, s 257)

Every individual who is resident in the UK is entitled to the basic personal allowance. This is often called the 'single person's allowance' – a throwback to the days when there was also a 'married man's allowance'.

The basic personal allowance for the current year is £4,385. Although this is an allowance for a year, it is not scaled down if the individual is born, or dies, halfway through a year of assessment.

## Example – Death during tax year

Suppose *A* died at the end of September 1999, by which time he had earned only half his annual salary. His tax bill for 1999–2000 would be:

|  |  | £ |
|---|---|---|
| Salary |  | 1,000 |
| Professional subscription paid |  | 135 |
|  |  | 9,865 |
| Personal allowance |  | 4,335 |
| Tax payable on |  | 5,530 |
| £1,500 | charged at 10% | 150.00 |
| £4,030 | charged at 23% | 926.90 |
| £5,530 |  | 1,076.90 |

Because the PAYE scheme assumes that personal allowances will be used in equal monthly (or weekly) instalments over the year, about £1,705 will have been deducted from *A*'s salary while he was alive. On request, the Revenue will therefore repay his executors the excess tax deducted (£1,705 less £1,076.90 = £628.10)

## 7.3.1 Higher allowances for the over-65s

Higher allowances are given to those who have attained the age of 65 and who are of limited means. The higher allowance is currently £5,790 for those between the ages of 65 and 74 and £6,050 for those aged 75 or more. If an individual attains the age of 65 (or 75) during a year of assessment, he is entitled to the appropriate allowance for the whole of that year. For example, a man born on 1 June 1933 will attain the age of 65 on 1 June 2000 and will be entitled to the higher allowance of £5,790 for the 2000–01 tax year.

The higher allowance is also given where the individual was alive on the first day of the tax year and would have achieved the age of 65 (or 75) within the tax year, had he not died.

However, the higher allowance is designed to assist only those of limited means. Therefore the allowance is reduced by £1 for every £2 by which the individual's 'total income' exceeds £17,000, until it falls back to the standard allowance for the under-65s.

Within this band, every £2 of income can cost 66p in tax (44p on the £2 itself, plus 22p on the £1 of allowances withdrawn). This is an effective percentage rate of 33%. For 1999–2000, the £1 for £2 reduction operated between 'total incomes' of £16,800 and £19,570 for those between the ages of 65 and 74 and between £16,800 and £20,090 for those aged 75 or more.

## Example – Reduced higher allowances

In 1999–2000, B was aged 70. He received a State pension of £4,500 a year, an occupational pension of £12,500 and rental income of £1,000. His 'total income' was £18,000 and his overall income tax liability for 1999–2000 is therefore:

|  | £ | £ | £ |
|---|---|---|---|
| Total income |  |  | 18,000 |
| Higher personal allowance |  | 5,720 |  |
| Total income | 18,000 |  |  |
| Income limit | 16,800 |  |  |
| Excess | 1,200 |  |  |
| Half of excess |  |  | 600 |
| Reduced higher personal allowance[1] |  |  | 5,120 |
| Tax payable on |  |  | 12,880 |

[1]This cannot be reduced below the standard personal allowance of £4,335.

| £1,500 | charged at 10% | £150.00 |
|---|---|---|
| £11,380 | charged at 23% | £2,617.40 |
| £12,880 |  | £2,767.50 |

The definition of 'total income' is, accordingly, very important, especially as in certain circumstances it is possible for an individual to rearrange his investments so that his 'total income', as defined by the Taxes Acts, is less than his real income. This is explained in 7.4 below.

## 7.4 CALCULATING 'TOTAL INCOME'
(TA 1988, s 835)

A person's 'total income', as defined by the Taxes Acts, differs from his real income, first because not all receipts count towards 'total income' and secondly because certain deductions can be made from real income in calculating 'total income'.

The first step in calculating 'total income' is to add together all the income which is assessable to tax. Income which is not assessable to tax is excluded. Examples include letting income exempt under the 'rent-a-room' scheme (see 4.4), the interest credited to an ISA or an existing TESSA (see 11.4), the dividends earned by a PEP (see 11.5) or a venture capital trust (see 11.7), the growth in value of National Savings Certificates (see 11.2.1) and amounts withdrawn from insurance bonds up to the 5% limit (see 12.3.3). A person whose income falls within the marginal age relief band would, therefore, clearly do well to consider placing his money in tax-exempt investments.

The second step is to deduct, from the sum of assessable income, the following outgoings:

(1) Interest paid, insofar as it qualifies for tax relief under the usual rules other than under MIRAS (see Chapter 9).
(2) All of the 'other outgoings' listed in Chapter 10, insofar as each qualifies for tax relief under the normal rules. (The 'other outgoings' which may qualify are payments for vocational training, charitable donations, certain covenanted payments and certain maintenance and alimony payments.)
(3) Contributions paid to an occupational or personal pension plan.
(4) Any tax-allowable loss arising from investment in enterprise zone property (see 11.8).

## Example – Total income

Suppose that $B$ in the example in 7.3.2 above received a windfall of £5,000. He decides to invest £1,000 in an Enterprise Zone Property Trust and the balance in National Savings Certificates. To celebrate his good fortune, he signed a deed of covenant for £200 a year (gross) in favour of his local church. Although $B$ is now clearly better off, his tax liability for the year 1999–2000 will in fact fall to £2,353.40, as follows:

|  | £ | £ | £ |
|---|---|---|---|
| Pension and interest received |  |  | 18,000 |
| Enterprise Zone property investment |  | 1,000 |  |
| Deed of covenant payment (gross) |  | 200 |  |
|  |  |  | 1,200 |
| 'Total income' |  |  | 16,800 |
| Higher personal allowance | 5,720 |  |  |
| Total income | 16,800 |  |  |
| Income limit | 16,800 |  |  |
| Excess | Nil |  |  |
|  |  |  | 5,720 |
| Tax payable on |  |  | 11,080 |
| £1,500 charged at 10% |  |  | 150.00 |
| £9,580 charged at 23% |  |  | 2,203.40 |
| £11,080 |  |  | 2,353.40 |

## 7.5 MARRIED COUPLE'S ALLOWANCE
(TA 1988, s 257A)

As previously announced this relief has been abolished with effect from 6 April 2000, though it still exists for married couples where either spouse was born before 6 April 1935.

### 7.5.1 Who could claim the allowance?

The basic rule was that a married man, whose wife was living with him, could claim the married couple's allowance. The couple had to be legally married. Where the parties were domiciled abroad, the test was whether they were legally married according to the laws of their country of domicile.

If a man was domiciled in a country where polygamous marriage is allowed, he could claim the married couple's allowance if he had one or more wives. However, he was entitled to only one married couple's allowance, irrespective of the number of wives he had.

A married couple were taken as living together unless they had signed a separation agreement, were separated by order of the court, or were living apart in such circumstances that the separation was likely to be permanent. Consequently, a couple were treated as living together even if they were temporarily apart, for example because one was working abroad, or was in hospital or in prison.

### 7.5.2 Amount of the allowance

The married couple's allowance for those under 65 was abolished from 6 April 2000. The allowance was £1,970 for 1999–2000, but relief was given only at 10%. For 1998–99 the allowance was given at 15%.

#### Example – Married couple's allowance

| | £ |
|---|---|
| A married man earns £10,000 a year. For 1999–2000 his liability was: | |
| Earnings | 10,000 |
| Personal allowance | 4,335 |
| Tax payable on | 5,665 |
| £1,500    charged at 10% | 150.00 |
| £4,165    charged at 23% | 957.95 |
| £5,665 | 1,107.95 |
| *Less*: married couple's allowance (£1,970 at 10%) | 197.00 |
| | 910.95 |

## 7.5.3 Year of marriage

The allowance was scaled down where marriage took place during the tax year. It was reduced by one-twelfth for every complete income tax month before the marriage. (An income tax month begins on the sixth day of one calendar month and ends on the fifth day of the next.)

### Example – Married couple's allowance in the year of marriage

*A* married *B* on 2 November 1999. By then, the first six income tax months of 1999–2000 had passed (the months ending 5 May to 5 October). *A* will therefore be entitled to a reduced married couple's allowance of £985, calculated as follows:

|  | £ |
|---|---|
| Full married couple's allowance | 1,970 |
| *Less* %₁₂ | 985 |
| Reduced allowance | 985 |

However, the allowance was not reduced if the parties ceased to live together, or if the marriage came to an end during the year of assessment, whether by divorce, annulment or death.

## 7.5.4 Transferring the married couple's allowance
(F(No2)A 1992, s 20 and Sched 5)

There have been two possible elections:

(1) A wife could claim half the married couple's allowance for herself; and
(2) Husband and wife could jointly elect for the whole of the married couple's allowance to be given to the wife.

A claim or election could be made on Revenue Form 18 (available from your local tax office). The claim or election had to be made before the beginning of the first year for which it was to have effect (so that the closing date for 1999–2000 elections was 5 April 1999), except that a claim or election for the year in which marriage took place could be made during that year (so that if a couple married in June 1999, they had until 5 April 2000 to submit Form 18).

Once made, a claim or election remained in force for future years, unless revoked. Where the couple elected to transfer the whole allowance to the wife, the husband may, without his wife's consent, claim back half the allowance. Revocations or amended claims had to be made before the beginning of the first year for which they were to have effect.

Again, following the abolition of married couple's allowance from April 2000, these elections are no longer relevant if the couple is aged below 65.

### 7.5.5 Husbands with excess allowances
(TA 1988, s 257B)

The ability to transfer the married couple's allowance ran alongside an existing provision, in force since the introduction of independent taxation in 1990–91, under which the married couple's allowance (or part of it) could be transferred to the wife if the husband had insufficient income to utilise that allowance himself. The older provision will remain relevant because relief does not depend on a claim being made before the beginning of the year of assessment. For 1996–97 onwards a claim must be made within five years of 31 January following the end of the tax year ie for the year ended 5 April 2000 by 31 January 2006.

Special rules apply when calculating the husband's available income (the income, that is, against which his personal allowances may be set). For further details see *Allied Dunbar Tax Handbook 1999–2000* at 7.5.5.

## 7.6 PENSIONER COUPLES
(TA 1988, s 257A)

A higher married couple's allowance is available if either spouse was born before 6 April 1935. The allowance for 2000–01 is £5,185 if the elder spouse is aged between 65 and 74 and £5,255 if he or she is aged 75 or more. Once again, relief is restricted to 10%.

For 1999–2000, the same rules applied as for the age-related personal allowances (see 7.3.1 above), namely that the higher allowance is due if the relevant age is attained during the year of assessment, or if it would have been attained had the individual not died. For example, suppose that a man was born on 1 January 1935 and his wife on 1 June 1935 (ie he will be 65 on 1 January 2000 and his wife on 1 June 2000). He may claim the higher (£5,125) married couple's allowance for 1999–2000 and this will not be withdrawn should he in fact die before his birthday.

For 2000–01 onwards, though the rules are modified in respect of individuals born before 6 April 1935 and aged less than 75 during the year of assessment, the same principle applies.

### 7.6.1 Pensioner couples – Transfer of excess allowances
(TA 1988, s 257B; F(No 2)A 1992, s 20 and Sched 5)

Subject to the normal rules (as set out in 7.5.5 above), the whole of a higher, age-related married couple's allowance may be transferred to the wife if the husband has insufficient income to use it himself.

### 7.6.2 Married couple's allowance

As mentioned previously, the married couple's allowance for people aged below 65 is to be withdrawn from 6 April 2000. The Chancellor has, however, confirmed that the allowance will continue for those entitled to higher allowance at 6 April 2000.

New claims for couples where one spouse reaches 65 will no longer be possible. However, where an individual born on or before 5 April 1935 gets married after 5 April 2000 he will be able to claim the allowance.

## 7.7 WIDOW'S BEREAVEMENT ALLOWANCE
(TA 1988, s 262)

### 7.7.1 Introduction

Where the husband died before the 6 April 2000 and provided the couple were living together at the time the husband died, a widow may claim (in addition to her basic personal allowance) a 'widow's bereavement allowance' of £2,000 for 2000–01 (£1,970 for 1999–2000). This allowance is given for the tax year in which her husband died and for the following year (but not for that following year if she remarries before the beginning of that year).

Although the allowance is equal to the standard married couple's allowance, it is not increased if the widow has (or her late husband had) attained the age of 65.

Another important point is that it is the widow's bereavement allowance; there is no corresponding relief for widowers. As such the Chancellor has deemed this discriminatory and the allowance was abolished from 6 April 2000. There are plans to compensate for this by the introduction of a 'bereavement payment' available to both widows and widowers in due course.

### 7.7.2 Rate of relief

As with the married couple's allowance relief is restricted to 10% for 1999–2000 and 2000–01 (see 7.5.2). Relief was restricted to 15% in 1995–96 to 1998–99.

## 7.8 ADDITIONAL PERSONAL ALLOWANCE
(TA 1988, ss 259–261A)

### 7.8.1 Introduction

Prior to 6 April 2000 the tax legislation recognised that single people with children have responsibilities equivalent to a married man. Therefore it provided the 'additional personal allowance' which may be claimed by a man or woman, who is either not married or is not living with his or her spouse, and who has care of a qualifying child. The allowance was £1,970 for 1999–2000 (and although this was equal to the married couple's allowance, it was not increased should the parent have attained his or her 65th birthday).

A child, to qualify, must have been living with the claimant, but need not have been the claimant's own son or daughter. For example, the allowance can be claimed by an unmarried aunt who is looking after her orphaned nephew. The detailed conditions are a little odd, however, in that they discriminate against natural children.

Any child qualified for any year of assessment which begins before his 16th birthday, or 18th if still in full-time education. For this purpose, 'education' includes an apprenticeship or similar arrangement, provided it lasts for at least two years. However, a child who has attained the age of 18 by the beginning of the year of assessment qualified only if he is in full-time education and is the claimant's legitimate or legitimated, adopted or stepchild.

The child does not have to reside with the claimant throughout the year – it will not affect entitlement to the relief if, for example, the child is sent away to school. Where a child's time is divided between two parents who are not living together, the additional personal allowance has to be divided between those parents either as they agree, or in default of agreement, by reference to the amount of time the child spends with each.

However many children a person is responsible for, he can only claim one additional personal allowance. However, if a separated couple have two children, and both children spend some time with each parent, each parent may claim half the allowance for both children (so that the result is the same as if each parent had claimed a single, full, additional personal allowance).

A household may consist of an unmarried couple and their children from previous marriages. If both the man and the woman were able to claim an additional personal allowance, they would in fact be better off than if they were married. Therefore the legislation provides that only one additional personal allowance may be claimed, and that it goes to the parent of the youngest qualifying child.

## 7.8.2 Rate of relief

Relief for 1999–2000 was restricted to 10% of £1,970 and as with similar reliefs the additional personal allowance was abolished from 5 April 2000.

## 7.8.3 Year of separation

The introduction of the rule allowing a husband to transfer the married couple's allowance to his wife (see 7.5.4) has been accompanied by specific provisions for those separating after 5 April 1993. Whichever spouse takes the child will be able to claim the additional personal allowance for the year of separation, but from that allowance must be deducted any married couple's allowance already allocated to that spouse.

### 7.8.4 Year of remarriage

If a 'single parent' father remarried, he was not able to claim both the additional personal allowance and the married man's allowance for the year of remarriage. As explained in 7.5 above, the married couple's allowance was scaled down if marriage took place after 5 May, so it was usually better to disclaim the married couple's allowance and take the additional personal allowance. However, if a 'single parent' mother remarried, she could claim the additional personal allowance for the year of remarriage without affecting her new husband's right to a married couple's allowance.

## 7.9 ADDITIONAL ALLOWANCE FOR DISABLED SPOUSE

There was one situation where a married person could claim both the full additional personal allowance and the full married couple's allowance. This was where the spouse was 'totally incapacitated by physical or mental infirmity throughout the year of assessment'. Four points should be noted:

(1) The allowance was (as is invariably the case with the additional personal allowance) available only where a 'qualifying child' (as defined in 7.8) was living with the claimant.
(2) The Revenue construes 'incapacitated' very strictly: simple blindness, for example, is not enough. The test is that the spouse must be quite unable to care for the child, in the sense of preparing his food and washing his clothes.
(3) The allowance was not given unless the spouse was incapacitated throughout the year of assessment. Therefore if a woman became paraplegic after a car accident in, say, May 1998, her husband could not claim the allowance until 1999–2000.
(4) The allowance was not due unless husband and wife were living together at least for part of the year of assessment. (Very often, by the time the wife is sufficiently ill to be 'incapacitated' under the Revenue's definition, she is so ill as to need the full-time care of a nursing home.)

For 1996–97 and previous years the allowance was only given where the wife was incapacitated. However, for 1997–98 and subsequent years the relief has been extended to situations where the husband is incapacitated.

This allowance was removed with effect from 5 April 2000.

# 7.10 BLIND PERSONS
(TA 1988, s 265)

A person who is blind may claim a special, additional, personal allowance of £1,250 for 1996–97, £1,280 for 1997–98, £1,330 for 1998–99, £1,380 for 1999–2000 and £1,400 for 2000–01. A person counts as 'blind' if:

(1) he lives in England or Wales and his name appears on the local authority's register of blind persons; or
(2) he lives in Scotland or Northern Ireland and is so blind that he cannot perform any work for which eyesight is essential.

This definition means that a person resident abroad can never, for tax purposes, count as blind – an odd rule which is strictly enforced by the Inland Revenue.

A person who becomes blind during a year of assessment may claim the full blind person's allowance for that year.

## 7.10.1 Married couples

If husband and wife are both blind, each may claim a separate blind person's allowance.

A blind husband with insufficient income to use all his personal allowances may be able to transfer the whole, or part of, his blind person's allowance to his wife (whether or not she also is blind). However, the transfer of the married couple's allowance took priority, so a transfer of blind person's allowance was only possible where the husband's income was insufficient to use his basic personal allowance and the blind person's allowance itself. Furthermore, the transfer of the blind person's allowance is subject to the same restrictions as a transfer of an unused married couple's allowance (see 7.5.5).

Similarly, a wife may transfer her unused blind person's allowance to her husband (whether or not he also is blind), but again subject to the point that she cannot, in calculating her income for this purpose, deduct the five prohibited items (see 7.5.5).

A claim to transfer a blind person's allowance to a spouse must be made, on Revenue Form 575, within five years of the 31 January following the end of the relevant year of assessment.

### Example – Blind married couple

*A*, who is sighted, earns £10,000 a year. His wife, *B*, who is blind, has a pension of £4,450. They live in a flat bought by *B* before their marriage, so the flat and the mortgage are in her sole name. The mortgage is within MIRAS and the gross interest payable for the current year is £2,000.

*B*'s 'total income' (as defined by the Taxes Acts) is £2,450 (ie £4,450 less mortgage interest paid £2,000 as explained in 7.4). However, in calculating the allowance which may be transferred, the mortgage interest is to be ignored. Therefore the position for 1999–2000 is:

| B | £ | £ |
|---|---|---|
| Pension | | 4,450 |
| Basic personal allowance | 4,335 | |
| Blind person's allowance | 1,380 | |
| | | 5,715 |
| Excess, transferable to husband | | 1,265 |
| | | |
| A | | |
| Salary | | 10,000 |
| Basic personal allowance | 4,335 | |
| Blind person's allowance | 1,265 | |
| | | 5,600 |
| Tax payable on | | 4,400 |
| £1,500 charged at 20% | | 150.00 |
| £2,900 charged at 23% | | 667.00 |
| £4,400 | | 817.00 |
| *Less*: married couple's allowance (£1,970 at 10%) | | 197.00 |
| | | 620.00 |

However, the couple will also have enjoyed £200 of tax relief under the MIRAS scheme (although the gross mortgage interest was £2,000, they will actually have paid only £1,800). Therefore their net contribution to the Exchequer is only £420.00.

## 7.11 WORKING FAMILIES' TAX CREDIT

Working Family Tax Credits (WFTC) and Disabled Person's Tax Credits (DPTC) are schemes administered by the Inland Revenue.

WFTC tops up the earnings of individuals with children. DPTC tops up earnings of a disabled person. In both cases, a childcare tax credit can be available to assist with the childcare costs incurred by a working parent.

WTFC can be claimed by couples or lone parents who are resident in the UK, have at least one child, work at least 16 hours per week, and do not have savings of more than £8,000. The tax credit is based on four elements:

(1) basic tax credit of £53.15;
(2) supplement of £11.25 for a person who works more than 30 hours per week

(3) tax credit for each child dependent on age:
  - age up to 11 – £21.25
  - age 11 to 16 – £21.25
  - age 16 to 18 – £26.35; and
(4) childcare credit of up to 70% of eligible costs up to a maximum of £100 per week for one child or £150 per week for two or more children.

The total award is calculated by adding all the credits together. If the family's income (after tax and NICs) exceeds £91.45 per week, the award is reduced by 55p for every £1 of excess. The credits are normally calculated at six-monthly intervals and occasional overtime may affect the calculation if it falls within the basis period for calculating the next six months' credits.

For further details, contact the Tax Credit Helpline on 0845 609 5000.

# 8

# THE TAXATION TREATMENT OF MAINTENANCE

(FA 1988, SS 36–40; F(NO 2)A 1992, SS 61–62)

This chapter covers the tax treatment of maintenance payments up to 5 April 2000, both from the standpoint of the payer and the recipient. The following aspects are covered:

(1) Definition of maintenance and alimony payments.
(2) Maintenance paid under an existing obligation.
(3) Maintenance under an existing obligation paid direct to a child.
(4) Increased payments under an existing obligation.
(5) Payer's relief for other maintenance payments.
(6) The Child Support Agency.

Revenue booklet IR93 (*Separation, Divorce and Maintenance Payments*, available at www.inlandrevenue.gov.uk/pdfs/ir93.htm) outlines the tax positions when married couples separate or divorce and also deals with the tax treatment of maintenance payments. From 6 April 2000, the position has been greatly simplified by the removal of relief for maintenance payments.

## 8.1 DEFINITION OF MAINTENANCE AND ALIMONY PAYMENTS

Maintenance payments (sometimes called 'alimony') may be received:

(1) by a woman from her husband or former husband and by a man from his wife or former wife;
(2) by a child from a parent (including an adoptive or step-parent);
(3) by a woman from the father of her natural child;
(4) by any other person who has care of a child, from a parent of the child (eg if the child's mother is dead and the father is considered unfit to care for the child, the court may grant custody to a grandparent but order the father to make a financial contribution).

The tax treatment of such payments was fundamentally changed on 15 March 1988. For tax purposes, payments of maintenance or alimony to a wife or former wife (or exceptionally to a husband or former husband), and similar payments for the support of children, have been divided into two categories: those which are, and those which are not, payments under an 'existing obligation'. As explained below, the tax treatment of payments under an existing obligation was far more generous until 6 April 2000 than that of payments under later obligations.

Essentially, an existing obligation is one which existed at the time the 1988 Budget Statement was made, but the statutory definition is a little more complex. A payment is made under an existing obligation if it is made:

(1) under a court order made no later than 14 March 1988; or
(2) under a court order made no later than 30 June 1988 in pursuance of an application made no later than 14 March 1988; or
(3) under a written agreement signed by the parties no later than 14 March 1988 and produced to an Inspector of Taxes no later than 30 June 1988; or
(4) under an oral agreement reached between the parties no later than 14 March 1988, written particulars of which were produced to an Inspector no later than 30 June 1988; or
(5) subject to limitations (as explained below), under a court order or written agreement replacing, amending or varying a prior order or agreement qualifying under (1)–(4) above.

Any other payment is not made under an existing obligation.

An order may qualify under (1), (2) or (5) whether it is made by a UK or a foreign court. There is no requirement for the payer to be UK resident: and a payment for the maintenance of a child may be made to the child himself, to his parent or guardian, or to a third party (such as the school at which the child is educated).

## 8.2 MAINTENANCE PAID UNDER EXISTING OBLIGATION

The following sections set out the rules as they have applied until 6 April 2000 when relief for payments under existing obligations was abolished in line with other related reliefs.

The position depended partly on the recipient's identity. Therefore, it was important to distinguish between an order (or agreement) under which an adult received a payment earmarked for the support of a child and one under which a payment was made in theory direct to the child, but in practice to an adult as his guardian. For example, if the order stated that payment was to be made to the mother for the child, then the mother was the recipient. However, if it stated payment was to be made to the child, then the child was the recipient, even if the mother in fact received the money on his behalf.

A payment to a spouse or former spouse under an existing obligation gave rise to a deduction from the payer's taxable income of an amount by which the payment exceeds the married couple's allowance. Normally this meant that the recipient was regarded as having taxable income of the same amount (but see the final sentence of 8.4.1). This is so whether the payment is for the wife's (or husband's) own maintenance, or for the maintenance of a child. Similarly, a payment to the mother of the payer's natural child is treated as a transfer of taxable income to the mother.

A payment direct to a child who had not attained his 18th birthday was treated as a transfer of income only if that payment was made under an existing obligation arising under a court order. Other payments to a child under the age of 18 were simply ignored for tax purposes. Payments to adult children are considered separately in 8.3.

At one time a 'net payment' system (similar to that used for charitable deeds of covenant) applied to most payments of maintenance but, from April 1989, virtually all maintenance and alimony has been payable gross (the sole exception relates to maintenance paid to children who have attained the age of 18 years – see 8.3).

### Example – Payment under existing obligation

In 1987, *A* was ordered by the court to pay his wife *B* maintenance of £300 a month and his son *C* (then aged 6) £200 a month (ie £6,000 for the tax year 1999–2000). This counted as an existing obligation, so *A* could deduct, in computing his taxable income for 1999–2000, £6,000 minus £1,970 (ie £4,030) and he can also claim relief of £1,970 at 10%. Therefore the sum paid out attracted tax relief of £4,030 at *A*'s top rate and £197.00 (£1,970 at 10%).

## 8.2.1 Maintenance paid under existing obligation

Where the recipient is the payer's spouse or former spouse, then the following rules applied (whether the payment was stated to be for the recipient's own support or for the support of a child living with him or her):

(1) Payment was made gross (ie the spouse making the payment paid the full amount he or she agreed or was ordered to pay and could not, as was once the case, deduct an amount in respect of income tax on the payment).

(2) Providing the recipient had not remarried, the first £1,970 received was exempt from tax in 1999–2000 (equivalent to the married couple's allowance for 1999–2000). Exemption was lost only if the recipient had remarried; cohabitation did not count. If the recipient remarried halfway through the tax year, the exemption was claimed only against payments falling due before the date of marriage.

(3) If the payment was made under a UK court order or agreement, the balance was taxable under Schedule D Case III, but on a current-year

basis. If it was made under a foreign order or agreement, it was taxable under Case V (see 6.5).

### 8.2.2 Late payments

It is not unusual for maintenance payments to fall into arrears, or even not to be paid at all. The recipient's assessment is limited to the amount actually received. If an amount due in one year is in fact paid in a later year, it will still be assessed as income of the year in which it should have been paid. (This avoids 'bunching' of income where payments are not made regularly and will usually be to the recipient's advantage.)

Suppose in the example in 8.2 that the husband had omitted to pay three months' maintenance in the tax year 1998–99. In his tax assessment for that year, he would be given relief only for the payments actually made (9 × £500 = £4,500). However, if in, say, December 1999, he makes good the payments omitted in 1998–99, relief will be given in the 1999–2000 self-assessment at the 1998–99 rates.

### 8.2.3 Maintenance paid under existing obligation to person (other than spouse) for support of child

A 'child' for this purpose is defined as a person under 21 years of age. Maintenance for a child may be payable by a parent, a step-parent or an adoptive parent.

Here we are concerned with payments other than to the child himself or to a spouse or former spouse. The payee may therefore be the child's natural mother or a relative, such as a grandparent, who has been given charge of the child. Such payments should always have been made gross and were fully taxable income in the payee's hands. They were taxed under Case III, if made under a UK court order or agreement, and under Case V, if made under a foreign order or agreement.

### 8.2.4 Relief from 2000–01 onwards

As from 6 April 2000, relief is due only under the rules set out in 8.5, ie the concept of payments under an existing obligation was abolished.

## 8.3 MAINTENANCE UNDER EXISTING OBLIGATION PAID DIRECT TO CHILD

Payments 'direct to a child' can include to an adult as guardian of a child. The tax treatment depended both on whether payment was made under a court order or under an agreement and on the child's age (at the time of each payment, not at the time the order or agreement was made).

## Payments under court order up to 5 April 2000

Payments had to be made gross until the child reached the age of 21; thereafter they had to be made under deduction of tax. While payments were made gross, the parent could for 1999–2000 claim tax relief at 20%, basic rate (23% for 1998–99) or 40% as appropriate. Once payments were made net, he could claim relief at the difference between 23% basic rate and 40% (if he was liable for the higher rate).

Payments counted as the taxable income of the child throughout. Although they were taxable in full, they were unlikely to exceed the child's personal allowance, so in practice it was rare for tax to be payable.

For the position where a court order was amended between 15 March 1988 and the child's 21st birthday, see 8.4.1.

## Payments under an agreement up to 5 April 2000

Such payments did not count as the child's taxable income until he attained age 18. Payment should have been made gross until that age was attained. However, once age 18 was attained, such payments counted as the child's taxable income (but for basic rate purposes only; by a quirk of the law, higher rate tax was never chargeable on maintenance received by a child under an agreement).

From age 18, payment should have been made under deduction of tax. For example, if the gross payment due was £100, the parent should have paid only £77. If the child was a taxpayer, that £23 covered his basic rate liability on the £100; if he was not a taxpayer (because his income did not exceed his personal allowance), he could have reclaimed the £23 from the Revenue.

## Example – Payments to children under existing obligations

In 1988, A was ordered by the court to pay £250 a month to his daughter, B, until she completed her education. B was 21 on 1 June 1999, but did not complete her university course until 2000.

The May instalment was paid gross, but in June A should have paid only £192.50 (£250 less basic rate tax). A kept the £57.50 deducted as his own basic rate tax relief (and B may be able to reclaim the tax deducted from the Revenue, as explained in 8.3). If A was a higher rate taxpayer, the higher rate relief due (17% of £250, or £42.50) would have been given in his tax assessment or PAYE coding.

## Payments due after 5 April 2000

All payments falling due for payment on or after 6 April 2000 should be made gross. They do not constitute taxable income for the recipient.

## 8.4 INCREASED PAYMENTS UNDER EXISTING OBLIGATION

An order or agreement which replaced an existing obligation counted as an existing obligation. For the exception, see 8.4.2.

However, payments made under a replacement order or agreement were only treated as made under an existing obligation to the extent that they did not exceed the payments due to be made (as distinct from the payments actually made) and allowed for tax purposes in the 1988–89 tax year.

Very occasionally, a pre-15 March 1988 court order or separation agreement provided for the amount payable to increase automatically – perhaps in line with inflation. In such a case, tax relief was similarly limited to the amount payable for 1988–89.

### 8.4.1 Reallocation of payments made under existing obligation

Suppose the existing obligation was a pre-March 1988 court order which provided for payments of £10,000 to be made to a former wife and £5,000 to a child until the child attained 21. If the court order was varied so that the whole £15,000 was paid to the former wife, the husband could claim tax relief up to £15,000 (ie the total amount paid under the existing obligation in 1988–89). Curiously, in such a case the former wife was still only taxed on £10,000 (ie the amount receivable by her in 1988–89).

### 8.4.2 Children who had attained 21 years

In one circumstance, an order or agreement which replaced an existing obligation did not count as an existing obligation. A 'replacement' order or agreement to pay maintenance to or for a child ceased to count as an existing obligation on that child's 21st birthday. Payments made on or after the child's 21st birthday have never been deductible in computing the payer's taxable income and were not assessable as income of the child.

## 8.5 PAYER'S RELIEF FOR OTHER MAINTENANCE PAYMENTS

Payments under court orders and agreements which did not count as existing obligations qualified for tax relief only if they were made to a separated or former spouse. Payments made direct to a child did not qualify, nor did payments to the mother of a natural child. However, payments made to an (ex-)spouse qualified even if they were earmarked for the maintenance of children.

Furthermore, a payment which was not an existing obligation did not qualify for relief unless it was due under a court order made in an EU/EEA member state or under a written agreement subject to the jurisdiction of a member state's courts. (Whether an agreement is subject to the jurisdiction of a particular court is a complex legal question outside the scope of this book. If you or your (ex-)spouse is domiciled abroad, or if the agreement was signed abroad, you should seek specialist advice on this point. Alternatively, you could submit your claim to the Revenue, disclosing all the relevant facts, and seek specialist advice only if your claim is refused.)

Tax relief for payments made otherwise than under an existing obligation was limited to an amount equal to the married couple's allowance (£1,970 for 1999–2000). Consequently, if a man was ordered to pay his former wife £300 a month, he must pay that sum gross, but can claim relief for £1,970 only in 1999–2000. Moreover, relief was due only at 10% (15% for 1998–99).

The man's entitlement to relief ended when his former wife remarried, even if the payments, being earmarked for the maintenance of children, continued. On the other hand, if the man remarried, he could have claimed the married couple's allowance for his new wife in addition to the relief for maintenance payments made by him.

The £1,970 limit was reduced, £1 for £1, by any maintenance paid which qualified under the existing obligation rules explained above, except that payments to children who had attained the age of 21 years may be ignored. (As mentioned above, these rules are not logical.)

Finally, the £1,970 limit was a global limit and was not increased even if a man was paying alimony to two or more ex-wives.

### 8.5.1 The payer's option
(FA 1988, s 39)

An individual paying maintenance under an existing obligation was entitled to disclaim existing obligation relief and elect instead to claim relief as if the relevant Order or agreement had been made after 14 March 1988. An election had to be made, under self-assessment on or before the first anniversary of the 31 January following the end of the first year of assessment for which it was to have effect (so that an election for 1999–2000 must be made by 31 January 2002).

## 8.6 THE CHILD SUPPORT AGENCY
(F(No 2)A 1992, s 62)

In April 1993 responsibility for determining how much maintenance should be paid for a child was (in most cases) transferred from the courts to the Child Support Agency (CSA). On request, the CSA will make a 'maintenance assessment' based on a published formula, taking into account factors such as the age(s) of the child(ren), the incomes of both parents, their housing costs and whether either has remarried or has responsibility for a 'second family'. The procedure is explained in some detail in a free booklet *For Parents Who Live Apart*, available from:

Child Support Agency
Freepost CL3349
PO Box 1032
Sudbury
Suffolk CO10 6BR
Tel: 0345 830 830
(calls charged at local rates from anywhere in the UK).

This address and telephone number is only for booklet requests. The CSA also operates an enquiry line service on 0345 133 133 (9.00 am to 6 pm, Mondays to Fridays: calls charged at local rates from anywhere in the UK). The CSA's website can be found at www.dss.gov.uk/csa/index.htm.

For tax purposes, a maintenance assessment made by the CSA was treated as if it were a court order. To the extent that it replaced a prior agreement or court order which was an existing obligation, the maintenance assessment could therefore count as an existing obligation, subject to the rules in 8.4.

# 9

# INTEREST ON QUALIFYING LOANS

PETER JUN TAI

Although at one time, tax relief was generally available on interest paid on borrowed money, there are now relatively few opportunities to claim relief for loan interest.

This chapter covers the following topics:

(1) MIRAS (abolished from 6 April 2000).
(2) Loans used to purchase investment properties.
(3) Loans used to invest in partnerships.
(4) Loans used to invest in close companies.
(5) Loans used to invest in employee-controlled companies.

## 9.1 MIRAS
(TA 1988, ss 369–370)

Mortgage Interest Relief At Source (MIRAS) was the mechanism by which income tax relief was allowed to the borrower on the interest payable on the first £30,000 of a mortgage loan. The relief was not withdrawn where the individual was not liable to tax because his income was too low for him to be liable for income tax.

For 1995–96 to 1997–98, relief was restricted to 15% except for loans taken out in connection with the purchase of an annuity (see 9.1.2). For 1998–99 onwards there was a further restriction to 10%. The relief was abolished altogether from 6 April 2000.

The availability of MIRAS on a home loan was not automatic. It was only allowed if all the following three conditions were satisfied:

(1) the interest had to be relevant loan interest;
(2) the borrower had to be a qualifying borrower; and
(3) the lender had to be a qualifying lender.

Relevant loan interest applied to loans used for the purchase of land, a caravan or a houseboat in the UK which was used wholly or substantially as the borrower's only or main residence.

### 9.1.1 Negative equity
(FA 1993, s 56)

The legislation allowed a loan to qualify where the individual had ended up with negative equity and had transferred his mortgage to a new property. Basically, a person was treated as if he had raised a new eligible amount on the new property. The amount of the eligible loan was the smaller of the purchase price of the new home and the amount of the outstanding loan.

### 9.1.2 Loans used to purchase an annuity from an insurance company

Interest has also been relevant loan interest if the borrower is aged 65 or over and at least 90% of the loan on which the interest is payable was used to buy an annuity for the remainder of his life. Once again, the loan had to be secured on the borrower's main residence.

Interest payable on these types of loan continues to attract basic rate relief despite the general restriction in MIRAS relief to 10% (see 9.1). Furthermore, the relief will continue at 23% after 5 April 2000 despite the general abolition of MIRAS and despite the reduction in basic rate to 22%.

### 9.1.3 Qualifying borrower
(TA 1988, s 376)

A qualifying borrower was any individual who paid relevant loan interest. However this did not include individuals who were employed in the UK but were exempt from UK income tax by virtue of some special exemption or immunity (eg diplomatic immunity).

### 9.1.4 Qualifying lender
(TA 1988, s 376)

This included the building societies, local authorities, insurance companies authorised to carry on long-term business, etc. It did not automatically include the banks, which had to be authorised by statutory instrument issued by the Treasury. In practice, most of the larger banks and specialist mortgage companies were authorised.

### 9.1.5 Administration

The application of MIRAS to a loan was not automatic. The procedure was for the borrower to complete a form, usually stocked and supplied by the lender, certifying that he was a qualifying borrower and that the interest was relevant loan interest. Alternatively, the Revenue may, if asked, notify the lender and borrower that the interest may be paid under deduction of tax.

If at any time after the application of MIRAS to a loan was established the borrower ceased to be a qualifying borrower or the interest was no longer relevant interest (e.g. because the borrower had bought another principal private residence), the borrower was required to inform the lender. Any excess MIRAS relief may be recovered by direct assessment.

## 9.1.6 Joint borrowers
(TA 1988, s 356C)

Before 1 August 1988, joint borrowers other than husband and wife were each entitled to a £30,000 limit on their qualifying borrowings. For example, if a brother and sister jointly bought a house for £100,000 with a deposit of £20,000 and a joint loan of £80,000, MIRAS relief was available on £60,000.

From 1 August 1988, the relief became residence-based so that only £30,000 was available per residence. This rule applied only to loans taken out after 31 July 1988 and pre-existing loans continued to attract full MIRAS relief.

## 9.1.7 Job-related accommodation
(TA 1988, s 356)

Where a person lives in job-related accommodation, he was entitled to claim MIRAS relief on a property which he owned provided that:

(1) the property was used as his main residence or was so used within 12 months after the loan was made, or
(2) the property was intended at that time to be used in due course as his only or main residence.

Living accommodation is job-related if it is provided to a person and is necessary for the proper performance of his duties or it is customary in that particular trade for employers to provide living accommodation or there is a special threat to security. Self-employed individuals could qualify in certain circumstances. Typical examples of people in job-related accommodation are public school teachers, army personnel, school caretakers and publicans.

## 9.1.8 Temporary absences

Tax relief on mortgage interest was strictly only available where, at the time the interest is paid, the property was used as the only or main residence. The Revenue has confirmed that tax relief will not be denied or withdrawn in the following cases:

(1) Temporary absences of up to a year.
(2) Where the taxpayer was required to move to another place in the UK or abroad because of his employment, tax relief on a property used as his

main residence before departure was preserved provided that its use as a main residence was expected to resume on return. This also applied where a property was purchased and the person was prevented by his move from occupying it.

The relief was not extended beyond four years. However, if the property was occupied as a main residence for at least three months after a four-year absence, a further four-year extension could be obtained. Further details may be found in ESC A27 (available at <u>www.inlandrevenue.gov.uk/leaflets/</u>).

### 9.1.9 Year of marriage

A married couple was only entitled to one limit in respect of mortgage interest paid after the date of their marriage. However, where bride and groom each owned a qualifying property before marriage and one spouse went to live in the other spouse's home, interest for the period in which the other property was vacant was allowed provided that it was sold within 12 months. For further details, see ESC A35 (available at <u>www.inlandrevenue.gov.uk/leaflets/</u>).

## 9.2 LOANS USED TO PURCHASE INVESTMENT PROPERTIES
(TA 1988, ss 354–355)

### 9.2.1 Position from 1995–96 onwards

FA 1995 fundamentally changed the position. Previous rules which enabled qualifying interest to be allowed as a charge against an individual's rental income were abolished. However, interest payments can still be allowed as a business expense, like any other allowable expense. The main consequence of all this is that the requirement under the pre-1995 legislation that the property should be let for at least 26 weeks in a period of 52 weeks no longer applies. Moreover, overdraft interest can also qualify for relief.

### 9.2.2 Tax relief pre-1995–96 on loans used to buy investment properties

See *Allied Dunbar Tax Handbook 1997–98* at 9.2.2 for details of this tax relief.

## 9.3 LOANS USED TO INVEST IN PARTNERSHIPS
(TA 1988, s 362)

Tax relief may be obtained on loan interest where the money is to provide capital into a partnership. Relief is available where the loan is applied:

(1) in purchasing a share in a partnership; or

(2) in contributing capital to a partnership or advancing money to a partnership where the money advanced is used wholly for the purposes of the partnership's trade, profession or vocation; or

(3) in paying off another loan the interest on which would have been eligible for tax relief.

In addition, the borrower must be a member of the partnership throughout the period (and not just as a limited partner) and he must not have recovered any capital from the partnership since raising the qualifying loan.

## 9.3.1 Recovery of capital
(TA 1988, s 363)

If at any time after the application of the proceeds of the loan, the partner recovers any amount of capital from the partnership, he is deemed to have used the withdrawal to repay the qualifying loan on which he is claiming interest relief. This is so whether or not he actually uses the proceeds in this manner. It is therefore advisable to segregate the partners' capital and current accounts in the partnership's books so that any withdrawal can be clearly identified.

## 9.3.2 Replacement capital

Where a partner has a surplus balance on either his current or capital account with a partnership and he does not already have a qualifying loan, he may withdraw the balance due to him (with the consent of his partners), use the money to pay off non-qualifying borrowings and then borrow further funds to introduce capital into partnership with tax relief.

### Example – Replacement capital

B is a partner in the XYZ partnership. He has a credit balance of £100,000 in his capital account. Outside the partnership, he has bought a yacht for his private use with the help of a £40,000 loan from his bank. In addition, he has a building society mortgage of £50,000 of which £30,000 was under MIRAS for 1999–2000.

B would withdraw £60,000 from his capital account in the partnership and use the money to make the following repayments:

|  | £ |
|---|---|
| Yacht bank loan | 40,000 |
| Building society | 20,000 |
|  | 60,000 |

This would leave B with outstanding borrowings of only £30,000 with his building society on which MIRAS relief is available.

Once these transactions have been completed, B would borrow £60,000 as a loan (not overdraft) and use the funds to reintroduce capital into the partnership with full tax relief on the interest payable.

Professional advice should be sought well in advance before setting up this sort of loan and the situation will of course now be varied with the abolition of MIRAS.

### 9.3.3 Other partnership loans

Another situation where it may be appropriate to restructure existing borrowings is where there is a partnership loan outstanding in the business's books. The loan might typically have been used to purchase goodwill or the property from which the practice/business is carried on.

In this situation, each partner is required to borrow privately his share of the partnership loan and introduce the monies raised into the partnership. The partner can then claim tax relief on the interest paid personally as a charge on his income on an actual basis.

The partnership collects the monies raised by each partner's loan and uses the funds to redeem the partnership loan. As a result, each partner's share of profits becomes correspondingly higher because no interest is now payable by the partnership. However the situation redresses itself because the higher profits must be used to finance the private borrowing.

### 9.3.4 Purchase of plant and machinery
(TA 1988, s 359)

Where a partner incurs capital expenditure in the purchase of plant and machinery which is used for the purposes of the partnership's business, and which is eligible for capital allowances, he can claim tax relief on interest paid if the plant or machinery is financed by a loan. The relief is only available in the tax year in which the loan is taken out and the following three tax years. Similar relief is also available for employees who are required to purchase plant or machinery for use in carrying out their duties.

#### Example – Use of loans to purchase plant and machinery

A partner borrowed £10,000 at 10% pa on 6 October 1997 to buy a car which is used for the partnership's business. His private use of the car is agreed at 25%.

Interest relief is available on £375 in 1997–98 and on £750 in 1998–99, 1999–2000 and 2000–01.

### 9.3.5 Property occupied rent free by partnership

Where a partner takes out a loan to purchase property which is occupied by the partnership for business purposes and the interest is paid by the partnership, no deduction is technically due to the partnership as the interest is not its liability but the partner's. However, SP4/85, issued in February 1985, regards the interest paid as rent so that it then becomes allowable as a deduction. In the hands of the partner, the rent is taxable but the interest paid will be allowed as a deduction provided it does not exceed a market rent.

### 9.3.6 Incorporation of partnership
(Extra-statutory concession A43)

Where a partnership is incorporated into a limited close company, any qualifying loan in existence at the time will continue to attract tax relief provided the conditions for relief in 9.4 below would be met if a new loan was taken out.

## 9.4 LOANS USED TO INVEST IN CLOSE COMPANIES
(TA 1988, s 360)

Where interest is paid on a loan used to purchase shares in a close company, or in lending money to such a company which is used for the purposes of the company's business, the interest will be eligible for tax relief, provided that the borrower meets one of two conditions:

(1) The borrower either alone or together with certain associates owns a material interest in the close company (defined broadly as more than 5% of the ordinary share capital).
(2) The borrower holds less than 5% of the ordinary share capital, but works for the greater part of his time in the actual management or conduct of the company or an associated company (a works manager, a production manager or a company secretary would normally satisfy this condition).

The company must exist wholly or mainly for one of the following purposes:

(1) To carry on a trade or trades on a commercial basis.
(2) To make investments in land or property which is let commercially to unconnected parties.
(3) To hold shares or securities or to make loans to 'qualifying companies' or an intermediate company, all of which are under its control. A qualifying company is one which is under the control of the close company and satisfies the conditions at (1) and (2) above.
(4) To co-ordinate the administration of two or more qualifying companies.

If the company holds property, the individual must not reside in it unless he has worked for the greater part of his time in the actual management or conduct of the company. For the definition of a close company see 24.12.1.

### 9.4.1 Close EIS and BES companies
(TA 1988, s 360(3A); FA 1989, s 47)

Loan interest relief is not available in respect of shares issued under the Enterprise Investment Scheme. Similar rules apply where an individual has used a loan to acquire shares on which relief was due under the Business Expansion Scheme.

## 9.5 LOANS USED TO INVEST IN EMPLOYEE-CONTROLLED COMPANIES
(ICTA 1988, s 361)

It is also possible for an individual to establish a qualifying loan where he uses it to acquire shares in an employee-controlled company, even if the company is not a close company. The conditions which need to be satisfied for a loan to qualify under this provision are:

(1) during the year of assessment in which the interest is paid, the company must either become employee-controlled for the first time or be employee-controlled for at least nine months;
(2) the individual or his spouse must be a full-time employee throughout the period commencing with the application of the loan and ending with the date on which the interest is paid. An individual can also continue to obtain relief for interest paid within 12 months of his having ceased to be an employee;
(3) the shares must be acquired before, or not later than 12 months after, the date on which the company first becomes an employee-controlled company; and
(4) the individual must not have recovered any capital from the company during the period from applying the proceeds of the loan to the payment of interest.

The legislation requires that the company be unquoted and resident only in the UK and either a trading company or the holding company of a trading group. A company is 'employee-controlled' if more than 50% of its ordinary share capital and voting power is owned by full-time employees or their spouses. If a full-time employee owns more than 10%, the excess is disregarded. For this purpose a spouse's holding is attributed to the employee unless the spouse is also a full-time employee.

# 10

# ANNUAL PAYMENTS WHICH ATTRACT TAX RELIEF

This chapter looks at the various types of 'annual payments' which attract tax relief. In the main, they are paid net of basic rate tax. It covers the following topics:

## Charitable donations

(1) Covenanted payments to charities.
(2) Gift Aid.
(3) Millennium Gift Aid.
(4) Gift of listed shares and securities.

## Non-charitable payments

(5) Deeds of covenant and annuities.

## Other payments which attract tax relief

There are various situations where tax relief can be taken at source, but at less than basic rate:

(6) Vocational training.
(7) Medical insurance.
(8) Trade union and friendly society subscriptions.
(9) Life assurance premiums.

## CHARITABLE DONATIONS: FINANCE ACT 2000 CHANGES

Following a two-and-a-half-year consultation period, the Government has finally introduced sweeping changes as part of FA 2000. The changes affect deeds of covenants and Gift Aid and introduce a new tax relief for individuals who give shares and securities to charities.

## 10.1 COVENANTED PAYMENTS TO CHARITIES
(TA 1988, s 660; FA 1989, s 59)

The Government has in the past encouraged charitable giving through tax relief for deeds of covenant. Under a deed of covenant, the donor enters into a written agreement to pay a regular weekly, monthly or annual contribution to the charity. Any payment interval may be specified, but there must be at least one payment a year. The agreement must be witnessed.

Prior to 6 April 2000, to qualify for tax relief the deed needed to run for at least three years and a day (though relief was not lost if payments ceased earlier by reason of events outside the donor's control (eg the winding-up of the charity or his own death)). As from 6 April 2000, relief will be given under the Gift Aid scheme (see 10.2) and tax relief will apply to any gift irrespective of size or regularity of payment.

### Example

> *B* covenants in 1999–2000 to pay £77 a year for five years to a recognised charity. The donation was treated as a gift of £100, from which basic rate tax has been deducted, and the charity may reclaim that tax from the Revenue.
>
> If *B* is a basic rate taxpayer, that is the end of the story: the Revenue has simply 'topped up' his £77 donation to £100. If he is a higher rate taxpayer, *B* may additionally claim the higher rate relief of £17. However, if he does not pay tax at all, the Revenue may ask him to make good the £23 it has paid to the charity.
>
> From 6 April 2000, the Revenue will not seek to collect tax from *B* unless the total amount of tax that he pays, whether at 10%, 20% or whatever, is less than the amount which it has repaid to the charity.

### 10.1.1 Conditions for relief

There is no requirement that the donor be UK resident, but the charity must be registered in the UK.

Relief was available only for donations in money (however, see 10.5 for gifts of listed shares and securities) and, in principle, relief was lost if the donor, or a member of his family, enjoyed any reciprocal benefit. However, it is quite common for those subscribing to charities to receive magazines or newsletters, or to be allowed free admission to places of interest managed by the charity. In determining whether any reciprocal benefit is enjoyed, the Revenue will therefore ignore any right of admission to wildlife sanctuaries or to buildings and land of historic or architectural interest, and any other benefit worth less than one-quarter of the subscription paid.

### 10.1.2 Deposit covenants

A popular arrangement for an individual wishing to make a single donation of, say, £200 to a charity was to covenant £50 (net) a year for four years and then to treat the £200 as the first £50 instalment due under the covenant plus a loan of £150. In each following year, there would be an exchange of £50 cheques (the payment of an annual instalment due under the covenant being matched by a partial repayment of the loan). Thus tax relief was generated for what was in truth a single lump-sum donation.

However, this arrangement is now unnessary following the abolition of the Gift Aid scheme limit from 6 April 2000.

## 10.2  GIFT AID
(FA 1990, s 25; F(No2)A 1992, s 26)

Gift Aid, introduced in 1990, is another way in which the Government seeks to encourage taxpayers to support charities. The scheme originally gave income tax relief only for substantial cash donations to charity. Prior to 6 April 2000 there was a minimum limit for gift to qualify under this scheme of £250. This limit was abolished from 6 April 2000.

### Example – Gift Aid donation

In 2000–01, *A* gives £780 to a recognised charity. Under the Gift Aid scheme, that will be treated as a donation of £1,000, from which basic rate tax of £220 has been deducted. The charity will be able to claim that tax from the Revenue, so it will receive a total of £1,000.

If *A* is a basic rate taxpayer, that is the end of the story: he has paid over £780 which the Revenue has 'topped up' to £1,000. If *A* is a higher rate taxpayer, he may claim higher rate relief on the gift, calculated as follows:

|  | £ |
|---|---|
| Gross donation made | 1,000 |
| Tax relief at 40% | 400 |
| *Less*: deducted when gift made | (220) |
| Reduction in *A*'s own tax liability | 180 |

If *A* is not a taxpayer at all, the Revenue will require him to make good the £220 it has paid to the charity, but if he has paid sufficient tax at the lower rates to cover the £220 this is sufficient.

Relief can also be obtained against an individual's capital gains in 2000–01 and subsequent years.

### 10.2.1  Qualifying donations

Several conditions have had to be satisfied before a donation could qualify under the Gift Aid scheme:

(1) The recipient must be a recognised charity established in the UK (ie the charity must be administered in the UK: it may carry out its charitable work anywhere in the world). However, many appeal funds and societies established for the public benefit are not technically charities. In case of doubt, intending donors should ask for evidence of charitable status or should consult:

> The Charity Commission
> 57–60 Haymarket
> London SW1Y 4QX

By way of exception, four bodies which are not technically charities are deemed to be charities for Gift Aid purposes: the British Museum, the National History Museum, the National Heritage Memorial Fund and the Historic Buildings and Monuments Commission for England.

(2) Until 6 April 2000, the donor had to be resident in the UK.
(3) The gift must be of money – it is not possible to claim Gift Aid relief for donated works of art, or even for goods (eg clothing or blankets) which will be used to assist distressed people. Also, it is not possible to give money on condition that it be used to buy something from the donor, a member of his family or a company in which he has an interest.
(4) The gift may be made in cash, by cheque or bank transfer, or by credit card. However, the Revenue does not accept that writing-off an existing loan to the charity is equivalent to a gift of money.
(5) There is no minimum or maximum donation.
(6) Any reciprocal benefit received from the charity (by the donor or a member of his family) must fall within prescribed limits (see 10.2.2 below).

## 10.2.2 Permissible benefits for Gift Aid donors

A charity may wish to give a token of its appreciation by way of a thank you to donors for their donations. Modest benefits received in consequence of making a donation will not stop the donation from qualifying as a Gift Aid donation, provided their value does not exceed certain limits. If a charity wishes to provide benefits to donors (eg as part of a membership scheme) it should consider whether the proposed benefits fall within the limits in the donor benefit rules. If they exceed the limits then the membership subscriptions cannot qualify as Gift Aid donations.

In order to decide whether a donation can qualify as a Gift Aid donation, the following need to be determined:

(1) whether the donor, or a person connected with the donor, receives any benefits in consequence of making the donation; and
(2) if so, whether the value of the benefits exceeds the limits in the donor benefit rules.

### 10.2.3 **What is a benefit?**

A benefit is:

- any item or service
- provided by you or a third party
- to the donor or a person connected with the donor
- in consequence of making of the donation.

### Acknowledgements

A mere acknowledgement of a donor's generosity in the charity's literature (eg a theatre programme) or on a plaque will not amount to a benefit, provided the acknowledgement does not take the form of an advertisement for the donor's business.

### Right of admission to view heritage property or wildlife

The benefit of a right of admission to the premises of certain charities is disregarded. This reproduces a relaxation that existed in the Deed of Covenant scheme. A free or reduced-price right of admission to property is disregarded if it is:

- to view property the preservation of which is the charity's sole or main aim, or
- to view wildlife the conservation of which is the charity's sole or main aim, and
- restricted to the donor and members of his or her family, and
- available to any member of the public who makes a similar donation.

This relaxation of the donor benefit rules does not apply if the benefit extends beyond a right of admission to view property or wildlife (eg a right of admission to a heritage property to attend a concert).

The relaxation also does not apply if the benefit extends beyond the donor and members of his or her family. For this purpose, 'members of the family' means the donor's parents, spouse, children and their spouses.

The Revenue accepts that rules that are intended to restrict the right of admission to family groups (eg a right of admission for the donor and up to two other adults and six children) satisfies the 'members of the family' test.

### Literature

Where a charity sends literature to donors, the Revenue will accept that the value is nil provided it is:

- not normally sold to the public, and
- produced for the purpose of describing the charity's work.

This means that literature such as newsletters, bulletins, annual reports, members' handbooks and programmes of events will generally carry no value for the purposes of the donor benefit rules.

### Charity auctions

When an item is purchased at auction, the sale price can normally be taken as the item's value. However, the Revenue recognises that when a person purchases a lot at a charity auction he may intentionally pay more than it is worth in order to support the charity. If the charity can show that the market value of a lot purchased at a charity auction is less than the sale price paid for the lot, it can take the lower figure as the lot's value.

For example, suppose a travel agent gives a weekend break that normally retails for £225 as a lot for a charity auction. Ms Smith purchases the weekend break with a bid of £9,600. As the value of the weekend break does not exceed the limit of £240 (ie 2½% of £9,600), the payment of £9,600 passes the relevant value test and so can qualify as a Gift Aid donation.

### Split payments

Where the value of benefits would exceed the limits in the donor benefit rules, the donor may specify that part of his payment is to be treated as payment for the benefits and part is to be treated as a donation. Provided the donor specifies this before or at the time of making the donation, the part of the payment that is specified as a donation may qualify as a Gift Aid donation, provided it satisfies all the conditions for the tax relief.

## 10.2.4 The donor benefit rules

The donor benefit rules contain two limits for the value of the benefits that a donor, or a person connected with the donor, may receive in consequence of making a donation. If the value of the benefits received:

- exceeds the limits in 10.2.5 (the relevant value test), or
- plus the value of any benefits received in consequence of any Gift Aid donations made by the same donor to the same charity earlier in the same tax year exceeds £250 (the aggregate value test),

the donation will not qualify as a Gift Aid donation.

## 10.2.5 **The relevant value test**

The limits for the relevant value test are:

| Amount of donation | Value of benefits |
|---|---|
| £0–100 | 25% of the donation |
| £101–1,000 | £25 |
| £1,001+ | 2½% of the donation |

These limits apply separately to each donation. However, special rules apply to 'annualise' the amount of certain donations and the value of certain benefits for the purposes of applying the limits. Broadly, in the case of subscriptions under a membership scheme the limits normally apply by reference to the amount of the annual membership subscription and the value of the annual membership benefits. This way:

(1) a charity can tell whether the benefits in its membership scheme will exceed the limit simply by looking at the annual membership subscription and the annual membership benefits; and
(2) the result will be the same whether the donor pays the subscription in a single payment, half-yearly, quarterly or monthly.

Annualising applies where a benefit:

(1) consists of the right to receive benefits at intervals over a period of less than 12 months;
(2) relates to a period of less than 12 months;
(3) is one of a series of benefits received periodically in consequence of making a series of donations at intervals of less than 12 months; or
(4) is a one-off benefit received in consequence of making a donation which is one of a series of donations made at intervals of less than 12 months.

In each of (1)–(3), the amount of the donation and the value of the benefit are annualised, so that the limits apply by reference to the annual amount and the annual value respectively. In the final category, the amount of the donation, but not the value of the benefit, is annualised, so that the limits in 10.2.2 apply by reference to the annual amount of the donation and the actual value of the benefit.

Annualising is done by:

(1) multiplying the amount of the donation or the value of the benefit by 365, and
(2) dividing the result by
   (a) the number of days in the period of less than 12 months, or
   (b) the average number of days in the intervals of less than 12 months.

In practice, where the period or the intervals are measured in calendar months, annualising can be done by reference to calendar months, rather than days.

## Example

> A makes four unconnected donations to a charity as follows:
>
> | Date | Amount | Benefits |
> |------|--------|----------|
> | 6 May 2000 | £30 | nil |
> | 21 June 2000 | £10 | nil |
> | 18 August 2000 | £25 | nil |
> | 5 February 2001 | £80 | book worth £30 |
>
> As no benefits are received in consequence of making any of the first three donations, they all pass the relevant value test.
>
> The book received in consequence of making the fourth donation does not fall into any of the categories mentioned above, so annualising does not apply. As the value of the book (£30) exceeds the limit of £20 (ie 25% of the £80 donation) the fourth donation fails the relevant value test and so cannot qualify as a Gift Aid donation.

## 10.2.6 The aggregate value test

In addition to satisfying the relevant value test, the value of the benefits received in consequence of a donation must also satisfy the aggregate value test if the donation is to qualify as a Gift Aid donation. In other words:

(1) the value of the benefits received in consequence of making the donation
(2) plus the value of any benefits received in consequence of any Gift Aid donations by the same donor to the same charity earlier in the same tax year
(3) must not exceed £250.

The aggregate value test is unchanged from the old Gift Aid scheme. In particular, the value of benefits is not annualised for the purposes of the aggregate value test. Thus it is the actual value, as opposed to an annual value, of the benefits that counts.

For example, suppose in the above example A makes two further donations to the charity in the tax year 2000–01 as follows:

| Date | Amount | Benefits |
|------|--------|----------|
| 11 March 2001 | £9,600 | weekend break worth £225 |
| 4 April 2001 | £4,000 | dinner for two worth £90 |

As the value of the weekend break does not exceed the limit of £240 (ie 2½% of the £9,600 donation), the fifth donation passes the relevant value test. Furthermore, it passes the aggregate value test (it is not aggregated with the benefit worth £15 received in consequence of the fourth donation, because that donation did not qualify as a Gift Aid donation).

As the value of the dinner for two does not exceed the limit of £100 (ie 2½% of the £4,000 donation), the sixth donation passes the relevant value test. However, it fails the aggregate value test, because the value of the dinner for two plus the value of the weekend break exceeds £250. Therefore, the sixth donation cannot qualify as a Gift Aid donation. The other five donations are unaffected.

### 10.2.7 Records to be maintained by the charity

This is covered at 28.1.9.

## 10.3 MILLENNIUM GIFT AID

This scheme was introduced in the March 1998 budget to encourage giving towards education and anti-poverty projects in the world's poorest countries. It ceased to have any relevance from 6 April 2000 when the £250 minimum for Gift Aid relief was abolished.

### 10.3.1 Outline of the scheme

The scheme applied to donations made in 1998–99 and 1999–2000. Individuals needed to make cash gifts of at least £100 to UK-registered charities for qualifying schemes. The £100 minimum could be achieved by making a series of smaller donations adding up to at least £100.

### 10.3.2 Qualifying scheme

A qualifying scheme was one which benefited inhabitants of countries which were designated as 'low income countries' by the World Bank. Only those charities which could demonstrate the necessary structure and expertise were allowed to operate qualifying schemes.

### 10.3.3 How relief was given

Individuals who gave £100 were treated as if they had made a 'gross' payment of £129.87 from which they had deducted £29.87 (ie 23%). Provided they paid tax at the basic rate they would not have to pay any more tax over to the Revenue than would otherwise have been the case and the charity would be able to recover the £29.87 from the Revenue. If the individual had been a higher rate taxpayer, he would receive higher rate relief of 17% of £129.87 (ie £22.07) so the net cost after tax relief of giving the charity £129.87 was reduced to £77.93.

## 10.4 GIFT OF LISTED SHARES AND SECURITIES

A new tax relief was introduced in FA 2000. From 6 April 2000 both individuals and companies that make gifts to charity of listed shares and securities are able to obtain tax in calculating their income for tax purposes. The new relief applies where the shares and securities listed on a recognised stock exchange (in the UK or overseas) are gifted or sold at undervalue to a charity. A gift of AIM shares can qualify.

The deduction will be equal to the market value of the shares or securities on the date of disposal (inclusive of the incidental cost of disposal) less any consideration received for or in consequence of disposal of the shares or securities.

### Example

A gives listed shares with a market value of £10,000 to a charity. The shares show an unrealised gain of £9,000. A obtains income tax relief of £10,000 and CGT relief of £9,000. For a 40% taxpayer this amounts to tax relief of £7,600.

# NON-CHARITABLE PAYMENTS

## 10.5 DEEDS OF COVENANT AND ANNUITIES
(TA 1988, ss 347A, 663 and 683; FA 1988, s 36)

A deed of covenant is basically a written promise to pay another person a certain sum of money each year (or each week, month or quarter, etc), either for a fixed number of years or for a period determined by events (for example, until the payer's or the payee's death). A covenant for the payee's life is a kind of annuity.

At one time, all deeds of covenant operated so as to transfer taxable income from the payer to the payee, so that the payer's taxable income was reduced by the amount of the covenanted payment and the payee's similarly increased. This could save a great deal of money where (as would usually be the case) the payee was subject to a lower rate of tax than the payer. As a result, deeds of covenant were often used to redistribute income around a family. Inevitably this has led to anti-avoidance legislation which has gradually become all-embracing.

The anti-avoidance legislation began over 30 years ago. FA 1965 provided that a deed of covenant signed after the beginning of the 1965–66 tax year would not transfer income for higher rate purposes unless the covenanted payment was made:

(1) to a recognised charity (see 10.1); or
(2) to support a divorced or separated spouse (see 8.1); or
(3) as part of the purchase price of a business; or
(4) by a partnership to a retired partner, or to the widow or other dependant of a former partner.

A covenant made today which falls within (1), (3) or (4) above will still operate to transfer taxable income from payer to payee, for both basic and higher rate purposes.

Following FA 1965, the position was that most types of covenanted payments counted as the recipient's income for basic rate, but not higher rate, tax purposes and that those payments reduced the payer's income for basic rate, but not higher rate, purposes.

Most such payments were made under deduction of basic rate tax, so that the payer took his relief by reducing the net payment actually made and the payee received his money tax paid. Where the payee had surplus personal allowances, he could claim a repayment from the Revenue.

This situation lasted until 15 March 1988. Payments under covenants made on or after 15 March 1988 (other than for charitable covenants, business purchase annuities and partnership annuities) are simply ignored for tax purposes and are deemed to be paid gross. Relief for existing covenants continued for a transitional period, but relief was abolished completely with effect from 6 April 1996.

### 10.5.1 Business purchase and partnership annuities

Business purchase and partnership annuities attract higher rate relief as well as basic rate. However, the payer can only deduct basic rate at source, and must claim the higher rate relief from the Revenue. For details of such annuities, see 6.11.

## 10.6 VOCATIONAL TRAINING
(FA 1991, ss 32 and 33)

Tax relief was available up to 5 April 2000 where an individual paid for his or her own vocational training, subject to the following conditions:

(1) Relief was available for registration, tuition, assessment and examination fees, but not for books, equipment, travel or other incidental expenses.
(2) Those fees had to be paid by the student himself and not, for example, by his employer.
(3) The student had to be UK-resident (but not necessarily ordinarily resident).
(4) The course had to lead to, or count towards, a National or Scottish Vocational Qualification (NVQ or SVQ) at levels 1–5 inclusive. (Level 5, which covers senior managerial and professional skills, was added with effect from 1 January 1994.) However, tax relief was also available for other courses where the individual was aged at least 30.
(5) The college or other body organising the course had to be registered with the Revenue as a 'training provider'.
(6) The student could not be entitled to claim tax relief for his training expenses in any other way.

(7)  The student could not be receiving public sector financial support (eg a local authority grant or a subsidised loan under the Career Development Loan Scheme).

(8)  The student had to be age 16 or over.

(9)  The student could not be in full-time education and qualify for relief unless he was over age 18.

There was no requirement that the course had to be relevant to the student's current job, or even that the student had to be in employment or in business on his own account. Accordingly, tax relief was available on equal terms to unemployed people keen to increase their chances in the job market, to those wishing to embark upon a new career path and to those seeking to update their skills with a view to returning to work after a career break.

Furthermore, provided the study unit could count towards an NVQ or SVQ, tax relief was available even if the student had no intention of pursuing the full qualification.

## 10.6.1 How relief was given

Basic rate relief was given by deduction at source: that is to say, if the course fee in 1999–2000 was £200, the college asked the trainee to pay only £154 and claimed the balance of £46 (23% of £200) from the Government. From the student's point of view, this system offered two advantages: first, relief was obtained immediately, and secondly the reduced fee was payable even if the student was not a taxpayer (eg was unemployed and so had no taxable income).

The college asked the student to sign a simple declaration that he fulfilled the qualifying conditions. For identification purposes, he was also required to state his national insurance number. The tax return form asked him to enter the 'name of the training organisation' and the 'net amount paid' – in the example above, the £154 actually paid to the college, rather than the full £200 fee.

No higher rate relief was due for 1999–2000. For earlier years, higher rate relief could be claimed so that if the student in the example above was a higher rate taxpayer in 1998–99, the higher rate relief would reduce the tax payable by 17% of £200. The Tax Office may require the student to produce an official college receipt to verify the fee paid.

## 10.7  MEDICAL INSURANCE
(FA 1989, ss 54–57)

With effect from 2 July 1997, payments on policies taken out or renewed ceased to qualify for tax relief. Premiums paid under an existing annual contract continued to attract tax relief, provided the premium was paid before 6 April 1999.

For further details see *Allied Dunbar Tax Handbook 1999–2000* at 10.6.

## 10.8 TRADE UNION AND FRIENDLY SOCIETY SUBSCRIPTIONS
(TA 1988, s 266(6) and (7))

Some trade unions provide pensions and/or death benefits (often called 'funeral benefits') for their members. Each member is entitled to tax relief on half of that part of his subscription which relates to the provision of such benefits. However, this relief is sometimes given by the Revenue making a block payment to the union and the union then charging reduced subscriptions to its members.

The members of some friendly societies also pay a subscription which covers both a death benefit and a sickness benefit. Half of the amount referable to the death benefit qualifies for tax relief.

There is a distinction between relief under the special arrangements for trade union subscriptions and 'mixed' friendly society policies (described above) and the general relief for life assurance premiums (see 10.9). Relief under the special arrangements is available only in the exact circumstances described – and not, for example, for a premium paid under a simple life assurance policy issued by a friendly society. Relief under the special arrangements is, however, available irrespective of the date the insurance came into force, whereas the general relief for life assurance premiums is available only for policies which entered into force before 14 March 1984.

## 10.9 LIFE ASSURANCE PREMIUMS
(TA 1988, s 266)

Most life assurance polices which came into force before 14 March 1984 qualify for a form of tax relief. (The operative date is the day the policyholder's proposal was accepted by the insurance company, not the day the policy was issued.) The Revenue makes a block payment to the insurance company, equal to half the basic rate of tax on the premiums payable on qualifying policies, and the insurance company correspondingly reduces the amount actually paid by the policyholder. For example, if the standard premium was £100, the Revenue would pay £12.50 and the policyholder only £87.50. That £12.50 is, however, the sum total of the relief available. No additional relief may be claimed if the policyholder is a higher rate taxpayer. Furthermore, relief will be lost completely if any material change is made to the policy – for example, if a term policy is converted into an endowment or if the insurance company makes a loan to the policyholder without charging a commercial rate of interest.

No tax relief is available for the premiums on life assurance policies which came into force on or after 14 March 1984. However, an alternative route to tax relief is to arrange your life cover through a personal pension plan as explained in Chapter 12.

# 11

# TAX EFFICIENT INVESTMENT

COLIN WALKER

There is a range of investments where the interest and any gains are exempt from tax. This chapter covers the following:

### Investments which provide a tax exempt return

(1) Individual savings accounts (ISAs).
(2) National Savings investments.
(3) Friendly society investments.
(4) TESSAs.
(5) Personal equity plans (PEPs).

### Investments which qualify for a tax deduction

(6) Enterprise investment schemes.
(7) Venture capital trusts (VCTs).
(8) Enterprise zone trusts.

## 11.1 INDIVIDUAL SAVINGS ACCOUNTS (ISAS)

### 11.1.1 Basic outline of scheme

ISAs are a scheme designed to encourage new saving. They are offered by financial institutions such as banks, building societies and insurance companies ('providers'). All UK resident and ordinarily resident individuals aged 18 or over are able to take out an ISA from 1999–2000 onwards. Key features of the scheme are:

(1) during 1999–2000 and 2000–01 the annual limit is £7,000 of which up to £3,000 can be kept on deposit and up to £1,000 in life assurance policies. The balance must be invested in stocks and shares, and unit trusts; and

(2) for 2001–02 and future years, the annual subscription is limited to £5,000 of which up to £1,000 can be kept on deposit and up to £1,000 invested in life assurance policies.

Investors in ISAs are exempt from income tax and CGT on their investments and the ISA manager can reclaim the 10% tax credit on UK dividends until 5 April 2004. This applies to shares both held directly within the ISA and which are held by an insurance company in a special fund for policies issued as part of an ISA.

Normally contributions to an ISA will be made in cash (but see below on shares acquired under approved schemes).

It is intended that this scheme will run for ten years, but the Government has indicated that it will be reviewed after seven years to decide whether any changes are necessary after the ten-year period has expired.

## 11.1.2 Transfers of shares into an ISA

It is possible to transfer into an ISA shares received from an approved profit-sharing scheme (see 3.12) or from an approved savings-related share option scheme (see 3.15.2). The market value of the shares transferred into the ISA will count towards the annual £7,000/£5,000 limit, but no CGT will be payable on the transfer. The transfer must take place within three years of the shares being appropriated in the case of a profit-sharing scheme and within 90 days of acquisition under a savings-related share option scheme.

It is not possible to transfer other shares into an ISA, eg shares acquired under a public offer or on a building society demutualisation (as was permitted with PEPs).

## 11.1.3 Withdrawals

It is possible to make withdrawals from an ISA at any time without loss of tax relief, but it is not possible to return sums to an ISA unless the amounts fall within the annual 'allowance'.

## 11.1.4 Practical aspects

The regulations permit an individual to take out a 'maxi' ISA or up to three 'mini' ISAs in a tax year. An individual is not allowed to take out a maxi and a mini ISA in the same year.

A maxi ISA can be wholly invested in quoted (but not AIM) shares, unit trusts, investment trusts and OEICs, gilts, and corporate bonds with a life of at least five years. This is sometimes called the 'equity' component, although the range of investments is wider than equities. Alternatively, the maxi may be split into three separate components with cash deposits of up to £3,000 and life assurance of £1,000 in 2000–01. With a maxi, you can 'top-up' the stocks and shares component so that if, for example, only £1,000 were put into the cash component, and £750 in life assurance, £5,250 could be put into the stocks and shares component. Once you have set up a maxi ISA with two or more components, you are stuck with it, as the rules do not permit internal transfers from one component to another.

Alternatively, it is possible for an individual to take out three mini ISAs, possibly with different managers, for each separate component. In this case it is not possible to top-up the stocks and shares component, so if you take out a £1,000 mini cash ISA and a £750 mini insurance ISA, you can still put in only £3,000 into a stocks and shares ISA.

### 11.1.5 CAT standards

The Government has introduced a system of voluntary standards. The standards are known as 'CAT' standards (Charges Access Terms). The standards vary according to the different types of ISA. For example, the CAT for mini cash ISAs requires seven-day access and interest of no less than base minus 2%; the CAT for mini insurance ISAs requires that annual charges should not exceed 3% and the surrender value after three years must be at least equal to the premiums paid.

The standards are voluntary, but providers have to inform potential investors whether their products meet or exceed the standards.

### 11.1.6 Consequences if rules are broken

With an ISA invested in stocks and shares, if the rules are broken (eg because the individual has taken out both a maxi and a mini ISA in the same year), the individual must report any capital gains.

With a cash ISA, the provider must withhold 20% tax and the individual must include the interest on his SA return and pay any higher rate tax which is due. In the case of an insurance ISA, the policy will be cancelled and the insurance company must deduct tax at basic rate. If the investor has made a profit, he will be liable for higher rate tax. An individual who has knowingly broken the rules may also be liable for a penalty.

## 11.2 NATIONAL SAVINGS INVESTMENTS

### 11.2.1 National Savings certificates
(TA 1988, s 46)

These are certificates which pay an accumulating rate of interest over a five-year period. All the returns are tax free. Index linked certificates accumulate at a rate related to the Retail Price Index. If held for the full five years a bonus is payable.

### 11.2.2 NSB ordinary account interest
(TA 1988, s 325)

The first £70 of interest paid on a National Savings Bank (NSB) ordinary account is exempt from tax (see 5.1.1).

## 11.3 FRIENDLY SOCIETY INVESTMENTS

Friendly societies issue qualifying insurance policies and there is no tax charge for investors when such policies mature. In this respect the position is no different from policies issued by insurance companies. The difference lies in the way that friendly societies are treated favourably for tax purposes in that they are not normally subject to tax on life assurance business; this has generally enabled them to produce attractive returns.

Friendly society policies are, however, essentially a long-term investment. For many years they were prevented from paying a surrender value within the first ten years which exceeded the amount of premiums paid, but this limitation was removed by FA 1995. However, this will often be academic since the surrender value can be very low where plans are cancelled or surrendered before the ten-year term has expired because penalties tend to be heavy and frequently the charges on friendly society plans are high.

The maximum premiums are still very low. The maximum permitted is £270 pa. Some societies do permit a lump sum investment to be made to cover the full ten-year plan. Most of the larger friendly societies are governed by the same investment regulations as life assurance companies. All investment income and capital gains within the fund are free of all UK tax which enhances the rate of return.

## 11.4 TESSAS
(TA 1988, ss 326A–326C)

An individual was permitted to open a Tax-Exempt Special Savings Account in 1998–99 and earlier years. This is basically a five-year plan under which an individual aged 18 or over can save up to £9,000. The sum must be held on deposit by a bank, building society or other institution authorised under the Banking Act 1987, but the regulations permit an investor to switch from one group to another. The resulting interest is not taxable provided the individual makes no withdrawals during the five-year period, or any such withdrawals do not exceed the amount of the interest credited to the account less tax at basic rate.

Up to £1,800 pa may be invested in a TESSA opened before 6 April 1999 provided that the total sums invested do not exceed £9,000.

Where a TESSA ceases to qualify, the interest credited to the TESSA becomes taxable income which is deemed to arise at that point in time.

### Second TESSAs

In order to encourage savings the Government increased the first year deposit limit for a second TESSA to the amount of the capital held in the first TESSA account (£9,000 maximum). It is therefore conceivable that an individual may have started two TESSAs in 1997–98 or 1998–99 and these will mature after 5 April 1999, with a total saving of up to £18,000 (2 × £9,000).

## Replacement by ISAs

No new TESSAs can be opened after 5 April 1999. It is, however, still possible to pay into a TESSA opened before 1999–2000. When existing accounts mature the capital can be transferred into the cash component of an ISA (see 11.1). Neither the annual subscriptions to TESSAs nor any maturing capital are treated as included in the annual subscription limit for the ISA.

# 11.5 PERSONAL EQUITY PLANS (PEPS)
(TA 1988, s 333)

An individual aged 18 or over who is resident and ordinarily resident in the UK was permitted to invest up to £6,000 in a PEP in 1998–99, the final year of the scheme. In addition, a further £3,000 could be invested in a single company PEP (see below).

The investments are held by a PEP manager and once again it is possible for a plan to be transferred to another authorised manager.

PEPs are intended to be a way of encouraging investment in shares. Up to £6,000 may be invested in shares in companies quoted on the Stock Exchange or shares quoted on the unlisted securities market (USM) or in authorised unit trusts or investment trusts which in turn invest at least 50% of their funds in UK equities or shares quoted on EU Stock Exchanges. A PEP manager is also allowed to invest in qualifying corporate bonds and convertible stocks (see below). As an alternative, up to £1,500 may be invested in any other authorised unit trust or investment trust. The balance of any investments over the £1,500 limit must then be invested in qualifying equities or in unit trusts or investment trusts which meet the 50% requirement.

An individual may also invest up to £3,000 a year in a single company PEP where the investment is restricted to shares in one particular company.

All income and capital gains arising within the PEP are exempt from tax. The plan managers can recover a 20% credit on UK dividends received in 1998–99 and a 10% credit on 1999–2000 dividends paid by UK companies cashed in.

## Replacement by ISAs

All PEPs held at 6 April 1999 can continue to be held as PEPs outside the new ISAs (see 11.1) but with the same tax advantages as the new account.

## 11.6 ENTERPRISE INVESTMENT SCHEMES
(FA1994, s 135 and Sched 14)

The scheme is intended to provide a 'targeted incentive' for new equity investment in unquoted trading companies and to encourage outside investors to introduce finance and expertise to a company. The reliefs were substantially increased by FA 1995, which enabled minority investors to secure 20% income tax relief and CGT deferral relief which could be worth up to another 40% of the amount invested.

The EIS was further extended by FA 1998 to enable some investors to secure EIS CGT deferral relief even though they do not qualify for the income tax relief (eg because they take a controlling stake in the company). This effectively replaced CGT reinvestment relief and subsumed this into a 'unified' scheme under which companies in which investors take up shares have to conform to a common set of rules.

### 11.6.1 Summary of main aspects

(1) Income tax relief may be given at 20% on the amount invested This relief is forfeited if there is a disposal within three years (five years for shares issued before 6 April 2000). CGT deferral relief may also be obtained so that in some situations total tax relief of 60% can be secured.

(2) EIS relief is due only if an individual subscribes for new shares in a qualifying company.

(3) Income tax relief is not available if the individual acquires a shareholding which exceeds 30%, but CGT deferral relief can still be available for investments made after 5 April 1998.

(4) There is a ceiling for investment by individuals who qualify for income tax relief under the EIS of £150,000 per tax year (£100,000 up to 1997–98). There is no ceiling for investments by individuals and trustees which qualify only for CGT deferral relief.

(5) Up to one-half of the amount invested by an individual between 6 April and 5 October in any year can be carried back to the previous tax year if the individual did not invest the full amount during that year (subject to a maximum of £25,000).

(6) Income tax relief is not available to an individual if he was previously connected with the company. This does not prevent a connected investor from qualifying for the CGT deferral relief.

(7) EIS relief is available only where the company has gross assets of less than £15m before and no more than £16m after the EIS share issue.

(8) Where EIS shares are sold at a loss, relief is available either against capital gains or against the individual's income by virtue of TA 1988, s 574 (see 15.2).

(9) Shares which attract the 20% income tax relief are exempt from CGT on the occasion of their first disposal, except to the extent that EIS relief has been withdrawn.

The Revenue publishes a most informative booklet, IR137, *The Enterprise Investment Scheme.*

## 11.6.2 Conditions which must be satisfied for EIS relief to be available

### Subscription for new shares in a qualifying company

Both EIS income tax relief and EIS CGT deferral relief are available only if an individual subscribes for shares. The shares must be ordinary shares which are not preferred in any way. EIS income tax relief is available only if the individual invests at least £500. The company must be a qualifying company.

### Certificate EIS 3

An investor must obtain certificate EIS 3 from the company before he can claim either type of EIS relief.

## 11.6.3 Qualifying companies

A qualifying company can be a UK resident or non-resident company, but it must be an unquoted company which either:

(1) exists wholly for the purpose of carrying on one or more qualifying trades (see 11.6.4) 'or which so exists apart from purposes capable of having no significant effect (other than in relation to incidental matters) on the extent of the company's activities'; or
(2) has a business which consists wholly of:
    (a) the holding of shares or securities of, or the making of loans to, one or more qualifying subsidiaries of the company; or
    (b) both the holding of such shares or securities, or the making of such loans, and the carrying on of one or more qualifying trades.

### Company must be unquoted

A company does not qualify if any of its shares or securities are dealt in on the Stock Exchange or USM. The fact that a company's shares are dealt in on the AIM does not disqualify it but the £15m gross asset test will rule out many AIM companies.

### Other conditions

There are also certain other conditions which need to be satisfied if it is to be a qualifying company:

(1) the company must not control another company apart from a qualifying subsidiary, either on its own or together with a connected person and

there must not be any arrangements in place under which the issuing company can acquire such control;

(2) the company must not be under the control of another company or under the control of another company and persons connected with it, and once again there must be no arrangements in place whereby such a company may acquire control of the issuing company.

## 11.6.4 Meaning of qualifying trade

There are certain trades which are excluded under s 297, ie the company's business must not consist to any substantial extent of any of the following:

(1) dealing in land, in commodities or futures or in shares, securities or other financial instruments;
(2) dealing in goods otherwise than in the course of any ordinary trade of wholesale or retail distribution;
(3) banking, insurance (but not insurance broking), money-lending, debt-factoring, hire-purchase financing, or other financial activities;
(4) oil extraction activities;
(5) leasing (except for certain short-term charters of ships) or receiving royalties or licence fees;
(6) providing legal or accountancy services;
(7) providing services or facilities for any trade carried on by another person (other than a parent company) which consists to any substantial extent of activities within any of (1)–(6) above and in which a controlling interest is held by a person who also has a controlling interest in the trade carried on by the company;
(8) any of the following property-backed activities where the shares were issued on or after 17 March 1998:
   (i) farming and market gardening;
   (ii) forestry and timber production;
   (iii) property development;
   (iv) operating or managing hotels or guest houses; and
   (v) operating or managing nursing or residential care homes.

### Wholesale and retail distribution trades

Wholesale and retail distribution trades qualify only if they are 'ordinary' trades. Section 297(3) states that a trade does not qualify as an ordinary trade of wholesale or retail distribution if:

(1) It consists to a substantial extent of dealing in goods of a kind which are collected or held as an investment; and
(2) A substantial proportion of those goods are held by the company for a period which is significantly longer than the period for which a vendor would reasonably be expected to hold them while endeavouring to dispose of them at their market value.

The following are taken as indications that a company's trade is a qualifying trade:

(1) The goods are bought by the trader in quantities larger than those in which he sells them.
(2) The goods are bought and sold by the trader in different markets.
(3) The company incurs expenses in the trade in addition to the costs of the goods, and employs staff who are not connected with it.

The following are 'indications' that the trade is not a qualifying trade:

(1) There are purchases or sales from or to persons who are connected with the trader.
(2) Purchases are matched with forward sales or vice versa.
(3) The goods are held by the trader for longer than is normal for goods of the kind in question.
(4) The trade is carried on otherwise than at a place or places commonly used for the type of trade.
(5) The trader does not take physical possession of the goods.

The above are only indications and are not conclusive that a company's trade is or is not a qualifying trade, but it will be difficult to persuade the Revenue that a trade qualifies if there are a number of indications to the contrary.

### 11.6.5 Definition of qualifying subsidiary
(ICTA 1988, s 308(2))

A qualifying subsidiary is one in which the issuing company or one of its subsidiaries holds at least 75% of the share capital. In addition, the company must meet one of the following tests:

(1) it must be carrying on a qualifying trade; or
(2) it must exist to hold and manage a property used by the parent company, or by a fellow 75% subsidiary, for the purposes of a qualifying trade; or
(3) it must be dormant.

It was necessary for the activities of each member of a group of companies to be a qualifying activity. This was relaxed with effect from 27 November 1996 so that a group's activities are considered as a whole, rather than on an individual company basis. The Revenue has stated that relief will no longer be withdrawn where the non-qualifying activities do not form a substantial part of the group's activities as a whole, but no indication has been given of what percentage is considered to be 'substantial'.

### 11.6.6 Reliefs available to an EIS investor
As already mentioned, there are two types of relief: income tax and CGT deferral relief. They are separate and either can be claimed without the

other. On the other hand, an individual who invests (say) £100,000 can claim both reliefs by reference to the same £100,000 invested.

Trustees can only claim the CGT relief.

## 11.6.7 Income tax relief

An investor is entitled to the lower of the income tax payable by him and relief at the lower rate (20%) on the amount invested up to a limit of £150,000 from 1998–99 (£100,000 for earlier years). For this purpose, an individual's tax liability is calculated without regard to the reliefs which are given as a reduction expressed in terms of tax, ie:

(1) the married couple's allowance, the additional personal allowance and the widow's bereavement allowance;
(2) qualifying maintenance payments; and
(3) MIRAS interest for years up to 1999–2000.

The investor's tax liability is also computed without regard to double taxation credits and basic rate tax deducted at source on annual payments.

### Example – Computation of EIS income tax relief

*J* is a married woman. Her gross income for 1999–2000 totals £75,000. During the year she inherits £100,000 which she invests in a qualifying EIS company. Her husband does not work and has no income whatsoever. For 1999–2000 her tax position is:

|  | £ |
|---|---|
| Total income | 75,000 |
| *Less:* Personal allowance | (4,335) |
|  | 70,665 |
|  |  |
| Tax thereon |  |
| 1,500 × 10% | 150 |
| 26,500 × 23% | 6,095 |
| 42,665 × 40% | 17,066 |
|  | 23,311 |
| *Less*: Married couple allowance |  |
| £1,970 × 10% | (197) |
|  | 23,114 |
| *Less*: EIS relief lower of |  |
| (a) £100,000 × 20% = £20,000 |  |
| (b) £23,311 | (20,000) |
|  | 3,114 |

If *J*'s income had been £50,000, relief would have been restricted to her tax liability before the married couple's allowance, ie £13,311.

## 11.6.8 **Further conditions for income tax relief**

There are extra conditions to be satisfied for an individual to qualify for the EIS income tax relief. Basically he must not be regarded as connected with the company.

### Individual must not be connected with the company

The legislation provides that an individual may be treated as connected with the issuing company, and therefore not entitled to EIS income tax relief, if he directly or indirectly possesses or is entitled to acquire more than 30% of:

(1) the issued ordinary share capital of the company, or any of its subsidiaries;
(2) the loan capital and issued share capital of the company or any subsidiary; or
(3) the voting power in the company or any subsidiary.

However, a connected individual can still be eligible for CGT deferral relief.

An individual is also regarded as being connected with the issuing company if he directly or indirectly possesses, or is entitled to acquire such rights as would, in the event of the winding-up of the company (or any of its subsidiaries), mean that he is entitled to receive more than 30% of the assets available for distribution to equity holders of the company.

Rights of 'associates' need to be taken into account. For these purposes, an 'associate' means partner, spouse, parent, grandparent, great-grandparent, child, grandchild, great-grandchild and certain family trusts.

An individual is also regarded as connected with the company if he possesses any loan capital in a subsidiary of the company.

### Individual must not be previously 'connected with the company'

An individual is deemed to be connected with the company if he is:

(1) a paid director of the issuing company or any of its subsidiaries; or
(2) an employee of the issuing company or any of its subsidiaries; or
(3) a partner of the issuing company or any subsidiary; or
(4) an associate of someone who is a director or an employee or a partner of the issuing company, or any of its subsidiaries.

An individual is disqualified if he falls into any of the above categories during the two years prior to the date that the EIS shares are issued. Furthermore, an individual will not qualify for EIS relief if he is connected with the issuing company at the time the shares are issued, unless he is a business angel who qualified for EIS relief on his original investment and is now acquiring additional shares and he is connected only because he is a paid director (see the flow-chart overleaf).

## Flowchart to demonstrate whether an investment by a 'business angel' investor is eligible for EIS reliefs.

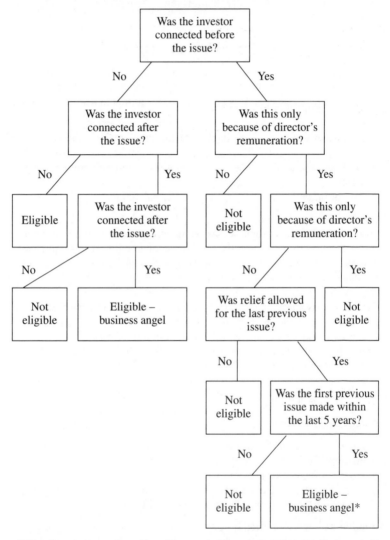

*This assumes there was only one issue of shares to the investor before he became a 'business angel'.

## 11.6.9 CGT deferral relief
(FA 1995, s 65 and Sched 13)

This relief involves a concept of deferred gain. Basically an individual who has realised a gain may secure deferral relief if he invests in the EIS during the period beginning one year before and ending three years after the disposal giving rise to the chargeable gain. However, the deferred gain is separately identified and will come back into charge if certain events happen (see 11.6.16).

### Example of EIS CGT deferral relief

G sold quoted shares for £20,000 in December 1999. The shares were originally purchased in January 1985 for £5,000. In June 1999 G had invested £10,000 in ordinary shares in an EIS company. The CGT position would be as follows:

|  | £ | £ |
|---|---|---|
| Proceeds | | 20,000 |
| *Less*:  Cost | 5,000 | |
|   Indexation relief (say) | 3,000 | |
|  | (8,000) | |
| Net gain | | 12,000 |
| *Less*: EIS CGT deferral relief | | (10,000) |
| Net chargeable gain for 1999–00 | | 2,000 |

*Note.* If G were a higher rate taxpayer the combined income and CGT relief could amount to 60% (20% income tax relief and 40% deferral of CGT).

The CGT deferral relief can be claimed even where the investor is 'connected' with the company (see 11.6.8).

## 11.6.10 Withdrawal of relief where company redeems share capital

All EIS investors lose a proportion of their relief if at any time during the investor's relevant period the company repays, redeems or repurchases any of its share capital which belongs to any member other than:

(1) the qualifying individual in question; or
(2) another EIS investor who thereby loses relief under the disposal of shares rule; or

the total relief withdrawn from EIS investors is the greater of:

(1) the amount receivable by the non-EIS investor; or
(2) the nominal value of the share capital in question.

The relief so lost is apportioned between the EIS investors in proportion to the amounts of the investments which have qualified for relief.

## 11.6.11 Withdrawal of relief where value is received from the company

Relief is withdrawn to the extent that an investor receives value from the company within five years of making his investment. An investor is regarded as having received value where he:

(1) Repays, redeems or repurchases any part of his holding of its share capital or securities, or makes any payment to him for the cancellation of rights.
(2) Repays any debt to him (other than a debt incurred by the company on or after the date on which he subscribed for the shares which are the subject of EIS relief).
(3) Pays him for the cancellation of any debt owed to him other than an ordinary trade debt, ie a debt incurred for a supply of goods or services on normal trade credit terms. The legislation specifically provides that normal trade credit does not allow for payment to be left outstanding for a period which exceeds six months.
(4) Releases or waives any liability of his to the company (the liability is deemed to have been waived if the liability is outstanding for more than 12 months) or discharges or undertakes to discharge any liability of his to a third person.
(5) Makes a loan or advance to him if this includes the situation where the individual becomes indebted to the company other than by an ordinary trade debt.
(6) Provides a benefit or facility for him.
(7) Transfers an asset to him for no consideration or for consideration less than market value.
(8) Acquires an asset from him for consideration exceeding market value.
(9) Makes any other payment to him except:
   (a) one which represents payment or reimbursement of allowable expenditure;
   (b) interest at a commercial rate on a loan from the individual;
   (c) dividends representing a normal return on investment;
   (d) payment for supply of goods by the individual to the company (provided that the price does not exceed the goods' market value);
   (e) reasonable and necessary remuneration for services rendered to the company where the individual is chargeable under Schedule D Case I or II (the last let-out does not cover remuneration for secretarial or managerial services).

In addition, an individual may receive value from a company if it is wound up and he receives a payment or asset in the course of the liquidation.

## 11.6.12 Withdrawal of relief where company ceases to be a qualifying company

EIS relief is withdrawn completely where any of the following events occur during the three-year relevant period.

(1)  it becomes a quoted company;
(2)  the company issues shares which are not fully paid up;
(3)  the company ceases to exist wholly for the purpose of a qualifying trade;
(4)  the company comes under the control of another company or under the control of another company and persons connected with that company;
(5)  arrangements come into being whereby another company could acquire control.

### Quoted companies

A company is regarded as quoted if any of its shares are dealt in on the Stock Exchange or USM. However, dealings on the AIM do not mean that a company is regarded as quoted.

## 11.6.13 Clawback of income tax relief where investor becomes connected with the company

EIS income tax relief (but not CGT deferral relief) is withdrawn completely where an individual becomes connected with the company during the investor's relevant period (five years from the date that the shares are issued).

### Definition of 'connected'

An individual is regarded as becoming connected with the company if he is:

(1)  the owner (directly or indirectly) of more than 30% of the company's voting shares, its issued ordinary share capital, or its loan capital and issued share capital taken together; or
(2)  the owner of rights entitling him to more than 30% of the company's assets available for distribution to equity holders;
(3)  entitled to acquire more than 30% of the company's voting shares, its issued share capital or its share and loan capital taken together;
(4)  entitled to acquire rights entitling him to more than 30% of the company's assets available for distribution to the company's equity holders;
(5)  the associate of a person who owns or is entitled to acquire more than a 30% interest;
(6)  the owner of any loan capital in a subsidiary of the company;

(7)  an employee of the company;
(8)  a partner of the company;
(9)  an associate of an employee or a partner of the company;
(10) a director of the company – unless he receives only 'normal and necessary' remuneration.

## 11.6.14 Withdrawal of income tax relief on disposal within three years

If a disposal takes place within three years (five years for shares issued before 6 April 2000), and the disposal is not to the investor's spouse, relief is withdrawn. If the disposal is anything other than a sale to an unconnected party at an arm's-length price, EIS income tax relief is withdrawn completely. Where the disposal is on an arm's-length basis, relief is withdrawn only on the sale consideration received by the investor.

The grant of an option during the relevant period may be treated as a disposal – ie where the exercise of the option would bind the grantor to purchase any EIS shares.

The receipt of a loan during the relevant period may also be treated as a disposal. This applies where the loan is made to the investor or an associate of his, if 'the loan is one which would not have been made, or would not have been made on the same terms' if the EIS investment had not been made.

## 11.6.15 Loss relief on an arm's-length disposal at less than cost

Where a loss arises on disposal or the company goes into liquidation within the three-/five-year period, further income tax or CGT relief may be due to the investor. In a case where the investor receives no payment whatsoever under the liquidation, the net amount of his investment may qualify as a capital loss.

### Example – EIS income tax relief

An individual invests £80,000 under the EIS. He receives income tax relief at 20% of £80,000, ie £16,000. If the entire investment has to be written off, he will be entitled to a capital loss of £64,000. This loss may be set against an individual's income or relieved against capital gains.

## 11.6.16 Clawback of CGT deferral relief

A gain which has been deferred is brought back into charge if any of the following events happen:

(1) the investor disposes of the shares other than to his or her spouse (unless the conditions for exemption set out in 11.6.18 are satisfied);

(2) the investor (or where there has been a transfer between spouses, the investor's spouse) ceases to be resident in the UK at any time within three/five years of the issue of the EIS shares;

(3) the company ceases to be a qualifying company for EIS purposes within three years of the issue of the shares, or within three years of the date that it starts trading if this happens later.

The rule in (2) above does not apply if an individual temporarily becomes non-resident because of his employment, and he returns to the UK within three years still owning the shares.

### Example of withdrawal of CGT deferral relief

During the year 1997–98 *R* realised a capital gain of £60,000 and made an investment into an EIS company of £55,000 in August 1997. *R*'s other income is sufficient to warrant full EIS relief.

For 1997–98 *R* received EIS relief of £55,000 × 20% = £11,000. *R* could also elect to defer gains of £53,500 (£60,000 less the annual exemption £6,500). This would defer a potential CGT liability of £21,400.

In July 2000 *R* decides to emigrate. This causes the deferred gain of £53,500 to be reinstated as if it were a 2000–01 capital gain.

## 11.6.17 Taper relief

Where a capital gain arising after 5 April 1998 has been reduced by taper relief (see 14.6), and the gain is deferred by an EIS investment, the gain which is clawed back on disposal is the original gain (ie no further taper relief). However, where EIS shares are issued after 5 April 1999, sold at a gain and the gain is reinvested in new EIS shares, extra taper relief may eventually be due.

## 11.6.18 Disposal after three/five years of shares which qualified for EIS income tax relief

Once shares which qualify for the 20% income tax relief have been held for three or five years (depending on when the shares were issued – see 11.6.14), there is no claw back of relief on a disposal of shares. Furthermore, these shares are then an exempt asset for CGT purposes so that no CGT will be payable on any gain. However, and in contrast to the rules which applied under the BES, a loss realised on the disposal of the shares after the three-/five-year period may still attract either income tax or CGT relief. Once again, the loss is calculated as the difference between the net of tax cost and the disposal proceeds (see 11.6.15).

CGT may still be payable on disposal to the extent that CGT deferral relief has been obtained (see 11.6.16) even though any capital gain may be exempt.

## 11.7 VENTURE CAPITAL TRUSTS (VCTS)
(TA 1988, s 842 and Sched 28)

### 11.7.1 Qualifying trusts

VCTs are companies broadly similar to investment trusts. The main conditions for approval will be that in its most recent accounting period, the VCT meets the following requirements:

(1) The VCT's ordinary share capital has been quoted on the Stock Exchange.
(2) The VCT has not retained more than 15% of the income that it derived from shares or securities.
(3) Its income must have been derived wholly or mainly from shares or securities.
(4) At least 70% by value of its investments comprise of shares or securities in qualifying holdings (see below). Securities can include medium-term loans for a period of at least five years.
(5) At least 30% by value of its qualifying holdings are made up of ordinary shares.
(6) No holding in any one company represents more than 15% of the VCT's investments.

A VCT may be given provisional approval provided that the 70% and 30% requirements will be met within three years and the other conditions will be met in the current or next accounting period. If the trust fails to meet the conditions within these time periods, provisional approval will be withdrawn.

#### Qualifying holdings

Qualifying holdings are defined as holdings in unquoted companies which exist wholly for the purpose of carrying on wholly or mainly in the UK one or more qualifying trades (defined as for the EIS).

VCTs may count annual investments of up to £1m in total in any one qualifying unquoted trading company as a qualifying holding. The gross assets of the unquoted company must not exceed £16m immediately after the VCT's investment.

VCTs will be able to treat certain quoted investments as qualifying holdings where the companies were unquoted at the time that the VCT made its investment, and no more than five years have elapsed since the company became quoted.

#### Finance Act 1998 changes

The rules which govern the types of companies in which VCTs may invest were aligned with the EIS rules (see 11.6) with effect from 17 March 1998. In addition:

(1) guaranteed loans and securities cannot qualify as part of the fixed pro-portion of qualifying investments which a VCT must hold in order to preserve its approved status; and

(2) VCTs are required to ensure that at least 10% of their total investment in any company is held in ordinary, non-preferential shares.

These latter changes apply to VCTs for accounting periods ending on or after 2 July 1997, but not in respect of funds raised by the issue of shares before that date.

### Finance Act 1999 changes

Some of the anti-avoidance rules were relaxed with effect from 16 June 1999.

It is now permissible for a VCT to exchange its shares in an unquoted company for shares in a new holding company where that holding company has a 100% interest in the original company and the share exchange is being carried out in order to facilitate a flotation. In broad terms, the VCT may treat its shares in the new holding company as a qualifying investment provided the VCT has the same interest in the holding company and the VCT's shares in the original company were a qualifying investment.

Similarly, where a VCT holds convertible loan stock or preference shares, and it exercises its conversion rights, the resulting shareholding can be a qualifying investment.

## 11.7.2 Income tax reliefs

There are two kinds of income tax relief available for investments in VCTs.

(1) Individuals aged 18 or more are exempt from income tax on dividends from ordinary shares in VCTs to the extent that the shares acquired each year do not exceed £100,000 in value (relief on distributions). As from 9 March 1999, this relief can be withheld if the Revenue can show that the VCT shares were acquired in order to avoid tax (eg where the shares were acquired shortly before the VCT paid a dividend and sold shortly afterwards).

(2) Individuals aged 18 or more who subscribe for new ordinary shares in VCTs are, in addition, entitled to claim income tax relief at 20%, subject to the amount subscribed in any one year not exceeding £100,000. This relief on investment will be withdrawn unless the shares are held for at least three years (five years for shares issued before 6 April 2000).

## 11.7.3 CGT reliefs

There are also two kinds of CGT relief available for investors.

(1) Individuals aged 18 or over are exempt from CGT on disposals of ordi-nary shares in VCTs in respect of which they qualify for relief on investments (relief on disposals).

(2) Individuals aged 18 or over who have subscribed for new ordinary shares in VCTs for which they have been given income tax relief on investment may also be able to defer tax on a chargeable gain arising from the disposal of any asset on or after 6 April 1995, providing the VCT shares for which the individual subscribes are issued in a period beginning 12 months before and ending 12 months after the disposal (deferred relief on reinvestment). The deferred gain is reinstated if and when any of the following events happens:

(a) the investor disposes of the shares other than to his or her spouse;

(b) the investor (or where there has been a transfer between spouses, the investor's spouse) ceases to be resident in the United Kingdom at any period within three/five years of the issue of the VCT shares;

(c) the company ceases to be a qualifying VCT within three years of the issue of the shares, or within three years of the date that it starts trading if this happens later;

(d) the investor ceases to qualify for the 20% income tax relief, or some event occurs as a result of which the income tax relief is withdrawn or reduced.

## 11.8 ENTERPRISE ZONE TRUSTS

It is possible to invest in properties in enterprise zones through a syndicate or 'enterprise zone property trust'. An individual who invests in the enterprise zone property trust is treated as if he had incurred a proportion of the trust's expenditure on enterprise zone properties. Similarly, rents (and sometimes interest) received by the trust are apportioned amongst the investors, ie the Revenue looks through the trust and treats the individual as if he had acquired an interest in the underlying properties.

Where an individual is treated as having acquired such an interest in an enterprise zone property, the allowances may be set against his other income (see 4.6.4). However, an individual who invests in an enterprise zone property trust is entitled to capital allowances only for the year in which the trust invests in enterprise zone properties. In some cases, there may be a delay in that an individual invests in a trust at the end of one tax year and becomes entitled to allowances only for the following year (because that is the year in which the trust acquires the relevant properties).

# 12

# LIFE ASSURANCE AND PENSIONS

## VINCE JERRARD AND STUART REYNOLDS

This chapter covers the tax treatment of life assurance and pensions plans and looks at the treatment of the contributions paid in the funds while they are invested, and the benefits paid out. It covers the following topics:

### Life assurance

(1)  Introduction.
(2)  Qualifying and non-qualifying policies.
(3)  Taxation of life policy proceeds.
(4)  Offshore life policies.
(5)  Annuities.
(6)  Permanent health insurance.
(7)  Life policies effected by companies.

### Pensions

(8)  Personal pension plans and stakeholder pensions.
(9)  Retirement annuity contracts (s 226 contracts).
(10)  Occupational schemes.
(11)  Free-standing AVC (FSAVC) schemes.
(12)  Unapproved schemes.
(13)  The State pension scheme.
(14)  Contracting out.

### Miscellaneous

(15)  Taxation of commission.

## 12.1 INTRODUCTION – LIFE ASSURANCE

A life assurance policy is simply the evidence of a contract between the individual policyholder and the life assurance company. The general principle is that the company is the collecting house for pooled investments and mortality risks, offering benefits directly to policyholders based on personal contracts.

Life assurance policies can be classified in a number of different ways but the most common, practical classification reflects the nature of the benefits provided under the policy and the periods for which they are provided:

(1) whole of life policies, where the sum assured is payable on the death of the life assured, whenever that occurs;
(2) term policies, where the sum assured is payable on death during the policy term only;
(3) endowment policies, where the sum assured is payable on death during the policy term, or on survival to the end of the term.

Each type of policy has its own characteristics in terms of the blend of life assurance protection and potential investment return. Term policies for a relatively short period are most likely to offer the highest sum assured for each pound of premium while, towards the other end of the spectrum, an endowment policy will have a greater investment element.

An important characteristic of life assurance policies is that they do not produce income, as such, but are essentially medium or long-term accumulators. While a policy is held intact, the income and gains arising from the underlying investments held by the life company are taxed in the hands of the life company itself. In general the policyholder's prospective tax liability generally arises only when he receives payment under the policy.

This chapter deals with the tax consequences on the policyholder paying premiums or receiving benefits under a life assurance policy issued by a UK company or a foreign insurer operating through a branch in the UK (for 'foreign' life policies see 12.4).

Over the years many changes have been made to this complex and technical area. Unless the contrary is clearly the case, this chapter deals with the current life policy tax regime which took effect from its 'appointed day' of 1 April 1976, and assumes enactment of FA 2000.

### 12.1.1 The company's tax position
(TA 1988, ss 76, 432 *et seq*; FA 1989, ss 82–89 and Sched 8; FA 1990, ss 41–48 and Scheds 6–9; and F(No2)A 1992, s 65(n))

Taxation of life companies is extremely (and increasingly) complex. Broadly speaking, in respect of their life assurance business, companies are generally taxed on the excess of their investment income and realised capital gains over management expenses (the 'I–E' basis). For proprietary companies there is a formula to determine the proportions of the company's income and gains which should be allocated to policyholders and shareholders, respectively. With effect from tax year 2000–01, tax is charged on the policyholder's share of income and gains at the rate of 22% (20% on some items, eg the income from directly-held equities and, since the tax year 1996–97, for the policyholders' shares of the investment returns corresponding to savings income). The company's profits attributable to shareholders are, on the other hand, chargeable to corporation tax at the usual rates.

To enable UK life companies to compete more equally for the business of residents of other EU states, companies are able to write such business in an 'overseas' life fund, broadly on a gross roll-up basis with no UK tax on the income and gains, but no relief for expenses.

Registered friendly societies are in a somewhat different position, being exempt from corporation tax in respect of tax-exempt life or endowment business. This is life and endowment business where total premiums under contracts do not exceed £270 pa, with effect from 6 April 1995. Policies which can be written on the tax-exempt basis are generally qualifying policies provided they satisfy a minimum sum assured test. Such policies can give tax-free proceeds even to higher rate taxpayers but non-qualifying friendly society policies are taxable at basic and higher rates. The remainder of this chapter does not deal specifically with friendly society business.

## 12.1.2 Review of life assurance taxation

In recent years the Revenue has conducted a review of life assurance taxation covering both taxation of life companies and of life policy proceeds.

The current I–E regime collects an aggregated tax in respect of both the company's trading profit and the bulk of the income and gains accruing to the individual's policy but an alternative would be a gross roll-up regime (similar to those found in most EU countries). Under such a regime life companies would be taxed on their profits with the remaining tax charge being levied directly on the individual policyholder when his policy comes to an end.

It was intended that decisions should be reached during 1995, but the timescales slipped somewhat, although the first results of the review (correction of some technical anomalies and the removal of what the Revenue saw as avoidance through the use of some reassurance arrangements) appeared in FA 1995. Implementation of any far-reaching changes still appears to be some years away.

Whatever the outcome of the life company tax review, it did seem likely that there would be changes to the life assurance qualifying rules in the next few years. The Revenue interpreted the EC 3rd Life Directive as requiring the removal of pre-certification of life policies (see 12.2.1), and the 1994 Budget announced consultations with a view to removing pre-certification and amending the policy tax regime for 6 May 1996. In fact, the Revenue's proposals were not published until after the 1996 Budget and consultation continued until the end of April 1997.

The proposals would have introduced an 'exit testing' regime under which the tax consequences of a policy coming to an end, or paying out benefits, would have been determined by looking at how the policy had been maintained previously. This contrasts with the current 'qualifying rules' approach under which the tax treatment of the policy proceeds is determined, to a significant extent, by reference to the policy design at outset.

The tests to be applied on 'exit' would have been similar to those used in the qualifying rules and under the new regime favoured policies would still have been able to pay tax-free proceeds, even to higher rate taxpayers.

However, the proposals had a number of significant drawbacks which the industry and other interested parties drew to the Revenue's attention. Among these are the following:

(1) *Complexity*   The aim was to produce a simpler regime but the 93 draft clauses published were far from simple.
(2) *Cost*   It was not the Revenue's aim to increase the tax-take from life policies. Against this background it was difficult to see the cost/benefit justification for the change, given that early industry estimates put the cost of implementing the new regime in the order of £1bn.
(3) *Legitimate expectations of existing policyholders*   As life policies are medium to long-term contracts, policyholders must be able to have confidence that subsequent tax changes, even if not actually retrospective, recognise and safeguard their reasonable expectations as to the benefits their policies will produce. The proposals provided for all policies to move on to the new regime, with little in the way of protection for existing policyholders – something the industry would have found difficult to accept.
(4) *Specific proposals*   As proposed, the new regime would have been disadvantageous to policies held in trust (both new policies and existing policies in existing trusts).

Later in 1997 it was announced that the wide-ranging reforms canvassed would not be introduced. FA 1998 contained clauses dealing with certain specific matters, namely 'dead settlor' trusts, the appointment of fiscal representatives by offshore life companies selling to UK residents, and changing the taxation of 'personal portfolio bonds' (see 12.3.12). Pre-certification has been retained.

## 12.1.3 Individual savings accounts (ISAs)

This new form of tax-favoured savings was introduced in April 1999. In outline, the scheme as it affects life insurance is as follows.

Life assurance policies will be permitted ISA investments but only to the extent of £1,000 of premium in any year, out of a personal subscription limit of £5,000 pa (£7,000 in the first two years of the scheme). ISA policies may not require payment of regular premiums, but it is anticipated that 'regular single premium' policies will be allowed to offer greater investment benefits, reflecting the duration of the policy and repeated investment in them. The proceeds of such policies will be free of tax and the funds to which the policies are linked will grow tax free, with the benefit of a 10% credit in respect of UK dividend income for the first five years of the scheme.

## 12.2 QUALIFYING AND NON-QUALIFYING POLICIES

For tax purposes, the key classification of policies is between qualifying policies and non-qualifying policies.

The distinction is only relevant to the *individual.* There is no differentiation between qualifying and non-qualifying policies in respect of taxation of the income and gains from the underlying assets, in the life company's hands.

Each of the three types of policy already identified (whole life, endowment and term assurances) is capable of being a qualifying or non-qualifying policy depending on its initial design and the way in which it is dealt with once in force.

### 12.2.1 Qualifying policies
(TA 1988, s 267 and Sched 15)

These are policies which satisfy the conditions set out in TA 1988, Sched 15, and do not fall foul of the various anti-avoidance provisions.

The main features of the qualifying rules are as follows:

#### Premiums

(1) must be payable for a period of ten years or more (though term assurances may be written for shorter periods) and must be payable annually or more frequently; and
(2) must be fairly evenly spread so that premiums payable in any one period of 12 months are neither more than twice the amount of premiums paid in any other 12 month period, nor more than $\frac{1}{8}$ of the total amount of premiums payable over the first ten years (in the case of whole life policies) or over the term of the policy (in the case of an endowment).

#### The sum assured

(1) for an endowment policy, must not be less than 75% of the total premiums payable during the term of the policy. This percentage is reduced by 2% for each year by which the life assured's age exceeds 55 years at the issue of the policy;
(2) for a whole of life policy, must not be less than 75% of the total premiums payable if death were to occur at the age of 75 years;

(3) for a term policy, which has no surrender value and ends before the life assured's 75th birthday, need not satisfy any minimum requirement.

### Benefits

(1) may include the right to participate in profits, the right to benefits arising because of disability or the right to a return of premiums on death under a certain specified age (not exceeding 16 years); but

(2) may not include any other benefits of a capital nature.

The rules for certain special types of policy may vary from those referred to above, eg mortgage protection policies, family income policies and industrial assurances.

Life assurers usually submit standard policy wordings to the Revenue so that they can be certified as satisfying the qualifying rules ('pre-certification'). Policies in those standard forms can then be marketed as qualifying.

Where a policy contains options by which the policyholder may, for example, increase the sum assured, or the premium, or extend the policy term, these options are tested at the outset to ensure that, however any options are exercised, the policy will still satisfy the qualifying rules.

## 12.2.2 Non-qualifying policies

Non-qualifying policies are all other life policies not satisfying the qualifying rules, and those which, although they may have satisfied the qualifying rules at the outset, have subsequently been changed in some way such that they no longer satisfy those rules.

The most significant category of policies which are non-qualifying are single premium investment contracts (usually referred to as bonds). These are written as whole of life contracts and provide for only a small amount of life cover, being primarily investment vehicles.

A decision of the High Court in mid-1994 had cast doubt on the status of some policies such as life assurance contracts where no (or possibly insubstantial) life cover is provided. In 1996 the Court of Appeal restored the previous industry understanding.

## 12.2.3 Taxation of premiums
(TA 1988, s 266 *et seq* and Sched 14)

No specific tax relief is available to an individual in respect of premiums paid under a non-qualifying life assurance policy.

Similarly, there is no specific relief for premiums paid under qualifying policies issued in respect of contracts made after 13 March 1984.

However, for qualifying policies issued before that date, Life Assurance Premium Relief (LAPR) is still available where the policy was issued on the life of the payer of the premium (or the payer's spouse) and where the payer is resident in the UK at the time premiums are paid.

Relief is given currently at the rate of 12.5% on premiums up to the greater of £1,500 or one-sixth of total income and is usually obtained by deducting the tax relief from the premiums payable to the life company. Relief is lost if the policy becomes non-qualifying or if the benefits secured by the policy are increased, or its term extended, after 13 March 1984.

Where an individual receives the benefit of LAPR but, in effect, recoups himself for his outlay in premiums by withdrawing money from the policy, there is a process by which some or all of the LAPR is 'clawed back' by deduction from the amount withdrawn by him.

## 12.3 TAXATION OF LIFE POLICY PROCEEDS
(TA 1988, ss 539–554)

In view of life policies' position as income accumulators, where liability for gains and income in respect of the underlying assets is dealt with by taxing the life company, the usual income tax principles are inappropriate to life policy taxation. Accordingly, the tax regime which applies to the individual policyholder has been specifically constructed for the purpose. It caters separately for qualifying and non-qualifying policies and for mortality and investment profits realised from policies.

It is first necessary to determine whether any particular action constitutes a chargeable event in respect of the policy. If it does not, no income tax consequence arises from that action, under the life policy regime. If it does, it is then necessary to calculate the 'gain', to determine the rate of tax applicable to the gain, and to determine who is liable to pay the resulting tax.

Despite references to 'chargeable events' and 'gains', it is the income tax regime which applies to life policies (for the CGT position, see 12.3.10).

For the tax treatment of life policies which qualify as an ISA investment see 12.1.3. For the taxation of personal portfolio bonds, see 12.3.12.

### 12.3.1 Chargeable events

#### Non-qualifying policy
(TA 1988, s 540)

For a non-qualifying policy, the five chargeable events are:

(1)  the death of the life assured;
(2)  the maturity of the policy;

(3) the total surrender of the policy;
(4) the assignment of the policy for money or money's worth;
(5) excesses arising on partial surrenders or partial assignments in any policy year commencing after 13 March 1975 (see 12.3.3).

No chargeable event occurs where an assignment takes place by way of security for a debt (or on the discharge of the security). Similarly, an assignment between spouses living together is not a chargeable event.

## Qualifying policy

For a qualifying policy, the chargeable events are the same but subject to the following amendments:

(1) death or maturity are only chargeable events if the policy has previously been made paid-up (ie premiums have ceased but the policy has remained in force) within the first ten years (or threequarters of the term of an endowment policy, if shorter);
(2) surrender, assignment for money or money's worth or an excess will only be a chargeable event if it occurs before the expiry of ten years (or three-quarters of the term of an endowment policy, if shorter) or if the policy was made paid-up within that period.

Three key consequences of the chargeable event rules are that:

(1) the gift (ie assignment of the whole policy with no consideration) of qualifying or non-qualifying policies is not a chargeable event and so triggers no income tax consequence;
(2) there is no chargeable event on death of the life assured under, or on the maturity of, a qualifying policy where all due premiums were paid prior to the event in question;
(3) there is no chargeable event on the assignment for value or surrender (in whole or part) of a qualifying policy where premiums have been paid for the first ten years (or three-quarters of the term), as appropriate.

Where there is no chargeable event in respect of a life policy, there is no charge to income tax under the specific life policy tax regime, irrespective of the tax position of the individual policyholder. In particular, points (2) and (3) above illustrate the key, current advantage of qualifying policies ie their ability to provide tax-free proceeds, even for higher rate taxpayers.

## 12.3.2 Calculating life policy gains
(TA 1988, s 541)

Broadly speaking, where the chargeable event is a maturity, total surrender or assignment for consideration, the chargeable gain is the investment profit made under the policy. This is calculated by reference to the value of the benefits being received as a result of the chargeable event, plus the amount of any 'relevant capital payments' previously received under the policy (ie any sum or other benefit of a capital nature, other than one paid as a result of an individual's disability), less the amount paid by way of premiums and any taxable gains as a result of previous partial surrenders.

This principle of charging tax only on investment gains also applies where the chargeable event is the death of the life assured. The exclusion of mortality profit from the taxable gain is achieved by using the surrender value of the policy immediately before death instead of the value of the benefits being received under the policy.

## 12.3.3 Partial surrenders
(TA 1988, s 546)

The fifth of the chargeable events listed in 12.3.1 creates a potential income tax liability on the policyholder surrendering part of his policy (often referred to as making 'withdrawals' from the policy). Partial surrenders include the surrender of a right to a bonus and loans made by (or by arrangement with) the insurance company to the policyholder (unless the policyholder's policy is qualifying and the loan bears a commercial rate of interest or is lent to a full-time employee of the insurer for the purposes of house purchase or improvement).

At the end of each policy year, the policy attracts a 'notional allowance' of 5% of the total premium then paid under the policy. This allowance is then set against the value of any partial surrenders made up to that date. If the value of those partial surrenders exceeds the current cumulative allowance, a chargeable event occurs; if the cumulative allowance is equal to or exceeds cumulative withdrawals, no chargeable event occurs. Allowances are given up to 100% of the total premiums paid so that, for a single premium investment bond, the allowances are given at the rate of 5% for 20 years.

Once an 'excess' (ie an occasion on which the cumulative partial surrenders exceed the cumulative allowances) has occurred the cumulative withdrawals and allowances up to that date are considered to have been used and the process of accumulating allowances and withdrawals starts afresh (subject to the '100% of premiums' limit which applies to the allowances).

## Example – Cumulation of allowances and withdrawals

X invests £10,000 in a single premium investment bond; £1,200 is withdrawn after four policy years, a further £4,500 after six policy years and £1,000 after eight policy years.

| Policy Years | A Cumulative Allowances | B Partial Surrender chargeable events | C Cumulative surrender between (C–A) | D Taxable Gain |
|---|---|---|---|---|
| | £ | £ | £ | £ |
| 1 | 500 (1 × 500) | 0 | 0 | 0 |
| 2 | 1,000 (2 × 500) | 0 | 0 | 0 |
| 3 | 1,500 (3 × 500) | 0 | 0 | 0 |
| 4 | 2,000 (4 × 500) | 1,200 | 1,200 | 0 |
| 5 | 2,500 (5 × 500) | 0 | 1,200 | 0 |
| 6 | 3,000 (6 × 500) | 4,500 | 5,700 | 2,700 |
| 7 | 500 (1 × 500) | 0 | 0 | 0 |
| 8 | 1,000 (2 × 500) | 1,000 | 1,000 | 0 |
| 9 | 1,500 (3 × 500) | 0 | 1,000 | 0 |
| 10 | 2,000 (4 × 500) | 0 | 1,000 | 0 |
| etc | | | | |

*Note:* (1)  A chargeable event occurs only when C exceeds A.

(2)  The value of the policy is irrelevant to these calculations so that it is possible to have a taxable gain under a policy at a time when the policy itself is worth less than the premiums paid.

When the final chargeable event occurs under the policy (ie death, maturity, final surrender or assignment for value) the total profit on the policy is brought into account. The profit is the final proceeds (excluding any mortality profit where the event is death), plus previous partial surrenders, less premiums paid and any taxable gains from previous partial withdrawals.

## Example – Total surrender after partial surrenders

Using the example immediately above, if the policy were totally surrendered at the end of the tenth policy year for £10,400, the taxable gain on that final encashment would be as follows:

£10,400 + £1,200 + £4,500 + £1,000 – (£10,000 + £2,700) = £4,400

*Note:*
If, on final termination, the 'gain' calculated in this way is a negative figure, it may be deducted from taxable income, for the purposes of higher rate tax only (see 12.3.4).

## 12.3.4 Taxing gains on chargeable events
(TA 1988, ss 547 and 550)

In the majority of cases where the policyholder owns the policy for his own absolute benefit, the gain is treated as the top-slice of his income and is taxed appropriately.

However, because the income and gains attributable to the underlying assets of the policy have already been taxed in the hands of the life company, life policy gains are not chargeable to income tax at the basic rate. This applies to both qualifying and non-qualifying policies. Despite the fact that, in effect, the gain is treated as having already suffered basic rate tax, there is no grossing up of the gain for the purposes of higher rate tax.

Accordingly, for an individual paying tax at the higher rate, the maximum rate of tax payable on life policy gains at present (tax year 2000–01) will be 18% (40% less 22%). An individual whose income (including the gain) is taxable at the basic rate only will have no further income tax liability on the policy gain. Non-taxpayers or those paying tax at the lower rate of 20% will not be able to make any reclaim in respect of tax notionally paid by the life company.

If the individual realises a loss under the policy, that loss is only available as a deduction from taxable income for the purposes of higher rate tax.

### Top-slicing

In view of the fact that the gain will have arisen over a period of years, the legislation recognises that it might be rather harsh to treat the total gain as part of the taxpayer's income in the year of receipt. A measure of relief is afforded by a process known as 'top-slicing'.

Top-slicing first requires calculation of the 'appropriate fraction' of the gain, more usually referred to as the 'slice'. Where the chargeable event in question is death, maturity, total encashment or assignment for value, the slice is calculated by dividing the gain by the number of complete policy years for which the policy has been in force. Where the chargeable event is caused by a partial surrender, the gain is divided by the number of complete policy years since the last excess caused by a partial surrender (or by the number of years for which the policy has been in force where the chargeable event is the first excess).

The slice (and not the whole of the gain) is treated as the top part of the policyholder's income and the average rate of tax applicable to the slice (less the basic rate) is calculated. That tax rate will then apply to the whole of the gain to determine the total income tax liability on the gain. The result is that relief is given to individuals whose other income would mean that they pay the tax at no more than the basic rate, but who would be taken into the higher rates of tax if the whole of the gain were added to their income.

## Example – No tax on the gain

A invests £20,000 in a single premium investment bond in May 1995 and cashes it in after five years for £27,500. The gain is therefore £7,500 and the 'slice' is £1,500 (£7,500 divided by five).

| | |
|---|---:|
| Taxable income (excluding policy gain) | 15,000 |
| 'Slice' | 1,500 |
| Taxable income | £16,500 |

The tax rate applicable to the 'slice' is therefore 22% less 22% = 0%.

## Example – Slice falling into basic and higher rate bands

B invests £12,000 in a single premium investment bond in May 1995. After five years he cashes it in for £17,000. The gain is £5,000 and the slice is £1,000 (£5,000 divided by five). In that year his other taxable income after reliefs is £27,400.

Tax calculation on gain:

| | | |
|---|---|---:|
| Taxable income + 'slice' | = | £28,400 |
| Tax Applicable to slice | | |
| On £600 (ie £27,400 to £28,000) at 0% (23%–23%) | = | Nil |
| On £400 (ie £28,000 to £28,400) at 17% (40%–23%) | = | £68 |
| Total tax on slice | = | £68 |
| Average rate on slice | | |
| $\dfrac{68}{1,000} \times 100$ | = | 6.8% |

The tax payable is £5,000 × 6.8% = £340.

To illustrate the effect of top-slicing, if it had not been available the calculations would have been:

| | | |
|---|---|---:|
| Tax applicable to the gain | | |
| On £600 at 0% (22%) | = | Nil |
| On £4,400 at 18% (40% – 22%) | = | £792 |
| Tax payable | = | £792 |

*Notes:*
(1) The whole gain (without top-slicing) is counted as income in determining whether any age allowance should be reduced.
(2) There is no top-slicing where the taxpayer is a company.
(3) Any business expansion scheme relief is left out of account when calculating top-slicing relief.
(4) For top-slicing purposes, total income is computed without reference to amounts chargeable in respect of loss of office or lease premiums chargeable as rent.
(5) The examples given in this chapter assume no reliefs or amounts as mentioned in (3) and (4).

### Age allowance for over 65s

If an individual is entitled to the higher personal allowance, the gain on a life policy can reduce (or eliminate) that additional allowance. Top slicing relief does not apply in respect of this reduction of the additional allowance. See 7.3.1 for an example of how higher allowances can be reduced.

## 12.3.5 Two policy gains in one tax year
(TA 1988, s 550)

Where an individual has two policies with chargeable gains in a tax year, tax is calculated as if the gains arose under only one policy, with a slice equal to the sum of the individual slices. Thus, if two policies are surrendered in the same tax year, one with a gain of £10,000 (having been in force for five years) and one with a gain of £24,000 (having been in force for eight years) tax on the gains is calculated as if one policy had been surrendered yielding a gain of £34,000 and with a slice of £5,000.

This approach can have the effect of increasing or decreasing the total tax payable (compared to disposing of the policies in separate tax years) depending on the individual's tax position and the performance of the relevant policies.

## 12.3.6 Persons liable for the charge
(TA 1988, ss 547 and 551)

Where a policy is held by an individual for his own benefit, the tax charge falls on him. The same applies to an individual where the policy is held as security for a debt owed by him.

If the policy is held in trust, the charge falls on the settlor, who can recover the tax paid from the trustees. If a policy is held by a trust created by a settlor who has since died, it is possible that gains realised by trustees in these circumstances may escape tax altogether in view of the impossibility of taxing somebody who has not been alive in the appropriate year of assessment. Although somewhat anomalous, this has been very useful if an individual owned a policy which would not come to an end on his death (eg a joint life policy paying out on the second death). By declaring a suitable trust of the policy in his Will, he may have been able to put future gains realised under the policy outside the income tax net.

FA 1998 included provisions to counter this by enabling the trustees, or perhaps even the trust's beneficiaries, to be taxed where the settlor is dead (or not UK-resident at the time of the chargeable event). The rules do not apply where the settlor had died before 17 March 1998 and the policy is not 'enhanced' after that date.

Where the policy is held by a company, or on a trust created by or as security for a debt owed by a company, the charge falls on the company (with the right for the company to recover the tax paid from the trustees where the policy is held on trust).

If a policy is assigned by way of gift, chargeable excesses arising during that policy year, but prior to the assignment, are taxed on the assignor. Future gains are taxed on the new beneficial owner.

## 12.3.7 Timing of the taxation of gains

Where the chargeable event is death, maturity, total surrender or assignment for value, the gain is treated as arising at the time of the appropriate event.

Excesses arising from partial surrenders, on the other hand, are generally only regarded as arising at the end of the policy year in which the excess occurs. Accordingly, if the policy was taken out in June 1993 and an excess occurs as a result of a partial surrender in February 2000, the gain resulting from that partial surrender is treated as arising in June 2000 and so is taxable in the tax year 2000–01.

## 12.3.8 Critical illness policies

A development in the UK life assurance market in recent years has been the ability to include critical illness or 'dread disease' benefits in a variety of policies. In general, this benefit pays a capital sum if the life assured is diagnosed as suffering from any of the specified 'dread diseases or events'. The diseases or events specified will vary from company to company but will usually include heart attack, stroke, cancer, heart by-pass surgery etc.

It is understood that the Revenue accepts that the payment of a benefit on the happening of a dread disease is not a chargeable event so that this benefit is paid free of tax under the life policy tax regime.

## 12.3.9 Chargeable event certificates
(TA 1988, s 552)

When a chargeable event occurs, the lite assurance company is required to provide the Revenue with a chargeable event certificate which gives the name and address of the policyholder, the nature and date of the chargeable event and information required for computing the gain.

## 12.3.10 Capital gains tax and life policies
(TCGA 1992, s 210)

A policyholder will have no personal liability to CGT on a disposal of the policy if he is its original beneficial owner, or if he is an assignee and acquired the policy other than for money or money's worth.

If a policy is in the hands of an individual who is not the original beneficial owner and who did acquire it for money or money's worth, the policy is an asset potentially liable to CGT. However, where the policy is issued in respect of an insurance made after 25 June 1982 the policy also remains subject to the income tax regime which applies to life assurance policies. This may also affect some policies issued before that date. The potential for double taxation (income tax and CGT) is resolved by TCGA 1992, s 37 which provides, broadly, that money or money's worth charged to income tax will be taken into account and excluded from the CGT calculations.

Where a life policy is subject to the CGT regime, the occasion of the payment of the sum or sums assured and the surrender of the policy are treated as disposals.

### 12.3.11 Guaranteed income bonds

In 1996 the Revenue raised questions concerning the taxation of some policies which could provide regular payments to the policyholder. Most common among these policies were guaranteed income bonds. The Revenue view was that such payments were interest or annual payments, rather than policy part surrenders. FA 1997 reinstated, with retrospective effect, the industry's understanding of the position, confirming such payments as part surrenders to be dealt with under the life policy tax rules.

### 12.3.12 Personal portfolio bonds

These are policies usually, but not exclusively, written offshore where the benefits due under the policy are – or may be – closely linked with the value of a portfolio of assets personal to the policyholder.

FA 1998 included the introduction of a new charge on such policies, which deems a gain of 15% of the total premiums paid to the end of each policy year and deemed gains from previous policy years chargeable under the new legislation. This is an additional charge but is not imposed in respect of any policy year ending before 6 April 1999. This charge does not apply to 'managed portfolio bonds', ie those which do not allow 'personalisation' by restricting the policy investment to pooled assets generally available to investors.

## 12.4 OFFSHORE LIFE POLICIES
(TA 1988, s 553 and Sched 15, paras 23–27; FA 1995, s 56)

In general, policies issued in respect of contracts made after 17 November 1983 cannot be qualifying unless they are issued by a UK insurance company or the UK branch of a foreign insurer. Before that date foreign policies could be qualifying, if they satisfied the normal qualifying rules.

Other amendments to the life policy tax regime, as it applies to such foreign policies, are as follows:

(1) The gain calculated on a chargeable event is reduced by reference to the

amount of time, during the life of the policy, the policyholder was not resident in the UK.

(2) In calculating the 'appropriate fraction' for top-slicing purposes, any complete years during which the policyholder was not resident in the UK are excluded.

(3) Taxable gains arising under such policies are charged to basic rate tax as well as higher rate tax, as appropriate. An exception to this applies where the insurer is taxed on the investment income and gains accruing for the policyholder's benefit at a rate of not less than 20%. In such cases the policy gains will not be liable to basic rate UK income tax. This exception will apply only to policies issued by EU or EEA insurers.

FA 1998 included a framework requiring certain categories of offshore life companies to appoint a fiscal representative in the UK to be responsible for reporting, to the Revenue, gains on life policies in accordance with TA 1988, s 552 (see 12.3.9). Discussions between the Revenue and the offshore insurers have resulted in regulations which enable insurers to comply with local secrecy laws while giving the insurers time to develop systems to comply with the reporting requirements.

## 12.5 ANNUITIES
(TA 1988, ss 656 and 685)

An annuity is an arrangement under which one person agrees to pay another a sum of money for a known period, or a period to be determined by some specified contingency.

Annuities may be immediate (ie the payment will start straightaway) or deferred (where payments will start at some predetermined point in the future). Many annuities are established to continue for the lifetime of the annuitant but temporary annuities will cease at the end of a fixed period or on the annuitant's death, whichever comes earlier. Annuities may be effected on the lives of two or more individuals and, for example, continue until the death of the last survivor. Annuities may be paid monthly, quarterly or annually, may be of a fixed amount or subject to some sort of index-linking. Annuities may also be written with a guaranteed minimum period, so as to reduce the loss which might otherwise be suffered by an individual who dies shortly after purchasing an annuity.

There are four main types of annuity:

(1) Purchased life annuities, where an individual pays a lump sum to an insurance company in return for the annuity.

(2) Annuities received as a gift (eg at one time it was common for testators to direct that annuities be paid out of their estates).

(3) Annuities paid as part of the purchase price of a business or by continuing members of a partnership to a former partner who has retired.

(4) Compulsory purchase annuities, eg those purchased out of pension funds.

Significant changes to the taxation of life companies in respect of general annuity business were made in FA 1991, with effect for accounting periods commencing after 31 December 1991. The changes apply to existing business, subject to transitional relief.

These changes brought the taxation of life company general annuity funds broadly into line with the regime which applies to ordinary life business. Previously, a general annuity fund was not taxed on its income and gains if annuities paid by the company during the tax year equalled or exceeded the investment income and realised gains of the fund.

For the annuitant, a purchased life annuity attracts a special relief in that amounts received by him will be treated in part as a return of the money paid for by the annuity (the capital element) and in part as interest on that purchase price. The capital element of each payment is calculated by reference to actuarial tables and is not taxable. This tax exemption applies even where the annuitant lives long enough for the capital element of annuity payments he receives to exceed the original purchase price of the annuity.

Other types of annuity do not receive this favourable treatment in respect of the capital element of annuity payments.

Purchased life annuities are also subject to an income tax regime similar to that previously described as applying to life policies (see 12.3.4).

Chargeable events for life annuities are total surrender, assignment for money or money's worth and 'excesses' (calculated in much the same way as in respect of life policy partial surrenders).

Where a gain arises on a chargeable event, the gain is not charged to basic rate tax where the company offering the annuity has been taxed under the new life company tax regime described above because of the 'credit' which is, in effect, given in respect of tax paid by the life company on the income and gains of its general annuity fund.

For capital gains tax purposes, deferred annuities are also treated in a similar way to life policies, with the effect that no chargeable gain accrues on the disposal of such a contract except where the person making the disposal is not the original beneficial owner and acquired the rights for consideration in money or money's worth.

## 12.6 PERMANENT HEALTH INSURANCE

### 12.6.1 Introduction

Permanent health insurance (PHI) policies provide a replacement income for an individual who is unable to work through illness or disability. Contracts are usually available to those aged between 16 and 60 but terminate on the insured reaching his normal retirement date.

Once the disability or illness arises, benefits commence on expiry of a deferred period, typically between one and twelve months, selected by the policyholder. The longer the deferred period, the fewer claims the insurer will expect to pay and so the lower the premium will be per £ of benefit.

PHI contracts can be written as life assurance policies – typically as non-qualifying policies to avoid provision of substantial sums assured payable on death. If structured as a life policy, payment of disability benefits is not treated as a surrender of rights for the purposes of life policy taxation.

## 12.6.2 Tax consequences

If an individual effects a PHI contract for himself, premiums are not deductible for tax purposes. If an employer effects a policy on an employee to enable him to continue to pay the employee's salary during a period of disability or illness, or if the policy covers a revenue loss during such a period, the employer might be able to claim the premiums as a business expense.

For tax year 1995–96, benefits received from an individual's own PHI policy were taxable under Schedule D Case III but received the benefit of ESC A26, which gave him a 'tax holiday'.

The tax holiday was a period of 12 months (before April 1996 the holiday ran for a complete tax year and so could have been up to 23 months). An individual's tax holiday commenced when he became entitled to claim appropriate benefits, so that if he had two PHI policies with different deferred periods, the tax holiday on the one with the longer deferral would be less than 12 months.

No tax holiday was available if the benefit did not compensate for loss of income from employment or self-employment.

Insurers had to deduct basic rate tax from payments to individuals where entitlement to those benefits arose on or after 6 April 1994 (even if the policy was effected before that date). Before April 1994, the industry practice was to pay benefits gross, even after the end of the tax holiday.

With effect from tax year 1996–97 benefits from most individually owned PHI policies are tax free.

If the contract is effected by an employer to maintain the employee's salary during the period of illness or disability, the income will be taxable in the individual's hands, in the same way as salary would have been.

## 12.7 LIFE POLICIES EFFECTED BY COMPANIES
(TA 1988, s 540)

There are a number of circumstances in which a company can effect a life policy. For example, it may do so on the life of a director or other key executive to provide the company with compensation for the death of that individual. Similarly, policies may be effected to provide funds to repay loans.

In general, if a company effects a term assurance for a short period (usually not more than five years), which does not acquire a surrender value and is effected solely to provide protection against the loss of profits resulting from the death of a key person, the premiums will be tax-deductible and the proceeds will be taxable in the hands of the company.

If, on the other hand, the policy is for a longer term, may acquire a surrender value, is effected for a capital purpose, or where the life assured has a material shareholding in the company, the premiums will not be tax-deductible but the proceeds are unlikely to be charged to corporation tax in the company's hands, other than by virtue of the life assurance chargeable event rules.

Prior to FA 1989, policies owned by companies could be qualifying policies (provided they satisfied the qualifying rules) and so could provide tax-free proceeds to the company, in the same way as for individuals. Gains from non-qualifying policies were also tax-free in the hands of the company, except where the company was a close company.

For policies effected after 13 March 1989 (or those effected before that date but subsequently varied to increase the benefits or the policy term) the rules changed. Such policies cannot be qualifying policies (irrespective of their compliance with the qualifying rules) if, immediately prior to the chargeable event, the policy was owned by a company or was held on trusts created, or as security for a debt owed by, the company. Gains from such policies are treated as the company's income and chargeable under Schedule D Case VI.

There is an exception to this denial of qualifying status where policies are used to secure company debts incurred in purchasing land to be occupied by the company for the purposes of its trade (or in constructing, extending or improving buildings occupied in that way). Broadly speaking, provided that the policy has been used for this purpose since its inception, the chargeable gain will only be the amount by which the policy proceeds exceed the lowest amount of the loan which has been secured by the policy.

## 12.8 PERSONAL PENSION PLANS (PPPs) AND STAKEHOLDER PENSIONS

### 12.8.1 Types of plan

All PPPs are money purchase schemes where the final benefits are determined by the contributions paid and the rate of investment growth. PPPs may take the form of life assurance and pension policies provided by life assurance companies. They may also be offered by banks, building societies and authorised unit trust schemes. It is also possible to adopt a self-administered approach with investment in a range of permitted assets. Where the PPP can invest only in life assurance and pension policies it need not be set up under a trust but a trust is necessary if the other types of PPP investment are used.

## 12.8.2 Eligibility

(1)   A taxpayer will be eligible to make contributions to one of these plans if he is in receipt of 'relevant earnings'. This means either earnings from non-pensionable employments, or from businesses, professions, partnerships, etc. For example, if there is a source of Schedule D Case I or II earnings, the taxpayer normally qualifies for relief from income tax in respect of contributions paid under a PPP approved by the Revenue. This relief is also available in respect of Schedule E earnings (including taxable benefits) from a non-pensionable employment, eg with a firm which does not provide a pension scheme or if the taxpayer is not a member of such a scheme for some other reason.

(2)   If an employer's pension scheme provides only a sum assured payable on death while in the employer's service and/or a pension to a surviving spouse, the earnings from that employment will still be regarded as 'relevant earnings'.

(3)   Where there are two sources of income, one being relevant earnings and the other arising from pensionable employment, it is possible to contribute to a PPP in respect of the non-pensionable earnings, subject to certain limits.

(4)   In two cases it is possible for an individual to have a PPP even though he is not eligible to make contributions to it. The first is that it is possible for an employee who is a member accruing pension benefits under his employer's occupational pension scheme to effect a PPP in order to contract out of SERPS (see 12.13). Such a PPP may not receive any contributions other than protected rights contributions from the DSS. The second is that a PPP can be established to accept a transfer payment from another approved pension scheme or arrangement.

(5)   Controlling directors of investment companies are not eligible for any form of PPP in respect of earnings from such a company nor are certain other controlling directors who are in receipt of benefits from their employer's occupational scheme.

## 12.8.3 Tax relief on contributions and limits

(1)   Individuals who have relevant earnings, and pay either single or regular contributions to a PPP within the limits mentioned below, enjoy full income tax relief on those contributions in the relevant years. Employees pay contributions net of basic rate tax (22% for the tax year 2000–01), under the Pensions Relief at Source (PRAS) system. Any higher rate relief is claimed either through the PAYE coding, by a repayment of tax already paid or in some cases a reduction in subsequent payments on account under self-assessment. The 10% tax band does not affect the rate at which the employee can deduct tax, which remains as the basic rate for the year in which the contribution is paid. The self-employed can set off contributions against their Schedule D income.

(2)   The current annual limits for contributions to PPPs (shown in (3) below) are expressed as a percentage of 'net relevant earnings' (NRE). This means relevant earnings from non-pensionable employment or business, etc less certain deductions such as expenses, trading losses, capital allowances, etc. Personal charges such as interest or payments under deeds of covenant are not deducted.

(3)   The PPP contribution limits since 1989–90 are as follows (for the limits for previous years see *Allied Dunbar Pensions Handbook*):

| Age at beginning of year of assessment | % |
|---|---|
| below 36 | 17.5 |
| 36–45 | 20 |
| 46–50 | 25 |
| 51–55 | 30 |
| 56–60 | 35 |
| 61 or more | 40 |

For example, a 48-year-old with net relevant earnings of £20,000 can contribute up to £5,000 pa to a PPP. A 58-year-old with the same net relevant earnings could contribute £7,000.

(4)   There is a limit on the maximum amount of net relevant earnings which can be taken into account in determining the contributions payable to a PPP. The limit was introduced in the 1989–90 tax year and it is normally increased each year in line with the Retail Prices Index (RPI), rounded up to the nearest multiple of £600. For the 2000–01 tax year, the figure is £91,800.

(5)   Larger contributions are not possible no matter how far net relevant earnings exceed £91,800. For example, in 2000–01 an individual aged 48 with net relevant earnings of £100,000 can contribute a maximum of £22,950 to a PPP (ie 25% of £91,800).

(6)   If an individual has two sources of income, one from pensionable employment, and the other being net relevant earnings, he may contribute up to the maximum limit in respect of his relevant earnings regardless of the level of pensionable earnings. For example, a 58-year-old with pensionable earnings as a company executive of £25,000 pa and net relevant earnings from a part-time consultancy of £8,000 pa can pay contributions to a PPP of 35% of £8,000 = £2,800.

(7)   An amount not exceeding 5% of net relevant earnings can be used to provide a lump sum payable from the PPP, in the event of death before age 75. Premiums used to provide this life cover must be included as part of the maximum contributions permitted.

(8)   If an employer pays contributions to an employee's PPP, these too must be taken as part of the maximum contribution which can be made to the PPP. Employer's contributions are not treated as the employee's income for income tax or national insurance contribution purposes.

(9)   Contributions paid to a PPP by the DSS to enable the individual to

contract out of SERPS (see 12.13) can be paid in addition to the maximum contribution payable by an individual and/or an employer.

(10)   An employee's relevant earnings can include profit-related pay even though this is normally exempt from tax. Thus an employee whose earnings consist of ordinary remuneration of £25,000 plus PRP of £4,000 can base his PPP contributions on total earnings of £29,000.

## 12.8.4 Year for which relief granted and 'carry-back'

(1)   Relief for contributions is normally only given against net relevant earnings of the tax year in which contributions are paid. However, it is possible to elect to have any contribution treated for tax purposes as if it had been paid during the preceding tax year; or, if the individual had no relevant earnings for the contribution to be relieved against in that year (eg, because of losses or retirement), then in the tax year before that; ie there is a 'carry-back' period of one or two years.

(2)   The amount of any claim for relief is calculated by reference to the tax payable in that year (or where carry back is used, for the year in which the contribution is treated as being paid). If the individual does not have any tax liability in that year he will not be able to utilize the tax relief available. The maximum relief available in any year is the amount of net relevant earnings for that year (or, where carry back is used, for the year in which the contribution is treated as being paid).

(3)   An election for carry back does not alter the rate of tax deducted under the PRAS system (see 12.8.3(1)) which always remains as the basic rate for the year in which the contribution is actually paid. For example, an employee who paid a £100 contribution on 6 April 2000 will have deducted tax of £22, paying a net contribution of £78. If he elects to carry back this contribution to the 1999–2000 tax year, the amount deducted will remain the same, but assuming the individual pays tax at the basic rate, a further £1 of relief may be claimed.

(4)   Claims to relief for carry back from 2000–01 to 1999–2000 (and earlier years) take effect, for self-employed persons, by an amendment to the self-assessment return. Claims can only be made by inclusion in the tax return or by a separate stand alone claim once the self-assessment return has been completed. Relief is not given by adjustment to the assessment for the earlier year but by a repayment of tax already paid or a set-off against outstanding liabilities. Carry back claims do not affect payments on account.

(5)   For employed persons adjustments are normally made through the PAYE coding.

## 12.8.5 Eligibility to pay contributions and 'carry forward'

(1)   To the extent that contributions paid in any year fall short of the permitted maximum of net relevant earnings, it is possible to carry forward

the shortfall for up to six years and use this (on a first-in first-out basis) to pay a contribution in a subsequent year which exceeds the maximum percentage limit of net relevant earnings for the year in which it is paid. (There are special rules where the tax liability for any year is determined after more than six years have elapsed.)

(2)    The earliest year's unused entitlement to pay contributions which may be utilised to permit payment of a contribution paid in 1999–2000 is that for 1993–94. The maximum payable by way of contributions in any tax year will be 17.5% (or the appropriate higher figure for those over 35 years old, based on the age in the appropriate previous year) of the net relevant earnings for that year plus any unused entitlement for the previous six tax years. For example, if an individual is aged 35 or under and pays a contribution of £3,000 in respect of the net relevant earnings of the current year, say £15,000, the first £2,625 (17.5% of £15,000) is permitted because of those relevant earnings, and the remaining £375 only by virtue of any unused entitlement brought forward. The Revenue's interpretation of the legislation is that the maximum contribution payable in any year is the amount of relevant earnings for that year (even where 'carry forward' would have suggested a greater eligibility to pay contributions).

## 12.8.6 Benefits payable and age at which they may be taken

(1)    The PPP scheme established by the pension provider can allow the individual to make more than one 'arrangement' under it. Multiple arrangements can give the opportunity to take benefits in stages.

(2)    The pension may start being paid at any age between 50 and 75. Normally this pension has to take the form of an annuity (but see (9) below). It is not necessary actually to retire before the annuity may commence. In certain occupations, the Revenue allow an annuity to start earlier than the age of 50 (eg, jockeys, motor racing drivers, cricketers, etc). The pension can also start to be paid before the age of 50 on retirement due to ill health. Under no circumstances may the annuity start later than the age of 75.

(3)    The annuity payable can take one of several forms: sterling or unit-linked, guaranteed or non-guaranteed, etc. In most contracts there is a provision that on death before the beginning of the annuity, an annuity is payable to any widow or dependants nominated by the individual or, alternatively, a lump sum could be paid, not exceeding the amount of the contributions plus a reasonable amount of interest or bonuses (this includes capital growth and income attributable to the contributions paid under a unit-linked plan).

(4)    The PPP can also incorporate a sum assured, so that on death an additional lump sum would be paid. This can be arranged to be free of inheritance tax by writing it in trust where the PPP scheme itself is not set up under trust.

(5)    Any annuity payable to a widow, widower, or dependant would be free of inheritance tax (IHTA 1984, s 152).

307

(6)   The whole of any annuity payable either to the individual, any spouse or dependants is currently treated and taxed as income under Schedule E (and not, as is the case with purchased life annuities, partly as income and partly as a return of capital). The PAYE system is applied to these payments.

Prior to 6 April 1995 all personal pension annuities were taxed under Schedule D and basic rate income tax was deducted at source when the pension was paid.

(7)   A lump sum may be taken from the PPP, between the ages of 50 and 75, up to a maximum of 25% of the fund excluding any part of the fund built up from contributions paid by the DSS. For PPPs effected prior to 27 July 1989, the value of the DSS contributions could be taken into account in calculating the cash lump sum available but any fund used to provide benefits for a widow(er) or dependants had to be excluded.

(8)   Instead of taking the annuity from the life company which issued the original pension contract, it is possible to use the fund built up to buy an annuity from any other company, thus obtaining the best terms then available ('open market option'). If the PPP is provided by an organisation which is not a life assurance company, the pension (and life assurance) must be provided by a life company.

(9)   With effect from 1 May 1995, it is possible for personal pension schemes to allow members to defer the purchase of the annuity up to age 75. Before the annuity is purchased, it is possible to take income withdrawals. These withdrawals are taxable under the PAYE system in the same way as annuity payments. The maximum amount of income withdrawal is set by reference to the amount of a level, single life annuity, using rates laid down by the Government, and must be reviewed every three years.

(10)   Where the option to defer the purchase of the annuity is exercised no further contributions or transfers can be paid to the personal pension arrangement. The fund will continue to grow free of income and capital taxes. If the member dies during the deferral period, withdrawals can continue to be paid to any surviving spouse or dependant up to the date when the member would have reached age 75. Alternatively the fund can be used to purchase an annuity or taken as a lump sum. Where the fund is taken as a lump sum there is a special charge to tax of 35% of the fund.

## 12.8.7 Cessation of approval

Where a member's arrangements under an approved personal pension scheme lose their tax approval on or after 17 March 1998 there is a special tax charge of 40% of the value of the assets attributable to the arrangements immediately before the cessation of approval. The tax charge is payable, in the first instance, by the scheme administrator or, in the event of non-payment, by the individual who made the arrangements.

## 12.8.8 Compensation for mis-selling of personal pensions

Following guidance issued by the Securities and Investments Board, investment firms are required to review sales of personal pensions and retirement annuity contracts made between 29 April 1988 and 30 June 1994. Under s 148 of FA 1996, lump sum payments of compensation for certain types of bad advice given between those dates are exempt from both income tax and CGT.

## 12.8.9 Stakeholder pensions

FA 2000 contains provisions which will take effect from 6 April 2001 when stakeholder pensions replace personal pensions. Stakeholder pension policies will be similar to PPPs and similar percentage limits will apply. However, there will be important differences:

(1) All types of taxpayer will make contributions to stakeholder pensions on a net of tax basis, ie self-employed individuals' contributions will be treated in the same way as employees are currently dealt with under the personal pension legislation, with contributions deemed to have had basic rate tax withheld at source. The pension provider will be able to reclaim this tax even where the individual did not actually have any tax liability for the year in question. The individual will be able to claim higher rate relief where he is a 40% taxpayer.
(2) There will be no carry-forward of unused relief.
(3) An individual will not need to show that he has any relevant earnings unless he makes contributions of more than £3,600 pa.
(4) An individual can base his contributions on the highest relevant earnings of the five years preceding the year in which he makes his contribution.

As at present, contributions may be made under s 226 retirement annuity policies and the rules on s 226 policies are not being changed.

## 12.9 RETIREMENT ANNUITY CONTRACTS (S 226 CONTRACTS)

Prior to the introduction of PPPs (on 1 July 1988), the self-employed and those in non-pensionable employment were able to contribute to retirement annuity contracts (often called s 226 contracts) which, while broadly similar to PPPs, had several important differences. Although no new s 226 contracts have been allowed since 30 June 1988, those in existence before then can continue much as before with contributions being paid and even increased on a regular basis.

The key differences between s 226 contracts and PPPs include the following:

(1) employers are not allowed to pay direct contributions into an employee's s 226 contract;

(2) the Pensions Relief at Source system does not apply to s 226 contracts;

(3) s 226 contracts cannot be used to contract out of SERPS; and

(4) the earliest age at which benefits could be taken was age 60 (except for those specific occupations where the Revenue permitted an earlier retirement age or in the case of ill health);

(5) annuities from s 226 contracts remain taxable under Schedule D and did not become subject to the PAYE system when the new rules on the taxation of personal pension annuities were introduced in the 1995–96 tax year;

(6) the rules allowing the purchase of an annuity to be deferred do not apply to s 226 contracts.

In addition, there are more favourable rules for determining the maximum lump sum cash which can be taken from a s 226 contract. Instead of being restricted to 25% of the fund, the lump sum can equal three times the annual annuity payable after the cash has been taken (but contracts entered into on or after 17 March 1987 are subject to a maximum cash lump sum of £150,000 per contract).

Section 226 contracts are not subject to the £91,800 cap on the earnings to be taken into account when determining maximum contributions but the maximum percentages of net relevant earnings are different. The current percentages are:

| Age at beginning of year of assessment | % |
|---|---|
| up to 50 | 17.5 |
| 51–55 | 20 |
| 56–60 | 22.5 |
| 61 or more | 27.5 |

Finally, if an individual has an existing s 226 contract he may also pay contributions at the same time to a PPP. However, the contributions to the s 226 contract reduce the amounts that can be paid to the PPP and care is needed to ensure that the interaction between the two sets of rules does not restrict the overall contributions that can be paid.

## 12.10 OCCUPATIONAL SCHEMES

(TA 1988, s 590 *et seq* and Sched 23; FA 1989, Sched 6)

### 12.10.1 Types of plan

(1) Occupational pension schemes may be either money purchase schemes or 'final salary schemes', where the benefits are determined as a fraction of the employee's salary at retirement. Final salary schemes are sometimes called 'defined benefit' schemes.

(2)   All occupational pension schemes require the involvement of an employer who will make some contribution to the scheme.

(3)   Occupational pension schemes may be insured, where all benefits are provided in the form of insurance policies either on a group or individual basis, or self-administered with investment in a range of permitted assets. There are special rules for Small Self Administered Schemes (SSAS) with 12 or fewer members.

## 12.10.2 Eligibility

(1)   All employees, whether part time or full time, are eligible for membership of an occupational pension scheme if their employer participates in such a scheme. There are special rules for employees of overseas employers and for employees who are temporarily seconded outside the UK.

(2)   Persons assessable under Schedule D (eg agents and consultants) are not eligible.

(3)   Directors are also eligible for membership of an occupational pension scheme but controlling directors of investment companies are normally not able to benefit from schemes approved under the Revenue's discretionary powers (see 12.10.3).

(4)   It is not possible for an employer to make membership of an occupational scheme (other than one providing death benefits only) compulsory. In general, leaving a good occupational scheme is unlikely to be wise except where its benefits are poor and expert advice should be sought if this is contemplated.

## 12.10.3 Approval of schemes

(1)   Approval of occupational pension schemes is given by the Pension Schemes Office (PSO) which is a branch of the Inland Revenue. 'Approval' will prevent contributions paid by the employer being taxed in the employees' hands as a benefit in kind.

(2)   In addition, 'exempt approval' will give the additional benefits of the gross roll-up in the fund and tax relief for the employee in respect of regular contributions he makes to the scheme. Exempt approval will also mean that the employer's contributions will be deductible business expenses without relying on the normal rules for deductibility applying to Schedule D income. In order to be exempt approved, the scheme must be set up under irrevocable trusts.

(3)   In most cases approval is given under the PSO's discretionary powers which are extremely wide-ranging. The main conditions for approval include the following:

(a)   The sole purpose of the scheme must be to provide 'relevant benefits' in respect of service as an employee. Relevant benefits, broadly speaking,

include most types of financial benefit given in connection with the termination of an employee's service with a particular employer.

(b) The scheme must be recognised by employer and employee and the
employee given written particulars of its essential features.

(c) The employer must contribute to the scheme although the employee
may indirectly provide the necessary funds by agreeing to a reduction
in salary, 'a salary sacrifice'.

(d) Pension benefits must be payable on retirement at any age between 50
and 75 and must not exceed a maximum permitted benefit calculated by
reference to the employee's final remuneration and the length of service
with that employer (see 12.10.5). Benefits may be available in respect of
early retirement at any earlier age where retirement is due to ill health.
There is also a maximum limit on the permitted pension which can be
provided for widows and dependants.

(e) No pension may be surrendered, commuted or assigned, save for commutation on retirement up to a maximum lump sum (see 12.10.5(7)).

(f) A scheme may also provide for a lump sum payment of up to four
times the employee's final remuneration on death in service and for a
return of the employee's contributions in certain cases.

## 12.10.4 Tax relief on contributions and limits

(1)   Contributions by the employer to an exempt approved scheme
are deductible business expenses, although relief in respect of
non-regular contributions may be deferred by being spread over a maximum
of five years.

(2)   The employee may make personal contributions up to 15% of his
remuneration subject to the £91,800 salary cap (see 12.10.5(6)). Personal
contributions attract tax relief at the highest rate paid by the individual.

(3)   Unlike PPPs there are no specific limits on the amount of
contributions which may be made to an occupational scheme other than
those applicable to personal contributions. Instead, the controls operate on
the level of benefits which is allowed. If a scheme becomes 'over-funded'
(ie, where the scheme has more capital than is necessary to meet its prospective liabilities), payment of further contributions may be restricted or capital
may have to be returned to the employer after deduction of tax of 40%.

(4)   Where a surplus arises from an employee's voluntary contributions any refund to the employee will have tax deducted at 32% (33% for
refunds made before 6 April 2000, and 34% for refunds made for the
period before 6 April 1997). The amount received by the employee is
treated as being paid net of tax at the basic rate. An employee who is a
higher rate taxpayer will be subject to a further charge on the equivalent
gross amount of the payment received taking the total effective rate to
approximately 47.8% (47.9% for payments received in the 1996–97 tax
year).

## 12.10.5 **Benefits**

(1)   The maximum pension benefits under an occupational pension scheme are expressed as a fraction of the member's final salary for each year of service with the employer. For example, many schemes provide a pension of one-sixtieth of final salary for each year of service so that the maximum pension of two-thirds of final salary is reached after 40 years' service.

(2)   The maximum rate at which pension benefits can accrue is one-thirtieth of final salary for each year of service. In order to obtain a maximum pension of two-thirds of final salary it is necessary to complete 20 years' service.

(3)   Final salary or 'final remuneration' must be calculated in a way which is approved by the PSO. The two permitted definitions are:

(a) the remuneration in any of the five years preceding retirement, leaving service or death (as applicable) together with the average of any fluctuating emoluments (bonuses, commissions etc) averaged over at least three consecutive years ending with the year in question; or
(b) the highest average of the total emoluments from the employer over any period of three consecutive years ending within ten years before retirement, leaving service or death (as applicable).
Company directors who are treated as controlling directors may only calculate final salary using the second permitted definition.

(4)   Final salary excludes any income and gains from shares and options acquired through share option, share incentive and profit sharing schemes. In addition, payments on the termination of employment (eg golden handshakes) cannot be used as part of the calculation of final salary.

(5)   It is possible to increase 'final salary' for previous years in line with the increase in the RPI up to the date when benefits are paid. This increase is known as 'dynamisation'.

(6)   There is a maximum amount of final salary which may be taken into account for pension purposes. For the tax year 2000–01 this amount is £91,800. The 'salary cap' is subject to the same rules relating to annual increases in line with the RPI as the limit on contributions to personal pension schemes (see 12.8.3(4)).

(7)   Instead of taking all benefits in pension form, the member may commute part of his pension for a tax-free cash lump sum. The maximum lump sum is three-eightieths of final salary for each year of service up to a maximum of 40 years' service or 2.25 times the pension available before commutation, if greater. The maximum lump sum is, therefore, one and a half times final salary.

(8)   A lump sum of up to four times final salary, together with a refund of the employee's personal contributions, can also be paid on the death of the employee in service. It is also possible to provide a pension for a spouse or dependant up to two-thirds of the maximum pension to which the

deceased would have been entitled at his normal retirement date. A pension of a similar amount can also be provided for a spouse or dependant on death after retirement.

(9)   Pensions payable are treated as earned income and taxed under Schedule E. The payments will be subject to the deduction of income tax under the PAYE system.

## 12.10.6 Cessation of approval

Where an approved occupational scheme ceases to be approved after 2 November 1994 there is a special tax charge of 40% of the accumulated fund valued immediately before the scheme ceases to be approved. This tax charge was introduced primarily to prevent avoidance of tax by the appointment of offshore trustees to Small Self Administered Schemes but the tax charge applies whenever a scheme ceases to be approved. From 17 March 1998 the tax charge was extended to apply where a scheme ceases to be approved and has received a transfer value from another approved scheme in respect of a controlling director of a company (or a person whose earnings were chargeable to tax under Schedule D). The tax charge is payable by the scheme administrator or, in the event of non-payment, by the employer or, from 17 March 1998, by the scheme members who were controlling directors (or whose earnings were chargeable to tax under Schedule D).

## 12.10.7 'Grandfathering'

The maximum limits on contributions to and benefits from occupational pension schemes have been restricted over the years. The most notable changes were in 1987 and 1989 when restrictions, including the introduction of the salary cap in 1989, were announced in the Budget. Members who joined schemes prior to the Budget Days in those years may continue to benefit from the old rules which have been preserved or 'grandfathered' for those members eligible. Minor changes have also been made to the Inland Revenue's discretionary practice at other times. Further details can be found in *Allied Dunbar Pensions Handbook*.

# 12.11 FREE-STANDING AVC (FSAVC) SCHEMES

## 12.11.1 Types of plan

FSAVC schemes are money purchase schemes which provide benefits in addition to the benefits provided by an employer's occupational pension scheme. They are similar to PPPs in that they may be offered by life assurance companies, banks, building societies and authorised unit trust schemes.

FSAVC schemes are occupational pension schemes for Revenue purposes and must be set up under irrevocable trusts for the sole purpose of providing relevant benefits of the type provided by occupational pension schemes.

## 12.11.2 Eligibility

An employee will only be eligible to contribute to an FSAVC scheme if he is a member of an occupational pension scheme to which his employer is currently contributing or is a member of a statutory scheme such as the Civil Service scheme. Contributions may only be paid to one FSAVC scheme in any tax year although if there are earnings from more than one employment separate contributions may be made to an FSAVC scheme in respect of each employment.

Directors who are treated as controlling directors are not eligible for membership of an FSAVC scheme.

## 12.11.3 Contributions

The maximum contribution is 15% of the employee's remuneration in any one tax year. In order to calculate the maximum contribution the contribution to the FSAVC scheme must be aggregated with the employee's contributions to his employer's scheme. The salary cap of £91,800 will apply if it applies to the benefits provided by the employer's scheme, so that the maximum contribution will be £13,770 in 2000–01 for an employee who is subject to the salary cap.

Where contributions to the FSAVC scheme exceed £2,400 pa the scheme's administrator must calculate the maximum contribution which is not likely to produce benefits in excess of the Revenue limits. To do this information is provided by the administrators of the employers scheme (or the member himself) about the benefits provided by that scheme. If necessary, contributions to the FSAVC scheme must be restricted.

Contributions to an FSAVC scheme must he paid net of basic rate tax under the PRAS system. Higher rate tax relief is obtained by either an adjustment to the employee's PAYE coding or to his end of year tax assessment.

## 12.11.4 Benefits

The benefits provided by an FSAVC scheme must be aggregated with the benefits provided by the employer's scheme to ensure that the limits on benefits provided by occupational schemes are not exceeded.

An FSAVC scheme may not provide a tax-free cash lump sum on retirement, although the pension provided may be used as part of the '2.25 times pension before commutation' calculation in order to enhance the tax-free lump sum provided by the employer's scheme where the rules of the employer's scheme allows this.

Where the funds accumulated in the FSAVC scheme are such that the maximum limits on benefits are exceeded, the excess must be returned to the employee after deduction of tax at 33% (34% for refunds made before 6 April 1997). The amount received by the employee is treated as being paid net of tax at the basic rate. An employee who is a higher rate taxpayer will be subject to a further charge on the equivalent gross amount of the payment received, taking the total effective rate to approximately 47.8% (47.9% for payments received in the 1996–97 tax year).

Pensions payable are treated in the same way as those from occupational schemes and are subject to the PAYE system.

## 12.12 UNAPPROVED SCHEMES

Unapproved occupational pension schemes were introduced to allow employers the flexibility to provide benefits for those employees who had earnings in excess of the salary cap. However, their use is not restricted to such employees and they may be used to provide benefits in excess of the normal two-thirds maximum pension benefit or to provide greater benefits for those with less than twenty years' service.

### 12.12.1 Eligibility

Any person in receipt of income taxed under Schedule E is eligible for an unapproved scheme. There is no requirement that the employee is also a member of an approved scheme.

### 12.12.2 Types of plan

Such schemes may be funded (ie contributions set aside in order to fund the promised benefits) or unfunded (ie at retirement the benefits will be paid by the company out of current income or investments). A funded scheme is often called a FURBS. There is no requirement that funded schemes are established under trust, but this is commonly the case.

### 12.12.3 Contributions

If the scheme is funded, the employer will obtain tax relief on the contributions as a normal business expense. There is no set limit on contributions that may be paid, although excessive contributions may be disqualified from tax relief.

The employee will be taxed on contributions paid by the employer as it they were emoluments. If no benefits are received by the employee it may be possible to reclaim some of the tax. Employee contributions will not be tax deductible and are to be avoided.

In an unfunded scheme there is no charge to tax on any reserves set up to provide for future benefits. Equally, the employer will not obtain any tax relief until the benefits are actually paid.

### 12.12.4 Taxation of scheme investments

Unapproved schemes do not benefit from 'gross, roll up' but are not subject to the special rate of income tax of 34% payable by trusts which accumulate their income. Tax is payable at 20% or 22%, depending on the type of income.

From 6 April 1998, the trustees of unapproved schemes will pay CGT on realised gains at the rate of 34% applicable to all trusts. Prior to 6 April 1998, realised gains were taxed at the basic rate (23% for the tax year 1997–98).

Prior to 30 November 1993, extra tax benefits could be achieved by establishing a funded scheme under an offshore trust, although care had to be taken to avoid the anti-avoidance legislation which applied to such trusts. FA 1994 effectively removed the tax advantage of offshore schemes, although existing schemes can continue unchanged.

### 12.12.5 Benefits

The scheme must be set up to provide relevant benefits but there are no set limits on the benefits which can be provided. Pensions from unapproved schemes, whether funded or unfunded, will be subject to income tax as earned income.

Lump sums paid from funded schemes may be paid free of tax but those from unfunded schemes are subject to income tax as earned income. Lump sums paid from funded schemes set up after 30 November 1993, or from schemes set up before then which are varied to provide a lump sum, may be taxed if they exceed the amount of the contributions on which the employee was taxed, where the scheme invests in assets which are not subject to income tax or CGT.

## 12.13 THE STATE PENSION SCHEME

The State scheme currently provides two types of pension; the basic pension and the State Earnings Related Pension Scheme.

### The basic pension

This is a contributory scheme which aims to provide a pension of approximately 20% of national average earnings. It is not related to salary but to obtain the maximum pension an individual must have paid (or have been credited with) national insurance contributions for about 90% of his expected working life. The pension (which is taxable as earned income if attributable to an individual's own contributions) is increased each year in line with the RPI.

### The State Earnings Related Pension Scheme (SERPS)

SERPS was introduced in 1978 and is based on national insurance contributions made by employers and employees on earnings between the lower and upper earnings limits (for 1999–2000 £66 and £500 per week respectively). The earnings between these two figures are often called 'band earnings'. The self-employed neither contribute towards, nor benefit from, SERPS.

SERPS provides a pension at state retirement age expressed as a percentage of band earnings. For those retiring in 2009–10 or later the percentage is currently 20% with those retiring before then receiving a higher percentage up to a maximum of 25% of band earnings. Band earnings are based on an average over the whole of your working life, although individuals retiring before 6 April 1999 can use their best 20 years to calculate band earnings.

State pensions do not provide any cash lump sum at retirement or any opportunity of retiring and receiving benefits before state retirement age. Benefits can be postponed for up to five years, in which case the pension will be increased.

The main benefit from the state scheme is a lifelong pension for the individual but SERPS can also, in certain circumstances, provide a widow's pension which will be of a reduced amount unless the widow is aged over 40 and has dependent children (or over 50 with no dependent children).

## 12.14 CONTRACTING OUT

It is possible to leave SERPS provided appropriate provision is made to replace the SERPS benefits with a suitable approved alternative. To encourage this, individuals and employers who 'contract out' in this way receive benefits in the form of reduced national insurance contributions and/or a direct payment into individual personal pension plans.

There are currently three ways in which an employee can be contracted out. These are:

(1) membership of an appropriate personal pension plan (APPP);
(2) membership of a contracted-out money purchase pension scheme (COMPS);
(3) membership of an occupational scheme providing guaranteed minimum pension (GMP) or from 6 April an occupational scheme which satisfies a 'Reference Scheme' test.

## 12.14.1 Appropriate personal pension plans (APPP)

These require no employer involvement at all and are open to all employees who are not contracted-out by another scheme, even those who are also members of an occupational scheme. In order to contract-out the employee and the chosen personal pension plan provider must complete a Joint Notice (Form APPI) which is submitted to the DSS. An individual can use only one APPP to contract out at any time and must contract out for a complete tax year.

Once the Joint Notice is accepted by the DSS payments are made, normally once a year, directly by the DSS to the pension provider. These payments, called protected rights contributions, consist of the National Insurance Rebate but both the employee and employer continue to pay the full rate of national insurance contributions. For the tax year 1997–98 and onwards a system of age-related rebates applies. For the tax years 1999–2000 to 2001–02 the age-related rebates range from 3.8% to a maximum of 9%.

The protected rights contributions must be used to provide a pension benefit at State Retirement Age, or a widow(er)'s or dependant's pension or a lump sum on death.

## 12.14.2 Contracted out money purchase schemes (COMPS)

These are occupational pension plans where the employer takes the initial decision to contract out, although the employer may allow individuals the choice of whether to contract out or not.

Both the employer and employee pay a reduced rate of national insurance contributions but this saving is balanced by the protected rights contributions which the employer must ensure are paid into the pension scheme on a monthly basis. Normally both the employer and the employee will contribute their respective shares of the protected rights contributions. In addition to the basic flat rate rebates the DSS pays an additional age-related payment after the end of the tax year. For the tax years 1999–2000 to 2001–02, the total rebates from all sources range between 2.2% and 9%.

The protected rights contributions must be used to provide benefits in the same way as those provided by an APPP.

## 12.14.3 Guaranteed minimum pensions

This method of contracting out involved an occupational pension scheme providing a guaranteed minimum level of pension equivalent to that provided by SERPS. Both the employer and employee benefited from a reduced level of national insurance contribution but the employer had to be prepared to provide the pension scheme with sufficient funds to enable it to meet the guarantee.

From 6 April 1997 no further guaranteed minimum pensions can accrue.

From then occupational schemes can be contracted out either on a money purchase basis (ie a COMPS) or by satisfying the 'Reference Scheme test'. The latter involves the scheme's actuary certifying that the pension benefits from the scheme are 'broadly equivalent' to the pension benefits of a standard 'Reference Scheme'.

The Reference Scheme is a basic scheme providing one-eightieth of earnings between the lower and upper earnings limit (for 1999–2000 £66 and £500 per week respectively) for each year of pensionable service for 90% of the scheme's membership.

Employees who contracted out using an APPP or a COMPS must consider whether the money purchase benefits provided by the protected rights contributions will exceed the likely benefits from SERPS. In general contracting out will be of benefit to younger people with older persons likely to benefit more from SERPS.

## 12.15 TAXATION OF COMMISSION, CASHBACKS AND DISCOUNTS

The Revenue published SP4/97, on the taxation of commission, cashbacks and discounts, further commenting on this subject in the *Tax Bulletin* Issue 33. The Revenue has offered its assurances to the 'ordinary retail customer' that there normally will be no tax liabilities on rebated commissions or discounts.

However, the position is more complex with regard to insurance products. SP4/97 states:

### Life insurance and personal pensions

*Qualifying life insurance policies*
**36**   Where commission in respect of a policy holder's own qualifying life insurance policy is received, netted off or invested, that policy will not be disqualified as a result of entitlement to that commission if the contract under which commission arises is separate from the contract of insurance. In practice, the Revenue will not seek to read two contracts as one in a way that would lead to the loss of qualifying policy status.

**37**   Where a policy holder pays a discounted premium in respect of his or her own policy, the premium payable under the policy will be the discounted premium. It is this amount that must be used for the purposes of establishing whether the relevant qualifying rules are met.

*Calculation of chargeable event gains in respect of life policies, capital redemption policies and life annuity contracts*
**38**   Chargeable event gains are computed by reference to the premiums or lump sum consideration paid. The amount paid will be interpreted as follows –
 - where a policy holder pays a gross premium and receives commission in respect of that policy, the chargeable event gain is calculated using the gross amount paid without taking the commission received into account;
 - where an amount of commission is received or due under an enforceable

legal right and subsequently invested in the policy, that amount is included as a premium paid when calculating the chargeable event gain;

- where a policy holder nets off commission from an insurer in respect of his or her own policy from the gross amount of premium payable and the commission is not taxable as income on the policy holder, the chargeable event gain is calculated using the net amount paid to the insurer;
- where a policy holder pays a discounted premium, the chargeable event gain is calculated using the discounted amount of premium paid;
- where extra value is added to the policy by the insurer (for example by allocation of bonus units), the premium for the purpose of calculating the chargeable event is the amount paid by the policy holder without taking the extra value into account.

*Tax relief in respect of personal pension contributions*
**39**　Tax relief for contributions to personal pension schemes is due in respect of 'a contribution paid by an individual'. The amount of the contribution will be interpreted as follows where the contract under which the commission arises is separate from the personal pension scheme contract –

- where a contributor pays a gross contribution and receives commission in respect of that contribution, tax relief is given on the gross amount paid without taking the commission received into account;
- where an amount of commission is received by, or is due under an enforceable legal right to, the contributor and subsequently invested in the personal pension that gave rise to the commission, tax relief is given on that amount;
- where a contributor deducts commission in respect of his or her own pension contribution from the gross amount payable, relief is due on the net amount paid;
- where a contributor pays discounted contributions, tax relief is due on the discounted amount paid;
- where extra value is added to the policy by the insurer (for example by allocation of bonus units), relief is due on the amount paid by the contributor without taking the extra value into account.

**40**　If commission were to be rebated to the contributor under the same contract as the personal pension contract, this would be an unapprovable benefit (since it would involve leakage of the pension fund to the member) which would jeopardise the tax-approved status of the arrangement.

**41**　The consequences of paying commission on transfers between tax-approved pension schemes may be different from those outlined if such payment is effectively a benefit not authorised by the rules of the pension scheme. Alternatively, the misrepresentation as an annual premium of any premium applied to new pensions business so that a higher rate of rebated commission is generated will call into question the bona fides of the pension arrangement and jeopardise its approval from inception.

The statement also encompasses the Revenue's two previous press releases by stating that:

(1) other commission rebates to ordinary customers will not be taxed; and
(2) cashbacks offered by banks and building societies as an inducement to take out a mortgage will not be regarded as chargeable to CGT.

## 12.15.1 Payments arising from trade or employment

If a cashback is received in the course of either the recipient's business or employment the cashback may be chargeable as income.

The income tax consequences of the new statement are that employees who receive commission arising from, and discounts in connection with, goods, investments or services sold to third parties are assessable regardless of whether the commission is passed on by them to the customer and whether the commission is paid by the employer or anyone else.

The Revenue takes the view that PAYE will apply in any situation where the commission etc falls to be taxed under Schedule E.

# 13

# CAPITAL GAINS TAX

This chapter deals with the following matters:

(1) Basic outline of CGT.
(2) Who is subject to CGT?
(3) What assets are chargeable assets?
(4) Which types of transaction may produce a chargeable gain?
(5) How gains may be deferred or 'rolled over'.
(6) Sales of shares to all-employee share trusts.

Unless otherwise stated, the statutory references refer to the Taxation of Chargeable Gains Act (TCGA) 1992.

## 13.1 BASIC OUTLINE OF CGT

Capital gains are assessed for a tax year. Under self-assessment the due date for the payment of the tax is 31 January following the tax year (ie for gains arising in the year ended 5 April 2000 tax is payable by the 31 January 2001).

The way in which chargeable gains are computed is quite different from the rules which determine assessable income for tax purposes. A range of exemptions and reliefs may apply and there is a major distinction between CGT and income tax in that capital gains may be reduced by indexation and/or taper relief.

The rate of CGT is now governed by whether the individual's income and capital gains are sufficient to put him into the 40% band.

### 13.1.1 Annual exemption
(TCGA 1992, s 3)

You cannot be liable for CGT for 2000–01 unless you make gains of more than £7,200. This is because there is an annual exemption, the amount of which for the past six years is as follows:

|         | £     |
|---------|-------|
| 1999–00 | 7,100 |
| 1998–99 | 6,800 |
| 1997–98 | 6,500 |
| 1996–97 | 6,300 |
| 1995–96 | 6,000 |
| 1994–95 | 5,800 |

## 13.1.2 No gain/loss on spouse transactions

Provided a couple have not separated on a permanent basis, there can be no chargeable gains on any assets transferred from one spouse to the other, whether by gift or sale. The asset is treated as passing across on a no gain/no loss basis, with the recipient acquiring it at his spouse's cost plus indexation to date (see 14.5 on indexation relief and 14.6 on taper relief).

## 13.1.3 Losses

Losses may arise as well as capital gains. The normal rule is that capital losses cannot be off-set against an individual's income but may be carried forward against capital gains of future years. However, losses arising from transactions involving connected persons may only be set against gains arising from transactions with the same person.

Brought forward losses do not need to be set against gains which are covered by the annual exemption. However, current year losses have to be set against capital gains before using the annual exemption.

## 13.1.4 Rate of tax
(TCGA 1992, s 4)

Once the gains for the year have been computed (net of any losses), the annual exemption is deducted. The balance is then added to the individual's taxable income and the CGT is normally ascertained by working out the additional income tax which would be payable if the capital gains had been taxable income.

### Example

B has 1999–2000 taxable income, after personal allowances, of £19,000. B's capital gains for the year are £17,000. After deducting the £7,100 annual exemption, this means adding in an amount of £9,900. The CGT payable would be computed as:

| Balance of basic rate band | £ |
|---|---|
| £28,000 – £19,000 = £9,000 at 20% = | 1,800 |
| £900 at 40% = | 360 |

| Total CGT payable | 2,160 |
| --- | --- |

However, if the individual had no taxable income at all, the calculation is slightly different. If the gains were again £17,000, the CGT payable would be:

| | £ |
| --- | --- |
| First £7,100 | Nil |
| £9,900 at 20% | 1,980 |
| | 1,980 |

As this example shows, capital gains are taxed as if they were income from savings so that the 20% rate applies until the aggregate of taxable income and capital gains exceeds £28,000 and the 40% rate starts to apply. This rule came into effect only from 1999–2000; however, any unused personal allowances for income tax purposes simply go to waste.

### 13.1.5 Tax rate for individuals with 2000–01 taxable income below £1,520

Where an individual did not use his 10% band in 1999–2000, this also went to waste, but from 2000–01 this is now also available. This means that the first £1,520 capital gains may be taxed at 10% where the individual has income which is covered by his personal allowance.

### 13.1.6 Trading losses

If relief for trading losses has been claimed against income from other sources for the year, any balance of loss may be set against capital gains for that year, or against income and capital gains of the preceding tax year.

A formal claim needs to be lodged with the Revenue by one year and ten months after the tax year of loss, ie a claim to utilise a 1998–99 trading loss must be made by 31 January 2001. Similar claims can be made for losses arising from letting furnished holiday accommodation, from post-cessation expenditure or from post-employment deductions (see 4.5 and 2.8).

## 13.2 WHO IS SUBJECT TO CGT?

An individual's residence and domicile status may have a crucial bearing on his liability to CGT.

### 13.2.1 Significance of residence status
(TCGA 1992, s 2)

An individual is subject to the CGT legislation only if he is either resident or ordinarily resident for the year in which relevant disposals take place.

Residence and ordinary residence are determined in the same way as for income tax (see 21.2).

There are two exceptions to the above. First, where a non-resident and non-ordinarily resident person has been carrying on a trade or profession through a branch or agency in the UK, CGT may be charged on a disposal of assets used in that branch despite the fact that the person would normally be outside the charge on capital gains. Secondly, an individual who has been resident or ordinarily resident in the UK for any part of at least four of the previous seven tax years, and who ceases to be resident for less than five complete tax years, may be taxed on his return to the UK (see 13.2.2 and 21.3.4).

## 13.2.2 What happens if an individual is non-resident for part of the tax year?

The rules changed with effect from 17 March 1998, but even before that date certain gains could be taxable even though the individual may have been non-resident.

Technically, an individual is resident or non-resident for the whole of a tax year. The Revenue practice of treating certain individuals as resident for only part of a tax year for income tax purposes is really no more than an extra-statutory concession. The 'split year' treatment (see 21.3.1) is therefore subject to two exceptions.

The first exception concerns the year of departure. Individuals who move abroad on or after 17 March 1998 are taxed on all capital gains for the year of departure, even if the gains are realised after the date that the individual leaves the UK. Different rules apply to individuals who left the UK before 17 March 1998: see *Allied Dunbar Tax Handbook 1998–99* at 13.2.2.

Secondly, the Revenue is able to assess capital gains where the individual concerned has returned to the UK during the year in question and he was non-resident for less than five years. In such a case, capital gains realised in the tax year in which the individual resumes UK residence may be charged to tax even though the disposals took place prior to the individual's return.

### Example – Non-residence for part of tax year

*A* was classified as non-resident in the UK from 1 January 1999 when she took up a job in the Middle East. She returned to the UK on 24 July 2003. For income tax purposes she is regarded as not resident and not ordinarily resident from 1 January 1999 to 23 July 2003. However, she would be subject to CGT for 1998–99 on disposals made during the period 1 January–5 April 1999.

Gains realised in the period 6 April 1999 to 5 April 2003 are not subject to CGT for the tax year concerned as *A* is neither resident nor ordinarily resident in those years. However, the gains will be taxed as if they were realised in 2003–04, ie the year in which *A* resumes residence in the UK. *A* will also be taxed on all her gains for 2003–04, not merely those realised after her return on 24 July 2003.

In some cases the provisions of a double taxation agreement may override the five-year rule and prevent the Revenue from taxing gains realised in the year in which the individual resumes UK residence. This is an area where specialist advice is essential.

### 13.2.3 Having a foreign domicile may make an important difference
(TCGA 1992, s 12)

(See 22.1 on domicile.)

An individual who is resident (or ordinarily resident) and domiciled in the UK is subject to CGT on a worldwide basis (ie on gains realised both in this country and abroad). By contrast, an individual who is not domiciled in the UK is charged tax on gains from foreign assets only if the proceeds are brought into this country (or, as the legislation puts it, the gains are 'remitted' to the UK). There are further details on the treatment of foreign domiciled individuals in 22.13. The rest of this chapter deals only with people who are domiciled in the UK.

## 13.3 WHAT ASSETS ARE CHARGEABLE ASSETS?

### 13.3.1 Assets within the scope of CGT
(TCGA 1992, s 21)

Gains on virtually all types of assets are potentially subject to CGT, subject to certain stated exceptions. TCGA 1992, s 21(1) states:

> All forms of property shall be assets for the purposes of this Act, whether situated in the United Kingdom or not, including:
> (a) options, debts and incorporeal property generally, and
> (b) any currency other than sterling, and
> (c) any form of property created by the person disposing of it, or otherwise coming to be owned without being acquired.

The asset does not have to be transferable or capable of being assigned. The term 'any form of property' is all embracing. For example, the courts have held that CGT was due on an employer's right to compensation from an employee who wished to be released from his service agreement. In another case, the right to compensation for property expropriated by the USSR in 1940 was held to be a form of property and therefore an asset for CGT purposes. Similarly, the High Court held in *Zim Properties Ltd v Proctor* [1985] STC 90 that the right to bring an action before the courts constitutes an asset which can be turned to account by the potential litigant negotiating a compromise and receiving a lump sum.

The conclusion therefore is that virtually all forms of property which can yield a capital sum are subject to CGT unless they are specifically exempt.

## 13.3.2 **What assets are specifically exempt?**

The following are the main categories of exempt assets:

(1) Principal private residence (see 14.13) [s 222].
(2) Chattels which are wasting assets, unless used in a business (see 14.9.1) [s 44].
(3) Chattels – where the sale consideration is less than £6,000. There is some alleviation of the charge when more than £6,000 is received (see 14.9.2) [s 262].
(4) Decoration for valour so long as sold by the original recipient [s 268].
(5) Foreign currency acquired for personal expenditure outside the UK. This includes money spent on the purchase or maintenance of any property situated outside the UK [s 269].
(6) Winnings from betting – for example the pools, horses, bingo and lotteries [s 51].
(7) Compensation or damages for wrong or injury suffered in a profession or vocation [s 51]. Certain compensation from foreign governments for property lost or confiscated by concession.
(8) Debts [s 251].
(9) National savings certificates and non-marketable securities, ie those which cannot be transferred or are only transferable with the consent of a Minister of the Crown or National Debt Commissioner [s 121].
(10) Gilt-edged securities and qualifying corporate bonds and any options to acquire or dispose of such investments [s 115]. A qualifying corporate bond is a loan stock which is not convertible and is not a relevant discounted security (see 5.7).
(11) Shares held in ISAs (see 11.1) and personal equity plans (see 11.5) [s 151].
(12) Shares issued by way of business expansion schemes after 18 March 1986 (see 11.9) provided the BES relief has not been withdrawn and the shares are sold etc by the original subscriber or his spouse.
(13) Shares issued under an enterprise investment scheme which qualified for income tax relief (see 11.6) provided the EIS relief has not been withdrawn.
(14) Shares in a venture capital trust (see 11.7).
(15) Motor cars – unless not suitable for use as a private vehicle or commonly used for the carriage of passengers [s 263]. Also veteran and vintage cars.
(16) Woodlands [s 250].
(17) Gifts to charities, gifts for national purposes to any one mentioned in the Inheritance Tax Act (IHTA) 1984, Sched 3 [s 257].
(18) Works of art where they are taken by the Revenue in lieu of death duties such as IHT (again see IHTA 1984, Sched 3) [s 258].
(19) Gifts to housing associations; a claim is made by both transferor and the association [s 259].

(20) Mortgage cash-backs – the Revenue conceded on 21 March 1996 that mortgagees who receive cash inducements from banks and building societies are not liable to CGT on such receipts.

(21) Compensation for missold personal pensions taken out as a result of disadvantageous advice given between 29 April 1988 and 30 June 1994.

(22) Life assurance policies, but only in the hands of the original owner or beneficiaries [s 210].

Where an asset is exempt no gain is assessable. Unfortunately, it follows that no relief is normally given for losses (losses on a disposal of shares in an enterprise investment scheme are an exception to this general rule).

## 13.4 WHICH TYPES OF TRANSACTION MAY PRODUCE A CHARGEABLE GAIN?
(TCGA 1992, s 28)

### 13.4.1 Introduction

The most obvious type of disposal is an outright sale with immediate settlement, but there are many other transactions which count as a disposal for CGT purposes, for example:

- Outright sale (possibly with payment by instalments)
- Conditional sale
- Exercise of an option
- Exchange of property
- Compulsory acquisition of asset by local authority, etc
- Sums payable as compensation or proceeds under an insurance policy
- Gifts
- Asset destroyed or becoming of negligible value.

The liability to CGT is determined by the tax year in which the date of disposal falls.

### 13.4.2 Outright sale
(TCGA 1992, s 28)

The date of disposal is the day on which the unconditional contract is entered into, which may, of course, be different from the date that the vendor receives payment.

#### Sale with payment by instalments

The date of disposal is fixed by the time that the parties enter into an unconditional contract. It may be possible to pay CGT arising from such transactions as the instalments come in over a period of up to eight years (provided the instalments are spaced over a period of at least 18 months: TCGA 1992, s 280).

The Revenue operates a concession where a purchaser defaults and the vendor takes back the asset in satisfaction of the sums due to him (see ESC D18). The disposal is effectively treated as if it has never happened.

### 13.4.3 Conditional sale
(TCGA 1992, s 28)

A conditional sale is a contract which does not take effect until a stated condition is satisfied.

#### Example

> A agrees to purchase B's shares in XYZ Ltd provided the local authority grants planning permission over land owned by XYZ Ltd by April 1997. Under this type of agreement, B remains the legal owner of his shares until the condition is satisfied. If the local authority does not in fact grant planning permission, A is under no obligation to buy B's shares.
>
> The date of disposal under such contracts is the day that the condition is satisfied and the contract becomes unconditional, eg in the above example, the date planning permission is granted.

### 13.4.4 Exercise of an option
(TCGA 1992, s 144)

A 'call' option is a legally binding agreement between the owner of an asset and a third party under which the owner agrees to sell the asset if the other party decides to exercise his option. The purchase price payable upon the exercise of the option is normally fixed at the outset and this constitutes one of the terms of the option.

A 'put' option is one where the other party agrees to buy the asset if the owner decides to exercise an option requiring him to do so.

The grant of either type of option does not constitute a disposal of the asset concerned. This happens only when the option is exercised and the day on which this happens is the date of disposal.

In some cases, payment is made for the option to be granted. This is treated as a disposal of a separate asset unless the option is subsequently exercised.

### 13.4.5 Exchange of property

An agreement to exchange an asset for another is a disposal of the old asset and an acquisition of the new asset. If there is any cash adjustment, this must also be brought into account. For example, if A exchanges his holding in ICI for *B*'s shareholding in Glaxo, *A* is treated as if he has disposed of the ICI shares for the market value of the Glaxo shares at the time of the exchange. This type of transaction commonly occurs where an individual transfers portfolio investments to a unit trust in return for units.

There is an important exception to the rule that an exchange constitutes a disposal which may apply where a shareholder takes securities offered to him on a company takeover (see 14.7.5 on such share exchanges). Provided certain conditions are satisfied, the exchange does not count as a disposal and the securities issued by the acquiring company are deemed to have been derived from the original shares, with the shareholder carrying forward his original acquisition value.

### Example – Exchange of shares on company takeover

*B* holds 1,000 shares in XYZ plc which he acquired in 1986 for £9,000. Another company, ABC plc makes a takeover bid and offers all XYZ shareholders a share exchange whereby they receive one ABC share (worth £30 each) for every two XYZ shares that they own. The offer document confirms that agreement has been obtained from the Revenue that TCGA 1992, s 136 applies.

If *B* accepts, he will receive 500 ABC shares worth £15,000. However, he will be deemed to have acquired them in 1986 for £9,000. No disposal is deemed to have occurred on the share exchange.

## 13.4.6 Compulsory acquisition of asset
(TCGA 1992, s 22)

The transfer of land to, for example, a local authority exercising its compulsory purchase powers is a disposal for CGT purposes. In some cases, once the compulsory purchase order has been served, contracts are drawn up and the land is transferred under the contract. In such a case, the rules in relation to outright sales and conditional sales apply.

Where the compulsory purchase order is disputed, the date of disposal will normally be the earlier of:

(1) the date on which compensation for the acquisition is agreed or otherwise determined, and
(2) the date on which the local authority enters the land in pursuance of its powers.

## 13.4.7 Sums payable as compensation or proceeds under insurance policy
(TCGA 1992, s 22)

In some cases, an asset (eg a building) may be destroyed or damaged and a capital sum is received as compensation for this. In such cases, the asset is deemed to have been disposed of at the date that the capital sum is received.

Similarly, where a capital sum is received from an insurance policy following such damage the receipt of the insurance monies is treated as constituting a disposal.

An extra-statutory concession was issued on 19 December 1994 which covers the receipt of compensation under the Foreign Compensation Act 1950, the Ugandan Expropriated Properties Act, compensation payable by the United Nations Compensation Commission for property lost during the Gulf War and compensation payable under German Law. The concession may provide exemption for a person who receives compensation for property which was lost or confiscated, eg because of the Nazis or under the East German regime.

### 13.4.8 Gifts
(TCGA 1992, s 17)

A gift is treated as a disposal at market value (except where the gift is from one spouse to the other: see 13.1.2). At one time it was possible for assets to be transferred at cost, but this general form of hold-over relief was abolished by FA 1989. In some cases the capital gains may still be held over such as where the gift involves business property or is a lifetime chargeable transfer for IHT purposes such as a gift to a discretionary trust (see 17.10) but not a PET (see 17.6.1). You should obtain a copy of Helpsheet IR295 if you make such a chargeable transfer.

A gift will often constitute a transaction between connected persons – see 20.9.

### 13.4.9 Asset destroyed or becoming of negligible value
(TCGA 1992, s 24)

The total destruction or entire loss of an asset constitutes a disposal. This could be physical destruction (eg by fire) or legal/financial destruction (eg bankruptcy or winding-up).

The legislation also permits a person to elect that he should be treated as having disposed of an asset which has become of negligible value. Normally, a capital loss will arise on such an occasion.

'Negligible value' is interpreted by the Revenue as meaning considerably less than small. For example, the Revenue will only agree that shares, loan stock and other securities are of negligible value on being satisfied that the owner is unlikely to recover anything other than a nominal amount on the liquidation of the company. The mere fact that shares have been suspended or de-listed by the Stock Exchange is not regarded as sufficient.

The legislation provides that a disposal is deemed to take place in the year during which the Inspector of Taxes agrees that the asset has become of negligible value. In practice the Revenue permits a claim to take effect up to two tax years prior to the claim provided that the asset was of negligible value in the prior year (see ESC D28).

In practice it is not always beneficial for an individual to claim the benefit of ESC D28 or indeed for a claim to be made until such time as there are gains against which the loss can be set (see 13.1.3).

## 13.5 HOW GAINS MAY BE DEFERRED OR 'ROLLED OVER'
(TCGA 1992, ss 164A–164N)

A roll-over relief was available up to 5 April 1998 whereby an individual (or trustee) who realised a gain on the disposal of an asset of any description could roll over the gain if he reinvested it in shares in a qualifying unquoted trading company. Where gains were rolled over they were not charged to tax, but the gain was deducted from the cost of acquiring the new asset (ie the unquoted shares).

An example of this relief would be if A sold quoted shares and realised a gain of £150,000. Provided he reinvested at least £150,000 in qualifying unquoted shares, and he claimed roll-over relief, the gain was not chargeable at all. If he reinvested only £95,000, the chargeable gain was limited to £55,000.

This relief is dealt with in detail at 15.4. From 6 April 1998, a similar relief is available under the Enterprise Investment Scheme (see 11.6 on EIS CGT deferral relief) and also in respect of Venture Capital Trusts.

## 13.6 SALES OF SHARES TO ALL-EMPLOYEE SHARE TRUSTS

Where an individual transfers unquoted shares to trustees who hold them for employees under an approved all-employee share scheme (see 3.14), the individual may roll over any capital gain arising from this transfer provided he reinvests in chargeable assets within six months. The all-employee trust must acquire at least a 10% interest in the company. The chargeable assets into which the individual's gain is rolled over cannot consist of shares in the company concerned or a property which is exempt as the individual's main residence.

# 14

# THE CALCULATION OF CAPITAL GAINS

The computation of a capital gain (or loss) is more complicated than it looks. Basically, a gain (or loss) is the difference between the disposal value and the original cost after certain expenses, allowances and deductions have been taken into account. However, there are a number of variables. This chapter deals with the following aspects:

(1)  Amount to be brought in as disposal value.
(2)  What costs are allowable?
(3)  Assets held at 31 March 1982 and 6 April 1965.
(4)  Other acquisition values.
(5)  Indexation.
(6)  Taper relief.
(7)  How gains are computed on quoted securities.
(8)  When may a chargeable gain arise on foreign currency?
(9)  Special rules for disposals of chattels.
(10) Specific rules which apply to disposals of land and investment properties.
(11) How the Revenue computes gains on unquoted shares.
(12) Disposal of foreign property.
(13) Main residence exemption.
(14) Possible restrictions on exemption.
(15) Living in job-related accommodation.
(16) Treatment where property has not been occupied throughout.

## 14.1 AMOUNT TO BE BROUGHT IN AS DISPOSAL VALUE

### 14.1.1 Market value
(TCGA 1992, s 17)

The general rule is that market value must be used unless the transaction is at arm's length. In the straightforward situation where a contract is entered into with a third party on a commercial basis, the disposal proceeds will be the actual sale proceeds. An individual is not penalised because he has made a bad bargain and sold an asset for less than it is really worth. On the other hand, if the bargain is not at arm's length and the individual deliberately sells the asset for an amount which is less than its true value, the legislation requires market value to be substituted. If the disposal is to a connected person such as a relative or the trustee of a family settlement or a family company, there is an automatic assumption that the bargain is not at arm's length and market value will always be substituted for the actual sale proceeds if the two amounts are different. There are three exceptions:

(1) Transactions between spouses (see 13.1.2).
(2) Gifts to charities and similar bodies (see 13.3.2).
(3) Situations where a hold-over election can be made (see 15.6).

### 14.1.2 Contingent liabilities
(TCGA 1992, s 49)

There may be occasions where the contract may require part of the proceeds to be returned at some time in the future. This is known as a sale with 'contingent liabilities'.

Suppose, for example, that a vendor receives £150,000 for the disposal of a plot of land, but is under an obligation to return £60,000 in certain circumstances. Will the capital gain be charged on sale proceeds of £150,000 or £90,000? In fact, s 49 provides that in these circumstances the capital gain must be computed in the first instance without any deduction for the contingent liability. However, if and when the vendor is required to refund part of the sale proceeds because the contingent liability has become an actual liability, the CGT assessment is adjusted accordingly.

### 14.1.3 Contingent consideration
(TCGA 1992, s 48)

In a similar way, it is possible that the contract may provide that additional sums may be payable if certain conditions are satisfied in the future. If it is possible to put a value on the further amount of consideration which is 'contingent' (ie which is payable only if certain conditions are satisfied) the full amount which may be received is brought into account at the date of disposal without any discount. If the conditions are not in fact satisfied, so that the further amounts are never received, an adjustment is made later to the CGT assessment.

The position is different where the contingent consideration cannot be ascertained at the date of disposal (this will normally be the situation where the contingent consideration may vary and is not a fixed amount). Basically, the legislation requires that the market value of the right to receive the future consideration should be regarded as the disposal proceeds. The difference between this amount and the amount eventually received forms a separate CGT computation for the year in which the final amount of the actual contingent consideration is determined. The treatment of contingent consideration, especially variable contingent consideration, is fairly complex. It normally arises in relation to either land or shares in private companies. This is an area where it is essential to take professional advice.

### 14.1.4 Deduction for amounts charged as income
(TCGA 1992, s 31)

In some cases the disposal of an asset may give rise to an income tax charge. Where this happens, the amount which is charged as income is deducted from the sale proceeds and only the balance is brought into account for CGT purposes. This commonly arises where a private company buys back its own shares and the transaction is treated as a distribution (see 5.9.7).

## 14.2 WHAT COSTS ARE ALLOWABLE?

### 14.2.1 Certain specific types of expenditure

The legislation permits only a limited range of expenses to be deducted in computing capital gains and losses. TCGA 1992, s 38(1) states:

> the sums allowable as a deduction from the consideration in the computation of the gain accruing to a person on the disposal of an asset shall be restricted to:
> (a)  the amount of value of the consideration, in money or money's worth, given by him or on his behalf wholly and exclusively for the acquisition of the asset, together with the incidental costs to him of the acquisition or, if the asset was not acquired by him, any expenditure wholly and exclusively incurred by him in providing the asset,
> (b)  the amount of any expenditure wholly and exclusively incurred on the asset by him or on his behalf for the purpose of enhancing the value of the asset, being expenditure reflected in the state or nature of the asset at the time of the disposal, and any expenditure wholly and exclusively incurred by him in establishing, preserving or defending his title to, or to a right over, the asset,
> (c)  the incidental costs to him of making the disposal.

### 14.2.2 The cost of the asset

The market value of the asset at 31 March 1982 or 6 April 1965 may be substituted for actual cost if the asset was held at those dates (see 14.3.1 and 14.3.4).

### 14.2.3 Incidental costs of acquisition

These are limited to:

(1)  fees, commission or remuneration paid to a surveyor, valuer, auctioneer, accountant, agent or legal adviser;

(2) transfer/conveyancing charges (including stamp duty); and
(3) advertising to find a seller.

## 14.2.4 Enhancement expenditure

The legislation permits a deduction to be claimed in respect of expenditure incurred in order to enhance the value of the asset provided that such expenditure is reflected in the state or nature of the asset at the time of disposal. The latter condition excludes relief for improvements which have worn out by the time that the asset is disposed of. Certain grey areas are worth mentioning:

(1) Initial expenditure by way of repairs to newly acquired property which is let may be allowable if no relief has been given in computing Schedule A income.
(2) Expenditure means money or money's worth. It does not include the value of personal labour or skill.

## 14.2.5 Expenditure incurred in establishing, preserving or defending legal title

The case law concerned with the allowable nature of this expenditure hinges on the inter-relationship between the words 'incurred' and 'establishing' etc. The High Court held in *IRC v Richards' Executors* (1971) 46 TC 626 that the cost of making an inventory and providing a valuation for a grant of probate was allowable under this head (see SP8/94).

## 14.2.6 Incidental costs of disposals

The following expenses may be deductible under this head:

(1) Fees, commission or remuneration for the professional services of a surveyor, valuer, auctioneer, accountant, agent or legal adviser.
(2) Transfer/conveyancing charges (including stamp duty).
(3) Advertising to find a buyer.
(4) Any other costs reasonably incurred in making any valuation or apportionment for CGT purposes, including in particular expenses reasonably incurred in ascertaining market value where this is required. Professional costs incurred in getting a valuation agreed with the Revenue are not allowable.

## 14.2.7 Part disposals
(TCGA 1992, s 42)

Where a person disposes of part of an asset, the cost is apportioned between the part disposed of and the part retained according to the formula $[A \div (A + B)]$ where A is the consideration received or deemed to have been received and B is the market value of the part retained.

### Example – Part disposals

> *B* holds 1,000 shares in XYZ Ltd which cost him £10,000. The company is taken over and he receives cash of £5,000 and convertible loan stock issued by the acquiring company worth £15,000 (assume that in this particular case no capital gain arises in respect of the loan stock because it is issued on the occasion of a takeover and the necessary Revenue clearances have been obtained (see 13.4.5 and 14.7.4)). *B*'s acquisition value will be apportioned as follows:
>
> $$£10,000 \quad \times \quad \frac{5,000}{5,000 + 15,000} \quad = \quad £2,500,$$
>
> ie the proportion of acquisition value which relates to the part sold. £7,500 is treated as the acquisition value of the part retained, ie it will be taken into account in computing any gain or loss as and when the loan stock is sold.

Special rules may apply where shares are sold out of a shareholding which includes shares held on 31 March 1982 and shares acquired after that date (see 14.7.3).

## 14.2.8 Small capital receipts
(TCGA 1992, s 122)

There are occasions where the formula $[A \div (A + B)]$ does not have to be used, and the amount received is simply deducted from the owner's acquisition value. The most common situation where this arises is where a shareholder sells his entitlement under a rights issue, normally on a nil paid basis. Provided that the amount received is less than £3,000 or is small as compared with the value of the asset, the receipt can be deducted from the owner's acquisition value. 'Small' in this context is interpreted by the Revenue to be an amount not exceeding 5% of the market value.

## 14.2.9 Capital sums applied in restoring assets
(TCGA 1992, s 23)

Under normal circumstances, an asset is regarded as having been disposed of for CGT purposes if it is lost or destroyed. However, where a capital sum is received from such an asset (eg the proceeds of an insurance policy), the owner may claim that the asset is not treated as disposed of if at least 95% of the capital sum is spent in restoring the asset.

## 14.3  ASSETS HELD AT 31 MARCH 1982 AND 6 APRIL 1965
(TCGA 1992, s 35 and Scheds 2–3)

### 14.3.1 General rebasing
(TCGA 1992, s 35)

The general rule is that where assets were held at 31 March 1982, it is to be assumed that the assets were sold on that date and immediately reacquired at their market value at that time. This is known as 'rebasing'.

The resulting gain or loss is then compared with the gain or loss calculated by reference to the original loss, with the following consequences:

| Original cost | March '82 value | For CGT |
|---|---|---|
| Gain | Gain | The lower gain is assessed |
| Loss | Loss | The lower loss is allowed |
| Loss | Gain | Nil assessed – no gain/loss |
| Gain | Loss | Nil assessed – no gain/loss |

However, original cost is ignored altogether if a universal rebasing election has been made (see below).

### 14.3.2 Universal rebasing election
(TCGA 1992, s 35(5))

If a person so elects, the rebasing rule is applied to all disposals made by him of assets held on 31 March 1982. In other words, original cost is ignored completely, and regard is had only for the value of the assets held at that date. In some cases, making this election will mean that losses can be claimed which would not otherwise be available (because of the no gain/no loss rule).

A universal rebasing election is precisely that. If the election is made the rebasing rule is applied to all assets held at 31 March 1982. Furthermore, once made, the election is irrevocable.

There is a time limit for making the election. The legislation requires it to be made within two years of the end of the year of assessment in which a disposal first takes place of assets which were held both at 6 April 1988 and at 31 March 1982. If no election has been made and assets held at 31 March 1982 have been disposed of during the period 6 April 1988–5 April 1998, it is now too late to make the election.

#### Married persons

The election may be made by each spouse separately. However, where assets pass from one spouse to another and the spouse who received the asset subsequently disposes of it, the gain or loss on that particular asset will be governed by whether or not the spouse who transferred the asset had made the universal rebasing election.

### 14.3.3 **Time apportionment for assets held at 6 April 1965**
(TCGA 1992, Sched 2, para 16)

Special rules apply to the disposal of assets which were held at 6 April 1965 and where a universal rebasing election has not been made and the assets concerned are not quoted shares or land with development value.

When CGT was first introduced in 1965, it was recognised that it would be unfair to charge tax on capital gains which had accrued before that date. For assets other than shares which were quoted at 6 April 1965 and land which (either at that time or subsequently) had development value, taxpayers were given the general right to compute gains on the basis that the appreciation had occurred at a uniform rate and to exclude the part relating to the period before 6 April 1965. This is known as the 'time apportionment' basis.

The capital gain computed on the time apportionment basis is arrived at by using the following formula:

$$\text{Overall gain} \quad \times \quad \frac{\text{Period between 6 April 1965 and date of disposal}}{\text{Total period of ownership}}$$

For example, if an asset had been acquired in, say, April 1960 and sold for an overall gain of £40,000 in April 2000, the time apportionment formula would produce the following result:

$$£40,000 \quad \times \quad \frac{\text{April 1965–April 2000 (35 years)}}{\text{April 1960–April 2000 (40 years)}},$$

ie a chargeable gain of £35,000. When using this formula, the fraction should be calculated by reference to months of ownership and the divisor cannot reflect a period prior to 6 April 1945.

Where land has development value at the date of disposal, it is not possible to time apportion the capital gain. One must either use the market value of the land at 6 April 1965 or its value at 31 March 1982.

### 14.3.4 **Market value at 6 April 1965**

There may also be circumstances where the fact that no universal rebasing election has been made means that the market value of an asset at 6 April 1965 can be used or must be used instead of original cost.

#### Quoted shares

Where an election was made under TCGA 1992, Sched 2, para 4 in respect of quoted securities held on 6 April 1965, either in respect of equity investments or fixed interest investments, all the securities falling into that particular category will be deemed to have been disposed of and reacquired on 6 April 1965 so that the original cost is not relevant. This election would normally have been made some years ago as the deadline was two years after the first relevant disposal which took place after 19 March 1968.

### Unquoted shares and other assets

In this situation, capital gains are calculated on the time apportionment basis unless a specific election is made within two years of the date of disposal, in which case the gain is computed by reference to the market value of the asset at 6 April 1965.

In practice, this election will be beneficial only where the market value of the asset at 6 April 1965 was higher than the value of the asset at 31 March 1982.

## 14.3.5 Assets acquired via a gift made between 1 April 1982 and 5 April 1988
(TCGA 1992, Sched 4)

This section may be relevant where all of the following conditions are satisfied:

(1) The asset was acquired as a gift or transfer from a trust during the period 1 April 1982–5 April 1988.
(2) The donor held the asset at 31 March 1982.
(3) The donor claimed hold-over relief so that the recipient was deemed to have acquired the asset at the donor's original cost.

When rebasing was first introduced, it was recognised that it would be unfair not to permit some relief where an asset had been transferred prior to 6 April 1988 and the gain had been held over. The person who received such a gift cannot claim rebasing because he did not own the asset concerned at 31 March 1982. To give rough and ready compensation for this, the legislation included provisions so that when the recipient of such a gift made a disposal after 5 April 1988, half of the held-over gain could be 'forgiven' or left out of account.

### Example – Transfer prior to 6 April 1988 with held-over gain

A received a gift of shares in August 1986 from his father B. At the time of the gift, the shares were worth £180,000. B's acquisition value was only £40,000, and indexation (see 14.5) amounted to £10,000. This would normally have meant that B would have had a chargeable gain of £130,000. However, he made a claim under the legislation prevailing at the time which permitted the capital gain to be held over. This meant that B did not suffer a CGT charge, but A was deemed to have acquired the assets with an acquisition value as follows:

|  | £ |
|---|---|
| Market value at date of gift | 180,000 |

| | |
|---|---|
| *Less*: held-over gain | (130,000) |
| Acquisition value | 50,000 |

When *A* disposes of the asset, his acquisition value is increased by 50% of £130,000 so that his acquisition value becomes £115,000.

### 14.3.6 Relief not automatic

A formal claim for the relief described in 14.3.5 must be made within two years of the end of the tax year in which the recipient makes his disposal.

## 14.4 OTHER ACQUISITION VALUES

### 14.4.1 Assets acquired via inheritance or family trust
(TCGA 1992, ss 62 and 71)

Where a person inherits an asset, he is generally deemed to have acquired it for its market value at the date of the testator's death (ie probate value). There is one exception to this. It is possible to claim a form of relief from IHT tax where quoted securities have gone down in value after the person has died (see 17.11.3). Where such relief has been claimed for IHT, a corresponding adjustment is made so that the person taking the assets concerned is deemed to have acquired them not at probate value, but rather at the value actually brought into account for IHT purposes after taking account of the fall in value.

Where assets have been acquired from a trust, the beneficiary's acquisition value is normally the market value at the time that the asset is transferred to him. However, the acquisition value may be lower than this where the trustees have claimed hold-over relief either under the general hold-over relief provisions which prevailed up to 5 April 1989 or under the more restrictive provisions which have applied subsequently (see 15.6).

### 14.4.2 Deemed acquisition value where income tax charged
(TCGA 1992, ss 120 and 141)

Where a person is subject to a Schedule E income tax charge when he acquires an asset (eg where he exercises a non-approved share option) he is deemed to have acquired the asset for an amount equal to the value taken into account in computing a Schedule E charge on him. Similarly, where a person acquires shares by way of a stock dividend (ie, where there is a choice as between a cash dividend or further shares issued by a UK company) the shares are deemed to be acquired for a consideration equal to the amount brought into account for income tax purposes by reason of the stock dividend (for further particulars see 5.8.5).

## 14.5 INDEXATION
(TA 1992, ss 53–57)

A person who makes a capital gain is allowed to deduct not only his actual acquisition value, but also a proportion which represents the increase in the RPI between the month of acquisition and the month of disposal. The formula used is $[(RD – RI) \div RI]$ where:

RD = retail prices index in month of disposal or April 1998, whichever is the earlier

RI = retail prices index for March 1982 or month in which expenditure incurred, whichever is the later.

Note that where the date of disposal is after 30 April 1998, indexation allowance is given only by reference to the April 1998 figure because of the introduction of taper relief from 1998–99 (see 14.6).

### Example

A acquired shares in X plc on 1 June 1991 for £20,000. He sells them in June 1997 for £30,000. He has a capital gain of £10,000 before indexation, and a gain of £6,520 after taking indexation into account. The indexation relief is computed as follows:

$$\text{Cost £20,000} \times \frac{\text{RPI for June 1997 – RPI for June 1991}}{\text{RPI for June 1991}}$$

That is $£20,000 \times (157.5 – 134.1) \div 134.1 = £20,000 \times 0.174 = £3,480$. The RPI figures are set out in Table 29.7 at the back of this book

### 14.5.1 Restriction to indexation relief
(FA 1994, s 93)

Indexation relief may only reduce or extinguish a gain; it cannot convert a gain into a loss or increase a loss. A different rule applied up to the November 1993 Budget, so that indexation relief may create or increase a loss in relation to transactions prior to 30 November 1993.

### Examples of restriction

Acquisition cost £4,000, indexation allowance to date of disposal 1 December 1994, £750.

|  | £ | £ | £ |
|---|---|---|---|
| Sale proceeds | 5,000 | 4,500 | 3,000 |
| *Less*: Cost | (4,000) | (4,000) | (4,000) |
| Unindexed gain/(loss) | 1,000 | 500 | (1,000) |
| Indexation allowance | (750) | (500) | Nil |
| Chargeable gain/(capital loss) | 250 | Nil | (1,000) |

## 14.6  TAPER RELIEF

### 14.6.1 Taper relief on gains between 6 April 1998 and 5 April 2000

For gains realised on or after 6 April 1998, indexation allowance is given for periods up to April 1998, but not thereafter. Where an asset was held at 6 April 1998 and disposed of after that date, indexation allowance will be computed only for the period from the date of acquisition (or the date the expenditure was incurred) to April 1998. For assets acquired on or after 5 April 1998, no indexation allowance will be available to reduce the chargeable gain.

Indexation has been replaced by taper relief. The taper reduces the amount of the chargeable gain according to how long the asset has been held for periods after 5 April 1998. The taper is more generous for business than for non-business assets. (The definition of business assets is covered at 15.4.) The rates of taper relief for gains realised between 6 April 1998 and 5 April 2000 are as follows:

| Number of complete years after 5 April 1998 for which asset held | Percentage of gain chargeable | |
|---|---|---|
| | Business assets | Non-business assets |
| 0 | 100.0 | 100.0 |
| 1 | 92.5 | 100.0 |
| 2 | 85.0 | 100.0 |
| 3 | 77.5 | 95.0 |
| 4 | 70.0 | 90.0 |
| 5 | 62.5 | 85.0 |
| 6 | 55.0 | 80.0 |
| 7 | 47.5 | 75.0 |
| 8 | 40.0 | 70.0 |
| 9 | 32.5 | 65.0 |
| 10 or more | 25.0 | 60.0 |

Assets which were acquired before 17 March 1998 qualify for an addition of one year to the period for which they are treated as held after 5 April 1998. This addition is the same for all assets, whenever they were actually acquired. So, for example, an asset purchased on 1 January 1998 and disposed of on 1 July 2000 will be treated for the purposes of the taper relief as if it had been held for three years (two complete years after 5 April 1998 plus one additional year). Therefore, a non-business held asset as at 17 March 1998 did not qualify for any taper relief until the current tax year.

Taper relief is given on the net gains that are chargeable after deduction of indexation allowance and any capital losses realised in the same tax year or brought forward from previous years. Where an individual has gains which attract no taper relief, losses are set against those first to produce the lowest tax charge.

## Table 14.1 – Computing your capital gains before taper relief

The following can be used as a 'pro-forma' when calculating capital gains (or losses).

| | | |
|---|---|---|
| Sale Proceeds (consider whether the market value provisions may apply) —see 14.1). | A | |
| Deduct incidental costs of disposal, see 14.2. | B | |
| Net sale proceeds (A – B). | | C |
| If the asset was acquired after 31 March 1982, enter cost. | D | |
| Amount of any enhancement expenditure. | E | |
| If the asset was owned at 31 March 1982 and a universal rebasing election is in force, enter value at 31 March 1982, see 14.3. | F | |
| If the asset was owned at 31 March 1982, but no universal rebasing election is in force, enter cost or value at 31 March 1982, whichever is the higher.[1] | G | |
| Enter the amount of enhancement expenditure—if 31 March 1982 value is entered at F or G, include only post-31 March 1982 enhancement expenditure. | H | |
| Enter the total of figures entered in any of D to H. | | I |
| Unindexed gain (C – I). | | J |
| Indexation relief on figure in D, F or G, see 14.5. | K | |
| Indexation relief on figure in E or H.[2] | L | |
| Enter total of K and L. | | M |
| Deduct M from J. The result is the indexed gain. | | N |

[1]Note that there will not be an allowable loss if there is an overall gain taking the original cost, but a loss taking the 31 March 1982 value.
[2]The figure of indexation relief cannot exceed the figure at J, except in relation to assets disposed of prior to 30 November 1993.

## 14.6.2 Period of ownership

Taper relief operates as follows in respect of periods of ownership after 5 April 1998:

(1) where there has been a transfer of an asset between spouses, the taper relief on a subsequent disposal is based on the combined period of holding by both spouses;

(2) for other no gain/no loss transfers and for situations where relief

applies, the taper operates by reference to the holding period only of the new owner;

(3) where a shareholding is increased by a bonus or rights issue, taper relief is given by reference to the date that the original shares were acquired;

(4) where a relief defers the gain on a disposal until a later occasion (such as the relief on reinvestment in a venture capital trust), the taper relief on the deferred gain relates to the period that the person owned the original asset (there is an exception to this where EIS shares issued after 5 April 1999 are sold for a gain and the gain is reinvested in new EIS shares); and

(5) where gains have been relieved under a provision which reduces the cost of a replacement asset (such as roll-over relief for business assets), the taper relief operates by reference to the period of ownership of the new asset.

### 14.6.3 Taper relief on business assets after 5 April 2000

The rate of taper relief in respect of business assets altered significantly in FA 2000. For business assets disposed after 5 April 2000, taper relief is now calculated according to the following table:

| Complete years of ownership | Taper relief % | Effective tax rate for a 40% taxpayer % | Effective rate under old rules % |
|---|---|---|---|
| 1 | 12.5 | 35 | 37 |
| 2 | 25 | 30 | 34 |
| 3 | 50 | 20 | 31 |
| 4 or more | 75 | 10 | 28 |

Under the new rules the period between 6 April 1998 and 5 April 2000 will count as a period of ownership, although the bonus year for assets held on 17 March 1998 is lost. The definition of what qualifies as a business asset has also been extended (see 15.4).

## 14.7 HOW GAINS ARE COMPUTED ON QUOTED SECURITIES

The term 'quoted securities' means shares, loan stock, warrants etc which are dealt in on the London Stock Exchange and other similar Stock Exchanges recognised by the Revenue as having similar rules and procedures to the London Stock Exchange. This section deals with the tax treatment of transactions such as:

- Sale of part of a shareholding.
- Bonus issues and rights issues.
- Takeovers and mergers.

## 14.7.1 Identification rules for 1998–99 onwards

Specific rules apply where a person sells part of his holding in securities of the same class. Securities are treated as being of the same class if they are treated as such under Stock Exchange practice. For example, all ICI ordinary shares are securities of the same class, whereas BP ordinary shares are not and form a different class.

The identification rules for disposals after 5 April 1998 are that shares disposed of should be matched with:

(1) acquisitions made on the same day;
(2) acquisitions within the next 30 days: if more than one acquisition is made in this period they are dealt with on a FIFO basis, ie the first shares acquired are deemed to be the ones sold;
(3) acquisitions made after 5 April 1998 on a LIFO (last in first out) basis; and
(4) shares held in a 'pool' at 5 April 1998.

## 14.7.2 Sale of part of a shareholding up to 1997–98
(TCGA 1992, ss 104–109)

For most quoted securities (see below for exceptions) the general rule for 1997–98 and earlier years was that on a disposal of part of a shareholding the securities sold were identified as follows:

(1) With securities of the same class acquired on or after 6 April 1982 which are deemed to form part of a 'new holding' (see below).
(2) With securities which are deemed to form part of a 1982 holding, ie securities held at 5 April 1982 other than securities held at 6 April 1965.
(3) With other securities on a LIFO basis (last in, first out). This applied only where a universal rebasing election was not made (see 14.3.2).

## 14.7.3 Pooling

Any securities of the same class acquired on or after 6 April 1982 and held at 6 April 1985 were 'pooled', ie treated as a single asset which grew or diminished as acquisitions and disposals were made. The technical term for this asset is a 'new holding' (to distinguish it from holdings at 31 March 1982).

Securities of the same class which were acquired for the first time after 5 April 1985 were pooled as a single asset in the same way.

Technically, the indexed cost of the pool needed to be recomputed every time there was an operative event, ie something which had the effect of either increasing or decreasing the qualifying expenditure.

## Capital gains tax share identification rules after 5 April 1998

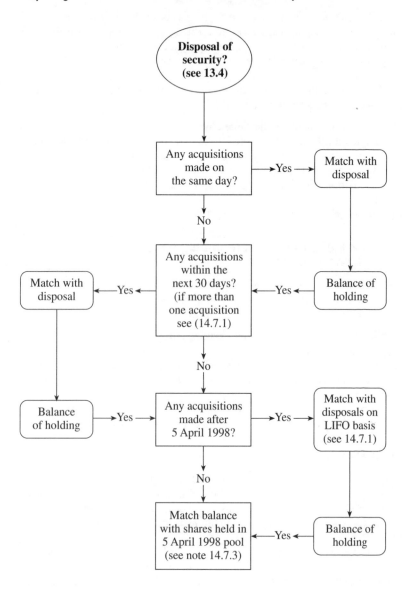

## Example – Securities acquired on or after 6 April 1982

*A* held 10,000 XYZ plc shares at 6 April 1985. They were all acquired in July 1984 at a cost of £3 per share. On 1 August 1989, *A* acquired a further 5,000 shares at a cost of £50,000 (£10 per share). *A*'s new holding had an indexed cost computed as follows:

|  | £ |
|---|---|
| 10,000 shares cost July 1984 | 30,000 |
| Indexation July 1984–August 1989 | 9,000 |
|  | 39,000 |
| 5,000 shares cost August 1989 | 50,000 |
| Indexed cost of 15,000 shares at August 1989 | 89,000 |

If *A* sold 5,000 shares in November 1997 the calculation is:

|  | £ |
|---|---|
| Indexed cost of pool at August 1989 | 89,000 |
| Indexation August 1989–November 1997 | 30,868 |
| Indexed cost of 15,000 shares at November 1997 | 119,868 |

$$\frac{5,000}{15,000} \times £119,868 = \text{Indexed cost of shares sold}$$

$$\frac{10,000}{15,000} \times £119,868 \text{ (ie the balance)} = \text{the indexed cost of the remaining shares}$$

Thus, the cost of the 5,000 shares sold would be taken as £39,956. *A* could not take as her cost the actual amount paid for the most recent acquisition of 5,000 shares.

## 1982 holdings

In much the same way, an individual's shareholding at 6 April 1982 was also treated as a single asset whose cost reduced as and when sales took place.

## Example – Assets held in 1982

*B* had 5,000 shares in XYZ plc at 31 March 1982. The shares cost £1 each in 1979. The value at 31 March 1982 was £2 per share. If *B* sells 1,000 shares in June 1997, the position is:

|  | £ |
|---|---|
| 5,000 shares 31 March 1982 value | 10,000 |
| Indexation 31 March 1982–30 June 1997 | 9,800 |
| Indexed cost at 30 June 1997 | £19,800 |

> Cost of 1,000 shares is taken as
> $$\frac{1,000}{5,000} \times £19,800 \text{ , ie } £3,960.$$
>
> The pool cost could increase because of rights issues which took place after 31 March 1982.

## 14.7.4 Bonus issues and rights issues before 6 April 1998

A bonus issue or rights issue was related to the shares which produced the entitlement.

### Example

C had acquired 4,500 shares in XYZ plc between 1982 and 1995 and also holds 13,500 shares which were acquired before 5 April 1982. The company provides a scrip issue of one new share for every three shares held. C would therefore acquire 6,000 new shares free of charge of which a proportion would be treated as an addition to her new holding with the balance being added to her 1982 holding, ie:

| | |
|---|---|
| Addition to new holding | 1,500 shares |
| Addition to 1982 holding | 4,500 shares |

Similarly, if D had a total of 40,000 shares in Y plc which was made up of a new holding of 10,000 shares and a 1982 holding of 30,000 shares, and the company announced a rights issue in March 1997 of one new share at £2 for every existing share held, D might acquire 20,000 new shares at a cost of £40,000. Only the cost of the rights shares which related to his new holding of 10,000 shares could be added to the indexed cost of the new holding. The other rights shares would be treated as forming part of the 1982 holding.

Shareholders sometimes dispose of rights nil paid. Sums received for such disposals were normally deducted from the indexed pool cost unless (exceptionally) the amount received exceeded 5% of the market value of the shareholding at the time of disposal (see 14.2.8).

## 14.7.5 Takeovers and mergers (pre- and post-6 April 1998)

There is a special relief which may apply where a company issues shares or securities in order to take over another company. The shareholders who accept this offer will not be treated as making a disposal provided they meet one of the following requirements:

(1) together with persons connected with them, they do not hold more than 5% of the company's share capital; or
(2) the Revenue is satisfied that the share exchange is a bona fide commercial transaction which is not entered into with a view to tax avoidance.

So far as quoted securities are concerned, the position is generally straightforward. The offer document forwarded to shareholders normally states whether clearance has been obtained from the Revenue under TCGA 1992, s 138 confirming that TCGA 1992, s 135 applies. Provided that this is the case, no capital gain will arise on the exchange of shares for securities issued by the company which is making the takeovers. Of course, matters may not be quite so simple.

## What happens if there is a mixture of shares and cash?

Suppose a shareholder in X plc is offered a share in Y plc plus cash of £1 in exchange for every share that he holds in X plc. If he accepts this offer there will be a part disposal. The value of the new Y plc shares on the first day of trading is taken and the following computation is required:

Amount received via cash element $\boxed{A}$

Take proportion of indexed cost of holding in X plc

$$\frac{\text{Cash received}}{\text{Cash + value of Y plc shares}} \times \text{indexed cost} \quad \boxed{B}$$

Capital gain/(loss) on cash element $\boxed{C}$

## What happens if there is a mixture of shares and loan stock?

Suppose the shareholder in X plc had instead accepted an offer of one share in Y plc plus £1.25 loan stock. Assume that when the new Y plc shares were first traded they had a price of £2.00 and the loan stock was traded at £80 for every £100 nominal. The cost of the two types of new securities would be determined like this:

## Example – Takeover by mixture of shares and loan stock

**Apportioned to Y plc shares:**

$$\frac{\text{Value of Y shares}}{\text{Value of Y shares + Y loan stock}}$$

ie $\dfrac{£2}{£2 + £1} \times$ cost of X shares = deemed cost of Y shares

**Apportioned to Y plc loan stock:**

$$\frac{\text{Value of loan stock}}{\text{Value of loan stock + shares}}$$

$$\text{ie} \quad \frac{\pounds 1}{\pounds 1 + \pounds 2} \times \text{ cost of X shares} = \text{deemed cost of Y loan stock}$$

This division of the indexed cost of the original holding in X plc will be relevant as and when there is a disposal of either the Y plc shares or loan stock.

### 14.7.6 Special rules where share exchange involves qualifying corporate bonds
(TCGA 1992, s 116)

Loan stock is often a type of qualifying corporate bond, ie an exempt asset for CGT purposes (see 13.3.2). The offer document sent to shareholders on a company takeover normally draws attention to whether the loan stock falls into this category. If it does, the investor is not entitled to indexation relief for periods after the takeover. Furthermore, the disposal of the loan stock creates a capital gain calculated according to values at the time of the takeover and not the value of the loan stock at the time that it is eventually sold or redeemed.

As a matter of fact, the deferred gain is triggered by any kind of disposal of the qualifying corporate bonds. For example, a gift of the loan stock causes the deferred gain to become chargeable. Indeed, a chargeable gain could even arise on a deemed disposal such as would apply if the company which had issued the loan stock went into liquidation.

## 14.8 WHEN MAY A CHARGEABLE GAIN ARISE ON FOREIGN CURRENCY?

There is an exemption for foreign currency provided that it was acquired for an individual's personal expenditure abroad. In all other situations, foreign currency is a chargeable asset and a gain (or loss) will arise when the currency is disposed of. A disposal may take place on the foreign currency being spent, converted into another foreign currency, or converted into sterling. In each of these situations, the sterling equivalent of the foreign currency at the date of acquisition is compared with the sterling equivalent at the date of disposal.

In theory, each separate bank account denominated in foreign currency counts as a separate asset. However, in practice, the Revenue does permit taxpayers to treat all bank accounts containing the particular foreign currency as one account (see SP10/84).

# 14.9 SPECIAL RULES FOR DISPOSALS OF CHATTELS
(TCGA 1992, s 262)

A chattel is defined by the legislation as a tangible, movable asset. Examples include a picture, a silver teapot, a first edition of a famous novel etc.

## 14.9.1 Chattels which are wasting assets
(TCGA 1992, s 45)

There are special rules which apply for chattels which also fall within the definition of wasting assets. A wasting asset is defined as an asset with a useful life expectancy of less than 50 years. These chattels are exempt regardless of the amount of the sale proceeds. Equally, there is no relief for any losses realised on the disposal of such chattels.

This exemption is not available for assets on which the owner was entitled to capital allowances because the asset had been used in a trade.

## 14.9.2 Other types of chattel
(TCGA 1992, s 262)

A gain arising on the disposal of a chattel which is not covered by the exemption in 14.9.1 is exempt only if the sale proceeds do not exceed £6,000. However, there is a form of marginal relief under which, if the sale proceeds are more than £6,000, the maximum chargeable gain cannot exceed five-thirds of the excess. For example, if a picture costing £900 is sold for £6,900, the chargeable gain cannot exceed $\frac{5}{3} \times £900$ ie £1,500.

In some cases, the marginal relief will not help. If the sale proceeds were £6,900, but the picture had cost £5,800, the chargeable gain would be computed on normal principles.

### Losses

A capital loss may arise on the disposal of a chattel. However, where the sale proceeds are less than £6,000, the loss has to be calculated on the basis that notional sale proceeds of £6,000 were received. For example, if an uninsured antique table costing £10,000 were destroyed by fire, the proceeds are taken to be £6,000, not nil.

### Assets forming a set

Several chattels may be deemed to form a single asset, for example a set of antique chairs and a table. Where such chattels are sold to the same person, or to persons acting in concert, they may be regarded as the disposal of a single asset. This rule may apply even though the sales take place at different times. As a consequence, gains which would otherwise be exempt because of the £6,000 limit may be brought into charge.

For example, someone may own four antique chairs each worth £6,000. If they were to be sold one at a time to the same person, the total sale would be regarded as the sale of a single asset for £24,000 and the £6,000 exemption would not apply.

## 14.10 SPECIFIC RULES WHICH APPLY TO DISPOSALS OF LAND AND INVESTMENT PROPERTIES

### 14.10.1 Will the gain be subject to income tax?

Speculative or short-term transactions in land may well give rise to a claim by the Inspector that the individual was dealing in land and therefore subject to tax under Schedule D Case I (see 2.2). Whether a trade is being carried on is a matter of fact. The following 'badges of trade' may be cited by the Inspector in support of an assessment under Schedule D Case I:

(1) Evidence that an asset was acquired with a view to its being resold in the short term.
(2) A large part of the purchase price being financed by borrowings, especially short-term borrowings such as an overdraft.
(3) The taxpayer has a background of similar transactions or has special expertise which assists in achieving a profit on disposal of the asset.

In *Kirkby v Hughes* [1993] STC 76, the court held that the taxpayer was carrying out a trade and the following were regarded as badges of trade:

(1) The properties were larger than would be expected for sole occupancy.
(2) The periods of occupancy were short.
(3) Another property was purchased while the taxpayer was still resident in the first without any clear intention of selling the first.
(4) There was no proof that the taxpayer had intended to acquire the first house as a personal asset.

Quite separately from the above, TA 1988, s 776 may enable the Inspector to assess a gain under Schedule D Case VI. Section 776 may apply where a capital gain is realised and UK land:

(1) was acquired with the sole or main object of realising a gain on its disposal; or
(2) is developed with the sole or main object of realising a gain on the disposal of the land when developed.

There are also circumstances where disposal of shares in a company which owns land may give rise to a Schedule D Case VI assessment (see 20.2.3).

Section 776 can apply whether or not the person is resident in the UK. Furthermore, the capital gain may be received by a third party and yet still give rise to an assessment under s 776 if an individual has transferred the opportunity of making a gain to the third party. Moreover, s 776 can apply to one or more transactions which form a scheme and any number of transactions may be regarded as constituting a single arrangement or scheme if a common purpose can be discerned in them, or if there is other sufficient evidence of a common purpose. For a fuller account of s 776, see 20.2.

The main disadvantage for UK-resident individuals who are assessed to income tax on gains from land, either under Schedule D Case I or VI, is that they will not be able to deduct either the indexation allowance or the annual exemption. Also, the fact that gains are assessed as income may mean that the individual cannot make use of capital losses which have been brought forward from earlier years or which have arisen during the same year on other transactions. On the other hand, where an individual has borrowed to acquire the land, he may be able to deduct the interest in calculating the gain for income tax purposes whereas no deduction will normally be available for CGT purposes.

However, the fact that since 6 April 1988 CGT is normally charged at the same rate as income tax means that it is now less common for Inspectors to argue that gains on land transactions should be assessed as income. The main circumstances where the Revenue is likely to argue on these lines is where the individual concerned is a builder or developer or estate agent or has entered into a large number of land transactions or the amounts involved in a particular transaction are substantial.

## 14.10.2 Specific points on computation of gains on transactions involving land
(TCGA 1992, Sched 8)

### Wasting assets

Where a person disposes of a wasting asset, his cost or acquisition value may need to be restricted. This applies where a person disposes of a leasehold interest in land and the lease has less than 50 years to run at the date of disposal. Table 14.2 below shows how the cost of a lease must be adjusted.

## Table 14.2 – Depreciation of leases

| Years | Percentage | Years | Percentage | Years | Percentage |
|---|---|---|---|---|---|
| 50 (or more) | 100 | 33 | 90.280 | 16 | 64.116 |
| 49 | 99.657 | 32 | 89.354 | 15 | 61.617 |
| 48 | 99.289 | 31 | 88.371 | 14 | 58.971 |
| 47 | 98.902 | 30 | 87.330 | 13 | 56.167 |
| 46 | 98.490 | 29 | 86.226 | 12 | 53.191 |
| 45 | 98.059 | 28 | 85.053 | 11 | 50.038 |
| 44 | 97.595 | 27 | 83.816 | 10 | 46.695 |
| 43 | 97.107 | 26 | 82.496 | 9 | 43.154 |
| 42 | 96.593 | 25 | 81.100 | 8 | 39.399 |
| 41 | 96.041 | 24 | 79.622 | 7 | 35.414 |
| 40 | 95.457 | 23 | 78.055 | 6 | 31.195 |
| 39 | 94.842 | 22 | 76.399 | 5 | 26.722 |
| 38 | 94.189 | 21 | 74.635 | 4 | 21.983 |
| 37 | 93.497 | 20 | 72.770 | 3 | 16.959 |
| 36 | 92.761 | 19 | 70.791 | 2 | 11.629 |
| 35 | 91.981 | 18 | 68.697 | 1 | 5.983 |
| 34 | 91.156 | 17 | 66.470 | 0 | 0 |

The fraction of the cost of the lease which is not allowed is given by the fraction

$$\frac{P(1)-P(3)}{P(1)}$$

where

$P(1)$ = the percentage derived from the table for the duration of the lease at acquisition

$P(3)$ = the percentage derived from the table for the duration of the lease at the time of disposal

## Example – Wasting assets

$C$ purchases a 48-year lease in 1986 for £10,000. In 1994 she spends £2,000 on improvements which are affecting the value of the lease. She disposes of it with 36 years left in 1998. Her allowable expenditure is therefore as follows:

Original cost £10,000 $\times \dfrac{(99.289 - 92.761)}{99.289}$ = £657

Additional £2,000 $\times \dfrac{(95.457 - 92.761)}{95.457}$ = £56

£713

Total allowable expenditure = £12,000 – £713 = £11,287

### Enhancement expenditure

It commonly happens that a person has spent money over the years on improvements. This expenditure can be taken into account provided the improvements are reflected in the state of the property when it is sold.

Where such enhancement expenditure occurred after 31 March 1982, the expenditure is added to the acquisition value and attracts indexation allowance from the time that it is incurred.

Enhancement expenditure prior to 31 March 1982 may be taken into account only if the universal rebasing election (see 14.3.2) has not been made and the total of original cost and pre-31 March 1982 enhancement expenditure exceeds the market value at 31 March.

Time apportionment and enhancement expenditure

Where a universal rebasing election has not been made, it may be possible to compute the capital gain on the time apportionment basis (see 14.3.3). This can be difficult where there has also been enhancement expenditure because the overall gain has to be split between the gain on the original cost and the gain relating to the enhancement expenditure. This is an area where professional advice is essential.

## 14.11 HOW THE REVENUE COMPUTES GAINS ON UNQUOTED SHARES

There are some special features to the way in which gains on unquoted shares are computed. Other aspects follow the principles already covered in this chapter. For example, the identification rules where a person disposes of part of a shareholding of unquoted shares are exactly the same as for quoted securities (see 14.7.2).

There are also practical considerations which do not arise in relation to quoted securities such as the need to negotiate a valuation of the shares at 31 March 1982. Retirement relief will also need to be borne in mind (see 15.9–15.11).

In the case of gifts, the value used for CGT purposes is normally the value of the asset taken by the acquirer, not the reduction in value for the person making the disposal. From this point of view, CGT works differently from IHT (see 17.3.3).

### 14.11.1 Shares held at 31 March 1982

Where an individual has made a universal rebasing election (see 14.3.2), the original cost is not relevant and the capital gain is computed only by reference to the value of the shares at 31 March 1982. Even where the election has not been made, it is often fairly clear that the market value at 31 March 1982 will be higher than either original cost or market value at 6 April 1965.

Inevitably, the market value at 31 March 1982 will be the subject of negotiation with the Revenue's Shares Valuation Division and professional advice should be taken. The shares' value will reflect factors such as the nature of the company, its assets and the size of the shareholding.

The general approach adopted by the Shares Valuation Division is to determine the value of the unquoted shares and securities by reference to a completely hypothetical market. It is assumed that any prospective purchaser will have available to him all of the information which a prudent prospective purchaser of the asset might reasonably require if he were proposing to purchase it from a willing vendor by private treaty and at arm's length. Open market value must be assumed and the yardstick is always the requirement of the willing and prudent purchaser and not the wishes etc of the directors of the private company.

The underlying assets of the company are largely irrelevant if a person has only a relatively small minority shareholding; there may be a more important consideration if he has control. Therefore, a quite different valuation might be placed upon shares which form, say, a 7% shareholding which allows the owner to retain control. In the former case the valuers will be looking at factors such as the level of dividends paid in the past and the likelihood of such dividends being paid in the future. At the other extreme, a 51% shareholder would place great value on a $\frac{1}{51}$ part of this shareholding as a disposal of such shares will cause him to lose voting control over the company.

On a practical aspect, it is possible to enter into negotiations with the Revenue in advance of filing your self-assessment tax return. If you wish to reduce any uncertainty to the minimum by trying to agree 31 March 1982 values before filing your return, ask the Revenue for form CG34.

## 14.11.2 Shares held at 6 April 1965

Where a universal rebasing election has not been made it may be possible (and beneficial) for the capital gain to be computed on the time apportionment basis.

### Example – Shares held at 6 April 1965

*B* acquired 1,000 shares in a family company on 1 April 1950 and they were then worth £10,000. He sold his shares on 1 April 2000 for £750,000. Assume for illustration purposes that indexation allowance amounts to £150,000. The capital gain on the time apportionment basis is:

$$\frac{\text{Period since 6 April 1965}}{\text{Overall period of ownership}} \times \text{gain of £600,000 (ie gain after indexation)}$$

The figures work out as follows:

$$\frac{420 \text{ months}}{600 \text{ months}} \times £600,000 = £420,000$$

The £420,000 gain may then be reduced by taper relief (and in some cases by retirement relief – see 15.9–15.11).

THE CALCULATION OF CAPITAL GAINS

### 14.11.3 Situations where time apportionment relief is not available

It is not possible to claim time apportionment relief on the disposal of unquoted shares if there was a capital reorganisation prior to 6 April 1965. A capital reorganisation would include a rights issue or a merger between two companies.

Furthermore, time apportionment relief may be severely restricted where an individual has, since 6 April 1965, transferred or sold a property to a company in which he holds shares. Once again, this is a situation where you should seek professional advice.

### 14.11.4 Retirement relief

This relief is covered in more detail at 15.9. It is frequently relevant to disposals of shares in family trading companies. It is not covered here since there are numerous other conditions which need to be fulfilled and there are therefore many situations where a sale of unquoted shares does not attract the relief (eg where the company concerned is an investment company).

## 14.12 DISPOSAL OF FOREIGN PROPERTY

### 14.12.1 Gains must be computed in sterling

Just as a chargeable gain may arise on the disposal of foreign currency, there may similarly be a currency gain on the disposal of certain foreign assets, such as a house or flat in a foreign country. Where overseas assets are disposed of, it is not correct to calculate the gain or loss in terms of the foreign currency and then convert that gain or loss into sterling at the time of the disposal. Instead, the following formula should be used:

| | |
|---|---|
| Market value of foreign currency received at sale (converted at exchange rate applying at that time) | $v$ |
| Deduct sterling equivalent of cost of asset on acquisition (converted at exchange rate applying at the time of acquisition) | $w$ |
| | $x$ |
| Deduct indexation relief | $y$ |
| Chargeable gain | $z$ |

## Example – Disposal of foreign property

A acquired a property in West Germany in 1984 for DM 1m (exchange rate DM 4 = £1) and sells it in 1998 for DM 1,350,000 (exchange rate DM3 = £1). The gain would be computed as follows:

|  | £ |
|---|---|
| Sale proceeds | 450,000 |
| *Less*: cost | (250,000) |
|  | 200,000 |
| *Less*: indexation on £250,000 – say | (150,000) |
| Chargeable gain | 50,000 |

This can produce some unexpected consequences. Suppose that A had borrowed the purchase price in deutschmarks. When she repaid the mortgage on selling the property, she might well be left with no cash in hand. In fact, the profit on the sale of the property in sterling terms was matched by the increase in the sterling value of her mortgage debt. However, there is no CGT relief for this increase and the gain of £50,000 would still be chargeable.

## 14.12.2 Relief for foreign tax
(TCGA 1992, ss 277–278)

Many overseas countries reserve the right to charge CGT on the disposal of real estate situated in that country, whether or not the owner is resident there. Where a UK resident has had to pay foreign tax in these circumstances, he may claim double tax relief. In effect, the overseas country's tax is available as a credit against the UK tax.

### Example – Relief for foreign tax

B has a property in Italy which cost 160m lire (at the time of purchase this was the equivalent of £90,000). The property is sold for 220m lire and there is a chargeable gain for UK tax purposes of £50,000 (assume that Italian CGT of £7,000 is payable). If B's £50,000 gain was chargeable to tax at 40%, the position would be:

|  | £ |
|---|---|
| UK CGT | 20,000 |
| *Less*: double tax relief | (7,000) |
| UK CGT actually payable | 13,000 |

However, there is no relief for any excess. Thus, if B had unrelieved losses brought forward such that his UK tax had been only £6,500, there would be no relief for the balance.

Sometimes there will be a liability for foreign tax, but no capital gains for UK tax purposes.

### Example – Foreign CGT only

*C* disposes of a property in Sierra Leone at a £40,000 loss in sterling terms. However, there was a gain in terms of local currency and the tax bill in Sierra Leone is £10,000. *C* can claim a deduction for this amount as if it were a deduction from his sale proceeds, and this would mean that his loss for UK CGT purposes would be increased from £40,000 to £50,000.

## 14.12.3 Foreign gains which cannot be remitted
(TCGA 1992, s 279)

Where a person realises a gain on the disposal of assets situated abroad, but is genuinely unable to transfer that gain to the UK because of restrictions imposed abroad or because the foreign currency is not convertible, the amount of the gain may be omitted from assessment for the year in which it arose. Instead, the gain will be assessed to CGT only when it becomes remittable. Claims to this relief have to be made within six years of the year in which the gain was realised.

## 14.13 MAIN RESIDENCE EXEMPTION

Despite the stagnation in house prices over recent years, the largest gain that most people realise is on the sale of their main (or only) residence. This is not surprising as, for the majority of the population, their home is their single largest investment. In the majority of circumstances, this gain is exempt from CGT provided certain conditions are satisfied.

## 14.13.1 Basic conditions which must be satisfied
(TCGA 1992, s 222)

There is a total exemption from CGT where a gain is realised by an individual on the disposal of a property which has been his sole or main residence throughout his period of ownership.

The legislation also provides exemption for land which forms part of the property (the garden or grounds) up to the 'permitted area'. The permitted area will always be at least 0.5 of a hectare (approximately one acre), but may be more where the land is required for the reasonable enjoyment of the property (see 14.13.3).

A married couple who are living together can have the exemption in respect of only one property for a particular period.

### 14.13.2 Occupation test

(TCGA 1992, s 223(3); Statement of Practice D4)

A delay of up to 12 months between a property being acquired and the owner taking up residence does not prejudice the exemption; the property is still treated as if it were his main residence. The 12-month period can be extended by up to a further 12 months if it can be shown that there were good reasons for the owner not taking up residence, such as the need to carry out alterations or building work, or there was an unavoidable delay in the owner being able to dispose of his previous residence.

The last three years of ownership are treated as qualifying for the exemption, whether the owner lives in the property or not, provided the property has previously been his main residence.

### 14.13.3 The permitted area

The legislation also provides exemption for a larger area of gardens or grounds than 0.5 hectare if it can be shown that it was 'required for the reasonable enjoyment' of the property as a residence. If the taxpayer and the Inspector cannot agree on this, the matter can be determined by the Commissioners.

Relevant factors here include considerations such as the extent to which other similar properties have gardens or grounds larger than 0.5 hectare, the need for an area of land to provide either privacy or a buffer between the property and (for example) a motorway and the need to have room for other facilities and amenities which are appropriate to the property.

The last-mentioned factor is often the most difficult to argue with the Revenue, which relies on a judgment by Du Parcq J in a 1937 compulsory purchase case, the so-called *Newhill* case [1938] 2 All ER 163:

> 'Required' . . . does not mean merely that the occupiers of the house would like to have it, or that they would miss it if they lost it, or that anyone proposing to buy the house would think less of the house without it . . . 'Required' means, I suppose, that without it there will be such a substantial deprivation of amenities or convenience that a real injury will be done to the property owner . . .

The Revenue's interpretation is not free from doubt, as the CGT legislation is worded differently from the compulsory purchase legislation, and the question has not yet been considered by the courts. This is an area where it is essential to take professional advice.

### 14.13.4 What is the residence?

There have been several cases which concerned a property where part of the premises were occupied by servants.

In *Batey v Wakefield* [1981] STC 521 the property consisted of the main house and a caretaker's lodge. The lodge was occupied (rent free) by the caretaker/gardener and his wife who was the owner's housekeeper. The main house and the lodge were separated by the width of a tennis court. The Court of Appeal upheld the taxpayer's claim that his residence consisted of the main house and all related buildings which were part and parcel of the property and were occupied for the purposes of the owner's residence.

At the other extreme, in *Lewis v Rook* [1992] STC 171 the Court of Appeal decided against a taxpayer who claimed the exemption should cover a gardener's cottage which was located some 170 metres away and which was not within the same curtilage as the taxpayer's house. Following that decision, the Revenue said that the exemption cannot apply to a separate building at all, regardless of how close it is to the house occupied by the owner.

This is another area where specialist advice should be taken if substantial sums are involved. The Revenue has set out its views in *Tax Bulletin* August 1994.

## 14.14 POSSIBLE RESTRICTIONS ON EXEMPTION

### 14.14.1 Part of property used for business purposes
(TCGA 1992, s 224(1))

If part of the property has been used exclusively for the purposes of a trade or business or a profession or vocation, the exemption does not cover the part of the gain attributable to that part. This restriction does not apply where the relevant rooms are used partly for business and partly for personal reasons. For example, if a journalist's living room doubles up as a work room from which he carries on business as a journalist, there will be no restriction under this provision.

### 14.14.2 Part of the property let out
(TCGA 1992, s 223(4))

Where the owner has let out part of his home, there may be a similar restriction. Thus, if the owner had let approximately one-third of her home, the exemption would normally be confined to two-thirds of the gain on disposal. However, the normal rule may be overridden if the lettings are as residential accommodation. The gain on the part of the property let out in this way may still be exempt up to the lesser of:

(1) the exemption on the part of the property occupied by the owner; and
(2) £40,000.

Where a husband and wife own a property jointly each of them can claim an exemption of up to £40,000 against their share of the gain.

## 14.14.3 Expenditure incurred with a view to gain
(TCGA 1992, s 224(3))

The exemption is not available if a gain arises from the purchase of property which was made wholly or partly for the purpose of realising a gain.

### Example – Expenditure with a view to gain

> *C* is a partner and has lived in a flat owned by his firm. He is offered the opportunity to buy it for £75,000 and he accepts because he knows that he will be able fairly quickly to find a buyer at £120,000. He realises a gain of £45,000. The Revenue is likely to argue that the gain is a chargeable gain because of s 224(3). Similarly, a person who holds a leasehold interest and who acquires the freehold because it will enable a better price to be obtained may suffer a restriction under s 224(3) if the Revenue can show that this was the only purpose of buying the freehold.

Some guidance on the circumstances in which the Revenue may seek to deny exemption on these grounds is contained in *Tax Bulletin* August 1994.

## 14.14.4 Sale of part of gardens

Special care is needed if it is decided to sell surplus land for development. In *Varty v Lynes* [1976] STC 508 the taxpayer had owned and occupied a house and the garden was less than one acre (the permitted area at that time). He sold the house and part of the garden in June 1971. Slightly less than 12 months later, he sold the rest of the garden to a builder and realised a substantial gain because he had secured planning permission in the meantime. He was assessed on the gain on the land sold to the builder and the High Court decided that the main residence exemption did not apply. Brightman J held that the exemption for the garden or grounds could apply only in relation to garden or grounds occupied as such by the owner at the date of sale. The Revenue has subsequently stated that it will invoke this only where land is sold with development value. The following principles should be borne in mind:

(1) A sale of land out of a parcel of land greater than 0.5 hectare may be vulnerable even where the owner remains in occupation. The fact that the owner continues to live in the property suggests that the surplus land was not required for the reasonable enjoyment of the property.
(2) A sale of land with development value at the same time as the owner ceases to live in the property is not open to attack in the same way as in *Varty v Lynes*.
(3) A sale of land with development value after the owner has moved out is likely to result in a tax charge.

### 14.14.5 What happens where there are two homes?

An individual may live in more than one property without necessarily owning both properties. The Revenue view is that a person has two residences if, for example, he owns a large house in Gloucestershire and rents a modest flat in Central London where he lives during the week.

If necessary, the Commissioners decide which of an individual's two or more residences is his main residence. The test is not necessarily where the individual lives most of the time, and it is often not clear in a particular case what view the Commissioners might take.

### 14.14.6 Taxpayer's right of election
(TCGA 1992, s 222(5))

Fortunately, the owner is able to settle the matter by formally electing that one property be treated as his main residence. The election may be varied from time to time, but only in relation to the last two years prior to the variation.

There is a time limit for a notice under s 222(5) of two years. The Revenue view has been that the time limit refers to the point in time that the individual starts to have a second residence. This interpretation was upheld by the High Court in *Griffin v Craig Harvey* [1994] STC 54.

There is one circumstance where the Revenue will accept an election outside the two-year time limit. ESC D21 provides that:

> Where for any period an individual has more than one residence, but his interest in each of them, or in each of them except one, is such as to have no more than a negligible capital value on the open market (for example a weekly rented flat or accommodation provided by an employer) the two-year time limit will be extended where the individual was unaware that such a nomination could be made. In such cases the nomination may be made within a reasonable time of the individual becoming aware of the possibility of so doing, and it will be regarded as effective from the date on which the individual first had more than one residence.

## 14.15 LIVING IN JOB-RELATED ACCOMMODATION

### 14.15.1 Meaning of job-related accommodation

Job-related accommodation is defined as accommodation provided for an individual or his spouse by reason of his employment where:

(1) it is necessary for the proper performance of his duties that he should live there; or

(2) it is provided for the better performance of his duties and the employment is one where employers customarily provide accommodation; or

(3) the accommodation is provided as part of the special security arrangements for the employee's safety.

## 14.15.2 **Right to nominate a property**
(TCGA 1992, s 222(8))

Where an individual is required to live in job-related accommodation, a house owned by him and intended to be occupied as his residence in due course is treated as if it were his residence. Such a house may therefore qualify for exemption even if the owner had let it and never actually occupied it himself before disposing of it, provided that he nominates it as his only or main residence.

## 14.15.3 **Similar provisions for self-employed individuals**

A self-employed individual who is required to live at or near his place of work (for example, a publican) can nominate a property under s 222(8) for eventual use as his main residence. This also applies if the individual's spouse is required to occupy such premises. Only periods after 5 April 1982 can qualify under this heading.

# 14.16 TREATMENT WHERE PROPERTY HAS NOT BEEN OCCUPIED THROUGHOUT

## 14.16.1 **Proportion of gain may be exempt**

The exemption under s 222 is not necessarily an 'all or nothing' test. The legislation makes provision for a proportion of the capital gain to be exempt where the necessary conditions are satisfied for part of the period of ownership. The exempt proportion of the gain is normally:

$$\frac{\text{Period of qualifying use}}{\text{Total period of ownership}} \times \text{ indexed gain}$$

## 14.16.2 **Periods prior to 31 March 1982 ignored**

A period of non-qualifying use is ignored if it is prior to 31 March 1982.

### Example – Incomplete period of occupation

A property was acquired in March 1975 and let as an investment until March 1984. Thereafter it is the owner's sole residence. It is sold in March 2000 for a gain of £340,000. The exempt proportion of the gain would be:

$$^{16}\!/_{18} \times £340,000 \quad = \quad £302,222$$

## 14.16.3 **Last 36 months of ownership**
(TCGA 1992, s 223(2))

Provided that the property has at some time qualified as the owner's main residence, the last three years of ownership will also qualify for exemption.

This still applies if the property is let or another property is nominated as his main residence for all or part of that period. It also applies even where the period when the property was occupied as the individual's main residence was before 31 March 1982.

The period was 24 months for disposals prior to 19 March 1991. The three-year period may be cut back in the future if the housing market improves.

### 14.16.4 Periods spent working abroad
(TCGA 1992, s 223(3)(b))

If, during a period when the owner's property was used as his main residence, the owner has to work abroad, the property will continue to be regarded as the owner's main residence (and therefore exempt from CGT) if the owner was employed abroad under a contract of employment and all the duties of the employment were performed overseas. The condition requiring the property to be the owner's only or main residence after working abroad is treated as satisfied if the individual is unable to resume residence because the terms of his new employment require him to work elsewhere (ESC D4).

### 14.16.5 Periods spent working elsewhere in UK

A period of up to four years during which the owner's employment necessitated his living elsewhere in the UK is also a qualifying period. A period (or periods) which in total exceed four years is covered to the extent of four years. Again, it is normally necessary that the period be followed by a period of occupation, but ESC D4 applies if the individual cannot resume occupation because his current employment prevents this.

### 14.16.6 Other periods which can qualify

A further period of absence of up to three years can be treated as qualifying for exemption, provided the period is both preceded and succeeded by a period of actual occupation.

### 14.16.7 Summary

Table 14.3 may help in computing the position in a particular case. The exempt gain is (X) + (Y).

### 14.16.8 Dependent relatives
(TCGA 1992, s 226)

In addition to the main residence exemption, an individual may qualify for exemption in respect of a property occupied by a dependent relative as his or her main residence provided the property was so occupied before 6 April 1988. To qualify for this exemption, the property must have been occupied by the dependent relative rent free, and without any other consideration.

A widowed mother (or mother-in-law) is automatically regarded as a dependent relative. In other situations, the relative is regarded as dependent only if prevented by old age or infirmity from maintaining himself or herself. The exemption is not available for a property acquired after 5 April 1988, even if the property is a replacement for another property previously occupied by a dependent relative.

In some cases, it may be appropriate to form a settlement with the trustees owning the property occupied by the dependent relative as the trustees may still qualify for exemption in respect of a property occupied by a beneficiary as his or her main residence (see 18.4.10).

## Table 14.3 – Computation of exempt gain on a main residence

| | |
|---|---|
| Number of complete months since 31 March 1982 when the property was actually occupied as the owner's main residence. See 14.13.2 | (A) |
| The lesser of 36 months or such part of the last 36 months which does not already fall within A (24 months for disposals prior to 19 March 1991). See 14.16.3 | (B) |
| Months spent working abroad when the property was not occupied as the individual's main residence provided that the individual resumed residence after his overseas employment ceased or would have done so if he had not been required to take up employment elsewhere in the UK. Note exclude any period which already falls to be included in B above. See 14.16.4· | (C) |
| Number of months spent living elsewhere because the individual's employment required him to live in another part of the UK (subject to a maximum of 48 months). Again, exclude any period already included in B. Note, an entry is appropriate here only if the individual resumed occupation of the property at the end of the period. See 14.16.5 | (D) |
| Any further period of absence which was both preceded and succeeded by the individual occupying the property as his main residence (subject to a maximum of 36 months). Again exclude any period already included in B. See 14.16.6 | (E) |
| Apply the following fraction to the overall gain which arose on the disposal of the property: $$\frac{A + B + C + D + E}{\text{months of ownership since 31 March 1982}}$$ | (X) |
| A further exemption may also be due where the property has been let. The additional exemption is the lesser of X or £40,000. See 14.14.2 | (Y) |

# 15

# CAPITAL GAINS TAX AND BUSINESS TRANSACTIONS

ROGER BLEASBY

This chapter focuses on the CGT aspects of various business transactions. It deals with the following matters:

(1) Loans to private businesses.
(2) Losses on unquoted shares.
(3) What is a business asset for taper relief purposes?
(4) Relief for replacement of business assets.
(5) Roll-over relief for reinvestment in unquoted shares.
(6) Hold-over relief for gifts of business property.
(7) Partnerships and capital gains.
(8) Transfer of a business to a company.
(9) Retirement relief – general provisions.
(10) Retirement relief and unincorporated traders.
(11) Retirement relief and full-time directors or employees.

## 15.1 LOANS TO PRIVATE BUSINESSES

A very common type of transaction is a loan to a sole trader or partnership (an 'unincorporated business') or to a private company. Almost as common are situations where a person gives a guarantee to a bank etc which makes a loan to a business. This section deals with the CGT position if a loan becomes written off or a person is required to make a payment under a bank guarantee that he has given.

### 15.1.1 Loans to unincorporated businesses
(TCGA 1992, s 253)

A CGT loss may be deemed to arise if the Revenue is satisfied that a loan has become irrecoverable. There are various conditions which need to be fulfilled:

(1) the borrower must not be the lender's spouse;

(2)  the borrower must be resident in the UK;

(3)  the borrower must have used the loan wholly for the purposes of a trade carried on by him. The trade must not have been a trade which consists of (or includes) lending money.

When a claim is submitted, the Inspector must satisfy himself that any outstanding amount of the loan is irrecoverable and that the lender has not assigned or waived his right to recover the loan.

Strictly speaking, relief is due only when a claim is made and admitted but, in practice, the Revenue permits claims to be made within two years of a year of assessment provided the other conditions were satisfied at the end of that year of assessment (ESC D36).

The allowable loss is restricted to the amount of the loan which is irrecoverable; there is no indexation relief in these circumstances (and this has always been the case, even where the disposal took place before 30 November 1993).

## 15.1.2  Loans to companies
(TCGA 1992, ss 253 and 254)

Similar provisions apply where a person has made a loan to a company which proves to be irrecoverable. The principal conditions which need to be satisfied are:

(1)  the company must be UK-resident;

(2)  it must be a trading company;

(3)  the lender must not be a company which is a member of the same group of companies.

In all other respects, the relief normally applies exactly as described in 15.1.1.

### Loan notes and debentures

There is an additional complication which may apply to a loss on a loan which constitutes a 'debt on a security'. A debt on a security is a special type of loan. In broad terms, such loans are usually evidenced by a debenture deed and are transferable, a typical example being a loan stock.

If a loan falls into this category, it is then necessary to ascertain whether it also falls into another sub-class, ie whether it is a qualifying corporate bond (see 13.3.2(9)). If it is a qualifying corporate bond then relief can be due as set out in 15.1.1 provided the disposal took place before 6 April 1998. No loss relief is available where the disposal of a qualifying corporate bond takes place after 5 April 1998. However, losses on other debts on security continue to attract relief.

### 15.1.3 **Payments under loan guarantees**
(TCGA 1992, s 253(4))

Instead of lending money to a relative or friend or his private company, a person may have given a guarantee to a bank etc. Similarly, a director of a company may have had to give personal guarantees in respect of bank loans to his company.

Where the borrower cannot repay the loan, the bank will call on the guarantor to pay the amount due. In these circumstances, the guarantor may be able to claim a CGT loss as if he had made a loan which was irrecoverable. The following conditions need to be satisfied for relief to be claimed in this way:

(1) payment has been made under a guarantee;
(2) the payment should arise from a formal calling in of the guarantee – a voluntary payment attracts no relief;
(3) the original loan met the requirements listed in 15.1.1;
(4) the amount paid under the guarantee cannot be recovered either from the borrower or from a co-guarantor.

## 15.2 LOSSES ON UNQUOTED SHARES
(TA 1988, s 574)

From time to time, an individual may invest in a private company, either as a working director/shareholder or perhaps as a 'passive' investor with a minority shareholding. Investments may also be made in companies which, whilst they are technically public companies as defined by the Companies Act, are not quoted companies.

### 15.2.1 **Special relief for subscribers**

A loss may arise on a disposal of shares in such a company. If the investor acquired existing shares by purchasing them, the loss is a normal CGT loss and the only way in which it can be relieved is as set out in 13.1.3. However, if the individual acquired his shares by subscribing for new shares, it may be possible to obtain income tax relief for the loss. Subject to certain conditions, the capital loss may be off-set against the individual's income for the year in which the loss is realised.

The following conditions need to be satisfied:

(1) First, the loss must arise from one of the following:
    (a) a sale made at arm's length for full consideration (this rules out a sale to a connected person); or
    (b) a disposal which takes place when the company is wound up; or
    (c) a deemed disposal where the shares have become of negligible value.

(2) Secondly, there are conditions which attach to the company itself. In particular:
   (a) the company must not have been a quoted company at any time during the individual's period of ownership; the fact that any class of shares has had a Stock Exchange quote rules out relief under s 574 even though the loss may have arisen on a class of share which did not have a quote;
   (b) the company must be a trading company, or the holding company of a trading group, at the date of disposal or it must have ceased to have been a trading company not more than three years prior to the date of disposal and it must not have been an investment company since that date;
   (c) the company's trade must not have consisted wholly or mainly of dealing in shares, securities, land, trades or commodity futures (further restrictions apply in relation to shares issued after 6 April 1998 so that the company must have met the conditions necessary to qualify for EIS relief; see 11.6);
   (d) the company's trade must have been carried on on a commercial basis.

## 15.2.2 Relief also available for subscriber's spouse

The spouse of a person who subscribed for shares may also claim relief under s 574 where he has acquired the shares in question through an *inter vivos* transfer from his spouse. However, shares which are acquired on the death of a spouse do not entitle the widow(er) to s 574 relief on a subsequent disposal.

## 15.2.3 Nature of relief

The loss is calculated according to normal CGT principles. If the loss is eligible for relief under s 574, the individual may elect within two years for the loss to be set against his taxable income. The loss may be set either against the individual's taxable income for the year of the loss, or his taxable income for the preceding year. Either claim may be made independently of the other. Where an individual has losses which are available for relief under s 574 and he is also entitled to relief for trading losses, he can choose which losses should be relieved in priority to the other.

Any part of the capital loss which cannot be relieved under s 574 can be carried forward for off-set against capital gains in the normal way.

## 15.3  WHAT IS A BUSINESS ASSET FOR TAPER RELIEF PURPOSES?

### 15.3.1  Rules for disposals between 6 April 1998 and 5 April 2000

As explained at 14.6, taper relief may reduce a chargeable gain realised after 5 April 1998. The rate of taper relief depends on whether the asset which has been sold is regarded as a business asset. A business asset is defined broadly as:

(1)  an asset used for the purposes of a trade carried on by the individual (either alone or in partnership) or by a qualifying company of that individual;

(2)  an asset held for the purposes of a qualifying office or employment to which that individual was required to devote substantially the whole of his time; or

(3)  shares in a qualifying company held by the individual.

A company is a qualifying company if it is a trading company or a holding company of a trading group, and the individual holds shares which entitle him to exercise at least:

(1)  5% of the voting rights in that company and the individual is a full-time working officer or employee of that company; or

(2)  25% of the voting rights in that company.

A company may be regarded as not being a trading company if a significant proportion of its assets are investments. This is an area where specialist advice should be sought.

The rules for business assets are extended to assets held by trustees and personal representatives (see 18.10). The status of an asset as a business asset is not jeopardised by the owner charging rent (eg where he lets premises to a qualifying company for use in its trade).

Where an asset has been used partly as a business asset and partly as a non-business asset the gain on the asset's disposal will be apportioned pro rata. Part of the gain will qualify for the business asset taper relief and the other part for the non-business asset taper relief. A switch to non-business asset use during the last ten years of ownership will always adversely affect the taper.

### Example of mixed use

> *A* has owned office premises since 1 January 1998. He rented the offices out until 5 April 2000, and then used them for his own business until 6 April 2001 when he sells them and realises a capital gain of £300,000. The gain will be split as follows:

**Non-business use:**

Period from 6 April 1998 to 5 April 2000 (⅔) =   £200,000
Qualifying period for taper relief is four years (including the bonus year), taper relief on this part of the gain is therefore 10%.

**Business use:**

Period from 6 April 2000 to 5 April 2001 (⅓) =   £100,000
Qualifying period for taper relief is four years (no bonus year), taper relief on this part of the gain is therefore 50%.

## 15.3.2 New rules from 6 April 2000

### Definition of business assets

The definition of business assets has been widened considerably with effect from 6 April 2000. All shareholdings in unquoted trading companies will rank as business assets (AIM will count as unquoted). Furthermore, all shares in quoted trading companies that are held by employees qualify whether the employee works full- or part-time.

Other individuals who hold shares in quoted trading companies will qualify for the business rate of taper relief provided that they hold at least 5% of the voting rights. This also covers trustees who hold a 5% interest.

Where shares did not qualify under the old rules, a capital gain will be time apportioned and business relief will apply only to the post-5 April 2000 proportion of the gain.

## 15.4  RELIEF FOR REPLACEMENT OF BUSINESS ASSETS
(TCGA 1992, ss 152–160)

Relief may be available where a person sells an asset which is used by him in a trade (or in certain circumstances, an asset which is used by his family company) and reinvests in replacement assets used for business purposes. This relief is termed 'roll-over' relief.

### 15.4.1 Nature of roll-over relief

A gain is said to be rolled over in that it is not charged to tax, but is deducted from the person's acquisition cost of the new assets. Note that the rolled-over gain is that which arises before taper relief.

### Example – Roll-over relief

A sells a farm for £450,000. His capital gain is £200,000. He starts up a new business and invests £500,000 in a warehouse. By claiming roll-over relief, A avoids having to pay tax on the gain of £200,000. The acquisition cost of his warehouse is reduced as follows:

|  | £ |
|---|---|
| Actual cost | 500,000 |
| *Less*: rolled-over gain | (200,000) |
| Deemed acquisition cost | 300,000 |

The relief is really a form of deferment since a larger gain will arise on a subsequent disposal of the replacement asset.

## 15.4.2 Conditions which need to be satisfied

The asset that has been disposed of must have been used in a business and must have fallen into one of the following categories:

(1) land and buildings;
(2) fixed plant and machinery;
(3) ships;
(4) goodwill;
(5) milk and potato quotas;
(6) aircraft;
(7) hovercraft, satellites and spacecraft;
(8) Lloyd's syndicate rights ('capacity');
(9) ewe and suckler cow premium quotas and fish quota.

The replacement asset must also fall into one of these categories.

It is not possible to claim roll-over relief on the disposal of shares in a family company, nor is it possible to claim s 152 relief for expenditure on such shares on the basis that this is replacement expenditure.

The replacement asset must normally be acquired within a period starting one year before the date of the disposal of the original asset and ending three years after the date of disposal. The time limit can be extended (at the Revenue's discretion) if the acquisition of the replacement asset within three years was not possible because of circumstances outside the person's control.

### Example – Full relief available only where all the sale proceeds are reinvested
(TCGA 1992, s 152(3)–(11))

Using the same figures as in 15.4.1, *A* sells his farm for £450,000, making the same capital gain of £200,000. He starts up a new business but invests only £400,000 in the new warehouse. The part of the £450,000 disposal consideration for the farm which is not applied in acquiring the warehouse is £50,000. This is less than the gain which arose on the disposal of the farm and the balance of the gain may be rolled over. The acquisition value of the warehouse is reduced by £150,000.

## 15.4.3 Old assets not used for business throughout ownership

If the old asset was not used for business throughout the period of ownership, s 152 applies as if a part of the asset used for the purposes of the trade was a separate asset to that which had not been wholly used for the purposes of the trade.

### Example – Old assets

In April 1999, *B* sells a warehouse for a gain, after taper relief has been calculated, of £50,000. It had originally been bought in April 1991 but had been used in his trade only since April 1993. The amount of gain which can be rolled over into the purchase of a new asset is calculated as follows:

$$\text{Chargeable gain £50,000} \quad \times \quad \frac{\text{period of trading use of old asset}}{\text{period of ownership}}$$

This equals £50,000 × %, ie £37,500. The balance of £12,500 (£50,000 – £37,500) is a chargeable gain.

## 15.4.4 Treatment where replacement assets are wasting assets
(TCGA 1992, s 154)

The roll-over relief is modified where the replacement expenditure consists of the purchase of a wasting asset (an asset with an expected useful life of less than 50 years) or an asset which will become a wasting asset within ten years. Plant and machinery is always considered to have a useful life of less than 50 years. Furthermore, the acquisition of a lease with less than 60 years to run will also constitute the acquisition of a wasting asset. Rather paradoxically, the goodwill of a business is not regarded as a wasting asset.

The capital gain in these circumstances is not deferred indefinitely, but becomes chargeable on the first of the following occasions:

(1) the disposal of the replacement asset; or

(2) the asset ceasing to be used in the business; or

(3) the expiry of ten years.

### Examples – Roll-over relief on wasting assets

> (1) *B* sells a factory and reinvests in a 59-year lease of a warehouse which he uses in his business. In the sixth year the warehouse is let as an investment property. The rolled-over gain would become chargeable in year six.
>
> (2) *C* also rolls over into a 59-year lease. He is still using the property after ten years, but because it has become a wasting asset within that period, the rolled-over gain becomes chargeable in year ten.

## 15.4.5 Reinvestment in non-wasting assets

On the other hand, if the person acquires new non-wasting replacement assets during the ten years, the capital gain which was originally rolled over into the purchase of the wasting assets can be transferred to the new replacement assets. Assume in example (1) above that *B* had bought the goodwill of a business in year five. He could transfer his roll-over relief claim to the new asset. No gain would then become chargeable in year six when he lets the warehouse.

## 15.4.6 Furnished holiday lettings

A property acquired for letting as furnished holiday accommodation (see 4.5) may qualify for roll-over relief and gains from the disposal of such properties may be rolled over.

## 15.4.7 Assets used by a partnership
### (Statement of Practice D11)

Roll-over relief can be secured where the replacement assets are used by a partnership in which the owner is a partner.

## 15.4.8 Assets used by a family company
### (TCGA 1992, s 157)

Relief can also be obtained where an individual disposes of a property etc which is used by his 'personal trading company', but only if the replacement asset is acquired by him and is used by the same company. A company is an individual's personal trading company if he personally owns at least 5% of the voting shares.

The individual need not be a director of the company, indeed he need not even be employed by it. Also, roll-over relief is not lost because he has charged the company rent (contrast the position for retirement relief, see 15.12.3).

### 15.4.9 Assets owned by an employee or office-holder

An employee or office-holder may claim roll-over relief where he disposes of an asset used in the employment. This condition may apply to a person such as a sub-postmaster who has an 'office' for tax purposes, but who generally owns the sub-post office premises. For further details, see SP5/86.

There are circumstances where these provisions can mean that a director of a family company who has sold an asset used by one company and bought new assets used by another family company is entitled to roll-over relief. However, this is a difficult area where professional advice is essential.

## 15.5 ROLL-OVER RELIEF FOR REINVESTMENT IN UNQUOTED SHARES
(TCGA 1992, s 164A)

Reinvestment relief made it possible for individuals and trustees to roll-over gains by reinvesting in ordinary shares in a qualifying unquoted trading company. The relief was abolished with effect from 6 April 1998 although similar relief can be available under the new Enterprise Investment Scheme (see 11.6).

Reinvestment had to take place within a period beginning one year before and ending three years after the disposal which had given rise to the capital gain. Most trustees were eligible for reinvestment relief. The main exclusion was where some of the beneficiaries of the trust were not individuals.

### 15.5.1 Qualifying companies

A company was a qualifying company only if it did not carry on a prohibited business (see below).

The fact that a company's shares were dealt in on the AIM did not mean that it was a quoted company and such shares could qualify. However, not all AIM companies carried on a qualifying trade.

Reinvestment relief was not available if the company was a subsidiary of another company. If the company had subsidiaries, it had to hold at least 75% of the subsidiaries' share capital. The company did not need to be a UK company but if it was a foreign company it had to carry on its business wholly or mainly in the UK.

Finally, reinvestment relief was not available where an individual had disposed of shares in a company and reinvests in the same company or in a subsidiary of it whose shares he had sold to realise his original capital gain.

### Table 15.1 – Prohibited activities of a company for reinvestment relief

(1) dealing in land, in commodities or futures or in shares, securities or other financial instruments;

(2) dealing in goods otherwise than in the course of any ordinary trade of wholesale or retail distribution;

(3) banking, insurance, money-lending, debt factoring, hire-purchase financing or other financial activities;

(4) leasing (including letting ships on charter or other assets on hire) or receiving royalties or licence fees;

(5) providing legal or accountancy services;

(6) providing services or facilities for any trade carried on by another person (other than a parent company) which consists to any substantial extent of activities within any of (1)–(5) above and in which a controlling interest is held by a person who also has a controlling interest in the trade carried on by the company.

*Note.* Property development and farming were also prohibited activities up to 29 November 1994.

## 15.5.2 Clawback of relief

The relief is clawed back where a company ceases to meet the qualifying conditions within three years of the reinvestment unless the company becomes quoted in which case the company's relevant period comes to an end. The mere fact that the company becomes quoted does not cause the relief to be withdrawn.

A clawback may also arise where the individual who has qualified for reinvestment relief ceases to be resident in the UK within the three-year period.

The gain which has been covered by reinvestment relief is clawed back by being brought into charge as if it were a gain arising at the point in time when the company breached one of the conditions or, where the individual emigrates, immediately prior to his becoming non-UK resident.

## 15.6 HOLD-OVER RELIEF FOR GIFTS OF BUSINESS PROPERTY
(TCGA 1992, s 165)

## 15.6.1 Background and nature of hold-over relief

Under the legislation which applied up to 5 April 1989, a UK-resident individual could transfer any asset to another UK-resident person on a no gain/no loss basis by claiming hold-over relief.

**HELP SHEET IR295**

*For the Capital Gains Pages*

## Claim for hold-over relief - Sections 165 and 260 TCGA 1992

**Transferor**

Name

Address

Tax Office

Tax reference

**Transferee**

Name

Address

Tax Office

Tax reference

Except in case of a gift in settlement, the claim must be made by both transferor and transferee. If the transferor or transferee has no Tax Office or reference please explain why.

We/I hereby claim relief under Section 165 / Section 260 TCGA 1992 in respect of the transfer of the asset specified below. The particulars given in this claim are correctly stated to the best of my/our information and belief.

Description of asset and date of disposal

one box

The gain held over is £ ___ A calculation is attached ☐

We apply for deferment of valuations and have completed the second page of the claim form. ☐

**We qualify for relief because**

one box

- the asset is used for the business of _____ ☐
  *Please insert name of person*
- the asset consists of unlisted shares or securities of a trading company or holding company of a trading group ☐

- the asset is agricultural land ☐

- the asset consists of listed shares or securities of the transferor's personal company or, where trustees are the transferors, a company in which they had 25% of the voting rights ☐

- the disposal was a chargeable transfer, but not a Potentially Exempt Transfer, for Inheritance Tax purposes ☐

- the disposal was exempt from Inheritance Tax under IHTA Section _____ ☐
  *Please insert Section number*

Signed _____ Signed _____

Date / / Date / /

### Example – Hold-over relief

B transferred shares in X plc to her brother C in 1988. They were both resident in the UK. B's shares were worth £29,000 and her capital gain would normally have been £13,000. By claiming hold-over relief, B could avoid having a chargeable gain of £13,000. C's acquisition value was then taken as:

|  | £ |
|---|---|
| Market value at acquisition | 29,000 |
| *Less*: held-over capital gain | (13,000) |
|  | 16,000 |

Hold-over relief was abolished in 1989 for gifts of most types of assets. However, the same type of hold-over relief can still be claimed on gifts of business property to a UK-resident person.

## 15.6.2 Definition of business property

Business property is defined for these purposes as:

(1) an asset used by the transferor in a trade, profession or vocation;
(2) an asset used by the transferor's family company in a trade;
(3) an asset used for a trade by a subsidiary of the transferor's family company;
(4) unquoted shares in a trading company;
(5) quoted shares if the company concerned is the transferor's family company (it will be very unusual for this condition to be satisfied);
(6) agricultural land which qualifies for the IHT agricultural property relief.

Hold-over relief cannot be claimed in respect of a gift of shares or securities to a UK company where the gift took place after 8 November 1999. The relief can, however, be claimed on a gift of an unincorporated business.

## 15.6.3 Claiming the relief

You should obtain a copy of Helpsheet IR295, which incorporates an election which needs to be signed by the donor and donee (see opposite).

## 15.7 PARTNERSHIPS AND CAPITAL GAINS

The way in which CGT affects partnership transactions can at times be complex. If you are a partner you should familiarise yourself with SP D12 – and take regular professional advice. The following section describes some key aspects.

### 15.7.1 Partnership's acquisition value

Although individual partners' entitlement to profits may vary over the years, the partnership's acquisition value for the firm's chargeable assets is not affected unless there are cash payments from one partner to another to acquire a greater interest in the firm or unless assets are revalued as part of the arrangements for changes in profit-sharing.

### 15.7.2 Assets held by the firm at 31 March 1982

The partnership may make a universal rebasing election for the values at 31 March 1982 to be used instead of cost (see 14.3.2). This is quite separate from the individual partners' position in relation to their personal assets when a disposal of an asset takes place. There may be partners who were not in the partnership at 31 March 1982, but this does not affect the computation of the gain.

### 15.7.3 Partnership gains divisible among the partners

Where a partnership asset is sold at a capital gain (or loss), the gain is divided amongst the partners in accordance with their profit-sharing ratios. Each partner is personally assessable on his share of the gain.

The partner's actual CGT liability depends upon his own situation, ie whether he has other gains for the year, has available losses, can claim roll-over relief or is entitled to retirement relief (see 15.9).

### 15.7.4 Revaluations and retirement and introduction of new partners

Problems may arise where a partnership has substantial assets which are chargeable assets for CGT purposes and which are worth more than their book value (ie the value at which they are shown in the firm's accounts). A revaluation to bring the book value of the assets into line with their market value can produce a liability for individual partners if there is a reduction in their profit-sharing ratios. This commonly happens when existing partners retire or new partners are introduced.

#### Example – Retirement of partner

A is a partner in a five partner firm and is entitled to 20% of the profits. He retires and his colleagues then share profits on the basis of 25% each. As part of the arrangements for his retirement, the book value of the firm's office block is increased from £150,000 to its current value of £750,000. The surplus is credited to each partner's account so that A is credited with £120,000.

A is treated as if he had realised a gain on the disposal of a one-fifth share of the building. This would be based on the £120,000. The remaining four partners are not treated as having made a disposal. Indeed, they each have made an acquisition of a 5% interest in the building for an outlay of £30,000.

### Example – Introduction of new partner

B and C are partners. Their premises are included in their firm's balance sheet at £200,000 (original cost), but are actually worth £500,000. B and C agree to admit D as an equal partner in return for his paying new capital into the firm of £700,000. They revalue the premises before admitting D as a partner, and the surplus of £300,000 is credited to their accounts. In this case, B and C will each be regarded as having made a disposal of a one-sixth interest in the premises. This is because D's new capital will go into the firm as a whole. After coming in, he effectively owns one-third of all the assets (and is responsible for one-third of the liabilities).

The former partners' ownership of the premises has been reduced from 50% to a one-third interest.

## 15.7.5 Retirement and introduction of partners with no revaluation of assets

There is no such problem where partners leave or come in and there is no revaluation of assets. In such a case, the remaining or incoming partners normally take over the outgoing partners' acquisition values for the firm's asset.

### Example – Change of partners with no revaluation of assets

A and B are in partnership. They own premises which have a book value of £94,000 (equal to cost in 1980). A retires and is replaced by C. The premises are not revalued. Later the premises are sold for £244,000. B and C are assessed on their share of the gain.

The gain will be computed by reference to the original cost (£94,000) or the premises' market value at 31 March 1982, not their value at the time that C became a partner. This does not apply where the partners are connected persons (perhaps because they are relatives), or where cash payments are made to acquire an interest in the firm. In either of these categories you should seek specialist advice.

## 15.8 TRANSFER OF A BUSINESS TO A COMPANY
(TCGA 1992, s 162)

Where a person transfers a business to a company (ie he 'incorporates the business'), there is a disposal of the assets which are transferred to the company. Not all the assets will necessarily be chargeable assets for CGT purposes, but a gain may arise on assets such as land, buildings and goodwill. Fortunately, there is a relief which may cover such situations.

## 15.8.1 Nature of relief

The main relief applies only where a business is transferred to a company in return for an issue of shares to the former proprietors of the business. Where the necessary conditions are satisfied so that s 162 relief is available, the gains which would otherwise arise on the transfer of chargeable assets are rolled-over into the cost of the shares issued.

### Example – Transfer of a business to a company

A transfers a business to X Ltd in return for shares which are worth £75,000. There are capital gains of £48,000 on the assets transferred to the company. If s 162 relief applies, A will not have any assessable capital gain, but her shares in X Ltd will be deemed to have an acquisition cost of £27,000 computed as follows:

|  | £ |
|---|---|
| Market value | 75,000 |
| *Less*: rolled-over gain | (48,000) |
|  | 27,000 |

## 15.8.2 Conditions which must be satisfied

In order for s 162 relief to be available, all the assets of the business other than cash must be transferred to the company. It is not acceptable to the Revenue for certain assets of the unincorporated business such as trade debts to be excluded, even though this might otherwise be advisable to save stamp duty.

Relief is available only in so far as shares are issued by the company instead of other forms of payment such as loan stock. The market value of the shares issued in return for the transfer of the business must be at least equal to the capital gains arising on the transfer of assets.

### Example – Limitations of s 162 relief

A transfers a business with a net value of £400,000 to Y Ltd, a new company specially formed for the purpose. Shares in Y Ltd are issued to him, and these have a value of £400,000. However, closer examination reveals that the business's value is depressed by heavy bank borrowings. Furthermore, capital gains of a total of £490,000 arise on chargeable assets transferred as part of the business.

Section 162 relief would be limited to £400,000. The balance of £90,000 would be taxable in the normal way.

## 15.8.3 Conditions which are not required

(1) Relief is not confined to a transfer of a business to a company by a sole trader; the same relief is available where a partnership transfers its business to a company.

(2) The shares which are issued need not be ordinary shares.

(3) Relief does not seem to be confined to a business which is classified as a trade which falls under Schedule D Case I or II. It is arguable that the relevant business might, for example, consist of letting a group of properties.

(4) There is no requirement that the company should be incorporated or resident in the UK. It can be both of these things, but relief is not prejudiced just because a foreign company is involved.

### 15.8.4 Relief may be due on proportion of capital gains

Some relief will still be available if the business is transferred to the company in return for a mixture of shares and loan stock, or shares and cash. The formula to be used is:

$$\text{Chargeable gain} \ \times \ \frac{\text{value of shares received}}{\text{value of whole consideration received}}$$

### 15.8.5 Alternative incorporation relief

It may sometimes be possible to transfer a business to a company and avoid any CGT liability by relying on the hold-over provisions (see 15.6). Professional advice is essential when implementing such arrangements.

## 15.9 RETIREMENT RELIEF – GENERAL PROVISIONS
(TCGA 1992, ss 163–164)

This is an important relief which may be available on the sale of a business, or an interest in a partnership, the disposal of assets used in a partnership, the sale of shares in a family company, the liquidation of such a company, or sales of assets used by such a company. The relief is available only if the individual is aged at least 50 (55 up to 28 November 1995) or is having to retire early because of ill health.

### 15.9.1 Nature of the relief

The maximum relief for 1998–99 was £250,000 plus a further amount of 50% of gains in excess of £250,000 (up to an overall ceiling of £1m). The relief is lower than this for disposals in 1999–2000 and 2000–01 (see 15.9.2 below).

The maximum relief is based on all of the requirements being met for a period of ten years. The relief is tapered using the 'appropriate percentage' which starts off at 10% for one year and rises to 100% for the full ten years.

## Example – Retirement relief

A, who is 57 years old and fulfils all of the criteria, disposes in May 1998 of his business in which he has been a full-time working director for 15 years. He realises gains qualifying for relief of £400,000. The relief is as follows:

| | |
|---|---|
| Appropriate percentage – 100% of first limit = | £250,000 |
| Excess of gains over this limit = | £150,000 |
| Relief on excess at 50% = | £75,000 |
| Therefore total relief = | £325,000 |
| Taxable gain | £75,000 |

The relief can be split between gains on disposals of two or more different businesses, but the aggregate relief will be restricted to the £250,000 and £1m limits. In some cases, the gains may arise in different tax years.

## 15.9.2 Relief being phased out

In view of the new taper relief rules for disposals of long held assets (see 14.6), retirement relief is being phased out from 6 April 1999 by a gradual reduction of the relief thresholds and will cease to be available altogether from 6 April 2003. The maximum retirement relief for each year in the transitional period will be as follows:

| Year | 100% relief on gains up to: | 50% relief on gains between: |
|---|---|---|
| 1999–00 | £200,000 | £200,001–£800,000 |
| 2000–01 | £150,000 | £150,001–£600,000 |
| 2001–02 | £100,000 | £100,001–£400,000 |
| 2002–03 | £50,000 | £50,001–£200,000 |

Relief will continue to be calculated in accordance with existing rules and to be given against chargeable gains computed after indexation allowance (available in respect of periods up to April 1998) but before any taper relief. Taper relief will be available on any gains which remain chargeable after retirement relief has been allowed. Where qualifying gains are not wholly covered by retirement relief, retirement relief will be applied so as to provide the maximum possible benefit from taper relief in respect of those gains that remain chargeable.

## 15.9.3 Retirement through ill health

The legislation provides that retirement relief should be available to an individual who is being required to dispose of his business because ill health makes it impossible for him to carry on.

In practice, the Revenue requires claimants to provide a medical certificate, signed by a qualified medical practitioner (whether or not the claimant's own general practitioner). The Board will take advice from the Regional Medical Service of the Department of Health, and in some cases a further medical examination by the Regional Medical Officer will be required.

The Revenue has made it clear that retirement relief will not be given to someone aged below 50 where he has ceased work because of the ill health of someone else, for example his spouse.

If you wish to claim retirement relief on these grounds, you should complete form CG85.

## 15.9.4 Conditions needing to be satisfied for ten years if full relief is to be available

The full relief is given only if the individual has satisfied various requirements for a period of ten years. During that period he must have been in business as a sole trader or partner or have been a full-time officer (eg a director) or employee of a personal trading company (see 15.4.8).

Separate periods during which an individual satisfied one of these requirements can be aggregated in certain circumstances.

### Example – Limited relief

| | |
|---|---|
| In the example at 15.9.1, if *A* had owned the business for six years, the relief would be as follows: | |
| Appropriate percentage of £250,000 | £150,000 |
| Excess of gain over £150,000 | £250,000 |
| 50% thereof | £125,000 |
| Total relief | £275,000 |
| Taxable gain | £125,000 |

## 15.9.5 Specific conditions for unincorporated traders and full-time directors and employees

There are a number of very specific requirements for disposals by sole traders, partners and full-time directors and employees of personal trading companies. These are dealt with separately at 15.10 and 15.11 respectively.

## 15.9.6 Retirement relief for trustees

There are certain circumstances where the sale by trustees of family settlements of business property or shares can attract retirement relief. This is an area where professional advice should be taken.

# 15.10 RETIREMENT RELIEF AND UNINCORPORATED TRADERS

The sale of a business may be broken down for tax purposes into the disposal of distinct assets (goodwill and buildings, plant and equipment, stock debtors and cash). The CGT position needs to be looked at separately in relation to each asset.

## 15.10.1 Retirement relief for sole traders

The legislation requires that a capital gain should arise on the disposal of a business or part of a business. There have been several cases concerning farmers where the individual concerned has disposed of part of his land. In each of these cases, the courts have held that retirement relief was not due since the asset disposed of was an asset used in the business rather than part of the business itself. A similar point would arise if a sole trader sold a warehouse or office block, but continued in business.

In practice, the Revenue resists relief for farmers unless the disposal concerns at least 50% or more of the total area being farmed. Problems sometimes arise even where this condition is satisfied.

## 15.10.2 Retirement relief for partners

A gain may attract retirement relief where it arises on a disposal which takes place on the introduction of a new partner or on some other change in profit sharing ratios combined with a revaluation of partnership assets (see 15.7.4). In some cases, a partner may own an asset which is used by his firm. Retirement relief is available to cover a gain arising from the disposal of such an asset provided the following conditions are satisfied:

(1) The disposal of the asset must take place as part of the withdrawal of the individual from participation in the business carried on by the partnership.
(2) Immediately before the disposal (or the cessation of the business) the asset must have been used for the purposes of the partnership business.
(3) During the whole or part of the period in which the asset has been in the ownership of the individual, the asset must have been used for the purposes of:
    (a) the business; or
    (b) another business carried on by the individual or by a partnership of which the individual concerned was a member; or
    (c) another business carried on by the individual's family trading company (in this instance, the individual must have been a full-time working director at the time).

The amount of retirement relief on the disposal of an asset of this nature may be restricted where the partner has charged his firm a commercial rent for use of the property.

## 15.11 RETIREMENT RELIEF AND FULL-TIME DIRECTORS OR EMPLOYEES
(TCGA 1992, ss 163–164, as amended by FA 1993, s 87)

This section focuses on the way in which the capital gain on the sale of shares in a personal trading company and assets owned privately by the shareholder may qualify for retirement relief.

### 15.11.1 Full-time working directors

It was necessary up to 15 March 1993 that the individual should have been a full-time working director if he were to qualify for retirement relief. For disposals after that date, it is sufficient for the individual to work for the company on a full-time basis in a managerial or technical capacity.

There is no statutory definition of what full-time means in this context. In practice, it is understood that the Revenue accepts that a director whose normal working week is 30 hours (excluding meal breaks) qualifies for relief. A person is required to devote more or less the whole of his time if that is what his job and service contract involve. Absence through illness does not prejudice entitlement to the relief.

In some cases, the individual will be working full-time for a group of related companies. Relief is available where a person is required to devote more or less the whole of his time to the service of a commercial association of companies which carry on businesses and which are of a nature that the business of a company and the associated companies taken together may be reasonably considered to make up a single composite undertaking.

This is clearly an area where professional advice may be required in the light of the circumstances of the particular case.

A director who has retired from full-time employment, but who continues to spend an average of at least ten hours per week in the conduct and management of the company's business may qualify for relief. However, his entitlement is based on the period of full-time service which he had up to the date of his retirement.

It is also a condition for an individual to qualify for retirement relief that he has a shareholding in the company of at least 5%. For disposals made prior to 16 March 1993, it was necessary that he should hold 25% or that he and his family should have held more than 50%.

### 15.11.2 **Possible restriction of retirement relief**

Where a company has investments as well as business interests, the gain which may attract retirement relief is restricted to the proportion of the gain determined by the following fraction:

$$\frac{\text{Chargeable assets used for business purposes}}{\text{Total chargeable assets}}$$

Where a company has disposed of business assets within six months of a disposal of shares, the individual may elect for the restriction to be computed by reference to the position if the company had not sold the assets concerned.

### 15.11.3 **Sale of premises etc used by company**

An individual who has been a full-time director or employee may own property or some other assets which are used by his personal trading company. Retirement relief may be claimed in respect of a disposal of such assets provided the following conditions are satisfied:

(1) the disposal of the asset must take place as part of the withdrawal of the individual concerned from participation in the business carried on by the company; and
(2) the asset must be in use for the purposes of the company's business at the time of the disposal or it must have been so used at the time that the company's business ceased; and
(3) the asset must have been used in the whole or part of the period in which the individual has owned it for the purposes of:
    (a) the business carried on by the company; or
    (b) another business carried on by the individual or by a partnership of which the individual was a member; or
    (c) another business carried on by a personal trading company.

Once again, relief may be restricted where the individual has charged rent (but see *Plumbly v Spencer* (1999) TLR, 5 July).

# 16

# SOME WAYS OF REDUCING CAPITAL GAINS TAX

Where a capital gain arises, the transaction tends to be an exceptional or 'one-off' event and the capital growth on an investment which may have been held for many years falls entirely into the tax year in which the disposal takes place instead of being spread evenly over the whole period of ownership. This can often mean that a large amount of tax is involved. There are a number of possible ways of mitigating tax and it is usually a good idea to take professional advice. The following suggestions should be borne in mind, but they are only suggestions rather than definitive advice.

(1) Make use of both spouses' annual exemptions.
(2) Realise gains to avoid wasting the annual exemption.
(3) Make sure you get relief for capital losses.
(4) Try to make gains taxable at 20% rather than 40%.
(5) Saving tax by making gifts to relatives.
(6) Roll-over relief and furnished holiday accommodation.
(7) Sale of a family company.

## 16.1 MAKE USE OF BOTH SPOUSES' ANNUAL EXEMPTIONS

### 16.1.1 Inter-spouse transfer can be a way of saving tax

All individuals are allowed to realise capital gains of £7,200 in 2000–01 before they become liable for CGT. This applies to husband and wife, but there are no provisions under which any unused amount may be transferred to a spouse.

### Example – Inter-spouse transfers

If $A$ has gains of £6,400 and his wife $B$ has gains of £8,000, the position is as follows:

| $A$ | $B$ | £ |
|---|---|---|
| No CGT | Gains | 8,000 |
| liability | *Less:* exempt | (7,200) |

| | |
|---|---:|
| Taxable | <u>1,800</u> |

There is often a way of avoiding this type of mismatch. If *B* had transferred assets to *A* before he sold them, she could effectively transfer her gain to him. A transfer between spouses does not count as a disposal for tax purposes and *A* would take over *B*'s base cost. So, with a little forethought, the position could have been:

| *A* | £ | *B* | £ |
|---|---|---|---|
| Gains | 7,200 | Gains | 7,200 |
| Exemption | (7,200) | Exemption | (7,200) |
| | Nil | | Nil |

# 16.2 REALISE GAINS TO AVOID WASTING THE ANNUAL EXEMPTION

Any unused annual exemption cannot be carried forward for use in a future tax year. Dealing costs may be a disincentive but, provided you expect to sell shares etc, at some time or other in the future, it can make sense to 'top up' any net gains to make full use of the £7,200 exemption.

The rules for matching sales and purchases within a period of 30 days mean that 'bed and breakfast' transactions will not achieve this. However, you may be able to realise gains and then have your ISA buy the same shares (ie 'bed and ISA'). Alternatively, your spouse or family trust can buy the shares.

A small word of warning, however: do bear in mind the effect on taper relief. If you sell and your spouse buys, he or she will have to start from scratch in building up a qualifying period for taper relief purposes.

# 16.3 MAKE SURE YOU GET RELIEF FOR CAPITAL LOSSES

It may be possible to save tax in a different way by a transfer of an asset between spouses before it is sold to an outsider. Capital losses for previous years attach to each spouse separately and can now be set only against that spouse's gain.

### Example – Relief for capital losses

If *A*'s wife *B* has losses of £35,000 and *A* has an asset which has appreciated by £50,000, it will make sense for him to transfer it to *B* before it is sold. Instead of the position being like this:

| | £ |
|---|---:|
| *A*'s gains | 50,000 |

| | |
|---|---:|
| *Less*: exemption | (7,200) |
| Taxable | 43,800 |

the position will be:

| | £ |
|---|---:|
| *B*'s gains | 50,000 |
| *Less*: capital losses | (35,000) |
| | 15,000 |
| *Less*: exemption | (7,200) |
| Taxable | 7,800 |

Of course, the ideal position would be achieved by *A* transferring part of the asset to *B*, so that they eventually make a joint disposal, use *B*'s losses and take full advantage of both of their annual exemptions.

### 16.3.1 Negligible value claims

You may have made an investment in the past which has gone badly. Indeed, you may have written it off in your own mind but, if you have not sold it, the loss is normally only a paper loss which is not allowable for CGT purposes. However, there is an exception to the normal rule whereby you may be able to establish an allowable loss even though there has been no disposal. If the Revenue can be persuaded that the asset has become of 'negligible value' (ie, virtually worthless) you can claim a loss (see 13.4.9). In practice, the Revenue issues lists of quoted shares which have been suspended and which are recognised to be of negligible value, so you should ask your Inspector whether your defunct investments are on the Revenue's list. It may also be possible to establish losses on unquoted shares and other investments.

### 16.3.2 Interaction with taper relief

If you have gains which qualify for taper relief and capital losses, the losses are set against gains before taper relief. In some cases, it may be better to defer realising losses until a later year.

Thus, if *A* has gains of £100,000 on disposal of business assets in 2000–01 and these gains qualify for 15% taper relief, *A* may be advised not to realise losses of £20,000 until after 5 April 2001. His 2000–01 chargeable gains will then be £85,000 rather than £68,000, but the full £20,000 capital loss can then be available to cover future gains which may not attract taper relief at all. As taper relief increases, the desirability of 'fine tuning' will become much greater.

Some married couples may approach matters differently by keeping all taper relief disposals in one name and putting all loss-making transactions through the other spouse who will then realise all their short-term gains.

### 16.3.3 Timing of disposals

Timing is going to be very important in some cases. Suppose that your position in 2000–01 is as follows:

|  | £ |
|---|---|
| Losses brought forward | 80,000 |
| Gains for 1999–2000 on disposals of business assets qualifying for 25% taper relief as asset owned on 5 April 1998 | 100,000 |

If matters stop there, the position will be as follows:

|  | £ |
|---|---|
| Gains | 100,000 |
| *Less*: losses | 80,000 |
|  | 20,000 |
| *Less*: taper relief | 5,000 |
| Taxable gain | 15,000 |

It will be rather sad if you then realise a gain of £90,000 which does not qualify for taper relief on 6 April 2001, making your combined taxable gains for the two years £105,000. If you had brought the disposal forward one day, the computation would be:

|  | £ | £ |
|---|---|---|
| Gains not qualifying for taper relief | 90,000 | |
| *Less*: loss brought forward | 80,000 | |
|  |  | 10,000 |
| Gains qualifying for taper relief | 100,000 | |
| Taper relief | 25,000 | |
|  |  | 75,000 |
| Total gains chargeable for 2000–01 |  | 85,000 |

It will probably be even better if you can postpone your disposal of the business assets until 2001–02 as one extra year's taper relief may be earned and the computation could then be:

|  | £ | £ |
|---|---|---|
| Gains not qualifying for taper relief | 90,000 | |
| *Less*: loss brought forward | 80,000 | |
|  |  | 10,000 |
| Gains qualifying for taper relief | 100,000 | |
| Taper relief (50%) | 50,000 | |
|  |  | 50,000 |
|  |  | 60,000 |

## 16.4 TRY TO MAKE GAINS TAXABLE AT 20% RATHER THAN 40%

The rate of tax depends upon the level of your income, rather than the amount of gain you make. If you have taxable income of more than £28,400 after deducting your personal allowances etc, the gains will be taxed at 40%. If you have little or no income, the first £28,400 of any capital gains will normally attract tax at a maximum rate of 20%. It can therefore make sense for you to transfer an asset to your spouse to sell and realise a gain if the gain will be taxed at a lower rate.

### Example – Transfers to reduce the rate of CGT

If A's wife has no income, A could transfer shares with a paper gain of £35,200 to her. If A sold them he would be taxed at 40%, but his wife's disposal will attract tax only as follows:

|  | £ |
|---|---|
| Gain | 35,200 |
| *Less*: exemption | (7,200) |
| Taxable | 28,000 |
| First £1,520 at 10% | 152 |
| Tax at 20% on £26,480 | 5,296 |
| Tax liability | 5,448 |

## 16.5 SAVING TAX BY MAKING GIFTS TO RELATIVES

If you are planning to sell unquoted shares it may be possible to save tax, but beware the effect of taper relief as hold-over relief applies to the gain before taper relief (see 14.6).

### Example – Sale of unquoted shares

A holds all the shares in a private trading company. He has reached broad agreement with a potential purchaser to sell his shares for £1,000 each which will produce a gain of £600 per share. The resultant capital gain will attract tax at 40% because of the level of A's other income and gains.

If A so wishes, he could transfer some shares to his son B, to enable him to use his annual exemption, ie A would give B 14 shares in the company and claim hold-over relief. No capital gain need arise for A on his gift to B who would then dispose of the shares to the ultimate purchaser. B's capital gain would then be as follows:

|  |  |
|---|---|
| | £ |
| Capital gain: $14 \times £600 =$ | 8,400 |
| *Less*: annual exemption | (7,200) |
| Taxable | 1,200 |

The overall effect is that *A*'s family saves tax of at least £2,880 (ie 40% of £7,200).

### Gifts of listed shares and securities

It is sometimes possible to achieve a similar saving by transferring quoted securities even though hold-over relief is not normally available unless a donor owns at least 5% of the voting shares. But you have to plan some way ahead.

The key point is that it is possible to claim hold-over relief where you make a chargeable transfer for IHT purposes, normally on your putting assets into a discretionary trust (see 13.4.8 and 17.10). The first thing to do is to either create such a trust or add property to an existing family trust and make a hold-over election under TCGA 1992, s 260 so that you do not have to pay any CGT. If the trustees subsequently appoint property in favour of the trust beneficiaries (such as your children, grandchildren etc), they can make a similar hold-over election to avoid any CGT charge on them. The overall effect will be that the trust beneficiaries will have taken the property that you put into trust at a value equal to your original acquisition cost plus indexation and if they do not have very much income or gains, a large part of the proceeds from their eventually selling the assets will have escaped CGT altogether.

You will need to take professional advice. Bear in mind that if transfers into a discretionary trust take your cumulative transfers over the nil rate band (at present £234,000), you may have to pay IHT at the rate of 20% on the excess. And do not try to do all this in rapid succession as the Revenue may well attack the transactions as a preordained scheme.

## 16.6 ROLL-OVER RELIEF AND FURNISHED HOLIDAY ACCOMMODATION

Where a person has realised a capital gain on the disposal of a business and does not wish to embark on further trading activities, roll-over relief may still be available. A particular type of property investment qualifies in this way because where a property is acquired for letting as furnished holiday accommodation, the owner is deemed to have acquired an asset for a trade and roll-over relief may be available. Two points are of particular interest:

(1) The property need not be located at the seaside. A property in (eg)

Central London could qualify provided that it is let for at least part of the year on a short-term basis (see 4.5 and 15.4.6).

(2) Roll-over relief may be obtained provided the property is let as furnished holiday accommodation for a period. If the property is subsequently let on a longer term basis or used for some other purpose (eg as a second home) the roll-over relief is not normally withdrawn. The one exception to this would be if the owner has acquired a leasehold interest on the property concerned and the lease has less than 60 years to run at the time that it is acquired. Taking such a property out of use as furnished holiday accommodation would mean that the deferred gain would become chargeable (see 15.4.4).

## 16.7 SALE OF A FAMILY COMPANY

### 16.7.1 Make the most of taper relief

It will often be advisable to defer a sale until shortly after the end of the tax year. For example, if A has owned all the shares in his family trading company since 6 April 1998, a sale on 5 April 2001 will result in a gain being taxed at 30%, whereas a sale on 6 April 2001 will be taxed at only 20%. But do not overdo this: it would be most unfortunate if you lost a very attractive and advantageous sale of your business just because you had delayed in order to increase taper relief.

### 16.7.2 It may pay to bring disposals forward into 2000–01

It will not have escaped some readers' attentions that retirement relief is being phased out. For 1998–99 the full relief was available, but in 1999–2000 the relief was reduced from £250,000 to £200,000. The relief has been further reduced in the current tax year to £150,000. There may be merit in realising a gain before 6 April 2001, possibly by transferring shares into a life interest trust under which you are the main beneficiary. You should discuss this with your accountant.

### 16.7.3 Avoid restrictions on retirement relief

This is a complex area, but consideration should be given to matters such as:

(1) careful planning in relation to disposals of assets which are owned by full-time working directors or senior employees and used in the company's business;

(2) transfer of shares between spouses if this will increase gains which are eligible for retirement relief;

(3) possible purchase by the individual shareholders from the company of all or some of its investments if this will avoid or reduce the restriction

imposed by the principle that only the following proportion of a gain on the sale of shares may qualify for retirement relief:

$$\frac{\text{Company's chargeable business assets}}{\text{Company's total chargeable assets}}$$

(See 15.11.2.)

## 16.7.4 Pre-sale dividend

In cases where the vendors of a private company do not qualify for the business rate of taper relief, it can make sense for them to take a dividend which is taxable as income, before disposing of their shares. Clearly, the purchaser will pay less, but the difference in the tax treatment of dividends and capital gains may mean that the vendors are better off.

### Example – Sale of a family company

A owns all the shares in X Ltd. He is planning to sell the shares for a total of £1.2m. The capital gain which would result is £900,000 and A will qualify only for 5% taper relief. However, his accountant advises him that no additional tax would be payable by X Ltd if a dividend were taken of £900,000. Assume that the payment of the dividend is acceptable to the purchaser (provided the price for the shares is reduced to £300,000). If A receives a dividend he will be liable only for higher rate tax ie:

|  | £ |
|---|---|
| Dividend | 900,000 |
| Tax credit | 100,000 |
|  | 1,000,000 |
| 32.5% income tax | 325,000 |
| *Less*: tax credit | (100,000) |
|  | 225,000 |

Because the sale price is reduced to £300,000 A has no CGT liability. If A had not taken the dividend his capital gain would have been £900,000 on which tax could be payable of £360,000 (40%). So by taking the dividend he has cut his tax bill by £135,000.

# 17

# INHERITANCE TAX AND INDIVIDUALS

## HILARY SHARPE

Inheritance tax (IHT) is a combined gift tax and death duty. It applies to gifts and deemed gifts made during a person's lifetime and to his estate on death. The first £234,000 of chargeable transfers (the 'nil rate band') is charged at 0% and is therefore free of IHT. Cumulative transfers in excess of this which take place either at death or within seven years of death are taxed at 40% (though the overall impact may be reduced on transfers that take place more than three years before death). On all other occasions when IHT is payable, the rate is 20%.

This chapter covers the following topics:

(1) Who is subject to IHT?
(2) When may a charge arise?
(3) Transfers of value.
(4) Certain gifts are not transfers of value.
(5) Exempt transfers.
(6) Potentially exempt transfers.
(7) Reservation of benefit.
(8) Business property.
(9) Agricultural property and woodlands.
(10) Computation of tax payable on lifetime transfers.
(11) Tax payable on death.
(12) Life assurance and pension policies.
(13) Heritage property.

## 17.1 WHO IS SUBJECT TO IHT?

An individual who is domiciled in the UK is subject to IHT on all property owned by him, whether it is located in the UK or overseas. By contrast, a person who has a foreign domicile is subject to IHT only on property which is situated in the UK. Domicile is a concept of general law and is distinct from a person being resident or ordinarily resident (see Chapters 21 and 22 on domicile, residence etc).

Section 267 of the Inheritance Tax Act (IHTA) 1984 contains a special rule which applies for IHT purposes whereby an individual may be deemed to be domiciled in the UK for a tax year if he has been resident in the UK for 17 out of the 20 tax years which end with the current year. However, this is overruled by provisions contained in a few of the UK's double taxation agreements.

## 17.2 WHEN MAY A CHARGE ARISE?

Inheritance tax can apply in the following circumstances:

(1) On a gift made by an individual during his lifetime.
(2) On a lifetime transfer of value which is regarded as a 'chargeable transfer'.
(3) On the death of an individual.

A person who has an interest in possession under a trust or settlement is normally regarded as if he were entitled to the capital. When the beneficiary dies the full value of the trust property is treated as part of his estate for IHT purposes (see 18.4.15).

Table 17.1 opposite indicates the circumstances under which a gift may be a chargeable transfer for IHT purposes.

## 17.3 TRANSFERS OF VALUE

### 17.3.1 Not all transfers are gifts
(IHTA 1984, s 3)

The legislation refers mainly to transfers rather than gifts. The reason for this is that all gifts are transfers of value but not all transfers of value are gifts. For example, where a person deliberately sells an asset at less than market value, he may not be making a gift but he is certainly making a transfer of value. Similarly, deliberately omitting to exercise a right can be a transfer of value but this is not a gift in the normal sense of the word. To give a third example, a transfer can even involve property which is not owned by the person since the IHT legislation deems a person to make a gift if his interest in possession under a trust comes to an end.

### 17.3.2 There must be gratuitous intent
(IHTA 1984, s 10)

IHT will not normally apply to a gift unless there is an element of 'bounty', ie there is a deliberate intention to make a gift. An unintentional loss of value (eg a loss made on a bad business deal) is not subject to IHT because there was no intention to pass value to another person.

**Table 17.1 – Is a gift a chargeable transfer?**

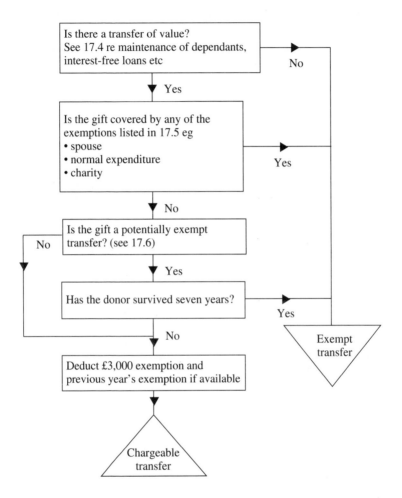

### 17.3.3 **How a transfer is measured**
(IHTA 1984, s 3)

The amount of any transfer of value is determined by the reduction in the donor's wealth. This is not necessarily the same as the increase in the recipient's wealth.

This can be shown by considering the situation where a person owns 51 out of 100 shares in a company. He has control because he has the majority of the shares. If he were to give two shares to his son, he would relinquish control of the company and his remaining 49 shares might be worth considerably less because of this. The two shares given to his son might not be worth very much in isolation, and the son may not have acquired a very valuable asset, but the father's estate would have gone down in value by the difference between the value of a 51% shareholding and the value of a 49% shareholding.

## 17.4 CERTAIN GIFTS ARE NOT TRANSFERS OF VALUE

Certain gifts and other transactions are not regarded as transfers of value so the issue of whether they are chargeable transfers simply does not arise. These include:

- Maintenance of dependants
- Waivers of dividends
- Waivers of remuneration
- Interest-free loans
- Disclaimers of legacies
- Deeds of variation.

### 17.4.1 Maintenance of dependants, family etc
(IHTA 1984, s 11)

The legislation specifically provides that the following lifetime payments are not transfers of value:

(1) Payments for the maintenance of a spouse or former spouse.
(2) Payments for the maintenance, education or training of a child or stepchild under the age of 18.
(3) Payments made to maintain a child over 18 who is in full-time education or training.
(4) Reasonable provision for the care or maintenance of a dependent relative, ie someone who is incapacitated by old age or infirmity from maintaining himself, or a widow or a separated or divorced mother or mother-in-law.

### 17.4.2 Waivers of dividends
(IHTA 1984, s 15)

A waiver of a dividend is not regarded as a transfer of value provided certain conditions are satisfied:

(1) The dividend must be waived by deed.
(2) The deed must not be executed more than 12 months before the right to the dividend has accrued.
(3) The deed waiving the dividend must be executed before any legal entitlement to the dividend arises.

The position is slightly different for interim and final dividends as the point in time at which entitlement may arise can be different.

### Interim dividends

A shareholder has no enforceable right to payment prior to the date on which a board resolution has declared that a dividend shall be payable. However, the directors can declare an interim dividend which is payable immediately, and without having to first seek shareholders' approval. Therefore, a deed waiving a dividend should be executed in good time before any board resolution is passed.

### Final dividends

A company might declare a dividend without stipulating any date for payment. In such circumstances, the declaration of the dividend creates an immediate debt and it is therefore too late to execute a waiver.

In other cases where a final dividend is declared as being payable at a later date, a shareholder may waive his entitlement provided that he does so before the due date for payment.

In practice, a final dividend will require the shareholders' approval and an individual shareholder may therefore waive a dividend provided that the deed is executed before the company's annual general meeting.

## 17.4.3 Waivers of remuneration
(IHTA 1984, s 14)

There is a specific provision whereby a waiver of remuneration does not constitute a transfer of value. The terms of this exemption are based upon the income tax treatment. In practice, the Revenue accepts that remuneration is not subject to income tax under Schedule E if it is waived and the Schedule E assessment has not become final and conclusive, and:

(1) the remuneration is formally waived (usually by deed), and
(2) the employer's assessable profits are adjusted accordingly.

## 17.4.4 Interest-free loans
(IHTA 1984, s 29)

The IHT legislation specifically provides that an interest-free loan is not to be treated as a transfer of value provided that the loan is repayable upon demand.

This exemption would not cover a situation where a loan was made for a specific period, with the lender having no legal right to call for repayment before that time. The grant of such a loan could be a transfer of value, with the Revenue assessing the transfer as the difference between the amount of the loan and the present market value of the loan if it were to be assigned.

### 17.4.5 Disclaimer of legacies
(IHTA 1984, s 142)

If a person becomes entitled to property under a Will or an intestacy or under a trust (eg on the death of a life tenant), he may disclaim his entitlement. Such a disclaimer is normally effective for IHT purposes and is not treated as a transfer of value provided that:

(1) no payment or other consideration is given for the disclaimer, and
(2) the person has not already accepted his entitlement, either expressly or by implication.

### 17.4.6 Deeds of variation
(IHTA 1984, s 142)

A deed of variation may be entered into where a person has died leaving property to a beneficiary, the effect being to redirect property. Where the necessary conditions are fulfilled, the revised disposition is treated as having taken place on the deceased person's death. Once again, a person who gives up an entitlement is not treated as making a transfer of value.

The following conditions need to be satisfied:

(1) The deed of variation must be executed within two years of a death and an election must be filed within six months of the deed being executed.
(2) The deed must be in writing and must specifically refer to the provisions of the Will etc which are to be varied.
(3) It must be signed by the person who would otherwise have benefited, and anyone else who might have benefited.
(4) Only one deed of variation in respect of a particular piece of property can be effective for IHT purposes.
(5) No payment or other consideration may pass between beneficiaries to induce them to enter into the deed of variation (except that a variation is permitted which consists of an exchange of inheritances and a cash adjustment).

The Revenue publishes a booklet IHT8, *Alterations to an inheritance following a death*. This can be obtained by calling the CTO's orderline 08459 000 404.

## 17.5 EXEMPT TRANSFERS

Even if a transfer takes place, it will not attract IHT if it is an exempt transfer. The full list of exempt transfers is as follows:

(1) Gifts to spouse.
(2) Normal expenditure out of income.
(3) £250 small gifts exemption.

(4) Annual £3,000 exemption.

(5) Exemption for marriage gifts.

(6) Gifts to charities.

(7) Gifts for national purposes.

(8) Gifts to political parties.

(9) Gifts to housing associations.

(10) Certain transfers to employee trusts.

### 17.5.1 Gifts to spouse
(IHTA 1984, s 18)

There is normally an unlimited exemption for transfers between husband and wife. For this purpose, a couple are regarded as husband and wife until a decree absolute has been obtained. The exemption covers outright gifts, legacies and a transfer of property to a trust under which the spouse has an interest in possession. (The transfer may either be a lifetime transfer or a transfer which takes place on death.)

The exemption is restricted in the case where a UK-domiciled spouse makes transfers to a foreign domiciled spouse. In this situation, the exemption is limited to £55,000. However, the deemed domicile rule which treats individuals as domiciled where they have been resident in the UK for 17 out of 20 years applies for all purposes of the IHT legislation except where expressly excluded. Consequently, a gift by a UK-domiciled individual to a spouse who has a foreign domicile, but who is treated as UK domiciled for IHT purposes under the 17-year rule, qualifies for the unlimited exemption.

### 17.5.2 Normal expenditure out of income
(IHTA 1984, s 21)

A lifetime gift is exempt if it is shown that the gift was made as part of the normal expenditure of the donor and comes out of income. The legislation requires that the gift should be normal ie the donor had a habit of making such gifts. The legislation also requires that by taking one year with another, the pattern of such gifts must have left the donor with sufficient income to maintain his normal standard of living.

Gifts which take the form of payments under deed of covenant or the payment of premiums on life assurance policies written in trust frequently qualify as exempt because of this rule.

### 17.5.3 £250 small gifts exemption
(IHTA 1984, s 20)

Any number of individual gifts of up to £250 in any one tax year are exempt. If a person wanted to, he could make 100 separate gifts of £250 per time. However, where gifts to a particular individual exceed £250, the exemption does not apply to these gifts.

### 17.5.4 **Annual £3,000 exemption**
(IHTA 1984, s 19)

This exemption is available to cover part of a larger gift. The exemption is £3,000 for each tax year. Furthermore, both husband and wife have separate annual exemptions.

If the full £3,000 is not used in a given year, the balance can be carried forward for one year only and is then allowable only if the exemption for the second year is fully utilised.

### Example

**Situation 1**

|  | £ | £ |
|---|---|---|
| Gifts made in Year 1 |  | 1,000 |
| Balance of exemption carried to Year 2 |  | 2,000 |
| Gifts made in Year 2 |  | 4,000 |
| Annual exemption for Year 2 | 3,000 |  |
| Part of unused exemption for Year 1 | 1,000 | (4,000) |
| Chargeable gifts |  | Nil |

The balance of exemption from Year 1 of £1,000 may not be carried forward to Year 3.

**Situation 2**

|  | £ | £ |
|---|---|---|
| Year 1 as in Situation 1 – unused exemption |  | 2,000 |
| Exemption for Year 2 | 3,000 |  |
| Gifts in Year 2 | 2,000 |  |
| Balance of Year 2 exemption to be carried forward to Year 3 | 1,000 |  |

The balance of the Year 1 exemption of £2,000 may not be carried forward to Year 3.

### 17.5.5 **Gifts in consideration of marriage**
(IHTA 1984, s 22)

Gifts made to the bride or groom in consideration of their marriage are exempt up to the following amounts:

| *Gifts made by* | *Maximum exemption* |
|---|---|
| Each parent | £5,000 |
| Grandparents (or great grandparents) | £2,500 |
| Bride or groom | £2,500 |
| Any other person | £1,000 |

Parents may make gifts to either party to the marriage – their exemption is not restricted to gifts made to their own child. This means that, for example, in relation to the groom each of the bride's parents may give up to £5,000. The gifts should be made so that they are conditional upon the marriage taking place.

### 17.5.6 Gifts to charities
(IHTA 1984, s 23)

Gifts to charities which are established in the UK are exempt regardless of the amount. A charity may be established or registered here even though it carries out its work overseas and the exemption covers gifts to such charities. However, donations made to a foreign charity which is established abroad do not normally qualify.

### 17.5.7 Gifts for national purposes
(IHTA 1984, s 25)

Gifts to certain national bodies are totally exempt. These bodies include colleges and universities, the National Trust, the National Gallery, the British Museum and other galleries and museums run by local authorities or universities.

### 17.5.8 Gifts to political parties
(IHTA 1984, s 24)

Gifts to 'qualifying political parties' are exempt only if certain conditions are satisfied. A political party qualifies if it had at least two Members of Parliament returned at the last general election, or if it had at least one member and more than 150,000 votes were cast for its candidates.

### 17.5.9 Gifts to housing associations
(IHTA 1984, s 24A)

Gifts of UK land to registered housing associations are exempt.

### 17.5.10 Certain transfers to employee trusts
(IHTA 1984, s 28)

Transfers by an individual to an employee trust of shares in a company can be exempt provided the following conditions are satisfied:

(1) The beneficiaries of the trust include all or most of the persons employed by or holding office with the company.
(2) Within one year of the transfer:

(a) the trustees must hold more than 50% of the ordinary share capital of the company and have voting control on all questions which affect the company as a whole; and

(b) the trustees' control is not fettered by some other provision or agreement between the shareholders.

(3) The trust deed must not permit any of the trust property to be applied at any time for the benefit of:

(a) a participator in the company (ie a person who holds a 5% or greater interest);

(b) any person who has been a participator at any time during the ten years prior to the transfer;

(c) any person connected with a participator or former participator.

A further restriction may apply where a company makes a transfer to an employee trust.

## 17.6 POTENTIALLY EXEMPT TRANSFERS
(IHTA 1984, s 3A)

### 17.6.1 Definition of a potentially exempt transfer

Irrevocable gifts made during an individual's lifetime may, provided certain conditions are satisfied, be 'potentially exempt transfers' (PETs). These gifts become actually exempt only if the donor survives seven years. If the individual dies during that period, the PET becomes a chargeable transfer. The tax payable depends upon the rates of IHT in force at the date of death. The donee is liable to pay the tax.

The main conditions that need to be satisfied for a gift to be a PET are that the gift is made to:

(1) an individual; or

(2) a trust under which an individual has an interest in possession (see 18.4.18); or

(3) a trust for the disabled (see 18.7); or

(4) an accumulation and maintenance trust (see 18.6).

A gift which is subject to a reservation of benefit (see 17.7) cannot be a PET. Furthermore, a gift to a discretionary trust is a chargeable transfer.

### 17.6.2 Taper relief
(IHTA 1984, s 7)

Where an individual makes a PET or chargeable transfer and dies within the seven-year period, taper relief may reduce the amount of tax payable. The tax payable on the transfer which has become a chargeable transfer is reduced so that only a proportion is charged. The proportion is as follows:

| Years between gift and death | Percentage of the full charge |
|---|---|
| Three to four | 80 |
| Four to five | 60 |
| Five to six | 40 |
| Six to seven | 20 |

Taper relief cannot reduce the tax on a lifetime chargeable transfer below the tax payable at the time that the transfer was made.

## 17.7 RESERVATION OF BENEFIT
(FA 1986, s 102 and Sched 20)

### 17.7.1 Introduction

Property which has been given away may still be deemed to form part of a deceased person's estate unless:

(1) possession and enjoyment of the property was bona fide assumed by the donee; and
(2) the property was enjoyed virtually to the entire exclusion of the donor and of any benefit to him by contract or otherwise.

The reference to the property being enjoyed virtually to the entire exclusion of the donor means that for all practical purposes this is an 'all or nothing' test. The Revenue's view is that the exception is intended to cover trivial benefits such as might arise where, for example, the donor of a picture enjoyed the chance to view it when making occasional visits to the donee's home.

The Act refers to a benefit reserved 'by contract or otherwise' and this is meant to refer to arrangements which are not legally binding but which amount to an honourable understanding. This might arise where a person gifts away a house but remains in occupation. A reservation of benefit would arise even if there is no legal tenancy and the donee could, in law, require the donor to vacate the property at any time.

The rules on gifts of land and buildings have been tightened up in FA 1999 in order to block the type of arrangements upheld by the House of Lords in *IRC v Ingram*. In this case, the late Lady Ingram carved out a 20-year lease which entitled her to occupy the property rent free and then gave away the freehold. It was decided that this did not constitute a GWR, but the law has been amended with effect from 9 March 1999 to block this loophole.

#### Starting date

The reservation of benefit rules apply to gifts made on or after 18 March 1986. Where a gift or transfer was made before that date, and the donor has reserved a benefit, the gift is effective for IHT purposes and the capital does not form part of that person's estate.

### 17.7.2 Two specific exemptions

The legislation specifically states that occupation of property or use of chattels does not count as a benefit provided the donor pays a market rent. The legislation also provides that a benefit enjoyed by a donor occupying property can be ignored where the donor's financial circumstances have changed drastically for the worse after the gift has been made.

**Table 17.2 – Is there reservation of benefit?**

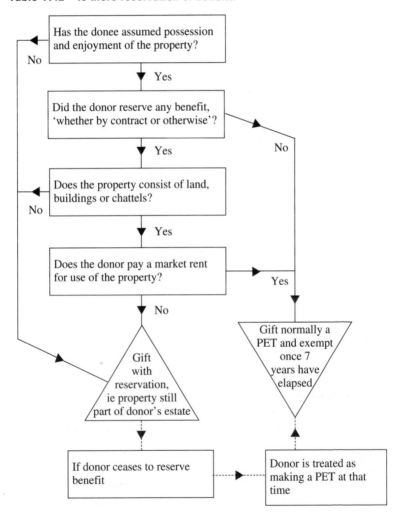

### 17.7.3 **Position where reservation of benefit ceases**

Where a person makes a gift and initially reserves a benefit, but then relinquishes that reservation, the donor is normally treated as making a PET at the time that he gives up the reserved benefit. The amount of the PET is governed by the market value of the property at that time.

#### Example – Giving up reservation of benefit

> *A* gives property worth £150,000 in July 1992 but reserves a benefit. The benefit is relinquished in July 1997 when the property is worth £220,000. *A* dies in October 1999.
>
> If no benefit had been reserved, the gift would have been completely exempt by August 1999 (ie seven years after the gift) but because a benefit was retained until July 1997, the seven-year period starts only from that date. The full £220,000 (ie the value at July 1997 when the reservation of benefit came to an end) would form part of *A*'s estate for IHT purposes.

### 17.7.4 **Settlements and trusts**

The position is less clear cut where a person has sought to reserve the possibility of a benefit, for example where an individual has created a settlement and he is a potential beneficiary. It is the Revenue's opinion that a benefit is reserved where the settlor creates a discretionary trust and is a member of a class of potential beneficiaries. This would also apply where the settlor may be added to a class of potential beneficiaries.

In contrast to this, the Revenue has confirmed that no reservation of benefit arises where a person creates a settlement and is a contingent or default beneficiary. This might apply, for example, where property is put into trust for the settlor's children but the property would revert to the settlor in the event of the children dying or becoming bankrupt.

The legislation does not require that the donor's spouse should be excluded from benefit and where a discretionary settlement is created it would be possible to include the donor's spouse, any future spouse or widow(er) as a potential beneficiary. However, if property were to be distributed to the donor's spouse from the trust and that property were then to be applied for the benefit of the settlor, the Revenue might well take the view that, looked at as a whole, there had been a reservation of benefit.

The Revenue has confirmed that a settlor may be a trustee of a settlement created by him without this constituting a reservation of benefit. Also, where the settled property includes shares in a family company, the settlor/trustee may also be a director of the company and may be permitted under the trust deed to retain his remuneration provided the remuneration is reasonable in relation to the services rendered.

## 17.8 BUSINESS PROPERTY
(IHTA 1984, ss 103–114)

### 17.8.1 Basic requirements

A special deduction is given against the value of business property where the following conditions are satisfied:

(1) The property must have been owned during the previous two years or it must have been inherited from a spouse and, when the spouse's period of ownership is taken into account, the combined period of ownership exceeds two years.
(2) Property must not be subject to a binding contract for sale.

(See also 17.11.10 replacement property.)

### 17.8.2 Rates of business property relief
(IHTA 1984, s 103)

#### Unincorporated businesses

A sole proprietor's interest in his business qualifies for a 100% deduction. A partner's interest in his firm also qualifies for 100% relief.

A 50% deduction is available for an asset owned by a partner but used by his firm.

#### Shares and debentures

Business relief is available on shares only where the company concerned is a trading company or the holding company of a trading group. The 100% relief is available on shares and debentures in an unquoted company. Where the company concerned is a quoted company 50% relief is due if (and only if) the person making the capital transfer had voting control before the transfer.

Shares dealt in on the USM were not regarded as quoted shares. Shares dealt in on the AIM are treated as unquoted.

Prior to 6 April 1996, the 100% relief was available for a transfer of shares in an unquoted trading company only if the transferor had control of more than 25% of the voting rights before the transfer. A 50% deduction was given for smaller shareholdings in unquoted trading companies.

Where a controlling shareholder transfers an asset which is used by his trading company, or where such an asset passes on his death, 50% relief is available.

### 17.8.3 Businesses which do not qualify

Business relief is not normally available where the business carried on consists wholly or mainly of dealing in securities, stocks or shares, land or buildings or in holding or making investments.

Where a transfer involves shares, business relief may be restricted if the company owns investments. The legislation refers to such investments as 'excepted assets', which are defined as assets which are neither:

(1) assets used wholly or mainly for the purposes of the business, nor
(2) assets required for the future use of the business.

Where a company has subsidiaries, it is necessary to look at the group situation (ie shares in subsidiaries may have to be treated as excepted assets if the subsidiaries are investment companies).

## 17.9 AGRICULTURAL PROPERTY AND WOODLANDS
(IHTA 1984, ss 115–124B)

Agricultural relief is available on the agricultural value of farmland in the UK, Channel Islands or Isle of Man.

### 17.9.1 Land occupied by the transferor

A 100% deduction is available where the individual has occupied the farmland for the two years prior to the date of the transfer. Where a farm has been sold and another farm has been acquired, the replacement farm normally qualifies for agricultural property relief provided that the owner has occupied the two farms for a combined period of at least two years in the last five years. Agricultural property relief is also available for land owned by an individual but occupied by a firm of which he is a partner or by a company of which he is the controlling shareholder for the two years preceding the date of the transfer.

### 17.9.2 Relief for other land

A 100% deduction is also available on land which is not occupied by the owner provided that he has (or had) the legal right to regain vacant possession within a period not exceeding 12 months. To qualify under this head, the individual must normally have owned the land for at least seven years.

### 17.9.3 Relief for tenanted farmland

A 50% deduction is available for farmland which is let on a tenancy granted before 1 September 1995 and where the owner cannot obtain vacant possession within 12 months. This would generally be the case where the land is let under an agricultural tenancy. Once again, the land must normally have been owned for seven years.

The 50% deduction is increased to 100% for land under a tenancy granted on or after 1 September 1995. This also includes a tenancy over property in Scotland acquired after that date by right of succession.

### 17.9.4 **Woodlands**
(IHTA 1984, ss 125–130)

The tax treatment of UK woodlands is largely beneficial as business relief is normally available after two years of ownership. In very unusual circumstances where business relief is not available, alternative relief may be due under s 125 after five years of ownership.

## 17.10 COMPUTATION OF TAX PAYABLE ON LIFETIME TRANSFERS

In practice, IHT is likely only to be paid during a person's lifetime for chargeable transfers made by him to a discretionary trust. The tax payable is calculated as follows:

### Initial calculation

| | | |
|---|---|---|
| Chargeable transfers made during the preceding seven years | | $\boxed{A}$ |
| *Add* | Amount of chargeable transfer | $\boxed{B}$ |
| | | $\boxed{C}$ |
| *Deduct* | Nil rate band | $\boxed{D}$ |
| | | $\boxed{E}$ |
| | IHT thereon at 20% | $\boxed{X}$ |
| *Deduct* | IHT on a notional transfer of $\boxed{A}$ minus $\boxed{D}$ as if it took place at the same time. | $\boxed{Y}$ |
| | IHT payable in respect of the chargeable transfer | $\boxed{Z}$ |

Position if the donor dies within three years

| | | |
|---|---|---|
| Chargeable transfers made during the previous seven years | | $\boxed{A}$ |
| *Add* | PETs caught by the seven-year rule | $\boxed{B}$ |
| | | $\boxed{C}$ |
| *Add* | amount of chargeable transfer | $\boxed{D}$ |
| | | $\boxed{E}$ |

*Deduct*   Nil rate band                                                                           $\boxed{F}$

$\boxed{G}$

IHT thereon at 40%                                                                     $\boxed{H}$

*Deduct*   IHT at 40% on a notional transfer of $\boxed{C}$ minus $\boxed{F}$         $\boxed{I}$

$\boxed{J}$

The donee is liable to pay additional IHT of $\boxed{J}$ minus the amount already paid under $\boxed{Z}$ above.

### Position if the donor dies during years four to seven

The above will be liable for additional IHT computed as $\boxed{J}$ above, but subject to the IHT on PETs caught by the seven-year rule being reduced by taper relief (see 17.6.2).

## 17.11 TAX PAYABLE ON DEATH

### 17.11.1 Normal basis of computation

The charge on death is normally computed as shown in the flowchart overleaf. The IHT will be the tax on the figure in box 6 minus the tax payable on a normal transfer equal to the amount in box 4 as if the notional transfer took place immediately prior to the death. Some taper relief may be due on the PETs caught by the seven-year rule (see 17.6.2).

However, there are a number of special reliefs which may be available.

### 17.11.2 Death on active service
(IHTA 1984, s 154)

Ever since the Second World War the death duty legislation has contained an exemption for a person who dies from wounds suffered whilst on active service. The exemption applies to the estates of those killed in the Falklands conflict and the Gulf War, and of members of the RUC killed by terrorists in Northern Ireland.

The exemption may well apply more often than people think. Death does not have to be immediate, nor need the wound be the only cause of death. The High Court held in 1978 that the exemption was owed to the estate of the fourth Duke of Westminster because serious wounds that he had suffered in 1944 contributed to his death in 1967.

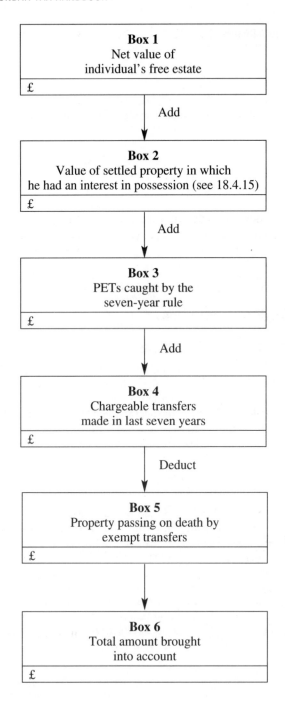

### 17.11.3 Sales of quoted securities at a loss
(IHTA 1984, ss 178–189, as extended by FA 1993, s 198)

Relief is given where quoted securities or unit trusts are sold at a loss within 12 months of death. Where shares are suspended, FA 1993, s 198 permits similar relief to be claimed by reference to the value of the shares when they return from suspension. It is not possible to pick and choose – the relief is confined to the amount of any overall loss. Executors must, in effect, elect that the total proceeds of any sales should be substituted for the value at date of death.

#### Example – Sale of quoted securities at a loss

*A* died on 1 October 1999. His estate included a portfolio worth £70,000. The executors had to sell some of the securities in December 1999 and realised an overall loss of £25,000. The estate can be reduced by this amount so that, in effect, only £45,000 is taken into account.

The overall loss of £25,000 may have been made up of a gain of £5,000 and losses of £30,000. Relief is, however, limited to the net figure.

### 17.11.4 Relief restricted where executors purchase quoted securities

Furthermore, the relief is restricted where the executors repurchase quoted securities within two months of the last sale.

#### Example – Restriction of relief on quoted securities

*A*'s executors sold the securities in December 1999. On 10 January 2000, they reinvested £10,000 in new securities. The £25,000 loss cannot be claimed in full, it has to be reduced by

$$\frac{10,000}{45,000} \ \times \ £25,000, \text{ ie } £5,556$$

### 17.11.5 Sales of land at a loss
(IHTA 1984, ss 190–198, as amended by FA 1993, s 199)

Relief is due where land and buildings are sold at a loss within four years of death, provided the loss is at least £1,000 or 5% of probate value (whichever is less). The net proceeds are substituted for the value at the date of death and the IHT is recomputed. However, this relief applies only where the property is sold to an arm's-length purchaser rather than to a connected person.

## 17.11.6 Debts which may be disallowed
(FA 1986, s 103)

There is a general rule that debts are not deductible where the deceased has made a capital transfer to the person who subsequently made a loan back to the deceased. This rule applies only to loans made after 18 March 1986 but there is no such time limit on the capital transfers. A debt may be disallowed because the deceased had made a capital transfer to the lender even though that capital transfer took place before 18 March 1986. It is also of no help that the loan was made on normal commercial terms and a market rate of interest was payable.

## 17.11.7 Legitim: special rules for Scotland
(IHTA 1984, s 147)

Where the deceased was Scottish, the 'legitim' rules need to be considered. Scottish law provides that a person must leave a set part of his estate to his children: their entitlement is called 'legitim'. If a person makes a will which does not take account of this, the children can have it set aside. In practice children often decide to renounce their right to legitim, especially where a person's will bequeaths all his property to his widow. The legislation provides that children who renounce their entitlement within two years of the death are not treated as making a chargeable transfer and the property is treated as passing to the widow in accordance with the will.

The deed renouncing the rights must satisfy the provisions as to variations, see 17.4.6.

Practical problems arise where children who are minors are involved. The IHT legislation provides that children under the age of 18 (at the date of death) may renounce their entitlement within two years of attaining 18 without this constituting a chargeable transfer by them. The property is then treated (for IHT purposes) as passing to the widow in accordance with the Will. As a child under the age of 18 does not have the legal capacity to renounce his entitlement, the executors have a difficult choice in such cases. They can either account for IHT on the basis that the child takes his entitlement or on the assumption that the child will renounce his rights when he reaches 18.

### Position where executors assume legitim rights are taken

IHT will have to be paid to the extent that the property which passes to the children exceeds the nil rate band. When each child attains 18, he may elect to renounce his rights so that the widow benefits. The spouse exemption will then mean that no tax should have been paid. The Revenue will then repay the IHT paid and pay interest.

### Position where executors assume that legitim will be renounced

No IHT will be paid in the first instance. However, if it turns out that one of the children decides not to renounce his entitlement, IHT on the death is recomputed and the tax payable attracts interest from the date that it should have been paid.

## 17.11.8 Quick succession relief
(IHTA 1984, s 141)

Suppose a person has recently inherited property from someone else. If he were to die and the full rate of IHT applied, the same property would have been subject to IHT twice within a relatively short period of time.

Quick succession relief is intended to alleviate this. The relief works by giving credit for a proportion of the tax charged on the first occasion against the tax payable on the second death. The proportion is set out below:

| Both deaths occur | Proportion |
| --- | --- |
| within one year | 100% |
| within two years | 80% |
| within three years | 60% |
| within four years | 40% |
| within five years | 20% |

### Example – Quick succession relief

*B* inherited property worth £150,000 in June 1996. Inheritance tax was paid on that estate at an average rate of 25%, so the grossed-up amount was £200,000 (£150,000 × $^{100}/_{75}$) and the tax suffered was £50,000. *B* dies in August 1999. The maximum amount on which quick succession relief can be claimed is:

$$\frac{150,000}{200,000} \times £50,000, \text{ ie } £37,500$$

This has to be reduced to 40% of £37,500 as three complete years have elapsed. The relief is not affected by the fact that property has been sold or given away before the second death takes place.

## 17.11.9 Treatment of gifts which are caught by the seven-year rule
(IHTA 1984, s 113A)

Tax on a PET which becomes a chargeable transfer because of the transferor's death is payable by the recipient of the gift. Business relief is available on a PET that becomes a chargeable transfer only if the conditions in 17.8 are satisfied both at the time of the gift and at the time of death.

### Examples – Business relief on PETs

(1) *A* owns all the shares in a family company. He gives his son a 24% share-holding. Three years later, the company is sold and the son receives cash for his shares. One year after that *A* dies.

Business relief will not normally be available as the necessary conditions are not satisfied by the donee at the time of *A*'s death. If the son had rein-vested the proceeds in another private company, business relief might have been available after all.

(2) In this case the basic position is as in (1) (ie *A*'s gift to his son of a 24% shareholding). However, this time the son retains his shares, but by the time that *A* dies the shares are quoted. No relief is due as the son does not control the company and his shares are quoted shares.

(3) The basic position is as in (1) but, in this case, the son retains the shares and they are still unquoted at the time of *A*'s death. The shares attract the 100% relief and this is not lost even if the son disposes of the shares shortly after *A*'s death.

## 17.11.10 Replacement property
(IHTA 1984, s 107)

Where a donee has disposed of business property, but acquires replacement property, the PET may still attract business relief provided the replacement property is acquired within three years of the disposal. Prior to 30 November 1993, the replacement property had to be acquired within one year. Similar rules apply for agricultural property.

## 17.11.11 Acceptance of property in lieu of IHT

The Revenue has power to accept certain types of property in satisfaction of inheritance tax liabilities. Such property includes pictures, prints, books, manuscripts, works of art, scientific objects and other items regarded as being of national, scientific, artistic and historic interest. However, the Revenue has to clear such arrangements with Heritage ministers and in practice only property which is regarded as of 'pre-eminent interest' is accepted.

Taxpayers who own such items which have been acknowledged as being first rate can enquire further about these arrangements by obtaining a copy of 'Capital Taxation and The National Heritage' from the Inland Revenue Reference Room, Room 8, New Wing, Somerset House, London WC2R 1LB, price £5.20.

# 17.12 LIFE ASSURANCE AND PENSION POLICIES

## 17.12.1 Life assurance

Life assurance is one of the best ways of providing for the payment of IHT, but the tax treatment of policies needs to be watched carefully. The following is only a summary of a complex area.

## 17.12.2 Death of policyholder

A life assurance policy beneficially owned by the deceased is property that is subject to IHT in the same way as any other property owned by him.

## 17.12.3 Gifts of policies

Gifts of policies may generally be made in two ways:

(1) Writing the policy in trust or making a subsequent declaration of trust.
(2) Assignment of the policy.

In either case subsequent premiums may be paid:

(a) by the donor direct;
(b) by the beneficiary out of cash gifts from the donor;
(c) by the beneficiary out of his resources;
(d) by a combination of the above.

In general, if the gift is to an individual, an accumulation and maintenance trust, a trust for the disabled or a trust in which there is an interest in possession, it will constitute a PET and will only be taxable if the donor dies within seven years of making the gift. Gifts to other trusts such as discretionary trusts may attract lifetime IHT.

If any of the usual IHT exemptions apply (see 17.5) neither the gift of the policy nor any gifts of premiums that have been made will be taxable, eg:

(1) The gift of the premium or policy falls within the annual exemption – currently £3,000 (note that if the policy is a qualifying policy and premiums are payable net of life assurance relief then it is the net premium that constitutes the gift; if the premiums are paid gross, it is the gross premium that constitutes the gift).
(2) The premiums come within the donor's normal expenditure out of income exemption (note that this applies to payment of premiums, not to the gift of an existing policy).
(3) The gifts fall within the marriage settlement exemption.
(4) The gifts fall within the small gifts exemption – outright gifts of not more than £250 per donee (eg a premium on a policy written in trust for the absolute benefit of a child).
(5) Policies written by husband or wife in trust for the other.

If none of the exemptions applies, IHT may be payable in respect of the gift of the policy or the payment of subsequent premiums (unless they fall within the £234,000 nil rate band).

If IHT is payable, the chargeable transfers are the premiums paid by the donor; or, if a gift of an existing policy is made by assignment or declaration of trust, the chargeable transfer is generally the greater of the total gross premiums paid or the market value of the policy (usually the surrender value).

If cash gifts have been made to enable the premiums to be paid by the beneficiary, the amount of the cash gifts will usually be PETs. The proceeds of the policy on death, maturity or surrender will not be subject to IHT in the hands of the recipient of the assignment or a beneficiary having an interest in possession in the trusts.

### 17.12.4 Life of another policies

On the death of the life assured the proceeds are totally free of IHT. Clearly they do not form part of the life assured's estate, as the policy is not owned by him. The surrender value will, however, be potentially chargeable in the policyholder's estate if he dies before the life assured.

If the policyholder is enabled to pay the premiums by virtue of cash gifts from the donor, the cash gifts will be taxable for the donor, unless the exemptions mentioned above apply, but the proceeds will be free of IHT in the policyholder's hands.

### 17.12.5 Use of policies

Life assurance policies can be used in two main ways in IHT planning:

(1) as a vehicle for making gifts to beneficiaries; and
(2) to create a fund for the eventual payment of the tax.

Thus they may help both to minimise the amount of tax payable and offer a means of paying any unavoidable liability whenever it arises.

### 17.12.6 Inheritance tax and pension plans

Although the legislation does not permit a policyholder to alienate his right to a retirement pension, it is possible to assign any death benefits provided under retirement annuity or personal pension plans, whether provided as a sum assured or as a return of the retirement fund. The IHT rules are broadly similar to those applicable to life policy assignments except that:

(1) discretionary trusts of these assignable benefits will not be subject to the usual IHT charging regime of ten-yearly and exit charges (see 18.5.12) provided the benefits are distributed within two years of the individual's death;
(2) the right to a pension is not treated as giving rise to an interest in possession in the pension fund;
(3) the gift of a 'return of fund' death benefit will usually be regarded as having no value, provided the individual is in good health. Similarly, subsequent contributions to the pension will be treated as being attributable to the provision of the pension benefits and not the death benefit, providing the individual is in good health at the time the contribution is made.

Occupational schemes are usually written under discretionary trusts and also achieve the same IHT exemptions on payment of contributions and distribution of benefits.

## 17.13 HERITAGE PROPERTY

It is possible to claim exemption for transfers of qualifying heritage assets such as chattels of museum quality, land of outstanding natural beauty or of historic or scientific interest, and buildings and amenity land deemed to be of outstanding historic or architectural interest. The exemption is currently conditional on the new owner undertaking to maintain and preserve the asset and to provide reasonable public access to it. It is no longer possible to restrict access by requiring a prior appointment with the asset's owner.

The rules for defining qualifying chattels have also been made more restrictive by FA 1998. Until recently there was no time limit for claiming heritage tax exemptions, but for tax charges arising after 16 March 1998 a claim for exemption will normally have to be made within two years of the date of the relevant chargeable event. In addition transfers made after 16 March 1998 no longer qualify for the special exemption previously available for gifts and bequests to certain non-profit making bodies.

# 18

# THE TAXATION OF TRUSTS

MARK FRANCIS

This chapter covers the taxation of trusts under the following headings:

(1) When are trustees liable to pay income tax?
(2) When are trustees liable for UK CGT?
(3) Bare trusts.
(4) Fixed interest trusts.
(5) Discretionary trusts.
(6) Accumulation and maintenance trusts.
(7) Trusts for the disabled.
(8) Protective trusts.
(9) Charitable trusts.
(10) Executors and personal representatives.

## 18.1 WHEN ARE TRUSTEES LIABLE TO PAY INCOME TAX?
(FA 1989, s 110)

A liability to pay UK income tax arises for all trusts which have at least one UK-resident trustee (even though there may be a majority of non-resident trustees) unless the trust was created by a person of foreign domicile, in which case the UK trustee is liable only in respect of UK income.

In the main, trustees are liable for tax at 20% on income from savings, with other income being taxed at the basic rate, but trustees of discretionary and accumulation trusts are subject to additional tax so that they pay an extra 14%.

A non-resident trust will be subject to tax on UK income such as interest taxed at source and dividends. Where the non-resident trust receives untaxed interest, there is in theory a tax liability, but in practice the trustees may escape tax because of ESC B13 (see 21.4.2).

Trustees are not entitled to personal allowances (see Chapter 7).

## 18.2 WHEN ARE TRUSTEES LIABLE FOR UK CAPITAL GAINS TAX?
(TCGA 1992, ss 2 and 69)

Trustees are subject to CGT only if the trust is resident in the UK. A trust is regarded as resident unless:

(1) the majority of the trustees are not resident in the UK; and
(2) the ordinary administration of the trust is carried on outside the UK.

This rule is therefore slightly different from that used for income tax purposes.

There is an exception to the above general rule in the case of property settled by a person of foreign domicile who was neither resident nor ordinarily resident in the UK at the time that the trust was created. Provided the UK trustees are professional trustees whose business consists of or includes the management of trusts, the facts that the majority of the trustees are UK-resident and the management of the trust is carried on within the UK do not make the trust resident in the UK.

### UK-resident trusts

In general trustees are responsible for reporting gains and paying tax, but this rule does not apply where either the settlor or his spouse can receive benefit. Capital gains made by trustees of such a trust are generally taxed as if they were personal gains of the settlor (see 20.12).

### 18.2.1 Annual exemption
(TCGA 1992, Sched 1)

For a number of years the annual CGT exemption available to trustees has been half the individual exemption, eg for 2000–01 £3,600 (half of £7,200).

Where a settlor has created a number of settlements since 6 June 1978, the annual exemption is shared equally. The minimum annual exemption for each settlement is currently £720 (ie $\frac{1}{10}$ of the annual individual exemption). An unused part of the exemption for one settlement cannot be utilised by another settlement.

Consequently, if a person created three trusts in 1975 and four trusts in 1989, the 2000–01 exemption for the 1975 trusts would be £3,600 each, and the four trusts created after 6 June 1978 would each have an exemption of £900. If all seven trusts had been created after 6 June 1978, each would have an annual exemption of £720.

### 18.2.2 Taper relief

Trustees may qualify for higher rate taper relief for business assets if they

425

own 25% of the voting rights in a trading company. Certain fixed interest trusts can also qualify where the trustees' shares are in a company which is the life tenant's qualifying company (see below).

## 18.3 BARE TRUSTS

A bare trust is one where trustees hold property on behalf of someone who is absolutely entitled to that property, or would be absolutely entitled if he were not a minor. Income and capital gains received by trustees of a bare trust belong to the person who is absolutely entitled to the property concerned. The trustees normally have no liability to tax.

Prior to 6 April 1996, the trustees of some bare trusts accounted for income tax at basic rate on the income which they paid over to the beneficiaries. These amounts became taxed income in the hands of the beneficiaries, who were required to give full details of that income in their tax returns, but were liable to pay further tax only if they were higher rate taxpayers. Conversely, they were entitled to a repayment of the tax paid by the trustees if they had no personal liability.

Under self-assessment, the Revenue will no longer allow trustees to account for tax in such circumstances because there is no entitlement in law for trustees to deduct tax from income arising to bare trusts. Any income which is received gross by the trustees must be paid gross to the beneficiaries. The only exception to this rule is that UK-resident trustees may be required, under the non-resident landlords scheme, to deduct and account for tax on the rental income of beneficiaries whose usual place of abode is outside the UK (see 21.3).

Trustees of bare trusts will not be required to complete self-assessment tax returns, or to make any payments on account. Beneficiaries will still be required to give details of all their income and gains from bare trusts in their own tax returns, and in addition will be required to account to the Revenue for the full amount of any tax due.

See 20.5.3 on the position where a parent gives money to a bare trust for his minor child.

## 18.4 FIXED INTEREST TRUSTS

A fixed interest trust is one where a beneficiary is entitled to receive income as it arises, either during his lifetime or for a specific period. A simple type of fixed interest trust would be a trust under which the beneficiary is entitled to receive all the income during his lifetime with the trust coming to an end on his death, perhaps with the capital then passing to the beneficiary's children. A beneficiary who is entitled to receive trust income in this way during his lifetime is called a 'life tenant'.

There may also be a situation where a life tenant is entitled to receive a proportion of the trust income, say 50%, with the other 50% being held upon different types of trust. It is also possible to have an entitlement to income (an 'interest in possession') for a specific period, so that a trust under which someone had a right to all of the income for a fixed period of ten years would be a fixed interest trust until the end of that period.

## 18.4.1 Income tax

Where property is held upon fixed interest trusts, income tax is charged on the trustees at the basic rate except in so far as the income is 'income from savings' which is taxed at only 20%. With effect from 6 April 1999 dividend income is taxable at 10% (the Schedule F rate). Prior to 1996–97 all income other than dividends was taxed at basic rate. There is no deduction for personal allowances (only individuals are entitled to them), but if a trust owns investment properties on which an entitlement to capital allowances arises, such capital allowances may be set against the trustees' income in the same way as for individuals. Similarly, if the trustees carry on a trade, any losses may be relieved against other income. Subject to this, the trustees will either suffer basic rate tax at source or be assessed to basic rate tax on all income arising to them, with the assessments being made under the different Schedules.

## 18.4.2 Ascertaining the beneficiary's income

It will not generally be possible for the trustees to pay over to a beneficiary the full amount of the income left to him after tax. Inevitably, there will be some expenses such as bank charges, interest, professional fees and so on, which are properly charged to income, and there may also be the trustees' own fees. Such expenses are not deducted in arriving at the trustees' taxable income, but they need to be taken into account in determining the amount of the beneficiary's income.

In broad terms, the proper procedure is to ascertain the trustees' taxable income for a year. The tax paid by the trustees for the year concerned should then be deducted, and a further deduction should be made for expenses which are properly charged against income. The net amount must then be 'grossed up' and this is the amount that the beneficiary will need to declare on his tax return.

### Example – Tax treatment of income from a fixed interest trust

The trustees of a fixed interest trust have taxable income of £20,000 for 1999–2000. They pay tax of £4,600 (23%). There are expenses of £1,700 which are properly chargeable against the income. The balance belongs to the life tenant. The life tenant's gross income will be ascertained as follows:

|  | £ |
|---|---|
| Trustees' taxable income | 20,000 |
| *Less*: basic rate tax | (4,600) |
|  | 15,400 |
| *Less*: expenses | (1,700) |
|  | 13,700 |
| £13,700 grossed up at basic rate = | 17,792 |

This income forms part of the life tenant's income for the year *whether or not it is actually paid out to him*. If the life tenant is subject to higher rate tax, he must pay the difference between the 40% rate and basic rate tax.

### 18.4.3 Income from savings
(FA 1993, s 79 and Sched 6)

From 1996–97 onwards, it is necessary to distinguish income from savings. The new, lower Schedule F rate of tax means that income from savings should be separated into that from dividends and that from other sources. Dividend income is taxable at 10% as opposed to 20% on other savings income. Trustees' expenses are deemed to be set first against UK dividend income, so as to minimise the restriction of the tax deemed to be withheld from the trust income.

### 18.4.4 Tax returns

The returns usually completed for trusts are forms SA900 and additional pages as necessary. For fixed interest trusts a tax deduction certificate (Form R185 (Non-discretionary)) should also be completed by the trustees or their professional advisers showing the appropriate gross, tax and net figures in respect of the beneficiary's income. It is necessary to show the different types of income separately on the certificate.

### 18.4.5 Income mandated to a beneficiary

Trustees sometimes take the view that it is simpler to mandate dividends and other income to the beneficiary so that such income does not pass through the trustees' hands. This does not alter the fact that the trustees are still the legal owners of the assets which produce the income.

Although this income can be entered directly in the beneficiary's personal tax return, care should be taken to ensure that it is entered in the correct section for trust income so as to avoid any confusion with the beneficiary's personal income. Where this happens, the Revenue will assess the beneficiary rather than the trustees. However, if the trustees incur expenses, these may not be deducted as in 18.4.2 above. This even applies where the beneficiary reimburses the trustees for such expenses later on.

## 18.4.6 Beneficiary's exempt income

It is sometimes possible for UK-resident trustees to take advantage of a beneficiary's tax exemption to avoid paying tax which the beneficiary would then have to claim back. For example, where a beneficiary is entitled to all the income of the trust and he is resident outside the UK, the trustees can agree with the Revenue that the income which arises outside the UK (and any other income which is exempt for a non-resident eg interest from exempt gilts – see 21.4.3) should not be taxed in the trustees' hands.

This treatment is not normally available where a non-resident beneficiary is entitled only to a proportion of the trustees' income.

## 18.4.7 Taxable income which is not income for trust purposes

Difficulties can arise where the trustees receive something which constitutes income for tax purposes, but is not income for trust purposes. For example, if trustees of a fixed interest trust receive a lump sum premium which is taxable income for Schedule A purposes (see 4.3) this is not income which belongs to the life tenant. Similarly, a distribution such as may arise on a company buying back its own shares may be income for income tax purposes (see 5.9.7) but is capital for trust purposes. In both these situations, the trustees must pay tax on such deemed income, but the amounts must be excluded when calculating the life tenant's income for tax purposes.

Another situation where taxable income, but not trust income, may arise is where trustees have acquired an enterprise zone building (or indeed any type of industrial building) and a balancing charge arises on a disposal. Such a balancing charge is taxed at basic rate only. Because it is a capital receipt, it is not normally possible for the trustees to pay it to a life tenant and it therefore does not constitute part of his income for tax purposes.

There are certain situations where the legislation makes special provision. Where trustees dispose of a loan stock cum-interest, the trustees will generally be subject to assessment under the accrued income scheme (see 5.6) in respect of the interest which has arisen on the loan stock during their period of ownership. However, this is not income which the trustees will be able to pay out to a beneficiary since a life tenant will be entitled only to actual income, not deemed income. In this specific case, the legislation provides that trustees should be taxed at 34% on income assessed under Schedule D Case VI in respect of the accrued income scheme.

A similar rule applies where trustees realise gains on the disposal of shares in an offshore roll-up fund (see 6.2) and also income distributions from a purchase of own shares on or after 7 December 1996.

Enhanced scrip dividends can give rise to special problems as the tax treatment depends upon the way that the dividend is treated for trust purposes (this may be affected by the way that the trust deed is worded). You should obtain a copy of SP4/94.

## 18.4.8 Exempt receipts which are income for trust purposes

The converse may happen. For example, a trustee may receive income in the form of a repayment supplement which is exempt. This will still constitute income for trust law purposes and the life tenant will generally be entitled to receive the full amount, but it is not taxable income for him.

The treatment of dividends arising from demergers (see 5.8.10) also gave rise to concern, but a test case involving the ICI demerger has established that such receipts by trustees are capital rather than income from the point of view of trust law so in this particular case the treatment for trust law and taxation will normally be the same. However, it is important to take professional advice where significant sums of money are involved as the Revenue distinguishes between different types of demergers (remind your accountant to refer to *Tax Bulletin* October 1994).

## 18.4.9 Capital gains tax

Trustees of fixed interest trusts are subject to tax at 34% on any capital gains. For 1996–97 and earlier years, the rate was the same as the basic rate of income tax. No further CGT (or income tax) liability will normally arise on the trustees distributing cash to a beneficiary after they have realised a capital gain by selling an asset.

## 18.4.10 Exemption for property occupied by a beneficiary
(TCGA 1992, s 225)

There is an exemption for trustees in respect of a property which is owned by them, but which is occupied by a beneficiary as his main residence (provided he is entitled to do so under the terms of the trust deed). The beneficiary may not also claim exemption for a property owned by him. Where an individual has more than one residence, and it is desired to elect that a property owned by trustees be treated as the individual's main residence, a joint notice needs to be given by the trustees and the individual concerned.

## 18.4.11 Disposals of business assets

Where trustees of a fixed interest trust dispose of an asset which has been used by an 'eligible beneficiary' for the purposes of a trade carried on by him, or by a firm in which he is a partner, the asset may be treated as a business asset for taper relief purposes (see 14.6). Similar provisions apply where trustees sell an asset used in a business carried on by an eligible beneficiary's qualifying company, or where they sell shares in the company itself.

An 'eligible beneficiary' is a beneficiary entitled to an interest in possession over the whole of the settled property or over a part of the settled property that included the asset concerned.

A company is the eligible beneficiary's qualifying company if he works for it on a full-time basis and he owns at least 5% of the voting rights.

Relief may be restricted where the eligible beneficiary has rights to only part of the income from the settled property. Professional advice should therefore be sought if the trust fund has more than one life tenant and some of the beneficiaries do not work full time for the company or they do not have the requisite 5% interest.

If the trustees own 25% of the voting shares, they may qualify for taper relief as business assets whether or not an eligible beneficiary works for the company.

## 18.4.12 Liability may arise on deemed disposals as well as actual disposals

A capital gain may arise on a deemed disposal such as where the trustees distribute assets to a beneficiary, or where a beneficiary becomes absolutely entitled to capital under the terms of a trust. Hold-over relief is available only if the disposal involves business property (see 15.6).

## 18.4.13 Transfer of capital losses to a trust beneficiary

The rules here have recently changed. Until 15 June 1999, where capital was distributed to a beneficiary by the trustees exercising their discretionary powers, or when he became absolutely entitled to the capital on attaining a certain age, capital losses which were attributable to the property to which he became entitled passed across and were available to cover capital gains realised by him in that year or a future year. Thus if the trustees had unrelieved capital losses of £100,000 and a beneficiary became entitled to one quarter of the trust capital, he would be treated as if he had personal CGT losses of £25,000.

Where a beneficiary becomes absolutely entitled on or after 16 June 1999, losses realised in the past by the trustees do not pass across. Furthermore, if a loss arises for the trustees on an asset passing across to the beneficiary, he may use this only against a capital gain that he may subsequently realise on a disposal of that asset.

## 18.4.14 Death of the life tenant
(TCGA 1992, s 73)

There is one type of deemed disposal which does not give rise to a CGT charge. Where an interest in possession ceases on a death, the assets are treated as having been disposed of and reacquired at their value at that date, but there is no chargeable gain for the trustees. This does not apply where the trustees hold assets which were subject to a hold-over claim by the settlor at the time that he transferred the assets to the trustees.

## 18.4.15 Inheritance tax
(IHTA 1984, s 49)

Where a beneficiary has an interest in possession, he is treated for IHT purposes as if he owned the trust capital. On death, the value of the trust capital is brought into account as part of the individual's estate and IHT is charged accordingly. However, the trustees are responsible for paying the IHT on the proportion of the tax attributable to the trust property.

### Example – IHT liability on a fixed interest trust

*A* died on 1 December 1998 owning property in his personal capacity worth £200,000 (this is called his 'free estate') and he is also the life tenant of a trust which has a capital value of £350,000. The total IHT payable is:

|  | £ |
|---|---|
| Free estate | 200,000 |
| Trust | 350,000 |
|  | 550,000 |
| *Less*: nil rate band | (223,000) |
|  | 327,000 |
| IHT thereon at 40% | 130,800 |

The inheritance tax is payable as follows:

$$Executors \quad \frac{£200,000}{550,000} \times 130,800 = £47,564$$

$$Trustees \quad \frac{£350,000}{550,000} \times 130,800 = £83,236$$

## 18.4.16 Exempt pre-13 November 1974 Will Trusts
(IHTA 1984, Sched 6, para 2)

These are trusts created by the will of a person who died before 13 November 1974 and left property in trust on the following terms:

(1) his surviving spouse was entitled to an interest in possession;
(2) the surviving spouse was not entitled to demand that the capital should be paid out to her.

These trusts are exempt from the normal charge that arises when the surviving spouse's interest in possession comes to an end. The reason for this is that prior to 13 November 1974, estate duty was levied on the death of an individual even if he left property in trust for his spouse. However, the estate duty legislation then provided an exemption on the death of the surviving spouse and this has been carried over to IHT.

Will Trusts which came into being after 12 November 1974 are treated differently because of the exemption which applies for IHT purposes where property passes to a surviving spouse. Property held in a post-12 November 1974 Will Trust is subject to IHT on the death of the life tenant.

## 18.4.17 No charge where a life tenant becomes absolutely entitled to the trust property
(IHTA 1984, s 53(2))

There are no IHT implications where a life tenant (or any other beneficiary entitled to an interest in possession) becomes absolutely entitled to the trust property. The reason for this is that the beneficiary was already regarded for IHT purposes as if he owned the capital concerned. All that has happened is that the beneficiary's interest has been enlarged and, whilst this may have CGT consequences, it does not give rise to an IHT charge.

## 18.4.18 Consequences of an interest in possession terminating during a person's lifetime
(IHTA 1984, ss 3A, 23 and 52)

Where a beneficiary's interest in possession comes to an end during his lifetime and he does not personally become entitled to the trust property, he is treated as making a transfer of value. The transfer is normally either a PET (see 17.6) or a chargeable transfer, according to what happens as a result of the interest in possession coming to an end.

### Potentially exempt transfer

If the effect of the beneficiary's interest coming to an end is that:

(1)  another individual becomes entitled to an interest in possession, or
(2)  another person becomes absolutely entitled to the trust property, or
(3)  the trust becomes an accumulation and maintenance trust,

the person whose interest in possession has terminated is treated as having made a PET. In such instances, IHT is charged if and only if the person dies within the following seven years. If this should happen, the trustees are liable to pay the IHT unless the settled property passes to a beneficiary through his becoming absolutely entitled on the termination of the interest in possession. In such a situation the person who becomes absolutely entitled is liable to pay any such IHT.

### Exempt transfer

Occasionally, the effect of a person's interest in possession coming to an end is that the spouse becomes entitled to an interest in possession. Where this happens, the person whose interest in possession has come to an end is treated as having made an exempt transfer. This treatment also applies if a trust becomes a charitable trust as a result of a beneficiary's interest in possession coming to an end.

## Chargeable transfer

Where a person's interest in possession comes to an end, and the trust thereby becomes a discretionary trust, the person is treated as having made a chargeable transfer. If the person's cumulative chargeable transfers bring him over the nil rate band, IHT is payable right away at the lifetime rate of 20%. If the person should then die within three years, the rate increases to 40% (see 17.10).

## 18.4.19 How the transfer of value is computed on a lifetime transfer

The legislation contains an anomaly. Where an individual makes a gift in his personal capacity, the transfer of value is deemed to be the amount by which his estate is reduced in value (see 17.3.3). This rule does not apply where a person's interest in possession comes to an end as, in this case, the amount of the transfer of value is taken as the value of the property in which the interest in possession has terminated.

### Example – Calculation of value of lifetime transfer

*A* owns 90% of a company in his personal capacity and is the life tenant of a trust which owns the remaining 10%. The value of a 100% shareholding in the company is worth £500,000. The value of a 90% shareholding is £450,000. However, a 10% shareholding valued in isolation is worth only £20,000. If *A* had made a gift of 10% out of his personal shareholding, his transfer of value would be taken to be:

|  | £ |
|---|---|
| Value of a 100% shareholding | 500,000 |
| *Less*: value of remaining 90% shareholding | |
| (taking his own shares and the trust together) | 450,000 |
| Reduction in value of his estate | 50,000 |

However, if *A* surrenders his life interest in the trust so that his interest in possession comes to an end, the value transferred is taken as £20,000.

## 18.5 DISCRETIONARY TRUSTS

In contrast to a fixed interest trust, a discretionary trust is one where the trustees can control the way in which the income is used. In some cases, the trustees have power to accumulate income, in which case it may be retained by them either with a view to its being paid out in later years or as an addition to the trust capital.

In other cases, the trustees have no legal right to accumulate income, but the trust is regarded as discretionary because no beneficiary has a fixed entitlement (ie the trustees must distribute the income, but they can choose how the income is distributed and which particular beneficiary should receive income).

A major change in the income tax rules came into effect from 6 April 1999.

## 18.5.1 Income tax for years up to 1998–99
(TA 1988, s 686)

Trustees of discretionary trusts were liable for tax at 34% for 1998–99, ie the 'rate of tax applicable to trusts'. They were also liable for 34% tax for 1996–97 and 1997–98. For 1995–96 and earlier years, the rate was 35%. Where part of the trust income is subject to a fixed interest trust and the balance was held on discretionary trust, the 34% rate is charged only on the income held on discretionary trusts.

In some cases, the trustees suffer basic rate tax at source and then pay an additional 11% (10% for 1996–97).

### Notional income which is left out of account

Certain types of income are not taken into account for additional rate purposes, ie sums which are capital profits under trust law such as:

(1) premiums treated as rent (see 4.3);
(2) profits on sale of certificates of deposit (see 6.1).

This income is subject to tax at only 23%. Income which is taxed under the accrued income scheme arising from a purchase of own shares on or after 7 December 1996 is charged at 34%. This comes to the same thing, but such deemed income is not technically subject to the additional rate.

## 18.5.2 Computing the trustees' liability to the rate applicable to trusts

The trustees' liability for basic rate tax and lower rate tax on income from savings is calculated in exactly the same way as for trustees of fixed interest trusts. A separate computation is then required for the purposes of the 34% rate.

Expenses paid out of net income are 'grossed up' and the resulting amount is then deducted. Examples of such expenses are:

(1) Bank charges

(2) Interest which does not qualify for tax relief
(3) The costs of administering the trust
(4) Charges made by professional trustees
(5) Deficits on properties where the deficiency cannot be relieved against other Schedule A income.

Costs such as premiums on an insurance policy (excluding fire insurance), or property expenses such as the cost of maintenance or insurance of a property or charges made for collecting rents, cannot be included directly as a deduction in computing liability for additional rate tax.

### Example – Calculating the additional tax on discretionary trusts

A discretionary trust receives income from savings of £15,000 in 1998–99. It has no other income. Expenses which are not allowable in computing income for basic rate tax purposes, but which are properly chargeable to income, amount to £960. The trustees' liability for tax at the 34% rate is computed as follows:

|  | £ |
|---|---|
| Income from savings | 15,000 |
| *Less*: expenses – grossed up | |
| £960 × $^{100}\!/_{80}$ | 1,200 |
| | 13,800 |
| Tax at 14% | 1,932 |

If the trustees had also received some other income which was not income from savings, this would normally be taxed at 11%, ie 34% less basic rate tax withheld at source. Administrative expenses are set off against income from savings first. Any balance is then grossed up at the rate of $^{100}\!/_{77}$ and then set against other income for the purposes of calculating the additional rate.

## 18.5.3 Income tax for 1999–2000 onwards

Trustees of discretionary trusts are still liable for 34% tax on income other than dividends in just the same way as described in 18.5.1–18.5.4. However, trustees will be taxed at 25% on UK dividend income received after 5 April 1999. This compensates for the reduction in the tax credit to 10% from 6 April 1999 (see 5.8.3). The actual amount of tax payable by the trustees should be almost exactly the same, ie:

|                                             | Up to<br>1998–99 | From<br>6 April 1999 |
|---------------------------------------------|------------------|----------------------|
|                                             | £                | £                    |
| Cash dividend received                      | 80.00            | 80.00                |
| Tax credit (²⁰⁄₀ and ¹⁰⁄₀)                  | 20.00            | 8.89                 |
| Taxable income                              | 100.00           | 88.89                |
| Rate applicable to trusts (34% and 25%)     | 34.00            | 22.22                |
| *Less*: tax credit                          | (20.00)          | (8.89)               |
| Tax payable                                 | 14.00            | 13.33                |

Furthermore, when the trustees distribute income to beneficiaries, they will be required to pay additional tax unless the distribution can be shown to have come out of a 'pool' which has suffered 34% tax.

Thus in the case of a new trust with only post-6 April 1999 dividend income, the trustees will be required to pay additional tax which brings the total tax paid by the trustees up to 34%. Therefore, in the above example, the trustees had dividend income of £80.00 on which they paid tax of £13.33, leaving them with £66.67. If they distribute the whole of this income to the beneficiaries, the trustees will have to pay further tax. The calculation is complicated and is as follows:

| Maximum distribution         | £52.80 |
|------------------------------|--------|
| Tax thereon                  | £27.20 |
| Gross income for beneficiary | £80.00 |

This income is regarded as having suffered 34% tax. The trustees then pay tax of £13.87 over to the Revenue so that they have paid a total of £27.20, ie:

| Tax payable on the dividend      | £13.33 |
|----------------------------------|--------|
| Tax payable on the distribution  | £13.87 |
|                                  | £27.20 |

Trustees should obtain a copy of *Tax Bulletin* February 1999 which covers all this in detail.

## 18.5.4 Income distributions in excess of the trustees' taxable income
(TA 1988, s 687)

There may be situations where trustees make distributions in excess of their taxable income. Such distributions also give rise to a liability for the trustees to account for tax at 34%. There are several situations in which such a liability can arise:

(1) A trust may have income on which income tax does not have to be paid. If such income is paid out to a beneficiary as an income distribution, the trustees must account for tax at 34%.
(2) Similarly, trustees may make payments of an income nature which are subject to tax as income in the hands of the beneficiary even though they come out of the trust capital. In practice, the Revenue would not normally assess such distributions unless they were made regularly.

If the income is fully distributed each year and foreign securities are held, there will be an additional liability to tax when the foreign income is distributed to beneficiaries. The liability is equal to the credit allowed against basic rate tax for double taxation relief.

## 18.5.5 Tax returns

One tax return (form SA900) is now completed whether the trust is a fixed interest trust or discretionary. There are supplementary forms to be completed for various types of income (SA901–SA904) and capital gains (SA905). If the trust is not UK resident, SA906 must be completed.

The Revenue provides a tax calculation guide for trusts and estates, but as the calculation layout is of Byzantine complexity the form is generally not used.

A tax deduction certificate form R185 should be completed by the trustees or their professional advisers showing the appropriate gross, tax and net figures.

## 18.5.6 The beneficiary's position

A beneficiary needs to include on his tax return the grossed up amount of any income distributed to him by the trustees during the tax year. Because the trustees are subject to the additional rate, the beneficiary's income is treated as net of 34% tax.

## 18.5.7 Accumulated income subsequently distributed as capital

A distribution of capital which represents income which has been accumulated is not normally taxable income for the beneficiary. Such a distribution is treated as a capital distribution though, of course, this presupposes that the trustees have power to accumulate income. In cases where they have no power to accumulate income, any distributions will remain as income.

### 18.5.8 Capital gains tax
(TCGA 1992, s 5)

All the capital gains of a discretionary trust are taxed at 34% except for the amount covered by the annual exemption.

As with a fixed interest trust, no further CGT (or income tax) liability will normally arise on the trustees' distributing cash to a beneficiary after they have realised a capital gain by selling an asset.

### 18.5.9 Exemption for property occupied by a beneficiary
(TCGA 1992, s 225)

The courts have held that trustees of a discretionary trust are entitled to this exemption where they permit a beneficiary to occupy a property as his main residence, even though the trust deed did not confer a right for the beneficiary to require the trustees to provide such a property.

### 18.5.10 Deemed disposals/hold-over relief
(TCGA 1992, s 71)

A capital gain may arise on a deemed disposal such as where the trustees distribute assets to a beneficiary, or where a beneficiary becomes absolutely entitled to capital under the terms of a trust. Hold-over relief is normally available where a disposal of the property arises on a capital distribution to a beneficiary.

### 18.5.11 Transfer of capital losses to a trust beneficiary

Where capital is distributed to a beneficiary, or when he becomes absolutely entitled to the capital, capital losses which are attributable to the property to which he becomes entitled pass across to the beneficiary and are available to cover future capital gains realised by him.

### 18.5.12 Inheritance tax
(IHTA 1984, ss 64–65)

By definition, no beneficiary has an interest in possession in a discretionary trust and it follows that the trust capital is not treated as forming part of his estate. There is therefore no IHT charge on the death of a beneficiary of a discretionary trust.

To make up for the absence of such a charge, the legislation imposes a lower charge every ten years (the 'periodic charge'). The theory is that a generation is approximately 30 years and the tax charged on three separate occasions by reason of the periodic charge will approximate to the tax payable on property passing down to the next generation.

There is also an 'exit charge' which applies where property leaves a discretionary trust. There are different rules for discretionary trusts created before and after 26 March 1974.

## 18.5.13 Trusts created after 26 March 1974

### Periodic charge
(IHTA 1984, s 66)

The periodic charge arises on the tenth anniversary of the creation of the trust and on every subsequent tenth anniversary. The maximum rate is at present 6%, computed as follows:

Tax payable at lifetime rate (20%) × 30%.

Actually, the computation is more complex and involves the following process:

| | |
|---|---|
| Amount of chargeable transfers made by the settlor in the seven years prior to the creation of the trust | A |
| Value of the trust property at the tenth anniversary | B |
| Add A and B | C |
| Deduct nil rate band | D |
| | E |

The next step is to compute the IHT payable on E and on A – D. The tax payable by the trustees on the periodic charge is 30% of the difference.

### Example – Periodic charge

*A* created a discretionary trust in June 1988. He had previously made chargeable transfers of £194,000. In June 1998 the trust is worth £160,000. The periodic charge is therefore computed as follows:

| | | £ |
|---|---|---|
| Amount of previous chargeable transfers | (A) | 194,000 |
| Value of trust property in 1998 | (B) | 160,000 |
| | (C) | 354,000 |
| Deduct nil rate band | (D) | 223,000 |
| | (E) | 131,000 |
| IHT on E | = | 26,200 |
| IHT at lifetime rates on A – D | = | Nil |
| | | 26,200 |

Periodic charge is 30% of £26,200, ie £7,860.

## 18.5.14 Trusts created prior to 26 March 1974

This type of trust is simpler in that there cannot have been any chargeable transfers made by the settlor prior to the creation of the trust. The computation is therefore:

| | |
|---|---|
| Value of the trust property at the tenth anniversary | X |
| Deduct nil rate band | Y |
| | Z |

Inheritance tax at lifetime rates on Z

Periodic charge is 30% of this amount.

## 18.5.15 Position where trustees have made capital distributions during preceding ten years

Where the trustees have made a capital distribution within the previous ten years or property has otherwise ceased to be held upon discretionary trusts (eg by reason of a beneficiary being entitled to an interest in possession) the value of the capital distribution must also be brought into account in arriving at the periodic charge. The computation is as follows:

| | |
|---|---|
| Amount of chargeable transfers made by the settlor in the seven years prior to the creation of the trust and capital distributions since the last periodic charge | A |
| Value of the trust property at the tenth anniversary | B |
| Add A and B | C |
| Deduct nil rate band | D |
| | E |

The next step is to compute the IHT payable on E and on A – D. The tax payable by the trustees on the period charge is 30% of the difference.

## 18.5.16 Treatment of undistributed income

The Revenue accepts that undistributed income which has not been accumulated should be excluded in arriving at the value of the trust capital at the tenth anniversary. The reason for this is that such income remains income held for the benefit of beneficiaries and is not capital.

Where income has been formally accumulated, it must be brought into account for the purposes of the periodic charge. However, such accumulated income is treated as if it were additional capital added to the trust at the date that the trustees resolved to accumulate it.

## 18.5.17 Exit charge (also known as the proportionate charge)

The way in which the exit charge is computed varies according to whether capital leaves a discretionary trust within the first ten years or only after there has been a periodic charge.

## 18.5.18 Exit charge during the first ten years
(IHTA 1984, s 68)

The position here is that a notional rate of charge should be computed which is the average rate of IHT which would have been payable if the settlor had made a chargeable transfer at the time that he created the trust equal to the value of the trust property at that time.

### Example – Exit charge during first ten years

A created a trust in February 1991 and the original trust property was worth £300,000. The entry charge would have been computed as follows:

|  | £ |
|---|---|
| Value of the trust property in February 1991 | 300,000 |
| *Less*: nil rate band at that time | (128,000) |
|  | 172,000 |
| £172,000 at 20% = | £34,400 |

Effective rate = $\dfrac{34,400}{300,000} \times 100$

The entry charge would therefore have been 11.47% and the tax payable if property leaves a discretionary trust within the first ten years is levied as a proportion of this rate. The exact proportion is determined by the number of complete periods of three months (or quarters) during which the trust has been in existence. Thus, if the exit charge occurred after the trust had been in being for six years and seven months, the charge would be at the rate of:

$\dfrac{26}{40} \times$ 30% of 11.47%.

## 18.5.19 Exit charge after a periodic charge
(IHTA 1984, s 69)

The position here is that the charge applies only to the proportion of the property which leaves the discretionary trust, with the proportion being determined by the following formula:

$$\frac{\text{Number of complete quarters since the periodic charge}}{40}$$

A distribution during the first quarter following the ten-year charge is entirely free of IHT.

The rate of tax charged is normally fixed by the effective rate charged on the previous periodic charge. However, the effective rate is calculated by using the scale of rates in force at the time that the exit charge arises. Thus, the notional effective rate may be slightly lower than the effective rate of IHT which actually applied on the last periodic charge.

## 18.6 ACCUMULATION AND MAINTENANCE TRUSTS
(IHTA 1984, s 71)

An accumulation and maintenance trust is a special form of discretionary trust which has been set up for a stated class of beneficiaries. The following conditions must normally be satisfied:

(1) One or more beneficiaries will become entitled to an interest in possession in the trust property on attaining a specified age which must not exceed age 25.
(2) Until one of the beneficiaries becomes beneficially entitled, the trust income must be held on a discretionary basis with income being applied only for the maintenance, education or benefit of the beneficiaries or accumulated for the benefit of such persons.
(3) The trust must have a life of not more than 25 years or it must be a trust for the benefit of grandchildren of a common grandparent.

Where an accumulation and maintenance trust was in existence at 15 April 1976, the 25-year period runs from that date, ie to 14 April 2001, and not from the date that the trust was created.

### 18.6.1 Taxation

The same rules apply, and the same returns and certificates need to be completed, for income tax and CGT as for discretionary trusts. There are, however, different rules for CGT hold-over relief and IHT.

### 18.6.2 Hold-over relief for trustees
(TCGA 1992, s 260)

Where trustees dispose of assets to a beneficiary, hold-over relief may be available if the property concerned is business property (see 15.6). As regards other assets, hold-over relief normally is available if the disposal takes place when a beneficiary becomes absolutely entitled to capital and income at the same date.

There is a problem area for trustees of accumulation and maintenance trusts in that many trusts provide that a beneficiary should become entitled to income when he reaches age 18, but capital vests only at age 25. If the beneficiary became entitled to the capital at age 18, there would be no problem but, because there is a gap in time between the accumulation period coming to an end and the beneficiary becoming absolutely entitled to the capital, it is not possible for trustees to claim hold-over relief (unless, of course, the trust property consists of business assets).

### 18.6.3 IHT privileges for an accumulation and maintenance trust

An accumulation and maintenance trust is not subject to the periodic charge described above. Furthermore, there is no exit charge on a beneficiary becoming entitled to an interest in possession under the trust or becoming absolutely entitled to trust property.

## 18.7 TRUSTS FOR THE DISABLED
(TCGA 1992, Sched 1; IHTA 1984, ss 74 and 89)

A trust for a disabled person is a type of discretionary trust which enjoys certain tax privileges. The trustees are entitled to the full CGT exemption of £7,100 for individuals (1999–2000 figure) and there is no liability for the IHT periodic and exit charges.

The terms of the trust must be such that not less than half of the settled property and income must be applied for the benefit of a disabled person who is treated as if he had an interest in possession. A disabled person is one who, at the time that the trust was created, was:

(1) incapable by reason of mental disorder within the meaning of the Mental Health Act 1983 of administering his property or managing his affairs; or
(2) in receipt of an attendance allowance under the Social Security Contributions and Benefits Act 1992, s 64; or
(3) in receipt of a disability living allowance under the Social Security Contributions and Benefits Act 1992, s 71.

The two conditions which need to be satisfied are as follows:

(1) not less than half of the property within the trust should be applied for the benefit of the beneficiary concerned; and
(2) the person should be entitled to not less than 50% of the income arising from the property (this condition is regarded as satisfied where the trust provides that no income may be applied for the benefit of any other person).

Income is deemed to be applied for the benefit of a person where it is held by the trustees for that person on protective trusts.

## 18.8 PROTECTIVE TRUSTS

This is a term under the Trustee Act 1925, s 33. The protective trust is one under which a person (known as the principal beneficiary) is entitled to an interest in possession in the trust unless he forfeits his interest, eg by assigning his interest or by becoming bankrupt. Protective trusts are normally worded so that if a principal beneficiary forfeits his interest, the trust property is held on discretionary trusts for a class of beneficiaries which includes the principal beneficiary.

### 18.8.1 The IHT position where principal beneficiary dies

The periodic charge does not apply whilst property is held on protective trusts because the principal beneficiary has forfeited his interest. However, an IHT charge arises on his death. The charge varies according to whether the principal beneficiary forfeited his interest before or after 12 April 1978.

Where the principal beneficiary forfeited his interest before 12 April 1978, the tax charged on his eventual death is calculated at a fixed rate on the value of the trust property according to the following formula:

|  | *Cumulative total* |
|---|---|
| 0.25% for each of the first 40 quarters | 10% |
| 0.20% for each of the next 40 quarters | 8% |
| 0.15% for each of the next 40 quarters | 6% |
| 0.10% for each of the next 40 quarters | 4% |
| 0.05% for each of the next 40 quarters | 2% |
| Maximum rate chargeable after 50 years | 30% |

The nil rate band is *not* available.

### 18.8.2 The position where principal beneficiary forfeited his interest after 11 April 1978

In this situation, the trustees are subject to a charge on the death of the principal beneficiary as if he had an interest in possession at the date of his death.

## 18.9 CHARITABLE TRUSTS

Provided that property is held for charitable purposes only, income and capital gains received by the trustees are normally exempt from tax.

### Exemption from income tax
(TA 1988, s 505)

There is total exemption from income tax for all income other than trading profits. The exemption is, however, dependent upon income being applied for charitable purposes.

### Exemption from CGT
(TCGA 1992, s 256)

There is also total exemption from CGT provided that the charitable trust applies the capital gains for charitable purposes.

## 18.9.1 Application for charitable purposes
(TA 1988, s 505)

A charity's exemption from tax may be restricted where income is not applied for charitable purposes. In particular, where a charity has income and capital gains which exceed £10,000 in a tax year, exemption is restricted where the following two conditions are satisfied:

(1) The charity's relevant income and gains exceed the amount of its qualifying expenditure.
(2) The trust incurs or is treated as incurring non-qualifying expenditure.

'Qualifying expenditure' for these purposes means expenditure actually made during the year for charitable purposes and commitments for such expenditure entered into during the year.

Payments made to bodies outside the UK count as qualifying expenditure only to the extent that the charity can show that it has taken such steps that are reasonable in the circumstances to ensure that the payments will be applied for charitable purposes. Expenditure for charitable purposes also includes reasonable administrative and fund-raising expenses.

Non-qualifying expenditure includes things such as political activities, trading expenses and excessive administration costs. Furthermore, the legislation specifically mentions certain types of investments or loans which are to be regarded as not being qualifying expenditure. This is intended to catch investments in a company controlled by a connected person (for example the settlor) or loans to such a company. Indirect arrangements may also be caught such as where a charity makes loans or investments which are used as security for borrowings by a connected person.

Where a charitable trust makes a payment to another connected charitable trust, this does not count as application of the income for charitable purposes unless the trust that receives the payment actually applies it for charitable purposes.

### 18.9.2 Inheritance tax position

Property held upon charitable trusts is exempt from the periodic and exit charges. If the property is held upon temporary charitable trusts, a charge arises on those charitable trusts coming to an end with tax being charged according to the same formula in 18.8.1.

## 18.10 EXECUTORS AND PERSONAL REPRESENTATIVES

### 18.10.1 Meaning

When a person dies, his assets vest in his executors/personal representatives. If he does not leave a will, it is normally necessary for letters of administration to be obtained and the person who acts in this way is treated for tax purposes as if he were an executor. The term 'personal representative' covers both executors in the case of a will and administrators in the case of an intestacy.

The fact that at least one personal representative is resident in the UK would normally mean that the estate is subject to UK tax. However, there is an exception to this where the deceased was not resident, ordinarily resident, or domiciled in the UK at the time of his death. In such a situation, provided that at least one of the personal representatives is not UK-resident, the estate is not regarded as UK-resident.

Personal representatives of a deceased person are treated as a single body of persons so that there is no tax implication if an executor retires or dies. The estate is treated as a single entity for tax purposes.

### 18.10.2 Income tax
(TMA 1970, s 40)

Personal representatives of a deceased person are liable to pay tax on income received by the deceased person up to the date of his death. The Revenue must issue the relevant assessments within three years following the tax year in which the person died. The tax is assessed in exactly the same way as if the individual were still alive, ie all the normal allowances and reliefs are due. The only difference is that the personal representatives are responsible for settling the tax (they are also entitled to any repayments).

Quite separately, personal representatives are also charged to tax on income received by them following the death. No personal allowances are given. During the administration period, the income is charged at 20% on income from savings, with other income being taxed at the basic rate; there is no higher rate liability for the personal representatives.

Although there are cases where income has to be apportioned pre- and post-death for legal purposes, for tax purposes any income received after a person's death is treated as income of the estate.

Where, under the terms of the Will, a trust evolves, the executors become trustees upon the completion of the administration period. Depending upon the type of trust, the trustees may become chargeable to additional rate income tax first on the balance of accumulated income at that date and second upon receipt of subsequent income. There is no date fixed by law to determine the completion of the administration period, but it is generally agreed that it is the date on which the residue is ascertained.

### 18.10.3 Beneficiary's position
(TA 1988, ss 695–696)

A beneficiary of a Will may receive an annuity. This income is taxable for the year in which it is payable unless, as a matter of fact, the annuity is paid out of capital in which case the annuity is income for the year in which it is paid.

Beneficiaries of specific legacies are normally entitled from the date of death to the income which arises on the property that they have inherited. Other beneficiaries will be entitled to the residue, either through a limited interest (eg a life tenant entitled to income arising from the residuary estate) or by an absolute entitlement.

During the administration period, sums paid to a beneficiary are normally treated as income for the year of payment. Different, and more complex, rules applied where the estate was administered before 5 April 1995 (see *Allied Dunbar Tax Handbook 1995–96* at 6.6.6–6.6.8).

Where income which has accrued to the date of death is treated as capital of the estate for IHT purposes and as residuary income, there is higher rate tax relief available to beneficiaries. Form 922 is used to calculate this relief.

### 18.10.4 Capital gains tax
(TCGA 1992, ss 3 and 62)

From 1998–99 onwards, personal representatives are subject to CGT at the rate of 34%. They are entitled to the full annual exemption due to an individual for the year of death and the following two tax years.

In computing capital gains, assets which were held by the deceased person at the date of his death are deemed to be acquired by the personal representatives at their market value at that date (the probate value). However, the probate value may need to be adjusted where securities are sold at a loss within 12 months of the death and relief from IHT has been claimed (see 17.11.3).

If a claim has been made to substitute the sale proceeds of property or land within four years of the date of death, the original probate value and not sale proceeds continues to be the acquisition value for CGT purposes.

Assets which are transferred to beneficiaries, either during the course of or on the completion of the administration period of an estate, do not give rise to a chargeable gain since the beneficiary is regarded as having himself acquired the asset at the date of the person's death and at the probate value.

Certain expenses incurred by the personal representatives in establishing legal title to assets are allowed in computing gains on the sale of the assets (see SP8/94).

Personal representatives of an estate in the course of administration are not entitled to an annual exemption if they realise capital gains after two full tax years have elapsed since the date of death. However, if a Will Trust evolves upon completion of the administration period, the trustees will then become entitled to their own exemption.

Losses made by personal representatives during the administration period, and not utilised, are not available to be transferred to residuary beneficiaries with absolute interests.

### 18.10.5 Property owned by the estate, but used by a beneficiary as his main residence

The Revenue treats the exemption for a property occupied by a beneficiary of a trust as his main residence as applying where personal representatives dispose of a property which has been used by a beneficiary of the estate as his only or main residence both before and after the deceased's death and he is entitled to at least 75% of the proceeds when the estate has been administered (see ESC D5 and *Tax Bulletin* August 1994).

### 18.10.6 Deeds of variation

Where the terms of a Will have been varied by a deed of variation (also known as a deed of family arrangement), there are important consequences so far as IHT is concerned (see 17.4.6). Basically, the revised way in which property passes to beneficiaries is read back into the Will and effectively treated as something done by the testator so far as IHT is concerned. However, the House of Lords held in *Marshall v Kerr* [1994] STC 813 that where the variation creates a trust, the person or persons who relinquish their original entitlement under the Will are treated as the settlor for CGT purposes.

The income tax treatment is also less favourable than the IHT treatment. Even where the deed specifically provides that all income is to be paid to a beneficiary named in the deed, this has no effect for income tax purposes for income which arose prior to the deed's execution. The original beneficiary or beneficiaries named in the will remain liable for any higher rate tax on such income which arose at a time when they were entitled to it. Furthermore, a person who gives up an entitlement under a will by executing such a deed is treated as a settlor for income tax purposes.

# 19

# DEDUCTING TAX AT SOURCE – AND PAYING IT OVER TO THE INLAND REVENUE

This chapter outlines the requirements imposed by law on employers etc to act as unpaid tax collectors on the Treasury's behalf. If you are caught up in this, the administrative burden can be onerous and the penalties for non-compliance severe.

(1) Employers.
(2) Contractors.
(3) IR35.
(4) Non-resident landlord scheme.
(5) Payments to non-resident sportsmen and entertainers.
(6) Other payments to persons not resident in the UK.

## 19.1 EMPLOYERS

An employer has an obligation to collect tax and operate the following schemes on the Revenue's behalf in respect of the following payments:

- PAYE/NICs
- Working Families Tax Credits (WFTC) and Disabled Persons' Tax Credit (DPTC)
- Student loans.

### 19.1.1 Payment of PAYE over to the Revenue

Employers are required to withhold tax under PAYE and NICs and pay them over to the Revenue on a monthly basis unless the PAYE and NICs do not normally exceed £1,500 per month, in which case it is possible to account for tax deductions on a quarterly basis. The £1,500 per month is inclusive of sums collected under the Student Loans scheme and sums paid out under the WFTC and DPTC schemes. At the end of the year, the employer must give employees form P60 showing the tax withheld from their earnings.

## 19.1.2 **Emoluments subject to PAYE**

All payments of 'emoluments' by a UK-resident employer to directors and employees are subject to Pay as You Earn (PAYE). Emoluments are cash payments (salary, wages, bonus etc) other than expense payments. The *Employer's Guide* lists the following payments as emoluments which are subject to PAYE:

Salary
Wages
Fees
Overtime
Bonus
Commission
Pension
Honoraria
Pay during sickness or other absence from work
Holiday pay
Christmas boxes in cash
Employee's income tax borne by the employer
Payments in respect of the cost of travelling between the employee's home and his normal place of employment
Payments for time spent in travelling
Cash payments for meals
Payments in lieu of benefits in kind
Certain lump sum payments made on retirement or removal from employment
Certain sums received from the trustees of approved profit-sharing schemes
Gratuities or service charges paid out by the employer.

On the other hand, PAYE cannot be deducted from certain benefits even though they are regarded as taxable income for Schedule E purposes. The *Employer's Guide* states that the following are income from which tax cannot be deducted:

Living accommodation provided rent-free or at a reduced rent
Gifts in kind such as Christmas hampers
Luncheon vouchers in excess of 15p per day
Employee's liabilities borne by the employer (even though such payments are earnings for NICs purposes).

The scope of PAYE was extended by FA 1994, s 127 and further extended by successive Finance Acts. FA 1994 required employers to account for PAYE when they pay their staff in 'tradeable assets' such as gold bars, commodities, fine wine or diamonds, or with non-marketable assets where the employer has made arrangements for the employee to convert them into cash. FA 1998 has replaced the concept of tradable assets with the yet more all-embracing term 'readily convertible assets'. This term includes (but is not limited to):

(1) money debts;
(2) property that is subject to a warehousing or fiscal warehousing regime;
(3) assets that give rise to cash without any action being taken by the employee; and
(4) assets for which trading arrangements come into existence in accordance with other arrangements or an understanding which is in place when the assets were provided to the employee.

PAYE may also have to be accounted for on gifts of shares in the employing company or profits realised on the exercise of non-approved share options (see 3.15).

### National insurance contributions

The PAYE and NICs rules have been largely aligned from 6 April 2000 and it is now unusual for a payment or benefit to be taxable under Schedule E but not subject to NICs. See further Chapter 23.

## 19.1.3 Anti-avoidance of PAYE and NICs

In 1997 the Government decided that PAYE would apply to assignments of trade debts by employers to their employees. Legislation was included in FA 1998 to bring remuneration in the form of trade debts within the scope of PAYE from 2 July 1997. Employers need to ensure that they have accounted for PAYE on assignment of trade debts to employees which took place on or after that date.

Under these provisions, the term 'tradeable assets' was replaced by a more all-embracing definition of 'readily convertible assets', the meaning of which includes items (1)–(4) in 19.1.2 above.

If an employee becomes liable under Schedule E on the exercise, assignment or release of an option for shares which are readily convertible assets, these provisions require the employer to operate PAYE. Similarly, PAYE will apply if the employee is rewarded by the enhancement of a readily convertible asset which he already owns. PAYE must be operated on a reasonable estimate of the income likely to be charged under Schedule E. Similar rules were also introduced for NICs.

## 19.1.4 Payment in shares

The Revenue's Personal Tax Division has issued guidance on the PAYE obligations for an employer where employees receive shares. The guidance refers to tradeable assets and trading arrangements whereas the legislation now refers to 'readily convertible assets' but this should not affect the advice contained in the following extracts.

## Background

Under [TA 1988, s 203F] employers are obliged to account for tax under PAYE whenever an employee is provided with assessable income in the form of trade-able assets. The November 1996 regulations extended the definition of tradeable asset to include certain 'own company' shares for the first time.

Shares in an employer or company which controls the employer will not be tradeable assets if they are acquired under the terms of a Revenue-approved share scheme or as the result of the exercise of options granted before 27 November 1996. All other shares will be tradeable assets if either:

(1) they are capable of being sold or otherwise realised on a recognised investment exchange; or

(2) trading arrangements exist in respect of them.

Trading arrangements are defined . . . as being

'arrangements for the purpose of enabling the person to whom the asset is provided to obtain an amount greater than, equal to or not substantially less than the expense incurred in the provision of the asset.'

### Q1. Does the exercise of a share option amount to the provision of assessable income?

Yes. The legislation applies where an employee is provided with 'assessable income'. If the exercise of an option gives rise to a liability to tax under Schedule E then there is assessable income. If the shares acquired are tradable assets then that assessable income has been provided to the employee in the form of tradable assets and the employer is obliged to account for tax under PAYE. The legislation does not, however, apply to charges under [TA 1988, s 162] because this liability can only be calculated after the end of the relevant tax year.

### Q2. Does *CIR v Herd* prevent the application of PAYE to share option gains?

No. *CIR v Herd* considered the application of PAYE to payments of emoluments within [TA 1988, s 203(1)]. Where income is provided in the form of tradeable assets there is no 'payment' of emoluments, actual payments of emoluments are specifically excluded from [TA 1988, s 203F by subs (4)(a)]. *CIR v Herd* does not prevent PAYE being applied to awards of tradeable assets.

### Q3. What code number should the employer use in operating PAYE?

The employer should use the code number that has been issued for the employee, even if this is code NT. Where the employer has to account for tax under PAYE in respect of an ex-employee he should account for tax at the basic rate . . .

### Q4. What about awards made by third parties?

When an employee is provided with an assessable income in the form of tradable assets an obligation to account for tax falls on the employer even if the shares are provided by a third party such as a parent company. It is the employer's responsibility to put in place arrangements to ensure that he has the information necessary to comply with his statutory obligations.

### Q5. On what figure should the employer operate PAYE?

Where the shares are tradeable assets because they are capable of being sold or otherwise realised on a relevant investment exchange, then PAYE should be operated on the amount obtainable.

Where the shares are tradeable assets because trading arrangements exist, PAYE should be operated on the amount obtained by the employee under those arrangements. There should therefore be no need for independent valuations for PAYE purposes.

Where assessable income is provided in the form of tradeable assets the employer is treated as having made a payment of that income and should not operate PAYE on an amount which exceeds the amount of that assessable income, namely the amount chargeable to tax under Schedule E. The total amount in respect of which the employer should deduct tax . . . and, where appropriate, account for tax . . . should also therefore be limited to the amount chargeable to tax under Schedule E.

### Q6. What happens where the employer cannot deduct the necessary tax because there is insufficient cash pay?

The employer remains responsible for accounting for the right amount of tax to the Collector within 14 days of the end of the income tax period. It is up to employers whether they make arrangements to recover this tax from the employees and if so how they go about this. If the employee does not make good to the employer the tax which could not be deducted within 30 days of the tradeable assets being provided then the amount of the tax will be treated as a benefit in kind . . . This charge . . . is not reduced nor eliminated if the employee makes good after the 30 day time limit has expired.

Note that FA 1998 also creates an obligation for an employer to account for PAYE where employees receive a cash sum in return for surrendering share options and the shares are readily convertible assets.

## 19.1.5 Payments to agency workers

Where the services of an individual are provided to a trader through an agency, and the manner in which the individual performs his work is controlled and supervised as if he were an employee, TA 1988, s 134 requires the trader to operate PAYE.

There are situations where the Revenue regards payments to a 'one man' company as caught by this provision so that the person paying the money to the company should deduct PAYE as if he had made payments to the individual worker concerned. This is increasingly relevant as many employers use service contracts to reduce their overheads and maximise the benefits available to the worker. The Revenue, however, is likely to apply the same criteria to payments made in such circumstances as those they apply to the self-employed, as covered in detail in 2.2.2.

## 19.1.6 Failure to operate PAYE

An employer who fails to operate PAYE takes a substantial risk. The primary liability to account for the tax rests with the employer and the scope of PAYE does not extend simply to deducting tax from the gross pay of an employee and remitting it to the Revenue. Instead, an employer must remember that PAYE can also apply to all forms of casual labour, which may or may not be paid through the payroll, and additionally to individuals who may be considered to be self-employed (see 2.2).

Another area frequently overlooked is that of expenses (see 3.4.1) which constitute part of an employee's emoluments and accordingly fall within the scope of PAYE. While genuine business expenses incurred wholly, exclusively and necessarily in the course of an employee's duties are allowed tax free, there remain several areas where employers are required to operate PAYE. These include the payment of all round sum allowances which have not been approved by the Inspector in the form of a dispensation, and the payment of unauthorised or unvouched expenses. Even the payment of travel expenses may not be permitted tax free in circumstances where the employee's workplace is deemed to be his normal place of work. As an example, a site-based employee living in London and working on a site in Aberdeen will be taxed on all his expenses for travel between London and Aberdeen. This shows that special attention needs to be paid to such payments and the circumstances surrounding them.

Whilst the Collector of Taxes will invariably seek to recover any unpaid tax from the employer in the first instance, the relevant Regulations (SI 1993/744) permit the Collector to direct that unpaid tax shall be recovered from the employee, but there is no legal requirement that the Collector should give such a direction. The Regulations make it clear that the Collector will make such a direction only if he is satisfied that the employer took reasonable care to comply with the PAYE regulations and the under-deduction of tax was due to an error made in good faith. Errors arising simply from confusion or ignorance of the rules are not, however, considered to be a reasonable excuse. In such situations, the Collector will not only seek recovery of all duties underpaid but is likely to add interest and penalties as well.

SI 1993/744, reg 42 provides that the Collector may pursue the employee if he has received his remuneration knowing that the employer has wilfully failed to deduct PAYE tax, but the Revenue will normally pursue this course of action only after it has endeavoured to collect from the employer.

All lump sum payments generally should be treated with caution in times when termination payments are increasingly common. Basically, if there is any contractual obligation or expectation, on the part of the employee, to receive a sum then the Revenue is likely to take the view that the employer should have deducted tax.

## 19.1.7 Interest and penalties for late payment of PAYE

Over recent years, the Revenue has progressively tightened its policing of employers operating PAYE schemes. The current position is as follows:

(1) Interest is charged on PAYE tax and employer's and employees' NICs not remitted to the Collector of Taxes by 14 days after the end of the tax year (that is to say, by 19 April 2001 for 2000–01).
(2) Penalties may be imposed on employers who do not submit their end-of-year returns (Forms P14 and P35) by 19 May following the end of the tax year. The maximum penalty is £100 per month per unit of 50 employees (rounded up, so that 51 employees count as two units).

These very substantial financial penalties mean that all employers must devote adequate resources to the preparation of PAYE returns.

## 19.1.8 Other returns required from employers

### Forms P46 (car)

These forms report details of changes in company car allocations. They are due quarterly within 28 days of the end of the periods ending 5 July, 5 October, 5 January and 5 April. Reportable events are when an employee or director:

- receives a company car for the first time;
- changes company car;
- receives an additional company car;
- gives up a company car; or
- exceeds the £8,500 threshold having been below it previously.

Late returns may be liable to penalties of up to £300 per return, plus a further £60 per day while the failure continues.

### Forms P11D and P9D

An employer must file forms P11D to report benefits and expenses for all employees earning £8,500 or more a year. Directors are automatically included in this category unless:

- they are full-time working directors or directors of a not-for-profit organisation; and
- they earn less than £8,500 pa; and
- they do not control directly or indirectly more than 5% of the company's ordinary share capital; and
- they do not have directorships in other businesses under the same control.

All benefits and expenses payments (including business expenses) must be reported, except those covered by dispensations. The amount is the cash equivalent (see 3.4–3.9 on taxation of benefits in general).

Except where special rules apply, the cash equivalent is normally the VAT-inclusive cost to the provider. Where the special rules apply, employers are responsible for calculating the cash equivalent and entering the appropriate amount on the P11D. The Revenue can supply the following P11D Working Sheets to assist you:

1 – Living accommodation and associated benefits
2 – Car and fuel benefits
3 – Vans available for private use
4 – Interest-free and low interest loans
5 – Relocation expenses.

If an arrangement has been made for someone else to provide benefits to the employees, the cash equivalents must be reported on P11D as though the employer provided the benefits itself. If the provider cannot or will not give details of the benefits to the employer, the employer must make a best estimate of the cash equivalent and notify the Revenue of this. Such arrangements are where an employer has guaranteed or facilitated provision of benefits or the benefits were part of a reciprocal arrangement with another employer.

P11D returns are due for submission to the Revenue by 6 July following the end of the tax year. Filing an incorrect return can result in a penalty of up to £3,000. Further, a penalty of £300 may be imposed for each form not submitted by 6 July, with a daily penalty of £60 per return if the forms are not submitted once the initial penalty has been imposed.

Details of taxable benefits must be supplied to employees by 6 July. Forms P9D may also be required for benefits provided to employees earning less than £8,500 pa.

The deadlines for submitting returns of Classes 1A and 1B NICs also need to be borne in mind (see 23.1.7–23.1.8).

### 19.1.9 Working Families Tax Credits and Disabled Persons Tax Credit

As from 6 April 2000, employers acquired a new responsibility as dispensers of tax credits to add to their existing duties as collectors of tax and NICs. The amounts paid by employers by way of tax credits are set against their PAYE tax and NICs liabilities due to the Revenue each month or quarter as appropriate. Where the employer has not collected enough PAYE and NICs to cover the tax credits payable for a particular period, application to the Revenue for additional funding may be made. At the end of the tax year, employers will be obliged to provide employees with details of the credits paid to them. This information will also need to be shown on payslips and P60 forms.

## Table 19.1 Summary of year-end deadlines

| Deadline | | Result of missed deadline |
|---|---|---|
| 19 April 2001 | Due date for all remittances of PAYE, Class 1 NICs and subcontractor deductions for 2000–01 tax year | Automatic interest charge |
| 19 May 2001 | Due date for submission of forms P35 and SC 35 detailing deductions made under PAYE and under the subcontractors scheme | Automatic penalties |
| 31 May 2001 | Forms P60 to employees in employment as at 5 April 2000 | Penalties |
| 6 July 2001 | Forms P11D and P9D to reach Revenue | Penalties of up to £300 per return |
| 6 July 2001 | Copies of P11D and P9D information to be given to employees, including any who have left the company since 5 April 2001 | Penalties |

## 19.1.10 Collection of student loans

Over recent years, student loans have become the main source of funding higher education. The Student Loans Company (SLC) remains responsible for recovering the repayment of loans made up to August 1998, loans made after that date are recovered via deductions from salary.

This new scheme came into effect from 6 April 2000. Unlike WFTC it is unlikely that payroll staff with be swamped with deduction start notices from this date. The majority of individuals who first took out loans after August 1998 will still be in higher education and the full effect of this new legislation will not be felt for some further years.

The system is similar to that for WFTC in that the employers will receive start and stop notifications from the Revenue. The employer is not responsible for either identifying employees who are liable to make these repayments or for answering questions from the employee on the loan. Such queries should be referred to the SLC. Only questions regarding operating the scheme should be referred to the Revenue.

The calculation of student loan repayments is very similar to that of

NICs. There is an annual limit of £10,000 pa (£833.33 per month) below which no deductions are made. This limit is non-cumulative as with national insurance so an employee who earns £800 in one month and £900 in the next will only be liable to deduction in the second month. The deduction made would be as follows:

| | | |
|---|---|---|
| £900 – £833.33 | = | £66.67 |
| Rate of deduction | = | 9% |
| Student loan repaid | = | £6.00 |

The initial rate of repayment has been set at 9% and this will be applied to those earnings that are subject to secondary Class 1 NICs. For any employees who are not liable to national insurance (eg employees working abroad in non-agreement countries) there will be no deductions due.

As mentioned above, an employer should only begin to make deductions when a start notice (form SL1) is received from the Revenue. This notice will give at least six weeks' notice before deductions should commence. Deductions should begin on the first pay day after this date.

An employer could receive notification of student loan repayments in another way. If a new employee hands over a P45 with a 'Y' in the SL box it means that the previous employer had received a start notice. Deductions should be made as soon as possible. However, if the P45 is received some time after the employee has started work no attempt should be made to deduct any arrears.

## 19.2 CONTRACTORS

The Revenue has seen the way in which contractors pay sub-contractors as an obvious area in which tax is being lost to the Treasury. Over the past few years measures have been introduced to tighten rules and ensure that taxes are accounted for. Payments made by a contractor (see below) will now be made:

- Net after the deduction of PAYE
- Net under the Construction Industry Scheme
- Gross under the Construction Industry Scheme.

### Construction industry

Changes in the rules dealing with construction workers were announced on 31 July 1997. Legislation which took effect from 6 April 1998 was then enacted as part of FA 1998.

From that date, construction workers supplied by employment agencies or other third parties were brought within the PAYE system. This aligned the tax and NICs treatment of such workers, who were in the past regarded as self-employed for tax purposes, but as employees for NICs purposes.

Note that this change does not only apply to agencies. Companies acting as 'in-house' agencies within the construction industry which supply labour to others, and anyone else who supplies construction workers to others, fall within the legislation.

## 19.2.1 Payments to sub-contractors in the construction industry

Where a person is carrying on a business which includes construction work, the payments to a sub-contractor in respect of 'construction operations' may be subject to a deduction of tax.

A contractor includes any person carrying on a business which includes construction industry operations even where these are not the main trading activity. If construction work is regularly commissioned on their own trading or investment properties, that person will be considered to be a contractor for the purposes of deducting tax if their expenditure exceeds £250,000 on average over a three-year period.

### Construction operations

The Regulations define construction so as to include the installation of heating, lighting or drainage, the internal cleaning of buildings in the course of their construction, alterations or repair work, internal or external painting, as well as the construction, alteration, repair or demolition of buildings.

### Construction Industry Scheme

With effect from 6 April 2000 the amount of tax deducted from a payment to a sub-contractor under the scheme was reduced to 18%. Prior to the 6 April the rate was 23%. Sub-contractors must hold one of the following:

- A registration card CIS4 (P)
- A temporary Registration card CIS4 (T)
- Certificate CIS6
- Certificate CIS5.

CIS4 and CIS6 have to be presented in person. Certificate CIS5 is only issued to companies which can show a turnover of at least £3m.

The certificates are issued by the Revenue and will determine the basis on which the contractor makes a payment to a sub-contractor or company.

### Payments to registration cardholders

If the sub-contractor holds either a valid CIS4(P) or (T) and the contractor is satisfied with the card then the payment is made under the Construction Industry Scheme with a deduction of 18% on the net payment after taking into account deductions for materials, VAT and Construction Board Levies where appropriate. The contractor must supply the sub-contractor with a

CIS25 voucher within 14 days of the end of the tax month in which the payment is made.

## Payments to certificate holders

If the contractor can answer 'Yes' to the three questions in advance of any payment then a payment is made gross and a voucher CIS6 supplied:

- Does the photo match the person?
- Is the certificate in date?
- Do you know the sub-contractor?

The certificate CIS5 is for payments to a company and once again the contractor must be satisfied that the certificate and person presenting it are genuine. To qualify for a CIS5 certificate, a turnover threshold is applied. Prior to the 21 March 2000 this was £5m; it is now £3m.

Regardless of the above, if the relationship between the contractor and sub-contractor is one of employer/employee, then the contractor is under an obligation to deduct PAYE. Any payments falling outside of the scheme should be made under the usual PAYE rules.

For further details on the operation of the scheme contact the Revenue or visit the CIS website www.inlandrevenue.gov.uk/cis.htm.

## Electronic filing

Contractors can file the tax payment voucher CIS (E), Construction Gross Payment Voucher (CIS23) and the end-of-year details for those two vouchers electronically. For further details e-mail the Inland Revenue Business Support Team at pms.ir.sh@gtnet.gov.uk.

## Payment of tax

The amounts of tax that a contractor should have collected from payments made to sub-contractors must be paid to the Revenue Accounts Office within 14 days of the end of the month to which the payment relates. For example, if the payment relates to the month 6 May 2000 and 5 June 2000, the payment must be made by 19 June 2000.

# 19.3 IR35

The revised version of the controversial rules and regulations on personal service companies came into effect as at 6 April 2000. These new rules use existing case law (see Chapter 2) to determine whether an individual performs services which would be taxed under Schedule E as employment income were it not for the fact that his services are provided through an intermediary such as a service company. Those caught by the new rules will pay approximately the same PAYE and NICs as an individual who is an employee of the end customer.

The Revenue has laid out a nine-point plan for determining the deemed Schedule E tax charge for a tax year:

*Step 1* determines that the starting point for the calculation is the total amount received by the intermediary during the tax year from relevant engagements. This figure will include any benefits in kind provided to the intermediary in respect of those engagements. This total amount is then reduced by 5%, which is an allowance for the running costs of the inter-mediary.

*Step 2* adds in any payments or benefits in kind received by the worker or his family in respect of any relevant engagements from anyone other than the intermediary, which are not otherwise taxable under Schedule E, but which would have been taxable under Schedule E if the worker had been employed by the client.

*Step 3* deducts any amounts spent by the intermediary, which could have been clamed as expenses against income tax if the worker had been an employee of the client and met them himself.

*Step 4* allows a deduction for any capital allowances that could have been claimed by the worker if he had been an employee of the client.

*Step 5* deducts any contributions paid by the intermediary to an approved pension scheme for the benefit of the worker.

*Step 6* deducts any employer's NICs (Classes 1 and 1A) paid by the intermediary in respect of salary or benefits in kind provided to the worker during the year.

*Step 7* deducts any amount of salary and benefits in kind provided by the intermediary to the worker during the year, which has already been sub-ject to Schedule E tax and Classes 1 and 1A NICs (excluding any amounts which have already been deducted at Step 3).

Note, if, after Step 7, the result is nil or a negative amount, there is no deemed Schedule F payment and no further tax or NICs will be payable. However, if the result is positive, then a deemed Schedule E payment must be calculated in accordance with Steps 8 and 9.

*Step 8* allows for a deduction of the employer's NICs payable on the deemed payment. So Step 8 requires the calculation of the amount which, together with the employer's NICs due on it, equals the result of Step 7.

*Step 9* states that the result after Step 8 is the amount of the deemed Schedule F payment.

Note that if the worker is within the Construction Industry Scheme (see above), then it is the amount before deduction of tax under that scheme that must be brought in at Step 1 of the calculation.

## Examples

Mr and Mrs A work through a service company in which they own all the shares. They each carry out some engagements during the year which fall within the new rules ('relevant engagements') and some which do not.

Assume the service company receives £20,000 in respect of relevant engagements for Mr A and £40,000 in respect of relevant engagements for Mrs A and that there is a further £40,000 income from other business activities which do not fall within the new rules. Assume the service company also incurs the following expenses during the course of the year:

| Expense | Mr A | Mrs A | Notes |
|---|---|---|---|
| Salaries | £20,000 | £20,000 | Paid in year. PAYE and NICs deducted and accounted for under normal provisions. |
| Employer's NICs | £1,913 | £1,913 | Paid in year. NICs calculated on an annual earnings period, as for directors. Assumes that the employer's threshold (£4,316) has been set against these earnings, and 12.2% paid on remainder. |
| Employer's pension contributions | £4,000 | £4,000 | To an approved scheme |
| Travel costs related to relevant engagements | £2,000 | £500 | All would be deductible under normal provisions relating to employees. |

Other expenses: £10,000 business expenses, all allowable for corporation tax purposes.

Under the new proposals, at the end of the tax year, the service company will have to calculate the amount of PAYE and NICs due on Mr and Mrs A's earnings. If they have not paid enough PAYE and NICs during the year, then PAYE and NICs will be payable on a 'deemed payment' on the last day of the tax year.

| Calculation of deemed payment | Mr A | Mrs A |
|---|---|---|
| Income from relevant contracts | 20,000 | 40,000 |
| Less: | | |
| Expenses | 2,000 | 500 |
| Employer's NICs paid in year | 1,913 | 1,913 |
| Pension contributions | 4,000 | 4,000 |
| Flat rate 5% relevant income | 1,000 | 2,000 |
| | 11,087 | 31,587 |

*Deduct*:

| | | |
|---|---|---|
| Salary paid in year | 20,000 | 20,000 |
| | No deemed payment | 11,587 |
| Employer's NICs on deemed payment | | 1,260 |
| Deemed payment | | 10,327 |

| *Company accounts* | £ | £ |
|---|---|---|
| Turnover | | 100,000 |
| *Less*: | | |
| Salaries (including deemed payment) | 40,000 | |
| Employer's NICs (including on deemed payment) | 3,826 | |
| Pension contributions | 8,000 | |
| Expenses | 12,500 | |
| | | 64,326 |
| Accounting profit | | 35,674 |
| Deemed payment | 10,327 | |
| Employer's NICs on deemed payment | 1,260 | |
| Profits for corporation tax purposes | | 24,087 |

**Summary**

Mr A brought in £20,000 from relevant contracts during the course of the year. The service company paid the whole of that amount onto him in salary and deducted and accounted for full PAYE and NICs. No further action is required.

Mrs A brought in £40,000 from relevant contracts during the course of the year and the service company paid £20,000 onto her in salary and deducted and accounted for PAYE and NICs on that salary. This left £20,000 from her relevant contracts on which PAYE and NICs had not been deducted and accounted for during the course of the year. Under the new rules this £20,000, less the deductions allowed, will be deemed to be paid to Mrs A as salary at the year end (on 5 April).

## Example of deemed payment for partnership

Mr and Mrs B work as members of a partnership, of which they are the two partners. They carry out relevant engagements during the year. Of the partnership income 50% arises from such engagements and 50% from other sources. Profits are split equally. Each is provided with a car, both of which are held as partnership assets. The private use proportion of the motoring expenses is 30%. Partnership accounts show the following results:

Year ended 5 April 2001

|  | £ |  |  |
|---|---|---|---|
| Income | 80,000 |  |  |
| Expenses | 17,000* |  |  |
| Profit | 63,000 |  |  |
| Tax adjusted profit | 65,000 | (reflects adjustments for depreciation, private expenses etc). |  |

\* includes motoring expenses of £3,000

| Calculation of deemed payment at 5 April 2001 | Mrs B | Mr B |
|---|---|---|
| Payments from relevant engagements: | 25,000 | 15,000 |
| Less: |  |  |
| 5% allowance | 1,250 | 750 |
| Schedule E expenses | 700 | 350 |
| Employer's NICs on deemed payment: | 2,031 | 1,036 |
| Deemed payment | 21,019 | 12,864 |

| Recalculation of partnership taxable profit | £ |
|---|---|
| Partnership profit: | 65,000 |
| Plus: disallowed expenses: |  |
| $(7,500 - (2,000 + 1,050))^1$ | 4,450 |
|  | 69,450 |
| Less: deemed payments | (33,883) |
| Taxable profit | 35,567 |

| Recalculation of personal liability | Mrs B | Mr B |
|---|---|---|
| Partnership profit: | 17,783 | 17,784 |
| Deemed payment | 21,019 | 12,864 |

[1] This amount reflects the difference between the expenses incurred in respect of the relevant engagements and the amounts allowed as part of the 5% allowance and Schedule E expenses.

### Payment of tax

Tax and NICs under IR35 regulations in respect of deemed payments are due for payment by 19 April following the end of the tax year. The first tax due under the scheme will be in respect of the current tax year and therefore the first payment will be due by 19 April 2001.

## 19.4 NON-RESIDENT LANDLORD SCHEME

If you rent a property from a non-resident landlord then you have an obligation to withhold basic rate tax and pay this over to the Revenue on a quarterly basis. There are two main exceptions to this rule. The first is where the rent paid is less then £100 per week, and the second is where you have received confirmation from the Revenue that you may make the payment gross.

If you are in this situation then you should contact the Revenue's Financial Intermediaries and Claims Office (FICO), St John's House, Merton Road, Bootle, Merseyside L69 9BB. They will forward you a form to complete within 30 days of the end of each quarter, explaining how the tax is calculated and how to make a payment to the Account's Office.

### Example – Calculation of quarterly payment

Tax is calculated at the basic rate on the rent due in quarter less allowable expenses. Therefore, if the rent due in the quarter to 31 March 2001 is £3,000 but during the quarter you have paid £300 out of this sum to repair a broken window, then the calculation would be as follows:

|  | £ |
|---|---|
| Rent | 3,000 |
| *Less*: Allowable expenses | 300 |
|  | 2,700 |
| Tax at 22% | 594 |

At the end of each tax year you have to provide a return including details of the rent paid, allowable expenses and tax deducted. This is to be provided by no later than 5 July. Within the same time frame you should also supply the landlord with a certificate of the tax deducted. The payments are dealt with by FICO (Non-Residents) at the address above.

## 19.5 PAYMENTS TO NON-RESIDENT SPORTSMEN AND ENTERTAINERS

Basic rate tax must be withheld from most payments made to non-UK resident sportsmen and entertainers for work performed in the UK. In addition, where benefits in kind are provided to them, the cost must be 'grossed up' for tax at the basic rate and accounted for. A tax voucher must be provided for each payment and the person making the payments needs to account for tax on a quarterly basis.

### 19.5.1 Payments caught by this scheme

Payments or benefits subject to these regulations include:

(1) Prize money.
(2) Appearance or performance fees.
(3) Endorsement fees where the individual has appeared in the UK

(whether or not his appearance is to promote the goods that he is endorsing).

(4) Payments which finance any of the above (such as commercial sponsorship).

Certain payments specifically excluded from the scheme are those:

(1)  subject to deduction of tax;
(2)  subject to PAYE;
(3)  solely for the use of copyright in words or music;
(4)  made to the Performing Rights Society;
(5)  made to UK residents and which are ancillary to a performance (this will include the cost of hiring a venue and payments for the services of UK-resident performers appearing with a non-resident);
(6)  which are royalties on the sale of records and tapes; and
(7)  amounting to less than £1,000 in a tax year. This *de minimis* limit applies to all payments made in a tax year in connection with the same event. Furthermore, payments made by the same or connected persons have to be aggregated and the £1,000 exemption applies only if the total is less than £1,000.

## 19.5.2 Special arrangements

It is possible for a payer to secure the Revenue's agreement to a lower rate of withholding tax provided an application is made at least 30 days in advance. Such authorisation may be given on the basis that:

(1)  the organiser can arrange that he is responsible for accounting for the tax; or
(2)  the sponsor can apply for clearance on the grounds that the tax will be collected from someone else; or
(3)  the payer can see authority to withhold tax at a lower rate, possibly to reflect the fact that the non-resident will have certain allowable expenses or perhaps because only some members of a group are non-resident.

## 19.5.3 Indirect payments also caught

The regulations provide that the withholding system should apply to payments made to any person:

(1)  who is under the control of the non-resident sportsman or entertainer;
(2)  who is:
    (a)  not resident in the UK; and
    (b)  not liable to tax in a territory outside the UK where the rate of tax charged on profits exceeds 22%;
(3)  in receipt of a connected payment or value transferred by a connected transfer;

who receives any connected payment or connected transfer where there is a contract or arrangement under which it is reasonable to suppose that the entertainer (or other person who is connected with him) is, will or may become entitled to receive amounts not substantially less than the amount paid.

## 19.6 OTHER PAYMENTS TO PERSONS NOT RESIDENT IN THE UK

### 19.6.1 Interest paid to a non-resident lender

Tax at 20% must normally be deducted where the interest is chargeable under Schedule D Case III and the lender is not resident in the UK. However, it may be possible for the lender to make a claim under a double taxation agreement. Where such a claim has been made, the Revenue may authorise payment of interest without deduction of tax.

### 19.6.2 Copyright royalties

Copyright royalties paid to a non-resident are normally subject to deduction of tax. Where the payment is made via a commission agent, basic rate tax has to be withheld for the net amount which is paid on to the non-resident. A statement made in the House of Commons in 1969 indicates that this obligation to withhold tax does not apply where copyright payments are made to professional authors who are resident abroad.

### 19.6.3 Purchase of British patent rights

There is an obligation for basic rate tax to be withheld where a person sells all or part of his patent rights and the vendor is not resident in the UK. Once again, the provisions of a double taxation agreement may override this, but a person making payment for such rights must deduct tax unless he is authorised not to do so by the Inspector of Foreign Dividends.

# 20

# ANTI-AVOIDANCE LEGISLATION

While the UK still does not have a GAAR (General Anti-avoidance Rule), there are numerous specific anti-avoidance provisions which must be borne in mind, especially when a tax planning exercise is being carried out. These provisions are generally intended to ensure that a person cannot reduce his tax liability by carrying out a given transaction in a roundabout way.

This chapter covers:

## Income tax

(1) Interest income.
(2) Transactions in land.
(3) Transactions in securities.
(4) Transfer of assets overseas.
(5) Trust income taxed on the settlor.
(6) Transactions involving loans or credit.

## Capital gains tax

(7) Bed and breakfast transactions.
(8) Disposals by a series of transactions.
(9) Transfers to a connected person.
(10) Qualifying corporate bonds.
(11) Value shifting.
(12) UK-resident settlements where the settlor has retained an interest.
(13) Offshore companies.
(14) Non-resident trusts.

## 20.1 INTEREST INCOME

### 20.1.1 Background

The Taxes Acts contain extensive legislation which is designed to prevent the conversion of taxable income into capital.

## 20.1.2 Sale of loan stock with right to purchase
(TA 1988, s 729)

At one time it was possible to enjoy the benefit of income in a capital form which was not subject to tax. This was achieved by selling loan stock or other interest bearing securities and retaining a right to repurchase them. For example, a person holding £1m $3^1/_2\%$ War Loan might sell the stock to a charity for £400,000 cum-interest while retaining the right to repurchase the War Loan once it had gone ex-interest for (say) £385,000, an overall profit of £15,000. He would have to forgo the income of £17,500 but that would be taxable and worth less than £15,000. The charity, however, would get the income tax free and so the transaction made sense to it.

There is now specific legislation designed to catch such arrangements. Where s 729 applies, the interest is treated as remaining taxable income of the person who sold the loan stock with a right to repurchase. Thus, in the above example, the interest payments actually received by the charity would be treated as income of the individual who had sold the War Loan stock with the right to repurchase it.

## 20.1.3 Sale of right to income
(TA 1988, s 730)

A variation on the above scheme worked for a number of years. It was common for individuals to sell to a charity or other exempt body the right to receive interest payments for a specified period of time, while retaining legal ownership of the securities themselves. This is now caught by TA 1988, s 730. If the loan stock is a UK security, the income which arises is assessed on the vendor. If it is a foreign loan stock, the proceeds of the sale are assessable as if they were income.

## 20.2 TRANSACTIONS IN LAND
(TA 1988, s 776)

### 20.2.1 Introduction

Section 776 was intended to prevent tax avoidance by persons concerned with land or development of land. Section 776 may apply where a capital gain is realised and one of the following conditions applies:

(1) The gain arises from UK land (or some other asset deriving its value from land) and the land was acquired with the sole or main object of realising a gain.
(2) The gain arises from the disposal of UK land which is held as trading stock.
(3) The gain arises from a disposal of UK land which has been developed

with the sole or main object of realising a gain on the disposal of the land.

Where s 776 applies, all or part of the capital gain is charged as income under Schedule D Case VI.

The definition of land includes buildings, and also assets deriving their value from land such as options. Consequently, s 776 could apply if a person received a lump sum for assigning the benefit of an option.

### 20.2.2 Exemption

There is an exemption for gains which arise on the disposal of an individual's principal private residence. This exemption continues to be available even where the CGT exemption is not due because the property was acquired with a view to realising a gain (see 14.14.3).

### 20.2.3 Sales of shares

Section 776 may apply where a person disposes of shares in a land-owning company. If a non-resident individual were to dispose of (say) a controlling shareholding in a company which itself owned a valuable UK property, the individual might be subject to tax under Schedule D Case VI on the whole of his capital gain.

There is a let-out in the case of a land-owning company which holds land as trading stock (ie a company which is a builder or developer or which deals in land as a trade). No liability arises under s 776 on a sale of shares in such a company, provided that the land held by the company is disposed of in the normal course of its trade and a full commercial profit from that land is received by the company.

Despite this let-out, s 776 may still be a problem on a sale of a land-owning company since the company may be an investment company (in which case it will not hold the land as trading stock).

### 20.2.4 Clearance procedure

It is possible for a person to apply for advance clearance from the Revenue that s 776 will not apply to a particular disposal. This clearance may be sought either for a sale of land or of shares in a land-owning company. The legislation requires that the person should supply full written particulars to the Inspector who must then make his decision within 30 days. Once clearance has been given, the Revenue cannot subsequently charge tax under s 776 unless the clearance application was invalid because it did not accurately set out all the facts.

# 20.3 TRANSACTIONS IN SECURITIES
(TA 1988, s 703)

## 20.3.1 Introduction

Legislation was originally introduced in 1960 to enable the Revenue to counteract tax advantages obtained by transactions in securities. The legislation is often applied by the Revenue to prevent tax savings being achieved because a right to income has been converted into a capital gain. An example of the type of transaction which might be caught in this way is where a person sells shares with a right to repurchase them for a lower amount after a dividend has been received by the purchaser (this is not caught by s 729 which has been mentioned at 20.1.2 above because that legislation applies only to loan stock and other fixed interest securities). However, the legislation also applies to other more devious types of transactions where the tax advantage is less obvious at first sight.

## 20.3.2 Conditions which must be satisfied before the legislation can apply

For s 703 to apply, the following three conditions must be satisfied.

(1) there must be one or more transactions in securities; and
(2) a person must have obtained, or be in a position to obtain, a tax advantage; and
(3) one of the prescribed circumstances set out in s 704 must have occurred.

If s 703 does apply, an income tax assessment may be made under Schedule D Case VI to counteract the tax advantage.

## 20.3.3 Transactions in securities

This term is widely defined so as to include transactions of whatever description relating to securities. It includes in particular:

(1) the purchase, sale or exchange of securities;
(2) the issuing of new securities;
(3) alteration of rights attaching to securities.

The term 'securities' is, in turn, defined as including shares and loan stock.

## 20.3.4 Tax advantage

In general, a tax advantage is deemed to arise if there is any increased relief, or repayment of tax, arising from transactions in securities, or if the transactions result in a reduction in the amount of tax which would otherwise be assessed.

The courts have taken the view that a tax advantage may arise wherever the Revenue can show that an amount received in a non-taxable form could have been received in a way which would have given rise to an income tax liability. Going back to the example given in 20.3.1 the Revenue would say that a tax advantage arises when a person sells shares and has a right to buy back at a lower price after a dividend has been paid because he could simply have retained the shares and received the dividend.

## 20.3.5 Prescribed circumstances

Section 704 lists five circumstances and at least one of them must apply before the Revenue can invoke s 703.

### Section 704A

This requires:

(1) the receipt of an abnormal dividend;
(2) a dividend should be received by someone entitled to an exemption or relief.

One example of this would be where shares are sold to a charity, the company then pays a dividend and the charity is able to reclaim tax because it is exempt from income tax. Another less obvious example of the circumstances caught under s 704A is where an abnormally large dividend is paid to an individual who is able to set losses against the dividend.

### Section 704B

This section applies in specific circumstances which are outside the scope of this book.

### Section 704C

This applies where a person receives consideration without paying income tax on it as a result of a transaction whereby another person subsequently receives an abnormal amount by way of dividend. The consideration received must represent:

(1) the value of assets which are available for distribution by way of dividends; or
(2) future receipts of the company; or
(3) the value of trading stock of the company.

### Section 704D

This sub-section applies where a person receives consideration which is not subject to tax and which represents:

(1) the value of assets which are available for distribution by way of dividend; or

(2) future receipts of the company; or

(3) the value of the trading stock of the company.

This sub-section is obviously similar to s 704C but s 704D can apply even though there has been no abnormal dividend.

Section 704D can apply only to transactions involving specified companies, ie:

(1) companies which are under the control of not more than five persons; or

(2) transactions involving any other unquoted company.

### Section 704E

Again, this section applies to special situations which are outside the scope of this book.

## 20.3.6 Exemption for bona fide commercial transactions

If there is a transaction in securities and the prescribed circumstances apply, a taxpayer may still avoid assessment if he can show that transactions were carried out for bona fide commercial reasons or in the ordinary course of making or managing investments, and that none of them had as their main object the obtaining of a tax advantage.

## 20.3.7 Clearances

Section 707 provides a procedure whereby a person can give details of the proposed transactions to the Revenue and request clearance that the Board will not apply s 703.

Once a written application has been made under s 707, the Revenue has 30 days in which to request further particulars; such further information must then be provided within 30 days.

The Revenue must give a decision either within 30 days of receiving the original application or within 30 days of receiving the further information.

Where the Revenue has notified someone that it is satisfied that s 703 should not apply, the Revenue may not subsequently change its mind. However, where information given in the application is incomplete or inaccurate, any clearance given by the Revenue may be void.

## 20.3.8 Situations where clearance should be sought

It is standard practice for vendors, or their advisers, to seek clearance under s 707 where a private company is being sold for a substantial amount. Quite apart from anything else, the vendor would otherwise be at the mercy of the purchaser who might extract an abnormal dividend and thus bring s 707 into consideration.

It is also advisable to seek clearance under s 707 where a company is liquidated, the reserves are extracted in a capital form and it is intended that the company's business should be carried on by a new company owned by the current shareholders.

## 20.4 TRANSFER OF ASSETS OVERSEAS

Legislation was originally introduced in 1936 to prevent tax savings for resident and ordinarily resident individuals arising from their transferring assets overseas. The legislation refers to avoidance of income tax. Capital tax avoidance is not subject to counteraction by s 739 or 740, although separate anti-avoidance legislation also exists for CGT (see 20.13).

### 20.4.1 Where the individual or his spouse can benefit

Section 739 applies where a UK-resident person has made a transfer and either he or his spouse may benefit as a result of the transfer of assets. A person is deemed to meet this test if he has 'power to enjoy' income which arises overseas. Power to enjoy income exists in the following circumstances:

(1) The income accrues for the benefit of the individual.
(2) The receipt of the income increases the value to the individual of any assets held by him or for his benefit.
(3) The individual may become entitled to enjoy the income at some future point in time.
(4) The individual is able in any way whatsoever, and whether directly or indirectly, to control the way in which the income is used.

Where s 739 applies, the transferor or spouse are assessed on the income as it arises, even if it is not actually paid out to them.

### 20.4.2 Exemption for bona fide transactions

Section 741 provides a clearance procedure. The individual must show to the satisfaction of the Revenue that:

(1) the purpose of avoiding tax was not one of the purposes for which the transfer of assets was carried out; or
(2) the transfer of assets, and any associated operations, were bona fide commercial transactions and not designed for tax avoidance.

### 20.4.3 Transfer of assets by non-resident individuals

The Revenue view has always been that s 739 could apply to income arising from a transfer of assets made by an individual at a time when he was not resident in the UK. The House of Lords found against the Revenue on this in *IRC v Willoughby* [1997] STC 995, but FA 1997 restored the position to what the Revenue always believed to be the case in relation to income arising on or after 26 November 1996.

## 20.4.4 Assessment of income caught by s 739

Income which is caught by s 739 normally is assessed under Schedule D Case VI. However, where the income is UK dividend income, or other income which has borne tax at source, relief is given for such tax and the assessment will be for higher rate tax purposes only.

## 20.4.5 Liability of non-transferors
(TA 1988, s 740)

A person may not be assessed under s 739 unless he or his spouse has made a transfer of assets. However, a UK-ordinarily resident individual may be assessed under s740 if he receives a benefit from a transfer made by another person. This particularly applies to beneficiaries of non-resident settlements created by someone other than the individual and his spouse. It is also arguable that s 740 might apply to a person who had made a transfer of assets but was not 'caught' by s 739, perhaps because he was not resident at the time of the transfer.

In contrast to s 739, a liability may arise under s 740 only when the individual concerned receives a benefit. The term 'benefit' is not specifically defined although the legislation states that it includes a payment of any kind. It is understood that an interest-free loan or the provision of accommodation are also regarded by the Revenue as constituting a benefit.

This is an area where professional advice is essential.

## 20.4.6 Matching income with benefits

The legislation provides for benefits to be matched with income received in either earlier or later years.

### Example

An overseas trust receives income of £10,000 in 1994–95. In 1996–97 a capital payment of £100,000 is made to a UK-resident and ordinarily resident individual. In the year 1998–99, the trustees receive further income of £120,000. If s 740 applies, the individual will be taxed as follows:

|  | £ |
|---|---|
| 1996–97 | 10,000 |
| 1998–99 | 90,000 |

## 20.4.7 An interest-free loan may constitute a benefit

The High Court decided in January 2000 that an interest-free loan which was repayable on demand gave rise to a benefit equal to interest at the 'official rate' (*Billingham v Cooper* [2000] STC 122).

## 20.4.8 Assessment under s 740

Where income is taxed under s 740, there is no credit for any UK tax suffered at source. This can give rise to double taxation. Thus, going back to the previous example, if the trustees' income represented dividends from UK companies, the total tax suffered would really be as follows:

|  | £ |
|---|---|
| Tax at source on dividends: £100,000 × $^{20}\!/\!_{00}$ = | 25,000 |
| Tax charged on beneficiary under s 740 = | 40,000 |
|  | 65,000 |

## 20.4.9 Clearances

Once again, it is possible to obtain clearance from the Revenue that s 740 should not apply because the transfer of assets concerned was not carried out for the purposes of tax avoidance.

## 20.4.10 Foreign domiciliaries

Where the income arising to the non-resident trust or company is foreign source income, no liability can arise for a foreign domiciled individual except to the extent that he remits such income to the UK (see 22.9).

## 20.4.11 Reporting income taxable under s 739 or 740

The relevant sections of your tax return are:

### Extract from Tax Return, page 2

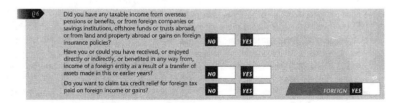

If you tick either YES box, you are required to complete a Foreign Schedule.

## Extract from Foreign Schedule, page F2

- Disposals of holdings in offshore funds, income from non-resident trusts and benefits received from overseas trusts, companies and other entities *see Notes, page FN10.*

  **6.5** £

  Tick box 6.5A if you are omitting income from boxes 6.4, 6.4A or 6.5 - *see Notes, page FN11*

  **6.5A**

## Extracts from Revenue notes to the Tax Return

If you have transferred, or taken any part in the transfer of, assets as a result of which income has become payable to a trust, company or other entity situated abroad **and,**

- you are ordinarily resident in the UK and you or your husband or wife may at any time enjoy any of that income (in whatever form), **or**
- you or your husband or wife have received or are entitled to receive a capital sum connected in any way with the transfer,

enter that income in columns A to E on Page F2 and include it in the total amounts in boxes 6.3, 6.3A, 6.4 and 6.4A **unless** you are ticking box 6.5A ...

### Benefits received from overseas trusts, companies and other entities

**boxes 6.5 and 6.5A** If someone else has made the same sort of transfer of assets ... the value of the payment or any other benefit you receive is treated as your income for tax purposes to the extent that the company, trust or other entity has 'unexpended income'. Unexpended income means income that has not already become that of another individual or that has not otherwise been spent by the company, trust or other entity. Income which arose before 10 March 1981 is not counted for this purpose. ...

... 'Benefits' include, for example, loans at less than a commercial rate of interest and the occupation or use of property at less than a commercial rental, the value of the benefit being the difference between the commercial rate of interest or rental and any amount actually paid to you.

A trust will be non-resident if all trustees are themselves resident outside the United Kingdom. A trust may also be non resident if at least one of its trustees is resident outside the United Kingdom – ask the trustees or your tax adviser if you are not sure whether the trust is treated as non-resident. 'Indirect' receipt must also be included, for example, if the capital or benefit came from a company controlled by the trustees or from a United Kingdom resident trust that has been, or has received funds from, an overseas trust.

If you received capital or benefit (other than income) from a trust which either is, or has been, non-resident, or which has received assets from a trust which either is or has been non-resident, enter that amount in box 6.5.

Enter in box 6.5 (unless you are ticking box 6.5A for the reason given below), the value of any payment or benefit received directly or indirectly to the extent that it is matched by unexpended income. If the payment or benefit is greater than the unexpended income, enter in box 6.5 the amount of the unexpended income. You may need to ask the overseas company, trust or other entity for this information. Include the value of any payment or benefit received in an earlier year if and to the extent that this was not taxed in earlier years. If the value of what you have received or benefited from exceeds the unexpended income that the overseas company trust or other entity has, you may be liable to Capital Gains Tax on the excess. You may need *Help Sheet IR301: Calculation of the increase in tax charge on capital gains from non-resident, dual resident and immigrating trusts* as well as the Capital Gains Pages; both are available from the Orderline. Otherwise that excess will need to be taken into account when completing your Tax Return next year. Also enter in the 'Additional Information' box on Page F3 the full name and address of the company or other entity receiving the income. Where the capital or other benefit has come from a resident trust in the circumstances described above, also give details of the circumstances including the full name of any other trust involved.

**box 6.5A** These provisions relating to transfers of assets do not apply if you can show that the purpose of the transfer and any associated operations was not to avoid tax. But if you are omitting income for this reason from columns A to E on Page F2 and boxes 6.4, 6.4A or 6.5 you must tick box 6.5A.

## 20.5 TRUST INCOME TAXED ON THE SETTLOR

### 20.5.1 Introduction

There are a number of separate provisions under which income on property which belongs to trustees may be taxed as if it were income which belonged to the settlor. FA 1995 re-cast these sections in relation to 1995–96 and subsequent years, but the overall effect of the new legislation (TA 1988, ss 660A–660J inserted by FA 1995, Sched 17) is virtually identical.

### 20.5.2 Trust where the settlor may benefit
(TA 1988, s 660A)

Legislation may catch income which arises to a trust under which the settlor or his spouse may benefit. The legislation provides that the settlor/spouse should be treated as capable of benefiting where they may benefit in any circumstances whatsoever except in one of the following exceptional cases:

(1) The bankruptcy of a person who is beneficially entitled under the settlement.
(2) The death under the age of 25 of a person who would be beneficially entitled to the trust property on attaining that age.
(3) In the case of a marriage settlement, the death of both parties to the marriage and of all or any of the children of the marriage.

The Revenue interprets this legislation rather literally. For example, if a person creates a trust for the benefit of his son, and the trust deed states that the property should revert to the settlor if the son dies before age 35, the

Revenue takes the view that s 660A applies because the let-out applies only where property reverts on the death of someone before he attains age 25.

Sometimes the trust deed is silent on a matter. For example, a person creates a trust for the benefit of his three children and the trust deed makes no reference to the capital coming back to the settlor. In such circumstances, the Revenue is apt to say that the property could revert to the settlor if all his children died and they left no children of their own. To avoid this kind of argument, it is normal for a trust to contain a clause which provides that the capital shall in no circumstances whatsoever come back to the settlor but shall be held for the benefit of (say) a charity in the event that all the named beneficiaries die before the capital is distributed.

The Revenue does not take the view that a person has reserved the benefit simply because his spouse may benefit after his death as his widow. On the other hand, cases have actually arisen where the settlor and his wife were excluded but the Revenue said that s 660A should apply because the settlor's current marriage might come to an end and he might marry someone who could benefit. Once again, it is best to make sure that the trust deed excludes such an interpretation by expressly providing that any future spouse of the settlor should be excluded from all benefit.

Where a settlor's spouse can benefit, the settlor is assessed on the trust income. This means that the benefits of independent taxation cannot be secured by putting capital into trust for a spouse.

FA 2000 has introduced a concession. Where a settlor is not totally excluded but one of the beneficiaries under the trust is a charity, income arising after 5 April 2000 which is actually paid out to the charity will not be assessable on the settlor under s 660A.

### 20.5.3 Settlements on minor children
(TA 1988, s 660B)

Where a person gives capital to his minor children, the resulting income may be taxed as if it belonged to the parent. This treatment applies where the following three conditions are satisfied:

(1) The child is a minor.
(2) The child is unmarried.
(3) The income exceeds £100 per tax year for each child.

Similarly when a person makes a settlement under which his minor children may benefit, income which is distributed to the children before they are 18 is treated as the settlor's income (subject to the £100 de minimis exemption). This applies even where the individual is separated or divorced and the children live with his former wife.

For the purposes of s 660B, a child includes an adopted child and illegitimate child. Once again, the Revenue interprets this legislation strictly and it has been known to tax a grandparent who set up a trust for his daughter's (illegitimate) child whom he subsequently adopted and brought up as his own child.

There are two circumstances where s 660B does not apply:

(1) Where the child has married.
(2) Where the settlor is not resident in the UK.

The legislation does not stop here. Any capital payments made to the children are also caught so far as the capital payments may be matched with accumulated income within the trust. This is less serious than in the past since trustees will normally pay 34% tax on accumulated income (see 18.5.1) so even if the income is then deemed to be the settlor's income because a capital sum has been paid out to the child, the additional tax payable cannot exceed 6% (ie the difference between the 40% top rate and 34% paid by the trustees).

Until recently there was a gap in the legislation so that if a parent made an outright gift of capital to a minor child, with the capital being held by a bare trustee, and the trustee did not pay out the income or pay it into a bank account in the child's own name, the income was not caught by the anti-avoidance legislation and was treated as the child's own income for all income tax purposes. The same treatment applied where a parent created a settlement under which a minor child had a life interest or other interest in possession. Provided that the resulting income was not paid out to the child, or paid into a bank account in the child's own name, the income was not assessed on the parent.

This loophole was closed in the March 1999 Budget, and the above treatment therefore applies only to parental gifts made before 9 March 1999.

### Roll-up funds

A way which remains open for achieving a tax saving may be for a parent to give capital to a minor child, with the money being invested in a roll-up fund or some other investment which does not produce taxable income. If the roll-up fund is cashed in shortly after the child's 18th birthday, the income will count as the child's income and not the parent's income. This may be a good strategy where a child is unlikely to have much income in his own right, perhaps because he will be in full-time education during the year in which he attains age 18.

## 20.5.4 Capital payments to the settlor
(TA 1988, s 677)

There is even a section which may apply to enable the Revenue to charge tax on income received by the trustees of the settlement under which the settlor and spouse are both totally excluded from benefit.

Section 677 may apply where the trustees of the settlement have accumulated income and they make a capital payment to the settlor. The capital payment is then treated as if it were income for the year in which the payment was made provided there is sufficient undistributed income.

If only part of the capital payment can be 'matched', the balance is matched with income for subsequent years, and amounts matched in this way are then taxable for those years.

### Example – Matching of capital payments

In 1996–97 *A* received a capital payment of £18,000 from a trust set up by him in 1985. The trust has net undistributed income of £30,000. *A* will be assessed under s 677 as if he had received gross income which after tax at the rate applicable to trusts (34%) would have left £18,000, ie £27,272.

In 1997–98 *A* receives a capital payment of £50,000. The trustees have undistributed income for that year of £20,000. The trustees make no further capital repayments but in 1998–99 and 1999–2000 they have undistributed income of £10,000 and £9,000. The following amounts are taxable under s 677:

|  |  | £ |
|---|---|---|
| 1996–97 | = | 27,272 |
| 1997–98 £32,000[1] grossed up | = | 48,484 |
| 1998–99 £10,000 grossed up | = | 15,151 |
| 1999–2000 £8,000 grossed up | = | 12,121 |

[1]ie balance of the undistributed income available at the end of the year 1994–95.

## 20.5.5 Income may be matched with capital payments made in previous 12 years

Undistributed income can be identified with past capital payments for up to 12 years. The only way to get round this is for the whole of the capital sum to be repaid by the settlor, but even doing this does not affect the position for past years and the year in which the capital sum is repaid.

## 20.5.6 Loans may also be caught

A loan from the trustees to the settlor or spouse may be treated under s 677 as if it were a capital payment. Furthermore, the repayment of a loan made by the settlor to the trust can also be treated as a capital payment.

### Example – Treatment of loans

In 1997–98 *A* makes a £150,000 loan to a trust created by him. The trustees repay the loan in full during 2000–01. At that time, the trustees have undistributed income of £45,000. *A* would be taxed under s 677 on £45,000 grossed up at 34% ie £68,181.

If the trustees had undistributed income of £30,000 for 2002–03 and £85,000 for 2003–04, the position would be that assessments could be made on £30,000 grossed up for 2002–03 and £75,000 grossed up for the year 2003–04.

## 20.5.7 Payments by companies connected with trustees

A liability could also arise under s 677 if a company which is connected with the trustees makes a capital payment to the settlor. There have to be three conditions here:

(1) The trustees must have undistributed income.
(2) There must be 'associated payments' by the trustees to the company. An associated payment may include a capital payment (eg a subscription for shares) or the transfer of assets at an undervalue by the trustees to the company.
(3) The company must make a capital payment to the settlor, or make a loan to him or repay a loan made by the settlor to the company. This event must occur within five years of the associated payment having taken place.

## 20.6 TRANSACTIONS INVOLVING LOANS OR CREDIT
(TA 1988, s 786)

Specific legislation exists to prevent any tax avoidance which could otherwise arise if a person who was liable to pay non-allowable interest found a way of converting his liability to pay interest into some other payment which is tax deductible. Section 786 may apply where a transaction is effected with reference to the lending of money. It can apply whether the transaction is between the lender and borrower or involves other persons connected with them.

(1) Section 786(3) states that if the transaction provides for payment of any annuity or other annual payment it shall be treated as interest for all purposes of the Taxes Act.
(2) Section 786(4) states that if the borrower agrees to sell or transfer to the lender any securities or other property carrying a right to income then the borrower may be chargeable under Schedule D Case VI on an amount equal to the income which arises from the property before he repays the loan.

(3) Section 786(5) refers to income being assigned, surrendered, waived or forgone and states that the person who has assigned, surrendered etc, may be charged to tax under Schedule D Case VI on the amount of income assigned, surrendered, waived or forgone.

In theory, s 786 could apply to interest-free loans. The Revenue has given some degree of comfort in that it has said that in the straightforward situation where one person lends money to another and then waives the interest, and there is no further transaction linked in any way to the arrangements, s 786 will not be invoked. There has been some concern, in the past, that s 786 could apply where, for example, a client deposited a large lump sum with his accountant on the basis that the accountant would not pay interest but would reduce his accountancy fees by the amount of the interest that would have been paid at commercial rates on the client's deposit. It is possible to read s 786(5) as permitting the Revenue to make an assessment in this way even though the type of transactions described are somewhat different from those envisaged when the legislation was originally enacted.

## 20.7  BED AND BREAKFAST TRANSACTIONS

For disposals of shares by individuals or trustees on or after 17 March 1998, any shares of the same class and in the same company which are sold and then repurchased within a 30-day period will be matched so that the gain or loss which would otherwise have arisen by reference to shares already held will not be realised. This blocks a widely used way in which individuals have realised losses and then brought back the same shares on the following day.

It would appear that it is still possible to circumvent this rule by one spouse selling and the other purchasing the same securities. However, the Revenue may attack this as an artificial transaction entered into solely for tax avoidance, especially if the purchasing spouse subsequently transfers the shares to the original owner.

## 20.8  DISPOSALS BY A SERIES OF TRANSACTIONS

### 20.8.1  Basic principle behind the legislation
(TCGA 1992, s 19)

There are certain assets which are worth more in total than the sum of their various parts. For example, a 55% shareholding in a private company will almost always be worth a great deal more than five times the value of an 11% shareholding since a 55% shareholder has control of the company. It follows from this that if there were not specific anti-avoidance legislation, a person could reduce his exposure to CGT on a gift to a relative etc by transferring the asset in stages.

In fact, in certain circumstances, the Revenue may look at the value transferred by a series of transactions and assess the value transferred by each separate transaction according to an appropriate part of the total value transferred.

## 20.8.2 Legislation may have wide application

The legislation can also apply in unexpected ways. For example, if an individual with a 75% shareholding in an investment company decided to give 25% to each of his brother's three children and even arranged to make the gifts over a period of two (or more) years, the Revenue could still apply s 19 so as to catch the total value transferred.

## 20.8.3 Circumstances which will cause s 19 to apply

The following circumstances may result in the Revenue applying s 19:

(1) A person disposes of assets to another person (or persons) who fall within the definition of connected persons.
(2) There are 'linked transactions' which fall within a period of six years.
(3) The disposals have all taken place since 19 March 1985.
(4) The aggregate value transferred by the series of linked transactions is greater than the total of the values transferred by the individual transactions.

A transaction may be caught by s 19 even if it is a sale rather than a gift.

## 20.8.4 Section 19 can result in retrospective adjustments

If the Revenue invokes s 19, it may result in assessments for previous years being reopened. For example, C may have made a gift to her father in 1993–94 of a 10% shareholding in X Ltd and the value of the shares may have been agreed with the Revenue as, say, £20,000. If C made a further gift to her brother in 1998–99 of a 70% shareholding, the position may have to be reopened. If the Revenue establish that an 80% shareholding is worth £800,000 at the time of the gift to C's brother, the effect of applying s 19 will be:

Deemed disposal proceeds on the 1993–94 gift     £100,000
Deemed disposal proceeds on the 1998–99 gift     £700,000

## 20.8.5 Hold-over relief may cover the position

In some circumstances, the donor may not have to pay extra tax because he and the donee may have agreed that the hold-over provisions should apply (see 15.6). However, hold-over relief will not always be available since the asset will not always fall within the definition of business property or the donee may not be resident in the UK.

Professional advice is clearly essential where a person is contemplating making a series of gifts to connected persons.

## 20.9 TRANSFERS TO A CONNECTED PERSON

Another potential pitfall arises from special rules which govern the way in which market value is to be determined when assessing a gain on a transaction between connected persons (whether the transaction is a gift or a sale).

### 20.9.1 Some restrictions may be taken into account
(TCGA 1992, s 18)

A gift or sale to a connected person may involve an asset over which the acquirer already has certain rights. Thus, A may own the freehold of a building and his daughter may have valuable rights as a tenant. Suppose that the freehold is worth £230,000 with vacant possession, but is worth only £180,000 if his daughter's lease is taken into account. When A sells the freehold to his daughter will the market value be taken as £230,000 or £180,000?

The legislation states that the market value shall be taken to be the market value of the asset less the lower of:

(1) the value of the interest held by the connected person who acquires the asset; or
(2) the amount by which the transferor's asset would increase in value if the connected person's rights did not exist.

Consequently, A would be deemed to make a disposal of an asset worth £180,000.

### 20.9.2 Some restrictions are ignored
(TCGA 1992, s 18(7))

Certain valuable rights may have to be left out of account. One example of this is an option. Suppose the facts set out in 20.9.1 had been slightly different so that A had vacant possession of a property worth £230,000, but his daughter had an option under which she could acquire it for £180,000. If A sells the property to his daughter or if she exercises her option he will receive only £180,000, but he may be assessed as if he had received £230,000.

This is because the legislation requires options to be ignored or left out of account when computing the market value of an asset. Similarly, legal rights which, if exercised, would effectively destroy or impair the asset also have to be ignored. Market value is determined as if such rights did not exist.

## 20.10 QUALIFYING CORPORATE BONDS
(FA 1997, s 88)

FA 1997 contains anti-avoidance provisions which took effect from 26 November 1996. They concern situations where an individual, or groups of individuals, dispose of their private company shares and take loan stock issued by the acquiring company as part of the sale consideration (referred to as 'rolling over' into loan stock since no capital gain normally arises until the loan stock is sold). Since 1984, legislation has made specific provision for the situation where a person receives qualifying corporate bonds in exchange for shares. The capital gain which would have arisen had the individual taken cash rather than qualifying corporate bonds is calculated but held over until such time as the individual disposes of the bonds. The legislation did not make express provision for the situation where the vendor receives loan notes which are not qualifying corporate bonds at the time of acquisition but become such bonds before a disposal takes place. As such bonds are normally an exempt asset for CGT purposes, the legislation seemed to allow a capital gain to escape a charge altogether, which gave rise to the term 'disappearing trick'.

The Revenue was sceptical that these arrangements succeeded in their objective. However, and without prejudice to litigation on past transactions, FA 1997 has clarified the position.

The CGT legislation has been amended so that when a loan stock changes from a non-qualifying corporate bond into a qualifying corporate bond the change is treated as a conversion of securities. This ensures that any gain which has been rolled over on an exchange of shares for loan stock is preserved and does not escape charge. The new rules apply to disposals after 25 November 1996 even where the loan stock was converted before the Budget.

## 20.11 VALUE SHIFTING
(TCGA 1992, s 29)

The legislation contains provisions which are intended to ensure that disguised gifts are assessed as a disposal at market value.

### 20.11.1 Type of transaction which may be caught

A controlling shareholder might exercise his control over a company to transfer value in an indirect way.

### Example – Value shifting

> *B* owns all the shares in Y Ltd. The company has 1,000 £1 ordinary shares in issue. Assume that the value of these shares is £300,000. If *B* allowed his son *C* to be issued with 2,000 £1 shares at par, he would not have made a disposal of his own shares. However, *C* would have acquired a valuable asset in that his 2,000 shares will probably be worth in excess of £200,000 compared with the £2,000 that he had paid to acquire them. Furthermore, *B*'s 1,000 shares will have gone down in value since he will have become a minority shareholder.
>
> Where the Revenue can apply s 29, the person who has transferred value (in this example *B*) is treated as if he had disposed of an asset.

## 20.11.2 An omission to exercise a right

There can be circumstances where s 29 is relevant because a person has failed to exercise a right. For example, if *A* and his grandson *D* were 50:50 shareholders in Y Ltd and the company announced a rights issue of three new shares for every one share already held and the amount payable for each share was £1 (par), s 29 would come into operation if *A* chose not to exercise his entitlement to the rights issue, as this omission would mean that after the rights issue the shares in Y Ltd would be owned as to:

|   |      |
|---|------|
| *A* | 20% |
| *D* | 80% |

Control would have thereby passed to *D*.

# 20.12 UK-RESIDENT SETTLEMENTS WHERE SETTLOR HAS RETAINED INTEREST

## 20.12.1 Introduction
(TCGA 1992, s 77)

Capital gains realised by trustees of a UK-resident settlement may be taxed as if they were the settlor's own gains if he is deemed to have retained an interest in the trust. The gains are simply added to his personal gains and he is responsible for paying the CGT. He can, however, reclaim the tax from the trustees.

This does not apply unless the settlor is resident or ordinarily resident in the UK for the tax year concerned. These provisions can apply to a settlement which was created some years before the introduction of this legislation in 1988.

### 20.12.2 Circumstances in which the settlor is deemed to have retained an interest

A settlor is regarded as having retained an interest if there are any circumstances whatsoever under which the property within the settlement or income arising to the trustees may become payable to him or his spouse. Furthermore, he may be deemed to have retained an interest if he or his spouse enjoys a benefit derived directly or indirectly from the settled property.

There are some circumstances in which a settlor is not deemed to have retained a benefit even though he might receive a benefit. These exceptions relate to the possibility of the settlor or spouse benefiting in the event that a beneficiary becomes bankrupt or dies under the age of 25 years or, in the case of a marriage settlement, the death of the married couple and their children.

### 20.12.3 Considerable care needed

There is no 'proportionality' here so the retention of even a very small interest could result in the settlor being taxed on considerable gains which he did not (and perhaps never could) enjoy. There are two areas of special concern: loans by a settlor and remarriage.

#### Loans by a settlor

If the settlor lends money to the trustees there is a risk that he might be said to have an interest in the settled property and this situation should therefore be avoided.

#### Remarriage

The possibility of the settlor's current marriage coming to an end and his remarrying may be remote, but will be considered by the Revenue to bring s 77 into operation if such a future spouse is not specifically excluded from benefiting under the settlement.

### 20.12.4 Death of the settlor

Once the settlor has died, s 77 ceases to apply. His widow cannot then be charged on the trustees' gains.

## 20.13 OFFSHORE COMPANIES
(TCGA 1992, s 13)

A person who is resident and ordinarily resident in the UK (see 21.2) may be liable for a proportion of capital gains realised by a non-resident company in which he has a shareholding.

## Example

> A owns all the shares in Z Ltd, a company incorporated and resident in Bermuda. The company realises a capital gain by disposing of a US property that it owns. The legislation enables the Revenue to assess A as if he made the capital gain himself. However, certain conditions need to be satisfied before the Revenue can assess a capital gain in this way (see 20.13.1).

## 20.13.1 Conditions which need to be satisfied

(1) The company must be controlled by five or fewer shareholders, or shareholder directors must between them own more than 50% of the company's shares.

(2) The individual concerned must be resident (or ordinarily resident) and domiciled in the UK (see 22.1 and 22.14).

(3) The individual and persons connected with him must between them have an interest in the company of at least 5%. Until 27 November 1995, the legislation could apply only if the individual was a shareholder who was entitled to at least 5% of the company's assets on a winding-up.

## 20.13.2 Certain gains not assessable under s 13

The legislation is really intended to catch gains on investment assets etc held through an offshore company. There is therefore an exemption under s 13(5) for gains arising:

(1) on the disposal of foreign currency where the currency represents money in use for a trade carried on by the company outside the UK;

(2) from the disposal of 'tangible property' used for the purposes of a trade carried on by the company wholly outside the UK;

(3) from disposals of assets used by a UK branch of the company.

## 20.13.3 Distribution test
(TCGA 1992, s 13(5)(d))

Where an offshore company has realised gains which are not exempt under 20.14.3, the individual may still escape assessment on gains realised before 28 November 1995 if he can show that the offshore company has distributed the gains within two years, either as a dividend or on the company being wound up. However, if the individual is resident in the UK at the time that he receives such a distribution, he will be assessed on it (either for income tax or, in the case of a liquidation, for CGT).

# 20.14 NON-RESIDENT TRUSTS
(TCGA 1992, s 86 and Sched 5)

## 20.14.1 Introduction

Trustees of a trust may be resident outside the UK and the administration of the trust may be carried out overseas. Provided both these conditions are satisfied, the trust is not resident and there will not normally be any liability for the trustees so far as UK CGT is concerned. However, there may be a liability for either the settlor (ie the person who set up the trust) or the beneficiaries (who may include the settlor).

## 20.14.2 Post-18 March 1991 offshore trusts
(TCGA 1992, s 86 and Sched 5)

The legislation refers to these type of trusts as 'qualifying settlements'. In fact, they qualify for an adverse CGT treatment in that the trustees' gains are deemed to be the settlor's personal capital gains. The conditions under which the trust's capital gains will be treated in this way are as follows:

(1) The settlor must be UK-resident or ordinarily resident for the year concerned.
(2) He must not have died during the course of the year.
(3) The people who benefit from the trust include one of the following:
    (a) the settlor;
    (b) the settlor's spouse;
    (c) the settlor's children (and spouses);
    (d) a company connected with the settlor;
    (e) for trusts created after 16 March 1998, the settlor's grandchildren.

## 20.14.3 Pre-19 March 1991 offshore trusts
(TCGA 1992, s 97(1))

Provided that the trust does not become a qualifying settlement (see 20.14.5), there will be no CGT liability for beneficiaries for years up to 1998–99 (see 20.14.6 on 1999–2000 and future years) until such time as 'capital payments' are received.

UK-resident and domiciled beneficiaries may be assessed for CGT purposes on a proportion of the trustees' capital gains which can be 'matched' with capital payments received.

The receipt of a benefit may count as a deemed capital payment (the rules are virtually the same as under s 740 – see 20.4).

### Example – Pre-19 March 1991 offshore trusts

Trustees of an offshore trust make capital gains in 1989–90 of £200,000. In 1989–90 to 1991–92 the trustees distribute income, but their doing this does not have any CGT consequences. In 1997–98 they make a capital payment of £50,000 to *A*, who is UK resident.

*A* would be assessed as if he had personally made capital gains of £50,000 for 1997–98. The tax actually payable will depend upon whether he has made other capital gains, whether he has capital losses available for off-set and his rate of tax.

## 20.14.4 Supplementary charge

A supplementary charge may be made of 10% of the tax for each complete year between 1 December following the year in which the trustees realised the gain and the time that the trustees make the capital distribution. The supplementary charge cannot exceed 60%.

## 20.14.5 Pre-19 March 1991 trusts can become qualifying settlements

A pre-19 March 1991 offshore trust may become a qualifying settlement if:

(1) property is added after 18 March 1991;
(2) the trust is varied so that a person becomes a beneficiary who previously could not have been expected to benefit.

## 20.14.6 Finance Act 1998 changes

### Protection for pre-March 1991 trusts removed

From 6 April 1999, the distinction between pre- and post-19 March 1991 trusts created by UK domiciliaries ceased to be relevant. If the settlor, his spouse or children can benefit, the trustees' gains may be taxed as if they had been realised by the settlor.

The only circumstances where this does not apply is where the trust is a qualifying settlement only because the settlor's children are potential beneficiaries and the children are under age 18. Once the children attain age 18, this protection is lost.

Where a qualifying settlement has gains in the period 17 March 1998 to 5 April 1999, they may be taxed on the settlor as if he had realised them on 6 April 1999.

UK domiciliaries can be taxed on capital payments from trusts created by foreign domiciliaries. With effect from 17 March 1998, UK-resident and domiciled beneficiaries can be assessed where they receive capital payments from a non-resident trust created by a foreign domiciled settlor.

However, this can apply only where payments made after 16 March 1998 can be matched with gains realised by the trustees after that date.

## 20.14.7 One particular avoidance scheme blocked

In addition to the changes set out above, ten days before the March 1998 Budget the Treasury announced a separate anti-avoidance rule to take effect from 6 March 1998. The change in the rules concerns beneficiaries of non-UK resident trusts which might have received the trust capital without any liability for CGT. Any gain realised on the disposal of an interest in a non-UK trust – or a trust which was non-resident in the past – is now a chargeable gain.

# 21

# RESIDENCE STATUS

This chapter covers the following:

(1) Consequences of residence in the UK.
(2) Various criteria for determining residence status.
(3) Ceasing to be resident in the UK.
(4) UK income and capital gains received by non-residents.
(5) Non-resident investment companies.
(6) When tax should be withheld from payments to non-residents.

## 21.1 CONSEQUENCES OF RESIDENCE IN THE UK

The basic principle of UK taxation is that an individual may be charged tax on his world-wide income if he is resident in the UK. If the individual is not resident in the UK he is still liable for tax on income that arises in the UK but not for tax on income which arises overseas.

There is an exception to this in that an individual who is resident in the UK but not ordinarily resident and/or not domiciled there may have to pay tax only on UK income. The concept of domicile is different from residence – for further details see 22.1.

The rest of this chapter proceeds on the basis that an individual has a UK domicile.

## 21.2 VARIOUS CRITERIA FOR DETERMINING RESIDENCE STATUS

### 21.2.1 Introduction

For the purposes of UK taxation, 'the UK' means England, Scotland, Wales and Northern Ireland. It does not include the Republic of Ireland, the Channel Islands nor the Isle of Man. A person may be resident in more than one country so the fact that an individual is treated as resident in, for example, the USA or South Africa does not necessarily mean that he is not resident in the UK.

A person is resident or not resident for a tax year. A person may also be ordinarily resident if he is habitually resident in the UK as opposed to simply being resident for one year in isolation.

Somewhat surprisingly the word 'resident' is not defined in the Taxes Acts. There is, however, considerable case law and the position is summarised below.

## 21.2.2 Two basic tests

An individual will always be treated as resident in the UK for a tax year if he is caught under either of the following tests:

(a) The six-month rule, ie the individual is present in the UK for 183 days or more during the tax year.
(b) The three-month average rule, where the individual is present in the UK for an average of 91 days or more per annum measured over a period of four tax years.

Days of arrival and departure are normally left out of account for these tests.

## 21.2.3 Existing UK residents

So far as a person who has been resident in the UK for a number of years is concerned, he is likely to continue to be regarded as UK resident despite temporary periods of absence from this country unless the following conditions are satisfied:

(a) he works full-time abroad, and the period spent overseas includes a complete tax year, or
(b) he has no accommodation in the UK and he lives abroad for at least one full tax year.

The treatment of UK residents who move overseas is covered at 21.3.

## 21.2.4 Foreign nationals coming to the UK

The residence status of individuals who come to the UK is now governed by the six- and three-month rules set out in 21.2.2. Individuals who regularly visit the UK, and are therefore caught by the three-month rule, are normally treated as ordinarily resident only from the fourth year. However, an individual may be regarded as ordinarily resident from year one if it is clear that he intended to spend an average of three months per annum in this country.

## 21.2.5 Visits for education

A person who comes to the UK for a period of study or education which is expected to last more than four years will be regarded as resident and ordinarily resident from the date of his arrival. If the period is not expected to exceed four years, he may be treated as not ordinarily resident, but this will depend on whether he:

(1) has accommodation available there, or
(2) intends to remain in the UK when his education is complete, or
(3) proposes to visit the UK in future years for average periods of three months or more per tax year.

If, despite his originally intending not to do so, the individual remains in the UK for more than four years, he will be treated in any event as ordinarily resident from the beginning of the fifth year of his stay. This applies both to a person who comes to the UK for his own education or a parent or guardian of a child who comes in connection with the child's education.

## 21.2.6 Double taxation agreements

The UK has entered into a large number of double taxation agreements (also known as double tax treaties) with other countries. Provisions of such an agreement may override UK tax law. Specifically, the agreement may provide exemption for certain income received by a person who is resident overseas even though the income arises in the UK. For example, most double taxation agreements provide that a resident of the foreign country concerned may claim exemption from UK tax in connection with interest income arising in the UK.

Most double taxation agreements also make provision for the situation that an individual may be resident in both the foreign country concerned and the UK. The agreements usually contain a clause along the following lines:

(1) If the individual has a permanent home in only one country, he is deemed to be resident in that country.
(2) If the position has not been resolved by (1), then the individual is treated as resident where he has the centre of his personal and economic interests.
(3) If the above tests do not resolve the position, the individual is treated as resident in the country where he has an 'habitual abode'.
(4) If the individual has an habitual abode in both countries he is deemed to be a resident of the country of which he is a national.
(5) If he is a national of both countries, or if he is not a national of either country, the Revenue authorities of the UK and the foreign country may settle the matter by mutual agreement.

These provisions apply only for the purposes of determining residence under the agreement. They are deeming provisions and, under UK law, an individual might still be regarded as resident in the UK even though he may be treated as resident in the foreign country for the purposes of the double taxation agreement. However, the terms of a double taxation agreement override UK tax law and, if an individual is deemed to be resident in a foreign country under the agreement, his liability to UK tax will then be computed in accordance with other provisions of the double taxation agreement.

## 21.3 CEASING TO BE RESIDENT IN THE UK

### 21.3.1 Working abroad

Up to 1992–93 there was an important distinction between individuals who worked full-time abroad and other people who lived overseas in that the legislation specifically provided that, where an individual worked full-time abroad, the fact that he had accommodation available for his use was not regarded as a relevant factor in determining his residence status. As from 6 April 1993, this distinction became less important as the legislation now provides that an individual shall not be regarded as resident just because he has available accommodation in the UK. Nevertheless, it is still easier to establish non-resident status if you are working overseas.

A key Revenue publication (IR20) states that if a person goes abroad for full-time service under a contract of employment and:

(1) all the duties of his employment are performed abroad or any duties he performs here are incidental to his duties abroad; and
(2) his absence from the UK and the employment itself both extend over a period covering a complete tax year; and
(3) any interim visits to the UK during the period do not amount to:
    (a) six months or more in any one tax year; or
    (b) an average of three months or more per tax year

he is normally regarded as not resident and not ordinarily resident in the UK on the day following the date of his departure until the day preceding the date of his return. On his return, he is regarded as a new permanent resident.

The treatment whereby a person is treated as not resident for part of a tax year is called the 'split year' concession. The latest edition of IR20 indicates that this concession will also apply to self-employed people who leave the UK to work full time in a trade, profession or vocation providing they are able to meet the conditions similar to those set out above.

### 21.3.2 Involuntary residence
(Statement of Practice SP2/91)

The Revenue operates a concession which covers individuals who are forced to spend time in the UK because of exceptional circumstances outside their control, eg someone who was working abroad in a Gulf state, but who had to return to the UK prematurely at the outbreak of the Gulf War, may be allowed some leeway when the Revenue apply the three-month average test. Similarly, where an individual spends days in the UK because of illness, these may be left out of account in certain circumstances.

These concessions do not apply where an individual returns to the UK because his employer has prematurely terminated his contract of employment. Also, and more fundamentally, the Revenue's concession does not affect the rule that an individual is treated as resident in the UK if he spends 183 days or more in the UK during a particular tax year.

### 21.3.3 Other individuals who live abroad

Different rules apply where a person does not work full-time abroad (eg where an individual moves to a foreign country on retirement), or where he works overseas but continues to perform duties in the UK which are not incidental to the work carried out abroad. A person who falls into this category will continue to be treated as resident where he spends an average of three months per annum in the UK over a four-year period.

### 21.3.4 Temporary non-residence

An individual who leaves the UK on or after 17 March 1998 and who

(1) has been tax resident in the UK for any part of at least four out of the seven tax years immediately preceding the year of departure, and
(2) becomes not resident and not ordinarily resident for a period of less than five tax years, and
(3) owns assets before he leaves the UK

remains liable to tax on any gains realised on those assets after departure from the UK. Gains made by such an individual in the year of assessment in which he leaves the UK are chargeable for that year. Gains made after that year are chargeable in the year of assessment in which the taxpayer resumes residence in the UK. Losses are allowable on the same basis as gains are chargeable. Gains of non-resident trusts and companies may also be taxed if they would have been taxable had the individual been resident (see 20.13).

Any gains made in the intervening years (ie the years between the tax year of departure and the tax year of return) on assets acquired by the taxpayer after becoming tax resident abroad will be exempt from the charge. This exemption will not apply to assets held in a non-resident trust or closely controlled non-resident company. Special rules prevent gains on assets held before departure from escaping the charge, where gains are rolled over or otherwise deferred on the acquisition of assets during the period of absence.

Certain double taxation agreements may protect a temporary non-resident from the five-year rule. It is essential to take specialist advice if you decide to rely on this.

## 21.4 UK INCOME AND CAPITAL GAINS RECEIVED BY NON-RESIDENTS

A person who is not resident in the UK for a tax year may still be subject to tax on UK source income, but is not liable to tax for income which arises abroad. The following types of income are deemed to arise within the UK and are therefore subject to tax even where the individual is not resident there:

(1) employment income which relates to duties performed in the UK;
(2) trading profits from a branch or permanent establishment in the UK;
(3) rents from UK properties;
(4) dividends from UK companies;
(5) interest paid by a person who is resident in the UK;
(6) 'annual payments' made by a UK-resident person.

Since 1995–96, tax charged on investment income of a non-resident individual has normally been limited to the tax deducted at source. This does not apply to income from property in the UK or income from trading in the UK through a broker or investment manager.

The provisions of a double tax agreement, or extra statutory concession, may also limit the tax charged on a non-resident individual.

### 21.4.1 Earned income

Where an individual is non-resident, profits from a trade carried on outside the UK are not subject to UK tax. Where such a person has a branch or permanent establishment in this country, a liability to UK tax may arise from profits earned by that branch. Provisions of a double taxation agreement may govern what type of presence in the UK is deemed to constitute a branch or permanent establishment.

Earnings from an employment may attract UK tax where the duties are per-formed in the UK (see 21.4.5 on double taxation agreements).

Where an individual works full-time abroad under a contract of employment, the resulting income will not be subject to UK tax even though the employer may be a UK company. However, a Crown employee or a member of the Armed Forces is regarded as performing the duties of his employment in the UK and he may therefore be subject to UK tax even though he performs all his duties overseas and is not resident in the UK.

Problems have arisen in recent years where an individual was granted a non-approved share option at a time when he was resident in the UK and subject to tax under Schedule E Case I, with the option subsequently exercised after the individual has ceased to be resident in the UK. The Revenue's view is that a liability may arise in these circumstances even if the individual is no longer employed by the company concerned.

Pensions paid by UK-resident persons are subject to tax unless the recipient can claim the benefit of a double taxation agreement (see 21.4.5).

## 21.4.2 Concession for bank and building society interest

In practice, certain income which arises from a UK source is not subject to UK tax. In particular, bank deposit interest is not subject to deduction of UK tax at source provided the non-resident person certifies that he is not ordinarily resident in the UK (TA 1988, s 481(5)(k)). The Revenue will not assess such income unless the account is managed or controlled by a UK-resident agent. This also applies to interest or dividends paid gross by a building society, discount (eg discount on deep discount bonds), gains on deep gains securities, and interest on certificates of tax deposit.

## 21.4.3 Exempt gilts

Interest paid on all British Government securities is exempt from UK tax where the person who owns the security is not resident in the UK (unless the interest forms part of the profits of a trade carried on in the UK). Different rules applied up to 5 April 1998 so that only some gilts were classified as FOTRA (free of tax to residents abroad); see *Allied Dunbar Tax Handbook 1998–99* at 21.4.3.

## 21.4.4 Income from property

Rental income received by an individual from a UK property is subject to UK tax even if the individual is not resident in the UK. A tenant who pays rent direct to a non-resident landlord should withhold basic rate tax at source where the rent exceeds £100 per week unless the Revenue has authorised the tenant to pay the rent gross. Where rent is paid to a UK agent, the tenant should pay the rent without deduction, but the agent must then deduct tax from the net rental income.

The Revenue will authorise a tenant or agent to make no tax deductions if the landlord has registered for self-assessment and his tax affairs are up to date. See leaflet IR140, *Non-resident landlords, their agents and tenants*.

## 21.4.5 Double taxation agreements

Where an individual is not resident in the UK but is resident in a foreign country which has a double taxation agreement, it may be possible for certain income which would normally suffer UK tax at source to be exempt from UK tax, or subject only to a lower rate.

### Remuneration for work performed in the UK

Most double taxation agreements provide an exemption from UK tax for employment income, provided the following conditions are satisfied:

(1) the recipient of the remuneration is present in the UK for a period not exceeding 183 days in aggregate in the tax year concerned; and

(2) the remuneration is paid by, or on behalf of, an employer who is not resident in the UK; and

(3) the remuneration is not borne by a permanent establishment or a fixed base which the employer has in the UK.

### Pensions

Double taxation agreements generally provide for exemption from UK tax in respect of a pension paid by a UK company or pension scheme, although such a pension will normally be subject to tax in the foreign country concerned.

### Interest

In general, most double taxation agreements provide for a person resident in the foreign country concerned to be exempt from UK tax on interest. The company etc which pays the interest can be given authorisation to pay the interest gross. In cases where tax has been withheld at source the individual may be entitled to a repayment.

### Dividends

A double taxation agreement will usually include a provision that the person who receives a dividend from the UK company will be entitled to the benefit of a reduced tax credit and any balance should be repaid.

### Royalties

Most double taxation agreements provide that where a royalty is received by a person resident in the foreign country concerned, the royalties shall be free from UK tax.

## 21.4.6 Allowances and reliefs

A British subject is entitled to full personal allowances for a tax year, even if he is not a UK resident.

Nationals of EU countries also became entitled to a full personal allowance from 1996–97 (in many cases such nationals may have been entitled to allowances for earlier years because of the provisions of the relevant double taxation agreement). This change also applied to nationals of the following EEA countries: Iceland, Norway and Liechtenstein.

A person who is resident abroad because of his employment, and who expects to return within four years, may continue to have MIRAS relief on mortgage interest.

A non-resident person is not generally entitled to repayment supplement so it is normally important that tax should not be overpaid where this can be avoided. However, EU nationals may be entitled to supplement even though they are not UK resident.

### 21.4.7 Capital gains

A non-UK resident is not normally subject to CGT except where capital gains arise from the disposal of assets used by a branch or permanent establishment of a business carried on by the non-resident in the UK (but see 21.3.4 on the taxation of gains realised by former UK residents who are non-resident for less than five complete tax years).

## 21.5 NON-RESIDENT INVESTMENT COMPANIES

A non-UK resident who has significant investment income arising within the UK may take certain steps to minimise his UK tax liability. In particular, where he cannot claim the benefit of a double taxation agreement, it may be advisable for UK assets such as real estate to be held through a non-UK resident company. This will mean that any tax liability will be confined to basic rate tax and there will be no question of any higher rate liability.

In such a case, it would still be sensible for some portfolio investments to be retained in the individual's own name if he is a British subject or is otherwise entitled to claim a personal allowance. Sufficient personal income should arise to use such an allowance as this will be wasted if all income arises within an offshore company.

In some cases, a non-resident landlord should form an offshore company to acquire UK properties already owned and let by him. The offshore company may raise a qualifying loan to purchase the properties from the individual concerned and interest payable on the loan may then be offset against the non-resident company's rental income. This is a way in which an individual who already owns a property which is not subject to a mortgage may create a situation where interest is payable on a qualifying loan which is deductible in computing Schedule A income.

## 21.6 WHEN TAX SHOULD BE WITHHELD FROM PAYMENTS TO NON-RESIDENTS

### 21.6.1 Payments to non-resident sportsmen and entertainers

A person paying a non-UK resident sportsman or entertainer for work carried out in the UK may be liable to withhold tax at basic rate and pay this over to the Revenue – see 19.5.

## 21.6.2 **Rent payable to a non-resident landlord**

A person who pays rent to a non-resident landlord is required to withhold tax at the basic rate and to account for this to the Revenue unless he has been authorised to pay gross (see 21.4.4). This obligation arises whether the payment is made within the UK or by payment out of a bank account held overseas.

Where a UK-resident person pays a premium to a non-resident landlord, the same requirement to withhold tax arises.

Where a tenant has failed to withhold tax, he may be required to account for it to the Revenue. In such circumstances, the tenant may withhold sums from subsequent payments of rent to cover the amounts paid over to the Revenue.

The obligation to withhold tax does not arise where the tenant pays rent to an agent in the UK. Also the Revenue would not normally pursue a tenant who had failed to deduct tax where the tenant could not have known that the landlord was non-resident and nothing had happened to put him on notice.

For further details, see 19.4.

# 22

# THE INCOME AND CAPITAL GAINS OF FOREIGN DOMICILIARIES

MIKE WILKES

This chapter deals with the tax treatment of individuals who are resident but not domiciled in the UK. The following subjects are discussed:

(1) Meaning of domicile.

## Earned income

(2) Foreign emoluments.
(3) Travelling expenses.
(4) 'Corresponding payments'.
(5) Overseas pension funds.
(6) Self employment.
(7) Partnerships controlled outside the UK.
(8) Pension benefits.

## Investment income

(9) The remittance basis for investment income.
(10) What constitutes a remittance?
(11) Position if foreign domiciliary acquires a UK domicile.
(12) Managing the remittance basis.

## Capital gains tax

(13) Remittance basis for capital gains on foreign assets.
(14) Use of offshore companies and trusts.

## Inheritance tax

(15) UK and foreign situs property.

# 22.1 MEANING OF DOMICILE

Domicile is a fundamentally different concept from residence and ordinary residence. It is not the same as nationality, although an individual's nationality may be one factor which is relevant in determining his domicile. The basic concept is that a person is domiciled in the country which he regards as his real home. The fact that an individual may be prevented from living in that country or may need to live elsewhere because of temporary reasons (such as business and/or employment) does not mean that the individual is domiciled in the country in which he resides. Under English law, an individual normally acquires his father's domicile at birth and he retains this domicile unless his father changes his own domicile before the individual attains age 16. The mother's domicile may apply instead where a child is illegitimate or the parents divorce. The domicile acquired in this way is called the individual's 'domicile of origin'.

An individual may change his domicile to a 'domicile of choice'. Normally this would happen by his leaving his country of origin and taking up permanent residence abroad with the intention of never returning to live in the country of origin on a permanent basis. An individual's domicile of origin will revive if his intentions alter and he decides not to make his permanent home in the new country after all.

## Married women

Where a woman married before 1 January 1974, she generally acquired her husband's domicile (this was referred to as a 'domicile of dependency'). This domicile continued after divorce or the death of the husband, although the woman could discard her domicile of dependency in which case she would regain her domicile of origin. A domicile of dependency in the UK may be discarded by the woman establishing that she no longer intends to remain permanently in that country and by her ceasing to be resident there. The mere intention is not itself sufficient. For example, an Australian woman who had acquired a domicile of dependency in England was held to be domiciled in the UK, despite her intention to return to Australia, because she had not ceased to be resident.

Where a couple have married after 31 December 1973, the law is somewhat different. The Domicile and Matrimonial Proceedings Act 1973 allows a woman to retain an independent domicile on her marriage.

## No changes likely for the time being

Following the publication of a report on the law of domicile by the Law Commission, the UK Government announced that it intended to introduce new legislation on the law of domicile 'when a suitable opportunity arises'. The draft Domicile Bill contained the following provisions:

(1) A child will be domiciled in the country with which he is, for the time being, most closely connected.
(2) On becoming an adult, a person retains the domicile he had immediately before becoming an adult.
(3) An adult will acquire a domicile in another country if he is both present there and intends to settle there for an indefinite period.
(4) The burden of proof to demonstrate a change of domicile will not be so great as it is under the present rules.

However, on 26 May 1993, a reply given by the Prime Minister to a written parliamentary question stated that the Government 'has no immediate plans to introduce legislation on this subject'. The Lord Chancellor's office indicated at the time that the reference to 'immediate' meant that legislation would not be introduced during the current parliamentary session, but no formal statement has ever been issued. So far as one can tell, the proposed changes have been quietly dropped.

### Registration as an overseas elector

FA 1996, s 200 states that where an individual registers as an overseas elector to vote in UK elections this is not to be taken into account in determining his domicile status for tax purposes.

## 22.2 FOREIGN EMOLUMENTS

### 22.2.1 Introduction

A foreign-domiciled individual who is employed by a UK-resident employer is basically treated no differently from a UK-domiciled individual in a similar position. The earnings from such an employment are taxed under Schedule E Case I or II according to whether the individual is ordinarily resident in the UK as well as resident there (for the taxation of such earnings, see Chapter 3).

However, where a person domiciled outside the UK is employed by a non-UK resident employer, the tax treatment is fundamentally different. Earnings from such an employment are called 'foreign emoluments'. Their tax treatment is as set out Table 22.1 opposite.

### 22.2.2 Employer's resident status need not be same as individual's domicile

It is not necessary that the employer should be resident in the same country as that in which the individual is domiciled (although this will often be the situation). An individual who is domiciled in (eg) Switzerland and who is employed by a company which is resident in the USA has foreign emoluments.

**Table 22.1 – Tax treatment under Schedule E of earnings by foreign domiciled individual from non-UK resident employer ('foreign emoluments')**

| | Duties of employment performed wholly or partly in the UK | | Duties of employment performed wholly outside the UK |
|---|---|---|---|
| | *In the UK* | *Outside the UK* | *outside the UK* |
| Employee resident and ordinarily resident in the UK | Liable to UK tax (Case I) | Liable to UK tax (Case I) | Liable if remitted to the UK (Case III) |
| Resident but not ordinarily resident | Liable to UK tax (Case II) | Liable if remitted to the UK (Case III) | Liable if remitted to the UK (Case III) |
| Not resident | Liable to UK tax (Case II) | Not liable | Not liable |

## 22.2.3 Earnings from Republic of Ireland-resident employer
(TA 1988, s 192)

There is one exception to the general rule that foreign emoluments arise from an employment by a person not domiciled in the UK from an office or employment with a non-UK resident employer. Where the employer is resident in the Republic of Ireland, the earnings are not regarded as foreign emoluments.

## 22.2.4 Earnings of person not ordinarily resident in UK

Where an individual has foreign emoluments and he is resident in the UK, but not ordinarily resident (see 21.2.1 for meaning of ordinary residence), it is necessary to divide the emoluments between those which relate to duties performed in the UK and those which are performed overseas. The remuneration which is referable to the UK duties is taxed on an arising basis under Schedule E Case II but the remuneration for the duties performed overseas is taxed on the remittance basis under Schedule E Case III.

## 22.2.5 Split contract needed for person resident and ordinarily resident in UK

A different rule applies where an individual is both resident and ordinarily resident in the UK. The earnings from an employment with a foreign employer are all subject to tax in the UK on an arising basis where all or any part of the duties are performed there. There are no provisions whereby remuneration can be split between earnings relating to work done in the UK and work performed overseas. However, if an individual has a contract of employment where all the duties are performed outside the UK, the earnings are taxed on the remittance basis under Schedule E Case III.

In practice, it is possible to take full advantage of this treatment by an individual having two separate contracts of employment, one covering duties performed in the UK and the other covering duties performed overseas.

Where a foreign national is given a right to tax equalisation in his service contracts, the amount charged on the UK employment may be carefully scrutinised by the Revenue. This is an area where you should take advice from a specialist.

## 22.3 TRAVELLING EXPENSES
(TA 1988, s 195)

There are special provisions which apply for individuals of foreign domicile. Certain travel expenses which are paid or reimbursed by an employer are not assessable income where all the following conditions are satisfied:

(1) The expenses must be paid during the five-year period which begins from the date of arrival in the UK.
(2) The expenses must relate to a journey between the individual's usual place of abode and the place in the UK where he works.
(3) The expenses must relate to journeys made by the employee, unless he is in the UK for a continuous period of 60 days or more for the purposes of performing duties. In this event, the expenses of a visit by his spouse or minor child will also be allowable, although there is a limit of two visits by any such person in a tax year.

In order to secure this exemption it is also necessary that the individual must not have been resident in the UK in either of the two tax years which precede the year in which he took up his UK employment.

## 22.4 'CORRESPONDING PAYMENTS'
TA 1988, s 192(3))

Certain payments made by an individual out of foreign emoluments qualify for tax relief where they are made 'in circumstances corresponding to those in which the payments would have reduced his liability to income tax' had they been paid in the UK. Payments which can be relieved under this heading include contributions to an overseas pension fund (see 22.5 below) and mortgage interest. Alimony and maintenance paid in 1999–2000 and earlier years under pre-15 March 1988 foreign court orders may also be deducted from foreign emoluments (see 8.2).

## 22.5 OVERSEAS PENSION FUNDS

An overseas pension fund will not normally be an approved retirement benefit scheme for the purposes of UK tax. However, where the benefits provided by an overseas pension fund are broadly similar to those which arise from UK-approved retirement benefit schemes, the Revenue may regard the employer's contributions as not constituting remuneration for the purposes of Schedule E and any contributions made by the employee may be deducted as corresponding payments (see 22.4). In some situations, the Revenue will accord this treatment only where the individual's rights under his overseas pension scheme are adapted or restricted. For example, a US national who has an individual retirement plan may be required to give notice to the US administrators so as to waive his ability to take a lump sum in circumstances where this would not be permitted under the rules which govern UK-approved retirement benefit schemes.

## 22.6 SELF-EMPLOYMENT

Where an individual is resident in the UK, any earnings from a business carried on as a sole trader are taxed under Schedule D Case I on the arising basis. This even applies in a situation where all the work is actually performed overseas. The basis for this interpretation by the courts is that a business is deemed to be carried on from where it is controlled and, in the case of a sole trader, control is located where the proprietor is resident.

A foreign domiciled individual who carries on self-employment and who performs a substantial amount of work overseas should consider forming a company. In particular, if an overseas company were to be formed and the company employed the individual and supplied his services outside the UK to customers, the earnings from that employment would constitute foreign emoluments. Provided that no work is performed in the UK under the contract of employment, interposing an offshore company in this way would mean that the individual could take full advantage of the remittance basis for earnings which are taxable under Schedule E Case III.

## 22.7 PARTNERSHIPS CONTROLLED OUTSIDE THE UK

Where a UK-resident individual is a partner in a firm which is controlled outside the UK, his earnings from that firm will be taxed as follows:

(1) *Profits from a UK branch*: under Schedule D Case I on the arising basis.
(2) *Overseas profits*: under Schedule D Case V under the remittance basis.

## 22.8 PENSION BENEFITS

### 22.8.1 Lump sums paid under overseas pension schemes
(Extra-statutory concession A10)

Income tax is not charged on lump sum benefits received by an employee (or by his personal representatives or any dependant) from an overseas retirement benefit scheme or an overseas provident fund where the employee's overseas service comprises:

(1) not less than 75% of his total service in the employment concerned; or
(2) the whole of the last ten years of his service in that employment (subject to the total service exceeding ten years); or
(3) not less than 50% of his total service in that employment, including any ten of the last 20 years, provided the total service exceeds 20 years.

If the employee's overseas service does not meet these requirements, relief from income tax is given by reducing the amount of the lump sum which would otherwise be chargeable by the same proportion as the overseas service bears to the employee's total service in that employment.

### 22.8.2 Pensions

An individual who receives a pension paid by a person who is not resident in the UK is subject to tax under Schedule D Case V on the remittance basis. However, there is no such reduction as exists for UK-domiciled individuals who are taxed on only 90% of such pensions. If the whole of the pension is remitted, tax arises under Schedule D Case V on the full amount.

## 22.9 THE REMITTANCE BASIS FOR INVESTMENT INCOME

### 22.9.1 Remittance basis

Chapter 6 covers the overseas investment income of an individual who is ordinarily resident and domiciled in the UK; such individuals are taxed under Schedule D Cases IV and V in respect of income as it arises. A completely different rule applies for individuals who are not ordinarily resident or not domiciled in the UK; their assessable income is fixed by reference to the amount of income remitted to the UK.

### 22.9.2 Exception for income arising within the Republic of Ireland
(TA 1988, s 68)

Where a foreign-domiciled individual has income which arises within the Republic of Ireland, the income is taxed as it arises and not on the remittance basis. The income is taxed on the current year basis.

## 22.9.3 Change from PY to CY basis

See *Allied Dunbar Tax Handbook 1999–2000* at 22.9.3–22.9.5.

## 22.9.4 No assessment can be made if individual ceases to have source of income

A Schedule D Case IV or V assessment can only be made for a tax year if the individual had the source of income during that year. Care needs to be taken as to what constitutes a source of income. Some advisors do not consider it prudent to rely upon this principle by closing a bank account and opening a new deposit account with the same bank, although the Revenue appears to accept that this represents the cessation of one source and the creation of another. It is however arguable that the source of income is represented by the debt due by that particular bank and so the individual continues to have the source of income in question.

## 22.9.5 Income from savings

Investment income assessed on the remittance basis cannot qualify for the 20% rate which applies to income from savings (see 5.1.6).

## 22.9.6 Relief for foreign tax
(TA 1988, s 793)

Where overseas income has borne foreign tax, credit may be claimed for this against the UK tax assessed on the same income.

# 22.10 WHAT CONSTITUTES A REMITTANCE?

## 22.10.1 General principles

A remittance arises where an individual brings money into the UK, either in cash or by transferring money to a UK bank account. However, no remittance occurs if money is spent abroad or if liabilities which fall due for payment overseas are settled directly from a foreign bank account.

## 22.10.2 Constructive remittances
(TA 1988, s 65)

The legislation deals with constructive remittances and states that a remittance is deemed to have occurred if an individual applies overseas income towards the satisfaction of:

(1) a debt (or interest thereon) for money lent to the individual in the UK;
(2) a debt for money lent to him abroad and brought to the UK;
(3) a loan incurred in order to satisfy such debts.

Case law also indicates that a constructive remittance is deemed to have occurred if an individual borrows from a UK bank but has his borrowings formally secured against money held in an overseas bank account.

The courts have held that a complex arrangement whereby money was transmitted between two South African companies, with the individual receiving a loan from one of them, constituted a constructive remittance of income. Since the courts are increasingly having regard for the overall consequences of a series of transactions, it would be unwise to rely upon an artificial scheme which enabled an individual to enjoy sums in the UK which could be matched with overseas income.

### 22.10.3 Unauthorised remittances

In one case, a bank remitted untaxed overseas income by mistake. Because the bank acted contrary to its customer's instructions, it was held that there was no liability under the remittance basis.

### 22.10.4 Gifts of unremitted income

The safest course of action is for a gift to take the form of a cheque to be drawn on a foreign bank account, with the recipient paying the sum into a foreign bank account. If matters are handled in this particular way, there can be no question of the gift constituting a remittance.

Where an individual makes a gift of foreign income, he is not affected by what happens subsequently. The money loses its income quality once it has been given away and the recipient can bring the money into the UK without any liability under the remittance basis. In principle, this rule ought also to apply to gifts between spouses, although one should expect the Revenue to carefully scrutinise such arrangements so as to ensure that there are no hidden arrangements which govern the way in which the recipient must use the money given.

## 22.11 POSITION IF FOREIGN DOMICILIARY ACQUIRES UK DOMICILE

Where an individual is assessable under the remittance basis, but then acquires a UK domicile of choice, the remittance basis ceases to apply and the individual's overseas income is taxable under the arising basis. No tax liability arises if he then remits money which would formerly have given rise to an income tax liability under the remittance basis. The Special Commissioners have held that this rule does not apply for CGT purposes and gains which are remitted after the time that the individual acquired a UK domicile continue to attract a tax liability.

## 22.12 MANAGING THE REMITTANCE BASIS

### 22.12.1 Maintaining separate bank accounts

Where a foreign-domiciled individual has substantial overseas income, it is normal for arrangements to be put in place so that remittances to the UK may be identified, as far as possible, with capital. The way that this is normally dealt with is by arranging for the individual to have three separate bank accounts, as follows:

(1) The first account is capital, ie the cash actually held by the individual at the time that he took up residence in the UK. It is normal for further sums to be paid into this bank account where the cash relates to the sale proceeds of assets sold at a loss for CGT purposes or the proceeds arise from the sale of exempt assets. The bank should be instructed that any interest on this bank account should not be credited to the account, but paid to a separate income account (see below).

(2) The second account should contain the proceeds of sales of assets which give rise to capital gains.

(3) The third account should be kept for income, including interest on the capital account and the capital gains account.

Clearly, in practice, an individual may minimise his liability under the remittance basis by taking remittances from the capital account in (1).

In some situations, it may be sensible to go one stage further and to keep two income accounts with one account containing income which has not borne tax at source (eg overseas bank deposit interest) and the other account containing income which has borne foreign tax. By organising matters in this way, remittances of income can come out of the account which contains income which has suffered foreign tax, and this will further minimise any UK tax liability.

There may be CGT savings from having different types of capital gains account (see 22.13.4).

### 22.12.2 Use overseas income accounts to fund expenditure outside UK

A foreign-domiciled individual should also organise matters so that all possible expenditure outside the UK is funded out of the income account and, where relevant, out of the income account which represents income which has not borne any foreign tax at source.

### 22.12.3 Closing bank account so source ceases to exist

Where an individual has a separate source of income (eg a bank deposit account) it may be possible to take full advantage of the rule that no assessment may be made for a tax year after the individual ceases to have the source of income concerned. This could be achieved by the individual's closing the bank deposit account, and transferring the cash to a new account (see 22.9.4). Remittances from that new account may then be made in the following tax year and no liability should arise under the remittance basis since such remittances will represent capital (even though the capital was built up out of income which arose whilst the individual possessed the particular source of overseas income concerned).

## 22.12.4 Trustees using unremitted income to buy investments from settlor

A further possibility whereby a foreign-domiciled individual may minimise the income he requires in the UK is for him to transfer unremitted income to foreign trustees who then use that income to make capital investments by buying property from the settlor.

### Example – Trustee's use of unremitted income

> *A* has accumulated overseas income of £45,000 which will become taxable if it is remitted to the UK. If *A* transfers the £45,000 to an offshore trust and then sells his main residence to the trustees, he should not be chargeable to tax under Schedule D Case IV or V as if he had remitted the income, even though the £45,000 is brought into the UK after the sale of the property. If *A* remains in occupation as a beneficiary of the trust, this will not of itself constitute a remittance or a deemed remittance.

## 22.13 REMITTANCE BASIS FOR CAPITAL GAINS ON FOREIGN ASSETS

### 22.13.1 Introduction
(TCGA 1992, ss 12 and 275)

A person of foreign domicile may be subject to CGT if he is either resident or ordinarily resident in the UK. Gains on UK assets are charged in the same way as gains realised by UK-domiciled individuals. However, gains realised on assets which are situated overseas are subject to UK CGT only if the proceeds are remitted to the UK.

The following rules determine whether an asset is deemed to be situated in the UK or abroad:

(1) Real estate and rights over such property are situated in the country where the real estate is located.
(2) Tangible movable property and rights over such property are situated in the country where the property is located.

(3) Debts are normally situated in the country where the creditor is resident.
(4) Stocks, shares and securities are generally situated in the country where the company maintains its principal register.
(5) Goodwill is treated as situated where the trade or business is carried on.
(6) Patents, trade-marks and designs are situated in the country where they are registered.

## 22.13.2 Definition of remittance

Capital gains are remitted if they are brought into the UK or enjoyed there. For example, payment of the disposal proceeds into a UK bank account counts as a remittance, as does a payment into a UK bank account from an overseas bank account containing such proceeds. Less obviously, the gains will be enjoyed in the UK if an individual has a large deposit account outside the UK and he formally secures a UK bank loan against this deposit account. However, if the money is spent outside the UK, it is not deemed to have been remitted. Payment of disposal proceeds into a bank account in the Channel Islands or Isle of Man does not constitute a remittance to the UK. An outright gift which takes place outside the UK will not normally be a remittance provided a cheque etc is paid into an overseas bank account for the recipient.

## 22.13.3 Losses not allowable
(TCGA 1992, s 16(4))

Where a loss arises on an overseas asset, a person of foreign domicile cannot claim a capital loss. In some situations this could give rise to hardship.

### Example – Losses not allowable

> *A* has gains of £90,000 on UK assets and capital losses of £60,000 on foreign assets. Unfortunately, there is no relief for the £60,000 losses so he would be taxed on gains of £90,000.

## 22.13.4 How to take full advantage of remittance basis

In some cases it may be that there is no likelihood of the individual needing to bring the proceeds of a sale of foreign assets into the UK. In such a situation the payment of CGT is something that the individual may or may not choose to do since he can control the amount of his chargeable gains. Where it is going to be necessary to bring money into the UK at some stage in the future, it is advisable for the individual to keep separate bank accounts.

One account should receive the proceeds of assets which have been sold at a loss when measured for UK CGT purposes. This account may be used to fund remittances to the UK which are not going to give rise to a CGT liability. A second account should contain the proceeds of sales of assets which are subject to foreign CGT. Remittances out of this account will give rise to a CGT assessment, but double tax relief will be due in respect of the foreign CGT which has been paid. Other sales of assets which have produced a gain should be kept in a third account, and should be remitted only as a last resort.

### 22.13.5 Position where foreign domiciliary acquires UK domicile

The law is not clear here. A Special Commissioners' decision indicates that a liability may arise for a UK-domiciled individual if he remits sums which would have been subject to CGT if they had been remitted before he acquired a UK domicile of choice. Caution is advisable.

## 22.14 USE OF OFFSHORE COMPANIES AND TRUSTS

The formidable range of anti-avoidance provisions covered in Chapter 20 do not have the same impact where a foreign domiciled individual is concerned.

### 22.14.1 Offshore companies

The anti-avoidance legislation contained in TCGA 1992, s 13 (see 20.13) does not apply to foreign-domiciled individuals and there are no other ways in which a person may be charged to tax on capital gains realised by an off-shore company, even though the UK-resident individual may own all of its share capital. Consequently, gains on UK assets may be taken outside the ambit of CGT if a foreign-domiciled individual makes his investments indirectly by setting up an offshore company which then makes the relevant investments. However, care needs to be taken to ensure that a company which is incorporated overseas is non-UK resident because central management and control are exercised there (see SP1/90).

It is also dangerous for the individual to occupy a property owned by an offshore company as the Revenue may seek to assess him under Schedule E as a 'shadow director'. The Revenue at one stage indicated that it might also raise assessments under transfer-pricing legislation introduced in FA 1998, but has now relented.

### 22.14.2 Offshore trusts

Offshore or non-resident trusts can be extremely tax-efficient where foreign-domiciled individuals are concerned. A settlement established by a foreign-domiciled individual after 18 March 1991 cannot be a 'qualifying settlement' which means that there are no provisions for charging a settlor to tax on gains realised by the trustees of his non-resident settlement.

The provisions of TCGA 1992, s 86 which charge beneficiaries when they receive capital payments had no application until 17 March 1998 where the settlor was not UK-domiciled and was not domiciled there at the time that gains were realised. Even if these exemptions do not apply, s 86 still does not come into force if a beneficiary who receives a capital payment is not domiciled there. There are no other provisions which may allow the Revenue to tax a beneficiary on gains realised by offshore trustees and so the creation of an offshore trust may enable a foreign-domiciled individual to escape from any CGT charge, whether on foreign or UK assets.

Professional advice should be taken to avoid potential pitfalls arising from income tax and other legislation.

## 22.15 UK AND FOREIGN SITUS PROPERTY

IHT may be charged on the death of an individual who is not deemed to be domiciled in the UK but only to the extent that his estate consists of property situated there. No charge arises on foreign situs property as this is classified as 'excluded property'. Table 22.2 below indicates which types of property are regarded as situated in the UK.

There is a special rule for IHT whereby an individual may be deemed to be domiciled in the UK if he has been resident for 17 of the 20 tax years ending with the current year.

### Table 22.2 – Assets chargeable to IHT

|  | Not chargeable | Chargeable |
|---|---|---|
| Channel Island property | ✔ | |
| Isle of Man property | ✔ | |
| Other foreign property | ✔ | |
| UK property | | ✔ |
| Bank deposits outside the UK | ✔ | |
| UK sterling bank deposits | | ✔ |
| UK foreign currency deposits | chargeable only if the owner is resident in the UK | |
| Shares in UK companies | | ✔ |
| Registered shares in foreign companies | ✔ | |
| Bearer securities | depends where the bearer certificates are held | |
| Debts owed by a UK resident person | | ✔ (normally) |
| Debts owed by foreign resident person | ✔ | |

# 23

# NATIONAL INSURANCE CONTRIBUTIONS AND SOCIAL SECURITY BENEFITS

SUDEEP GANGULI

This chapter covers the following topics:

(1) Class 1 contributions.
(2) Class 2 contributions.
(3) Class 3 contributions.
(4) Class 4 contributions.
(5) Social security benefits.
(6) Tax credits.

Where rates are quoted, they are the 2000–01 figures.

## 23.1 CLASS 1 CONTRIBUTIONS

### 23.1.1 Introduction

Individuals who are employed are liable for Class 1 NICs. No contribution is payable unless the employee earns more than £76 a week although entitlement to benefits will start for earnings in excess of £67. If he earns more than £76, contributions are calculated at 10% on the excess amount over £76 on earnings between £76 and £535 a week (eg on weekly earnings of £84, employee NICs due are £84 – £76 = £8, × 10% = 80p). No employee contribution is payable on earnings in excess of £535 (the 'upper limit'). Lower contributions of 8.4% apply if the individual is contracted out of SERPS.

Women who married on or before 6 April 1977 and who have chosen to pay a reduced rate are subject to pay NICs of only 3.85%. This right is lost if the woman is divorced, but is not lost if she is widowed.

Contributions are normally assessed by reference to weekly earnings, but if the employee is paid less frequently, contributions are calculated on the corresponding figures for a monthly basis or whatever other period is covered by the payment to the individual.

An individual's liability to NICs is not affected by a previous period of unemployment during the year. Each 'earnings period' is looked at in isolation and there is no principle which corresponds to the cumulative method used for income tax where a tax year is looked at as a whole. There is a slight exception to this for company directors (see 23.1.3) but this is basically an anti-avoidance provision.

On 1 April 1999 the Contributions Agency transferred from the Department of Social Security to the Inland Revenue to become the Inland Revenue National Insurance Contributions Office (NICO). NICs, statutory sick pay (SSP) and statutory maternity pay (SMP) are now handled by the Revenue including responsibility for NICs policy and appeals.

During the 1999–2000 tax year, new arrangements were introduced so that most NICs, SSP and SMP appeals can be heard by an independent tribunal in the same way as tax appeals. Previously, the Secretary of State was asked formally to determine one of a range of 'questions' via the Office for the Determination of Contribution Questions (ODCQ) based in Newcastle. However, appeals on contracting-out pensions issues and working families tax credit will not be heard by tax tribunals.

## 23.1.2 Deferment

Where an individual has more than one job, and the total earnings are likely to exceed the upper limit, he may apply for deferment so that NICO may authorise certain employers not to withhold contributions from his remuneration (form CA 2700). The deferment application is made on Form CF379. Ideally this form should be submitted before the start of a tax year for which deferment is sought. In any event, deferment will not be granted for 2000–01 unless NICO receives the application by 14 February 2001. NICO is also reluctant to grant deferment for a year in which the individual will reach pensionable age. Where a deferment application is made, the individual cannot choose which earnings should be subject to deduction for NICs. In addition, NICO will always defer contributions at the non-contracted out rate if any of the employments are not contracted out.

After the end of a tax year, the position is reviewed. It may be that the individual has not had the anticipated level of earnings from a particular employment and this may mean that the liability for the year has not been satisfied. In such a case, NICO will apply for payment of the balance and this falls due for payment within 28 days of NICO making such a demand.

There is an entitlement to a repayment of contributions withheld from the remuneration, where they exceed the maximum for the year, even if the individual has not applied for deferment.

## 23.1.3 Company directors

Remuneration paid to a company director is normally assessed for NICs as if it arose on a yearly basis. Therefore, a large lump sum payment of fees or a bonus could attract the maximum contributions for a year, rather than the maximum contributions for one week or one month.

## Example – Assessment on lump sum payments

A weekly paid company director receives remuneration of £28,000 paid in a single sum. The liability for contributions is the liability for the year, ie

$52 \times 459 \ (£535 - 76) \times 10\%$ ie                                    £2,386.80

It is not just the maximum for one week's earnings, ie 10% of £459.

Since 6 April 1999, a new administrative arrangement for the assessment and payment of NICs for directors came into effect (Social Security Act 1998). Regulation 6A of the Social Security (Contributions) Regulations 1979 still ensures that the earnings period is annual, but it is possible to make payments on account. When the last payment is made to the director in the tax year, the employer is required to reassess the NICs due on the total earnings for the tax year on an annual, or pro rata annual, earnings period, as appropriate.

To qualify for these new arrangements the following three conditions must be satisfied:

(1) the director agrees to NICs being assessed this way;
(2) the director normally receives his earnings in a regular pattern; and
(3) those payments normally exceed the lower earnings limit for the pay period.

## Example – Alternative administrative arrangement for directors' NICs

A director receives a monthly salary of £2,000 and in June 2000 receives a bonus of £10,000 in addition to his £1,000 salary.

| | | £ |
|---|---|---|
| Months 1, 2 and 4–11 | £1,000 – £291 (monthly LEL) × 10% = | 70.90 |
| Month 3 | £11,000 exceeds UEL for month of £2,319, therefore maximum NICs for month applies = | 199.00 |
| Total paid | (to date) = £70.90 × 10 months + £199.00 in month 3 = | 908.00 |
| Month 12 | Based on annual earnings period, NICs due on £22,000 (12 × £1,000 + £10,000) = £22,000 ÷ 12 = £1,833.33 – £291 (monthly LEL) × 10% = £154.23 × 12 months = | 1,850.76 |
| Total due | (in month 12) = £1,850.76 – £908.00 = | 942.76 |

From 6 April 1999, directors (and officers) may be held liable for the employer's contributions where it has failed to pay NICs on time and the failure appears to be attributable to fraud or neglect by the culpable officers.

## 23.1.4 Definition of earnings

'Earnings' for NICs purposes include all cash remuneration. Contributions are also payable on sick pay, holiday pay etc. The NICs definition of 'earnings' is quite different from that used for income tax purposes. For example, NICs are assessed on an individual's pay before pension contributions and before any charitable donations made under a payroll deduction scheme. Profit-related pay was another type of earnings which was exempt for income tax purposes, but gave rise to a liability for NICs.

Where an employer settles an employee's pecuniary liability, the sum paid is treated as earnings for NICs purposes even though it is not pay for PAYE purposes. Previously only certain types of benefits in kind which could easily be converted into cash were liable to NICs. For example, premium bonds and national savings certificates are regarded as earnings for NICs purposes because they may be encashed by the holder surrendering them. However, in the March 1999 Budget the Chancellor announced that NICs would be extended to all taxable benefits in kind with effect from 6 April 2000 (see 23.1.8).

Since 6 April 1999, non-cash vouchers have been treated as earnings with the following exceptions (see 3.4.7 and 3.4.8):

- Transport vouchers where the employee earns less than £8,500
- Transport vouchers for the disabled
- Transport vouchers for the armed forces
- Vouchers exchangeable for the use of sports or recreational facilities
- Vouchers associated with long service awards
- Vouchers in respect of staff functions (less than £75 per person)
- Vouchers exchangeable for meals provided on employer's premises or a staff canteen
- The first 15p per working day of luncheon vouchers (maximum £1.05 per week)
- Incentive awards up to £150 per year per donor
- Childcare vouchers for children up to the age of 16.

For some years, financial instruments such as gilts, unit trusts, quoted shares, equities, certain life assurance policies etc, have been treated as earnings for NICs purposes, as have derivative instruments such as warrants and options. In order to close the legislative loophole allowing NICs to be avoided, a succession of new regulations were introduced making the avoidance of NICs increasingly difficult and financially risky. Gold bullion and other tradeable commodities and vouchers exchangeable for gold or commodities were brought into charge for NICs purposes from 30 November

1993 and gemstones and certain alcoholic liquors were similarly blocked from 23 August 1994.

A more decisive regulation brought all 'tradeable assets' into charge for NICs purposes with effect from 6 April 1995. The term 'tradeable assets' covers a broad but undefined range of goods or services for which a market value or 'trading arrangements' may exist. From 6 April 1998, the term is 'readily convertible asset'.

In the March 1998 Budget, the Chancellor announced the introduction of new provisions to ensure that artificial schemes created to avoid NICs would be tackled and regulations introduced to mirror the tax changes on anti-avoidance of PAYE.

NICO will seek NICs on an employer's contribution to a FURBS established for a specific individual. Therefore, in general, if a Schedule E charge arises, there will be an NICs charge on the employer's contributions to the scheme.

Since 6 April 1999, all share options granted on or after that date were liable to NICs on the same amounts chargeable to tax (TA 1988, s 135). There are no NICs liability on the grant of the option, except where the option can be exercised more than ten years after the date of the grant.

NICs ought not to arise where a director receives a dividend, or interest on a loan made to the company, or rent for a property used by the company. Investment income of this nature is clearly not earnings but there may be borderline cases where a so-called dividend is really remuneration which has been given a misleading label. NICO may have a point if the dividend payment does not conform with company law requirements.

### 23.1.5 Problem areas

One major problem area concerns directors' drawings. NICO takes the view that where a director arranges for a personal liability to be settled by the employer and charged to his drawings account, the payment constitutes earnings for NICs purposes unless the drawings account is in credit.

#### Example – Directors' drawings

*A* has a drawings account with his company which is £60 in credit. The company pays a personal bill for *A* of £100 and debits his drawings account with £100, thus turning the credit balance into an overdrawn balance of £40.

NICO takes the view that £60 of the payment of the £100 bill is a repayment of a loan and attracts no NICs, but the balance of £40 is a payment of earnings and the grossed up amount is subject to NICs.

### 23.1.6 Loans from the employer

Curiously, NICO takes the view that if an individual arranges for a loan from his employer and the loan is used to settle a personal liability, there is no liability for NICs unless (and until) the loan is written off by the employer. Considerable care should be taken when dealing with any documentation and the structure of such arrangements to minimise liability for NICs.

## 23.1.7 Employer's NICs

In addition to the 'primary' contributions paid by the employee, employers are also required to pay 'secondary contributions'. There is no ceiling on the amount of an employee's earnings which attract secondary contributions. No liability for secondary contributions can arise unless there is a liability for primary contributions, except when an employee with other employment has a deferment form CA 2700 or is a pensioner (Table C or S). An employee can agree to pay his employer's NIC on profits from the exercise of non-approved share options after 19 May 2000. The NIC borne by the employee is then deducted in arriving at his Schedule E income (see 3.14.2).

Employers are also liable for Class 1A contributions where the employee has benefits in kind (see 23.1.8). For company cars, the cash equivalent used for income tax purposes is treated as if it were additional earnings subject to secondary contributions. A further charge may arise if the employee is provided with fuel for private mileage, with the Class 1A charge again being based on the scale benefit used for income tax purposes.

Since 6 April 1998, Class 1A NICs on cars are due on unremunerated employees and directors (Social Security Act 1998, s 52). This section states that the person liable to pay Class 1A NICs in these circumstances is the person who would normally have been liable to pay secondary Class 1 NICs had the benefit of the car been earnings.

Unfortunately for employers, although the statutory instrument (SI 1998, No 2209) made this new provision operative only from 8 September 1998 to 5 April 1999, since Class 1A is an annual liability, if the car was available for the whole of the year, a Class 1A liability existed for the whole of 1998–99. The issue was clarified in the Employer's Budget update pack, despite the fact that in the Employer's Bulletin sent out by the Revenue in February 1999 the start date is given as 6 April 1999.

In the 1995 Budget, the Chancellor introduced NICs 'holiday' for employers who engage people who have been unemployed for two years or more. This was designed to help the long-term unemployed by giving employers an NICs rebate for up to a year per person and came into effect on 6 April 1996. For employments starting on or after 1 April 1999, the NICs holiday will no longer be available, although will continue to run to 31 March 2000 for holidays already in place. This scheme was replaced by the New Deal in April 1999; instead of employer rebates, the employee is given a direct grant.

On 15 November 1996, the Secretary of State for Social Security announced that proposals would be made to align NICs with the Inland Revenue treatment of tax under PAYE Settlement Agreements (PSAs). With effect from 6 April 1999, Class 1B NICs are payable on PSAs entered into for the 1999–2000 tax year onwards and is payable at the same time as the tax (19 October 2000). Class 1B NICs are currently payable at 12.2% on the total value of:

(1) all items covered by the PSA which would give rise to a Class 1 or 1A liability, and
(2) the tax payable by the employer under the PSA.

## 23.1.8 Class 1A NICs

As mentioned above, Class 1A NICs already apply to company cars and fuel, but from 6 April 2000, Class 1A NICs have been extended to include most benefits in kind. The payment date of Class 1A NICs is 19 July after the end of the year of assessment. Payment of the increased charge will therefore first arise on 19 July 2001.

The amount of the charge is normally equivalent to the highest rate of employer's secondary Class 1 NICs, which is currently 12.2%. Although the Chancellor of the Exchequer has announced a reduction to 11.9% from 6 April 2001, the 12.2% rate will still apply to the Class 1A NICs payment to be made by 19 July 2001 since it relates to the tax year 2000–01.

The principal effect will be to increase the cost of taxable benefits and the additional Class 1A NICs charge will be an above inflation cost increase. Class 1A NICs is an employer's charge only and is a tax-deductible expense. The charge will not be payable by employees or directors and there will still be scope for savings by providing benefits in kind, as compared with paying additional salary to enable employees to make purchases out of taxable income.

Class 1A NICs will not be charged if:

(1) they are already due (eg on expense payments);
(2) the expense payment or benefit in kind is covered by a P11D dispensation, extra-statutory concession or specific exemption;
(3) the expenses payment or benefit in kind is included in a PAYE settlement agreement (PSA) (where Class 1B NICs will be payable); or
(4) the benefit in kind is provided to an employee earning at a rate (inclusive of benefits) of less than £8,500 pa.

To reduce the reporting requirements, the Revenue has announced an exemption from income tax and NICs for the following:

(1) tools and equipment provided for work use where there may be a small amount of private use in the home, workplace or elsewhere;
(2) qualifying beneficial loans (as a result of the withdrawal of tax relief on house purchase loans from 6 April 2000, these loans will no longer be qualifying);

(3) general welfare counselling (but not private medical treatment or consultation); and

(4) refreshments provided by employers.

The current method of reporting Class 1A NICs on the end-of-year returns, Form P14 and P35, will cease after 1999–2000 and Class 1A NICs reports will be merged with the existing forms P11D. The simpler Alternative Payment Method, which will become compulsory, will require an employer to register with NICO and to send a payment with an annual return for the benefits in kind and the amount due.

## 23.2 CLASS 2 CONTRIBUTIONS

### 23.2.1 Introduction

A self-employed individual is liable to Class 2 NICs of £2.00 per week unless his earnings are less than £3,825 pa and he has applied for a Certificate of Exemption.

The Class 2 contributions for sharefishermen is £2.65 per week and for volunteer development workers is £3.35 per week.

### 23.2.2 Earnings from employment and self-employment

Where an individual has income from both employment and self-employment, both Class 1 and Class 2 NICs will be payable unless he applies for deferment. However, the maximum that an individual may pay for any year is an amount equal to the maximum Class 1 primary contributions on 53 weeks' earnings. Consequently, for 2000–01 the maximum is £2,432.70. A repayment may be claimed if an individual has paid a mixture of Class 1 and Class 2 NICs in excess of this amount.

### 23.2.3 Small earnings exception

A person may avoid paying Class 2 NICs by applying in advance for the small earnings exception. The amount of the limit for small earnings exemption for 2000–01 is £3,825.

Earnings for this purpose are measured by reference to actual earnings for the tax year. For example, if a trader makes up accounts to 30 September, the small earnings exception will be available only if his earnings for 2000–01 are less than £3,825 when computed as follows:

$$\text{\textsuperscript{6}/12} \times \text{profits for the year ended 30 September 1999}$$
$$\text{\textsuperscript{6}/12} \times \text{profits for the year ended 30 September 2000}$$

An individual may apply for repayment if Class 2 NICs have been overpaid. The repayment claim must normally be made between 6 April and

31 December following the end of the tax year and thus the deadline for making a repayment claim for 2000–01 will be 31 December 2000.

### A false economy?

In general, choosing not to pay Class 2 NICs could prove a false economy as entitlement to benefits such as pensions and sick pay may be affected.

## 23.3 CLASS 3 CONTRIBUTIONS

These are a type of voluntary contribution. A person who is neither employed nor self-employed (or whose earnings fall below the exemption) may pay voluntary Class 3 NICs to secure the State retirement pension. The weekly rate is set at £6.55 for 2000–01.

## 23.4 CLASS 4 CONTRIBUTIONS

These are payable by self-employed individuals according to the level of their profits as determined for income tax purposes. At present, Class 4 NICs are levied at the rate of 7 per cent of Schedule D profits between £4,825 and £27,820. A change introduced for the 1996–97 tax year means that there is no longer a deduction against profits for 50% of the Class 4 contribution.

Where an individual pays interest on a business loan or has suffered trading losses, such amounts may be set against his earnings for the purposes of assessing liability for Class 4 NICs. This situation applies even where the losses have been relieved for income tax purposes by way of off-set against his other income.

## 23.5 SOCIAL SECURITY BENEFITS
(TA 1988, s 617)

The following types of benefit are taxed as earned income under Schedule E:

● Incapacity benefit ● Income support when paid to unemployed and strikers (see below) ● Industrial death benefit (if paid as pension) ● Invalid care allowance ● Invalidity allowance when paid with retirement pension ● Job release allowance ● Jobseeker's allowance (contributions-based) ● Old person's pension ● Retirement pension ● Statutory maternity pay ● Statutory sick pay ● Unemployment benefit ● Widowed mother's allowance ● Widow's pension.

(*Note*: The jobseeker's allowance was introduced from 7 October 1996. The payments are dependent on the NICs record and/or the income.)

The following benefits are not taxable:

● Attendance allowance ● Child benefit ● Child dependency additions paid with widow's allowance, widowed mother's allowance, retirement pension, invalid care allowance, unemployment benefit or supplementary benefits ● Child's special allowance ● Christmas bonus for pensioners ● Disability living allowance ● Disability working allowance ● Employment rehabilitation allowance ● Fares to school ● Guardian's allowance ● Home improvement, repair and insulation grants ● Invalidity allowance when paid with invalidity pension ● Invalidity pension ● Job search allowances ● Maternity allowance ● Mobility allowance ● One parent benefit ● Severe disablement allowance ● Sickness benefit ● Employment training allowance ● War orphan's pension ● War widow's pension ● Widow's payment ● Youth training scheme allowance.

## Means-tested benefits

● Educational maintenance allowance ● Family credit ● Hospital patients' travelling expenses ● Housing benefit ● Jobseeker's allowance (income-based) ● Income support ● Social fund payments ● Student grants ● Uniform and clothing grants.

(*Note*: The jobseeker's allowance was introduced from 7 October 1996. The payments are dependent on the NICs record and/or the income.)

## War disablement benefits

Disablement pension, including: Age allowance ● Allowance for lowered standard of occupation ● Clothing allowance ● Comforts allowance ● Constant attendance allowance ● Dependant allowance ● Education allowance ● Exceptionally severe disablement allowance ● Invalidity allowance ● Medical treatment allowance ● Severe disablement occupational allowance ● Unemployability allowance.

## Industrial injury benefits

Disablement benefit, including: Constant attendance allowance ● Exceptionally severe disablement allowance ● Reduced earnings allowance ● Retirement allowance ● Unemployability supplement ● Industrial death benefit child allowance.

### Adoption allowances
(Extra-statutory concession A40)

Sums paid under schemes approved under the Children Act 1975, s 32 are exempt from income tax.

## 23.6 TAX CREDITS

### 23.6.1 Introduction

In the Chancellor's pre-Budget report (November 1998), he announced that family credit and disability working allowances were to be replaced by working families' tax credit (WFTC) and disabled person's tax credit (DPTC). The new benefits came into effect from October 1999. Both of these credits are now paid through the individual's employer from April 2000. The employer is informed by the Revenue how much the payments should be and when they should start. The Revenue will also notify the employers when the payments should cease. If an employer is not paying the credit, either because the credit has just started or the employment has ended, then payments will be made direct from the Revenue.

### 23.6.2 Working families' tax credit

The WFTC is available to families (ie couples, married or unmarried or single parents with at least one child). In addition, at least one family member should be working at least 16 hours a week. The family should be resident in and entitled to work in the UK and have savings of less than £8,000. Couples who apply for WFTC are allowed to choose which partner receives the tax credit.

Basic tax credit has been set at £53.15 per week and it is per family. Where one earner works at least 30 hours per week there is additional credit available of £11.25 per week. The child-related credits are shown in Table 23.2. There is also available a child care tax credit. This varies depending on the costs of the child care, but is expected to be 70 per cent of eligible child care costs up to £100 per week for one child and £150 per week for two or more children.

The relevant amounts that correspond to a family's individual circumstances are totalled to reach the qualifying amount; the amount actually payable is calculated based on the family's net earnings and other income after tax and NICs have been deducted. Where net income is less than £91.45, the full WFTC is payable. Where net income is more than £91.45 per week, the amount of qualifying credit is reduced by 55p for each pound of income over the £91.45 threshold.

## 23.6.3 **Disabled person's tax credit**

This is paid to people who have an illness or disability which puts them at a disadvantage for getting a job. Like WFTC, claimants must be resident and entitled to work in the UK and must be working at least 16 hours per week. More generously than WFTC, the savings threshold is £16,000. In addition, they must be eligible for one of a number of qualifying benefits for disability, or have been receiving them up to 182 days prior to their application.

- Basic tax credit is £55.15 per week for a single person and £84.90 per week for a couple.
- A 30-hour tax credit of £11.25 per week in addition.
- Child-related credits are given for each child in the family according to his age, as shown in Table 23.3:
- The same child care tax credit applies as for the WFTC.

An award of the tax credit will be effective for 26 weeks at a time, although when employers begin to distribute the tax credits they will be paid at the same intervals as pay (eg monthly or weekly).

## 23.6.4 **The role of employers**

From October 1999 to end of March 2000, the WFTC and DPTC was paid directly to claimants by the Revenue. From April 2000, the order book or girocheque has been replaced by the payslip and employers will take on a new role of dispensers of tax credits to add to their existing duties as collectors of tax and NICs. The amounts paid by employers by way of tax credits will be set against their PAYE tax and NICs liabilities due to the Revenue each month or quarter as appropriate. Where the employer has not collected enough PAYE and NICs to cover the tax credits payable for a particular period, application to the Revenue for additional funding may be made. At the end of the tax year, employers will be obliged to provide employees with details of the credits paid to their employees. This information will also need to be shown on payslips and P60 forms.

If the applicant is self-employed, he will continue to receive his credits directly from the Revenue. It will not usually be necessary for the recipients of the tax credit to have to complete a tax return unless they are required to do so for some other reason. If an applicant does not agree with the Revenue's decision about qualification or the amount awarded, he will be able to ask for the case to be reviewed. If he still disagrees, he will be able to appeal to the Unified Appeals Tribunal.

ALLIED DUNBAR TAX HANDBOOK

## Table 23.1 – Taxable social security benefits

|  | 1999–2000 (£) | 2000–01 (£) |
|---|---|---|
| *Retirement pension* | | |
| Single | 66.75 | 67.50 |
| Adult dependant | 39.95 | 40.40 |
| *Incapacity benefit\** | | |
| Long-term benefit | 66.75 | 67.50 |
| increase for age higher | 14.05 | 14.20 |
| increase for age lower | 7.05 | 7.10 |
| Short-term benefit | | |
| under pension age | | |
| lower rate | 50.35 | 50.90 |
| higher rate | 59.55 | 60.20 |
| Short term benefit | | |
| over pension age | | |
| lower rate | 64.05 | 64.75 |
| higher rate | 66.75 | 67.50 |
| *Income Support* | | |
| Single/lone parent | | |
| – under 18 | 30.95 | 31.45 |
| – 18 to 24 | 40.70 | 41.35 |
| – 25 or over | 51.54 | 52.20 |
| Couple | | |
| – both under 18 | 61.35 | 62.35 |
| – one/both 18 or over | 80.65 | 81.95 |
| *Invalidity allowance (transitional)* | | |
| lower rate | 4.45 | 4.50 |
| middle rate | 8.90 | 9.00 |
| higher rate | 14.05 | 14.20 |
| *Statutory sick pay* | | |
| Earnings threshold | 66.00 | 67.00 |
| Standard rate | 59.55 | 60.20 |
| *Statutory maternity pay* | | |
| Earnings threshold | 66.00 | 67.00 |
| Lower rate | 59.55 | 60.20 |
| *Jobseeker's allowance (contribution based)\*\** | | |
| Single people under 18 | 30.95 | 31.45 |
| Single people 18–24 | 40.70 | 41.35 |
| Single people 25 and over | 51.40 | 52.20 |

*Widow's benefit*

| | | |
|---|---|---|
| Widowed mother's allowance | 66.75 | 67.50 |
| Widow's pension (standard) | 66.75 | 67.50 |

\* Incapacity benefit replaced invalidity benefit and sickness benefit from 6 April 1995. It is taxable (under Schedule E) *except* for short-term benefit payable at the lower rate.
\*\*The jobseeker's allowance was introduced from 7 October 1996 and replaced unemployment benefit.

## Table 23.2 – Non-taxable social security benefits

| | 1999–2000 (£) | 2000–01 (£) |
|---|---|---|
| *Attendance allowance* | | |
| Higher rate | 52.95 | 53.55 |
| Lower rate | 35.40 | 35.80 |
| *Child benefit* | | |
| First or only child | 14.40 | 15.00 |
| Each subsequent child | 9.60 | 10.00 |
| *Severe disablement allowance* | | |
| Basic rate | 40.35 | 40.80 |
| Age-related addition | | |
| higher rate | 14.05 | 14.20 |
| middle rate | 8.90 | 9.00 |
| lower rate | 4.45 | 4.50 |
| *Widow's payment* | | |
| Single lump sum | 1,000.00 | 1,000.00 |
| *Christmas bonus* | | |
| Single annual payment | 10.00 | 10.00 |
| Family credit ⎫ | amount | amount |
| Housing benefit ⎭ | varies | varies |

## Table 23.3 – Working families' tax credit (WFTC) and disabled person's tax credit (DPTC) weekly amounts and thresholds 2000–01

| | April 2000 (£) | June 2000 (£) | Oct 2000 (£) |
|---|---|---|---|
| *WFTC* | | | |
| basic tax credit | 53.15 | 53.15 | 53.15 |
| *DPTC* | | | |
| single person | 55.15 | 55.15 | 55.15 |
| lone parent/couple | 84.90 | 84.90 | 84.90 |
| 30 hours tax credit | | | |
| (WFTC and DPTC) | 11.25 | 11.25 | 11.25 |

Child tax credits
  (WFTC and DPTC)

| | | | |
|---|---|---|---|
| – Under 11 | 21.25 | 25.60 | 25.60 |
| – 11–16* | 21.25 | 25.60 | 25.60 |
| – 16–18* | 26.35 | 26.35 | 26.35 |
| Disabled child tax credit – WFTC** | – | – | 22.25 |
| Disabled child tax credit DPTC | 22.25 | 22.25 | 22.25 |
| WFTC threshold | 91.45 | 91.45 | 91.45 |
| DTPC threshold |
| single person | 71.10 | 71.10 | 71.10 |
| lone parent/couple | 91.45 | 91.45 | 91.45 |

* The 11–16 and 16–18 chld tax credits apply from the September following the 11th and 16th birthday respectively.
** The disabled child tax credit in the working families' tax credit is to be introduced from October 2000.

# 24

# TAX AND COMPANIES

PETER HARRUP

This chapter looks at the taxation of companies under the following headings:

(1) Who pays corporation tax?
(2) How 'profits' are defined.
(3) Accounting periods, rates and payment of tax.
(4) Companies' capital gains.
(5) Loan relationships.
(6) Dividends.
(7) Losses.
(8) Self-assessment.
(9) Double taxation relief on foreign income.
(10) Groups of companies.
(11) Investment companies.
(12) Close companies
(13) Corporate venturing
(14) Research and Development tax credits
(15) Claims and elections.
(16) Should you operate via a company?

## 24.1 WHO PAYS CORPORATION TAX?
(TA 1988, ss 11–12; FA 1988, s 66)

Corporation tax is levied on the chargeable profits of companies resident in the UK for tax purposes. A company is generally defined as meaning any body corporate or unincorporated association, but does not include a partnership, local authority or local authority association. The definition also extends to authorised unit trusts, the detailed provisions for which are set out in TA 1988, s 468.

Corporation tax also extends to non-resident companies carrying on a trade in the UK through a branch or agency. Such companies are chargeable to tax on any income attributable to the branch or agency and on any capital gains arising on the disposal of assets used in the UK for the purposes of the branch or agency trade. Any income of a non-resident company from sources within the UK which is not charged to corporation tax is liable to income tax.

A company which was incorporated in the UK is regarded as resident there regardless of where the directors exercise their management and control. However, some of the double taxation conventions negotiated with other countries override this in practice and treat a dual resident company as if it were not resident in the UK.

A company which was incorporated overseas may still be regarded as resident in the UK on the basis that its central management and control is exercised there. Questions relating to the residence status of a foreign incorporated company are usually determined by reference to the guidelines set out in SP1/90 dated 9 January 1990.

## 24.2 HOW 'PROFITS' ARE DEFINED

### 24.2.1 Computation of profits
(TA 1988, s 6)

The income and chargeable gains of a company, collectively termed 'chargeable profits', are chargeable to corporation tax. The computation of chargeable profits can be a very complex process bearing in mind the detailed tax legislation and extensive case law. There are also myriad Inland Revenue Statements of Practice, press releases and extra-statutory concessions which may need to be borne in mind when calculating chargeable profits upon which corporation tax is payable.

The general principles of profit adjustment closely follow the rules for income tax and the assessment of income under the various schedules is computed on an actual or arising basis.

### 24.2.2 Special computational rules for companies

#### Rental income

With effect from 1 April 1998 all income from UK rental activities will be treated as arising from one source and taxed along the same lines as trading profits taxable under Schedule D Case I. Any losses will be relieved first against other income and gains of the same period, and any excess will be available for carrying forward against all future income, or may be surrendered as group relief (subject to certain restrictions).

The old Schedule A rules apply in relation to rental income received before 1 April 1998. These rules are set out in *Allied Dunbar Tax Handbook 1998–99* at 4.9.

## Forex transactions

Special rules apply for foreign exchange profits and losses and professional advice should be taken if the company has significant foreign assets or borrowings in foreign currency.

## Loan relationships

Specific rules govern the treatment of loan relationships such as gilts and other fixed interest investments in relation to accounting periods ending after 31 March 1996. Basically, any profits on disposal of such assets are taxed as income and any losses are allowed against the company's income. It is necessary to revalue gilts and fixed interest investments at the end of each accounting period. Any increase compared with the market value at the start of the period (or the date of acquisition where the gilt etc was acquired during the course of the year) is taxable income, any reduction in value is an allowable loss.

## Capital allowances
(CAA 1990, s 144)

Although depreciation is not regarded as an allowable expense for tax purposes, tax relief is given for expenditure on qualifying capital assets by means of capital allowances. The principles follow very closely those which apply in the case of individuals (see 2.5) and therefore the main provisions are not covered in detail here. Capital allowances for a trade carried on by a company are regarded as trading expenses for the accounting period in which they arise. They are therefore taken into account in arriving at the chargeable profits or overall tax loss for the accounting period.

Capital allowances for non-trading activities are primarily deductible from the income arising from that source. Any surplus allowances may be carried forward against similar source income arising in later accounting periods or deducted from overall chargeable profits for the accounting period in which they arise.

## Annual payments
(TA 1988, s 338)

Unlike individuals, a company is liable to account to the Revenue for certain annual payments which it makes (as well as annual interest). Such annual payments (termed 'charges on income') are deductible from a company's profits in arriving at the amount assessable to corporation tax. The basic principle is that these charges on income are offset against the total profits of the payer, not merely against a particular source of income with which the payment is connected.

A payment will count as a charge on income only if the following conditions are met:

(1) It has been made out of the company's profits brought into charge to corporation tax.
(2) It is made under a liability incurred for a 'valuable and sufficient consideration' (or the payment is a covenanted donation to charity).
(3) The payment must not be one charged to capital or one not ultimately borne by the company.
(4) It must not be in the nature of a dividend or distribution made by the company.

Payment must actually be made in the accounting period for it to count as a charge for that period.

Where the total profits for an accounting period are insufficient to absorb charges on income, excess charges in respect of payments made wholly and exclusively for the purposes of the company's trade may be carried forward and utilised against future trading income of the company. Non-trade charges may not be carried forward in this manner and no further relief is available.

## 24.3 ACCOUNTING PERIODS, RATES AND PAYMENT OF TAX

### 24.3.1 Accounting periods for tax purposes
(TA 1988, s 12)

Companies pay corporation tax by reference to their accounting periods and the income included is assessed on an actual or accruals basis. Accounting periods may straddle two financial years (which for corporation tax purposes run from 1 April to 31 March and are named after the year in which it begins). If this is the case, the chargeable profits are apportioned on a time basis for the purposes of determining the rate of tax to apply to the overall profit.

An accounting period begins for corporation tax purposes when:

(1) the company comes within the charge to corporation tax either by becoming resident in the UK or acquiring a source of income; or
(2) the company's previous accounting period ends without the company ceasing to be within the charge to corporation tax.

An accounting period runs on for a maximum of 12 months from its commencement. It will end earlier if the company's own accounting date falls within the 12 months and it will also end if the company:

(1) ceases to trade;
(2) begins or ceases to be resident in the UK; or
(3) ceases to be within the charge to corporation tax altogether.

Where accounts are made up for a period of more than 12 months, the income is usually apportioned on a time basis to the relevant accounting period.

However, where a more appropriate basis of apportionment is available, the Inspector may apply that basis instead (*Marshall Hus & Partners Ltd v Bolton* [1981] STC 18). In some instances, the accounts year end may vary slightly for commercial reasons (eg where accounts are made up to the last Friday of a specified month). Provided the variation is not more than four days from the 'mean' date it will normally be acceptable to treat each period of account as if it were a 12-month accounting period ending on the mean date.

### 24.3.2 The corporation tax rates
(TA 1988, s 6)

The rate of corporation tax is fixed for each financial year which, for these purposes, starts on 1 April. The rate of tax for the financial year 1999 (ie 1 April 1999–31 March 2000) is 30%. Profits include both income and capital gains.

### 24.3.3 Small companies rates and associated companies
(TA 1988, s 13)

A reduced rate of corporation tax (known as the 'small companies rate') applies to the profits of a company where those profits do not exceed a minimum level. The rate of tax for the financial year 2000 (ie 1 April 2000–31 March 2001) is 20% and the current profit level below which the small companies rate applies is £300,000. This rate and limit have applied since 1994.

Where profits exceed the maximum profit limit for small companies rate purposes, an element of marginal relief is given for profits between £300,000 and £1,500,000. This relief operates on a tapered basis by charging the profits to the full corporation tax rate but gives an element of credit for the reduced corporation tax rate which would have been applicable to the initial tranche of profit.

The profit limits applicable to small companies relief are restricted, based upon the existence of any 'associated' companies which the company has during the accounting period concerned. A company is an associated company of another if they are under common control or one has control of the other. 'Control' for this purpose is defined as the ability to exercise direct or indirect control over the company's affairs and in particular:

(1) the possession or entitlement to acquire more than 50% of the share capital or voting rights in the company;
(2) entitlement to receive the greater part of income distributed among the shareholders;
(3) entitlement to receive the greater part of the assets of the company in the event of a winding-up.

For example, if a company has one associated company, the small companies profit limits are divided by two, ie one plus the number of associated companies. However, an associated company which has not carried on any trade or business at any time during the accounting period concerned would be disregarded. Where a company's accounting period straddles more than one financial year and the marginal relief limits for each financial year differ, the 12-month period is treated as separate accounting periods for the purpose of calculating marginal relief.

### 24.3.4 10% rate for very small companies

A 10% rate for companies with profits of up to £10,000 was introduced with effect from 1 April 2000. The new starting rate is on taxable profits of up to £10,000, and companies with profits of between £10,000 and £50,000 are subject to an effective marginal rate of tax, so that the overall rate for a small company (a company with taxable profits of less than £300,000) does not exceed 20%. For example, a taxable profit of £25,000 would give rise to a corporation tax charge of £5,000 for 1999 (20%), but this would be only £4,375 for 2000 on the same level of profit.

The following table, comparing the company tax years starting on 1 April 1999 and 1 April 2000, demonstrates how the new starting rate works for companies with profits between £5,000 and £50,000:

| Total taxable company profit £ | Year 2000 corporation tax payable £ | Year 1999 corporation tax payable £ |
|---|---|---|
| 5,000 | 500 | 1,000 |
| 10,000 | 1,000 | 2,000 |
| 15,000 | 2,125 | 3,000 |
| 20,000 | 3,250 | 4,000 |
| 25,000 | 4,375 | 5,000 |
| 30,000 | 5,500 | 6,000 |
| 35,000 | 6,625 | 7,000 |
| 40,000 | 7,750 | 8,000 |
| 45,000 | 8,875 | 9,000 |
| 50,000 | 10,000 | 10,000 |

### 24.3.5 Payment of tax
(TA 1988, s 10)

Corporation tax for an accounting period ending after 30 September 1993 automatically becomes due and payable nine months and one day from the end of the accounting period. Since 1 July 1999 large companies with taxable profits over £1.5m must pay corporation tax by instalments. The payments commence 14 days after the first six months of the year in question, and are due in four equal quarterly instalments. A company with a year end of 31 December will pay on 14 July, 14 October, 14 January and 14 April.

There are transitional rules where the company pays 60% of the liability due by instalments in year one, with the balance due nine months after the year end. This increases gradually from 60% to 72% in year two, 88% in year three, and 100% in year four.

Interest will be charged on any unpaid tax due and will be an allowable deduction, and will be payable to the company on any overpayments – this interest will be taxable.

## 24.4 COMPANIES' CAPITAL GAINS

### 24.4.1. Computation of gains

Capital gains made by companies are included in their chargeable profits and are subject to corporation tax. CGT therefore does not apply to companies, although chargeable gains and losses are computed in accordance with the detailed provisions of CGT. The main differences between CGT and corporation tax on chargeable gains for companies are, first, that provisions which clearly apply only to individuals (eg annual exemption) have no application as far as companies are concerned, and secondly, that computations of chargeable gains are prepared on an accounting period basis rather than by income tax years of assessment. Furthermore, taper relief does not apply to companies but they remain entitled to indexation allowance on increases in the RPI after 31 March 1998. The total chargeable gains for an accounting period less a deduction for allowable losses are brought into charge to corporation tax in the same way as any other source of income.

Capital losses can only be off-set against chargeable gains; they cannot be offset against trading or other income. On the other hand, it is possible for a company which realises a loss after 31 March 2000 to surrender its loss to another group company for it to off-set against its chargeable gains.

### 24.4.2 Roll-over relief
(TCGA 1992, ss 152–158 and 175)

Roll-over relief is available where the proceeds on the disposal of a qualifying asset are reinvested in further qualifying assets. It operates as a deferral of the corporation tax liability arising on the chargeable gain if the proceeds are fully reinvested in qualifying assets within a period of 12 months before and three years after the date of disposal.

Where the proceeds are only partly reinvested, a proportion of the gain is deferred or 'rolled over' and the balance (equivalent to the amount of proceeds not reinvested) is brought into charge. The element of gain deferred or rolled over is deducted from the base cost of the new asset for capital gains purposes. This, of course, will operate to increase the potential gain on the eventual sale of the new asset acquired, hence the term 'roll-over relief'.

Qualifying assets for this purpose are freehold and leasehold land and buildings, goodwill, ships, aircraft and hovercraft, fixed plant and machinery, satellite space stations and spacecraft and certain agricultural quotas. Expenditure on an asset acquired from a group company (see 24.10) does not rank as qualifying expenditure for roll-over relief.

The Government is presently consulting with professional bodies on an extension to the roll-over rules to enable gains on sales of shares in trading companies to be eligible for roll-over. If the rules are widened, they will probably apply only to shares in which the disposing company had at least 30% of the equity. The change is not expected to take effect before 1 April 2001.

## 24.5 LOAN RELATIONSHIPS

In broad terms, for all accounting periods ending after 31 March 1996 the tax treatment of profits and losses from loan relationships follows the accounting treatment. The new rules introduced in FA 1996 affect the tax treatment of items such as interest received and paid, premiums and discounts.

### 24.5.1 Scope of legislation

The legislation applies to all UK-resident companies and UK branches of overseas resident companies. The commencement date for the new regime is the start of a company's first accounting period ending after 31 March 1996 for interest, and 1 April 1996 for gains and losses on debt.

### 24.5.2 'Loan relationships'
(FA 1996, s 81)

The legislation refers to 'loan relationships' rather than loans, and these can arise as follows:

(1) where a company is a debtor or creditor in respect of a money debt, and this debt arose as a result of a transaction for the lending of money; or
(2) where an instrument is issued for the purpose of representing security for, or the rights of a creditor in respect of, a money debt.

Loan relationships therefore include bank loans, director's loans, gilts, intercompany accounts and debentures. Even where a money debt does not fall within the definition (eg trade creditors and debtors) the interest charged on such debts falls within the new regime.

### 24.5.3 Tax treatment
(FA 1996, s 84)

In general, the income and expenditure will be taxed or allowed in the year it is credited or debited to the profit and loss account or, if appropriate, reserves. However, the company's accounting treatment must comply with an 'authorised accruals' accounting policy. Where a company accounts for debt using normal accounting practice (as set out in FRS4, *Capital Instruments*) this should satisfy the authorised accruals accounting policy.

Banks are also permitted to use an authorised market to market basis where loan relationship is brought into account in each accounting period at the fair value.

### 24.5.4 Taxation of corporate debt
(FA 1996, ss 82–83)

The tax treatment of corporate debt depends on whether the item arose from the trade. Debits and credits arising in an accounting period from loan relationships entered into for the purposes of the company's trade are treated as forming part of its trading profits or losses, whereas any debits and credits arising from activities outside the company's trade are aggregated in coming to a profit or loss on non-trading loan relationships.

Where any expenditure or income arises partly from trading and partly from non-trading, it is split on a pro rata basis.

#### Taxation of non-trading profits and losses
(FA 1996, s 83)

Net profits from non-trading loan relationships are taxed under Schedule D Case III. If there are net losses then these can be relieved in a number of ways:

(1) by offset against the company's profits chargeable to corporation tax for that accounting period; or
(2) by surrender as group relief to other group companies; or
(3) by carry back against the last three year's profits from non-trading loan relationships, setting off the loss against later years before earlier years; or
(4) by carry forward against all profits, other than trading profits, of the next period; or
(5) by carry forward against future profits from non-trading loan relationships.

Claims must be made within two years of the accounting period in which the loss arose for (1)–(3), and two years of the next period for (4). No claim is required for losses carried forward under (5).

### 24.5.5 Connected parties
(FA 1996, s 87)

Special rules apply when the other party to a loan relationship is a connected company. A company and another party are connected for these purposes if

they are under the same control, or one controls the other, in that accounting period or in the two years before. A person controls a company by
owning the greater part of the shares, voting rights, or other capital giving
entitlement to more than one-half of the assets in a winding-up.

The same rules also apply if the other party, or its 'associate', is a 'participator' in the accounting period or was at any time in the two years
before. In general participators are shareholders, and associates are relatives,
partners or trustees of settlements where a relative or the participator is or
was the settlor.

### 24.5.6 Late interest
(FA 1996, s 87)

If two parties are connected, then interest is only allowable on an accruals
basis when paid to a connected party where the recipient is liable to UK corporation tax on the full amount of interest received, or the interest is paid
within 12 months of the end of the accounting period. Therefore, if the
recipient is an individual, trustee, non-resident company or exempt body
such as a charity, the interest must be paid by the anniversary of the
accounting period if a deduction is to be obtained.

### 24.5.7 Bad debts and waivers
(FA 1996, Sched 9)

No tax relief is available for any bad debts on connected party loan relationships, and conversely no liability to tax arises when a debt is waived.

### 24.5.8 Annual charges
(TA 1988, ss 338–339)

Apart from interest, a company may make annual payments in respect of
annuities, royalties, covenanted payments etc which are available for off-set
as charges on income against the chargeable profits of the company on a
paid basis.

### 24.5.9 Income tax deduction at source

Companies must deduct and account to the Revenue for income tax on
payments of annual interest and other charges on income, with the exception of annual interest paid to a UK bank. A return Form CT61 is required
to be submitted on a quarterly basis detailing payments made and computing the income tax payable to the Revenue. In arriving at the income
tax liability due, any income tax suffered on income received under
deduction of tax may be off-set. Where the income tax suffered on income
received exceeds the income tax payable on annual charges, the surplus
may be carried forward to the next quarterly return. If at the end of the

accounting period it has not proved possible to obtain credit against income tax payable, credit may be obtained against the corporation tax liability for the accounting period (and if there is no or insufficient corporation tax liability to offset any income tax credit, a repayment may be obtained from the Revenue).

## 24.6 DIVIDENDS
(TA 1988, ss 238–241)

### 24.6.1 Taxation of company distributions

Company distributions are defined as any dividends, and any other distribution out of assets of the company, paid by a company in respect of shares in the company. The main exception to this is that any repayment of share capital is not regarded as a distribution of assets.

UK recipients of the distribution are entitled to a tax credit. This aggregate amount is described as a 'franked' payment and, as far as individuals are concerned, represents the gross equivalent of the dividend received. This amount is taxable income, but the shareholder may set the tax credit against his tax liability on the 'grossed-up' amount.

Dividends received by a company from another UK company are termed franked investment income. This income is regarded as having already borne tax and does not form part of the chargeable profits of a company and is therefore non-taxable.

### 24.6.2 Advance corporation tax (abolished from 6 April 1999)
(TA 1988, s 238)

Until 5 April 1999, a liability to account for ACT arose when a company made a qualifying distribution to its shareholders. The rate was 20/80 of the dividend, ie 20% of the 'grossed up' amount. As its name suggests, ACT was treated as an advance payment of corporation tax and relief was obtained by deduction from the mainstream corporation tax liability payable on the profits for the accounting period in which the distribution had been made.

The collection of ACT on dividends and other distributions made by a company was undertaken on Inland Revenue Form CT61. The company was required to submit this return on a quarterly basis to the Revenue in respect of the ACT liability arising on dividends and other distributions made during the three-month period. ACT was then payable 14 days after the end of the quarterly period concerned.

ACT was abolished with effect from 6 April 1999.

## 24.6.3 **Relief for payment of ACT**
(TA 1988, s 239)

The maximum relief against mainstream corporation tax for ACT paid on distributions made in an accounting period was equivalent to the ACT which would have been due on a franked payment equal to the profits chargeable to corporation tax. Where the ACT exceeded this maximum, relief could be obtained in the following ways:

(1) It could be carried back to accounting periods beginning in the six years preceding the accounting period in which the surplus ACT arose, taking later years before earlier years. A claim had to be lodged within two years of the end of the accounting period in which the surplus ACT arose.

(2) It could be carried forward and treated as ACT payable for the next accounting period. If it cannot be utilised in the next accounting period, it was treated as surplus ACT in the following accounting period and carried forward indefinitely until utilised (see below for accounting periods ending after 5 April 1999).

(3) It could be surrendered to a 51% subsidiary company resident in the UK. It is then treated as ACT paid by the subsidiary (see 24.10.3). A claim to surrender ACT had to be made within six years of the end of the accounting period in which the ACT was paid and required the consent of the subsidiary or subsidiaries concerned.

Even after the abolition of ACT on 6 April 1999, surplus ACT remains available for relief. However, the company will have to calculate the ACT which would have been due on any distributions after 5 April 1999. This fictitious ACT is referred to as 'shadow ACT'.

## 24.6.4 **Shadow ACT**

Shadow ACT is not actually payable to the Revenue, but merely serves as a method to calculate the extent to which surplus ACT can be set off against future corporation tax liabilities.

The Shadow ACT position has to be computed for each accounting period ending on or after 6 April 1999 as if ACT were still payable on dividends and the Shadow ACT were then set against mainstream corporation tax according to the rules covered in 24.6.2 above.

Shadow ACT is relieved in priority to surplus ACT brought forward from before 6 April 1999. Where there is spare capacity (ie where the Shadow ACT does not amount to the maximum which may be offset against mainstream corporation tax), surplus ACT brought forward from before 6 April 1999 will be set against the company's mainstream corporation tax.

Any unrelieved Shadow ACT will be carried forward and must be 'utilised' before actual unrelieved ACT.

Some companies may abandon the struggle and simply accept that they will never access unrelieved ACT. If they take this line they will not be required to carry out Shadow ACT calculations.

### 24.6.5 Foreign Income Dividend (FID) scheme

Only a dividend paid before 6 April 1999 can be an FID. The FID scheme was designed to assist companies resident in the UK with surplus ACT arising from double taxation relief for foreign tax paid on their foreign profits (see 24.9.2 for interaction of double taxation relief and ACT). If a company elected for a dividend to be paid as an FID, ACT was paid in the normal way. However, provided it is shown that the FID was paid out of foreign profits, any surplus ACT was repayable to the company.

Special rules applied to international headquarters companies (IHCs) which did not need to account for ACT at the time an FID was paid. A company qualified as an IHC if it was owned either directly or indirectly by a foreign quoted company.

## 24.7 LOSSES

### 24.7.1 Losses arising in accounting period
(TA 1988, s 393)

When a company makes a tax loss in respect of its trading activities for an accounting period, it may claim that the loss arising may be off-set against other profits including chargeable gains arising in that accounting period. A tax loss is computed in the same manner as taxable profits, but is restricted to losses arising from trading activities carried out on a commercial basis and with a view to the realisation of profit.

### 24.7.2 Utilisation of loss relief

There are a number of ways in which a trading loss may be relieved for tax purposes apart from being off-set against other profits arising in the accounting period. The loss can be carried forward to off-set against trading profits from the same trade arising in succeeding accounting periods. Losses can be carried forward indefinitely in this manner for as long as the company carries on the trading activity which generated the loss. A loss may also be carried back.

Losses incurred after 1 July 1997 can be carried back and offset against profits in the 12 months immediately preceding the accounting period in which the loss was incurred. Losses before 2 July 1997 can be carried back three years. Where a loss is incurred in an accounting period straddling 1 July 1997 the loss is apportioned accordingly. Normally the apportionment is on a time basis.

The company must have been carrying on the relevant trade in the earlier periods. Partial relief claims are not allowed, and relief is obtained for later years before earlier years. Relief must be obtained for the loss against other profits of the accounting period before computing the balance of the loss available for carry-back.

### 24.7.3 Capital losses

Capital losses, like capital gains, are computed in accordance with CGT rules although the net capital gains are subject to corporation tax as part of the overall chargeable profits for the accounting period. Capital losses may be off-set against capital gains in computing net chargeable gains, and capital losses which cannot be relieved in this way may be carried forward and off-set against gains arising in subsequent accounting periods without limit. The carry-forward of capital losses is not dependent upon whether or not the company continues to carry on its trading activity, and may be off-set against gains arising on trade and non-trade assets.

### 24.7.4 Surplus charges on income
(TA 1988, s 393(9))

Relief for charges on income is generally given as the last of all reliefs other than group relief (see 24.10). It is given against the total profits of the period in which the charges are paid. If profits are insufficient to absorb the charges, the amount of charges paid wholly and exclusively for the purposes of the company's trading activities may be carried forward to the next accounting period and treated as a trading loss to be off-set against future trading income of the company. Non-trade charges on income may not be so carried forward and therefore relief will be lost.

### 24.7.5 Terminal losses
(TA 1988, ss 393A and 394)

A trading loss arising in the accounting period in which the trade ceases may be carried back and off-set against profits of the three years ending immediately before the commencement of the final period of trading. Charges on income paid wholly and exclusively for the purposes of the trade are treated as trading expenses for the purpose of computing the terminal loss available for carry-back.

### 24.7.6 Changes in company ownership
(TA 1988, s 768)

There are anti-avoidance provisions designed to ensure that trading losses carried forward can only be utilised against future trading income from the trading activity which generated the losses. Losses may not be carried forward if:

(1) within any period of three years there is a change in the ownership of the company preceded or followed by a major change in the nature or conduct of the trade carried on by the company; or
(2) there is a change in ownership of the company at any time after the scale of activities in a trade carried on by the company has become small or negligible, and before any considerable revival in the trade.

A 'change in ownership' means a change in more than 50% of the ownership of the ordinary share capital in the company. A 'major change in the nature or conduct of a trade' includes a major change in the type of property dealt in, or the services or facilities provided in, the trade or in customers, outlets or markets. The Revenue has issued guidelines on some of the factors which will be relevant in determining whether or not there has been a major change in the nature or conduct of a trade or business (see SP10/91).

Similar provisions apply for surplus ACT and for excess management expenses brought forward by an investment company.

## 24.8 SELF-ASSESSMENT
(TA 1988, ss 8 and 10; FA 1989, s 102; FA 1990, ss 91–103 and Scheds 15–17)

Self-assessment applies to all companies with accounting periods ending on or after 1 July 1999. This is a similar system to that already in operation for individuals and trustees.

Where a company has taxable profits for such an accounting period, and it also had such profits in the preceding year, it will be required to make four payments on account of its expected corporation tax liability for the year.

Self-assessment for companies brings with it extensive record-keeping obligations.

A copy of the relevant manual, *A Guide to Corporation Tax Self-assessment* (CTSA/BK2), can be obtained from the Revenue.

## 24.9 DOUBLE TAXATION RELIEF ON FOREIGN INCOME
(TA 1988, ss 788–806)

### 24.9.1 The main reliefs
A UK-resident company may claim a credit for foreign tax paid on income or capital gains arising from any overseas source. Credit is available against the corporation tax liability payable on the same income or gains. Relief may be due either under the provisions of a double taxation agreement

between the UK and the overseas country concerned, or under the general rules for 'unilateral relief' as provided in TA 1988, s 790. Where credit is due under a double taxation agreement, the relevant agreement takes precedence over UK domestic legislation.

For most types of income and gains, the full amount is brought into charge for the purpose of computing the corporation tax liability on chargeable profits for the accounting period. Any overseas tax suffered is then off-set by way of credit against the corporation tax liability. The amount of credit which is available is limited to the corporation tax liability on the source of income or gain which has suffered overseas tax. No relief is due for the excess foreign tax paid.

Further relief may be available for dividends received. In addition to relief for withholding or other taxes suffered on payment of the dividend, relief may also be available for the foreign tax suffered on the profits out of which the dividend has been paid. This is known as 'underlying tax', for which relief is given automatically if the UK-recipient company controls 10% or more of the voting share capital in the overseas company paying the dividend. The dividend taxable in the UK is grossed up at the rate of underlying tax applicable to the profits out of which the dividend has been paid. This, together with any withholding and other taxes suffered on payment of the dividend, can then be off-set against the corporation tax liability arising on the grossed up equivalent of the dividend received (subject to the restriction that underlying tax relief cannot exceed the corporation tax liability on the same income).

Where double tax relief would be lost (eg where no corporation tax liability arises for the accounting period) it is possible to obtain relief for overseas tax paid by treating the tax as an expense in computing profits for the purposes of Schedule D Case I.

## 24.9.2 Interaction between double tax relief and ACT for periods up to 5 April 1999
(TA 1988, s 797)

Double tax relief for overseas taxes paid and underlying tax is given by way of credit against the corporation tax liability arising on the same income. In arriving at the corporation tax liability arising on the overseas income or gains, it is possible to take account of the following:

(1) Charges on income may be allocated against other sources of income in priority to overseas income and gains which have suffered overseas tax.
(2) Double tax relief is off-set against the attributable corporation tax liability in priority to ACT.

If double tax relief cannot be obtained by way of credit against the corporation tax liability arising on the same income or gains, it may be advisable to claim the tax paid as an expense deduction in computing the profit or loss arising for Schedule D Case I purposes.

### 24.9.3 Unremittable income

Where an overseas source of income is taxable on an arising basis but it is not possible to remit the income due to Government actions in the overseas territory, it is possible to make a claim to defer the corporation tax liability until such time as sufficient funds are remitted to the UK to satisfy the liability. A claim under these circumstances may be made to the Revenue at any time within six years of the end of the accounting period in which the income arises.

## 24.10 GROUPS OF COMPANIES

### 24.10.1 Group relationships
(TA 1988, s 402)

There are special rules which apply to groups of companies. For corporation tax purposes, a group relationship exists between two companies if one company holds not less than 75% of the ordinary share capital of the other, or if both companies are 75% subsidiaries of a third company. Before 1 April 2000, the companies concerned had to be UK-resident 75% subsidiaries of a UK-resident parent company, but FA 2000 has now amended the rules to allow UK-resident subsidiaries of non-resident companies to constitute a group for UK tax purposes.

### 24.10.2 Use of losses
(TA 1988, ss 402–413)

Where one company in a group makes a tax loss for an accounting period, it may 'surrender' that loss to a member of the group for off-set against that company's taxable profits. For this purpose, losses available for surrender include charges on income to the extent that they exceed profits chargeable to corporation tax. Where the accounting periods of the surrendering and claimant companies do not coincide, the amount of loss to be surrendered is restricted on a time basis reflecting the length of the accounting periods common to both companies.

For group relief purposes, the requirement for a 75% shareholding relationship is extended so that the company owning the shares must also be beneficially entitled to 75% or more of the profits available for distribution to equity shareholders, and of assets available for distribution in a winding-up.

### 24.10.3 ACT surrenders
(TA 1988, s 240)

Where a company has paid ACT on a dividend distribution to shareholders prior to 6 April 1999, it may surrender the ACT to a 51% subsidiary which is resident in the UK. The 51% relationship refers to ordinary share capital and the shareholding relationship must subsist throughout the whole of the accounting period during which the dividend was paid. If a surrender of ACT is made, the subsidiary is treated as if it had itself paid both the dividend and the ACT. It may therefore off-set the ACT against its own corporation tax liability for that accounting period, or carry it forward to subsequent accounting periods. It is not possible to carry back surrendered ACT, although for the purpose of determining the amount of surplus ACT to be carried forward or back, surrendered ACT is off-set against the subsidiary's mainstream corporation tax liability before ACT paid by the subsidiary itself.

### 24.10.4 Transfers of assets between group companies
(TCGA 1992, ss 171–174)

Where a trading activity is transferred from one group company to another, relief is available under TA 1988, s 343 to ensure that the company transferring the trade does not suffer balancing charges on assets which have qualified for capital allowances. The successor company merely takes over the tax residue for capital allowances purposes relating to those assets. It is also possible to elect under CAA 1990, s 158 that properties may be transferred between group companies at tax written-down value for the purpose of industrial buildings allowances.

Section 343 can also apply where a trade is transferred to another company which is under common control, even though it is not a member of a group.

### 24.10.5 Payment of interest
(TA 1988, s 247)

The payment of interest by one company to another normally involves the payer having to account for income tax on the interest payment. Where the two companies concerned are members of the same group for tax purposes, relief is available from this procedure by lodging an election with the Revenue under TA 1988, s 247. This is effective for as long as both companies remain resident in the UK and one company beneficially owns more than 50% of the ordinary share capital of the other.

### 24.10.6 Capital gains
(TCGA 1992, ss 171 and 175)

For the purposes of capital gains, chargeable assets may be transferred from one group company to another without tax consequences. Such transfers are treated as if made at a 'no gain/no loss' price and the recipient company will take over the capital gains base cost of the asset concerned from the transferor company.

For assets held on 31 March 1982, it is possible for the principal company of a group (normally the holding company) to make an election on behalf of all companies in the group that assets held on 31 March 1982 should be subject to the general rebasing rule for capital gains purposes (see 14.3). Such an election is required within two years of the end of the accounting period in which the first disposal occurs after 5 April 1988 of an asset held on 31 March 1982 by a group company.

For roll-over relief purposes, all the trades carried on by group companies are treated as a single trade and therefore it is possible to roll over a gain made on qualifying assets by one member of a group against qualifying expenditure incurred by another member of the group within the appropriate timescale. Roll-over relief is generally available only for trading companies within a group although, concessionally, relief is also available for a property holding company where the properties concerned are used for trading purposes by the other members of the group.

TCGA 1992 does not allow losses of one company in a group to be set off against gains of another group company. However, from 1 April 2000 two members of a group may jointly elect that an asset which has been disposed of outside the group by one of them may be treated as if it had been transferred between them immediately before that disposal. Previously the asset had to be actually transferred to the company with the losses.

## 24.11 INVESTMENT COMPANIES
(TA 1988, ss 75 and 130)

An investment company is any company whose business consists wholly or mainly of the making of investments and the principal part of whose income arises as a result of that activity. The expenses of managing a UK-resident investment company are deductible in computing its total profits for corporation tax purposes. Where management expenses exceed the company's chargeable income and gains for an accounting period, the surplus may be carried forward and treated as management expenses incurred in the next succeeding accounting period, and may continue to be carried forward until relieved. Surplus management expenses may also be surrendered as group relief from one group company to another. Expenses brought forward from previous periods are not available for surrender as group relief. Unrelieved management expenses of an accounting period may also be off-set against surplus franked investment income by a claim under TA 1988, s 242(2), for the purposes of claiming repayment of the tax credit attaching to it.

## 24.12 CLOSE COMPANIES
(TA 1988, s 13A)

### 24.12.1 Definition
(TA 1988, ss 414–415)

Companies which are under the control of five or fewer persons, or under the control of their directors, are known as 'close companies'. There are special provisions which are designed to ensure that such individuals cannot take undue advantage of corporation tax legislation by virtue of their positions of influence over a company's affairs.

A person controls a company if, in fact, he is able to exercise control directly or indirectly over its affairs by owning the greater part of its share capital, voting capital, or other capital giving entitlement to more than half the assets on a winding-up. Shareholders and certain loan creditors in a close company are known as participators.

## 24.12.2 Loans to participators
(TA 1988, s 419)

Where a close company makes a loan or advances any money to a participator, or an associate of a participator, there is a liability to account for an amount of tax equal to 25% of the loan.

This tax falls due nine months after the end of the company's accounting period in which the loan is made. However, no tax will need to be paid if the loan is repaid before the tax falls due. Where the loan is repaid after the tax falls due, the repayment of tax will not be due until nine months after the accounting period in which the loan is actually repaid.

For accounting periods ending before 31 March 1996, the tax liability is due within 14 days after the end of period for the purposes of interest on overdue tax. If the loan is repaid, the tax is repaid accordingly.

Regardless of when the loan was originally made, if it is wholly or partly written off or released, the borrower is treated as receiving, as part of his total income, an amount equal to the amount so written off, grossed up at the lower rate of income tax. While no basic or lower rate tax liability arises, there may be a further liability to higher rate tax.

## 24.12.3 Close investment-holding companies
(TA 1988, s 13A)

A close company carrying on specific investment-holding activities. For this purpose, investment-holding activities do not include the carrying on of a trade on a commercial basis, property holding, or holding shares in companies carrying on either of these activities.

A close investment-holding company does not qualify for the small companies rate of corporation tax.

The Revenue has also been able to restrict repayment of tax credit to shareholders receiving dividends from a close investment-holding company where it appears that arrangements have been made for the distribution of profits, the main purpose of which is to enable the individual shareholder to obtain the tax repayment. This will of course, be academic from 6 April 1999 now that such credits cannot be reclaimed by individuals.

## 24.13 CORPORATE VENTURING

Companies which subscribe for new ordinary shares in EIS-type companies (see 11.6) after 31 March 2000 may qualify for tax relief at 20% on the sum invested. This relief is dependent on the shares being retained for three years. The investment may also attract a capital gains deferral so that if the company invests £50,000 it may defer £50,000 of capital gains realised during the preceding three years or the following 12 months. These gains are then brought into charge as and when the company disposes of the shares or if the qualifying conditions are breached within a three-year period.

If all or part of the investment eventually has to be written off, the loss may be set against any of the company's profits for the year in which the loss is realised or the preceding accounting period.

The company in which the investment is made must meet basically the same tests as apply under the Enterprise Investment Scheme (see 11.6), ie its gross assets must not exceed £15m before the investing company subscribes for its shares, nor exceed £16m after that subscription.

The investing company must not have more than 30% of the equity. Furthermore, at least 20% of its shares must be held by individuals.

## 24.14 RESEARCH AND DEVELOPMENT (R&D) TAX CREDITS

Small and medium-sized companies qualify for 150% relief on sums invested in R&D after 31 March 2000. If the company eventually pays the 30% rate of corporation tax this amounts to relief at an effective rate of 45%.

Furthermore, an SME can surrender its right to relief for a cash sum payable by the Treasury if it does not have sufficient profits to utilise the relief. A company paying corporation tax at the small companies rate can receive a cash sum equal to 24% of the amount invested subject to this not exceeding the amount paid over to the Revenue for PAYE and NICs during the year.

An SME is defined for these purposes as a company with turnover not exceeding £25m. It must spend at least £25,000 on R&D to qualify for the increased rate of relief.

## 24.15 CLAIMS AND ELECTIONS

Throughout the Taxes Acts there are various claims for relief from corporation tax which must be lodged with the Revenue and, in practice, are made to the Inspector dealing with the company's affairs. Unless otherwise specified by legislation, claims must be made within six years of the end of the accounting period to which they relate. The most common claims and elections are set out below together with the time limit by which the claim or election must be made. The Inspector does not generally have discretion to accept claims made after the time limit has expired for a particular claim unless the legislation (or Revenue practice) allows otherwise.

Relief may be claimed within the normal six-year time limit against any over-assessment to corporation tax due to an error or mistake in, or an omission from, any return or statement. No relief is due where the information was not used to form the basis of an assessment, or where the assessment was made in accordance with practice generally prevailing at the time of issue. An error or mistake claim under TMA 1970, s 33 should be made to the Revenue.

For accounting periods ended after 30 September 1993, group relief and capital allowances claims are no longer made by submitting formal claims to the Inspector. Such claims are made in the pay and file return Form CT200, as are claims for repayment of tax deducted at source.

| Claim | Time limit for submission | Reference |
|---|---|---|
| Trading losses carried forward | 6 years | TA 1988, s 393 |
| Trading losses off-set against other income of accounting period | 2 years | TA 1988, s 393A |
| Trading losses carried back | 2 years | TA 1988, s 393A |
| Terminal loss relief | 2 years | TA 1988, s 393A |
| Disclaimer of capital allowances | 2 years | CAA 1990, s 24 |
| Group relief | 2 years | TA 1988, s 412 |
| Surrender of ACT | 6 years | TA 1988, s 240 |
| Carry back of ACT | 2 years | TA 1988, s 239 |
| Rollover relief | 6 years | TCGA 1992, s 152 |
| CGT rebasing at 31 March 1982 | 2 years after the end of the accounting period in which the first relevant disposal is made after 31 March 1988 | TCGA 1992, s 35 |

## 24.16 SHOULD YOU OPERATE VIA A COMPANY?

There is no simple answer to this question. There are both advantages and disadvantages in carrying on business through a limited company rather than operating as an unincorporated business. Some of the considerations arise from commercial rather than tax aspects. Limited liability may be an important consideration, either for the proprietors of the business or in order to attract finance from an outside investor. However, the apparent protection given by limited liability is often illusory since banks or other lending institutions will normally require personal guarantees from directors for any bank loans made to the company.

## 24.16.1 Tax considerations

### Lower rate of tax on profits

Having a company means that a lower rate of tax will apply to retained profits. The small companies rate of 20% applies to profits up to £300,000 provided there are no associated companies. If there are associated companies, the threshold at which profits attract tax at either the normal 30% rate or the marginal small companies rate will be reduced. If there are no associated companies, the small companies rate can produce a very substantial saving.

### Example – Tax saving through incorporation

|  | £ |
|---|---|
| Profits of an unincorporated business | 400,000 |
| Tax and NICs (assuming single personal allowance) | 154,696 |
| Profits of a company before director's remuneration | 400,000 |
| *Less*: director's remuneration and NICs (say) | (150,000) |
|  | 250,000 |
| Corporation tax at 20% | 50,000 |
| Tax and NICs on director's remuneration | 64,840 |
| Total tax and NICs on profits of £400,000 | 114,840 |
| Saving in tax through operating via a company | 39,856 |

## 24.16.2 Other tax considerations

### Timing difference

There is a useful timing difference where a business is carried on through a company in that remuneration can be deducted from the profits of the company even though it is not paid (and is not taxable income of the individuals until it is paid). Provided that the remuneration is actually paid within nine months of the company's year end, the company is normally entitled to a deduction in arriving at its profits.

### Example – Timing of tax payments

If a company draws up accounts to 31 March 2001, it may secure a deduction for director's remuneration of £150,000 even though the remuneration is not paid until 31 December 2001 in which case PAYE tax does not have to be paid over until 14 January 2002. Contrast this with an unincorporated business where tax needs to be paid on account on 31 January 2001 and on 31 July 2001, with a balancing payment on the following 31 January.

### Pension contributions

Another aspect which favours having a company is that it is generally possible for a company to fund pensions for directors at a greater rate than the legislation permits them to make personal pension contributions.

### Payment of remuneration may prevent personal allowances going to waste

Where an unincorporated business operates at a loss, and the individuals have no other private income, the benefit of their personal allowances is lost forever. By trading through a company, it is possible to vote remuneration equal to the individuals' personal allowances and the remuneration voted in this way will increase the amount of the company's loss which can be carried forward and set against subsequent profits.

## 24.14.3 Possible disadvantages

Possible disadvantages of operating through a company include the following:

### Extra administration

There are more statutory requirements concerning the keeping of books, filing of annual accounts, disclosure etc. An unincorporated business does not normally need to file annual accounts at all, whereas a company must file accounts with Companies House, and make an annual return.

### IR35 Regulations

Some companies may fall foul of the new regulations on personal service companies (see 19.3).

### Admitting future partners

If profits are retained, this may make it increasingly difficult for individuals who come up through the business to become shareholder directors.

For example, if a company has 100 £1 shares in issue and the company retains profits after tax of £15,000 per annum for ten years, each share will be worth £1,500 more at the end of the ten years than at the start of the period. In order for an individual to acquire a 10% shareholding, he must find sufficient finance to purchase shares which reflect this. The problem does not arise in the case of a partnership, since the normal procedure is to allocate past profits to partners' capital accounts and then admit a new partner on the basis that he would share in future profits at a specified percentage.

## Tax savings may only be a deferment

The traditional analysis has been that tax will generally become payable by the shareholders on their share of retained profits, either when the shareholders sell their shares and realise a capital gain, or as and when they extract retained profits by taking a dividend. On this analysis, the saving of tax on retained profits is often little more than a deferment of tax. However, there can be a true saving following the changes in the taxation of capital gains which will mean that up to 75% of any gain can be received tax free because of taper relief. The traditional analysis is therefore no longer valid since shareholder directors are generally able to enjoy the full value of the shares on the sale or liquidation of the company.

## Increased liability for NICs

A company is required to pay Class 1 NICs on all amounts paid as remuneration. There is no ceiling such as applies to the employees' own contributions. This can give rise to a substantially increased burden for a company as compared with an unincorporated business. Comparing an unincorporated business owned by four equal partners with a company which has four 25% shareholders (and it is assumed that in both cases the individuals will have income of £75,000 each), the national insurance bill for 2000-01 is as follows:

| | Partnership £ | | Company £ |
|---|---|---|---|
| Class 2 | 416.00 | employees' Class 1 | 9,552.00 |
| Class 4 | 6,561.80 | employer's Class 1 | 34,460.12 |
| | 6,977.80 | | 44,012.12 |

While the benefits payable to employees are better than those received by the self-employed (a larger pension because of SERPS and entitlement to unemployment benefit) the higher NIC costs can be a very expensive way of financing such benefits.

## Work in progress

In principle, a professional firm should not include partner time in arriving at the cost of work in progress. This means that the figure brought into account should be lower because of this. However, if a business is carried on by a company, time put in by a director should be included when valuing work in progress.

## Treatment of wives' earnings

If a wife is a partner in an unincorporated business, it is most rare for the Revenue to dispute the level of profits allocated to her. In this regard, unincorporated businesses are treated more favourably than companies where the Revenue regularly argues that a wife's remuneration is excessive and part of the remuneration should be disallowed in computing profits.

## Potential double charge for capital gains

Where a valuable asset is held within a company, a tax liability may arise at two stages before the shareholders can enjoy the sale proceeds. For example, if a company acquired a property at a cost of £100,000, and five years later it is worth £550,000, there might be a gain for the company (after indexation) of £400,000. The company will pay tax on this capital gain either at the marginal small companies rate or at 30%. If a tax charge at 30% is assumed, the company will have net funds available after paying tax of £330,000 ie

|  | £ |
|---|---|
| Profits for accounting purposes | 450,000 |
| *Less*: tax on gain (£400,000 at 30%) | 120,000 |
|  | 330,000 |

If the company is then wound up, and the cash distributed to the shareholders, they are likely to have a personal CGT liability on the £330,000. If retirement relief is not available, the CGT payable by them could be £132,000 (ie £330,000 at 40%). This figure assumes that other assets and retained profits within the company are such that there would have been capital gains for the shareholders in any event, even if the company had not held the property concerned.

However, once again, the traditional analysis is open to question. If the company had paid a dividend to transmit the £330,000 cash to shareholders, their personal liability could not exceed £82,250. Furthermore, taper relief is likely to mean that capital gains tax is paid at less than 40%. Consequently, while it is not generally good policy to have appreciating assets within a company, the extent of the extra tax payable is not as great as it was in the past. While some additional tax is likely to be payable if an appreciating asset is held within a company, this is not an argument in itself against a business operating through a company. Correctly analysed, the treatment of capital gains within a company is an argument in favour of shareholder/directors holding such assets in their personal capacity rather than through a company.

### 24.14.4 Conclusion

The question of whether an individual should operate via a company is a complex question which needs professional advice.

# 25

# OUTLINE OF VAT

RICHARD HEAP

Value added tax was introduced by FA 1972 and became operational on 1 April 1973 when it replaced purchase tax and selective employment tax. In concept, it is a simple tax, although various exclusions from a VAT charge and the European influence have resulted in a simple concept becoming one of the most complicated taxes of all time.

This chapter covers some of the detail of VAT under the following headings:

(1) Introduction.
(2) Legal authorities.
(3) Liability to VAT.
(4) Practical implications.
(5) Anti-avoidance measures.
(6) Special schemes.
(7) Control and enforcement procedures.
(8) Fraud.
(9) Appeals.

## 25.1 INTRODUCTION

The introduction of VAT was a pre-condition of the acceptance of the UK into what was then known as the European Economic Community (EEC) which, as a result of the European Communities Act 1982, became the European Community (EC) and is now commonly referred to as the European Union (EU). Part of the EU philosophy is the harmonisation of taxing statutes, particularly those that affect cross-border trading activities. For example, customs duty is an EU tax and is payable when goods enter the EU and is charged at the same rate when or wherever the goods enter the Community.

Once customs duty is paid the goods are in free circulation and can move freely between member states without the payment of any further duty or being subject to Customs' controls. The legislative authority for customs duty is to be found in EC Regulations which, once agreed by the EC Commission, have immediate direct effect in each member state.

The harmonisation of VAT has been the subject of much discussion by the EC Commission in the recent past. This has resulted in the introduction of transitional rules with effect from 1 January 1993 and commonly referred to as The Single Market Legislation. These implement a degree of harmonisation on the VAT accounting requirements of the movement of goods between member states. The EC Commission has proposed a staged work programme to introduce complete harmonisation for EC VAT. The Commission has agreed that the system will not take effect until two years after the measures have been adopted by the European Council. The present transitional system will therefore remain until at least 2001.

The ultimate legal authority for VAT is a number of EC VAT directives, which must be reflected in the national legislation of each member state. To that extent, directives have direct effect. For example, if the national law is not in accordance with a directive and thereby disadvantages the taxpayer, it is possible for the taxpayer to argue his case, using the directive, in the national court, which must recognise the directive and with the ultimate right of an appeal to the European Court of Justice.

The administration of VAT was given to HM Customs and Excise, which introduced a completely new system of tax enforcement to the majority of businesses and the accounting profession. Customs, which is steeped in the history of duty enforcement, brought with it its practical approach to controlling the taxpayer. For the first time, many businesses and their professional advisers had to justify, face to face with the enforcement agencies (the VAT control officer), what had been declared in the VAT return and the amounts shown in the annual accounts.

In principle, for the majority of businesses VAT is *not* a tax on profits. It is a tax on the consumer that is collected in stages throughout the business chain and is collected, eventually, by the business person supplying the consumer, whether that be an individual or a business which is not registered for VAT. If a business fails to charge and account for VAT correctly, it will have to account for both the VAT and any penalties from its own resources and thereby, by default, VAT becomes a charge on profits. Put simply, the business person is a tax collector.

## 25.2 LEGAL AUTHORITIES

There is no single piece of legislation covering the administration and collection of VAT. The VAT legislation is described briefly below.

### 25.2.1 The VAT Act 1994 (VATA 1994)

This is a consolidation Act which brought together the VATA 1983 and subsequent Finance Acts amending the original legislation. VATA 1994 deals with the administration of the tax and provides for certain aspects to be dealt with by delegated legislation.

## 25.2.2 VAT (General) Regulations 1995

This consolidates 60 sets of existing regulations and amendments introduced since 1972. It deals with a wide range of administrative procedures which must be complied with, eg the detail to be shown on tax invoices, the method of recovering VAT when a VAT registered person is not entitled to a full recovery of VAT paid to its suppliers, and special VAT accounting procedures for particular transactions.

## 25.2.3 Treasury orders

Certain Treasury orders describe amongst other things what is or is not chargeable to VAT and also give legal authority to certain organisations being able to recover VAT which would otherwise not be recoverable. Occasionally, Treasury orders are published only in the *London Gazette*.

## 25.2.4 Customs notices and leaflets

The general principle is that VAT public notices are not part of the law. Certain notices, however, are published pursuant to VATA 1994 and VAT Regulations 1995 and, thereby, *are* part of the law. As such they have the same status as an Act of Parliament and are legally binding upon the taxpayer. For example, Notice 700 (General Guide) is principally Customs' interpretation of the law, but the section that deals with the maintenance of accounting records *is* part of the law as is the Public Notice on the special VAT Retail Schemes (Notice 727).

Customs' leaflets are not strictly part of the law but certain leaflets which explain the Commissioners' requirements for particular types of transactions are, in practical terms, legally binding. This applies to relatively few of the leaflets, the vast majority being simply the Commissioners' interpretation of the law.

## 25.2.5 EC directives

All VAT law has its roots in the EC Sixth VAT Directive which has direct effect in the UK and other EU countries through their respective national laws. There are a number of other EC directives that deal with specific aspects such as that which, on 1 January 1993, introduced VAT harmonisation in the Single Market and others which provide the right to recover VAT incurred in other countries.

## 25.3 LIABILITY TO VAT

The basic rule is that VAT is chargeable on the supply of any goods or services (for a consideration) in the UK when supplied 'in the course or furtherance of any business'. Supplies made outside the UK are outside the scope of UK VAT. There are complex rules for determining the place of supply. The rules are different depending on whether the supply concerned is one of goods or services, and it is recommended professional advice be obtained if unsure as to the place of supply of a transaction.

### 25.3.1 Business
(VATA 1994, s 94)

Business has not been defined but has been interpreted to have a very wide meaning and covers all organisations that carry on an activity in a businesslike way. This has resulted in a number of organisations which do not consider themselves to be carrying on a business (such as clubs and associations, charities etc) having to conform with the VAT legislation and, where appropriate, register and account for VAT on their business income. If it can be demonstrated that the activity is purely and simply a hobby, there is no requirement to charge VAT on any resulting income. An employee's services to an employer in return for a salary meets the definition of a supply of services but the law specifically provides that such services are not in the course or furtherance of a business and, therefore, are outside the scope of VAT.

### Charities

There is no automatic relief from VAT for supplies either to or made by charities. If a charity is carrying on a business activity it is required to register and account for VAT on its business income the same as any commercial organisation.

There is relief from VAT by means of zero-rating for certain supplies to charities, but these are mainly in the health and welfare area and new commercial property which would otherwise be subject to a VAT charge and which is used wholly for charitable non-business activities, known as 'qualifying buildings'. If a qualifying building is to be used for both non-business and business use the purchase price will be apportioned between the standard and zero-rated elements.

Zero rating has been extended in FA 2000 to include supplies of advertising when made to charities and all costs incurred in producing the advertising material when supplied with advertising.

## Clubs and associations
(VATA 1994, s 94(2)(a))

Many local clubs and associations, including those formed by local residents, consider they are not carrying on a business, but this is not correct. The law specifically provides that the admission to premises for a consideration and the provision of benefits to members in return for a subscription or other payment is a business activity.

Certain trade and professional organisations either consider they are not in business, or qualify for exemption as professional associations, and consequently have no requirement to register for VAT. Such organisations generally provide other benefits to their members and, possibly, non-members which are not within the exemption and, therefore, there may be a liability to register for VAT.

## Admission to premises
(VATA 1994, s 94(2)(b))

The admission of persons to any premises in return for a payment is a business activity. Any person carrying on such an activity will be required to register and account for VAT if the income exceeds the registration threshold. To avoid the risk of penalties all clubs, associations and similar organisations should review their activities to ensure that they meet their VAT obligations at the correct time.

## 25.3.2 Supplies

The application of VAT differs depending upon whether there is a supply of goods or a supply of services.

A supply of goods is where legal title to the goods is, or is to be, transferred to another person. This includes, for example, the transfer of title in land by means of a freehold sale or a lease exceeding 21 years.

Anything which is not a supply of goods that is done for a consideration is a supply of services and, therefore, subject to the VAT regime. A VAT charge will only arise where consideration is present and, accordingly, a free supply of services is outside the scope of VAT. Care is required, because what may appear to be free is not necessarily so in real terms and a hidden VAT liability could arise.

With effect from 1 January 1996, processing work carried out on goods is treated as a supply of services. Prior to the aforementioned date processing work was treated as a supply of goods in the UK. The change is due to the adoption by all member states of the EC Second Simplification Directive.

It has been agreed that zero rating (see below) will still apply to such processing services carried out on goods which are themselves zero-rated.

## Zero-rated supplies

The zero-rated supplies are exports of goods to places outside the EU (VATA 1994, s 30) and those listed in VATA 1994, Sched 8. There are 16 groups in Sched 8:

(1) Food for human consumption
(2) Sewerage services and water (this does not include bottled water)
(3) Books and newspapers etc
(4) Talking books and wireless sets for the blind
(5) Construction and sales of new dwellings
(6) Approved alteration of listed residential buildings and listed buildings used by charities for non-business purposes
(7) International services (the services qualifying under this heading were greatly reduced on 1 January 1993)
(8) Transport
(9) Caravans and houseboats
(10) Gold
(11) Bank notes
(12) Drugs, medicines, aids for the handicapped etc
(13) Imports, exports etc
(14) Tax-free shops
(15) Charities (certain supplies to or by charities)
(16) Clothing and footwear (childrens and protective)

The VAT liability of supplies can fall into three main headings.

## Taxable

These are supplies that are subject to VAT at either the zero (see above) or the standard (currently 17.5%) rate. Supplies of fuel and power are taxable at 5% when supplied for domestic use or for use by a charity otherwise than in the course or furtherance of a business.

## Exempt

These are supplies that are exempt from VAT by statute, ie those that are listed in VATA 1994, Sched 9 (see 25.4.4). Exemption and zero-rating must not be confused because the overall effect on a business is totally different. As will be seen later, zero-rating gives entitlement to recover VAT on underlying costs whereas exemption does not.

## 'Outside the scope'

Certain supplies or business activities are 'outside the scope' of VAT. This includes an employee's services to an employer but can also include what, on the face of it, are normal trading activities of the organisation. For example, the supply of goods that are situated outside the UK, although part of the UK business activities, are outside the scope of UK VAT. Similarly, with effect from 1 January 1993, certain services that are either physically performed or are to be received outside the UK are deemed to have been supplied outside the UK and, therefore, outside the scope of UK VAT.

Generally speaking, 'outside the scope' activities of an organisation do not permit the recovery of VAT on related costs. The exception to this general principle is where a VAT-registered person supplies goods or services outside the UK that would be subject to VAT if supplied in the UK.

### 25.3.4 Imports

VAT is normally charged on the importation of goods into the UK from outside the EC. VAT is normally paid at the time of importation, but can be deferred, provided approval for deferment is obtained. The VAT payable can be recovered as unpaid tax, subject to the normal rules.

### 25.3.5 European Community

The terms 'imports' and 'exports' have been replaced by 'acquisitions' and 'supplies' respectively for transactions with other EC member states. It is not necessary to make an import declaration on an acquisition of goods from a supplier in another EC country.

Subject to certain conditions (eg showing the Customs VAT number on each invoice), supplies to a customer registered for VAT in another EC country can be zero rated. VAT is chargeable if the conditions cannot be met, and on supplies to non-registered customers.

### 25.3.6 Commercial property

The sale of the freehold of a new commercial property (ie a property that is less than three years old) is subject to VAT at the standard rate. The grant of the freehold of old commercial property or the grant of a leasehold interest is exempt from VAT, but the landlord has the right to elect to waive the exemption and charge VAT on rental payments, commonly known as the option to tax. The major advantage of making an election is that a landlord can recover VAT on costs relating to an elected property. The tenant can of course recover VAT charged on rent provided he or she is using the property for taxable purposes.

With effect from 17 March 1998 the option is not available for certain supplies where, at the time of the grant of the interest, there is an intention or expectation that the land will become 'exempt land'. In broad terms, exempt land is land or buildings used wholly or mainly for non-VATable purposes.

# 25.4 PRACTICAL IMPLICATIONS

The administration of VAT is by a system of VAT registration, the submission of regular VAT returns and control verification visits (now known as assurance visits) by Customs.

## 25.4.1 VAT registration

Registration is required where a business or any other organisation makes taxable supplies over a pre-determined limit. The limits, which are based on gross turnover, are increased each year, generally in line with inflation.

It is the person who is registered, not the business activity. Once registered, all business activities must be reflected in the VAT accounting records; for example a solicitor VAT-registered as a sole proprietor must also include his farming or writing income in his VAT accounts.

Currently registration is required when one of the following two conditions is satisfied:

(1) When, at the end of any month, the gross taxable turnover during the previous 12 months, on a rolling basis, exceeds £52,000 with effect from 1 April 2000 (previously £51,000). Such a liability must be notified within 30 days and registration is effective from the first of the month following the month in which a liability to notify arose.

For example, where taxable turnover in the 12 months to 31 January 2000 is, say, £53,000, notification must be made within 30 days and registration is effective from 1 March.

There is no VAT liability for income received prior to the effective date of registration.

(2) As soon as there are reasonable grounds to believe the value of taxable supplies to be made during the following 30 days will exceed £52,000. Registration is due immediately.

Before March 1990, different rules applied and a liability to register was then based, in general, on either a historic quarterly or annual turnover limit. These rules still apply when determining whether or not there is a past liability to register for VAT prior to the aforementioned date.

It is only *taxable* turnover (ie goods or services liable to VAT at either the zero or standard rate) that is taken into consideration when determining whether or not there is a liability to register for VAT. Income which is exempt or outside the scope of VAT is ignored.

### Voluntary registration

There is an entitlement to register voluntarily for VAT even if the taxable turnover is below the VAT registration limits. This could be an advantage to an expanding or small business as VAT on costs would be recoverable and this, providing the charging of VAT on supplies does not reduce demand for the product, would increase profitability. Similarly businesses based in the UK which do not make any supplies there but make what would be taxable supplies overseas are entitled to register and are thereby able to recover VAT on UK costs.

## VAT groups

Incorporated companies under common control may register for VAT as a single unit – a VAT group. All supplies between the companies in the VAT group are disregarded for VAT purposes, ie no VAT or other consequence arises. One company is nominated as the representative member and is responsible for submitting the VAT returns and accounting for VAT on all supplies to or received from persons outside the VAT group. However, there is a joint and several liability on all companies within a VAT group for any VAT due to Customs.

## 25.4.2 VAT returns

Once a business is registered, VAT returns have to be submitted on a regular basis. Each VAT registered person is allocated a three-monthly VAT accounting period, but it is possible to request a particular VAT period (for example to coincide with the business's financial year). It is also possible to request monthly returns if the business will be regularly recovering VAT from Customs and Excise.

VAT returns must be submitted with full payment by the end of the month following the end of the VAT accounting period. A failure to submit returns and make full payment by the due date is subject to penalties (see 25.7.2).

The VAT chargeable on supplies made during the period (known as output tax) must be declared on the VAT return (VAT 100) which is provided automatically each period by Customs. Output VAT is due on all tax invoices issued during the period, irrespective of whether or not the invoices have been paid. There are special schemes available to ease this particular requirement for certain classes of business as explained in 25.6. In addition, VAT is also due on all monies received for supplies made during the period and for which a tax invoice has not been issued, eg scrap sales, vending machine income, emptying telephone boxes, staff canteen sales, certain deductions from salaries for supplies to staff, etc.

For businesses which do not issue tax invoices, such as retailers, VAT is due on the gross taxable income received during the VAT period.

With effect from 1 January 1993, VAT on the value of goods which have been both supplied by other EU VAT registered persons and have been received from another EU country must be declared as output tax in Box 2 of the VAT return.

## Payments on account

With effect from 1 October 1992, those businesses which normally pay more than £2m annually to Customs are required to make monthly payments on account with a balancing payment when the three-monthly VAT return is submitted.

The monthly payments of businesses required to make payments on account are $\frac{1}{24}$ (before 1 June 1996, $\frac{1}{12}$) of their annual VAT liability. Businesses have the option of paying their actual monthly VAT liability instead of the set amount. It is compulsory for businesses to pay their VAT liability by electronic means. Unfortunately payments on account are subject to the default surcharge (25.7.2) and the seven-day period of grace given to taxpayers who pay their VAT liability by electronic means does not extend to businesses which have to pay on account.

## 25.4.3 VAT recovery

VAT registered businesses may off-set any VAT paid to suppliers (known as input tax) against the output tax declared, subject to the following conditions:

(1) Goods/services have been *supplied to* and have been, or will be, used by the business to make taxable supplies.
(2) Documentary evidence of the supply received, ie a tax invoice to the business by the supplier, is obtained and retained. If there is no tax invoice or other documentary evidence, the VAT officer will refuse claims for input tax.

However, Customs has discretion and may accept alternative evidence of VAT paid.

Supplies of zero-rated goods or services are taxable supplies with an entitlement to recover VAT on related costs whereas there is no such entitlement in respect of exempt supplies.

With effect from 1 August 1995, VAT is recoverable on the purchase of a motor car used wholly for business purposes, including leasing. 'Wholly for business purposes' is being interpreted very strictly, and in practice most businesses will still be unable to recover the VAT on the purchase of a car. Prior to 1 August 1995, subject to certain exceptions, VAT on the purchase of a motor car was non-recoverable as input tax (VAT (Car) Order 1992 (SI No 3122) and VAT (Input Tax) Order 1992 (SI No 3222)). A new SI will be introduced in 2000 to allow for the treatment of all items on which input tax deduction was blocked to be treated as exempt from VAT. This follows an ECJ decision against the Italian Government in favour of an appeal made by a taxpayer.

VAT is not recoverable on business entertainment expenses. In addition VAT on goods or services received by the VAT registered person which are

ALLIED DUNBAR TAX HANDBOOK

used for a non-business activity, transactions outside the scope of VAT or private use is not recoverable as input tax. Many people believe that merely because a VAT registered person pays an invoice, there is an automatic entitlement to recover the VAT shown on the invoice. This belief is not correct and to do so may give rise to penalties.

The recovery of VAT by businesses which make both taxable and exempt supplies is described in 25.4.4.

### Bad debt relief

A claim for bad debt relief may be made for any debt that is more than six months old whether or not the debtor has gone into formal bankruptcy, liquidation or winding-up. Prior to 1 April 1989 there had to be a formal insolvency before VAT bad debt relief was available and these rules still apply to any supplies made before that date.

Where a claim for bad debt relief relates to a supply made after 26 November 1996, the debtor will have to repay to Customs VAT previously reclaimed as input tax. The claimant has to notify VAT-registered debtors of his claim within seven days of making the claim. With effect from 17 December 1996, the time when bad debt relief can be claimed is six months from the time payment is due. Prior to the aforementioned date the timescale is six months from the date of supply, normally invoice date.

Once a debt is six months old and providing the VAT has previously been accounted for to Customs the debt may be written off by being entered in a Refund for Bad Debt Account (ie not written off in the accounting sense, as for corporation tax). The VAT is recovered by including the sum in the input tax recovery box of the VAT return (Box 4). Any payment received after the claim has been made is VAT inclusive and the VAT element must be repaid to Customs. VAT bad debt relief is not available for businesses which use either a retail or the cash accounting scheme; such relief is built into the scheme.

### 25.4.4 Three-year cap

On 18 July 1996, the Treasury announced that, with immediate effect, claims for refund of overpaid VAT will be limited to a period of three years. Following a consultation process, the measures were introduced in the 1996 Budget. One welcome change from the original announcement is that Customs' power to issue assessments for underdeclared VAT will also be limited to the three-year period. However, the 20-year limit remains in cases of fraud.

### 25.4.5 Partial exemption

A business that makes both exempt and taxable supplies is known as partially exempt and will generally be unable to recover all VAT paid to its suppliers. However, if the VAT on costs relating, directly and indirectly, to the exempt activities (known as exempt input tax) is below prescribed limits (known as *de minimis* limits), all the VAT is recoverable in full. The current limits are that the exempt input tax must not exceed £625 per month on average, and 50% of the total input tax incurred. This entitles a business to incur approximately £42,800 of costs, each year which relates to its exempt activities without having to restrict its recovery of input tax provided the 50% qualification is not breached. Once the exempt input tax limit is exceeded in any VAT year (the VAT year ends March, April or May depending upon the business's VAT return period), *all* the relevant VAT is irrecoverable ie the £625 per month is not an automatic entitlement.

The limits described above apply to VAT years commencing on or after 1 December 1994. In earlier years the *de minimis* rule was that exempt input tax must not exceed £600 per month on average in the VAT year, and there was no qualifying percentage.

Note that prior to 1 April 1992, the *de minimis* rules were more complex involving both monetary and percentage limits.

There are other minor limits that apply in particular circumstances. The rules are complex and it is advisable to obtain professional advice. Full details may be found in the VAT Regulations 1995 (SI No 2518), regs 99–109 and Customs VAT Notice 706.

Goods and services which are exempt from VAT are listed in VATA 1994, Sched 9. The main headings are:

(1) Land (with a number of exceptions, and see 25.3.2)
(2) Insurance
(3) Postal services
(4) Betting, gaming and lotteries
(5) Finance
(6) Education (when provided by eligible bodies). This heading also includes supplies by youth clubs
(7) Health and welfare
(8) Burial and cremation
(9) Trade unions and professional bodies
(10) Sports competitions, sport and physical education
(11) Works of art etc (in limited circumstances)
(12) Fundraising events by charities and other qualifying bodies
(13) Cultural services.

As the headings are a general description and the rules for exemption are extremely complicated, it is advisable to take professional advice before exempting a particular transaction.

## 25.5 ANTI-AVOIDANCE MEASURES

There are a number of anti-avoidance measures available to Customs. These include the following.

### 25.5.1 Business splitting

Where a business activity has been divided amongst a number of legal entities (eg a series of partnerships with a partner common to all) and the reason for such a division is to avoid having to account for VAT, Customs may issue a direction informing all the businesses that they are registered as a single unit and that VAT must be accounted for on all taxable income. The direction can only be from a current or future date.

With effect from 19 March 1997, Customs no longer has to demonstrate that the reason for dividing a business is the avoidance of VAT registration. Customs can treat connected businesses as one for VAT purposes, whether or not there is genuine commercial reason for the division.

### 25.5.2 Sales to connected parties

Where a VAT registered business supplies goods or services at below market value to a connected party which is not entitled to a full recovery of input tax, Customs may direct, during the three years following the supply, that the open market value is used.

### 25.5.3 Self supplies etc

In certain circumstances, an output VAT charge will arise on normal business activities which are not supplies made to third parties ie a VAT charge arises on business expenditure (usually referred to as 'self supplies'). The value of such self supplies is taken into consideration when determining a liability to register for VAT; the more important ones are described below. The reasons behind such a liability are both anti-avoidance and to reduce possible trade distortion.

#### Stationery

If an exempt, or partially exempt, business prints its own stationery there is an output VAT liability on the total printing cost (including all overheads). If the in-house printing costs of an otherwise exempt business exceed the VAT registration threshold there is a liability to register and account for VAT on such costs.

#### Reverse charges

Certain professional and intellectual services purchased from overseas persons give rise to an output tax liability on the recipient. The services are deemed to be both supplied by and received by the UK organisation ie there is an output tax liability and the VAT may also be recovered under the normal rules (restricted if partially exempt). The services include royalty and/or licence payments; financial, insurance advertising, legal, accountancy and consultancy services; and the hire of staff or equipment.

### 25.5.4 Transfer of a business

Where the assets of a business are transferred to another person who intends to use them to carry on the same kind of business as the vendor, the transaction is not subject to a VAT charge. However, where a VAT group which is partially exempt (ie not entitled to a full recovery of input tax) acquires assets in these circumstances, there is a deemed taxable supply by the VAT group and output tax must be accounted for on the VAT group's return. The corresponding input tax will be restricted by whatever method has been agreed with the local VAT office.

### 25.5.5 Group registration

Customs has been given new powers for the treatment of VAT group registrations. They can direct, in exceptional circumstances, that VAT is charged on intra group supplies, which are normally disregarded for VAT purposes. In addition, Customs can treat an associated company as part of a VAT group retrospectively from a particular date or remove a member of a VAT group from that group with effect from a particular date.

The new powers are used only where to group structure will result in a loss to the Revenue; they are designed to have an effect only in cases involving VAT avoidance. Customs consulted with professional bodies and issued a statement of practice in May 1996 which gives examples of proposed structures where the new powers will be used.

More widespread powers are to be granted to Customs. They will be able to remove from a VAT group companies which are no longer eligible and companies presenting a revenue risk. This is in addition to the powers granted in May 1996 which apply in specific circumstances.

Overseas companies, which subject to certain conditions had been eligible to be included in VAT groups, will no longer qualify unless they have a branch or substantial establishment in the UK.

### 25.5.6 Election to tax commercial property

The election, or option, to tax the grant of freehold or leasehold interests in commercial property is no longer available in certain circumstances if the purchaser or tenant does not use the property wholly or mainly for taxable purposes. The Customs' view is that 'wholly or mainly' means more than 80%.

The change, which was announced in the 1996 Budget, does not apply to leases granted prior to 26 November 1996 and took effect from 19 March

1997. The changes are beyond the scope of this book; those entering into property transactions should seek professional advice.

Landlords and vendors of commercial property must enquire about a tenant's or purchaser's legal relationship with the vendor, the financing arrangements and likely use of the property as, if the election is disapplied, this may effect the landlord's or vendor's right to recover VAT on related costs. Indemnity clauses may therefore need to be inserted into leases and agreements.

## 25.6 SPECIAL SCHEMES

There are a number of special schemes which are either designed to simplify accounting for VAT or reduce the VAT liability.

### 25.6.1 Retail schemes

These are special schemes for use by retailers, ie businesses which sell, hire or repair goods direct to the general public rather than to other VAT-registered businesses and which are in trade classification Groups 24 (Retail Division) and 28 (Miscellaneous Services). Generally it is those who deal direct with the public on a cash basis and who do not normally issue tax invoices.

However it was announced in the 1996 Budget that the future use of retail schemes will be restricted. Taxpayers are only be allowed to use a retail scheme when normal VAT accounting is not possible. The measures are being implemented on an individual basis as part of Customs' normal VAT assurance visit programme.

As retailers normally account for VAT on the receipt of payment, retail schemes provide automatic bad debt relief. However, with effect from 1 March 1997, retailers have to account for VAT on all credit sales at the time of sale.

### 25.6.2 Secondhand schemes

Prior to 1 January 1995 there were a number of special secondhand schemes which provided for VAT to be charged on the profit, if any, as opposed to the full selling price. Schemes were available for:

(1) Cars
(2) Motor cycles
(3) Caravans/motor caravans
(4) Works of art, antiques and collector's items
(5) Boats and outboard motors
(6) Electronic organs
(7) Aircraft
(8) Firearms
(9) Horses and ponies.

Special stock recording and records are required.

The scheme was extended by FA 1995 to cover all secondhand goods, works of art, antiques and collectors' items except precious metals and gemstones.

It has been recognised that dealers in low value, high volume goods will have difficulty maintaining the detailed records required. A simplified method of accounts for VAT has been introduced, known as 'Global Accounting'. Under the system 'eligible businesses' are able to account for VAT on the difference between total purchases and sales in each tax period rather than on individual items.

### 25.6.3 Cash accounting

The general principle is that VAT must be accounted for on all tax invoices issued whether or not the customer/client has paid for the supply. Businesses that cannot use a retail scheme, and whose turnover is less than £350,000 (excluding VAT) annually, may use the cash accounting scheme, provided certain conditions are satisfied. The conditions are laid down in regulations as described in C&E Notice 731, which in this respect has the force of law. Output VAT is not due until payment has been received but, similarly, input tax on purchases/expenses cannot be recovered until the supplier has been paid and a receipt obtained.

### 25.6.4 Annual accounting

To avoid having to submit returns quarterly, businesses with an annual turnover not exceeding £300,000 (excluding VAT) may be authorised, in writing, by Customs to use the annual accounting scheme. Nine payments, based on the previous year's VAT liability, are made by direct debit and a final, balancing payment is made with the VAT return at the end of the second month following the allocated VAT year.

Businesses with a turnover below £100,000 can make quarterly interim payments of 20% of the previous year's net VAT liability. Where the net tax liability is below £2,000 businesses can choose whether to make interim payments.

### 25.6.5 Tour operators' margin scheme

This scheme must be used by any VAT registered business which supplies packaged travel/accommodation services. As the name implies, VAT is accountable on the margin, if any, on the taxable element of the package. Special record keeping and an annual calculation are required.

### 25.6.6 Agricultural flat rate scheme

This is a special scheme, introduced on 1 January 1993, under which farmers, and other agricultural businesses need not register and submit VAT returns in order to recover VAT on overhead expenses, etc. Instead, the farmer charges VAT at a nominal 4% on all his supplies which he retains (in lieu of input tax) and the recipient is entitled to recover as input tax under the normal rules. The scheme requires authorisation by Customs and is not applicable to all farmers. Farmers who would benefit by more than £3,000 compared to being VAT registered are not entitled to join the scheme.

## 25.7 CONTROL AND ENFORCEMENT PROCEDURES

### 25.7.1 VAT visits

Customs officers regularly visit VAT registered businesses to verify the returns submitted. Their powers are extensive and include the right to see any documents, accounts etc relating to the business activities and the right to inspect (but not search) the business premises. The frequency of visit depends upon a number of factors such as the size of the business, types of business activity and compliance history. Visits can range from half a day every few years for the smaller business to several weeks a year for the multi-nationals.

Where errors are discovered, the visiting officer will raise an assessment for any VAT previously under-declared and, where appropriate, impose penalty and interest charges (see 25.7.2). It is advisable, therefore, to have all assessments independently reviewed. Customs collect over £1,000m by the way of additional assessments from approximately 450,000 visits each year but most visits do not result in assessments being issued. If the accounting records have been well kept and have been independently reviewed regularly no problem should arise at the visit.

### 25.7.2 Penalties

There are a number of penalty provisions which Customs may impose automatically, and arbitrarily, for a failure to comply with the many complex VAT regulations. These were introduced with the view to improving compliance and reducing the amount of VAT outstanding at any one time.

#### Late registration
(VATA 1994, s 67(1))

Failure to notify and register at the correct time (see 25.4.1) will result in Customs imposing a financial penalty. With effect from 1 January 1995, the penalty is a percentage of between 5% and 15% (depending upon the length of the delay) of the net tax due between the date notification was required and the actual date of notification.

## Late returns
(FA 1994, s 59)

With effect from 1 October 1993, if one payment is submitted late in any period of 12 months, Customs will notify the VAT registered person that payments submitted late during the following 12 months will be subject to a default surcharge. Prior to 1 October 1993, the business would be notified if two returns or payments were submitted late in any 12 months.

If a payment is submitted late during the 12-month surcharge period, a 2% penalty is imposed and the surcharge period extended for a further 12 months. The surcharge rises for each successive late payment to 5% and by increments of 5% to a maximum of 15%. If payments have been submitted by the due dates for 12 months, the business is removed from the default surcharge regime and the cycle starts again.

The surcharge is waived if it is assessable at the lower rate and below a minimum amount of £200.

## Misdeclaration penalty
(FA 1994, s 63)

If a VAT officer discovers an under-declaration which exceeds specified limits, he will assess a serious misdeclaration penalty of 15% of the additional VAT assessed. The penalty, which is based on each individual period (ie it is not accumulative), is imposed where the additional VAT assessed exceeds the lesser of:

(1) £1m; and
(2) 30% of the gross amount of tax due for the appropriate return period.

## Interest
(VATA 1994, s 74)

An interest charge will be imposed on assessments for additional tax issued by VAT visiting officers. The rate of interest is the prescribed rate as enacted by Treasury order and is not deductible for income or corporation tax. However, Customs has stated that interest may not be imposed where there is no overall loss of revenue eg where a supplier has failed to charge VAT to a customer who would have been entitled to recover the VAT charge. Customs has indicated that each case will be decided on its merits, but that officers have been made aware of the need to consider whether or not there has been a loss of revenue.

## Other penalties

There are a number of other penalty provisions such as failure to maintain or produce records, unauthorised issue of a tax invoice (by non-registered persons), persistent incorrect returns etc. There are, in fact, over 60 regulatory offences which could give rise to a penalty.

## 25.8 FRAUD

In VAT law there are two forms of fraud: civil and criminal.

### 25.8.1 Civil
(FA 1994, s 60)

If, after an investigation, Customs is satisfied there has been an element of dishonesty it may seek to impose a civil fraud penalty of 100% of the tax involved. If there has been full co-operation by the taxpayer, Customs, or (on appeal) a VAT tribunal, may reduce the penalty by whatever percentage is considered reasonable.

In a civil fraud investigation, Customs has only to prove on a balance of probabilities that a fraud had been committed in order to impose a penalty.

### 25.8.2 Criminal
(VATA 1994, s 72)

The more serious cases are dealt with under the criminal law with penalties of up to three times the VAT involved, or imprisonment, or both. In these cases Customs must use the criminal rules of evidence etc and prove beyond reasonable doubt that a fraud has been committed deliberately.

## 25.9 APPEALS

### 25.9.1 VAT tribunals

There is a right of an appeal to an independent VAT tribunal on a number of matters including:

(1) Assessments which are considered to be incorrect or not issued to the Commissioners' best judgement.
(2) Liability rulings by Customs in respect of a specified supply.
(3) Penalties, other than the interest charged for errors, if there is a reasonable excuse for the error. The law does not define reasonable excuse but does state that the insufficiency of funds or the reliance on another is *not* a reasonable excuse.
(4) The amount of the reduction, if any, of a penalty for a civil fraud where the taxpayer considers he has provided full co-operation with the investigating officers.

The details of appeal procedures are outside the scope of this book.

However, the procedure for lodging an appeal to a VAT tribunal (which must be made within 30 days of the appealable event) is straightforward. It is prudent, however, to obtain professional advice before doing so and it is advisable to be represented at the tribunal hearing which in many ways resembles a court hearing, although less formal.

A decision of the VAT tribunal may be appealed to a higher court on a point of law and, in limited circumstances, an appeal may be referred to the ECJ for a ruling.

## 25.9.2 Departmental reviews

Many disputes are settled by negotiations with Customs by formally requesting a departmental review of the disputed ruling/assessment within the 30-day time limit. This allows discussions to continue without the loss of the right to appeal to an independent VAT tribunal. The departmental review may become compulsory. Taxpayers will not be able to lodge an appeal to a VAT tribunal until a departmental review has been completed. The Commissioners, if requested, will usually review an assessment after the 30-day limit has expired and will, where appropriate, reduce the amount assessed. In certain circumstances it is also possible to make an application to a VAT tribunal to hear a case that is out of time.

# 26

# STAMP DUTY

Stamp duty is a tax charged on the documents by which certain types of property are transferred to new owners – eg it is charged on the conveyance of a freehold house. It is important to emphasise that stamp duty is not charged on the sale of the house, but on the document by which that house is conveyed to the purchaser.

The relevant document has to be submitted to a Revenue Stamp Office with the appropriate payment. An official stamp is embossed on to the document – to confirm that duty has been paid – and it is then returned to the person presenting it for stamping. Documents are usually submitted by post, but a counter service is available in 11 major cities (Belfast, Birmingham, Bristol, Cardiff, Edinburgh, Leeds, Liverpool, London, Manchester, Newcastle and Nottingham).

This chapter looks at stamp duty under the following headings:

(1) Documents liable to duty.
(2) Sanctions where duty is not paid.
(3) Avoiding or reducing duty.

## 26.1 DOCUMENTS LIABLE TO DUTY

Stamp duty was first introduced in 1694 and the law has not been redrafted since the Stamp Act of 1891. In some cases, stamp duty is charged on the value (ie ad valorem); in other cases the duty is a fixed duty of £5 (50p for documents executed before 1 October 1999).

Numerous amendments have been made over the years (to block loopholes or to grant new reliefs) and the result is legislation which is archaic, exceptionally complex and difficult to follow, and in which the detailed exceptions are more important than the broad general rules. For example, the scheme of the legislation is not to impose duty on documents implementing the sale of certain types of property, but to impose duty on all documents implementing the sale of any type of property and then to provide a series of exceptions.

The practical effect of this legislation is to impose stamp duty on documents implementing the sale of:

(1) shares and other securities;

(2) freehold land and buildings and the grant or assignment of leases;

(3) certain types of business property, such as goodwill and patent rights.

This is not a comprehensive list but it does include all the charges likely to be incurred by an investor or business proprietor. (There is, for example, also a duty on life annuity policy documentation, but this is paid by the assurance company and so is not of direct concern to the annuitant.)

Ad valorem stamp duty is charged only on sales and not (since 1985) on gifts which generally attract duty at a fixed rate of £5. Nor is any duty payable when assets are put into trust. However, a sale is defined to include the exchange of property for shares or securities, or the exchange of one block of shares for another. Similarly, if A gives a property worth £200,000 to his son on condition that the son assumes responsibility for a £150,000 mortgage, this is treated as if the property were sold for £150,000.

Strictly speaking, a document should be stamped before it is executed (signed), though in practice the rule is that it must be presented for stamping within 30 days of execution. Late stamping attracts a substantial financial penalty (see 26.2).

### 26.1.1 Sale of shares or other securities

Stamp duty is charged on documents transferring ownership of shares (in both quoted and private companies), debentures, unit trust units and other securities. The rate of duty is one half of 1%, rounded up to the next 50p (eg the duty on a sale for £325 would be £2). British Government stocks ('gilts') and stocks issued by certain international bodies (such as the EU) are exempt from duty.

The stamp duty is borne by the purchaser and is shown as a disbursement on the broker's contract note. It counts as part of the cost of the holding for CGT purposes.

Where one block of shares is exchanged for another, the transaction is treated as two sales, so both participants must pay the usual duty.

In certain circumstances it is possible for shares to be sold without a stampable document being created. This most commonly happens where a block of shares, traded on the London Stock Exchange, changes hands several times in the space of a few days. In such circumstances, Stamp Duty Reserve Tax (SDRT) is charged on the transaction. SDRT is equal in amount to the stamp duty that would otherwise have been paid and so, from the investor's point of view, it is immaterial which tax is paid.

In 1990 the Government announced that stamp duty on share transfers (and, indeed, on all transactions other than sales and leases of land) would be abolished once the London Stock Exchange had introduced 'paperless' share dealing under its TAURUS computer project. Unfortunately, in the Spring of 1993, the Stock Exchange announced that, because of technical difficulties, it was obliged to abandon TAURUS. It is still not clear how this will affect the Government's plans to abolish stamp duty on share transfers.

## 26.1.2 Sale of land and buildings

Stamp duty is charged on the conveyance of freehold land or buildings, normally at 1% of the price paid, rounded up to the next whole pound. It is paid by the purchaser. Stamp duty is calculated in exactly the same way whether the property in question is residential or commercial. In both cases, where the sale price does not exceed £60,000, no duty is payable (ie if the sale price is £60,000, no duty is payable; but if the sale price is £60,250, the duty is £603).

Higher rates for more expensive properties were introduced in July 1997, as follows. These rates are not tiered, so a purchaser has to pay the rates indicated on the entire purchase price.

| Price | Rate |
| --- | --- |
| £0–£60,000 | exempt |
| £60,001–£250,000 | 1% |
| £250,001–£500,000 | 1.5% |
| over £500,000 | 2% |

Further increases were announced in the March 1998, 1999 and 2000 Budgets and the current position is as follows:

| Price | Rate |
| --- | --- |
| £0–£60,000 | 0% |
| £60,001–250,000 | 1% |
| £250,001–500,000 | 3% |
| £500,001 or more | 4% |

These rates came into force on 28 March 2000.

### Stamp duty on leases

The stamp duty payable on an assignment of an existing lease is calculated in exactly the same way. It is the capital sum paid for the lease that determines the amount of stamp duty; the amount of rent payable under the lease is irrelevant.

However, when a new lease is granted, stamp duty is charged both on the premium and on the annual rent. The duty on the premium is 1% of the premium paid. The premium will however be exempt if it does not exceed £60,000 and the annual rent does not exceed £600.

The duty on the rent depends on the length of the lease and (subject to minor rounding-up) is:

| Length of lease | Duty (as % of annual rent) |
|---|---|
| Seven years or less | 1[1] |
| Seven years and one day to 35 years | 2 |
| 35 years and one day to 100 years | 12 |
| More than 100 years | 24 |

[1] Nil if the annual rent does not exceed £500. Also, if a dwelling is let furnished for less than a year, no stamp duty is payable if the total rent for the period of letting is less than £500. If it is £500 or more, a fixed duty of £1 applies.

### Example – Stamp duty on a lease

A ten-year lease is granted at a premium of £50,000 and an annual rent of £1,000. Because the rent exceeds £600, the premium is not exempt and the total duty payable is:

| | |
|---|---|
| Duty on premium: 1% of £50,000 | £500 |
| Duty on rent: 2% of £1,000 | £20 |
| Total duty payable | £520 |

Sales and rentals of some commercial property may be subject to VAT. In such cases, stamp duty is charged on the VAT-inclusive sale price, premium and/or rent. Moreover, in certain circumstances the landlord may have the right to add VAT to the rent at a later date: in such a case again the VAT-inclusive figure must be taken.

## 26.1.3 Sale of goodwill and other business assets

Land and buildings may of course be business assets and the rules explained above apply equally to commercial and residential property.

An exemption came into effect from 28 March 2000 for transfers of intellectual property such as patents, trade marks, registered designs, copyrights and licences to exploit such assets.

Other types of property likely to be included in the value of a business for stamp duty purposes include plant and machinery, stock-in-trade and book debts. Depending on the way in which the purchase agreement is drawn up, all these may have to be taken into account in calculating the stamp duty payable on the purchase of a business as a going concern. This is a complex area requiring the advice of a solicitor experienced in business transactions.

Because the stamp duty definition of a sale includes an exchange of property for shares, the incorporation of a sole trader's or partnership business is treated as a sale of that business in exchange for shares in the new company. Stamp duty is charged according to the value of the shares received by the proprietor or the partners which will, effectively, be an amount equal to the value of the business as a going concern.

## 26.2 SANCTIONS WHERE DUTY IS NOT PAID

As a general rule, the Revenue cannot enforce the payment of stamp duty by taking court proceedings (though it can enforce the payment of SDRT). Nevertheless, a number of effective sanctions do exist, which mean that in practice it is usually best to ensure that a stampable document is indeed stamped:

(1) Although the Revenue cannot take civil proceedings to enforce payment of stamp duty, it can prosecute a purchaser or lessee who fails to produce for stamping a conveyance of freehold land, or the grant or transfer of a lease for seven years or more. The maximum fine is £1,000.
(2) HM Land Registry will not accept any document which is not duly stamped and it is very unwise not to register a purchase of land at the Registry.
(3) A transfer of shares or debentures cannot be registered unless the transfer document has been properly stamped. (Any purported registration by the company will simply not be valid in law.)
(4) An unstamped document will not be accepted in any court proceedings. An unstamped document required in court could always be stamped, but there is a penalty where a document is presented for stamping outside the permitted 30-day period, plus interest from the time the document should have been stamped. The penalty for late stamping of documents executed after 30 September 1999 depends on whether the delay exceeds 12 months. If it does not, the penalty is the lessor of £300 or the duty. If the delay exceeds 12 months, the penalty is the greater of £300 or the duty. A lower level of penalties apply in relation to documents executed before 1 October 1999.

## 26.3 AVOIDING OR REDUCING DUTY

### 26.3.1 Sale of shares or other securities

The opportunities to avoid or mitigate duty are circumscribed by the rule that a company may not register a transfer of shares or debentures unless the transfer document has been duly stamped. Beneficial ownership may, of course, be transferred without any change in the registered owner of the shares (as where the shares are registered in the name of a nominee company) and beneficial ownership of shares in certain UK quoted companies, registered in the name of American banks, are traded free of stamp duty in the form of 'American Depositary Receipts' (ADRs). Practical difficulties mean, however, that ADRs are suitable only for institutions such as life assurance companies and pension funds and they are not normally held by private investors.

There is a limited statutory relief for the stamp duty payable on the documentation arising out of certain company reconstructions: this is an area in which proper professional advice is essential.

One widely used scheme for avoiding duty on the sale of a private company was closed by the November 1996 Budget. The scheme involved the company issuing shares in bearer form or issuing bearer share warrants. An issue of such securities has normally attracted 1.5% duty but there has been a specific let-out for bearer shares which were denominated in foreign currency.

With effect from 26 November 1996, the issue of such foreign currency bearer securities attracts 1.5% SDRT. The same charge applies to the issue of bearer loan stock which is convertible into shares or which carries a return of an equity nature. Convertible loan stock which is in registered, rather than bearer, form remains liable to 0.5% stamp duty on transfer.

Attempts to circumvent the new rules by issuing the foreign currency bearer securities with only a nominal value, and then increasing their value by changing the rights attached to the various classes of shares, will not succeed. With effect from 26 November 1996, there is a 1.5% SDRT charge on any such increase in value of bearer securities.

## 26.3.2 Sale of land and buildings

A way of mitigating stamp duty was closed some years ago. If two owners exchange houses, stamp duty is now payable on the market value of the properties as well as on any cash adjustment.

Stamp duty is not charged on that part of the agreed purchase price which is allocated to items such as carpets, curtains and domestic appliances which are to be left in the house. This is because ownership of such items is transferred, not by the conveyance, but by the vendor physically handing them over to the purchaser (the legal term is 'delivery'). However, do-it-yourself conveyancers should be warned that it is possible to transfer ownership of goods by conveyance rather than by delivery, so that if the documentation is faulty, stamp duty can be charged on the price paid for the carpets and other house contents.

To reduce duty, purchasers are sometimes tempted to apportion an unrealistically high percentage of the agreed overall price to the contents – especially where this will bring the price allocated to the house itself below the threshold and so avoid duty altogether. The Stamp Offices are, of course, alive to this temptation and will refuse to stamp a conveyance if the valuations used cannot be justified.

A suggestion sometimes put forward is that a purchaser wishing to buy a brand new house should buy the site and then contract separately with the builder for the construction of the required dwelling. Certainly, if the buyer buys a building plot and then contracts with an unrelated third party for the construction of a house, stamp duty is payable only on the 'site value' price actually paid. A recent court case suggests that the same holds true if the buyer buys a plot from the builder and then commissions him to build a house on that site provided that the site is conveyed to the purchaser before a substantial start is made on the building work.

At first sight, this means that all developers should sell bare sites coupled with agreements to build houses, but in practice there would be problems. The developer probably would not want to convey the site until he had received the full price for the completed house, but at the same time the purchaser would not be willing to pay for a house that had yet to be built. Moreover, if (as would usually be the case) the purchaser needed a mortgage to buy the house, he would almost certainly find that the building society would not make the money available until the house was at least virtually complete. Solutions to these difficulties could no doubt be found, but would probably cost more than the stamp duty saving.

Finally, where a long lease at a substantial rent is proposed, it is sometimes possible to save duty by splitting the period between two shorter leases eg instead of a 50-year lease with stamp duty of 12% of the annual rent (see 26.1.2) at the outset sign two leases, one for 20 years and the second for 30 years (commencing on the expiry of the first) with the duty on each lease then being only 2% of the annual rent.

For legal reasons, the first lease must be for less than 21 years and so counts as a short lease which cannot be registered at the Land Registry.

### 26.3.3 Sale of goodwill and other business assets

The assets of a business sold as a going concern will typically include buildings, goodwill, plant and machinery and stock-in-trade. As for house contents, duty can be saved if the vendor transfers ownership of plant, machinery and stock-in-trade to the purchaser by physical delivery rather than by conveyance.

Generally speaking, the ownership of buildings and goodwill can only be transferred by a written document and so duty has to be paid. There are however ways of avoiding or reducing duty, though they are usually only practicable where vendor and purchaser trust each other completely.

(1) Stamp duty is payable on a conveyance of freehold land although the contract is sufficient to transfer ownership to the purchaser. Therefore, if vendor and purchaser sign and exchange contracts, but never 'complete' by conveyance, no duty is payable. This was upheld by the courts as long ago as 1889 and the Government has never blocked the loophole. The drawback is that, without a stamped conveyance, the purchase cannot be registered at the Land Registry, and this means that this is not normally a practical proposition where the purchaser is raising a mortgage.

(2) Where substantial amounts of money are at stake, advantage may be

taken of the rule that a document executed (signed) outside the UK need not be stamped until it is brought into the UK. (The document may be stamped without penalty provided it is presented at a Stamp Office within 30 days of being brought to the UK, but interest will run from 30 days after the date that the contract was executed.) The usual procedure is to take a day trip to Jersey or Guernsey, sign the documents, and leave them in a local safe deposit or bank vault.

Stamp duty is payable where a sole trader's or partnership business is incorporated, because the trader or the partnership is treated as having sold the business in exchange for shares in the new company (see 26.1.3). Where the successor company is a limited company, its proprietors must produce to the Registrar of Companies a properly stamped copy of the contract by which the business was sold to the company. It is therefore necessary to pay stamp duty, not only on the value of the goodwill, but also on that of the plant, machinery and stock-in-trade. No stamped contract is however required where a business is transferred to an unlimited company and it is possible to transfer a business to an unlimited company by means of an unstamped contract (eg one kept outside the UK) and then to re-register that company as a limited company.

## 26.3.4 Groups of companies
(FA 1995, s 140)

Statutory exemption from stamp duty applies, subject to conditions, where property is transferred from one member of a group of companies to another. For this purpose, a 'group' consists of a holding company and its 75% subsidiaries. The holding company can be a foreign company.

The definition of a group changed with effect from 1 May 1995. Only ordinary shares are now taken into account whereas previously the test was applied by reference to issued share capital of any class. On the other hand, up to 30 April 1995, the requirement was that the holding company should have a 90% interest; this has now been reduced to 75%.

Suppose that you have a situation like this:

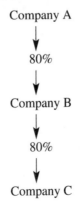

A Ltd can transfer an asset to B Ltd and claim protection from the group rules. However, if A Ltd transfers the asset to C Ltd, stamp duty will be payable as A Ltd has only a 64% interest in C Ltd. Rather oddly, there does not appear to be anything which prevents A Ltd selling to B Ltd and B Ltd then selling on to C Ltd, with this then qualifying for group relief.

The group relief rules are subject to anti-avoidance provisions where the transferee company is going to leave the group. For further details, see SP3/98.

FA 2000 contains further anti-avoidance provisions which prevent the avoidance of stamp duty by the use of redeemable shares to create a group relationship. Also, the definition of a group now follows the definition which applies for capital gains purposes so that the parent company must have 75% of the nominal ordinary share capital and at least 51% economic ownership.

# 27

# SOME SPECIAL TYPES OF TAXPAYER

This chapter gathers together special tax provisions and Revenue practices which are relevant only to specific occupations. The chapter covers:

(1) Authors.
(2) Barristers.
(3) Doctors.
(4) Dentists.
(5) Farmers.
(6) Lloyd's Names.
(7) Ministers of religion.
(8) Members of Parliament
(9) Business economic notes

## 27.1 AUTHORS

### Spreading lump sums
(TA 1988, s 534)

There is a special relief for authors and playwrights. Normally, where they assign a copyright for a lump sum, that amount will be taxable in full as a receipt for the year in which the copyright is assigned. However, where the author was engaged in producing the work over a period of more than 12 months, he may spread the lump sum.

Where the period during which the author was working on the piece did not exceed 24 months, the effect of making a claim to spread the lump sum is that one-half is treated as having been received on the actual date of receipt, and the other half is treated as having been received 12 months earlier.

If the author was working on the book for longer than 24 months, then the effect of a claim is that one-third of the lump sum is treated as income arising at the time it was actually received, one-third is treated as having been received 12 months prior to that date, and one-third is treated as having been received two years before that date.

A claim to spread copyright receipts in this way must be made within 22 months of the end of the tax year concerned.

## 27.2 BARRISTERS

Detailed notes on the requirements following FA 1998 for barristers to produce accounts on an earnings basis are available from the General Council of the Bar, 3 Bedford Row, London WC1R 4TB. Bear in mind that barristers' accounts may be produced on the cash basis for the first seven years. (See also 2.4.14.)

## 27.3 DOCTORS

### 27.3.1 Locum and fixed practice expenses insurance

The Revenue formerly resisted claims for such premiums. However, this policy changed on 30 April 1996 and the premium should now be treated as an expense in the doctor's accounts. If any claim is made under the policy, the amounts paid out by the insurer are treated as taxable receipts. See *Tax Bulletin* August 1996.

### 27.3.2 Pension contributions

Doctors engaged as general practitioners (GPs) are actually independent contractors to the NHS. However, rather uniquely, GPs are entitled to a pension under the NHS pension scheme as if they were employees. The NHS withholds 6% of the GPs' NHS salary as a contribution towards these pension benefits and this is normally treated as an allowable deduction from a GP's earnings.

The strict position is that a GP's contributions to the NHS pension scheme are allowed only by virtue of an extra statutory concession (ESC A9). The GP can therefore insist on the legal basis whereby no relief is due in respect of his NHS pension contributions and he can then make contributions under a personal pension policy.

Where a GP renounces relief for his NHS contribution, he can do so in relation only to one particular tax year, ie the GP does not have to take an irrevocable decision in relation to later years.

As an alternative to making personal pension contributions, a GP can continue to claim relief for his NHS pension contributions and make additional voluntary contributions. These may take the form of the purchase of pension rights for past years (ie added years) or the GP may make FSAVC payments of up to 6% of his NHS earnings.

### 27.3.3 Capital gains tax

Many GPs have a surgery which is either attached to or part of their main residence. Where the property is sold, that part of any capital gain which relates to the surgery will not normally be covered by the principal private residence exemption. However, it should be possible for the GP to claim roll-over relief (see 15.4) where he purchases another property to be used as a surgery. Also, if the GP is over 50 and retiring, the gain relating to the surgery should qualify for retirement relief.

The position is more complex where a GP is over 50 and a partner in a practice. If he disposes of his interest in the surgery when he retires, or he takes a material reduction in his share of the profits of the practice, he should qualify for retirement relief provided he has not charged a market rent to the practice.

Note that the notional rent reimbursed by the health authority to the practice as a whole is not rent for these purposes as it is merely a 'grant' to cover part of the doctor's expenses.

If a capital gain arises on a qualifying business asset for taper relief purposes (see 14.6 and 15.3), then the GP will benefit from the accelerated taper relief introduced in FA 2000.

## 27.4 DENTISTS

Relief is due in respect of insurance premiums paid to secure locum cover (see 27.3.1 above). Self-employed dentists are given tax relief for their contributions to the NHS superannuation scheme contributions by ESC A9, in the same way as doctors (see 27.3.1); they too can renounce relief for these.

## 27.5 FARMERS

There are a number of tax provisions which are specific to farmers.

### 27.5.1 All farming a single trade
(TA 1998, s 53)

The legislation specifically provides that all farming activities carried on by an individual within the UK are treated as a single trade. However, where an individual is a sole trader but also a partner in a farming partnership, the two activities are regarded as separate and distinct trades for tax purposes.

### 27.5.2 What counts as farming income?

There have been cases where the Revenue has argued that profits arising from farm shops form a separate venture and are not part of the farming activity. This depends upon the facts and, in particular, on the extent to which the produce sold in the farm shop is bought in rather than produce of the farm itself.

Where farmers engage in ancillary activities such as providing bed and breakfast accommodation or self-catering facilities for holidaymakers, the

Revenue will normally regard the resulting profits as forming part of a separate business unless the profits are relatively modest, in which case they may be included in the profits of the farming business for administrative convenience.

### 27.5.3 Farmhouse

It was normal practice for many years to claim that one-third of the farmhouse expenses were an allowable expense in computing the Schedule D Case I profits of the farm. However, the Revenue has moved away from this practice and has emphasised that regard should be had to the actual usage of the farmhouse (see *Tax Bulletin* February 1993).

### 27.5.4 Valuation of stock

If you are dealing with the accounts of a farming business, the Revenue's booklet BEN 19 is required reading. This booklet is one of a series produced for Revenue staff on 'Business and Economic Notes' to give Inspectors of Taxes some background on the commercial practice of different industries.

### 27.5.5 Herd basis

The effect of a herd basis election is that the herd is treated as a fixed asset. The original cost of the herd and any additions are excluded in arriving at the farm's profit for tax purposes. If the whole herd (or a substantial part of it) is disposed of the proceeds are not treated as a trading receipt. There is a free Revenue booklet IR9, *The Tax Treatment of Livestock – The Herd Basis*. Advice should be sought from an accountant about the mechanics of the herd basis.

### 27.5.6 Treatment of set-aside payments

Where farmers receive payments under the Government's set-aside scheme, the way in which such payments are taxed depends on the use to which the land is put. If the farmer allows the land to become fallow, income received under the set-aside scheme is normally treated as farming income. In contrast, where the land which has been set aside is used for non-agricultural purposes, income received under the set-aside scheme is not regarded as farming income, but rather as Schedule A rental income.

### 27.5.7 Averaging
(TA 1988, s 96)

It is possible for a farmer to make a claim under which his profits of two consecutive years of assessment are averaged. However, this election cannot be made where the profits of the lower year exceed three-quarters of the other year's profits.

Where the profits of one year are no more than 70% of the other year's profits, the results of the two years are simply averaged. Where the profits of the lower year are between 71 and 75% of the other year, the averaging is done as follows:

Take three times the difference between the two
years' profits                                      A
Deduct 75% of the profits for the higher year       B
                                                    ___
                                                     C
                                                    ===

Take the resulting figure (C) away from the taxable
profits for the higher year and add it to the profits
for the lower year

## 27.5.8 Capital gains tax

The availability of retirement relief where a partner sells part of his farmland is a difficult and contentious matter. At one time the Revenue's yardstick was that retirement relief would be available if the farmer disposed of more than half of his land, but the position is not now clear cut even here. It is very much an area where a farmer should seek specialist advice. However, with the phasing out of this relief over the next few years this point becomes less important as the land will normally qualify as a business asset for taper relief purposes.

## 27.6 LLOYD'S UNDERWRITERS ('NAMES')

The taxation of Lloyd's Underwriter's (Names) has always been a complicated area of the tax legislation, partly because of the specialised nature of the underwriting business. The restructuring of Lloyd's after a series of disastrous underwriting results in the late 1980s and early 1990s has led to a review of the way in which the whole business is structured. Names, who in the past had written on an unlimited liability basis, known now as natural Names, have looked for a way to limit their exposure in years of loss. The past few years have therefore seen the emergence of NameCos (small corporate entities), SLPs (Scottish Limited Partnerships) and LPVs (large pooled vehicles such as SOC Group plc).

The taxation of Names has been complicated by arguments with the Revenue over reinsurance to close (RITC). This dispute has now been settled by the Revenue accepting the General Commissioners' decision in respect of the 1994–1997 Accounts, but changing the rules from the 1998 Account onwards. This means that Names affected will be faced with amending the 1998 and 1999 self-assessments which included the 1994 and 1995 Account results respectively, both declared on a provisional basis.

The tax legislators have also been slow in coming to terms with the concept of syndicate capacity (the right to participate on an underwriting account), though capacity now has the advantage of being a 'business asset' for taper, IHT and roll-over relief purposes.

It is beyond the remit of this book to cover the taxation of Underwriters' in any depth, although the following sections act as a general guide.

## 27.6.1 General principles

An individual who is a Name at Lloyd's is deemed to carry on a trade whose profits are charged to tax under Schedule D Case I. For years up to 1992, profits from Lloyd's were treated as earned income only if the Name spent 75% of his time working at Lloyd's but, with effect from the 1993 underwriting year, all underwriting profits (including syndicate and other Lloyd's investment income and syndicate capital appreciation) is treated as earned income. Although the Contributions Agency originally took the view that any profits arising to individuals who had previously been regarded as non-working Names were not liable to Class 2 or 4 NICs, it has now revised this view. As a result Class 2 contributions are payable by all Names with effect from 5 January 1997, and Class 4 contributions from 1997–98, unless they are already paying maximum NICs on other sources of earned income.

There is a time lag in that Lloyd's syndicates make up their accounts only after a period of two years has elapsed. This means that the results for Lloyd's account 1997 (ie the year ended 31 December 1997) were known only in the later stages of 1999. The basis of assessment of individual Names changed for the 1994 and subsequent accounts. The profits will be assessed for the year of assessment in which the profits are declared and not for the year in which they arose. Thus, 1996 profits will be assessed for 1999–2000.

## 27.6.2 Allowable deductions

A deduction may be claimed for the following personal expenses borne by the Name (strictly on a calendar year cash basis for all expenses paid after 5 April 1993):

(1) Premiums for insurance policies (known as Personal Stop Loss policies) paid to minimise a Name's exposure to underwriting losses. The premiums are allowable as a deduction for the calendar year in which they are paid. Any recovery from the insurance company will in turn be treated as additional underwriting income for the year of the loss to which the recovery relates.

(2) The annual cost of maintaining a letter of credit or bank guarantee.

(3) Interest on a loan raised to finance an underwriting loss and on money borrowed to fund the Lloyd's deposit and personal reserves (and Lloyd's expenses).

(4) Personal accountancy fees. The Inland Revenue takes the view that only fees relating to the agreement of income tax assessments or to the earning or calculation of profits for the Name are allowable (and, therefore, those relating to the computation of transfers to the special reserve fund or the submission of loss claims are not). The deduction is on a cash basis.

(5) Premiums paid to an estate protection plan (an insurance arrangement intended to facilitate the winding-up of a Name's estate following death).

(6) Subscriptions to the Association of Lloyd's Members and certain expenses of attending meetings.

(7) Purchase of Lloyd's 'blue book' (annual listing of syndicate members), Chatset tables (Lloyd's league tables) and certain other publications.

(8) Subscriptions to Names' Action Groups, eg Outhwaite.

(9) Central Fund payments, Members Agency fees and commissions and personal run off contract premiums.

## 27.6.3 The special reserve fund
(FA 1993, Sched 20)

The purpose of the special reserve fund is to enable Names to set aside some of their Lloyd's income, free of tax, as a reserve against future liabilities. Subject to the rules set out below, the amount transferred (if any) is entirely at the Name's discretion.

### Transfers to the special reserve fund

The new fund operates as follows:

(1) Transfers into and withdrawals from the fund are made gross rather than net of tax at basic rate.

(2) Payments into the fund are deducted as a trading expense and withdrawals are taxed as trading receipts.

(3) A transfer into the fund is permitted of up to 50% of the profits for an underwriting year provided the value of the fund at the end of the year does not exceed 50% of the Name's overall premium limit.

(4) Transfers are voluntary and must be made by the earlier of:
   (a) the date in which the balance of the Name's profit is paid to him; or
   (b) 31 October of the year of distribution.

(5) Income and gains on the investments in the fund are exempt from income tax and capital gains tax.

(6) If an underwriting loss is sustained, a withdrawal must be made from the fund of the lower of the loss and the amount of the fund.

(7) If a cash call is made, a withdrawal must be made of the lower of the cash call and the amount of the fund and, if the cash call is greater than the ultimate loss, the excess must be transferred back.

(8)  The fund is valued each year at 31 December and if the value of the fund exceeds 50% of the premium limit for that year, the excess must be withdrawn.

(9)  When a Name ceases to underwrite, the balance of the fund is repaid to him or his estate. This repayment may take the form of money or money's worth. Where assets are transferred, the Name (or his personal representatives) acquire the assets at market value for capital gains tax purposes.

(10) The fund managers can claim repayment of tax suffered by deduction and payment of tax credit, because it is a gross fund. However, following changes introduced in the first Labour budget in July 1997, it is not possible to reclaim tax credits on dividends after 5 April 1999.

(11) Although funds accumulate tax free in the fund, there is a potential tax liability on withdrawal and this is on the full value of the fund.

(12) If a withdrawal is made when a Name ceases to underwrite, the payment is treated as a trading receipt received immediately after the end of the year preceding the one in which his Lloyd's deposit is repaid to him, ie normally it is a receipt of his final year.

### 27.6.4 Payment of tax

New rules applied to the 1994 account, which was the first underwriting year where all underwriting profits fell within self-assessment. Basic rate tax is not deducted at source from syndicate profits payments on account in respect of the 1996 Account, which was declared in summer 1999, would have been made under self-assessment based upon the 1995 Account profit, declared in 1998–99, on 31 January 2000 and 31 July 2000. The balance of any tax will fall due for payment on 31 January 2001.

### 27.6.5 Treatment of underwriting losses for UK taxation purposes
(TA 1988, ss 380–381, 385; FA 1994, Sched 1(2))

Underwriting losses for an underwriting year arise where a Name's total syndicate net claims and expenses (including reinsurance costs and personal allowable expenses) exceed his total syndicate income from premiums, investments, capital gains and personal Lloyd's income (including stop loss recoveries). A formal claim for the relief of such losses must be made by the Name to the Inspector of Taxes not later than 31 January following the end of the tax year after the year of the loss and would normally be incorporated in the self-assessment tax return. Thus a loss arising from the 1996 underwriting account (ie a loss for the tax year 1999–2000) must be claimed by 31 January 2002.

## Order of set-off

Such losses are set off against the claimant Name's income in the following order from 1997–98:

(1) Other income of the same, or the previous, year of assessment. Unlike earlier years, there is no requirement to set losses against the current year first. This means that a loss arising from, say, the 1997 account can be set against other income for 2000–01 or 1999–2000.
(2) Any balance of loss can only be carried forward under TA 1988, s 385 against future underwriting income and investment income from the Lloyd's deposit, special reserve fund and personal reserves (but not personal capital gains). Consequently, if beneficial, a Name can choose to carry forward all losses against future Lloyd's income.
(3) Underwriting losses can be set-off against a Name's capital gains in certain circumstances.

New Names have the option, in any of their first four years of underwriting, to carry back any loss under TA 1988, s 381(1) against any income of the three years immediately preceding that in which the loss arose (taking the earlier year first) (see 2.9.5).

## 27.6.6 Capital gains tax

A Name may have several sources of capital gains as a result of his participation in Lloyd's, and it is necessary to distinguish between each type in order to determine the correct tax treatment.

Capital gains or losses which arise within each of the syndicates in which a Name participates are not subject to CGT, but are charged or allowed as Lloyd's syndicate income or expenses. They form part of a Name's Lloyd's trading income for the year of account in which the disposal takes place.

Capital gains or losses which arise within the new Lloyd's special reserve fund are free of all taxes while in the fund, but are effectively taxed on withdrawal as trading income.

By contrast, capital gains or losses which arise from the disposals of assets held in a Name's Lloyd's deposit or personal reserves (other than the special reserve fund) are treated as personal gains or losses for the tax year in which the disposal takes place. They are therefore added to any other personal gains or losses arising during the same fiscal year.

Similarly, the sale or transfer of syndicate capacity is treated as a personal disposal and any gain or loss arising has to be included with other capital gains or losses for the tax year in which the disposal takes place. Some Names write insurance through Members' Agent Pooling Arrangements (MAPAs) which allows them to buy into a pre-selected portfolio of syndicates, rather than participate directly in a much smaller number of syndicates. This enables them to spread the risk of their underwriting activities. FA 1999 gave Inland Revenue practice a statutory basis in treating a

MAPA as a single asset for CGT purposes. Effectively a capital gains tax liability will only arise when there is a distribution form the MAPA manager of surplus funds (normally at the time of the annual auctions) or if the MAPA Name withdraws from the MAPA.

FA 1999 extended the classes of assets which qualify for roll-over relief to include syndicate capacity whether held directly or through a MAPA.

Capacity is treated as a business asset for taper relief purposes and additional investment in an existing syndicate or MAPA is treated as enhancement expenditure (ie the taper will run from the date of the original purchase, not the date of the additional expenditure).

### Example

> *J* purchases £50,000 capacity in the 1999 auctions in syndicate 2121. In the following auctions in 2000 *J* purchases another £20,000 in syndicate 2121. The taper on the total capacity held of £70,000 will run from 1999, not 2000.

It is therefore important to consider the use of taper relief and enhancement expenditure as an alternative to claiming roll-over relief.

### 27.6.7 Inheritance tax

The value of a Name's underwriting interests at Lloyd's is potentially chargeable to inheritance tax (IHT) when transferred on death. The valuation of these interests is normally based on the insolvency statement for the underwriting account ending with the calendar year preceding that in which the death occurs, and includes the value of investments held as funds at Lloyd's, underwriting profits or losses for open and running off accounts, and undistributed profits or losses for closed accounts.

Normally, underwriting interests qualify for business property relief (currently 100%) but the Capital Taxes Office investigates all claims for relief, and may seek to reduce the relief where it believes that a Name's combined reserves are excessive in relation to the amount and nature of the underwriting activities.

## 27.7 MINISTERS OF RELIGION

### 27.7.1 No tax on rent-free accommodation

A clergyman is not normally liable for tax in respect of his occupation of a vicarage or other living accommodation provided by the church, charity or ecclesiastical body for carrying out his duties (TA 1998, s 332).

ESC A61 also provides exemption for payment or reimbursement of the heating, lighting, cleaning and gardening expenses. However, this does not apply if the clergyman is a P11D employee because his earnings exceed £8,500 pa (see 3.4.1).

Where the minister's earnings exceed £8,500, any tax charge on such 'service benefits' in respect of his vicarage or manse is limited to 10% of the net emoluments (after deducting expenses). All this is covered in Helpsheet 124.

If the clergyman pays his wife wages for cleaning the part of the house used for official duties, this may be treated as a tax deductible expense for him.

### 27.7.2 Allowable expenses

The following expenses which are commonly incurred by clergy are allowable deductions under TA 1988, s 198:

- stationery, postage and use of telephone for clerical duties
- secretarial costs (including wages paid to the clergyman's wife for providing such assistance provided this is separate and distinct from work she performs as an active member of the church)
- travelling in the course of his duties (including the 12p per mile for 'business use' of a bicycle)
- cost of repair or replacement of robes
- communion expenses
- cost of providing a locum
- reasonable entertainment on official functions.

*White v Higgingbottom* [1983] STC 143 decided that a clergyman was not entitled to allowances for an OHP and screen which he paid for personally.

### 27.7.3 Capital gains tax

Where a clergyman buys a property, he can often nominate it as his main residence for CGT purposes on the grounds that his work requires him to live elsewhere (see 14.15.1).

For further background information, contact the Churches Main Committee, Fielden House, Little College Street, London SW1P 3JZ for a circular, *The Taxation of Ministers of Religion.*

## 27.8 MEMBERS OF PARLIAMENT

As one would expect there are special rules which apply to Members of Parliament, Members of the Scottish Parliament and Members of the Welsh Assembly. MPs are dealt with by a central Inland Revenue office in Cardiff. They complete a supplementary form SA101 (MP) which is available on the Revenue's website, together with help notes. The Revenue also publishes a leaflet, *MPs, Ministers and Tax.*

## Additional costs allowance

MPs receive a tax-free additional costs allowance which covers the additional costs of living away from home while engaged in Parliamentary duties either in London or in the MP's constituency (s 200 ICTA 1988). This means that an MP can effectively receive tax relief on interest on a mortgage to buy a second home in London, as the allowance is calculated to allow for the payment of either rent or mortgage interest in the case of a property owned by the MP.

## Travel

MPs are issued with rail/air warrants. No taxable benefit arises where these are used to travel from Westminster to a home in the constituency. Where the MP's home is not in the constituency, the extent to which a benefit is taxable is as follows:

- where the MP's home is not more than 20 miles from the constituency, no amount is taxable
- where the home is within 20 miles of Wesminster, no amount is taxable
- in other cases, the cost of the rail/air warrant is taxable

Where a warrant is used for travel to/from the constituency via home, only the excess cost over a direct journey from Westminster to the constituency is taxed. This treatment depends on the MP staying at home for only one night unless the journey spans a weekend.

The position of car allowances is complex because the cash mileage reimbursement that the MP receives from the Fees Office includes the cost of travel between the MP's home and Westminster, or between home and constituency. All this ranks for tax purposes as private travel. In strictness, the car mileage allowance paid by the Fees Office is assessable as an emolument and an expenses claim should be made. However, for practical purposes the allowance is not taxed. The rates for 1999/2000 were

| First 20,000 miles | Additional miles |
|---|---|
| 51.2p | 23.6p |

Incidental travel costs in London, such as taxi fares between London rail and air terminals and Westminster, and in visiting ministers on parliamentary business, are allowable expenses.

## Office costs allowance (OCA)

MPs receive an allowance for office, secretarial and research expenses, currently around £50,000 a year. This is taxable, but a deduction is made for the actual costs of any secretarial and clerical assistance, general office expenses and research assistance undertaken in the proper performance of the MP's parliamentary duties. Such expenses include the normal costs of office accommodation such as rent, heat and light, including the use of part of the home as an office and the costs of repairs and renewals of office equipment. Telephone, stationery and postage costs, if not provided free, are also allowable. An MP's secretary is paid direct by the Fees Office rather than the MP receiving the salary as part of a claim for office expenses, and PAYE is operated by the Fees Office.

### Incidental expenses

An MP can claim a deduction for the following:

- costs of hiring a room to meet constituents
- costs of expenses incurred in participation in delegations organised by all-party Parliamentary organisations such as the Parliamentary Group for European Unity
- payments to a local agent or party organisation for assistance in constituency work
- extra cost of meals taken while travelling on parliamentary business.

### Pensions and Retirement Lump Sums

Parliamentary pensions accrue at the rate of $\frac{1}{50}$ final remuneration for every year of service. MPs can buy extra years pension by making regular contributions or by paying a lump sum within 12 months of election to the House of Commons.

Ministers are able to pay contributions into a personal pension scheme if their ministerial salary is not pensionable under the Parliamentary Pension Scheme. Terminal grants to a person who is ceasing to be an MP are regarded as tax free up to £30,000.

## 27.9  BUSINESS ECONOMIC NOTES

Even if there is no special legislation which governs the way in which your particular occupation is taxed, you may well find it interesting to see the background information which the Revenue provides to its staff.

The Revenue publishes a series of Business Economic Notes which are primarily intended to aid Inspectors in the examination of accounts. The notes, listed below, are available for purchase from the Inland Revenue, Room 28 New Wing, Somerset House, Strand, London, WC2R 1LB.

| No | Subject | Date of issue |
|----|---------|---------------|
| 26 | Confectioners, Tobacconists and Newsagents | November 1997 |
| 25 | Taxicabs and Private Hire Vehicles | July 1997 |
| 24 | Independent Fishmongers | June 1997 |
| 23 | Driving Instructors | June 1997 |
| 22 | Dispensing Chemists | May 1995 |
| 21 | Residential Rest & Nursing Homes | November 1994 |
| 20 | Insurance Brokers & Agents | August 1994 |
| 19 | Farming – Stock Valuation for Income Tax Purposes | April 1993 |
| 18 | Catering – Fast Foods, Cafes and Snack Bars | October 1990 |
| 17 | Catering – Restaurants | October 1990 |
| 16 | Catering – General | October 1990 |
| 15 | Veterinary Surgeons | October 1990 |
| 14 | The Pet Industry | October 1990 |
| 13 | Fish and Chip Shops | October 1990 |
| 12 | Antique and Fine Art Dealers | March 1990 |
| 11 | Electrical Retailers | 1989 |
| 10 | Jewellery Trade | 1989 |
| 9 | Licensed Victuallers | May 1988 |
| 8 | Florists | September 1987 |
| 7 | Dentists | July 1987 |
| 6 | Funeral Directors | May 1987 |
| 5 | Waste Materials Reclamation and Disposal | March 1987 |
| 4 | Hairdressers | February 1987 |
| 3 | Lodging Industry | February 1987 |
| 2 | Road Haulage | February 1987 |
| 1 | Travel Agents | February 1987 |

Further details can be obtained over the Internet at www.inlandrevenue.gov.uk/bens/.

# 28

# CHARITIES AND NOT FOR PROFIT ORGANISATIONS

Most of this book is concerned with paying tax. However, there are many organisations who enjoy exemptions and whose main involvement with the Inland Revenue is in reclaiming tax.

We look at the following

(1) Charities.
(2) Mutual associations.
(3) Holiday clubs and thrift funds.
(4) Investment clubs.

## 28.1 CHARITIES

Charities are dealt with by

> Inland Revenue
> FICO (Charity Repayments)
> St John's House
> Merton Road
> Bootle
> Merseyside L69 9BB
> Tel: 0151 472 6036/6037.

In Scotland, the address is

> FICO (Scotland)
> Trinity Park House
> South Trinity Road
> Edinburgh EH5 3SD
> Tel: 0131 551 8127.

### Review of charity taxation

A thorough review of the tax regime for charities gave rise to important changes in FA 2000. We cover:

(1) exemption from income tax and CGT;
(2) tax credits on dividends;
(3) trading profits;
(4) Gift Aid scheme and record-keeping requirements; and
(5) payroll giving schemes.

## 28.1.1 Exemption from income tax and CGT

Charities are exempt from income tax on all income other than trading income (see 28.1.3), provided the income is applied for charitable purposes. Similarly, charities are exempt from CGT.

The exemption can be restricted in a year in which the charity accumulates income of more than £10,000 which is not reasonably required for application for charitable purposes in the foreseeable future or if it incurs non-qualifying expenditure. In practice, the rule on non-qualifying expenditure is most likely to arise where a private charity makes loans to a company connected with the settlor, especially if the loans are not on proper commercial terms. Professional advice should be obtained in such circumstances. (See further 18.9.1.)

## 28.1.2 Tax credits on dividends

Although tax credits on UK dividends are not normally reclaimable, it is possible for a charity to make a claim for transitional relief. The claim must be made within two years of the year in question. The charity will then be entitled to relief as follows:

| | |
|---|---|
| Dividends received in 1999–00 | 21% |
| Dividends received in 2000–01 | 17% |
| Dividends received in 2001–02 | 13% |
| Dividends received in 2002–03 | 8% |
| Dividends received in 2003–04 | 4% |

## 28.1.3 Trading profits

Trading income is exempt only if the trade is exercised in the course of carrying out a primary purpose of the charity or if the work is carried out mainly by its beneficiaries. A major problem area in the past has been the tax treatment of profits from other types of trading.

### Small fundraising events

ESC C4 has applied for many years and exempted profits from most fundraising activities. The concession states:

> Bazaars, jumble sales, gymkhanas, carnivals, firework displays and similar activities arranged by voluntary organisations or charities for the purpose of raising

funds for charity may fall within the definition of 'trade' in ICTA 1988, s 832, with the result that any profits will be liable to corporation tax. Tax is not, however, charged on such profits provided all the following conditions are satisfied:

(1) The organisation or charity is not regularly carrying on these trading activities;
(2) The trading is not in competition with other traders;
(3) The activities are supported substantially because the public are aware that any profits will be devoted to charity; and
(4) The profits are transferred to charities or otherwise applied for charitable purposes.

Profits from lotteries are exempt provided the profits are applied solely for charitable purposes and the lottery is promoted and conducted in accordance with the Lotteries and Amusements Act 1976.

However, it was argued that the terms of the concession were too restrictive and as from 1 April 2000, a wider exemption applies for trading profits from fundraising events provided:

(1) the public are aware that the purpose of the event is to raise funds for charity; and
(2) the event does not last for more than four days; and
(3) the charity holds no more than 15 events of a similar type in the same location each year. Small-scale events with gross takings of up to £1,000 per week do not count towards this total.

### New exemption for charity's trading profits

From April 2000, there is a new tax exemption for the profits of certain small trading and other fundraising activities carried on by a charity that are not otherwise already exempt from tax. This will mean that, for tax purposes, a charity no longer has to set up a trading company to carry on these activities.

The Charity Commission has confirmed that if a charity is governed by one of the Commission's model governing documents – which contain prohibitions on 'any substantial permanent trading activity' – it may lawfully carry on the activities falling within the new tax exemption without having to set up a trading company. If the charity has some other governing document, it should check that it permits it to carry on a fundraising trade before doing so.

The new exemption will apply to the profits of all trading activities, and most other incidental fundraising activities, that are not already exempt from tax, provided:

(1) the total turnover from all of the activities does not exceed the annual turnover limit, or
(2) if the total turnover exceeds the annual turnover limit, the charity had a reasonable expectation that it would not do so, and
(3) the profits are used solely for the purposes of the charity.

## The annual turnover limit

The annual turnover limit is:

(1) £5,000, or
(2) if the turnover is greater than £5,000, 25% of the charity's 'incoming resources', subject to an overall limit of £50,000.

For this purpose, 'incoming resources' has a very wide meaning. It means the total receipts of the charity for the year from all sources (grants, donations, investment income, etc).

## Example

A charity sells Christmas cards to raise funds and the sales in the year total £4,000. Assuming this is the only taxable fundraising activity, any profits will be exempt from tax because the turnover does not exceed £5,000.

However, suppose the sales in the year total £40,000 instead of £4,000. Any profits will still be exempt from tax provided the charity's incoming resources are at least £160,000, because the turnover does not exceed either:
(1) 25% of the incoming resources (£160,000 @ 25% = £40,000), or
(2) the overall limit of £50,000.

Even if the charity's incoming resources are below £160,000, so that the turnover exceeds the annual turnover limit, the profits will still be exempt from tax if it had a reasonable expectation at the start of the year that the turnover would not exceed the limit. Thus, in the above example, suppose the sales in the year total £60,000. This exceeds the overall annual turnover limit of £50,000. However, any profits will still be exempt from tax if there was a reasonable expectation at the start of the year that the turnover would not exceed the limit.

## The reasonable expectation test

If the total turnover of the taxable fundraising activities for any tax year exceeds the annual turnover limit, any profits will still be exempt from tax if it can be shown that, at the start of the tax year, it was reasonable to expect that the turnover would not exceed the limit. This might be because:

(1) the turnover was expected to be lower, or
(2) the charity's incoming resources proved to be lower than expected.

The Revenue will consider any evidence the charity may have to satisfy this test. For example, if a charity has carried on an activity for a number of years, it might be able to show that the turnover increased unexpectedly compared with earlier years. If it started carrying on the fundraising activity in the year, it might be able to show that the turnover was higher than forecast when it was decided to start the activity. Alternatively, it might be able to show that the charity's incoming resources were lower than forecast, perhaps because a grant it was expecting to receive was not paid in the year. Evidence might include minutes of meetings at which these matters were discussed, copies of cash flow forecasts and business plans and copies of previous years' accounts.

### Trading profits not covered by the new exemption

If trading profits are not likely to be covered by the above exemption, consideration should be given to the establishment of a company which would carry on the trading activities and then pay away the profits to the charity by a Gift Aid donation. Professional advice should be taken on this.

### 28.1.4 Other changes following the review of charities

From 1 April 2000 companies – including companies owned by a charity and unincorporated associations, such as clubs and societies – no longer:

(1) deduct tax from their Gift Aid donations; or
(2) have to give charities a Gift Aid declaration.

This applies to all Gift Aid donations by a company made on or after 1 April 2000 – including covenanted payments (even if under a Deed of Covenant executed before that date). For example, suppose a Deed of Covenant executed on 1 April 1999 provides for a company to make covenanted payments of 'such an amount as after deduction of tax equals £1,000'. While the basic rate is 22%, the company is required to make gross payments of £1,282 (£1,282 – tax at 22% = £1,000). From 1 April 2000, the company simply pays this gross amount and claims tax relief for it when calculating its profits for corporation tax.

Therefore, a charity should *not* reclaim tax on donations received from a company on or after 1 April 2000. If a company incorrectly deducts tax from its donation, the charity should inform the company of the correct position and ask it to pay over the sum it has incorrectly deducted.

Individuals still have to deduct tax from their Gift Aid donations and provide a Gift Aid declaration. The guidance below regarding tax reclaims and Gift Aid declarations applies only to donations by individuals.

### 28.1.5 Simpler paperwork: Gift Aid declarations

From 6 April 2000, Gift Aid certificates have been replaced by new, simpler and more flexible Gift Aid declarations. Before a charity can reclaim tax on a donation by an individual, it must have received a Gift Aid declaration from the donor containing certain information and confirming that the donation is to be treated as a Gift Aid donation. Companies will no longer have to give a Gift Aid declaration in respect of their donations.

Donors can give a declaration:

(1) in advance of their donation, at the time of their donation, or at any time after their donation (subject to the normal time limit within which a charity can reclaim tax – normally around six years)

(2) to cover a single donation or any number of donations

(3) in writing (eg by post, by fax or electronically through the Internet) or orally (eg over the phone).

The amount of information required on a Gift Aid declaration has been kept to the minimum consistent with proper administration of the tax relief and the need for the charity to be able to show an audit trail. A charity can design its own Gift Aid declaration. However, it should ensure that it satisfies all the requirements set out below and any other legal requirements under the Data Protection Act, the Charities Act, etc. There is no need to get the Revenue's approval for an own-design declaration, but FICO will be happy to approve it if required.

## What a Gift Aid declaration must contain

All Gift Aid declarations must contain:

- The donor's name
- The donor's address
- The charity's name
- A description of the donations to which the declaration relates
- A declaration that the donations are to be treated as Gift Aid donations

and, except in the case of a declaration given orally:

- A note explaining the requirement that the donor must pay an amount of income tax or CGT equal to the tax deducted from his donations
- The date of the declaration.

There is no requirement for a declaration to contain the donor's signature.

In the case of a written declaration, the charity may pre-print the information on the declaration form. For example, it can pre-print the charity's name. In the case of an oral declaration, the information may be recited to the donor for him to confirm it, rather than asking the donor to recite the information.

## Written records of oral declarations

If a charity receives an oral declaration it must send the donor a written record of the declaration showing:

(1) all the details provided by the donor in his oral declaration;

(2) a note explaining the requirement that the donor must pay an amount of income tax or CGT equal to the tax deducted from his donations;

(3) a note explaining the donor's entitlement to cancel the declaration retrospectively;

(4) the date on which the donor gave the declaration; and

(5) the date on which the written record was sent to the donor.

An oral declaration will not be effective unless and until the donor is sent the written record. This means that a charity cannot reclaim tax in respect of a donation covered by an oral declaration until it has sent the written record. Once it has sent the written record, it can reclaim tax in respect of any donations covered by the declaration, even if it received them before sending the written record.

### Cancellation of declarations

Donors are entitled to cancel their declaration at any time. They may do so by notifying the charity in any form of communication. The charity should keep a record of the cancellation of a declaration, including the date of the donor's notification. Cancellation of a declaration has effect only in relation to donations received by the charity on or after:

(1) the date on which the donor notifies the cancellation, or

(2) such later date as the donor may specify.

The charity must not reclaim tax in respect of such donations. Any donations received by before the date of the donor's notification will still qualify as Gift Aid donations.

If a donor who has given an oral declaration cancels it within the period of 30 days of being sent the written record, the cancellation will have retrospective effect, so that it will be as if the declaration had never been made. The charity does not have to wait for the 30-day period to expire before reclaiming tax in respect of donations received. But if it reclaims tax and the donor subsequently cancels his or her declaration within the 30-day period, it must pay the tax back to the Revenue. It may be possible for the charity to pay the tax back to the Revenue by deducting it from its next tax reclaim and it should contact FICO on this.

## 28.1.6 Gift Aid donations by partnerships

In England, Wales and Northern Ireland a partnership does not have legal personality, so a donation by a partnership is treated as made by the underlying partners. One partner may make a Gift Aid declaration on behalf of all the partners, provided he has the power to do so under the terms of the partnership agreement, in which case it will be sufficient for the declaration to show the name and address of the partnership. Otherwise, it will be necessary for each partner to make his own Gift Aid declaration, in which case he may do so on the same declaration form, provided it lists all the partners' names and addresses.

In Scotland a partnership has legal personality, so in all cases one of the partners may make a Gift Aid declaration on behalf of the partnership, showing the name and address of the partnership.

In order to claim higher rate relief, the partners should enter their share of the donation on their own self-assessment returns. How the donation is apportioned between the partners is a matter for them, but normally will be in accordance with their share of the partnership profits.

## 28.1.7 Deeds of covenant – Transitional arrangements

From 6 April 2000 there is no longer any separate tax relief for payments made under a deed of covenant; all tax relief for such payments is now given under the Gift Aid scheme. As a transitional measure, the charity does not have to get a Gift Aid declaration in respect of payments under a deed of covenant that is already in existence before 6 April 2000. The deed of covenant will stand in place of the Gift Aid declaration. However, any donations made outside the terms of, or after expiry of, the deed must be covered by a Gift Aid declaration.

Payments made under a deed of covenant executed on or after 6 April 2000 must be covered by a Gift Aid declaration.

## 28.1.8 New simpler forms for claiming repayments

A new, simpler claim form and schedules have been produced to enable charities to reclaim tax on Gift Aid donations (including covenanted payments which fall within the Gift Aid scheme) by individuals received on or after 6 April 2000. FICO issues them automatically when it receives a tax reclaim. Alternatively, charities can obtain them from the Forms Orderline 0151 472 6293.

A charity no longer has to complete separate schedules for Gift Aid donations and covenanted payments – in future there will only be one type of schedule for all donations. It will have to enter the following details on the new schedule for each donor:

- The donor's name
- The date of the donation, or, where the claim covers more than one donation by the donor, the date of the last donation
- The total amount of donations by the donor on which you are claiming in the schedule.

The charity will have to complete a separate schedule for each tax year, or part tax year, included in the claim. It will no longer be necessary, however, for you to calculate the tax relating to each donation separately. The charity can simply calculate the total tax reclaimed for all the donations shown on each schedule.

## 28.1.9 Keeping records

A charity must keep sufficient records to show that its tax reclaims are accurate. In other words, it must keep records that enable it to show:

(1) an audit trail linking each donation to an identifiable donor who has given a valid Gift Aid declaration; and

(2) that all the other conditions for the tax relief are satisfied.

If a charity does not keep adequate records it may be required to pay back to the Revenue tax it has reclaimed, with interest. It may also be liable to a penalty.

The form of records that must be kept is not prescribed in the legislation and has not changed significantly as a result of the new Gift Aid measures. In practice, it will depend on the size of the charity, the number of donors and the kind of systems used.

In the event that FICO audits a tax reclaim, the auditor will usually ask to see in respect of a donation:

● Any written Gift Aid declaration
● In the case of an oral Gift Aid declaration, a copy of the written record sent to the donor
● Any correspondence to or from the donor which relates to the donation, including
    – any notification of a change of name or change of address
    – any notification of the cancellation of the Gift Aid declaration
● The charity's bank statements
● Its paying-in book stubs showing details of cheques and cash banked
● Statements received from credit card companies showing details of credit card donations
● A cash book recording the receipt of cash donations
● If the charity uses envelopes to collect cash donations, a sample of the envelopes and a record of the sums enclosed
● Any other records kept relating to the donation.

A charity does not have to keep records on paper. They may be held on the hard drive of a computer, floppy disc or CD ROM, or stored on microfiche.

Revenue Code of Practice 5, *Inspection of Charities' Records*, explains how FICO carries out its audit inspections. In particular, it explains a charity's rights, and promises that it will be treated fairly and courteously. It also promises that FICO will provide help where appropriate. A copy of COP5 will be issued to the charity before any audit inspection.

## How long must records be kept ?

If the charity is a charitable trust, it must keep records until the later of:

(1) the 31 January next but one after the end of the tax year to which the tax reclaim relates (eg if it makes a tax reclaim for the tax year 2000–01, until 31 January 2003);

(2) one year after it makes its tax reclaim, rounded to the end of the next

quarter (eg in the case of a tax reclaim on 25 May 2002, until 30 June 2003); or

(3) when FICO completes any audit it has commenced.

If the charity is a company, it must keep records until six years after the end of the accounting period to which the tax reclaim relates.

These are the minimum periods for which a charity must keep records. In the event that FICO audits a tax reclaim and the auditor identifies errors, he may reopen tax reclaims for earlier years. Therefore, it may be in the charity's interests to keep records for longer than the minimum period.

### Using envelopes to collect cash donations

A charity may choose to collect cash donations in envelopes (eg church stewardship envelopes) so that it can show an audit trail linking the donation to the donor. For one-off donations, it may choose to pre-print the Gift Aid declaration on the envelope for completion by the donor. If the donor is a regular supporter, the charity may already hold his Gift Aid declaration, in which case the envelope need simply contain either:

● The donor's name, or
● Some other unique identifier, such as a reference number which can be cross-referenced to a donor register.

Where a reference number, is used, this should be unique to the donor. In practice, where envelopes containing the same unique identifier are used by the donor and his spouse and minor children, a charity can assume that all the donations are from the donor.

When the envelope is opened and the contents are counted, an official of the charity should record the sum that it contained:

● on the envelope, and
● in a donor record.

A charity should retain for all envelopes on which a Gift Aid declaration is printed for the periods set out above, together with a sample of other envelopes (normally for one month of the year) and the donor record.

## 28.1.10 Donations from joint bank accounts, etc

If a charity receives a donation drawn on a joint bank account, and it has not been given a Gift Aid declaration by all of the account-holders, it will need to determine whether the donation is from a donor who has given a Gift Aid declaration. It is normally safe to assume that the donation is from the account-holder who signs the cheque, debit card slip or direct debit mandate or standing order mandate. In the case of a donation received over the phone or through the Internet, a charity can normally assume that the donation is from the account-holder who authorises the transaction.

Similarly, if a charity receives a credit card donation drawn on an account in respect of which there is more than one authorised signatory, it can normally assume that the donation is from the authorised signatory who signs the credit card slip. In the case of a donation received over the phone or through the Internet, it can normally assume that the donation is from the person who authorises the transaction.

If there is any doubt whether the donation is from the person who signs the cheque, etc or authorises the transaction, the charity should ask him to confirm whether the donation is from him.

## 28.1.11 Payroll giving schemes
(TA 1988, s 202)

Under a payroll giving scheme an employee asks his employer to deduct an amount from his wage or salary and pay that amount over to a charity (usually a clearing house such as the Charities Aid Foundation). PAYE is then operated by the employer as if the employee's wage or salary had been the amount remaining after the charitable donation, which has the effect of granting tax relief at the highest rate paid.

An employer is not obliged to offer a payroll giving scheme and, if a scheme is offered, employees may decide individually whether they wish to participate. Usually each employee will specify particular charities to the clearing house, but in some cases the money is paid into a fund administered by a workplace committee. However, such funds can cause difficulties, especially where the name of the fund suggests that it was established by the generosity of the employer, rather than the employees themselves.

The maximum donation an individual could make under payroll giving arrangements was £1,200 (£900 up to 1995–96). This ceiling was abolished with effect from 6 April 2000 and in addition the Government is giving a 10% supplement on all donations made under the scheme between 6 April 2000 and 5 April 2003. The 10% supplement will be distributed to charities by payroll giving agencies along with payroll giving donations. Agencies will not deduct any administration fee from the supplement.

Some payroll giving agencies issue vouchers to employees in respect of their donations, which they can then give to the charities of their choice to redeem from the agency. To simplify the administration of the 10% supplement, agencies may add the supplement to the employee's donation account, in which case the amounts shown on vouchers given to charities will include the supplement.

## 28.2 MUTUAL ASSOCIATIONS

Mutual trading arises where a company or association (eg a club) trades with its members. Profits from such trading are exempt from tax under

ICTA 1988, s 491; thus, if a member receives a dividend paid out of profits from mutual trading, he is not liable for tax on it.

Problems are apt to arise if there is a mixture of mutual trading (exempt) and trading with non-members (which is taxable), eg a golf club which also receives green fees from non-members and makes bar profits from them. The Revenue's views are set out in an article in *Tax Bulletin* December 1997. You should consult an accountant if you are responsible for running a mutual company or association and the level of turnover is starting to become substantial.

If a company or association receives investment income, it will be subject to corporation tax in the normal way.

### CGT roll-over relief
(Extra statutory concession D15)

Roll-over relief may be due to a unincorporated association, whose activities are not wholly or mainly carried on for profit, if it replaces an asset (eg a hockey club which sells its ground and uses the proceeds to purchase fresh headquarters). Where an asset is owned by a company 90% of whose shares are held by such an unincorporated association or its members, roll-over relief may be due provided the other conditions are satisfied.

## 28.3 HOLIDAY CLUBS AND THRIFT FUNDS

In strictness, a holiday club might be regarded as an unincorporated association. However, where the club is formed on an annual basis, income which is earned on deposits etc is simply apportioned among the members (for further particulars, see ESC C3).

## 28.4 INVESTMENT CLUBS

Capital gains and allowable losses are apportioned among the members and should be included in their tax returns. Provided that all the following conditions are satisfied the secretary can apply for the gains and losses to be agreed by the tax district in which he lives (form 185-1 must be used when applying for this treatment):

- There are no more than 20 members
- The average amount invested is not more than £5,000
- The annual subscription does not exceed £1,000
- Total annual gains are not more than £5,000.

The Revenue will then accept each member's share of the gains without further enquiry.

# 29

## TAX TABLES

### Table 29.1 – Rates of income tax

| | Rate | Taxable Income £ | Cumulative Tax £ |
|---|---|---|---|
| *2000–01* | | | |
| Lower rate | 10% | 0–1,520 | 152 |
| Basic rate | 22% | 1,521–28,400 | 6,065.60 |
| Higher rate on dividends | 32.5% | (see *Note*) | |
| Higher rate | 40% | over 28,400 | |
| *1999–2000* | | | |
| Lower rate | 10% | 0–1,500 | 150 |
| Basic rate | 23% | 1,501–28,000 | 6,245 |
| Higher rate on dividends | 32.5% | excess | |
| Higher rate | 40% | excess | |
| *1998–99* | | | |
| Lower rate | 20% | 0–4,300 | 860 |
| Basic rate | 23% | 4,301–27,100 | 6,104 |
| Higher rate | 40% | over 27,101 | |
| *1997–98* | | | |
| Lower rate | 20% | 0–4,100 | 820 |
| Basic rate | 23% | 4,101–26,100 | 5,880 |
| Higher rate | 40% | over 26,101 | |
| *1996–97* | | | |
| Lower rate | 20% | 0–3,900 | 780 |
| Basic rate | 24% | 3,901–25,500 | 5,964 |
| Higher rate | 40% | over 25,500 | |
| *1995–96* | | | |
| Lower rate | 20% | 0–3,200 | 640 |
| Basic rate | 25% | 3,201–24,300 | 5,915 |
| Higher rate | 40% | over 24,300 | |
| *1994–95* | | | |
| Lower rate | 20% | 0–3,000 | 600 |
| Basic rate | 25% | 3,001–23,700 | 5,775 |
| Higher rate | 40% | over 23,700 | |

*Note:* The rates of tax applicable to dividends are 10% for income below the basic rate and 32.5% for income above it.

## Table 29.2 – Personal allowances and reliefs

| Allowances (£s) | 1994–95 | 1995–96 | 1996–97 | 1997–98 | 1998–99 | 1999–2000 | 2000–01 |
|---|---|---|---|---|---|---|---|
| Single person – under 65 | 3,445 | 3,525 | 3,765 | 4,045 | 4,195 | 4,335 | 4,385 |
| – 65 plus | 4,200 | 4,630 | 4,910 | 5,220 | 5,410 | 5,720 | 5,790 |
| – 75 plus | 4,370 | 4,800 | 5,090 | 5,400 | 5,600 | 5,980 | 6,050 |
| Married couple's allowance: | | | | | | | |
| – under 65 | 1,720* | 1,720* | 1,790* | 1,830* | 1,900* | 1,970* | –[1] |
| – either spouse 65 plus[3] | 2,665* | 2,995* | 3,115* | 3,185* | 3,305* | 5,125* | 5,185 |
| – either spouse 75 plus | 2,705* | 3,035* | 3,155* | 3,225* | 3,345* | 5,195 | 5,255 |
| Age allowances—reduced by: | | | | | | | |
| – £1 in £2 for income over | 14,200 | 14,600 | 15,200 | 15,600 | 16,200 | 16,800 | 17,000 |
| Additional personal allowance | 1,720* | 1,720* | 1,790* | 1,830* | 1,900* | 1,970* | –[1] |
| Widow's bereavement allowance | 1,720* | 1,720* | 1,790* | 1,830* | 1,900* | 1,970* | 2,000 [1,2] |
| Blind person's allowance | 1,200* | 1,200 | 1,250* | 1,280 | 1,330 | 1,380 | 1,400 |

*Allowance where relief is restricted to 20% for 1994–95 and to 15% from 1995–96 to 1998–99 and to 10% for 1999–2000 and 2000–01.

[1] The married couple's allowance for couples where neither partner has reached age 65 before 6 April 2000 and the associated reliefs (additional personal allowance, widow's bereavement allowance and relief for maintenance payments) are withdrawn from April 2000.

[2] Women who were widowed during 1999–2000 keep their widow's bereavement allowance in 2000–01 for the second year of their entitlement, unless they remarry before 6 April.

[3] Age 65 before 6 April 2000.

## Table 29.3 – 'Official rate' of interest for beneficial loans

|  | Average rate (%) |
|---|---|
| 2000–01 | 6.25 * |
| 1999–00 | 6.25 * |
| 1998–99 | 7.16 |
| 1997–98 | 7.08 |
| 1996–97 | 6.93 |
| 1995–96 | 7.79 |
| 1994–95 | 7.70 |

The rate on 6 April 1998 was 7.25% and on 6 April 1999 was 6.25%.

\* Now fixed in advance.

## Table 29.4 – Personal pension schemes maximum contributions by individuals 1994–95 to 2000–01

| Age at the beginning of the Tax Year | Percentage of net relevant earnings |
|---|---|
| up to 35 | 17.5 |
| 36–45 | 20 |
| 46–50 | 25 |
| 51–55 | 30 |
| 56–60 | 35 |
| 61 or more | 40 |

Note – there is a 'cap' on relevant earnings as follows:

|  | £ |
|---|---|
| 2000–01 | 91,800 |
| 1999–00 | 90,600 |
| 1998–99 | 87,600 |
| 1997–98 | 84,000 |
| 1996–97 | 82,200 |
| 1995–96 | 78,600 |
| 1994–95 | 76,800 |

## Table 29.5 – Retirement annuity premiums

*From 1995–96*

| *Age at beginning of tax year* | *Percentage of net relevant earnings* |
| --- | --- |
| Up to 50 | 17.5 |
| 51–55 | 20 |
| 56–60 | 22.5 |
| 61 or more | 27.5 |

*1994–95*

| *Age at beginning of tax year* | |
| --- | --- |
| Up to 50 | 17.5 |
| 51–55 | 20 |
| 56–60 | 22.5 |
| 61 or more | 27.5 |

**Table 29.6 – Rates of capital gains tax**

| | 2000–01 | 1999–00 | 1998–99 | 1997–98 | 1996–97 | 1995–96 | 1994–95 |
|---|---|---|---|---|---|---|---|
| *Annual Exemptions* | | | | | | | |
| Individuals | 7,200 | 7,100 | 6,800 | 6,500 | 6,300 | 6,000 | 5,800 |
| Trusts | 3,600 | 3,550 | 3,400 | 3,250 | 3,150 | 3,000 | 2,900 |
| | | | | | | | |
| *Rates of Tax* | | | | | | | |
| *Individuals* | | | | | | | |
| Gains are effectively taxed as top slice of taxable income: | | | | | | | |
| Gain less than lower rate limit | 10% | 20% | 20% | 20% | 20% | 20% | 20% |
| Gain less than basic rate limit | 20% | 20% | 23% | 23% | 24% | 25% | 25% |
| Gain greater than basic rate limit | 40% | 40% | 40% | 40% | 40% | 40% | 40% |
| | | | | | | | |
| *Trusts* | | | | | | | |
| Discretionary (including Accumulation and Maintenance) | 34% | 34% | 34% | 34% | 34% | 35% | 35% |
| Interest in possession | 34% | 34% | 34% | 23% | 24% | 25% | 25% |
| Where the settlor (or settlor's spouse) has retained an interest | Chargeable on settlor at his personal rate (see Individuals, above) | | | | | | |

## Table 29.7 – Taper relief

| Number of complete years after 5 April 1998 for which asset held* | Percentage of gain chargeable Business assets | Non-business assets |
|---|---|---|
| 0 | 100.0 | 100 |
| 1 | 92.5 | 100 |
| 2 | 85.0 | 100 |
| 3 | 77.5 | 95 |
| 4 | 70.0 | 90 |
| 5 | 62.5 | 85 |
| 6 | 55.0 | 80 |
| 7 | 47.5 | 75 |
| 8 | 40.0 | 70 |
| 9 | 32.5 | 65 |
| 10 or more | 25.0 | 60 |

*Assets which were acquired before 17 March 1998 will qualify for an addition of one year to the period for which they are treated as held after 5 April 1998. This addition will be the same for all assets, whenever they were actually acquired. So, for example, an asset purchased on 1 January 1998 and disposed of on 1 July 2000 will be treated for the purposes of the taper as if it had been held for three years (two complete years after 5 April 1998 plus one additional year).

*Business Assets*
(1) For disposals on or after 6 April 2000, the new four-year taper for business assets will apply for holding periods from 6 April 1998. The gains charged to tax will be reduced as set out in the table:

| Period asset held (years) | Percentage of gain chargeable (%) | Equivalent rate for higher rate CGT payer (%) |
|---|---|---|
| 0–1 | 100 | 40 |
| 1–2 | 87.5 | 35 |
| 2–3 | 75 | 30 |
| 3–4 | 50 | 20 |
| more than 4 | 25 | 10 |

(2) For business assets, the additional year for assets held at 17 March 1998 will be consolidated into the new four-year taper so that it will not be added for disposals on or after 6 April 2000. All CGT payers holding business assets will benefit from the enhanced taper relief.
(3) For non-business assets, the existing 10-year taper, together with the additional year for assets held at 17 March 1998, will continue to apply.

## Table 29.8 – Capital gains tax indexation allowance

### RETAIL PRICE INDEX FIGURES

|       | 1982  | 1983  | 1984  | 1985  | 1986  | 1987        |
|-------|-------|-------|-------|-------|-------|-------------|
| Jan   |       | 325.9 | 342.6 | 359.8 | 379.7 | 394.5/100.0¹ |
| Feb   |       | 327.3 | 344.0 | 362.9 | 381.1 | 100.4       |
| Mar   | 313.4 | 327.9 | 345.1 | 366.1 | 381.6 | 100.6       |
| Apr   | 319.7 | 332.5 | 349.7 | 373.9 | 385.3 | 101.8       |
| May   | 322.0 | 333.9 | 351.0 | 375.6 | 386.0 | 101.9       |
| June  | 322.9 | 334.7 | 351.9 | 376.4 | 385.8 | 101.9       |
| July  | 320.0 | 336.5 | 351.5 | 375.5 | 384.7 | 101.8       |
| Aug   | 323.1 | 338.0 | 354.8 | 376.7 | 385.9 | 102.1       |
| Sep   | 322.9 | 339.5 | 355.5 | 376.5 | 387.8 | 102.4       |
| Oct   | 324.5 | 340.7 | 357.7 | 377.1 | 388.4 | 102.9       |
| Nov   | 326.1 | 341.9 | 358.8 | 378.4 | 391.7 | 103.4       |
| Dec   | 325.5 | 342.8 | 358.5 | 378.9 | 393.0 | 103.3       |

|       | 1988  | 1989  | 1990  | 1991  | 1992  | 1993  | 1994  |
|-------|-------|-------|-------|-------|-------|-------|-------|
| Jan   | 103.3 | 111.0 | 119.5 | 130.2 | 135.6 | 137.9 | 141.3 |
| Feb   | 103.7 | 111.8 | 120.2 | 130.9 | 136.3 | 138.8 | 142.1 |
| Mar   | 104.1 | 112.3 | 121.4 | 131.4 | 136.7 | 139.3 | 142.5 |
| Apr   | 105.8 | 114.3 | 125.1 | 133.1 | 138.8 | 140.6 | 144.2 |
| May   | 106.2 | 115.0 | 126.2 | 133.5 | 139.3 | 141.1 | 144.7 |
| June  | 106.6 | 115.4 | 126.7 | 134.1 | 139.3 | 141.0 | 144.7 |
| July  | 106.7 | 115.5 | 126.8 | 133.8 | 138.8 | 140.7 | 144.0 |
| Aug   | 107.9 | 115.8 | 128.1 | 134.1 | 138.9 | 141.3 | 144.7 |
| Sep   | 108.4 | 116.6 | 129.3 | 134.6 | 139.4 | 141.9 | 145.0 |
| Oct   | 109.5 | 117.5 | 130.3 | 135.1 | 139.9 | 141.8 | 145.2 |
| Nov   | 110.0 | 118.5 | 130.0 | 135.6 | 139.7 | 141.6 | 145.3 |
| Dec   | 110.3 | 118.8 | 129.9 | 135.7 | 139.2 | 141.9 | 146.0 |

|       | 1995  | 1996  | 1997  | 1998  | 1999  | 2000  |
|-------|-------|-------|-------|-------|-------|-------|
| Jan   | 146.0 | 150.2 | 154.4 | 159.5 | 163.4 | 166.6 |
| Feb   | 146.9 | 150.9 | 155.0 | 160.3 | 163.7 | 167.5 |
| Mar   | 147.5 | 151.5 | 155.4 | 160.8 | 164.1 | 168.4 |
| Apr   | 149.0 | 152.6 | 156.3 | 162.6 | 165.2 | 170.1 |
| May   | 149.6 | 152.9 | 156.9 | 163.5 | 165.6 | 170.7 |
| June  | 149.8 | 153.0 | 157.5 | 163.4 | 165.6 |       |
| July  | 149.1 | 152.4 | 157.5 | 163.0 | 165.1 |       |
| Aug   | 149.9 | 153.1 | 158.5 | 163.7 | 165.5 |       |
| Sep   | 150.6 | 153.8 | 159.3 | 164.4 | 166.2 |       |
| Oct   | 149.8 | 153.8 | 159.5 | 164.5 | 166.5 |       |
| Nov   | 149.8 | 153.9 | 159.6 | 164.4 | 166.7 |       |
| Dec   | 150.7 | 154.4 | 160.0 | 164.4 | 167.3 |       |

¹*Note:* At January 1987 the index base was changed to 100.0. This means that an adjustment must be made where an asset was acquired before 1987 and sold after 31 Dec 1986. Thus where an asset was acquired in January 1986 and sold in January 1995, RD will be 379.7 × ¹⁴⁶/₁₀₀.

## Table 29.9 – Rates of interest on overdue tax/repayment supplement

| | |
|---|---|
| 6 January 1994 to 5 October 1994 | 5.5% |
| 6 October 1994 to 5 March 1995 | 6.25% |
| 6 March 1995 to 5 February 1996 | 7.0% |
| 6 February 1996 to 31 January 1997 | 6.25% |
| | |
| *Rates from 1 February 1997–5 August 1997:* | |
| For overdue income and capital gains tax | 8.5% |
| For overpaid income and capital gains tax | 4.0% |
| | |
| *Rates from 6 August 1997:* | |
| For overdue income and capital gains tax | 9.5% |
| For overpaid income and capital gains tax | 4.75% |
| | |
| *Rates from 6 January 1999:* | |
| For overdue income and capital gains tax | 8.5% |
| For overpaid income and capital gains tax | 4.0% |
| | |
| *Rates from 6 March 1999:* | |
| For overdue income and capital gains tax | 7.5% |
| For overpaid income and capital gains tax | 3.0% |
| | |
| *Rates from 6 February 2000:* | |
| For overdue income and capital gains tax | 8.5% |
| For overpaid income and capital gains tax | 4.0% |

Note that different rates apply for late payment/repayment of inheritance tax. The current rate is 5 per cent.

**Table 29.10 – Rates of corporation tax**

| Financial year commencing 1 April | 1994 &1995 | 1996 | 1997 | 1998 | 1999 | 2000* |
|---|---|---|---|---|---|---|
| Full rate | 33% | 33% | 31% | 31% | 30% | 30% |
| Small companies rate | 25% | 24% | 21% | 21% | 20% | 20% |
| Starting rate | | | | | 10% | 10% |
| Small companies rate – profit limit | £300k | £300k | £300k | £300k | £300k | £300k |
| Small companies marginal relief profit limit | £1.5m | £1.5m | £1.5m | £1.5m | £1.5m | £1.5m |

* Year commencing 1 April 2000, a 10% rate applies to companies with profits up to £10,000, and for companies with profits between £10,000 and £50,000 a lower average rate applies.

Marginal relief will ease the transition from the starting rate to the small companies rate for companies with profits of between £10,000 and £50,000. The fraction for calculating this marginal relief will be 1/40. Marginal relief will also apply to companies with profits of between £300,000 and £1.5m. The fraction for calculating this marginal relief will also be 1/40.

**Table 29.11 – Rates of inheritance tax**

| Cumulative chargeable transfers net | TRANSFERS ON DEATH Rate on gross %age | Rate on net fraction £ | Cumulative tax £ | GROSS Cumulative chargeable transfers £ | LIFETIME TRANSFERS Rate on gross %age | Rate on net fraction | Cumulative tax £ | GROSS Cumulative chargeable transfers £ |
|---|---|---|---|---|---|---|---|---|
| *from 6 April 1992* | | | | | | | | |
| 0–150,000 | nil | nil | nil | 0–150,000 | nil | nil | nil | 0–150,000 |
| over 150,000 | 40 | 2/3 | – | over 150,000 | 20 | 1/4 | – | over 150,000 |
| *from 6 April 1995* | | | | | | | | |
| 0–154,000 | nil | nil | nil | 0–154,000 | nil | nil | nil | 0–154,000 |
| over 154,000 | 40 | 2/3 | – | over 154,000 | 20 | 1/4 | – | over 154,000 |
| *from 6 April 1996* | | | | | | | | |
| 0–200,000 | nil | nil | nil | 0–200,000 | nil | nil | nil | 0–200,000 |
| over 200,000 | 40 | 2/3 | – | over 200,000 | 20 | 1/4 | – | over 200,000 |
| *from 6 April 1997* | | | | | | | | |
| 0–215,000 | nil | nil | nil | 0–215,000 | nil | nil | nil | 0–215,000 |
| over 215,000 | 40 | 2/3 | – | over 215,000 | 20 | 1/4 | – | over 215,000 |
| *from 6 April 1998* | | | | | | | | |
| 0–223,000 | nil | – | nil | 0–223,000 | nil | nil | nil | 0–223,000 |
| over 223,000 | 40 | – | – | over 223,000 | 20 | 1/4 | – | over 223,000 |
| *from 6 April 1999* | | | | | | | | |
| 0–231,000 | nil | – | nil | 0–231,000 | nil | nil | nil | 0–231,000 |
| over 231,000 | 40 | – | – | over 231,000 | 20 | 1/4 | – | over 231,000 |
| *from 6 April 2000* | | | | | | | | |
| 0–234,000 | nil | – | nil | 0–234,000 | nil | nil | nil | 0–234,000 |
| over 234,000 | 40 | – | – | over 234,000 | 20 | 1/4 | – | over 234,000 |

# INDEX

Entries are indexed by paragraph number except for the opening section of the book which does not have paragraph numbers; page numbers have been given instead for this section and these are in bold.